TELEVISION

For over two decades, *Television* has served as the foremost guide to television studies, offering readers an in-depth understanding of how television programs and commercials are made and how they function as producers of meaning. Author Jeremy G. Butler shows the ways in which camera style, lighting, set design, editing, and sound combine to produce meanings that viewers take away from their television experience.

Highlights of the fifth edition include:

- An entirely new chapter by Amanda D. Lotz on television in the contemporary digital media environment.
- Discussions integrated throughout on the latest developments in screen culture during the on-demand era, including the impact of binge-watching and the proliferation of screens (smartphones, tablets, computer monitors, etc.).
- Updates on the effects of new digital technologies on TV style.

Jeremy G. Butler is Professor of Journalism and Creative Media at the University of Alabama. He has taught television, film, and new media courses since 1980 and is active in online educational resources for television and film studies.

TELEVISION

Visual Storytelling and Screen Culture

Fifth Edition

Jeremy G. Butler
with a contribution from Amanda D. Lotz

NEW YORK AND LONDON

Fifth edition published 2018
by Routledge
711 Third Avenue, New York, NY 10017

and by Routledge
2 Park Square, Milton Park, Abingdon, Oxon OX14 4RN

Routledge is an imprint of the Taylor & Francis Group, an informa business.

First edition published 1994 by Wadsworth Publishing Company.

Fourth edition published 2012 by Routledge.

The *LIFE* magazine photograph on the cover illustrates the variety of channels that were available to "community antenna TV" (CATV) subscribers in 1966. CATV was the first form of "cable television" in the U.S. and would eventually lead to the vast profusion of cable channels in the 1990s. In turn, the proliferation of cable networks came to disrupt the dominance of over-the-air broadcast networks—harbinger of future upheaval caused by on-demand streaming services.
Photo credit: Arthur Schatz.

Library of Congress Cataloging-in-Publication Data a
Names: Butler, Jeremy G., 1954- author. | Lotz, Amanda D., 1974- author.
Title: Television : visual storytelling and screen culture / Jeremy G. Butler ; with a contribution from Amanda D. Lotz.
Description: Fifth edition. | New York : Routledge, 2018. | Includes bibliographical references and index.
Identifiers: LCCN 2017038602 | ISBN 9781138744004 (hardback) | ISBN 9781138743960 (pbk.)
Subjects: LCSH: Television—Psychological aspects. | Television—Semiotics. | Television broadcasting—United States. | Television criticism.
Classification: LCC PN1992.6 .B86 2018 | DDC 302.23/45—dc23
LC record available at https://lccn.loc.gov/2017038602

ISBN: 978-1-138-74400-4 (hbk)
ISBN: 978-1-138-74396-0 (pbk)
ISBN: 978-1-315-18129-5 (ebk)

Typeset in Interstate
by Apex CoVantage, LLC.

Visit the companion website: www.routledge.com/cw/butler

Printed and bound in the United States of America by Sheridan

CONTENTS

PREFACE

Should we take television seriously?

Should we take television seriously as a cultural or aesthetic medium, as a *text* capable of producing meaning? Should we take *The Real Housewives of Orange County* seriously? Should we commission studies on *The Wire*'s visual style? Should an interpretation of the discourse of *The Beverly Hillbillies* be permitted in an academic journal? And, most pertinent to this book, should there be college courses on these programs? Should *The Simpsons* be allowed in today's syllabi?

Yes, we should study television in school. And, yes, we should take television seriously. Why? Because television provides meanings, many meanings, as it entertains. There is little doubt that it is the predominant meaning-producing and entertainment medium of the past 70 years. As such it demands our scrutiny. In order to dissect the pleasures and meanings that television affords us, we need an understanding of *how* narrative is structured, and *how* commercials persuade, and *how* sets are designed, and *how* the camera positions the viewer's perspective, and *how* sound interacts with image.

Television: Visual Storytelling and Screen Culture (formerly subtitled *Critical Methods and Applications*) supplies the student with a whole toolbox of implements to disassemble television. It explains how television works, how television programs and commercials are made, and how they function as fertile producers of meanings. *Television* does not attempt to teach taste or aesthetics. It is less concerned with evaluation than with *interpretation*. It resists asking, "Is *The Bachelor* great art?" Instead, it poses the question, "What meanings does *The Bachelor* signify and how does it do so?" To answer this question brings viewers closer to understanding television as a meaning-producing phenomenon and thus helps them stay afloat in a sea of frequently contradictory meanings.

The form of analysis stressed here asks the viewer, first, to explore the structures of narrative, non-narrative, and commercial television material. Second, *Television* questions how those structures emphasize certain meanings (and repress others) to viewers, who approach television with many varying understandings of how the world works. And third, it considers how television's images and sounds work together to create its programs, commercials, and assorted on-screen flotsam and jetsam. Thus, this textbook works from the very concrete (light and shadow on an illuminated screen, accompanied by sound) to the very abstract (discourses on many aspects of the human experience)—and back again.

Accordingly, Part I of this textbook introduces the student to the principles organizing television's narrative, non-narrative, and commercial content and the industrial organization of network-era TV and today's on-demand media. Part II explains how that content is communicated to the viewer through the medium's style—its manipulation of image and sound. And it accounts for how the American TV industry generates that style through two main modes of production: single-camera and multiple-camera. Part III departs from *Television*'s consideration of television texts to survey the critical approaches—the methods of television studies—that have been applied to the medium. This part of the book first grounds the student in methods of analyzing programs themselves and then outlines methods of examining how TV's meanings are received by viewers and produced by TV-industry workers. Additionally, Appendix I provides guidance for writing papers about TV. It outlines how the principles of textual analysis that are developed over the previous chapters may be applied to a specific program. Appendix II discusses approaches to television from social-scientific or empirical methods, which contrast with the television-studies approach advocated in the bulk of the book.

Television's first edition was written during the year that websites evolved from a relatively primitive, text-only format to one that accommodated images and sounds (1993, when the Mosaic browser was released). We're excited about the possibilities for TV analysis that online platforms provide, and we've developed a companion website for *Television* at tvcrit.com. Here you'll find sample student analyses, color versions of all the illustrations (larger than reproduced in print, too), and many additional television materials that cannot fit between the covers of a book—specifically, audio and video clips. Parts of the site are reserved for *Television* users and require the following account name and password:

Account name: tvcrit
Password: tvcrit4u

Television, this book, was born of the author's frustration as a teacher of television studies in the 1980s and early 1990s. Many television textbooks from that era deal with the history and structure of television as an industry, but few offer students a way to analyze that industry's products from a critical perspective. Other TV textbooks emphasize the "nuts-and-bolts" of video production (how to operate cameras, microphones, and the like) to the extent that they seldom have space to consider television meanings and how they are generated by those nuts-and-bolts. Textbooks that do address television analysis as part of "mass communication" research and theory rely largely upon empirical methods drawn from psychology and sociology. They often neglect the issue of critical interpretation.

Aside from Appendix II, *Television* does not engage extensively with the mass-communication research tradition. Instead, its authors draw upon nonempirical models for their inspiration. Much of *Television* will look familiar, for example, to readers who have encountered film-studies textbooks. Moreover, *Television* also bears the marks of nonempirical disciplines such as literary criticism, semiotics (the study of signs and meaning), and ideological criticism. It refers to these approaches where appropriate, but the authors are concerned above all else to analyze television *as television* and not as a test case for a particular research method. As such, this textbook fits within the still developing field of "television studies"—a label that was firmly established in the early 2000s with the publication of about a dozen books with it in their titles (see p. 311 for specific titles). The core principles of television studies remain a bit fuzzy, but Part III will attempt to bring them into focus.

This, the fifth edition of *Television* (prepared 2017–18), arrives at a time when screen culture is evolving rapidly. For many viewers, especially younger ones, the smartphone has become the screen with which they spend the most time—sometimes supplanting the old-fashioned TV set in front of the living room couch and sometimes serving as a second screen that can distract from or enhance what's on that TV set. We live in a time of a plenitude of screens: one constantly in our pocket, one in the living room, one in the doctor's waiting room, a dozen in the sports bar, and on and on. The programming on all these screens is sometimes unique to one technology, the way that Snapchat only works on phones; or, it can slide from one screen to another, the way a humorous monologue on TV monitors later shows up on your smartphone. Our 4K television sets can offer us a visual experience rivaling a movie theater, and smart TVs can provide an interactive user interface much like a desktop computer. Our phones can amuse us with cat videos, but they can also tell us the weather, entice us to play games, allow us to communicate with our friends via social media, or play us the latest tune from Beyoncé. Screen technology in the twenty-first century continues to mutate, blurring the functions of specific devices and offering possibilities that at times seem endless.

This is not just a time of great technological shifts. There have also been huge changes in the economics of television—particularly in the United States. The broadcast networks are under siege from online, video-on-demand (VOD) portals such as Netflix, Hulu, and YouTube. These VOD systems have significantly disrupted old broadcasting models by providing new ways for getting storytelling video from a producer to a viewer. It is obvious that conventional television no longer commands our attention as it did from the 1950s to the 1970s. Some critics have even proclaimed an end to the "broadcast era" or "network era" of television, but the mode of production associated with broadcast television is far from dead. Despite the appearance of television programs on mobile devices such as smartphones and tablets, the distribution of television via over-the-air or cable/satellite networks is still the engine that powers the television machine. Television originated as a commercial, network medium in the years after World War II and will continue to have an impact as such for the foreseeable future. Just how much longer this will hold true is currently the subject of much speculation.

Television does not pretend to be a comprehensive guide to deconstructing everything that appears on a video screen. No single volume could. We spend little time, for example, on video gaming or the cultural discourse on social media. Rather, we here emphasize storytelling with sound and image as it originated in the cinema and network-era television and as it remains, perhaps surprisingly healthy, on streaming services. *Television* helps students understand television's various manifestations, emphasizing the ever-present, ever-flowing, network-era television system and its many descendants.

New to the Fifth Edition

Readers familiar with previous editions will note the following changes:

- An entirely new chapter by Amanda D. Lotz on television in the contemporary media environment.
- Discussions integrated throughout on the latest developments in screen culture during the on-demand era, including the impact of binge-watching and the proliferation of screens (smartphones, tablets, computer monitors, etc.).
- Updates on the effects of new digital technologies on TV style.
- The online availability of previously eliminated "special-topics" chapters: "A History of Television Style" (tvcrit.com/find/history), "Music Television" (tvcrit.com/find/musictv), and "Animated Television" (tvcrit.com/find/animation).
- Additional video examples, to which short links are provided.
- Dozens of newly added or updated still illustrations—eliminating ones from shows no longer generally available and incorporating new ones from recent shows.

ACKNOWLEDGMENTS

Blaine Allan and Gary Copeland each wrote a *Television* chapter that appeared in previous editions, but their contributions to this project go far beyond that. They were there for the original conceptualization of the project, helped shepherd it through various drafts and rewrites, furnished key examples when my mind went blank, and generally illustrated just how collegial colleagues can be. Daniel Goldmark stepped up and rewrote much of the "Animated Television" chapter for the third edition.

I thank my original editor, Linda Bathgate, for her diligence in bringing this project to fruition and for supporting it through multiple editions and Erica Wetter for assuming editing duties on the current edition. I am also grateful to Routledge for its continuing efforts in the area of television studies.

Several persons read and provided useful comments on previous editions: David Bordwell, Jim Castonguay, Brent Davis, Maureen Furniss, Carolyn Hales, Chad Harriss, Michele Hilmes, Lynne Joyrich, Chuck Kleinhans, Tara McPherson, Ellen Seiter, Greg Stroud, Lang Thompson, Robert M. Young, Kristen Warner, Mark J. P. Wolf, and Shuhua Zhou. Among the television-industry workers I have consulted are Tom Azzari, Tom Cherones, Aaron Greer, Dean Holland, Ken Kwapis, Michael Laibson, Chuck Meyers, Bryan C. Fails, Michael Parnes, and Craig Pettigrew. I am grateful for all of their time and insights.

The Center for Public Television and Radio at the University of Alabama; its current director, Elizabeth Brock; and its former director, Tom Rieland, graciously assisted with the preparation of illustrations. Videographer Preston Sullivan set up several illustrative shots, with the help of Brent Davis, Dawn Haskew, Jim Holliman, Glen Richard, and Jason Ruha. Additionally, Catherine May assisted with photographs of a CPT&R editing suite, with accompanying screen shots.

Most screen shots in this book were created by digitally capturing individual frames from videotapes, DVDs, video files, Blu-ray discs, and mobile devices (as technology has marched on). Barry Smith ably assisted in this task originally. Details on the process are provided in a tutorial on tvcrit.com. Nathan Dains (and his son) kindly provided a screen shot from *Pokémon Go*. Other illustrations were created by Laura Lineberry (drawings), and Rickey Yanaura (photographs). Our narrative charts were inspired by a diagram created by Victoria Costley. Figure 5.9 is courtesy of MTV. Figure 9.51 is courtesy of The Weather Channel and photographer Richard Grant. The STEADICAM® photo in Figure 9.37 is courtesy of The Tiffen Company. STEADICAM® is a registered trademark of The Tiffen Company. Tables 6.2 and 7.1 are courtesy of Nielsen Media Research. Figures 8.28–8.30 are courtesy of Steven DiCasa, co-founder of Rethink Films.

Rosemary McMahill diligently compiled the glossary for the first edition and also provided valuable assistance with the word processing of the manuscript.

My students at the University of Alabama were the first to be exposed to this text, while still a manuscript. I thank them for their patience in dealing with *Television* in photocopied form—missing an illustration here and there and lacking a binding that would properly hold it together for a 15-week semester. Their responses and comments helped make this a much more readable book.

Not all support for this book was academic. Jeremy, Penelope, and Reid Butler took me under their wings during *Television*'s initial development—allowing me the privilege of writing time unfettered by concerns of room and board. Marysia Galbraith supports my writing efforts in so many ways, even though my love of *Rick and Morty* perplexes her. My 14-year-old son's interest in *Overwatch* gameplay videos on YouTube reminds me on a daily basis that "television," if we can call it that, is not the television with which I grew up. And that's mostly for the best. During the time since the last edition, my mother and father passed away. He was a part-time announcer for KBUN-AM radio in the 1950s and she was one of Arizona's first women sports reporters in the 1970s, at the *Arizona Republic*. Clearly, media are in my DNA because of them. This edition of *Television* is therefore dedicated to Jeremy E. and Penelope W. Butler.

Part I

Television Structures and Systems

1 An Introduction to Television Structures and Systems

Ebb and Flow in the Network Era

Television is dead. According to various pundits, it was killed by cable TV and the VCR in the 1980s; by the Internet and video games in the 1990s; by Netflix, TiVo, and the iPod in the 2000s; and by smartphones and the iPad in the 2010s.

Considering its multiple deaths, television's corpse is remarkably active. The "television household universe," to use a TV-rating term, still contains 118.4 million homes in the United States—accounting for 96 percent of all U.S. households.[1] Perhaps surprisingly, the number of TV households has actually increased during most of the twenty-first century—dipping during 2010 to 2013 but then resuming its growth.[2] And upwards of 20 million Americans continue to watch TV's most popular recurring programs on conventional broadcast networks each week. This dwarfs the numbers that go see a particular movie, play a video game, check out individual videos on YouTube or Netflix, or stream a movie to a cell phone. Despite assaults on their primacy, broadcast networks—ABC, CBS, CW, Fox, NBC, and PBS—and cable/satellite networks—ESPN, AMC, USA, Lifetime, TNT, HBO, and so on—are not prepared to concede defeat. Television remains the principal medium through which most people obtain visual entertainment and information and through which advertisers reach the largest audiences.

Yet, there is no denying that overall viewership is declining precipitously, television-viewing habits are changing rapidly, and advertisers are getting very nervous. While the number of TV viewers remains enormous, it is dropping quickly as viewers find other screens—principally, of their digital devices—more compelling. Advertisers are particularly anxious about new technologies that grant viewers increased control over programming. The remote control and VCR were just the beginning of this trend. TiVo and other digital video recorders (DVRs), as well as video-on-demand (VOD) services streamed via the Internet, not only let viewers time-shift programs; they also permit the pausing and rewinding of live broadcasts and fast-forwarding through commercials. And **Internet-distributed television** supports both time-shifting and *location*-shifting as viewers can watch *Walking Dead* while commuting on a bus instead of parked on their living room couch, tuned into the AMC channel at 10:00 p.m. Sundays.

What does all this mean for the study of television? Is a book such as the one you're holding useless and outdated? Obviously, we do not think so. As Lynn Spigel writes in *Television After TV: Essays on a Medium in Transition*,

> [W]hile mutated in form television remains a central mode of information and entertainment in our present-day global culture, and it appears that it will continue to do so for many years to come. Understanding what is new about the medium thus demands an understanding of both its past and present.[3]

To this end, we begin our study of television with a consideration of the medium's structure circa 2018, which still greatly resembles how it has worked for the past 60 years. This is an "age of uncertainty" for television, however.[4] And so Amanda D. Lotz will offer some thoughts on the impact of Internet-delivered TV in the next chapter. It is inaccurate, however, to assume that Internet-delivered TV has wholly replaced **network-era television**. We are not yet in a post-network era, as some scholars have suggested. Once the dust settles after this current stage of upheaval, it may even be that network-era TV and other **legacy media** survive as choices among a profusion of other options. After all, in the 1950s television usurped many of radio's functions (and a lot of its advertising revenue), but radio persists in various forms in the present day. Fortunately, most of the analytical methods in the following chapters may be easily adapted to whatever form television takes in the future.

Television's Not-So-Distant Past: The Network Era

"Network-era television" refers to that time, in the not-so-distant past, when television broadcasting in the U.S. operated through a system in which three networks dominated general programming. Over the years, the number of networks multiplied—exploding to dozens of channels in the 1980s, with the widespread acceptance of cable and satellite delivery. For the sake of convenience, we will initially lump together TV shows that originate on over-the-air (a.k.a. "terrestrial") broadcast networks with those that come into our home via cable and satellite systems. Viewers born in the 1980s and after likely grew up receiving both broadcast networks and cable-originating channels from cable and satellite distribution services such as Comcast and DirecTV, respectively. Although the rules governing broadcast networks and the nature of their businesses are very different from cable channels, they are all based on the idea of "casting" a single program at a time toward their viewers and attempting to entice those viewers to tune in while that broadcasting is actually happening. Programs are *pushed* toward viewers, and the viewers then decide whether to accept the networks' invitations to watch at a particular time. Internet-distributed TV, in contrast, is where an individual viewer seeks a show and then *pulls* it toward them—on-demand, whenever they wish. Within the television industry, these two types of viewer experiences are known as **linear** and **nonlinear television**. The former consists of programs broadcast toward viewers at a specific time and as part of an ordered schedule of other individual programs—one after another, as in a line. The latter denotes programming that is acquired with no regard for the order in which it was provided on VOD services such as Netflix, YouTube, and Hulu.

The principles behind linear television are illuminated by the program guides displayed in cable/satellite user interfaces and printed in newspapers and magazines such as *TV Guide*. These venues find it convenient to represent the television schedule as a spreadsheet-like grid. In most of them, the channels run vertically down the left side of the grid, while half-hour time slots run horizontally along the top. (Table 1.1 shows one such grid—limited to over-the-air, linear channels—for a typical Sunday evening in November 2016.) The reasoning behind this array is obvious. At a glance, we can fix our location in the grid, noting the axis of channel (say, channel 9) and the axis of time (say, 7:00). After figuring that location, we can quickly see what will follow the current program in linear time (horizontal) and what is happening on other channels at that same time (vertical). Interactive, on-screen grids provided by Comcast, DirecTV, et al. also allow us to scroll horizontally and vertically to explore our current and upcoming options.

Grids such as these may help us understand the basic structure of network-era TV and the current experience of today's linear television. Most listings emphasize programming time slots as much as the individual programs themselves. Television programs are positioned by network programmers and experienced by viewers as one program within a linear sequence of other programs in an ongoing series of timed segments. Further, programs are also associated—potentially linked—with other programs by their shared time slot. During the time that a television set is on in American households—over five hours per day, on average—we are carried along in the horizontal current of linear television time, flowing from one bit of TV to the next. Equally important, we may move vertically from one channel to another, creating associations among concurrent programs. A listing grid depicts visually these two axes of television's structure: sequence (one thing after another) and association (connections among simultaneous programs).

We begin with this brief consideration of program listings because it illustrates the fundamental principle of network-era television's linear structure. As Raymond Williams first argued in 1974, television differs crucially from other art forms in its blending of disparate units of narrative, information, and advertising into a never-ending **flow** of television.[5] Although we often talk of watching a single television program as if it were a separate discrete entity, during the network era we more commonly simply *watched television*. The set was on. Programs, advertisements, and announcements came and went (horizontal axis). Mere fragments of programs, advertisements, and announcements flashed by as we switched channels (vertical axis). We stayed on the couch, drawn into the virtually ceaseless flow. We watched television as television more than we sought a specific television program. Or, at least, that is how TV watching worked during the peak of the network era and how linear TV can still work in numerous situations today. The pursuit of flow underpins linear networks' programming of similar programs in succession—as when ABC scheduled four comedies in a row for Tuesday and Wednesday nights during the 2017-18 season. Many viewers—especially older viewers accustomed to network-era television—continue to experience linear TV flow in their homes, and TV sets in public spaces such as restaurants, doctors' waiting rooms, and airport lounges flow programming in the direction of their captive audiences. As we'll see in the next chapter, DVRs and Internet-distributed VOD TV challenge and disrupt this essential concept of flow, but its conventions refuse to be eliminated entirely.

The maintenance of television flow dominates nearly every aspect of the structures and systems of network-era television and its descendants. It determines how stories will be told, how advertisements will be constructed, and even how television's visuals will be designed. Every chapter of this book will account in one way or another for the consequences of television flow. Before we start, however, we need to note three of this principle's general ramifications:

1. polysemy
2. interruption
3. segmentation.

Polysemy, Heterogeneity, Contradiction

Many critics of television presume that it speaks with a single voice, that it broadcasts meanings from a single perspective. Sometimes television's significance becomes part of a national debate. During the 1992 presidential election campaign, Vice President Dan Quayle repeatedly advocated a return to traditional "family values," an ideologically loaded term for conservative beliefs about the family. In one frequently discussed speech he singled out the TV pregnancy of an unwed sitcom mother—Murphy Brown (Candice Bergen)—as indicative of television's assault on the family. He claimed she was "mocking the importance of fathers by bearing a child alone and calling it just another 'lifestyle choice.'"[6] For Quayle, the meanings presented on TV had systematically and unambiguously undermined the idea of the conventional nuclear family: father, mother, and correct number of children; the father working and the mother caring for children in the home; no divorce; no sex outside of marriage; and no single or gay parenthood. The phrase "family values" quickly became a rallying cry for conservatives, and today, over twenty years later, it is still invoked by right-wing politicians such as Sarah Palin and former President George W. Bush. Such individuals often accuse television of eroding family values. One conservative lobbying organization, the American Family Association (AFA), contends that television and other entertainment media have "played a major role in the decline of those values on which our country was founded and which keep a society and its families strong and healthy."[7] Television's discourse on the family has become too liberal—even decadent—according to Quayle, Palin, Bush, the AFA, and their supporters.

What these individuals and organizations fail to take into consideration, however, is the almost overwhelming flow of programs on television. *Murphy Brown* (1988–98) is but one show among the hundreds that comprise TV flow. And its endorsement of single parenthood, if such indeed is the case, is just one meaning that bobs along in the deluge of meanings flooding from the TV set. The many meanings, or **polysemy**, that television offers may be illustrated by excerpting a chunk of the television flow. Look at the Sunday-night prime-time schedule reproduced in Table 1.1, which we selected largely at random. A typical household could have started its prime-time viewing with *Bob's Burgers* (2001–) and *The Simpsons* (1989–) on Fox, caught a bit of NBC's *Sunday Night Football* (2006–; the Kansas City Chiefs at the Denver Broncos), but become bored with the game and returned to Fox for *Family Guy* (1999–) and then the second half of ABC's *Secrets and Lies* (2015–16). The household might have concluded its prime-time viewing by bouncing back to the football game when Mom saw on Facebook that it was a nail-biter that went into overtime (the Chiefs won with a field goal that bounced off the goalpost before going through). What meanings surrounding the U.S. family, we might ask, do these programs present? Or, in Quayle's terms, is television destroying family values?

Let's start with a program that has frequently been attacked by conservative groups: *Family Guy*, an animated show that is rated TV 14 DLSV for "suggestive dialogue, [coarse] language, sexual situations" and "violence" and is not intended for viewing by children under 14. Considering the program's rating, the lyrics of its theme song are obviously presented with heavy irony:

> It seems today that all you see
> Is violence in movies and sex on TV.
> But where are those good old-fashioned values
> On which we used to rely?
> Lucky there's a family guy!
> Lucky there's a man who
> Positively can do
> All the things that
> Make us laugh and cry.
> He's . . . our . . . Fam . . . ily . . . guy!

Produced as a parody of a splashy song-and-dance number, with the cast wearing top hats (Figure 1.1), the theme song sets us up for a show that ridicules "family guys," in particular, and "those good old-fashioned [family] values," in general. The Parents Television Council (PTC), a

Figure 1.1 The Griffin family sings and dances in the overblown title sequence of *Family Guy*.

conservative advocacy group, has often taken issue with *Family Guy* and has filed numerous indecency complaints against it with the Federal Communications Commission. Indeed, the PTC website's "Action Center" features prepared electronic forms to enable its users to automatically submit a complaint with the FCC.[8]

The episode that aired on our sample Sunday, "The Peanut Butter Kid," contains enough references to anal sex, defecation, and drug use by a child to rankle the PTC, and in terms of polysemy it presents a radically dysfunctional family.[9] The storyline centers on the parents exploiting their infant son, Stewie (Seth MacFarlane), by forcing him to perform in commercials. They prepare him for auditions by giving him "acting juice," which contains enough cocaine to make him bounce off the walls. At one audition, Peter (Seth MacFarlane), the father, adds "a little molly" [the drug MDMA] to the acting juice, saying to Stewie, "We'll go out clubbing afterwards." Lois (Alex Borstein), the mother, warns Stewie, "If you screw this up, Mommy is going to kill all of your toys." The show's anthropomorphic, talking dog, Brian (Seth MacFarlane), reveals to Stewie that he's being used. Stewie then intentionally screws up his next commercial shoot, ruining his budding career. After seeing the disastrous results of Stewie's performance, the parents come to realize their mistakes and acknowledge that giving cocaine and MDMA to a baby might be a bad idea.

The show clearly exaggerates bad parenting in order to parody it, to wring humor from the extremely inappropriate behavior of its parents. Underlying the parody, however, is an undeniably dark view of the conventional nuclear family. The father is an incompetent dolt who engages in child abuse. The Griffin family members don't support each other, but, rather, they do terrible, violent things to one another. In this episode, Peter is thrown through a plate-glass window by his other son, Chris (Seth Green), with little provocation, and later Peter generates a live wolf with a 3D printer to attack Chris. In both instances, the characters appear battered and bloodied, but no remorse is shown for either attack. "The Peanut Butter Kid" ends with the parents regretting their behavior toward Stewie, but the damage has already been done.

Stewie admits, "That acting stuff was a bit much for me, but I did quite enjoy the dancing and the cocaine." The scene then flashes forward to a future in which Stewie is a heavily tattooed weight lifter, addicted to cocaine. *Family Guy* presents a world in which family life is perverse, brutal, and abusive. Its many layers of parody still cannot effectively counteract this negative perspective on family life. The PTC tends to focus on specific instances of indecency in the program, but it's clear that they should be fundamentally appalled by the show's representation of the American family.

Family life is equally troubled on the drama that overlapped with *Family Guy* on our sample Sunday night. In the *Secrets and Lies* episode from that night, "The Racket," two brothers are at each other's throats because one, Eric (Michael Ealy), erroneously believes the other, Patrick (Charlie Barnett), killed his wife, Kate (Jordana Brewster). In fact, the entire second season of *Secrets and Lies* is about a family in severe crisis. Brother is pitted against brother, and, by the time of the season's finale, we learn that the brothers' father was a bigamist with a secret second family and that, furthermore, Eric accidentally killed his own mother while he was a child—pushing her down a staircase while trying to protect his sister, Amanda (Mekia Cox). Even worse, it is eventually revealed that the murderer of Eric's wife is not his brother—or his stepbrother from his father's other family—but instead it is actually Amanda. The season finale reveals that she and Kate were in a shoving match on a roof and Kate fell to her death. *Secrets and Lies* is a melodrama—a genre known for conflict among family members. In a sitcom such as *Family Guy*, bad behavior has few consequences; when people do wrong in a melodrama, they are punished for it. The finale of *Secrets and Lies'* second season follows the conventions of its genre. Most of the evildoers are in jail or under arrest and most, but not all, feel remorse for their actions. In the episode shown during our sample Sunday night, however, the final reckoning is still two episodes off. Instead, in this episode we are presented with arguments and conflicts within a wealthy, successful family. The episode suggests that the elite American family is breaking apart, that money and success inevitably lead to secrets and lies.

Our sample Sunday night contains a show that contradicts the bitterly satiric and darkly melodramatic representations of the family in *Family Guy* and *Secrets and Lies*, respectively. *Bob's Burgers* centers on members of a middle-class family—mother, father, and three kids—who run a small hamburger restaurant. In this show, the nuclear family is far from disintegrating, dysfunctional, or oppressive. There may be occasional friction within its quirky family, but in the final analysis family provides an enclave, a safety zone, of affection and nurturing. "The Last Gingerbread House on the Left" episode, which aired on our sample Sunday, tells two Christmas stories and emphasizes the Belcher family's low economic status and lack of funds for gifts. It begins with the kids obsessing greedily over gifts and the father, Bob (H. Jon Benjamin), feeling very anxious about their long wish lists. The mother, Linda (John Roberts), tries to cheer him up, which leads to this exchange:

Linda: "Know what the greatest gift of all is? Family!"
Bob: "*You* say that to the kids with a straight face."
Linda: "Yeah, I know. I was just trying it out. What about 'Christmas is for closers'?"
Bob: "Um, needs a little work."

After gently poking fun at the common Christmas homily that family is the greatest gift, the episode tracks two story arcs. Bob attends a strange gingerbread-house competition hosted by his landlord, Calvin Fischoeder (Kevin Kline), while Linda, the kids, and their friend Teddy (Larry Murphy) go caroling in an unfamiliar neighborhood. The participants in the competition refer to themselves as the "Gingerbread Gentlemen"—an eccentric group of wealthy men with no emotional attachment to their families. When Bob asks them what their Christmas plans are, one replies, "I'm going to treat myself to a new penis!" The Gingerbread Gentlemen wind up destroying each other's gingerbread houses in a blaze of gunfire and Bob wins the competition by default. The prize is a special visit to the local zoo to cuddle with a rare albino polar bear, which Bob shares with his kids and thus provides them with the "best Christmas ever," as Linda exclaims. Bob provides the final moral of the episode, though, when he addresses the Gingerbread Gentlemen at the end of the competition (sentimental music underscores the scene): "Under that rich loner exterior, you're all a bunch of softies who care about each other. You're like a weird little family.... I mean, it may sound cheesy, but you know what the greatest gift of all is? Family." *Bob's Burgers* contains genuine moments of sentiment, even though it hedges its bets slightly—as when Bob qualifies his sentiment by saying, "it may sound cheesy." Still, it would be accurate to say that the Belchers signify much that is positive about the conventional nuclear family structure. *Bob's Burgers* often tells stories of the family members' misadventures that, in the end, confirm their love and affection for one another.

If we assemble *Family Guy*, *Bob's Burgers*, and *Secrets and Lies* as a group—as elements within an evening's flow of linear television in a hypothetical household—we can identify stories that confirm "family values" as well as those that radically subvert them. If we add *The Simpsons* to this list, we'll find a show that has an ambivalent relationship to the conventional nuclear family. Much like *Family Guy*, which has been accused of plagiarizing *The Simpsons*, *The Simpsons* has numerous examples of bad parenting and children misbehaving. Indeed, in its 620 episodes (and counting!), one can imagine few terrible things that Homer (Dan Castellaneta), Marge (Julie Kavner), Bart (Nancy Cartwright), Lisa (Yeardley Smith), and Maggie have *not* done to each other—especially if one includes the show's annual, bloody Halloween specials. This has led some conservatives to condemn the program. Early in its run, Republican president George H. W. Bush singled it out, contending that "We're going to keep trying to strengthen the American family, to make them more like the Waltons [from a homespun TV show of the '70s] and less like the Simpsons."[10] However, a more nuanced viewing of *The Simpsons* reveals a mother who is a thoughtful, caring parent, although she must often undo the parenting catastrophes caused by her husband. And the Simpsons' middle child, Lisa, is a voice of reason that is frequently counterposed to Bart's unruliness.

"Orange Is the New Yellow," the episode rerun on our Sunday night, illustrates these dynamics when Marge, the responsible parent, is wrongly accused of being a negligent mother because she allows Bart to go to the playground unsupervised. In a direct critique of overly protective laws and policies regarding the safety of children, she is incarcerated for her "crime." Ironically, she enjoys her time in prison as it gives her a break from the drudgery of housework and childcare. Of course, Homer quickly proves to be incompetent at taking care of the kids on his own. As he explains in court, he is an awful father—so terrible that his "email password is 'bad dad.'" Eventually, Marge returns home to a family that is freshly appreciative of all she does. In an image of family love, they all wind up together, hugging in their pantry (Figure 1.2). In this manner, *The Simpsons* is able to contain seemingly contradictory meanings (good parenting vs. bad parenting) within a single episode.

As this small portion of the television flow illustrates, network-era television contradicts itself frequently and haphazardly. It presents many heterogeneous meanings in any one night's viewing. This polysemy contributes to television's broad appeal. As Lauren Graham, an actor in the family-centered program *Gilmore Girls*, has said, that program's "strength is that it's a family

Figure 1.2 The Simpsons share a moment of family togetherness after Marge is released from prison for the "crime" of letting her children play unsupervised.

show that does not pander or condescend to families. It's not so soft that your grandmother could watch it with her dentures out."[11] That, in a nutshell, illustrates the power of polysemy: conflicting meanings reside within the same program and facilitate the viewing pleasure of a broad range of individuals. With so many different meanings being signified, we are bound to find some that agree with our world view. Does this mean that television can mean anything to anyone? And how are these meanings constructed? Three axioms will guide our approach to linear television.

Axiom 1

A segment of the television flow, whether it be an individual program, a commercial, a newscast, or an entire evening's viewing, may be thought of as a television **text**—offering a multiplicity of meanings or polysemy. We may interpret the Belchers' actions as signifying, among other things, "an unconventional family can nurture loving relationships." In its broadest sense, a "text" is any phenomenon that pulls together elements that have meaning for readers or viewers or spectators who encounter it. Just as we read and interpret a book's organization of words in sentences, so we view and interpret a television program's sequence of sounds and images. Thus, narrative and non-narrative structures, lighting and set design, camera style, editing and sound design, and so on, may be thought of as television's textual elements—those basic building blocks that the makers of television use to communicate with their audience. This book will present ways for students to better understand how these textual devices mount potential meanings for the viewer's consideration.

Axiom 2

The television text does not present all meanings equally positively or strongly. Through dialogue, acting styles, music, and other attributes of the text, television emphasizes some meanings and de-emphasizes others. When the Simpsons family is seen hugging in a closet, the text is obviously suggesting that family togetherness and generational harmony are positive meanings. But although television is polysemic, not all meanings are equal. TV is not unstructured or infinitely meaningful. Or, as John Fiske writes, "[Television's] polysemic potential is neither boundless nor structureless: the text delineates the terrain within which meanings may be made or proffers some meanings more than others."[12] The crucial work of television studies is to analyze the medium's hierarchy of meanings. Which meanings does the text stress? *How* are they stressed? These are key questions for the television critic. To answer them requires an awareness of the cultural codes of class, gender, race, and such that predominate in a society. As Stuart Hall has noted, "Any society/culture tends, with varying degrees of closure, to impose its classifications of the social and cultural and political world. This constitutes a *dominant cultural order*, though it is neither univocal nor uncontested."[13] Television always has been a medium encoded with the meanings prevalent in the society to which it appeals. In contemporary American society, many meanings circulate, but some are given greater weight than others by the dominant cultural order. Correspondingly, although television is polysemic, it must be stressed that it is a **structured polysemy**. There is a pattern or structure implicit in the meanings that are offered on television. That structure tends to support those who hold positions of economic and political power in a particular society, but there is always room for contrary meanings.

Axiom 3

The act of viewing television is one in which the **discourses** of the viewer encounter those of the text. "Discourse" is a term that can have many meanings. We will here rely on Fiske's definition:

> a language or system of representation that has developed socially in order to make and circulate a coherent set of meanings about an important topic area. These meanings serve the interests of that section of society within which the discourse originates.[14]

But what does he mean by this? Let's examine his definition in detail.

Fiske's discourse is a group or "set" of meanings: for example, a working-class discourse might include the meanings "unions protect workers' rights," "capitalists are evil," "the economy is based on workers' labor," and so on. Discourses contain meanings that arise from a certain segment or section of society. Unions and other representatives of workers, for example, are sources of many meanings associated with working-class discourse, and those meanings serve their interests. Thus, we come to a TV text with belief structures—discourses—shaped by the social environment in which we grew up: schooling, religion, family, class, gender. And the TV text, too, has meaning structures that are governed by ideology and television-specific conventions. When we "read" the text, our discourses overlay those of the text. Sometimes they fit well, and sometimes they don't.

Discourses do not advertise themselves as such. As Fiske suggests, discourse "works ideologically to naturalize those meanings into common sense."[15] He contends that the dominant discourse is so pervasive that it disappears into common sense, into the taken-for-granted. Consider the common presumption that in America everyone can become financially successful if they work hard enough. Most Americans believe this to be a truth, "just" common sense—despite the fact that statistics show that the economic class and education level of your parents virtually guarantees whether or not you'll succeed financially. The notion of "success for all" thus has a rather tenuous connection to the real world of work. However, it has a very strong connection to the discourse of corporate capitalism. If workers, even very poor workers, believe they may succeed if they work hard, then they will struggle to do good work and not dispute the basic economic system. So we may see that the commonsensical "truth" of the Horatio Alger success story is a fundamental part of a dominant discourse. As critics of television it is our responsibility to examine these normally unexamined ideals.

Interruption and Sequence

Up to now we have depicted television as a continuous flow of sounds and images and meanings, but it is equally important to recognize the discontinuous component of linear TV watching and of TV itself—the ebb to its flow.

On the Sunday-night grid in Table 1.1, we can move horizontally across the table and see, obviously, that an evening's schedule is interrupted every half hour or hour with different programs. One program's progression is halted by the next program, which is halted by the next and the next. Within programs the flow is frequently interrupted by advertisements and announcements and the like. And on an even smaller level, within narrative programs' storylines there tend to be many interruptions. A melodrama such as *Secrets and Lies*, for example, often presents scenes in which characters are interrupted just as they are about to commit murder, discover their father's second family, or consummate a romance that has been developing for months or years.

The point is that linear television is constantly interrupting itself. Although the flow that gushes from our TV sets is continuously television texts, it is not continuously the same type of texts. There are narrative texts and non-narrative texts and texts of advertising and information and advice, and on and on it goes. Furthermore, we as viewers often interrupt ourselves while watching television. We leave the viewing area to visit the kitchen or the bathroom. Our attention drifts as we check Snapchat or Twitter or argue with friends and family. We doze.

All of these forms of interruption—from television's self-interruptions to the interruptions we perform while watching—are not a perversion of the TV-viewing experience. Rather, they *define* that experience. This is not to suggest, however, that television does not try to combat the breaks in its flow. Clearly, advertisers and networks want viewers to overcome television's fragmentary nature and continue watching their particular commercials/programs. To this end,

Table 1.1 Sunday, November 27, 2016, Prime-Time Schedule CST, Broadcast Networks

<table>
<tr><th>Network</th><th>6:00</th><th>6:30</th><th>7:00</th><th>7:30</th><th>8:00</th><th>8:30</th><th>9:00</th><th>9:30</th></tr>
<tr><td>ABC</td><td colspan="2">America's Funniest Home Videos</td><td colspan="2">Once Upon a Time…</td><td colspan="2">Secrets and Lies</td><td colspan="2">Quantico</td></tr>
<tr><td>CBS</td><td>NFL Overtime</td><td colspan="2">60 Minutes</td><td colspan="2">NCIS: Los Angeles</td><td colspan="2">Madam Secretary</td><td>Elementary (until 10:30)</td></tr>
<tr><td>Fox</td><td>Ice Age: A Mammoth Christmas</td><td>Bob's Burgers</td><td>The Simpsons</td><td>Son of Zorn</td><td>Family Guy</td><td>The Last Man on Earth</td><td>Local News</td><td>Local News</td></tr>
<tr><td>NBC</td><td colspan="2">Football Night in America</td><td colspan="6">Sunday Night Football</td></tr>
<tr><td>PBS</td><td colspan="4">Masterpiece Classic: Downton Abbey</td><td colspan="2">Masterpiece: Poldark</td><td colspan="2">Inside Poldark (until 10:30)</td></tr>
<tr><td>CW</td><td>The Big Bang Theory</td><td>The Big Bang Theory</td><td colspan="5">To Catch a Thief (1955 movie)</td><td>2 Broke Girls</td></tr>
</table>

storylines, music, visual design, and dialogue must maintain our attention to hold us through the commercial breaks, to quell the desire to check out another channel, or, worse still, to turn off the TV or wholly direct our attention to our phone's screen.

In today's atmosphere of proliferating screens and constant distraction, interruptions have become more intrusive and more frequent; but they were also a part of television during the time when the broadcast networks were predominant. Many of the strategies used by network television to keep our eyes glued to the TV screen are still implemented in the contemporary media environment where video-on-demand has radically disrupted the premise of television flow. When viewers actively seek programs and *pull* them down to their screens, the traditional linear flow that networks *pushed* toward us during their primacy is ruptured and has to be reinvented. YouTube and other VOD services, for example, immediately transition into a new video when the one you're watching ends. This is one example of a twenty-first-century form of flow. In our next chapter, Amanda D. Lotz will further consider how the ascendency of Internet-delivery technology has significantly altered, but not destroyed, what Spigel calls network-era TV's "industrial formations, government policies, and practices of looking."[16]

Segmentation

Network-era television's discontinuous nature led to a particular way of packaging narrative, informational, and commercial material that persists and is heightened by the abundance of screens in today's media environment. The overall flow of television is segmented into small parcels, which often bear little logical connection to one another. A shampoo commercial might follow a *Family Guy* scene and lead into a station identification. One segment of television does not necessarily link with the next in a chain of cause and effect. In Fiske's view, "[Television] is composed of a rapid succession of compressed, vivid segments where the principle of logic and cause and effect is subordinated to that of association and consequence to sequence."[17] That is, fairly random association and sequence—rather than cause and effect and consequence—govern TV's flow.

TV's segmental nature peaks in the 30-second (and shorter) advertisement, but it is evident in all types of programs. News programs are compartmentalized into news, weather, and sports segments, then further subdivided into individual 90-second (and shorter) "packages" or stories. Game shows play rounds of a fixed, brief duration. Narrative programs must structure their stories so that a segment can fit neatly within the commercial breaks. After all, to the television industry, programs are just filler, a necessary inconvenience interrupting the true function of television: broadcasting commercials.

The construction of these television segments and their relationship to each other are two major concerns of television's advertisers, producers, and programmers. For it is on this level that the battle for our *continuing* attention is won or lost. We should also be mindful of TV's segmental structure because it determines much of how stories are told, information presented, and commodities advertised on linear television. Moreover, video has only become shorter and more segmented when presented on Internet-delivered television—as YouTube's reliance on short videos confirms.

Summary

Television flow—Raymond Williams's term for television's sequence of diverse fragments of narrative, information, and advertising—defines the medium's fundamental structure during the network era and in our current experience of linear television. This flow facilitates the multiplicity of meanings, or polysemy, that television broadcasts.

Our consideration of television flow grows from three rudimentary axioms:

1. Television texts (programs, commercials, entire blocks of television time) contain meanings.
2. Not all meanings are presented equally. Textual devices emphasize some meanings over others and thus offer a hierarchy of meanings to the viewer. TV's polysemy is structured by the dominant cultural order into discourses (systems of belief).
3. The experience of television watching brings the discourses of the viewer into contact with the discourses of the text.

Linear television flow is riddled with interruptions, despite its progression of one thing after another. TV continually interrupts itself, shifting from one text to the next. And as often as the text interrupts itself, so too do we disrupt our consumption of television with trips out of the room or simple inattention. These constant interruptions lead linear television to adopt a segmented structure, constructing portions of TV in such a way as to encourage viewer concentration.

The aspiration of this book is to analyze television's production of meaning. We set aside the evaluation of television programs for the time being in order to focus on TV's structured polysemy and the systems that contribute to its creation: narrative and non-narrative structures, mise-en-scene, camera style, editing, sound. The chapters that follow analyze television's implementation of that polysemy and those systems—recognizing its roots in the network era but aware of how network-era conventions have been disrupted in the twenty-first century. An important challenge to linear television's supremacy is currently evolving: the potential for viewers' increased interactivity and agency in a video-on-demand media environment. We believe that much of what holds true for network-era television will also hold true for future mutations of it. There is, of course, no way of knowing for sure, but in the next chapter Amanda D. Lotz provides some thoughts on where television is now and where it is going.

Notes

1 "Nielsen Estimates 118.4 Million TV Homes in the U.S. for the 2016–17 TV Season," August 26, 2016, *Nielsen*, tvcrit.com/find/nielsen2016, accessed November 22, 2016. "Nielsen's national definition of a TV household states that homes must have at least one operable TV/monitor with the ability to deliver video via traditional means of antennae, cable set-top-box or satellite receiver and/or with a broadband connection."

2 "Number of TV Households in the United States from Season 2000–2001 to Season 2016–2017 (in Millions)," *Statista*, tvcrit.com/find/tvhouseholds, accessed December 23, 2016.

3 Lynn Spigel, "Introduction," *Television After TV: Essays on a Medium in Transition* (Durham, NC: Duke University Press, 2004), 1.

4 John Ellis, *Seeing Things: Television in the Age of Uncertainty* (London: I. B. Taurus, 2000).

5 Raymond Williams, *Television: Technology and Cultural Form* (New York: Schocken, 1974), 86.

6 Dan Quayle, "Address to the Commonwealth Club of California (On Family Values)," May 19, 1992, *Vice President Dan Quayle*, tvcrit.com/find/quayle, accessed December 22, 2010.

7 "General Information," The American Family Association, January 13, 2006, tvcrit.com/find/afa. They continue:

> For example, over the last 25 years we have seen the entertainment industry 'normalize' and glorify premarital sex. During that time we have suffered a dramatic increase in teen pregnancies, sexually transmitted diseases such as AIDS and abortion as a means of birth control.
>
> (Ibid.)

8 For example, a form at the following URL is populated with complaint data about a *Family Guy* episode from November 10, 2013 titled "A Fistful of Meg."

9 "The Peanut Butter Kid" was the 11th episode of *Family Guy*'s 14th season. It was originally broadcast on Fox on January 10, 2016, and rerun during the 15th season on November 27, 2016.
10 Nick Griffiths, "America's First Family," *The Times Magazine*, vol. 5, no. 16 (April 15 2000), pp. 25, 27–28.
11 Ibid.
12 John Fiske, *Television Culture*, Second Edition (London: Routledge, 2011; originally published in 1987), 15–16.
13 Stuart Hall, "Encoding/Decoding," in *Culture, Media, Language*, Stuart Hall, Dorothy Hobson, Andre Lowe, Paul Willis, eds. (London: Hutchinson, 1980), 134.
14 Fiske, 14.
15 Ibid.
16 Spigel, 2.
17 Fiske, 105.

Further Readings

The basic principle of television flow stems from Raymond Williams, *Television: Technology and Cultural Form* (New York: Schocken, 1974). This short book is one of the fundamental building blocks of contemporary television studies.

John Corner, *Critical Ideas in Television Studies* (Oxford: Clarendon Press, 1999), devotes an entire chapter to the notion of flow. John Fiske, *Television Culture*, Second Edition (London: Routledge, 2011; originally published in 1987), and John Ellis, *Visible Fictions: Cinema: Television: Video* (Boston: Routledge, 1992), both elaborate upon the concept. Fiske is also concerned with articulating television's meanings and how they may be organized into discourses. Todd Gitlin confronts television's role in advocating a society's dominant or "hegemonic" discourse in "Prime Time Ideology: The Hegemonic Process in Television Entertainment" in *Television: The Critical View*, Horace Newcomb, ed. (New York: Oxford University Press, 2000), 574–94.

Further discussion of how meaning is produced in television texts may be found in the writings of British television scholars associated with the Centre for Contemporary Cultural Studies (University of Birmingham, England). This school of analysis is summarized in Fiske's *Television Culture* and in his "British Cultural Studies and Television" chapter in *Channels of Discourse, Reassembled*, Robert C. Allen, ed. (Chapel Hill: University of North Carolina Press, 1992). Students interested in the seminal work in this area should read Stuart Hall, "Encoding/Decoding," in *Culture, Media, Language*, Stuart Hall, Dorothy Hobson, Andrew Lowe, Paul Willis, eds. (London: Hutchinson, 1980).

The implications of Dan Quayle's comments about Murphy Brown are examined in Rebecca L. Walkowitz, "Reproducing Reality: Murphy Brown and Illegitimate Politics," in *Feminist Television Criticism*, Charlotte Brunsdon, Julie D'Acci, Lynn Spigel, eds. (New York: Clarendon, 1997). Walkowitz is concerned with the ideology of "family values" and the representation of women working in television news.

2 Television in the Contemporary Media Environment

Amanda D. Lotz

Television, and understandings of television, have evolved a lot in just a few years. It is easy to think that this change in television is a recent development or that recent changes are far more significant than those of the past. The ability to distribute television using Internet protocols has unquestionably introduced sizable, maybe even revolutionary, change to television, but it is also important to keep in mind that television changed considerably during the 50 or so years before Internet distribution as well.

The core of this recent change, as suggested in the first chapter, has been television's expansion from being available only as a flow of programming provided by a few networks that viewers could not control to one that has steadily allowed greater *choice* of programming and *control* over when and where its programming is viewed. As the final section of this chapter discusses, it is even the case that creating "television" has become possible for those outside the television industry.

Although television networks tried to enforce a "flow" of viewing that kept viewers tuned to their channel, various technological developments have made this task more difficult. The remote control first made it easier for viewers to deviate from a network's chosen flow, though of course the viewer still experienced a sequence of programs as a flow. The remote made it easier for viewers to select—or choose among—bits and pieces from that flow. Remote controls, videocassette recorders (VCRs), and basic cable all became common in U.S. homes in the 1980s and brought the first disruption to networks' scheduling practices and control over how viewers experienced television. DVDs and DVRs then expanded viewers' capabilities and choices in the early 2000s.

On-demand access to television introduced a more profound break from these earlier norms of the television experience around 2010. **Video-on-demand** (VOD)—or technologies that allow viewers to select a video from a library of programs and have it delivered to their set upon request—was technologically possible for cable services in the early 2000s. It largely went unused for over a decade, however, because networks and studios were unwilling to make current shows available. As a result, pay-per-view movies were the most common form of on-demand content for the first decade of this technology's availability.

Also by 2010, the capacity to distribute television programming using Internet protocols that allow on-demand distribution using the Internet rather than the VOD offered by cable providers became significant. This was the year that Netflix introduced its streaming service and HBO enabled its subscribers to access its library of programs using HBO Go. As the new competitors such as Netflix and Hulu began to change the competitive landscape, by 2013 networks and studios allowed episodes of their current season of programs to populate cable services' VOD libraries.

These technologies allow a considerable change in viewers' experience of television time. Now, when viewers sit before their television sets and mobile devices, they do not have to choose programming from what is showing at that time (as someone with a traditional remote control does). Rather, they choose from a library of programming and construct their own schedule. Beyond the ability to select programs, we now largely take for granted further abilities, such as the ability to pause or rewind programs.

Of course there was considerable experimentation with Internet-distributed television in the first decade of the twenty-first century, but it involved mostly failed experiments or noncommercial endeavors. During these years television viewers also grew familiar with downloading songs and reading blogs and newspapers distributed online. But uncertainty about how the Internet would affect television persisted. As the last chapter notes, the common expectation was that the Internet would "kill" television. Some even forecast that the videos shot by ordinary people might destroy the television industry when YouTube gained popularity and its amateur videos attracted attention.

By 2018 it no longer seemed likely that amateur creators would overthrow the professional television industry, but YouTube certainly created a new sector of the television industry. It became clear that as far as video was concerned, the Internet wasn't really a medium—a thing—like television or radio but more a mechanism for sending, sharing, and accessing messages. Those messages might be texts, web pages, MP3s, or television shows. Rather, the Internet was more comparable to *distribution technologies* such as over-the-air broadcasting or wired cable delivery than the *medium* of television, with its schedule of programs.

Internet-distributed television—such as the series delivered by Netflix, Hulu, and Amazon Video—may seem very different from television because of the difference in viewers' relationship to the content. The ability to choose what to watch is much different than being limited to what is on, but there is also considerable commonality across network television shows. Of course most of the series watched on these Internet-distributed services were created for a broadcast network or cable channel. And the series created for these services, such as *Transparent*, *13 Reasons Why*, and *Stranger Things*, look and feel very much like television. The differences in how we access and experience Internet-distributed television—the ability to search libraries, the services' recommendation engines, and their ability to offer viewers personalized displays, as shown in Figure 2.1—introduce new questions to the study of television and issues to consider. They require reconsideration of concepts such as flow and of the ability of networks to lead audiences from one program to another (see Chapter 1), but they haven't yet fundamentally changed the nature of television shows.

Internet-Distributed Television: Digital Endemic and Legacy Media

New communication services have developed quickly in recent decades. Often **legacy-media** industries—those industries that existed before digital distribution—provided these services, while others are **digital endemic**—or those that exist only in digital form. For example, the CBS television network is an example of a legacy-media service. Notably, its owner, CBS Corporation, has also entered into Internet distribution of its content with the CBS All Access service. In contrast, we'd likely classify Netflix as digital endemic because it did not have a stake in the legacy media of the broadcast or cable television industries.

The pace of new services and technologies, and increasing blending among legacy and digital-endemic media, has led to a lot of confusion. Media companies, viewers/users, and creators have muddled through nearly 20 years of perpetual change. Though there is much more

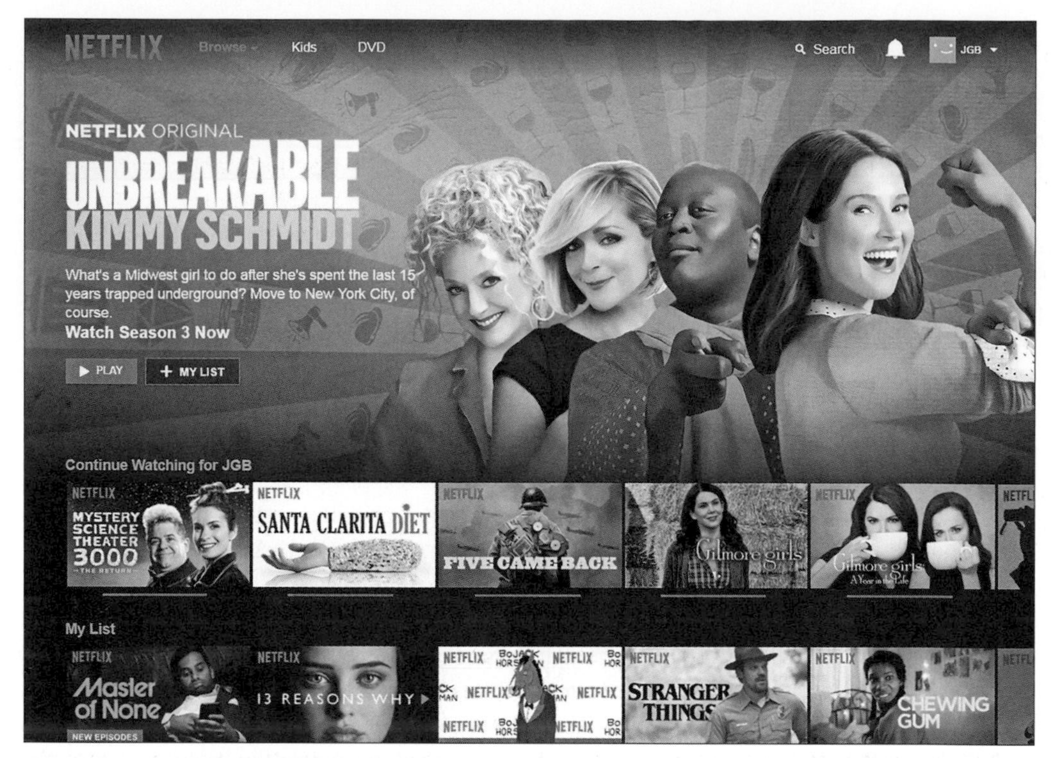

Figure 2.1 Internet-distributed television services such as Netflix display viewing options very differently from the linear schedule listings (as seen in Table 1.1). This image from Netflix features information about the show *Unbreakable Kimmie Schmidt* as well as other personalized suggestions from its library of shows.

change to come, we can now develop understandings of how digital distribution has initially changed television.

Starting out, it is helpful to be clear about what "digital" means and why digital distribution has been so disruptive to legacy-media industries. Digital technologies speak in a common language of ones and zeros and have different capabilities than analog media. Legacy-media industries developed based on analog media and their capabilities and limitations. Many facets of television have been significantly affected by digital technologies. Later, in Chapter 9, we'll discuss digital cameras and production techniques that changed as a result of switching from film cameras. In this chapter, we are focused on digital distribution—and a very particular aspect of digital distribution. In the twenty-first century, nearly all television is transmitted digitally—whether by digital broadcast signal, digital cable, or Internet. The most consequential of these digital distribution technologies is that of using Internet protocols because this technology enables viewer selection rather than a set schedule of programming.

Over-the-air broadcast signals, cable wires, and satellite transmissions are different technologies that have been used to distribute television shows. For the most part, these technologies can send only one message—or show—at a time, a technological limitation that led to television being organized by a schedule. Networks, channels, and stations were needed to organize that schedule, and, over the decades, the programmers who devised schedules developed extensive knowledge about different practices that would best draw and maintain viewers.

Video distributed by Internet was initially perceived as more separate from television than it actually was. Most people first encountered Internet-distributed video from YouTube. In these early years, some of the most watched videos were things like a delirious 5-year-old returning from a dentist appointment and other such personal videos. In fact, the very first video uploaded to the service, posted on April 23, 2005, was a home movie of one of its founders, Jawed Karim, at the San Diego Zoo (tvcrit.com/find/karim). Soon after its launch, YouTube also permitted the uploading of clips of television shows, films, and music videos—many of which attracted the attention of copyright attorneys. At first, there wasn't much advertiser funding in YouTube, but advertising eventually became quite lucrative and enabled the financial success of stars such as Bethany Mota and Hank Green, who created a new commercial television industry sector by distributing self-made videos.

Before Internet-distributed television became common, many who studied television wondered whether shows and videos watched on a screen other than a television set would still be "television." At that time, the most common household screens were television sets and desktop computer monitors—which partly explains why television on a screen other than a television set seemed so difficult to comprehend. As it happened, just as services such as HBO and Netflix began using the Internet to distribute content recognized as "television" in 2010, Apple introduced the iPad tablet, laptop sales overtook those of desktop computers, and smartphones—introduced three years earlier—grew increasingly common. Despite a decade of considerable uncertainty about what would happen to television once compression technologies made it easy for long-form video files to be streamed, in 2010 new screen technologies and services for distributing television programming made the transition to viewing television on many possible screens seamless.

Understandings of television and its relationship to new media consequently began to change in 2010 for these two reasons. New screen technology such as tablets and smartphones expanded the screens for viewing, and legacy and digital-endemic companies began delivering programs people wanted to watch on these devices.

Internet-distributed television came later to the U.S. than other places. The BBC launched its iPlayer service—somewhat like Netflix, but with only recent BBC content—in 2007. As a public service broadcaster, the BBC realized that making its programs easier to access was part of its mission. In the U.S., studios were terrified of eroding the revenue that could be earned from selling television series in various domestic and international **release windows** and locked down programs from Internet distribution. A viewer in the U.S. would be lucky to find clips from favorite shows on cbs.com or abc.com; finding a whole episode was rare until Hulu launched in 2008.

Netflix dominated the early years of Internet-distributed television in the U.S., though, in these years, most continued to think of it as separate from television. Of course Netflix began as a film on DVD by-mail service and continued to distribute films after focusing its streaming business more on television (as of summer 2016, 70 percent of content streamed by Netflix was television). Netflix and Amazon Video became important distributors of both film and television and further blurred increasingly porous boundaries between these two once-distinct industries.

Importantly, both companies soon moved beyond merely distributing content and began making or licensing original programs. Both recognized that businesses based only on redistributing programs produced for other networks wasn't sustainable in the long run and began financing production of original television series as early as 2011. By the time a significant number of viewers became accustomed to using Netflix to watch television shows—whether those it licensed after they were developed for another channel, such as *Mad Men*, or those original series it paid to have created, such as *House of Cards*—it became clear that Netflix was certainly part of television.

But I Don't Have a TV

Probably the biggest changes introduced by Internet-distributed video are in how and where we now view television. Distribution technologies such as broadcast signals were capable of sending only one "message" at a time. What made broadcast television—like radio before it—a "mass medium" was its ability to transmit a signal that carried a show to anyone with a receiving device that was within range. Each station's transmitter could deliver one show at a time to those with sets in range of receiving the signal. These broadcast technologies had expanded from point-to-point technologies such as the telegraph or telephone, which could transmit messages over a distance but only from one sender to one receiver. Broadcast technologies' limited capacity of sending a single signal required creating a schedule to organize the content transmitted (see Table 1.1). Also, someone needed to develop that schedule. As a result, stations and networks became important gatekeepers of television through their work deciding what would be on television and when it would air.

Broadcasting's technological attribute of scarcity—being limited to sending a single signal to all—led to many norms of television that came to seem inherent to the medium itself, although they were actually characteristic of television as distributed by broadcast signal. These technological features then combined with business strategies and regulatory policy to create the norms of the network era. Networks developed to take advantage of **economies of scale** that motivated broadcasters to seek as broad an audience as possible to sell to advertisers. Also, the Federal Communications Commission organized the broadcast spectrum to allow for only two VHF channels in each area. Though additional UHF stations could be licensed, the inferior quality of the UHF spectrum and the inability of many sets to receive them discouraged competition.

Internet distribution, in contrast, has different capabilities from other technologies that have been used to distribute television. It doesn't have the same capacity limitations. Internet communication can be one-to-one—as in the case of an email or a text—or one-to-many—as in the case of popular sites or widely shared tweets. But Internet transmission also allows different signals to be sent in that one-to-many communication, as when Netflix sends different shows, started at different times, to its many subscribers, making an "on demand" experience possible.

Internet-distributed television isn't restricted to a schedule—anything can be "on" at any time. Consequently, Internet-distributed services develop libraries of content instead of schedules. Such libraries still need organization. Just as channels and networks organize broadcast and cable distribution, **portals** such as Netflix, HBO Now, Amazon Video, and many others organize Internet-distributed television. Like channels and networks, portals select the content available in their service—whether paying for its creation (*Orange Is the New Black*) or licensing content previously created for a network or channel. In addition to curating a library of programming, technological attributes that allow different user experiences also distinguish portals. For example, many portals automatically play the next episode or pick up from where a viewer left off when they log in.

The business strategies of portals differ from networks and channels in many ways. We are in an early time of considerable experimentation and strategy building that makes it difficult to be certain which of today's practices are preliminary trials and which may become established norms. Still, it is clear that changes in distribution technology have encouraged adjustments and experiments with form and storytelling found on television, as will be discussed in the next chapter.

In many cases, the portals don't differ from broadcasting and cable only in terms of their distribution technology; they also rely on a different—or previously uncommon—revenue model. Many of the most common portals are subscriber funded. Viewers pay a monthly fee for access to the program library rather than having advertisers subsidize the program costs in exchange for viewers' attention. Subscriber-funded television is not new—HBO and Showtime have used this revenue model for more than a quarter of a century. But it is very different from the advertiser-supported norm that has dominated U.S. linear television.

Even though we can see how NBC, HBO, and Netflix all provide television, the different ways they make money lead them to be surprisingly different businesses. Advertiser-supported television services, such as broadcast and cable networks that air commercials, are foremost concerned with creating programming that will attract audiences that can be sold to advertisers. As a result, they develop programs with the aim of finding content that will gather the most advertiser-desired viewers; advertisers typically insert commercials into the midst of those programs.

In contrast, subscriber-funded services, whether cable channels such as HBO and Showtime or Internet-distributed services such as Netflix and Amazon Video, must provide programming of such value that people are willing to pay for it directly. This often leads to different programs and programming strategies than are typical of advertiser-supported television. This difference was particularly apparent in the late 1990s when HBO began making original television series that were unlike those on broadcast television. Subscriber-funded services need to provide programs unlike those that viewers find for "free" on advertiser-supported television, or they won't pay for the service. To entice subscribers, the subscriber-funded portals offer a distinctive, on-demand viewing experience and often distinctive programs as well.

Notably, a portal such as YouTube differs significantly from subscriber-funded portals. Rather than a deliberately curated library, YouTube functions more like an "open access" portal—meaning it is a distribution service that allows users to share content rather than the portal itself seeking out and curating the content it makes available. As a result, it functions more like social media that rely on behaviors like sharing, liking, and following that aren't as characteristic of broadcast or cable television or even that distributed by Netflix. YouTube also doesn't significantly invest in the cost of creating or licensing videos, which also makes its business model very different from those of other portals. Creating programs is very expensive, and avoiding these costs has allowed it to be advertiser-supported and profitable.

Television increasingly must be understood to be made up of many different sectors based on the technologies that distribute its content and the revenue models that support it. These industrial characteristics are important because they set the parameters of the programming that is created.

We Can All Make Television

Among the changes and blurred distinctions introduced by digital production and distribution technologies is an expansion of who can make and share television. Digital camera technologies have made sophisticated recording devices more affordable and accessible than film technology ever could. Many of these technologies have become ubiquitous, even embedded in the mobile phones we now carry in our pockets every day. The greater accessibility of recording devices and open access portals such as YouTube for sharing recordings have created a vast world of an abundance of things to watch.

Initially, lines were drawn between "amateur" and "professional" in sorting content. A video of your cat was amateur content, but a music video or a clip from a late night show was professional. But as YouTube grew in popularity, various stages in between these amateur and professional poles developed. Soon, new storytellers emerged that drew sizable fan bases to their so-called amateur videos. Some earned substantial advertising revenue from YouTube and also sponsorship support that made their enterprises difficult to classify as amateur. Yet this content is also distinctive from the content produced by the elaborate infrastructure associated with the professional industry.

An open access distribution technology such as YouTube expands the boundaries of television in important ways. Though new industrial sectors have emerged that must be considered in relation to the businesses of broadcast stations and cable channels, YouTube has also created an important nonindustrial space. Creators can share videos that are simply art for art's sake—not aimed at any commercial goal. This is very important for community building and activism and for helping groups still invisible in commercial television to tell their stories.

At this point, few shared understandings or classifications of Internet-distributed television exist—arguably because the sector of the industry reliant on YouTube remains very dynamic. In the coming years, media scholars will continue to discuss and debate structures for understanding the practices and relationships characteristic of emerging sectors of media industries. Importantly, we must not use technology alone to categorize different industrial sectors. Revenue models, whether based on subscriber funding, advertiser support, or, more common outside the U.S., public service funding, all lead to very different opportunities and outcomes for what we see on our screens. Flexibility in thinking and categorization is helpful in periods of such pronounced change such as this.

Summary

Many assumed that new media technologies would imperil television. Though change continues, it is clear that new ways of distributing television have forced many adjustments in television's industrial practices, but much remains unchanged. Moreover, the change has not uniformly been detrimental. Digital production and distribution technologies have also brought new opportunities—especially for types of television storytelling marginalized in the past—and made it possible for many more to make and circulate television.

Although Internet-distributed television has been part of the television ecosystem for the last decade, we remain in the early stages of identifying and understanding practices that continue to evolve. It is difficult to know much with certainty, but it is important to recognize the considerable continuity that remains despite the disruption.

Further Readings

Significant changes in television that occur before the arrival of Internet-distribution are explored and theorized in many essays and books, among them: John Ellis, *Seeing Things: Television in the Age of Uncertainty* (London: I. B. Taurus, 2000); Jostein Gripsrud, ed., *Relocating Television: Television in the Digital Context* (New York: Routledge, 2010); Amanda D. Lotz, *The Television Will Be Revolutionized*, 2nd ed. (New York: New York University Press, 2014); Lynn

Spigel and Jan Olsson, eds., *Television After TV: Essays on a Medium in Transition* (Durham, NC: Duke University Press, 2004); Graeme Turner and Jinna Tay, eds., *Television Studies After TV: Understanding Television in the Post-Broadcast Era* (London: Routledge, 2009); James Bennett and Niki Strange, eds., *Television as Digital Media* (Durham, NC: Duke University Press, 2011); and a special issue of *The Journal of Film & Television* appropriately titled "Mixed-Up Confusion: Television in the Twenty-First Century" (guest editors Ron Simon and Brian Rose; 38, no. 2 [2010]).

The most substantive consideration of the cultural impact of the media convergence hastening network-era TV's presumed demise is Henry Jenkins, *Convergence Culture: Where Old and New Media Collide* (New York: New York University Press, 2006); but one article that attempts to delineate the specific convergence of television and digital forms is Jeremy Butler, "VR in the ER: *ER*'s Use of E-Media," *Screen* 42, no. 4 (Winter 2001), 313–31.

Preliminary examination of Internet-distributed television can be found in Amanda D. Lotz, *Portals: A Treatise on Internet-Distributed Television* (Ann Arbor: Maize Publishing, 2017); Amanda D. Lotz, *We Now Disrupt This Broadcast: How Cable Transformed Television and the Internet Revolutionized It All* (Cambridge: MIT Press, 2018); a special issue of Media International Australia, "TV Now" (guest editors Sue Turnbull, Marion McCutcheon, and Amanda D. Lotz, 161, no. 1 [2017], 10–20); and Stuart Cunningham, David Craig, and Jon Silver, "YouTube, Multichannel Networks and the Accelerated Evolution of the New Screen Ecology," *Convergence* 22, no. 4 (2016), 376–91.

Amanda D. Lotz is Professor of media studies at the University of Michigan and Fellow at the Peabody Media Center. She is the author of several books about television and its changes from the 1990s through the present.

3 Narrative Structure

Television Stories

When asked if he thought films should be a slice of life, director Alfred Hitchcock is reported to have said, no, they should be a slice of cake. We might well pose the same question about television: Is it a slice of life or a slice of cake? The images we see on the screen show us real people and objects, and the sounds we hear are taken from our real experience, with dialogue spoken in a language and idiom with which we are familiar. Often we suspend disbelief and imagine that television characters are real persons, with tangible pasts and a future toward which time is carrying them. We might muse, "I wonder what happened to Jesse Pinkman after *Breaking Bad* ended." It seems as if we just dropped in on these TV people and tasted a slice of their lives.

But we should be aware that, for all their seeming reality, the stories we watch are actually slices of television confections. As if making a cake, the screenwriters and directors follow storytelling "recipes" that suggest the proper ingredients and their proper amounts for creating a television program. They mix those ingredients in conventionally prescribed ways—adding a chase scene here and a romantic clinch there—to maximize viewer pleasure. Just like the frosting on the top of a birthday cake, a television narrative has been blended to satisfy our appetites.

To understand television narrative, then, we must look beyond the appearance of reality the medium promotes and understand the recipe that created that reality. We may ask of any program, "How is this story put together? What are its narrative components and how do they relate to one another?" As we begin to look at television's narratives, we will notice a limited number of basic structures, a finite set of recipes for mixing story ingredients. Historically, there have been three principal narrative modes on television:

1. the theatrical film (originally shown in theaters)
2. the series program
3. the serial program.

This chapter charts these three structures and explores the differences and similarities among them. It also briefly considers how television's convergence with video-on-demand (VOD) services is necessitating new narrative forms. Later chapters look at how storytelling influences other aspects of television, such as reality TV and the news.

The Theatrical Film

From Antagonism to Alliance

When television experienced its first growth spurt in the years after World War II, the U.S. motion-picture studios and the television industry antagonized each other. TV, an upstart medium, stole the cinema's customers and undermined the studio system that had dominated North America's narrative market. Indeed, the entire world depended on Hollywood for its stories. But the 1950s would be the last decade that U.S. viewers would rely so heavily upon the cinema for their entertainment. By 1960 television had replaced the cinema as America's primary form of entertainment, and many within the film industry were bitter about this loss of control. While film executives resented television's intrusion into their domain, their counterparts in the television industry were hesitant to deal with the film studios. Television producers wanted to create their own material and not have to depend upon the whims of the film industry for their product.

What began as antagonism between the film studios and the television industry soon evolved into a wary alliance. Television was hungry for narrative product; the studios controlled thousands of movies. After their initial runs, these films were warehoused, seldom heard from again, and thus not a financial asset. RKO, Monogram, and Republic—three of the smaller studios—were the first to begin leasing their older movies to television. Soon the major studios were compelled to join in. It wasn't long before newer and newer films began making their way to television more and more quickly. The ratings success of NBC's *Saturday Night at the Movies* (1961) led to all of the broadcast networks featuring "nights at the movies." By the end of the decade there were recent theatrical films running on television just about every night of the week.

Since that time, the relationship between theatrical filmmaking and television has only become more complex. Today's theatrical film studios and television networks are mostly owned by the same few transnational media corporations, blurring the economic distinctions between the two media. And, technologically speaking, film and television were brought even closer together when theatrical film releases began to be offered on **videocassette**, **DVD**, and **Blu-ray disc** (**BD**) players, which were introduced to the U.S. home market in 1976, 1997, and 2006, respectively. And, of course, most recently the predominant method for distributing theatrical films is via VOD portals such as Netflix, Hulu, and Amazon—as well as cable and satellite television's own VOD options (see Chapter 2). In fact, ever since the late 1980s, when videocassette rental revenues first surpassed theatrical box-office receipts, the bulk of the money earned by a "theatrical" film has been acquired after a film's theatrical run has ended.

In today's complicated media environment, a theatrical release of a film still manages to command the lion's share of the marketing budget and to set audience expectations for it. After a movie makes a big splash on its theatrical release (or doesn't), it is then distributed through other platforms according to a specific schedule. **Release windows**, as they are called in the industry, are the limited times during which a film is available fairly exclusively on those specific platforms and in other ancillary markets. They used to be rigidly fixed, with movies only appearing on television screens months after their theatrical release; but the blurring of the divisions between film and television has disrupted those old standards. Moreover, the timing for individual films' releases may vary considerably, and much of this timing is open to negotiation among the major players, especially as release-window timing is rapidly evolving. For now, however, a film's release windows follow fairly standard stages (see Sidebar3.1).

SIDEBAR 3.1 Theatrical Film Release Windows

1. Day-and-date theatrical and video-on-demand window. Nonlinear VOD rental access to a theatrical film is sometimes made available on the same day as its theatrical release.

2. Standard VOD and DVD/Blu-ray window. Nonlinear VOD rentals and sales of video downloads (on iTunes, Amazon, etc.) and optical media (DVDs and Blu-ray discs) offer exclusive access to films during this window.
3. Nonlinear, subscription VOD services and linear "premium" cable channels window. Subscription VOD (a.k.a. SVOD) providers allow subscribers to watch titles in their library on-demand (e.g., Netflix, Hulu, and Amazon Prime). Premium TV channels are those for which cable/satellite-TV customers pay extra (prominently, HBO and Showtime). The length of this window depends largely on licensing deals the providers strike with the producers.
4. Ad-supported, nonlinear VOD window. Providers such as Hulu offer free or low-cost on-demand access to films. Licensing deals determine the length of this window.
5. Linear, over-the-air, network television (ABC, CBS, NBC, et al.) and "basic," nonpremium cable networks (e.g., TNT, USA, TBS, etc.) window. Licensing deals determine the length of this window.
6. Television syndication window.

(This outline is largely based on a 2015 article in *Indie Wire*.)[1]

The most recent addition to the release-window mix are the various VOD services—from cable/satellite companies' on-demand offerings to Netflix's online streaming and the like. Just where VOD fits into the release schedule is currently a point of much contention. Initially, it came after DVD releases, but more and more services are now releasing movies simultaneously on VOD and DVD/BD.

The main point here is that theatrical films continue to play a major role in what we view on our televisions—whether it's a linear-TV network programming a movie into a specific time slot or we viewers popping a BD into a player connected to our home-theater system. The notion of ancillary markets is changing, however, and has been strongly affected by the consolidation of media outlets. Nowadays, a corporation like Viacom might own both a home-video distributor (e.g., Paramount) and a television network (e.g., Comedy Central). Media outlets have vested interests in *all* of these markets, unlike the early days of television broadcasting when film studios and television networks were competing for our leisure time. Today, media corporations are only "competing" within themselves. The staggered release schedule of a theatrical film remains important in order to build marketing buzz, but it's likely to change radically as on-demand services become more dominant.

Although VCR/DVD/BD/VOD technologies, shifting ancillary markets, and corporate consolidation have radically changed the way we view/consume movies on television and virtually eliminated programs such as *Saturday Night at the Movies*, we still spend much of our television-viewing time watching films originally shown in theaters. Moreover, the narrative structure of the theatrical film is still used as a standard by which other TV programs are judged. It is important, therefore, to consider how the theatrical film structures its stories and how those structures are modified when they appear on broadcast television or in a movie of the week.

The Classical Paradigm

The theatrical cinema was not always a powerful narrative machine. Around the turn of the nineteenth century, film stories were in a rather primitive state. Some early movies told no stories at all: a baby is fed, a train arrives at a station, a wall falls over. Viewers were so enthralled with the mere sight of movement on the screen that characters and plot were superfluous. However, cinema viewers soon developed an obsession with narrative, and the young film industry was more than willing to provide it. When D. W. Griffith's milestone *The Birth of a Nation* was released in 1915, the cinema had already established itself as an accomplished, mature art form, a specifically narrative art form. The popularization of sound a little over a decade later threw the industry into upheaval and forced the cinema to readjust its storytelling methods. But by 1934 American movies had settled upon a certain way of constructing stories as well as a conventional style of editing, visual composition, dialogue and music, and so on. This filmmaking method and the industry that supported it have come to be known as the **classical Hollywood cinema**, or, more simply, **Hollywood classicism**. Classical narrative structure is the concern of the present chapter. Classical visual and sound style are discussed in Part II.

In order to avoid one possible point of confusion, it is important to note that "classical" film, in this sense, does not refer simply to well-established and admired films that have maintained their appeal over the decades. Calling *Casablanca* (1942) or *Gone With the Wind* (1939) a "classic" is not using the term as we will be using it here. Rather, classical in our sense refers to a specific mode of filmmaking and can be applied to almost all films made in Hollywood since the 1930s. *Casablanca* and *Gone With the Wind* are classical films, but so are *What! No Beer?* (1933), *Ishtar* (1987), and *Fifty Shades of Grey* (2015), not to mention its sequel, *Fifty Shades Darker* (2017). Moreover, of the theatrical films shown on broadcast television, only the very rare exception is not a classical film. Nonclassical films find a home on cable channels such as Sundance, the Independent Film Channel, Bravo, and Arts and Entertainment (A&E). The foreign-language "art" and U.S. "independent" (that is, independent of the major studios) films are often aggressively anti-classical. Although they have little impact on network narrative television, one can see their influence in music videos, television commercials, and quirky premium cable channel programs such as *Girls* (2012–17).

What binds together the thousands of classical films that have been made over the decades? The seven basic components of classical narrative structure are listed below. As we outline these components we will illustrate them mostly with examples from *Raiders of the Lost Ark* (1981). *Raiders* was chosen because it is one of the most widely viewed films in the history of the cinema and because it exemplifies classical principles so clearly.[2] Its exemplary status was recognized by the Library of Congress when it added the film to the National Film Registry in 1999.[3] Also, you may wish to study the film's narrative structure by examining its screenplay, which is available online (see tvcrit.com/find/raidersscript).[4]

Single Protagonist

The protagonist is the central character in a film, book, TV program, or other fictional mode. The story revolves around them. Classicism has usually limited a movie's protagonist to just one or, at most, two characters. Filmmakers reason that this facilitates viewer identification and streamlines the narrative action. Viewers can identify with one person more readily than with a dozen and can comprehend a single character more quickly than several mixed together at the beginning of the film.

This seems commonsensical enough, but narratives do occasionally use more than a single protagonist. Serial dramas such as daytime soap operas and *Game of Thrones* (2011-) usually feature a dozen protagonists at any particular point in the story. Russian silent filmmakers such as Sergei Eisenstein argued that an entire class of people could be the protagonist. In Eisenstein's *Strike* (1924) and *Potemkin* (1925), masses of people serve as the narrative focus. Of course, there are classical films that break this "rule" of the single protagonist, but, instead of splintering the story, these films often unite several characters with a single purpose so that they function as a united force within the narrative. The "ghostbusters" in the films of the same name (1984 and 2016), for example, work together to destroy the ghosts.

Exposition

The exposition introduces the viewer to two components of the story:

1. the principal characters' personas, their "personalities";
2. the space or environment the characters inhabit.

Every story must have an exposition, but not necessarily at the beginning of the film. Many movies, especially murder mysteries, start in the middle of the action and then later explain who the characters are and what their space entails. Stories that open in such a fashion are said to begin ***in medias res***. *Raiders of the Lost Ark* starts *in medias res*. The opening shot, beneath the credits, presents the hero as a mysterious silhouette (Figure 3.1; tvcrit.com/find/raiders01). Shortly afterwards, he is nearly crushed by a huge rolling boulder and is then pursued by angry natives. All of this occurs before we know who Indiana "Indy" Jones (Harrison Ford) is and why he is doing what he's doing—although a title does tell us that it is "South America 1936." Once Indy escapes from the jungle the film's exposition begins. His profession and motivation are established when we see him lecturing about archeology; and the entire story (its characters and their locations) is mapped out by the government bureaucrats who visit Indy and pique his interest in the Ark of the Covenant.

Motivation

In any classical story, something must catalyze events. The action must have motivation. Here the importance of the single protagonist is re-emphasized, for classical narrative is motivated

Figure 3.1 The opening shot of *Raiders of the Lost Ark* begins the film in the middle of the action.

by the desire of a single character to attain a goal or acquire something (or someone). *Raiders of the Lost Ark* illustrates this unequivocally: Indy desires to acquire the Ark of the Covenant. The protagonist's desire—his or her lack of something or someone or some emotion—catalyzes the story, provides a reason for events to happen, and establishes the narrative's central enigma.

Narrative Enigma

Early in any classical film a question is explicitly or implicitly asked. This question forms the central enigma of the classical story. In *Raiders* the question is, Will Indy find the Ark and prevent the Nazis from using it? There may be secondary enigmas (What is in the Ark? Will Indy get together with Marion [Karen Allen]?), but every other aspect of the story stems from the one central enigma. It is essential to classical narrative that the enigma must not be solved immediately. If it were, there would be no story. Imagine how short *Raiders of the Lost Ark* would be if Indy found the Ark in the first ten minutes. Consequently, *Raiders of the Lost Ark* and all classical narratives rely upon a series of delays that forestall the solution of the enigma.

Chief among the delaying tactics of the classical cinema is the introduction of a character who blocks fulfillment of the protagonist's desire—and, thus, blocks the resolution of the narrative enigma. This blocking character is known as the **antagonist**. The antagonist can be as simple as a solitary character with whom the protagonist battles or competes—for example, Belloq (Paul Freeman), Indy's nemesis, to whom he loses an idol in the opening scene (Figure 3.2). Or, the antagonist may take the shape of the character's environment: for example, the Civil War in *Gone with the Wind*, North Atlantic icebergs in *Titanic* (1997), or the monsters on Skull Island in *Kong: Skull Island* (2017). Some classical films even pose the antagonizing force as being within the protagonist—as in *Batman Begins* (2005), where the title character (Christian Bale) wrestles with inner demons and faces moral dilemmas. These narrative conflicts are not mutually exclusive. A film may contain a combination of them, as when, in *Ordinary People* (1980), Conrad (Timothy Hutton) deals with his internal conflicts about his brother's death at the same time he works through his antagonism toward his mother (Mary Tyler Moore).

In any case, the conflict created by the antagonist delays the resolution of the enigma until the end of the film. These delays form the basis of the chain of cause-effect actions that comprise the main body of the film.

Cause-Effect Chain

Once the exposition has established the characters and their space, and the protagonist's desire has sparked the forward movement of the story, the narrative begins a series or chain of events that are linked to one another and occur over time. Events do not occur randomly or in arbitrary order in classical films. One event causes the next, which causes the next, which causes the next, and so on (Figure 3.3). *Raiders of the Lost Ark* illustrates this: The visit by the bureaucrats causes Indy to go looking for the Ark, which causes him to track down Marion Ravenwood to find a clue to the Ark's location, which causes him to become realigned with her and take her to Cairo, which causes them to battle the Nazis in the Cairo market, and so on. Link by link the narrative chain is built.

Each single narrative event is commonly called a **scene** or sequence. A scene is a specific chunk of narrative that coheres because the event takes place in a particular time at a particular place. The space of a scene is consistent, and time passes in a scene as it does in real life. Contemporary narrative theory has renamed the scene the **syntagm**. The order in which the scenes or syntagms transpire is the film's **syntagmatic structure**.

Figure 3.2 *Raiders of the Lost Ark*: Belloq serves as the antagonist to Indy's protagonist.

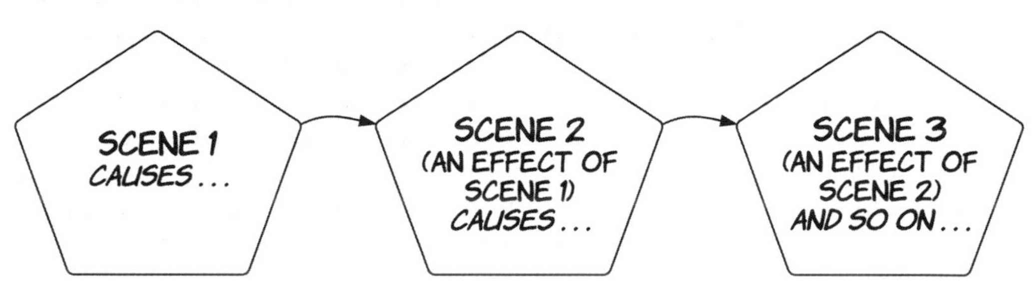

Figure 3.3 The cause-effect narrative chain.

In a single scene, time is continuous, as it is in life; but as we make the transition from one scene to another, the potential for manipulating time arises. Time in film does not match time in reality. If it did, it would take months to watch *Raiders of the Lost Ark*. **Story time**—several months, in this case—is rarely equivalent to **screen time**—*Raiders of the Lost Ark*'s 115 minutes. To maximize narrative impact, the duration and order of story time are manipulated as it is converted into screen time. Most commonly, screen time's duration is shorter than that of story time. Very few films last as long as the actions they represent on the screen. Obviously, films must compress time in order to tell their stories without taxing the viewer. Only occasional oddities equate screen time with real time. For example, in *High Noon* (1952) 82 minutes in the life of a sheriff are presented in 82 minutes; and *Rope* (1948) and *Birdman* (2014) are presented as if they were one long, continuous shot. Further, screen time is not always shorter than story time. This is less common than the reverse, but certainly not unheard of. In *Fantastic Voyage* (1966), a tiny submarine passes through a human heart in 57 seconds of story time, as we are told by the characters. But this 57 seconds of story time elapses over three minutes of screen time. Thus, the duration of time may be manipulated to maximize narrative effect.

The order of screen time may be similarly manipulated. In most classical films, the events shown in the second scene occur after those that appear in the first scene; those in the third scene occur after the second; and so on. That is, the temporal structure is normally chronological. However, it is not uncommon for films to use **flashbacks** or, less often, **flashforwards**, to rearrange a story's temporal structure. In classical film these departures from chronological order are clearly marked with visual effects so that we are certain when we are shifting into the past: the image goes wavy; the focus shifts; smoke appears before the lens; or the character's voice fades out. In nonclassical films, such as those by Alain Resnais, Luis Buñuel, and Christopher Nolan, the past is jumbled up with the present and the future in challenging and sometimes contradictory ways. Nolan's *Memento* (2000) even manages to tell its story in reverse, and his *Inception* (2010) takes us in and out of the past and dream time in ways that test viewer comprehension of the narrative.

Also important to consider is the increasing intensity of the cause-effect chain's events, the basic dynamic force of the narrative. As the enigma's resolution is delayed again and again, narrative intensity escalates. As Indy comes closer to the Ark, his battles become more and more death defying. Eventually, this results in the film's climax.

Climax

At a classical film's climax the narrative conflict culminates—necessitating a resolution. The film's central enigma, which has been delayed for 90 minutes or more, demands to be solved. At the climax of *Raiders of the Lost Ark*, the conflict between Indy and Belloq peaks as Indy and Marion are tied to a stake while Belloq and the Nazis open the Ark. The central enigma (Will Indy find the Ark and prevent the Nazis from using it?) and its subsidiary (What is in the Ark?) are solved in this scene: apparently the wrath of God is contained in the Ark and consequently the Nazis are destroyed when they open it. More specifically, Indy's antagonist, Belloq, is obliterated—thus resolving their long-standing competition (Figure 3.4; tvcrit.com/find/raiders02).

Climaxes are the most concentrated moment of the narrative conflict, but typically they are not the very end of the film. Classical films normally incorporate a short resolution to answer any outstanding questions.

Resolution/Denouement

Up to the point of the resolution, the enigmas have been consistently delayed and the narrative action has constantly risen. In the resolution, in contrast, the enigmas are solved and the narrative action (or conflict) declines. After the apocalyptic destruction of the Nazis, *Raiders of the Lost Ark* resolves its narrative by showing us Indy and Marion getting together for a drink and, in the very last shot, the Ark being stored in an anonymous crate in a huge warehouse (Figure 3.5; tvcrit.com/find/raiders03). The questions about the Ark's contents and the Nazis' use of it are answered. The battle with Belloq is finished. Also answered is a subsidiary question about whether Indy and Marion will reunite. There is a strong sense of **closure** at the end of this and most classical films. The enigmas that had been opened at the start of the film are now closed off, secured. The narrative's questions are answered and the tension between protagonist and antagonist diminishes. And yet, there is some residual tension. Indy and Marion have been through a traumatic experience and are changed by it. Thus, if we diagram the rising and falling action of the classical film (as in Figure 3.6), we can visualize how a protagonist's motivation results in mounting conflict that only begins to decrease with a film's climax and resolution.[5]

If a narrative concludes without answering its questions and the ending is ambiguous or open, this is an instance of narrative **aperture**. For the most part, narrative aperture exists

Figure 3.4 The climax of *Raiders of the Lost Ark* brings the narrative conflict to a peak.

Figure 3.5 Raiders of the Lost Ark: Storing the Ark in a huge warehouse is part of the film's narrative closure.

only in nonclassical films. Jean-Luc Godard's *Vivre sa Vie* (1962), for example, concludes with the protagonist being suddenly shot and killed, with no subsequent explanation. There are very few films that follow classical conventions up until the very end and then tantalize us with an ambiguous finish. The horror genre contains most of these films. *Halloween* (1978), with the mysterious disappearance of the killer's body, and the indeterminate endings of the *Underworld* films (2003–16), are two examples among many. There are, of course, economic reasons for the openness or aperture of horror films. An open ending facilitates the return of the killer in sequels. But aperture also suits the horror film's raison d'être, which is to call into question the stability of rational life. An ambiguous ending undermines the narrative equilibrium that is the goal of most classical films. The horror film does not share that goal.

Theatrical Films on Television

The transition from movie theater to linear, broadcast television can have significant effects on theatrical film narrative—although many of these issues are not pertinent to premium cable

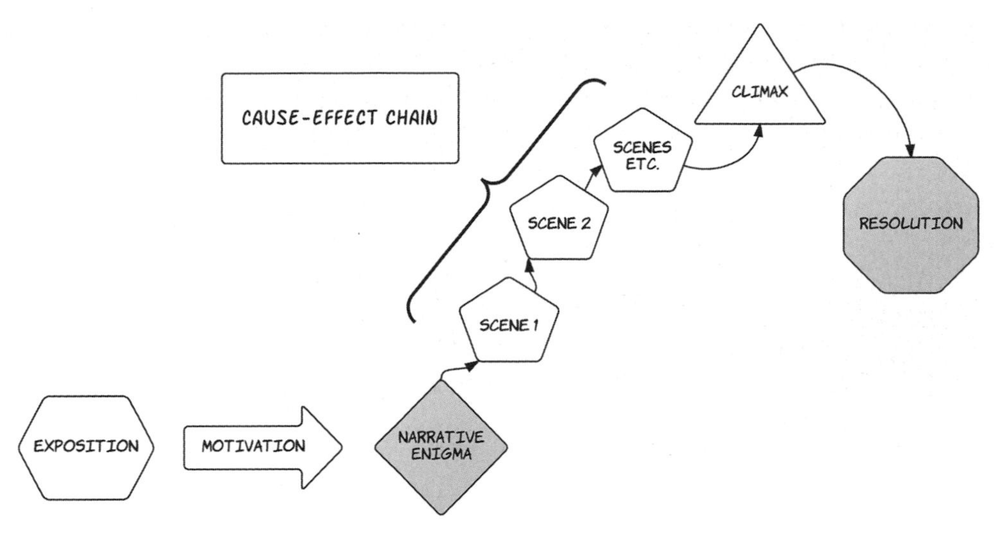

Figure 3.6 The rise and fall of the narrative action is highly conventionalized in classical film.

channels or streaming services. The most drastic of these effects is the shortening of a film to fit it into a commercial-based television time slot. Large parts of the narrative are excised in this process. A Chicago station once ran the 118-minute *From Here to Eternity* (1953) in a 90-minute time slot. Subtracting more time for commercials, station promotional materials, and other interruptions left about 75 minutes for the film itself. The Artists Rights Foundation tracks the time cut from theatrical films.[6] It notes, for example, how *The Silence of the Lambs* (1991) lost 29 minutes when broadcast on the WB network. Obviously, cutting this much time from any film is going to affect severely the coherence of its narrative chain. Characters appear and disappear unpredictably, and entire subplots cease to exist. The cause-effect linkage of classical films is disrupted, sometimes to the point of incomprehensibility, when films are edited in this fashion.

Movies shown on broadcast television are also shortened for reasons other than time concerns. Typically, broadcast standards for television are stricter than U.S. obscenity laws for motion pictures. Images, language, and even entire scenes that television networks deem unfit for family viewing will be cut. *Slap Shot* (1977), *Raging Bull* (1980), and the originally X-rated *Midnight Cowboy* (1969) have all been ravaged when broadcast on commercial television.[7] Even when movies are shown on cable premium channels there is no guarantee they will not be edited. When Showtime—a pay service that boasted running films "uncut and uninterrupted"—presented *Montenegro* (1981), it removed a sexually suggestive scene involving a motorized toy tank.

Thus, various bits and pieces of theatrical films are missing when they are presented on linear, commercial television. Of course, the portions of the film that remain are not presented without interruption—except on rare occasions (for example, the initial screening of *Schindler's List* [1993]). U.S. television inherited from radio the convention of interposing commercials within the body of movies and programs. Commercials and their impact will be considered in Chapter 6; but we may note here that the appearance of TV commercials within classical films adds a distracting, narratively detrimental element. Theaters used to be devoid of these distractions, but several years ago they started presenting commercials before films begin. Even though the commercials do not interrupt the movies themselves, but they can still be an annoying intrusion into one's movie-going experience—especially considering the price of admission to the theater.

The abbreviation and interruption of classical film narrative are not the only ways that film stories are modified on television. In uncommon circumstances, theatrical films are sometimes actually lengthened when presented on television. Network TV added 49 minutes to *Superman* (1978) and 19 minutes to *Superman III* (1983) when they were originally telecast.[8] In one of the strangest of such incidents, a 1980s telecast of *Rear Window* (1958) extended its running time by presenting the credits in slow motion and inserting a dream sequence that had not existed in the original film! The narrative effect of such alterations varies from film to film, but it is seldom beneficial. Narrative can be a fragile component of the movies and often is distorted beyond recognition in the transition from theater screen to television screen.

The Television Series

Early television drew upon a variety of sources for its programming material: theatrical movies, sports events, vaudeville-style music and comedy skits, and such. In many regards the infant medium relied most heavily upon its broadcasting predecessor, radio, for programming strategies and narrative forms. Indeed, the influence of radio was so strong, and the television image in the 1940s so poor, that early television was little more than radio accompanied by fuzzy, indistinct, black-and-white pictures—with the emphasis on sound rather than image. Television has changed a good deal since then, but the basic narrative form that TV inherited from radio endures to the present day: the **series**.

There are precedents for the television series in both literature and the cinema. Literary series have been published that center on figures such as Tarzan, the Hardy Boys, and Nancy Drew; and theatrical film series have featured a variety of characters: Tarzans (dozens since Elmo Lincoln first did the role in 1918), homicidal maniacs (Freddy Krueger of *Nightmare on Elm Street*, beginning in 1984), sports heroes (Rocky, beginning in 1976), superheroes (Superman, Batman, Spiderman, et al.), and so on. Even so, the series has never been as important to literature or film as it is to television. What are the characteristics of the narrative television series, and how is the series particularly well suited to the form of television? We can begin to answer these questions by examining the series' narrative structure.

Narrative Structure

The television series is a narrative form that presents weekly episodes with a defined set of recurring characters. Each week's episode is basically self-contained. Although they will occasionally have two-part episodes or a narrative arc that recurs, the narrative of a series does not consistently continue from one week to the next. Each episode does not begin where the previous one ended, as episodes do in the television **serial**. For example, during the 2016–17 broadcast season the most popular series included a trilogy of "Chicago" shows—that is, *Chicago Fire* (2012–), *Chicago Med* (2015–), and *Chicago P.D.* (2014–)—as well as the long-running *NCIS: Los Angeles* (2009–). Crime and medical series such as these, which typically deal with one major incident in each episode and resolve that incident within the course of the hour, follow "series" narrative conventions. In contrast, other popular shows during this season carry story arcs across several episodes and thus they are more accurately labeled "serials"—including *Grey's Anatomy* (2005–), *Scandal* (2012–), and *Stranger Things* (2016–). However, the series and the serial forms have gotten progressively closer to one another over the years.

Friends (1994–2004) exemplifies this. It's a program where narrative arcs (such as Ross's [David Schwimmer] numerous marriages) do persist over the course of several episodes, but the bulk of the issues raised on it each week are resolved by the end of the episode. It is thus considered a series even though it contains some serial aspects. We'll use it as our principal source of examples as we discuss the characteristics of the series.

In some respects, the television series resembles the classical film. After all, series do present chains of events driven by enigmas. But the pressures of commercial interruption and of repetition, of a weekly appearance before the viewer, force the television series to rely on some distinctly different narrative strategies. These strategies were forged during the network era of broadcast television, but a surprising number of them persist in an era when it is often possible to binge-watch an entire season's worth of episodes in one sitting.

Multiple Protagonists

Many series center on a single protagonist: Mary Richards (*The Mary Tyler Moore Show* [1970–77]) or Jessica Fletcher (*Murder, She Wrote* [1984–96]), for example. But it is more common for a TV series to use a pair of protagonists or even an ensemble cast of five or six main characters. Christine Cagney (Sharon Gless) and Mary Beth Lacey (Tyne Daly) hold equal narrative importance as the title characters on *Cagney and Lacey* (1982–88), as do the central characters on *The Big Bang Theory* (2007–) and *Friends*. The main function of these multiple protagonists is to permit a variety of plots within the same environment. One week *Friends* is concerned with Phoebe (Lisa Kudrow) giving birth to triplets (October 8, 1998). The next week Joey (Matt LeBlanc) appears on a PBS telethon, disappointed that he isn't hosting it; Ross decides to move to London to marry Emily (Helen Baxendale); and Phoebe's triplets are nearly forgotten. Narrative emphasis shifts from one episode to the next, but the core characters remain the same.

Exposition

The constancy of the series' central figures means that each episode needs only a brief exposition. Most of the characters and their space are known to the viewer from previous episodes, and often they are re-established in the program's theme song: for example, "Come and listen to my story about a man called Jed, a poor mountaineer, barely kept his family fed . . ." (*The Beverly Hillbillies* [1962–71]). Only the particulars of the current episode's characters and any new locations must be established. We rely upon the consistency of characters and space; it is part of what makes the show comfortable to watch. We know that every day in syndication the characters of *Friends* will congregate at the Central Perk coffee house and that Andy Taylor (Andy Griffith) and Barney Fife (Don Notts) will preside over their jail (*The Andy Griffith Show* [1960–68]). Only new characters and new locations need be established in the exposition. Obviously, this is quite different from a one-time presentation such as a theatrical film, which must acquaint the viewer with an unknown cast of characters and an unfamiliar setting. And it also explains why TV **pilots** are often heavily loaded with exposition, which becomes unnecessary over the course of a series' run.

Series characters have a personal history of which we are usually conscious and to which references are occasionally made. On most series programs, however, these personal histories are rather vague and ill defined. The past is a murky region in series television. The present tense of a specific episode is usually all that matters. In the 1986–87 season of *Miami Vice*, detective Larry Zito (John Diehl) is murdered—a narrative event important enough to warrant a two-episode story. Subsequent episodes of the program, however, seldom mention Zito. That segment of the program's past virtually ceases to exist, except in reruns. Thus, series characters do have an established past, and their characters do not need re-establishing each week; but they often misplace this past and, in any event, it is usually not necessary for our enjoyment of a specific episode for us to know the details of the characters' pasts.

If we examine a specific episode of *Friends*, we can see how series narrative is structured and how it is being blended with the serial structure discussed in detail below. In "The One With Chandler's Work Laugh" (January 21, 1999), the exposition begins before the credits. In a short scene, Rachel (Jennifer Aniston) pumps Joey for more information about Monica (Courteney Cox) and Chandler (Matthew Perry) getting together (Figure 3.7; tvcrit.com/find/friends01). As she quizzes him, the viewer is provided with background information, and one story arc for this episode is established. After the general program credits end, and while the credits for this specific episode are superimposed over the image, two more story arcs are begun: Ross announces that an ex-wife of his is getting married and expresses his frustration at being alone, and Monica and Chandler attend an office party at which he kowtows to his boss and is heard doing his fake "work laugh" (Figure 3.8; tvcrit.com/find/friends02).

Monica and Chandler's and Ross's stories are rooted in the past and depend upon viewer knowledge of previous episodes. Consequently, they qualify as serial-style storylines (see below). But the storyline based on Chandler's work behavior, from which the episode takes its title, has only vague connections to *Friends'* narrative history. For the longest time, the series didn't even show Chandler at work, so his behavior there has not been very important to the program. In this episode, however, it becomes a point of contention between him and Monica, with her criticizing the "work Chandler" as a "suck-up." Thus, the office-party scene serves as exposition for the storyline of Chandler's work behavior, which is woven into the storyline of Chandler and Monica's romance.

Motivation

The constancy of a series' characters and setting establishes a narrative equilibrium. A state of balance or rest exists at the beginning of each episode. However, if this balance were to

Figure 3.7 In the exposition of a *Friends* episode, Rachel asks Joey for key narrative information, which he cannot provide.

Figure 3.8 More *Friends* exposition: A secondary storyline develops between Monica and Chandler.

continue, there would be no story. Something needs to disturb the balance to set the story in motion, to catalyze it.

The most common narrative catalyst, as in the classical cinema, is the lack or desire of the protagonist. Since the series incorporates multiple protagonists, this permits it to shift the narrative-catalyst function from one character to another. The desire of one protagonist may dominate one week; the desire of another may arise in the next episode. In "Chandler's Work Laugh," several characters have desires which motivate the narrative: Will Rachel discover Monica and Chandler's secret romance, and will that affect their friendship? Will Monica continue to love Chandler despite his "suck-up" demeanor around his boss? Will Ross find true romance? Each lack (of the truth, of commitment in a relationship, of romance) raises the question of whether the protagonist's desire will be satisfied. In short, each raises a narrative enigma.

Narrative Problematic

Questions such as the above underpin the narrative of a series and capture our attention (if they are successful). But, of course, as in all narrative forms these enigmas must not be immediately resolved. There must be a counterforce that prevents their instantaneous resolution, or there would be no story to tell. In the *Friends* example, there are several counterforces. Monica functions as the antagonist for Rachel's desire for the truth—lying to her and concealing the relationship. Chandler's boss and his behavior around the boss are counterforces to Monica's commitment to him. And Janice (Maggie Wheeler)—an ill-suited date for Ross—delays his attainment of love. As with the classical film, the counterforce need not be a single individual. It may also be the protagonist's environment or an internal, psychological element within the protagonist. The main point is that protagonists' acquisition of their goals must be postponed, deferred, so that the narrative may develop further complications.

Thus, the narrative focus shifts from one week to the next, but it is important to recognize that these individual desires and enigmas exist within a larger **narrative problematic**. Because fundamentally the series is a repeatable form, there must be some narrative kernel that recurs every week. In effect, the program must ask the same question again and again to maintain consistency and viewer interest. Of course, we wouldn't watch exactly the same material each week (although the number of times we view a particular episode in syndication or streaming on Netflix contradicts this), so there must be some variation within that consistency. But, still, every series must have some recurring problematic, some dilemma with which it deals in every episode.

For *Friends* the ongoing dilemma revolves around issues confronting friends in their twenties—just out of college, but not yet fully settled into a career. We might think of that dilemma as, Will the friends' camaraderie be disrupted? That is, Will the friends stop being friends? Related questions include: Will Chandler/Joey/Monica/Phoebe/Ross/Rachel find romance? Will Chandler/Joey/Monica/Phoebe/Ross/Rachel find fulfilling work? Almost every week the program tests the bond among these six friends. To take another example—this time from a police drama—the problematic of *Miami Vice* is, Will Crockett and/or Tubbs surrender to the temptations they are immersed in and become villains? Individual episodes counterpose various antagonists against Crockett and Tubbs, but overriding these specific concerns is the more general issue of their moral character.

Each episode, drawing on the multiplicity of protagonists in series TV, poses a slightly different narrative enigma. As John Ellis has noted, "The basic problematic of the series, with all its conflicts, is itself a stable state."[9] Specific enigmas come and go—briefly igniting the viewer's interest—but the fundamental problematic remains firm, sustaining the viewer's ongoing attachment to the program. The particulars of Ross and Janice's situation and Chandler's work laugh are the embodiment of the program's underlying problematic on January 21, 1999. In the following week's episode, these particulars disappear, but the program's problematic returns. In sum, most series have a single, stable narrative problematic, which is embodied in numerous different narrative enigmas on a week-to-week basis.

Cause-Effect Chain

As in the classical film, events do not happen randomly in series television. One scene leads into the next, and the next, and the next. A cause-effect chain is erected scene by scene. However, in broadcast television this chain must be broken at least once during a half-hour program and at least three times during an hour-long program for the insertion of commercials. The TV chain is not continuous as it is in the cinema or on streaming services.

The series deals with this discontinuity by segmenting the narrative. That is, the story is broken into segments that fit between the commercial breaks. These between-commercial segments, often called **acts**, consist of one or more scenes that hold together as strongly as classical scenes do. They end with their own small climax, which leads into the commercial break. The function of this pre-commercial climax is not to resolve narrative dilemmas but instead to heighten them, to raise our interest in the narrative as we flow into the commercials. New, minor enigmas may even be posed just before the segment ends.

In "Chandler's Work Laugh," for example, Ross is despondent about his failed marriage to Emily. As act one ends, Monica, Joey, Rachel, and Phoebe quiz him about being out all night. He is evading their questions when Janice enters the room—revealing that Ross was with her. As the segment fades to black with a shot of an embarrassed Ross (Figure 3.9; tvcrit.com/find/friends03), the viewer is left with an enigma: Were Ross and Janice romantically involved the night before? Following the commercials, this question is answered in the very first scene (yes, they were) and the narrative chain resumes (Figure 3.10, the first shot after the break).

In sum, the segmentation of the series narrative interrupts the rising curve of increasingly intensified action that we see in classical cinema and replaces it with portions of narrative equipped with their own miniature climax—in a sense, several upward curves linked together. In this way, television narrative more closely resembles the play, with its division into separate

Figure 3.9 Friends: Ross looks guilty during the instant before a commercial break...

Figure 3.10 ... and everyone stares at him during the instant right after it.

acts, or the mystery novel that ends each chapter on a note of suspense. The chain is slightly ruptured, but not sundered by the so-called commercial breaks.

Climax

Series episodes do have a final climax, where the action finally peaks and asks for some form of resolution. In the final scene of "Chandler's Work Laugh," Ross's whining annoys Janice and she breaks off their relationship. However, series programs' climaxes are undercut by one main factor: the repeatability of the program, its need to return the following week with the same problematic. The conflict reaches its peak, but there is no final resolution.

Resolution/Denouement

Series episodes can have no final resolution, no narrative closure, because to do so would mean the end of the series itself. If there were no more threats to the friends' camaraderie, if they were all happily coupled up and satisfied with their jobs, or if the moral character of Crockett and Tubbs were permanently assured, there would be no more conflict upon which to base *Friends'* and *Miami Vice*'s narratives. Consequently, the ending of each episode must leave us in doubt as to the ultimate resolution of the series' overarching conflict. There must be a sense of narrative openness, a limited aperture. In "Chandler's Work Laugh," we learn that Ross and Janice's relationship is over, but we don't know about Ross's future romances or the possibility of Janice reappearing on the show. The small question: "Will Ross find romance with Janice?" is answered. Larger questions such as "Will Ross *ever* find romance?" or "Will romance and marriage take him away from his friends?" are not fully resolved. The last shot of the episode shows Janice teasing Joey, the one male "friend" with whom she has not slept, that he might be next (Figure 3.11, final shot before the end credits; tvcrit.com/find/friends04). And so future complications are already being seeded.

Figure 3.11 Friends: The final shot before the end credits opens the possibility of a union between Joey and Janice.

On rare occasions, television series will conclude the program's run by providing true narrative closure. *M*A*S*H* ended the fictional doctors' and nurses' conflict with the Korean War by presenting a two-and-a-half-hour episode (February 28, 1983) of the war's end. With no more war to play antagonist to the medical protagonists, the narrative motor of the program ran out of fuel. Its repeatable problematic had finally been resolved—after 11 years and hundreds of episodes. Most series, however, do not close in this fashion. One moment they are part of the weekly schedule and the next they are gone. Their abrupt departure sustains their narrative aperture, which is helpful if they are sold into stripped syndication, where their problematic is *re*-presented daily. When *Friends* concluded its ten-year run with a two-part finale—titled, significantly, "The Last One" (May 6, 2004)—it parceled out some closure by resolving long-running storylines such as Ross and Rachel's on-again-off-again romance, but it still left some storylines unresolved. Notably, Joey's future was left open so that he might move to Los Angeles, where the character's "life" could continue to be chronicled in a new sitcom the following season (*Joey* [2004-06]).

Thus, if we return to our diagram of classical-film narrative and modify it to visualize the narrative structure of a 30-minute, commercial-supported sitcom, we must recognize the increased complexity of the rise and fall of its narrative action and the changes necessitated by its repeatable format (Figure 3.12). Further, this diagram has been simplified—leaving out common sitcom elements such as the cold open and the tag just before the end credits. And, naturally, hour-long series have more than two acts and just a single commercial break. However, the basic principles of commercial-supported narrative structure are represented in Figure 3.12.

The Television Serial

The serial is another form of storytelling that successfully made the transition from radio to television. Even before radio made use of the serial, there were examples of it in literature and the cinema. Nineteenth-century novels, such as those by Charles Dickens, were often originally published chapter by chapter in magazines. Silent movie serials such as the hugely popular *Fantômas* (1913) in France and *The Perils of Pauline* (1914) in the U.S. entertained audiences during radio's infancy. Neither of these forms, however, would reach an audience as enormous as the TV serial's.

Narrative Structure

Unlike the *series*, the *serial* expects us to make specific and substantial narrative connections between one episode and the next. In the series, the link between each week's programs is rather vague. In the serial, the connection is fundamental to its narrative pleasures. The main difference between the series and the serial is the way that each handles the development of the narrative from episode to episode. In years past, the serial, in the form of the soap opera, dominated daytime television but had little impact upon prime-time schedules, with the significant exceptions of *Dallas* (1978–91) and *Dynasty* (1981–89). But the late 1990s and 2000s saw a surge in popularity of the prime-time serial that has continued to the present day. Critical favorite *Twin Peaks* (1990–91, resurrected in 2017) and ratings champion *ER* (1994–2009) led the way and have been followed by well-regarded, complex serials such as *The Sopranos* (1999–2007), *24* (2001–10, 2014), *The Wire* (2002–08), *Lost* (2004–10), *Grey's Anatomy*, and *Stranger Things*.

The television serial used to be the least respected narrative form. There was a creeping sexism in this attitude, for it assumed that soap opera and serial storytelling were something that only "housewives" could find interesting. The wealth of prime-time and streaming serials and the blurring of the distinction between serial and series have proven that the form may be

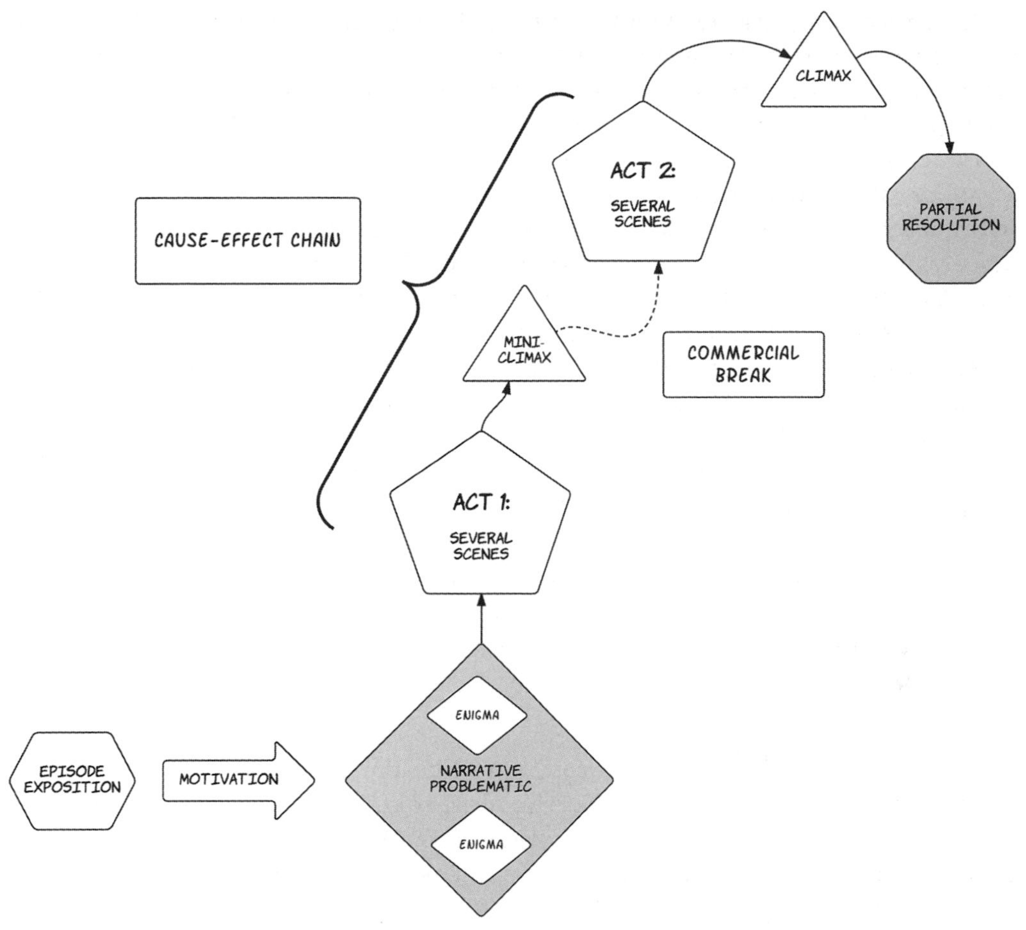

Figure 3.12 In the linear-TV series, narrative structure must accommodate commercial interruptions and allow for a repeatable narrative problematic.

used to create sophisticated and quirky television. Consequently, it is important to examine how it is that serials tell their stories. What is their narrative structure, and how does it differ from both the classical cinema and the television series? In the discussion that follows, we will focus on the daytime serial, the soap opera. Although it is a genre in decline, it still provides the best example for analysis because it remains the purest, most extreme form of serial television. Once narrative analysts come to understand the soap opera, they will be better able to dissect both daytime, prime-time, and streaming serials.

Multiple Protagonists

In our discussion of series programs, we noted an increased tendency toward multiple protagonists. The serial—especially the daytime serial—uses an even larger number of protagonists, each of whom is equally important to the narrative structure. Hour-long soap operas typically have 15 to 20 central characters—many more than the classical film, and even more than multiple-protagonist series such as *Friends* (whose main characters number just six). Soap-opera casts are the largest of any program on television—including most prime-time serials. The plot recap for the December 6, 2005 episode of *All My Children* (1970–2011), as published on its official website, indicates that no less than 16 central characters are involved in this one episode's events (see Sidebar 3.2).

The multiplicity of protagonists permits a variety of simultaneous storylines within the narrative world of a serial. And, more importantly, the high number of characters decreases the importance of any one character. Indeed, soap-opera characters lead a precarious existence. They come and go with a swiftness that is uncommon in other fictional forms. This is due partly to economics. Most soap-opera actors work under contracts that may be canceled every 13 weeks. If the producers feel that actors are not generating enough viewer interest, they may suddenly disappear, along with their characters (although characters are also frequently recast). However, economics is not the only reason for the large number of protagonists. Soap opera relies upon a multiplicity of characters to create a narrative web in which most characters are connected with one another.

Exposition

As does *Raiders of the Lost Ark*, the television serial begins each episode *in medias res*. The story has already begun, the action joined in progress. On the episode of *All My Children* that aired December 6, 2005, the first scene is Del (Alec Musser) and Babe (Alexa Havins) discussing her child-custody fight with J.R. (Jacob Young), while he (J.R.) eavesdrops on the two of them. In fact, the very first shot is of the eavesdropper, before any other context is established (Figure 3.13; tvcrit.com/find/amc01). The two men are working together in a scheme to set her up. We, the viewers, are dropped into the middle of a complicated storyline that has been running for months. The scene serves as episode-specific exposition by establishing characters and a location that will recur through this particular episode. The original exposition of *All My Children* began over 40 years ago when it was first broadcast (January 5, 1970). The "lives" of its characters were initially constructed then, and the story continued until it ceased production in 2013. Other soap operas' original expositions also date from decades ago. Similarly, *Guiding Light* developed its story on radio and television for more than 70 years—making its radio debut on January 25, 1937, and concluding its television run on September 18, 2009. If these were classical films they would have lasted thousands of hours and their exposition would have occurred years ago!

SIDEBAR 3.2

Kendall suspects either Greenlee or Jonathan left her in the hammock but Ryan feels Zach could be responsible. Meanwhile, Julia and Aidan try to stop Zach's attack on Jonathan. Lily becomes very agitated to see Zach pummeling Jonathan. Zach apologizes to Lily. Jonathan doesn't tell Ryan about Zach's attack. Kendall admits to Ryan she doesn't feel as though she's ready to be a mother. Ryan tells Kendall he will support any decision she makes regarding the baby. Di succeeds in getting Greg to hire her as his new receptionist. Tad decides to trust Di and use her as a spy in Greg's office. Tad explains to Di that he found a file on the Martin family in Greg's closet. Tad is hit with a wave of emotion when Di covers herself with a blanket Dixie had made. Babe doesn't fall for JR's trap and cleverly turns the tables on him. Amanda tells Josh about her blackouts and fears what she might have done during them. Josh offers Amanda a job as his assistant at New Beginnings and deliberately gives her wrong information for a meeting she is to set up for Erica.[10]

Figure 3.13 The opening shot of an *All My Children* episode begins the program in the middle of the action; J.R. eavesdrops on two characters.

Few, if any, viewers could listen to and watch every single episode of long-running series such as *Guiding Light* and *All My Children*. Additionally, the programs are always adding new viewers. So how do serials cope with viewers who have missed episodes or are new to the program? The answer is that serials, particularly the long-running soap operas, contain a large quotient of redundant narrative information. Character A has coffee with character B and they discuss how C has fathered a child with D. This narrative fact is now established. But in a later scene (the next day, perhaps) we will see character B at the nurses' station discussing the situation with two more characters. The information is redundant to the regular viewer, but serves as exposition for the viewer who has missed the previous scene. A small example from the December 6th episode illustrates this. In the very last line of a scene between Ryan (Cameron Mathison) and the pregnant Kendall (Alicia Minshew), she challenges him, saying, "I might not even have this child." Her first line following the commercials is the redundant "I might terminate this pregnancy!" Through repetitions such as these the soap opera constantly *re*-establishes its characters and their situations.

Part of the redundant information that is regurgitated in the serial is the pasts of the characters. Serial characters carry a specific, significant past—much more so than do the series characters. In the series, the past is obscure and indefinite; but in the serial, characters constantly refer to it. Previous love affairs and marriages, murders and double-crossings, pregnancies and miscarriages, are layered on top of the current goings-on. For the regular viewer in particular this creates a remarkably dense, multilayered narrative. A casual remark between two characters can be loaded with repressed, unspoken associations. A kiss hello can signify years of ill will or unrequited lust. In the December 6th episode, Di (Kelli Giddish) becomes indignant about an injustice done to Tad (Michael E. Knight). He interrupts her and says, "In light of things that have happened between you and me, I would consider it a personal favor if you would try to stop acting like Dixie." No further explanation is offered as to what those "things" might be. The regular viewer, however, knows that Tad is referring to Di's attempt to pretend to be Dixie,

Tad's (seemingly) dead wife. So it is that a complex weave of character relationships exists from the very first second of a day's episode of a daytime serial and extends back into decades of complicated, previously told storylines.

This is not to say that new characters are never introduced on serials. Obviously, they must be, to keep the narrative fresh and interesting. These characters all undergo a conventional exposition, as does a character entering a classical film. However, daytime soap operas commonly abbreviate this exposition by providing familial associations for the new character. Often, the new character will be someone's never-before-seen cousin or uncle, or even sister or mother. The use of familial relations quickly incorporates new characters into the storylines associated with that family. This narrative tactic is illustrated by the character "bios" (biographies of the characters, written as if they were real people) on *All My Children*'s official website. Each of the biographies begins with the character's complicated family connections. For example, the character of Di, who was introduced relatively recently, is situated thus:

Father:	Seabone Hunkle
Siblings:	Del Henry, Dixie Martin (half-sister; deceased), Will Cortlandt (half-brother; deceased), Melanie Cortlandt (half-sister; deceased)
Nephew:	J.R. Chandler
Brother-in-law:	David Rampal[11]

Her character is established as being similar to, or different from, the rest of the family's overall character—particularly Dixie's as she was pretending to be her.

Motivation

Like the exposition, the original catalyst for long-running television serials took place years ago. In the episodes we watch day after day or week after week, the many protagonists' desires and lacks are mostly already established. Only the occasional new desire/lack is introduced to maintain the narrative diversity. In most daytime and many nighttime serials, these lacks/desires normally concentrate on heterosexual romance and familial relations (especially paternity). Over the past three decades, however, the serial has diversified, with *Dallas* leading the serial into themes of corporate greed, and *General Hospital* (1963–) introducing international intrigue and science fiction (the "ice princess") into the soap opera world. The 2000s has even seen political thrillers (*24*) and crime dramas (*The Wire*) rendered in serial form.

Narrative Enigma

The serial is saturated with enigmas. It thrives on them. The multiplicity of protagonists ensures that several—up to a dozen or so—enigmas will be running on any one program at any one time. On December 6th, *All My Children*'s enigmas include:

- Will Kendall have her baby?
- Will Ryan and Kendall get together since she is carrying his child?
- Is Jonathan still a psychotic killer or has he been cured?
- Will Babe get custody of her baby from J.R.?
- Will Krystal and Adam make their fake marriage a real one?
- Did Amanda attack Babe, pushing her down the stairs? And what evil is Janet, Amanda's mother, up to?

Unlike the classical film or the TV series episode with their one central enigma, the serial nurtures multiple enigmas. They are its foundation. The multiplicity of enigmas ensures that serials will never lose their narrative momentum. If one enigma is solved, many others still remain to slowly pull the story forward.

Cause-Effect Chain

The narrative chain of daytime serial television is interrupted more frequently than that of series television. There are more commercial breaks per program minute in daytime soap operas than there are in nighttime series. (It is no coincidence that soap operas were the most consistently profitable programs on television until cheaply produced game shows and talk shows displaced them.) In an hour-long episode, approximately 20 minutes are taken up with commercials and other non-narrative material. Indeed, barely six minutes of story material elapse during the acts between commercial interruptions.[12]

Serials adapt to this constant interruption much the same way that series do. They segment the narrative. Each serial narrative segment ends with a small climax, which raises new enigmas rather than leading to resolutions. We enter, or "flow" into, a commercial break on the heels of a narrative question mark. Sometimes the break is preceded by a literal question, as in the December 6th episode when Ryan says to Kendall, "You are carrying my child. So, what the hell are we going to do about that?" The director, Angela Tessinari, ends the scene with a close-up of Kendall as this line is spoken (tight, scene-ending close-ups are a common convention of soap opera; Figure 3.14; tvcrit.com/find/amc02). Cut to commercial. After we return from the world of commerce, Kendall provides an evasive answer to that question. Her first line of dialogue is: "You forget, you and I are not the 'we' I was planning on with this baby. It was supposed to be me and Greenlee [her friend and stepsister]" (Figure 3.15). The program has teased us into waiting through five minutes of commercials by promising an answer to Ryan's question. We don't really get one, however, and the overarching enigma is sustained. As we have seen in all the narrative structures on television, they operate principally by delaying answers to enigmas.

Figure 3.14 All My Children: Kendall is framed in a tight close-up just before a commercial break. She has been asked what she will do about her controversial pregnancy...

Figure 3.15 ... and after the break she avoids providing a full answer.

Climax

Eventually, individual storylines do climax on serials. If they didn't, we would probably stop watching out of total frustration. So we do have fairytale weddings in which long-separated lovers are united and climactic gun battles in which evil characters are dispatched. But these climaxes never result in narrative resolution.

(The Lack of) Resolution

Almost by definition, serials cannot have total resolution. If they did, there would be no reason to tune in the next day. Climaxes don't generate resolutions. They just create new enigmas. In characteristic fashion, the December 6th *All My Children* episode is dealing with the repercussions of a resolved storyline. For months, the program focused on a mysterious series of murders. Then, the mystery was solved: it was Jonathan who killed three people, and what caused him to do so was a tumor pressing on his brain. Surgeons successfully removed the tumor—thereby both curing him and bringing the storyline to a conclusion. Or did they? Zach, the son of one of the murder victims, has turned to alcohol to ease the pain and he vows to kill Jonathan. Will he do so and/or will he get his life back in order? And is Jonathan truly cured, or is he just faking it? The attack on Kendall that begins the December 6th episode raises questions about Jonathan's rehabilitation. As is always the case in serials, the resolution of one storyline opens up new questions, new enigmas.

Even death is not a certainty—as was illustrated by Bobby Ewing's (Patrick Duffy) return to *Dallas* after "dying" in front of Pam's (Victoria Principal) eyes. (Apparently it was just a dream of Pam's—a dream that lasted an entire TV season!) And Jonathan (Jeff Branson), on *All My Children*, managed to return to the narrative after having been shot and having had a bomb he created explode, which caused a mining cave to collapse on top of him. Furthermore, many serial characters have returned from (presumed) death two and three times—as did James Stenbeck (Anthony Herrera) on *As the World Turns*. So even death is not a permanent resolution on the soap opera.

On the extremely rare occasions when a serial storyline does achieve relative narrative closure—say, a couple marries and leaves the program—it is still of little consequence to the enigma structure of the program because of the abundance of other enigmas. The sixth season of *ER* ends with major character Carol (Julianna Margulies) joining Doug (George Clooney) in Seattle—the conclusion of a very rocky relationship spanning several years. (Since both actors left the show, there would be no further developments in their relationship.) But *ER* hardly missed them and had no lack of ongoing enigmas in the following seasons. With numerous protagonists, someone is certain to be lacking or desiring someone or something at any point in time on television serials. The one imperative of the serial is that the story must continue.

In terms of individual episodes, the serial ends as it begins: in the middle of the action. The *All My Children* episode that begins *in medias res* in the child-custody storyline ends in the midst of the same storyline—with very little narrative development between start and finish. In the last shot of the day, Babe watches J.R. leave the boathouse, then grins at her success in turning the tables on him and Del. "Gotcha!" she says triumphantly to herself, concluding the day's episode (Figure 3.16; tvcrit. com/find/amc03). Her exclamation contains an implied tease: Will she trick J.R. and regain custody of their son? Tune in tomorrow to (perhaps) find out.

The narrative structure of a serial such as *All My Children* only partially maps onto the series-narrative diagram in Figure 3.12. A serial's beginning and ending are quite different from those of a series, and the cause-effect chain departs from the relatively simple progression of series such as *Friends*. Figure 3.17 accounts for the unique elements of the serial. As you examine the series

Figure 3.16 All My Children: The last shot of this episode provides no narrative resolution as Babe plots further schemes.

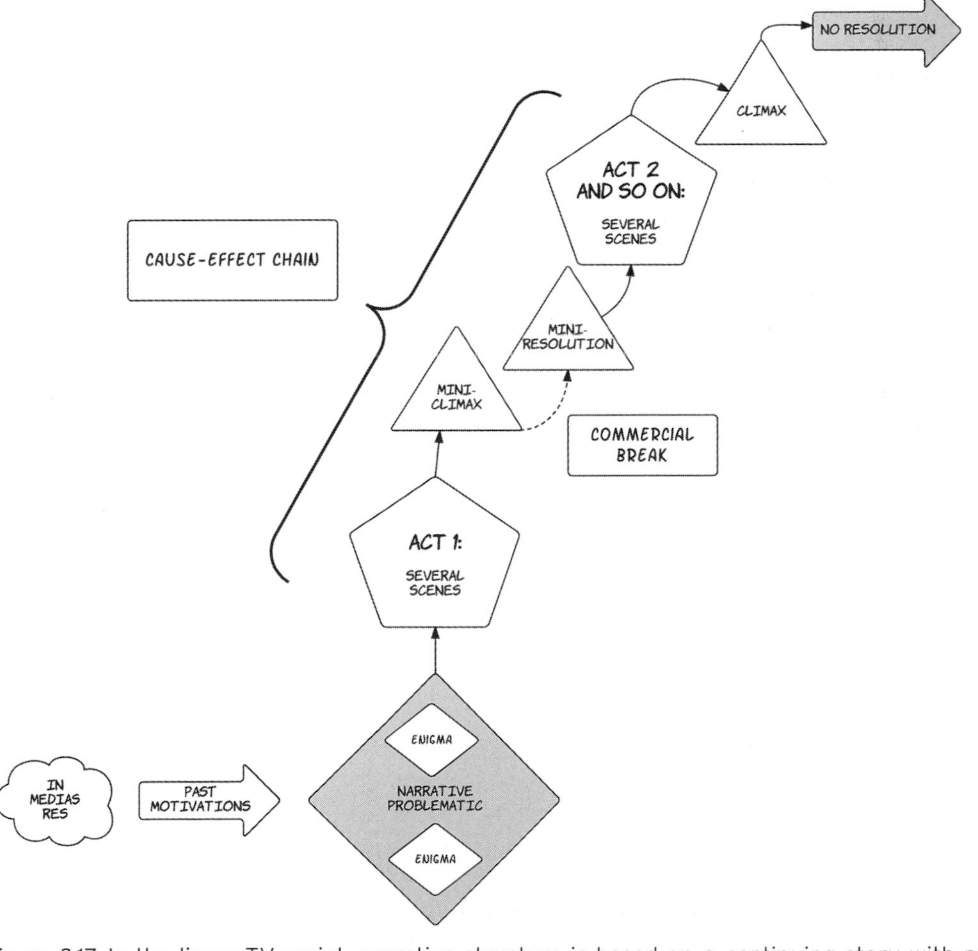

Figure 3.17 In the linear-TV serial, narrative structure is based on a continuing story with no foreseeable resolution and an exposition lost in the past.

and serial diagrams, look for the distinguishing features of the two television forms. And the next time you watch a serial, see if you can identify the components that are visualized in this diagram.

Transmedia Storytelling and Binge-Watching

Before leaving our consideration of narrative we should discuss **transmedia storytelling** and **binge-watching**. Both have changed how viewers consume television stories, and both have the potential to enhance and disrupt the traditional TV experience.

All television programs have some sort of companion online presence—websites, Facebook fan pages, Twitter feeds, and so on. Many programs have taken to including additional information about their characters in short webisodes, blogs that are written from the characters' perspective, and other more creative features. NBC's *The Office* (2005–13), for example, expanded its narrative beyond what we saw weekly on TV. The program's paper company, Dunder Mifflin, had its own fake website at dundermifflin.com (now taken down; see tvcrit.com/find/dunder) and several employees wrote blogs—including Ryan's (B. J. Novak) photo-blog titled *Thousand and One Words*.[13] Most significantly, in terms of *The Office*'s narrative, the program's online-only webisodes expanded and elaborated on the story presented on television. In one series of video segments, for example, Angela (Angela Kinsey) mentors Erin (Ellie Kemper) to become an accountant. By building a narrative world that existed both on television and online, the producers of *The Office* engaged in **transmedia storytelling**.

Transmedia storytelling in this example from *The Office* is a one-way street. Narrative elements from television travel to the Web and are elaborated upon there, but not the other way around. That is, *The Office* webisodes do not have an impact upon the television show's narrative; they function primarily as promotional material for the show. For example, the narrative action of the Angela–Erin webisode did not have any significant impact on Angela's or Erin's character on the television show. However, more significant experiments with transmedia storytelling have developed since the late 1990s. NBC augmented the later seasons of its police show, *Homicide: Life on the Street* (1993–99), with an online series titled *Homicide: Second Shift* (1997–99).[14] On television, *Life on the Street* showed one shift of homicide detectives while on NBC's website, *Second Shift* showed another. Mostly, the two shifts did not overlap, but, in an episode broadcast February 5, 1999 titled "Homicide.com," characters from the webisodes do appear and influence the narrative. However, NBC did not fully commit to transmedia storytelling. As the executive producer of the Web series, Thomas Hjelm, explains, "The [TV] episode on Friday is self-contained and makes sense by itself, but if you go online for the (continuing) *Second Shift* chapters, it just makes *more* sense."[15]

More fully developed transmedia worlds may be found in the realm of fantasy, science fiction, and animation. Henry Jenkins, one of the leading transmedia theorists, has chronicled how *The Matrix*'s (1999) narrative world has been constructed through theatrical movies, animated shorts, comics, video games, and various online materials.[16] And he contends that two of the most successful transmedia franchises are *Pokémon* (on American television 1998–) and *Yu-Gi-Oh!* (on American television 2001–06), which began as video games and have evolved across the media of television, theatrical film, and trading cards. Video games and trading cards that also involve game play introduce an intriguing, innovative aspect of transmedia storytelling: the ability of viewers to control the narrative themselves, to navigate through the narrative world along a path that they choose. This clearly has potential to disrupt the cause–effect chain upon which so much television narrative relies. The transmedia experience transforms the viewer into a "viewer/user/player" or VUP, as Stephen Dinehart has termed it.[17] In other words, the transmedia viewer both consumes and produces story elements. Jenkins provides an example from *Lost* (2004–10) where viewers captured a frame of a map from one episode, posted it online, and then used the "collective intelligence" of online fans to construct theories about the Hanso Corporation and what was transpiring on the island.[18] Thus, fans become VUPs, helping to fabricate a narrative world instead of being led along a predetermined cause-effect pathway. Such narrative world building can now lead users into the real space outside their homes—as was illustrated by the release in 2016 of *Pokémon Go*. In this **augmented reality** (AR) game, Pokémon characters appear over the live video from a smartphone's camera (Figure 3.18), allowing players to pursue them in the physical world. In true transmedia fashion, Pokémon narrative elements have transferred into users' worlds and entice them to hunt game characters in real spaces, not entirely unlike Indiana Jones seeking the Ark of the Covenant. When *Pokémon Go*

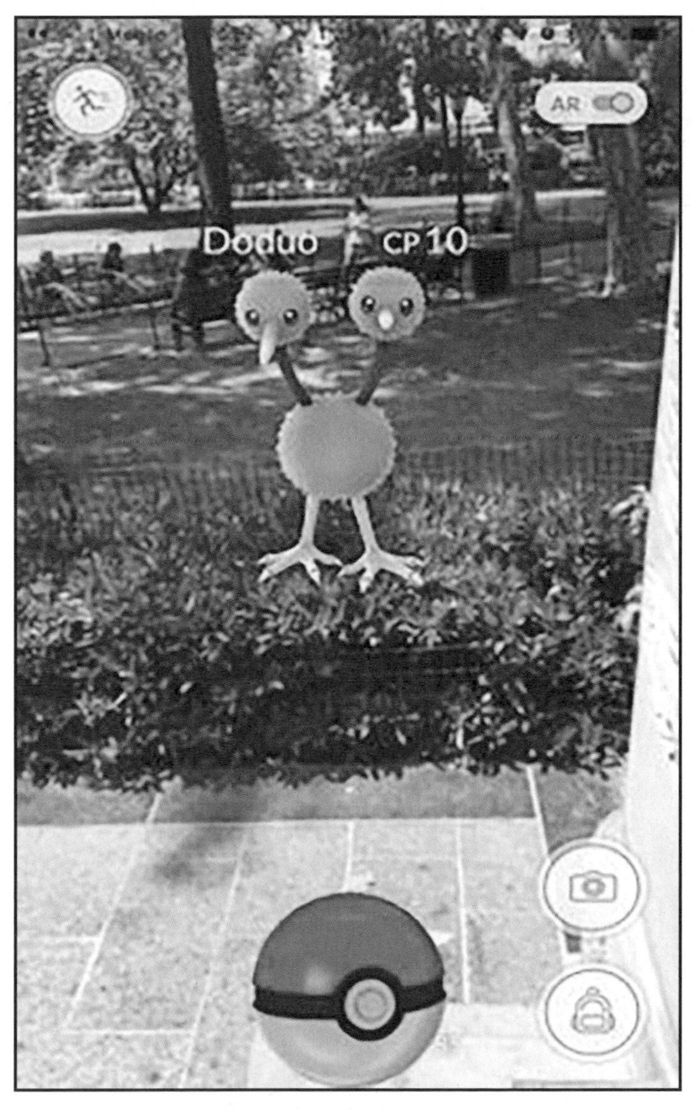

Figure 3.18 In the augmented reality game, *Pokémon Go*, game characters appear over real-life settings.

players search for Pokémon in the wild, they are authoring their own narratives, becoming part of a story's development that they themselves determine.

In our example from *The Office*, we see the most common transmedia use related to television narrative: the further elaboration of characters and their stories. This could put an end to narrative closure because it means that there is always the potential for the story to be continued—whether from official online episodes or fan-generated fiction. The serial television form was built on a similar lack of closure, and one could see how soap operas and other serials could benefit from never-ending transmedia storytelling. The series form, however, relies on narrative pleasure derived from repeatable narrative closure—the resolving of narrative lines week after week. Continuing these lines past their on-television closure could cause ruptures in the texts and generate displeasure and uneasiness. However, a transmedia franchise might also "steal" the core narrative problematic of a television series and shift it to other media or an augmented reality. For example, the forensic crime-fighting problematic of *CSI* has already been adapted for graphic novels.

The *CSI* graphic novel, along with the examples above from *The Matrix*, *Pokémon*, *Pokémon Go*, and *Yu-Gi-Oh!*, illustrate one seemingly undeniable fact of transmedia storytelling: the viewer/user/player has many entry points into a transmedia franchise's narrative world. These entry points may be television programs, but they could just as easily be video games, theatrical films, a blog, or even trading cards. Thus, we can no longer presume that television's stories *originate on television*. As Jenkins notes, "Any given product is a point of entry into the franchise as a whole. Reading across the media sustains a depth of experience that motivates more consumption."[19] Conceivably, narrative exposition could be encountered in another medium before the viewer watches the first episode of a TV program—as was the case of *Pokémon* fans who played the game before seeing the TV show. This could change how episodes or entire programs initiate their narratives, but few attempts have yet aggressively tested this potential.[20] The impact that transmedia storytelling will have on conventional television narrative is still being sorted out. It certainly has the capacity to change every aspect of narrative structure: its expository beginning, cause-effect middle, and semi-closed end. Will this result in the death of television and a revolutionary new transmedia form? It is still too soon to tell.

Just as transmedia storytelling provides viewers with new power over the ways they construct a TV narrative, so does binge-watching a TV program alter the broadcast-era experience of consuming narrative in weekly or daily installments. Binge-watching was a relatively limited phenomenon during the DVD era, when enthusiastic fans of a show might purchase a DVD set of an older program's entire season and blast through the episodes in short order. However, binge-watching gained new cultural currency in the 2010s when streaming VOD portals began releasing entire, season-long runs of original episodes all at once. Netflix has been a leader in this regard and has dropped entire seasons of original programming such as *House of Cards* (2013–) and *Orange Is the New Black* (2013–) to great fanfare. In fact, it is estimated that when *House of Cards'* second season came out on a Friday in 2014, hundreds of thousands of Netflix subscribers watched its nearly 11 hours of narrative over that weekend.[21] "Binge-watching" officially entered the Zeitgeist in 2013 when the Oxford Dictionaries declared it one of the runners-up to "Word of the Year" (the winner was "selfie").

To date, original programming on Netflix, Amazon Video, Hulu, and so on, has stuck with the episodic structure of broadcast-era television—that is, narratives built in 30- or 60-minute installments. Moreover, 30-minute comedies have mostly maintained the structure of the series as we discuss above—complete with a repeatable narrative problematic. And 60-minute dramatic serials have deviated very little from the open-ended structure we saw in the broadcast-era soap opera. However, the ability to watch two or three or more episodes in quick succession has the potential to change series/serial television's narrative formats. Episodes are becoming more and more like chapters in a novel, with viewers able to immediately turn a virtual page and move on to the next chapter. It's too soon to tell how television's "binge-ability," as it were, is going to affect narrative structure. Will it lead to more and more complex storytelling over longer forms? Or will it just mean that viewers will consume insubstantial stories much more quickly and distractedly—greedily gorging themselves on the plenitude of television in the twenty-first century?

Summary

Narrative forms must share linear-television time with all sorts of other material: news, commercials, game shows, public service announcements, sports, and so on. And yet, stories are what principally draw us to television. Theatrical films, series programs, and serial programs lure us with the promise of entertaining stories. These television narratives share certain characteristics. They all present protagonists—established by an exposition—in a chain of events motivated by desire. There are always antagonists—individuals, environments, or internal—that prevent the attainment of that desire. The chain in each narrative mode is comprised of actions connected to one another by narrative enigmas that pull the story toward a climax. All of these aspects are necessary for conventional storytelling, though their order and emphasis may differ from mode to mode.

However, important distinctions separate the narrative modes. Series and serials rely upon a viewer foreknowledge of characters that is not possible in individual theatrical films. The series and the serial adapt themselves to television's constant interruptions through narrative segmentation, to which theatrical films are not accustomed. Each mode handles enigmas and resolutions somewhat differently—depending upon whether the mode must be continued the next week/day or not. On one end of the spectrum is the classical film, with its firm narrative closure; on the other is the serial drama, with its never-fully closing narrative aperture.

We should resist the impulse to use the classical film as our yardstick to measure these individual narrative modes. Instead, we should understand them on their own terms as television narratives. Every narrative form on linear TV must somehow conform to television's flow, interruption, and segmentation. The daytime serial—with its extreme segmentation, multiple protagonists, multiple enigmas, and lack of full resolution—owes the least to the classical film and is perhaps the most televisual of the narrative modes. The theatrical film is, obviously, the least suited and consequently suffers the most. The series has its own way of accommodating the medium. And still, all are television stories.

The future of television narrative will probably involve some permutation of transmedia storytelling, where viewers encounter narrative worlds on many different narrative platforms through a variety of entry points. Exactly what format this storytelling will take is still a matter of contention, but it is likely that today's VOD, streamed, and binged-watched media will necessitate some new narrative approaches.

Notes

1 Melanie D. Miller, "Attention, Filmmakers: Here's Everything You Need to Know About Release Windows," *Indie Wire*, January 14, 2015, tvcrit.com/find/windows, accessed February 28, 2017.

2 Until 2015, it was one of the top 20 box office leaders of all time, but was bumped to number 21 that year by *Star Wars: The Force Awakens*. *Gone With the Wind* (1939) has been number one for over 70 years. Source: "Domestic Grosses: Adjusted for Ticket Price Inflation," *Box Office Mojo*, February 23, 2017, tvcrit.com/find/boxoffice.

3 Each year, 25 films deemed "culturally, historically or aesthetically significant" are added to the National Film Registry, which works to preserve them. "Film Registry," Library of Congress, February 23, 2017, tvcrit.com/find/nfr.

4 Lawrence Kasden, "Raiders of the Lost Ark," August 13, 2010, tvcrit.com/find/raidersscript.

5 Nineteenth-century German playwright Gustav Freytag was among the first to diagram dramatic structure. His "pyramid" inspired this diagram. Gustav Freytag, *Freytag's Technique of the Drama: An Exposition of Dramatic Composition and Art*, translated and edited by Elias J. MacEwan (Chicago: Scott, Foresman and Company, 1894). Available online at tvcrit.com/find/freytag.

6 "Film Victim of the Month," *Artists Rights Foundation*, January 1999, November 6, 2000, www.artistsrights.org. The Artists Rights Foundation has been subsumed under the Film Foundation and its website has changed to www.film-foundation.org.

7 *Midnight Cowboy* is so butchered when it is shown on television that Leonard Maltin advises, "[P]lease don't watch it on commercial TV: the most lenient prints run 104 m. [out of an original running time of 113 minutes] and are ludicrously dubbed to remove foul language." *TV Movies and Video Guide* (New York: Signet, 1990), 719.

8 Ibid., 1081-2.

9 John Ellis, *Visible Fictions: Cinema: Television: Video* (Boston: Routledge, 1992), 156.

10 "Recaps: 12/6/05," *All My Children*, December 7, 2005, tvcrit.com/find/amcrecap.

11 "Character Bios," *ABC*, December 7, 2005, tvcrit.com/find/amcbios.

12 For more specifics regarding soap-opera timing, see Jeremy G. Butler, *Television Style* (New York: Routledge, 2010), 48–53.

13 Ryan Novak, "Thousand and One Words," tvcrit.com/find/novak, originally accessed August 17, 2010.

14 See "Multidirectional Digital Flow and 'Second Shift' Programming," in John Thornton Caldwell, *Production Culture* (Durham, NC: Duke University Press, 2008), 279–82.

15 Josh Wolk, "*Homicide* Welcomes Its Website Cast to the Show—a First Step in NBC's Plans to Nab TV Defectors," *Entertainment Weekly*, February 5, 1999, tvcrit.com/find/homicideweb.

16 Henry Jenkins, "Searching for the Origami Unicorn: *The Matrix* and Transmedia Storytelling," in *Convergence Culture: Where Old and New Media Collide* (New York: New York University Press, 2006), 93–130.

17 Stephen Dinehardt, stephendinehart.com, August 16, 2010.

18 The concept of "collective intelligence" comes from Pierre Lévy. Henry Jenkins, "Transmedia Storytelling 101," *Confessions of an Aca-Fan*, March 22, 2007, tvcrit.com/find/transmedia, accessed February 23, 2017.

19 Jenkins, *Convergence Culture*, 96.

20 Experimental endeavors such as the University of Southern California's Labyrinth Project have explored transmedia's potential to a greater degree than the broadcast networks. For more information, see tvcrit.com/find/labyrinth.

21 Alexis Kleinman, "An Insane Number of Americans Binge-Watched 'House Of Cards,'" *The Huffington Post*, February 21, 2014, tvcrit.com/find/binge, accessed March 16, 2017.

Further Readings

The most cogent overview of television narrative, especially as it compares with the narrative of other related media, is John Ellis, *Visible Fictions: Cinema: Television: Video* (Boston: Routledge, 1992), although his references are becoming dated. A more current perspective on the complexities of television narrative in today's on-demand, transmedia world of storytelling is offered by Jason Mittell, *Complex TV: The Poetics of Contemporary Television Storytelling* (New York: New York University Press, 2015), which has an online version that includes video examples (see tvcrit.com/find/complextv). One anthology that assesses the broad-ranging transmedia world of *Star Wars* is Sean Guynes and Dan Hassler-Forest, eds., *Star Wars and the History of Transmedia Storytelling* (Amsterdam: Amsterdam University Press, 2017). Readers interested in constructing their own transmedia storytelling could consult Andrea Phillips, *A Creator's Guide*

to Transmedia Storytelling: How to Captivate and Engage Audiences Across Multiple Platforms (New York: McGraw-Hill Education, 2012); or Carolyn Handler Miller, *Digital Storytelling: A Creator's Guide to Interactive Entertainment*, 3rd ed. (Burlington, MA: Focal Press, 2014).

An overview of TV narrative theory is provided by Sarah Kosloff's chapter, "Narrative Theory and Television," in *Channels of Discourse, Reassembled*, Robert C. Allen, ed. (Chapel Hill, NC: University of North Carolina Press, 1992). Kosloff includes an annotated bibliography of narrative theory of literature, film, and television. Nick Lacey, *Narrative and Genre: Key Concepts in Media Studies* (New York: Palgrave Macmillan, 2000) covers general principles of genre and then applies them to both television and film. Genre studies often focus on narrative—as can be seen in two TV-genre overviews: Jason Mittell, *Genre and Television: From Cop Shows to Cartoons in American Culture* (New York: Routledge, 2004); and Glen Creeber, ed., *The Television Genre Book* (London: British Film Institute, 2001). Using *Star Trek*'s holodeck as a portent of the future, Janet H. Murray details the development of narrative in various formats of science fiction in *Hamlet on the Holodeck: The Future of Narrative in Cyberspace* (Cambridge, MA: MIT Press, 1997). Other discussions of specific television genres and formats include Robert C. Allen, *Speaking of Soap Operas* (Chapel Hill, NC: University of North Carolina Press, 1985); and Paul Attallah, "The Unworthy Discourse: Situation Comedy in Television," in *Interpreting Television: Current Research Perspectives*, Willard D. Rowland, Jr., and Bruce Watkins, eds. (Beverly Hills: Sage Publications, 1984).

Analyses of the narrative structures of film and literature can often provide insights into those of television. David Bordwell and Kristin Thompson have written frequently on narrative systems in film. Their *Film Art: An Introduction*, 11th ed. (New York: McGraw-Hill, 2016) offers chapters that summarize their work elsewhere. Bordwell also maintains an informative blog that often analyzes narrative elements: tvcrit.com/find/bordwell. Thompson has addressed the specifics of television narrative in *Storytelling in Film and Television* (Cambridge, MA: Harvard University Press, 2003). David Bordwell, Janet Staiger, and Kristin Thompson, *The Classical Hollywood Cinema: Film Style and Mode of Production to 1960* (New York: Columbia University Press, 1985) is a meticulous analysis of the evolution of classical film narrative form as a mode of production. Edward Brannigan, *Narrative Comprehension and Film* (London: Routledge, 1992) examines both narrative structure and our interpretation of it in film. Seymour Chatman's *Story and Discourse: Narrative Structure in Fiction and Film* (Ithaca, NY: Cornell University Press, 1978) provides a summary of narrative analysis in those two media.

4 Building Narrative

Character, Actor, Star

Chapter 3 discusses television narrative as if the characters involved were pieces in a jigsaw puzzle, depersonalized components fitted into abstract patterns. This is misleading. While it is, of course, important to understand narrative structures, it is equally important to understand the characters that inhabit those structures. In a sense, these characters can exist even before the narrative action begins. The first time we see Don Draper (Jon Hamm) in the opening shots of *Mad Men*'s pilot episode (2007), we immediately begin to construct an idea of his character: an overworked businessman in the 1960s (Figures 4.1–4.3). Even before this character *does* anything in the plot structure, we begin to make assumptions based on setting, props, and his appearance. Furthermore, characters such as Draper exist *after* the narrative action concludes each week. For instance, when we pick up a copy of *Us Weekly* because we respond to a picture of Jon Hamm as Draper, we are carrying Draper's significance beyond the storylines of *Mad Men*. Draper has begun to take on a "life" of his own. Of course, such magazine coverage of television introduces us to the actors who embody the roles, and it nurtures the process of turning common actors into genuine stars. Typically, the *Us Weekly* issue is more about actor Jon Hamm than it is about character Don Draper.

To put it bluntly: Without characters there could be no television narrative and no television stars. Correspondingly, without actors there could be no characters. Characters, actors, stars: these three intertwining phenomena will be the focus of this chapter. We will begin by charting the mechanisms used to construct characters on television. Among these is the performance of the actor, which will be discussed in terms of contrasting acting strategies. The significance of the actor does not end with their performance within a television text, however. An actor, such as Hamm, may also appear in other **media texts**: magazines, movies, online blogs, Twitter posts, *Saturday Night Live* guest hosting, public appearances at movie premieres, and so on. As the image multiplies, the actor evolves into a television star.

Building Characters

Because characters typically assume human form, because they look like us, talk like us, and, in some sense, behave like us, it is easy to mistake characters for real people, with real lives beyond the boundaries of their television programs. Most of us realize that Daenerys Targaryen is not a real person, that writers have designed her words and directors have chosen camera angles to present her. But still we willingly set that knowledge aside, suspending disbelief while watching *Game of Thrones* (2011–). Or, more accurately, the program endeavors to hide the work that went into creating Daenerys, to render invisible the making of a character. If it succeeds, we accept Daenerys as a plausible human being (even if her dragon-taming actions

Figure 4.1 In the opening shots of *Mad Men*, the audience is introduced to Don Draper.

Figure 4.2 Don's appearance and costuming set the time period and hint at his character.

Figure 4.3 Props also help to set up Don's character.

may seem fantastic). If it fails, we respond with annoyance: "Daenerys's use of the Dothraki language sounds awkward and weird." Annoyance at television's implausibility, its "fakery," is a first step toward viewing the medium critically. However, to systematically analyze TV, we must channel the occasional awareness of television's "fake," constructed nature into a systematic critique of how those narrative constructions operate. In this case, we need to ask how characters are manufactured and how we come to understand the meanings associated with them.

Fabricating characters is the day-to-day work of writers, directors, producers, production designers, and other craftspersons. Indeed, it's the principal work of the entire television medium–creating **signs of character** that signify the character to us. Character signs, as explained by Richard Dyer, are all those aspects of a character that communicate their nature and personality to us.[1] We viewers interpret or read these signs according to a variety of factors:

1. our understanding of the world, of television, of genre;
2. the context (i.e., program) in which the character appears;
3. the viewing situation itself. (Did we have a large meal just before turning on the television? Is the room too brightly lit? How large is the television? And so on.)

All these variables can influence how we perceive a character. They make character construction an imprecise science. Still, we can better understand how characters are constructed if we identify the types of signs that signify character and investigate the **code** of character construction. This code is comprised of certain "rules" that govern what meanings a character signifies to us and how those meanings are created.

Both producers and consumers of television have learned this code. In fact, we learn it so well that we take it for granted. Television producers (and writers and directors) unthinkingly use this code to construct characters; and television consumers (we, the viewers) incorporate it into our commonsense understanding of the medium. Producers and consumers alike understand, for example, that a female character who wears eyeglasses is supposed to be more "intellectual" than other female characters (see our discussion of Tina Fey's *30 Rock* character, Liz Lemon, below). If another smokes, she will likely be evil or immoral. These conventions of costuming and props are part of a code that is so taken for granted as to become nearly invisible. It is the analyst's task, then, to make it visible again. In so doing, it is important to remember that this so-called code is both *historical* and *cultural*. That is, it changes over time and is not fixed; and it differs from one culture to another and is not universal. For example, in television programs produced in the 2010s in the United States, cigarette smoking signifies "evil" to viewers; but in films produced in the 1930s in France there was no such association. Indeed, the changing cultural associations with smoking are something that *Mad Men*'s producer, Matthew Weiner, has had to address in interviews–defending the frequent smoking in the program as essential to establishing its time period (note the ashtray in Figure 4.3). If *Mad Men* had been produced in 1960, cigarette smoking would have been culturally invisible.

Although the historical and cultural nature of the code is true of all aspects of character construction, it is most obvious in the case of costuming. The skinny ties worn by Sergeant Friday in the 1950s and 1960s program *Dragnet* (1952–59, 1967–70) were part of a total costuming style that signified moral and political conservatism. When that same style of tie was worn by new-wave musicians such as Elvis Costello in music videos in the early 1980s, it had liberal and hip connotations. Time had changed the meaning of that visual signifier (the tie). As well as being bound to a certain time, such specifics of costuming are also culturally determined. The width of

Sergeant Friday's or Elvis Costello's ties would not mean much to a traditionally attired African, for instance, whose code of dress does not normally include neckwear.

To provide a less frivolous example of the cultural significance of dress, consider that in the Western world black is recognized as the color of mourning. It has come to signify death. In contrast, in Asian countries mourners wear white. Hence we may see that no costuming convention is universal. The code changes from one culture to another.

As we begin to examine the conventionalized code of character construction, we will rely heavily on a typology of character signs articulated originally by Dyer in his studies of cinema stars.[2] Most of Dyer's comments on film characters may be imported into our consideration of television characters, but television is not the cinema, and the following typology alters Dyer's scheme where appropriate.

A Typology of Character Signs

Viewer Foreknowledge

Before watching a single episode of a television program, we are provided with signs that signify the characters to us. Advertising on television, online, and in print describes and promotes the program in terms that capitalize on our familiarity with the program's genre, its stars (if famous enough), and, in the case of programs spun off other programs, its parent show. If a program is advertised as a new police drama, then we can expect certain genre character types: the foolish rookie, bitter veteran, helpless victims, and so on. If it features Andy Griffith—as when he appears in *Matlock* (1986–95)—then we are prepared for a character articulated by Griffith's homespun star image. And if the program is a spinoff, such as *Better Call Saul* (2015-), then we have already seen some of the characters in previous stories, although in a different context (*Breaking Bad* [2008–13]). Such aspects of genre, star, and parent program generate a **narrative image** of the program—an enticing representation of what the program's characters will be like—that functions to lure us to a new program.[3]

Of course, once the program has been on for a few weeks, viewer foreknowledge before each individual episode rises to the point where the characters become as familiar as figures from literary and cinematic series, such as Frankenstein's monster or Harry Potter. An established program often plays upon our familiarity by using its credit sequence to rehearse character relationships. The credit sequence of the original TV run of *Gilmore Girls* (2000–07), for instance, presents us with all of the major characters and their milieus (Figures 4.4–4.7). It emphasizes the mother-daughter relationship at the heart of the show (Figure 4.6), reinforced by Carole King singing, "Where you lead, I will follow, anywhere that you tell me to." And it ends by placing them in one of the most frequently used settings, Luke's Diner (Figure 4.7). Even though we are, most likely, already familiar with these characters, this short pre-narrative segment re-presents the program's cast and setting and diminishes the need for a full exposition to establish the characters. Of course, when *Gilmore Girls* was revived on Netflix nine years after its initial run, its narrative image was so strong that hardly any credits or exposition were necessary. The first episode of *Gilmore Girls: A Year in the Life* (2016) begins with simple white letters over black (no character images) and audio clips from the previous episodes. Not even the program's title is necessary because, presumably, the viewer has just clicked through to it from a Netflix menu with the show's title. Credit sequences are often telling indications of both characters and themes the program emphasizes, and tracking their changes over different seasons also illuminates how the show is positioning itself for us.

Figure 4.4 The title sequence of *Gilmore Girls* reacquaints us with Lorelei...

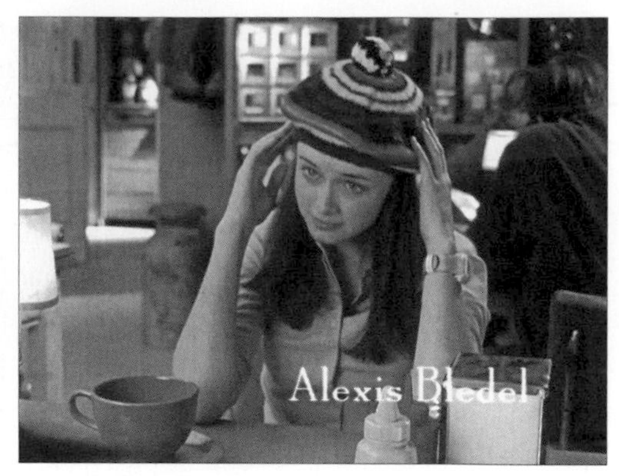

Figure 4.5 ... and her daughter Rory.

Figure 4.6 At the heart of the show is the mother-daughter relationship, which is emphasized in this shot...

Figure 4.7 ... and is continued in a shot that shows them in one of the program's most familiar settings, Luke's Diner.

Character Name

A character's name distinguishes them from the rest of the cast and, more important, signifies certain character traits to us. These traits may be as program specific as the character's familial bonds: Rory Gilmore is obviously related to Lorelei Gilmore on *Gilmore Girls*, but, further, Rory's given name is Lorelei, as is her grandmother's. Thus, the program has three "Lorelei Gilmores" and uses the name to suggest the very close connection among them. Even the program's title is stressing and playing off the family name. Names also carry significance within the general culture. The name Ricky Ricardo (*I Love Lucy* [1951–61]) carries Latino connotations. Howard Wolowitz (*The Big Bang Theory*) conveys Jewish associations. Each of these names raises expectations that the character will either fit into ethnic/religious stereotypes, defeat those stereotypes, or perhaps select particular stereotypical connotations while rejecting others.

Character names connote meanings other than religion and ethnicity, too. On *Murphy Brown*, the title character's name is distinctive enough within U.S. culture (a family name, Murphy, used as a first name) to imply an extraordinary woman: unusual name = unusual character. And, on the same program, the name Corky Sherwood is used to diminish that character's seriousness by using the diminutive and, for a broadcast journalist, overly familiar -y ending (compare with Buffy, Penny, Tippy, Candy). Further, when Corky marries a man named Forrest she becomes Corky Sherwood Forrest—the pun on her married name creating humor at the character's expense.

Appearance

Appearance can be broken down further into three components: the face (and hairstyle), the body (build and posture), and costuming.

Television's reliance upon the close-up favors the face as a signifier of character. Unfortunately for the purposes of analysis, the meanings of facial characteristics are ephemeral and difficult to pin down. It is hard to particularize the meanings of a face—although we unthinkingly make these interpretations a thousand times a day. What does Burt Reynolds's moustache "mean"? What does David Letterman's tooth gap signify? These are questions that cannot be answered with any rigor. And yet, there are some facial characteristics that become significant because of their difference from facial norms: Farrah Fawcett's copious amount of blond hair on *Charlie's Angels* (1976–77) signifies "blondness" and a specific type of "sex symbol" to many viewers (Figure 4.8). Her blond hair links her to other female sex symbols and thus signifies a certain sexual availability and vulnerability in the Marilyn Monroe tradition. It is the variation from the norm that not only makes a characteristic noticeable but also creates meaning. In Fawcett's case, its meaning has persisted but shifted over the decades—from signifying sexuality to signifying nostalgia or disdain for the 1970s. It has even become a punchline, as in "The Witch" episode of *Buffy the Vampire Slayer*, which features this exchange:

Buffy, to her mother, as they look at a yearbook photo of her:	"I've accepted that you've had sex. I am not ready to know that you had Farrah hair."
Joyce, her mother:	"This is Gidget hair. Don't they teach you anything in history?"

Gidget was played by Sandra Dee in film and Sally Field on television; and she had similarly distinctive—and distinctly signifying—hair. The hairstyles of Fawcett, Dee, and Field illustrate just how much meaning can be attached to appearance.

Corporeal (bodily) attributes carry clearer meanings than facial ones. 50 Cent's muscular, tattooed physique conveys strength and masculine sexuality in film/TV roles, video games, and music videos like *I'm the Man*, *Candy Shop*, and *In Da Club* (Figure 4.9; tvcrit.com/find/50cent). In contrast, Roseanne Barr's physique during the early years of her sitcom (*Roseanne*, 1988–97) associated her with the "mammy" stereotype—the overweight woman who is sexually neutral but an expert at caring for others (Figure 4.10). These actors' physiques and the way they carry them quickly signify aspects of their characters to the viewer.

As we have mentioned already, costuming is a significant component of character construction. Within television there are two very active overlapping codes determining our understanding of costume: the code of dress predominant in a specific culture at a specific time and the code of dress specific to television and television genres. Our earlier example of skinny ties in *Dragnet* and music video is one instance of a fashion element that was part of the culture at large and was incorporated into television programs. Narrow ties would have existed with or without TV. Certain genres, however, develop a code of costume that is not shared by the contemporary culture. Westerns, private-eye shows, and science fiction programs each have

Figure 4.8 Farrah Fawcett's hair (and implications of "blondness" and "sexuality") was a major feature of *Charlie's Angels*.

Figure 4.9 50 Cent's appearance conveys masculine sexuality in the *Candy Shop* music video.

Figure 4.10 In U.S. culture, Roseanne's physique connotes a woman who excels at mothering but is sexually neutral.

developed clothing items that hold specific meaning. The gambler's fancy vest in the Western, for example, has come to signify his greed and untrustworthiness. Costuming is closely related to, and often overlaps with, our next sign of character.

Objective Correlative

An objective correlative is an object (or sometimes an animal) that is associated with a character and conveys something about them. Objective correlatives include the environment that is the home or workplace of a character. The living room, neighboring junkyard, and storefront of *Sanford and Son* (1972–77) help establish Fred Sanford's social class and lifestyle (Figure 4.11; tvcrit.com/find/sanford), just as the setting of the Bada Bing! strip club in *The Sopranos* establishes Tony Soprano's (Figure 8.1). Sitcoms, in particular, rely heavily on a limited number of sets; and those settings come to be as familiar to the regular viewer as their own living room.

Even more distinctive than these sets are objective correlatives that are individual objects linked to characters: Ricky Ricardo's conga drum in *I Love Lucy*, Bart Simpson's skateboard in *The Simpsons* (1989–), the sheriff's badge worn by Seth Bullock in *Deadwood* (2004–06), and so

Figure 4.11 The setting of *Sanford and Son* contributes to building its characters.

Figure 4.12 Bart Simpson's skateboard is an objective correlative of his reckless character.

on. In each instance, the object comes to signify something about the character. Ricky's drum establishes him as a specifically Latino musician. Bart's skateboard connotes that he's reckless and brash (Figure 4.12). And Bullock's badge identifies him as a lawman in the notoriously lawless town of Deadwood.

Dialogue

What a character says and what other characters say about them determine a good deal about our understanding of that character. These meanings range from the direct (character A saying that character B is a murderer) to the oblique (the inflections of Charlie Sheen's voice as he cracks a joke). In each case, meaning about the character is communicated to the viewer.

Lighting and Videography or Cinematography

Some of the more technical aspects of filming or video recording an actor also contribute to our sense of character. These are discussed more fully in the chapters on visual style (Part II), but we may note here a few ways that television technique affects character.

Deviations from the standard of broad, even lighting have come to signify aspects of character. When actors are lit from below, their characters are thought to be sinister (Figure 8.27). When they are lit entirely from behind, the resulting silhouette conveys a sense of mystery (Figure 8.28). Other, more subtle lighting effects also serve to represent character. In a scene from *ER*'s pilot, where Dr. Mark Greene sleeps in a hospital bed and is awakened by a nurse (Figures 4.13 and 4.14), the repeated intrusion of light into the dark hospital room (also note the nurse's silhouette in Figure 4.13) and the strong sidelighting of Dr. Greene contribute to the sense of his discomfort and annoyance.

Similarly, camera lenses and other technical devices may influence character development (see Chapter 9). A close-up of someone taken with a wide-angle lens may distort the person's features, making her or him appear strange or goofy. The odd, low camera angle of Dr. Greene (Figure 4.13), for example, emphasizes his feet and his reclining position but conceals his face until we cut to the high-angle shot (Figure 4.14). Similarly, in the *Mad Men* scene above (Figures 4.1–4.3), the camera comes to rest on a close-up of the back of Draper's head,

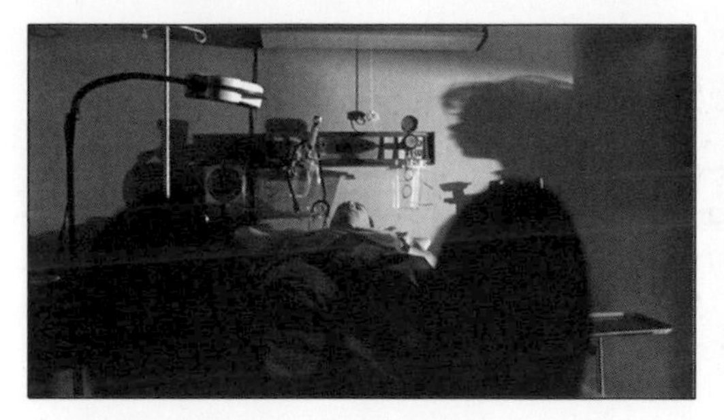

Figure 4.13 Heavy shadows contribute to the mood of an *ER* scene...

Figure 4.14 ... and can also signify the mood of the characters in the scene.

emphasizing his slicked-back hair and hiding his face until the reverse-angle shot. Remember, these are the very first shots of these programs' first episodes; we have absolutely no prior knowledge of these characters or their situations. These opening shots pique our curiosity about the characters and pull us into the programs' narratives.

Most viewers are not actively aware of such technical manipulations. Nonetheless, they do affect our understanding of character, and it is the analyst's responsibility to remain sensitive to these uses of television style.

Action

What characters do in stories—that is, their actions—determine in the final analysis what a character means. Simply enough, a character who does evil things comes to signify evil.

Building Performances

We have discussed the character as a fairly static object: a human being of a certain appearance, associated with certain objects, who is presented in a certain way and fits into a narrative structure. What we have ignored thus far—and what is frequently overlooked in television studies in general—is the work of the actor in the creation of character. Acting and performance, as we will use the terms, refer to how a line of dialogue is spoken and how a gesture is made and how a smile is smiled. It is what the actor does that is distinguishable from the scriptwriter's lines or the director's positioning of the camera. Consequently, performance is often difficult to isolate from other aspects of character and is even tougher to describe.

Our approach here, first of all, scraps any attempt to evaluate or judge acting. The evaluation of acting is clouded by ever-changing criteria of good and bad acting and the mercurial psychology of the individual viewer or critic. What is considered good acting at one time and place seems strange or exaggerated at another. Moreover, acting is not like the physical sciences; there is no such thing as progress in the art of acting. Acting does not get better and better. There are only different types of acting and different eras and different cultures that view certain types as better than others. For instance, there is a long-standing prejudice within U.S. culture that rates television acting below that of the theatrical film, and both television and film acting below that of the live theater. (And acting in daytime television is rated below that of prime time.) While there may be minor distinctions among the performances in these media, the main determinant in these judgments is a cultural elitism underscored by economic class prejudice; only relatively wealthy persons can afford to see live theater today. Consequently, television and film have become the cultural upstarts that have undermined the theater's dominance of the acting arts.

Elitism aside, the judgment of acting is a subjective business—inevitably anchored in deep-rooted prejudices and desires of which the viewer-critic is barely aware. In this book we will set aside the elitism and the subjectivity of judging acting in favor of trying to understand how we interpret acting and how performance conveys meaning. To this end, we will start with the raw material of acting—what Dyer calls the **signs of performance**—and then we will consider some of the strategies of performance that greatly determine how we interpret acting.[4]

A Typology of Performance Signs

When actors construct performances, they have two raw materials to work with: voice and body. How these materials are used is what defines the performance. Further, in studying performance it is useful to divide these materials into four types of performance signs:

1. vocal
2. facial
3. gestural
4. corporeal (the body).[5]

It may appear that there is some overlap here between performance signs, which depend on the actor's body, and the previously discussed character signs. The difference between the two is that performance signs deal with how the raw material is used; the discussion of character signs focuses on what material is selected and how it appears, even before being animated through performance. Thus, 50 Cent's and Roseanne Barr's body shapes are character signs that communicate aspects of the characters they portray on television, but the ways that these actors move and the postures in which they hold those bodies are performance signs.

Before considering briefly some of the specific ways that performance signs function, we should note that actor performance, more than any one character sign, contains the principal signifiers of a character's presumed emotional state. The way an actor talks or moves or smiles signifies how the character feels. In television, unlike the novel, we seldom have direct access to a character's emotions. The novel may represent emotions simply by describing them verbally: say, "Christine felt sad the day she murdered Bob." But a television program must signify these emotions mainly through performance signs—unless its characters talk about their mental health or voiceover narration explains what they're feeling (as in *Grey's Anatomy* [2005-]).

It is worth reiterating, however, that characters are not real people, that they do not feel emotions. Instead, emotions are represented through character and performance signs, which the viewer interprets as signifiers of emotion: a particular look in Christine's eye (a performance sign) while she murders Bob represents sadness. This difference between the emotions of characters and the emotions of real people is more than just wordplay. It is a distinction we must keep in mind to distance ourselves far enough from character emotions so that we can analyze how they function in the narrative structure, how they motivate the story.

Vocal Performance

There are a number of vocal qualities that may be manipulated in the construction of a performance: principally, **volume**, **pitch**, and **timbre** (a French word, pronounced "TAM-burr"). Just as in a musical performance, these qualities may be organized for specific affect.

The meanings of **volume** are varied. Loudness may signify strength, or it may signify shrillness or terror. Softness may signify meekness, or it may signify a control so total that speaking loudly is not necessary (see tvcrit.com/find/meek, tvcrit.com/find/control). As usual, context determines meaning.

- Pitch in music is how high or low a note is. Vocal pitch within our culture tends to convey gender-oriented meanings. A higher pitch is associated with the feminine and a lower pitch with the masculine. Higher voices are also linked with childlike characters. The deep bass voice of William Conrad helped create the tough, masculine character of detective Frank Cannon (*Cannon* [1971-76]) and earned him many jobs doing voiceover work for commercials (tvcrit.com/find/cannon). Actor Georgia Engel's high voice contributed to character Georgette Baxter's femininity in *The Mary Tyler Moore Show* (1970-77; tvcrit.com/find/engel). The gender significance of pitch is rooted in obvious biological differences between men's and women's vocal chords, but gender is also culturally determined. Individual men's voices are not necessarily lower than individual women's, and vice versa. And since pitch significance is part of culture, not just nature, female actors may use lower pitch to signify masculine characteristics, while male actors may use higher pitch to signify feminine ones. The final aspect of vocal quality that actors use in creating a performance is timbre, which is the most difficult to describe. Timbre is the tonal quality of a sound. Aside from being high or low, soft or loud, is a sound harsh or mellow or nasal or smooth? In short, what type of tone does it have? The harsh, nasal tone of Maggie Wheeler contributed to the annoying nature of Janice in the *Friends* episode discussed in Chapter 3 (tvcrit.com/find/friends03)—just as a similarly voiced Fran Drescher used her voice in *The Nanny* (1993-99; tvcrit.com/find/drescher). Sharon Gless's throaty delivery underlines the sexual potential beneath the police detective exterior of Chris Cagney (*Cagney and Lacey* [1982-88]; tvcrit.com/find/gless). Different tonal qualities convey a myriad of connotations within our culture. To describe them all would be nearly impossible, but still, the analyst needs to remain alert to them.

In addition to vocal quality, the performance of dialogue is also affected by the rhythm of the speech. Bob Newhart's trademark of halting, interrupted speech signifies his character's lack of confidence (in *The Bob Newhart Show* [1972-78] and *Newhart* [1982-90]; tvcrit.com/find/newhart). Peter Falk's slow delivery of crime scene analysis in *Columbo* (1971-77; tvcrit.com/find/falk) masks his quick and clever deductive skills. Lauren Graham's rapid-fire delivery of dialogue in *Gilmore Girls* marks her quirky spunkiness. In each case the rhythm of the vocal performance conveys meaning to the viewer (tvcrit.com/find/graham).

Facial Performance

Facial performance is the way that facial appearance is used. Facial appearance is a character sign—for example, Fawcett's hair in Figure 4.8. We may also think of it as a performance sign in terms of how Fawcett moves her hair. Fawcett's hair is not just larger than normal, it is also emphasized by the performer, which accentuates its significance. With each toss of Fawcett's head, the meaning of these signs (Fawcett's "blondness") is re-emphasized.

Most facial performance is not as large as Fawcett's, obviously. Minuscule movements of facial muscles can have significance. The viewer easily distinguishes the different meanings suggested by tiny variations in facial movement. A certain type of smile can mean amusement, while another can mean condescension or disbelief. In one *Charlie's Angels* scene, Fawcett's smile signifies flirtation as she plays dumb with a group of men Charlie's Angels are investigating. Her exaggerated performance in this scene also signifies to the viewer that her flirtation is a put-on, that it is just part of her disguise. In contrast, Marlon Brando's smile in *A Streetcar*

Named Desire is quite predatory as he sizes up his sister-in-law (discussed on p. 69, Figure 4.20; tvcrit.com/find/streetcar). Of all the performance signs, the facial presumably signifies the most about character emotions.

Gestural Performance

The significance of human gestures to a performance has been discussed since at least the nineteenth century, when a French teacher of elocution, François Delsarte (1811–71), codified gestures into the Delsarte system of performance. In the Delsarte system there is a strict vocabulary of gesture. Figure 4.15 shows three hand gestures that he particularized. The center gesture, labeled "Normo-normal," is the neutral, relaxed way to hold the hand and it signifies "calm repose" in Delsarte's system. In contrast, the "Concentro-normal" gesture means "approbation, tenderness" and the "Excentro-normal" gesture expresses "indifference, prostration, imbecility, insensibility, or death"![6] (Delsarte observed the latter gesture in many corpses.) However, the meanings of gestural performance are not as clear-cut or universal as Delsarte maintained. Instead, gestures convey meanings in more ambiguous fashion and in a way that changes over time and from culture to culture. Hand gestures, in particular, differ markedly from one country to another. In the United States, most people would indicate the number one by holding up their first finger, but in Poland they use their thumb, which in the U.S. would typically signify "Okay." Despite the inherent ambiguity of human gestures, Delsarte's codification system was commonly taught to stage actors as the twentieth century began and had a notable impact on the performance style in early, silent film, too.

The use of gestures is clearly one of the actor's main resources. Loretta Devine's performance as Cynthia Carmichael on *The Carmichael Show* (2015–), for instance, feature gestures that are so broad and active that they sometimes catch camera operators by surprise. In one shot she enthusiastically describes a protest she just attended and does it so broadly that her hand extends beyond the frame of the image (Figure 4.16; tvcrit.com/find/carmichael). What meaning are we to assign to this arm movement? Perhaps we can say that this broad gesture contributes to the passionate quirkiness of her character and her fiery spirit in this scene, but that is nowhere near as precise as Delsarte's strict code of gesture.

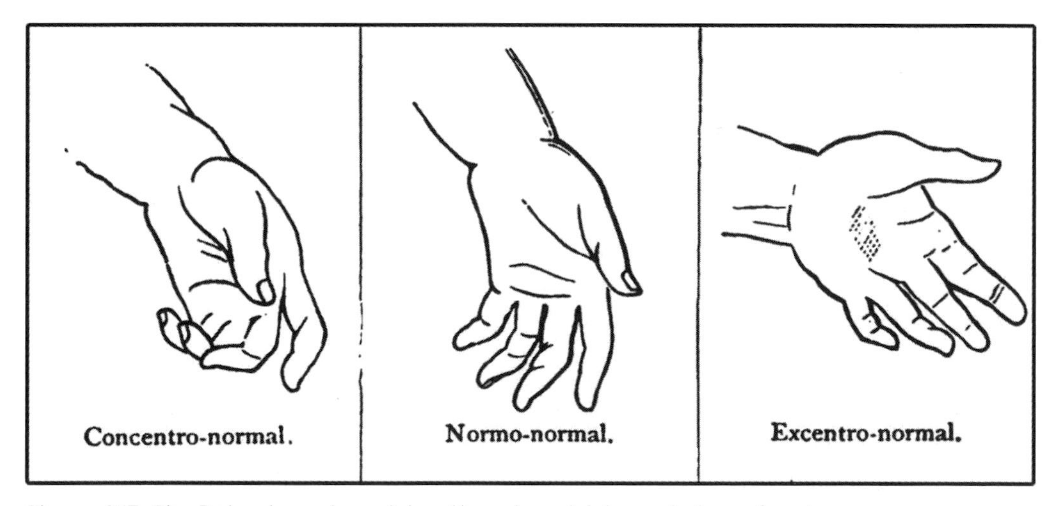

Figure 4.15 The Delsarte system claims there is a strict vocabulary of gesture.

Figure 4.16 Loretta Devine gestures broadly, forcing the camera operators of *The Carmichael Show* to struggle to keep her hands in frame.

Corporeal Performance

The stance and bearing of an actor's body communicate meaning to the viewer that, obviously, ties in with the actor's gestures. Jim Parsons's performance as Sheldon Cooper in *The Big Bang Theory* uses stiff, upright posture to emphasize his character's rigid attitude toward life. He is seldom seen running or moving quickly. Parsons's corporeal performance is contained and constrained–much like Sheldon's emotions (Figure 4.17). Moreover, Parsons's corporeal performance contrasts with those of his co-stars, who are substantially shorter than him and who move about more freely. In one scene from the first season, Sheldon, Howard (Simon Helberg), and Rajesh (Kunal Nayyar) discuss a road trip (tvcrit.com/find/bigbang). Sheldon stands stiffly next to the two of them, his arms behind his back. When they decide to leave, Howard and Rajesh bolt out the door, leaving Sheldon to follow them in his gangly gait (Figures 4.18 and 4.19). Leonard (Johnny Galecki) then hurries after them in his own distinctively jerky, hesitant movement. The only *Big Bang Theory* actor who regularly uses a fluid, active corporeal style is Kaley Cuoco as Penny, which suits her character's earthy sensuality.

Strategies of Performance

Most of the time, we do not concern ourselves with the work that the actor does to create the performance. Indeed, television programs erase the marks of that work by emphasizing the characters as "real" human beings rather than constructed collections of character and performance signs. However, our understanding of performance signs is often affected by presumptions of how the actor came to create those attributes. And discussions of acting inevitably return to questions of performance strategies: principally, how did the actor create the performance? As this is also the main concern of acting schools, it seems appropriate to deal with this issue here. To best understand the different approaches to acting, it is necessary, however, to place acting strategies into a historical context–since one style often reacts against another. It also becomes necessary to stray into the related media of film and live theater to place performance history in context.

Figure 4.17 Jim Parsons's body posture and gesturing help construct the constrained, rigid character of Sheldon Cooper in *The Big Bang Theory*.

Figure 4.18 The postures of Kunal Nayyar (Rajesh) and Simon Helberg (Howard) suggest more relaxed personas.

Figure 4.19 Differences among characters are also seen in their movements.

The danger in studying strategies of performance, however, is that it presumes that what is going on in the actors' minds is going to be evident in the way they perform. This, obviously, is a hazardous interpretive leap. Actors may be performing emotionally charged scenes and be thinking about what they will have for lunch that day. There is no way we can truly know an actor's mental processes. And yet, what we assume about those processes can be a key element in understanding how we interpret acting. Fundamentally, there are two approaches to performance in fiction television: **the naturalistic** and the **anti-naturalistic**. In naturalistic performance styles, actors struggle to create performances that we will accept as a "plausible," "believable" characters—as human beings, and not actors trying to look like someone they are not. Anti-naturalistic performance styles reject the notion of a believable character, but they do so for a broad variety of reasons that will be discussed in due course.

The Naturalists

There are many schools of thought regarding the production of a naturalistic performance. Limiting our scope to the nineteenth and twentieth centuries, we will consider two types of naturalistic performance: **repertory** and **Method**. It must be noted at the outset, however, that these two strategies do not exist in pure form. Any performance is an impure mixture of approaches.

Repertory Performance

In repertory theater, a set group of actors performs a series of different plays during a season. One week the group might do Henrik Ibsen's *A Doll's House* and the next week William

Shakespeare's *Macbeth*. As a result, the actors are constantly assuming new roles. To facilitate this ongoing change of roles, a repertory-style performance sees acting as a process of selecting particular gestures and spoken dialects and constructing a performance from them, although it does not rely upon a code of gestures set out in an acting manual (as in the Delsarte method, in specific, and pantomime, in general). The work of the actor is to study human movement and speech and to borrow gestures and dialects from life in the construction of characters. Repertory actors are dispassionate in this assemblage of actions and accents. They don't become emotional while acting, but they signify emotion through these movements and gestures.

For example, when Larry Drake began the role of the mentally challenged Benny Stulwicz on *L.A. Law* (1986–94) he observed psychiatric patients to see how they moved and spoke. Armed with this information, he could signify intellectual disability by reenacting the gestures and speech patterns of the mentally challenged. Some film actors are also particularly well known for this performance strategy—Laurence Olivier and Meryl Streep, for example.

Even though repertory acting today does not rely upon Delsarte's codified system of pantomime, it would be inaccurate to say that repertory performances are not in a sense "coded." True, there is no clearly delineated code such as Delsarte believed in, but repertory acting does draw upon the rather flexible code of human gesture and dialect that operates in a society at a particular time. An actor's selection from life of gesture and dialect depends upon certain commonsense presumptions about how people move and speak. Even when an actor such as Drake takes special pains to study a certain type of person, his perception is still filtered through assumptions of which gestures and dialects are significant and which are not. So-called body language follows certain conventions that shift over time and cultures.

Method Performance

The style of performance most generally known in the U.S. is called simply "the Method." Method acting differs sharply from the repertory style. Rather than stressing the selection and assembling of gestures and dialects, Method acting encourages the actor to become the character, to fuse their personality with the role, to relive the character. Method teachers argue that once the actor becomes the role, then the gestures and dialects necessary for the performance will organically grow out of that union of actor and character. Repertory performers are accused of mechanical acting by Method believers, because non-Method performance relies on a machine-like fitting together of techniques.

Three tactics that Method actors use to encourage the actor-character fusion are **emotional memory** (or affective memory), **sense memory**, and **improvisation**. Using emotional memory, actors draw upon their memories of previous emotions that match the emotions of the characters. To encourage those memories, actors can use sense memory to remember the physical sensations of a particularly emotional event. Was it hot or cold? How did the chair they were sitting on feel? Thus, sense memory is used to generate emotional memory. Improvisation is mostly used during rehearsal in Method acting. Actors imagine their way into the "minds" of characters and then place those characters into new situations, improvising new lines of dialogue based on this actor-character union.

According to Method advocates, if actors successfully tap into deep-rooted emotions and "become" the characters, then their performances will express a higher degree of "truth" because the actor is feeling what the character is feeling and behaving appropriately. For better or worse, this has become one of the principal criteria for judging acting: Do the actors appear to be fully submerged into the characters? Do they feel what the characters feel? Judging performance in this fashion can be dangerous. It rests upon the ability to read the actor's mind during a performance—an impossible task. For this reason, the evaluation of acting based on Method acting criteria remains questionable.

Method acting initially came to the attention of the U.S. public at about the same time that television enjoyed its first growth spurt: the late 1940s and early 1950s. At that time, director Elia Kazan brought Marlon Brando to the stage and then to the screen in *A Streetcar Named Desire* (1951, Figure 4.20; tvcrit.com/find/streetcar), which was followed by *On the Waterfront* (1954). Brando was the most visible of several distinctive new actors who were advocating the Method. He, James Dean, Montgomery Clift, Julie Harris, and others had been trained by Method teachers such as Lee Strasberg (at the Actors Studio) and Stella Adler (Brando's principal teacher). However, the Method was being taught in the live theater long before this crop of actors made their impact on U.S. cinema. The technique originated in Russia at the end of the nineteenth century, when Constantin Stanislavski founded the Moscow Art Theater in 1897. Stanislavski disdained any acting other than that of the live theater. He barely tolerated film actors and died in 1938 before television became a mass medium. Still, the impact of the Stanislavski system on television has been immeasurable.

The Method made a remarkably early incursion into television performance. The musical variety programs, Westerns, sitcoms, and soap operas—and, moreover, the bulk of 1950s television—had little to do with the Method, but 1950s television also hosted the so-called golden

Figure 4.20 A Streetcar Named Desire, the play and then the film, introduced the Method acting of Marlon Brando and others to the American public.

age of live television drama. Stage-trained actors and theatrical productions were imported into television to be broadcast live on programs such as *Playhouse 90* (1956–61) and *Philco Television Playhouse* (1948–55). The latter was initially sponsored by the Actors' Equity Association (the principal theatrical actors union in the U.S.) and dealt directly with Method-influenced performers. One such actor was Rod Steiger, who trained alongside Brando at the Actors Studio and brought the Method to the title role of *Marty*—broadcast live on *Philco Television Playhouse* May 24, 1953 (Figure 4.21; tvcrit.com/find/marty).

In some respects, the 1950s live television dramas more closely resembled theatrical presentations than did the cinema of that time. In both theater and live television, each scene was played straight through, not broken apart and then edited together as it would be in a film production. And 1950s television drama was also shot on an indoor sound stage—equivalent to the theatrical stage—rather than the location work that was becoming popular in film at that time. In many respects, 1950s actors must have felt more comfortable in a television studio production than on a movie set. As suggested above, however, *Playhouse 90* and the like were not typical of programs on the infant medium, and Method acting was definitely the exception rather than the rule. Since that time, though, Method acting has found a home on television in dramatic programs such as *Hill Street Blues* (1981–87) and *Law & Order* (1990–2010) and, in diluted form, many others. Vincent D'Onofrio, Detective Robert Goren on *Law & Order*, is one example of a television performer who studied the Method at the Actors Studio.

In theory, emotional and sense memories may be used to access a broad range of emotions, both negative and positive. The history of Method performances in television and film, however, has been heavily weighted toward darker emotions, anxieties, and quirky neuroses. It is no small coincidence that the Method was popularized at roughly the same time as Freudian psychology—psychoanalysis—became part of everyday language. Just as in Freud, the Method presumes that negative emotions are somehow more authentic than positive ones; that sorrow, depression, and doubt are more realistic than joy, elation, and self-confidence. This, however, is a dubious assumption, because positive emotions appear in reality also; they are thus no less

Figure 4.21 Rod Steiger brought Method acting to television in a production of *Marty* that was broadcast live in 1953.

real. Nonetheless, the Method's emphasis on emotional discord is a large part of the reason it has not been used much outside of television drama. These sorts of emotions find little expression in sitcoms and the like.

Aside from the emphasis on gloom and melancholy, Method performances historically also have been marked by a specific use of performance signs. In the 1950s, the vocal performance of Brando, Dean, Clift, et al., was often remarked upon. In comparison to contemporary acting norms, they used odd speech rhythms (offbeat, faltering); overlapped dialogue; and slurred or mumbled their lines (tvcrit.com/find/streetcar). Their movements were similarly offbeat and quirky when compared to the norm of the time. Thus, Method acting was initially described as a technique that actors used to create a performance, but it has also developed its own conventions, its own code of performance. It has come to rely on the creation of negative emotions and has been marked by odd performance signs.

The Anti-Naturalists

Naturalism can thus be seen to dominate how most people—critics and everyday viewers alike—think about acting. But it would be wrong to assume that we always demand naturalism from television performers. Sometimes it's quite clear that the actors are "faking" it, that they are separating themselves from the roles they play and pointing to the mechanics of their performances. It's as if they were winking at the viewer and implying, "You and I both know that I'm not really this character. I'm only performing this role." When actors distance themselves from their roles, they reject the basic tenet of the Method. They don't become the characters, they just present them to us. This style of performance can be traced back hundreds of years to broad comedy traditions in the theater, but we'll limit this overview to two twentieth-century anti-naturalistic approaches: vaudeville and Bertolt Brecht's theory of epic theater.

Vaudeville Performance

Vaudeville was a style of theatrical presentation that was built around song-and-dance numbers, comedy routines, and short dramatic skits and tableaux (the cast freezing in dramatic poses). Vaudeville was at its most popular in the late nineteenth and early twentieth centuries, but by the 1920s it was eclipsed by the competing mass entertainment forms of radio and the movies. Even though vaudeville as a medium no longer exists, the style of performance it used survives in many television forms. (For more on vaudeville, see the Library of Congress's multimedia anthology titled "American Variety Stage," tvcrit.com/find/vaudeville.)

Significantly, vaudeville performance does not demand that we forget the presence of the actor within the guise of the character. That is, vaudeville performance frequently reminds us that we are watching a performance and that the characters before us are not real people. This is largely achieved through the direct address of the viewer. Vaudeville actors often look straight at the audience, perform toward them, and even make comments to them—as can be seen in Figure 4.22, from a 1920s silent film in which the Gonzalez Brothers direct their dance routine to the audience while standing in front of a painted backdrop (tvcrit.com/find/gonzalez). Vaudeville's direct address violates the theatrical concept of an invisible "fourth wall" that separates audience from characters. In conventional theatrical performances, we observe the action without the actors recognizing our presence in the theater. In vaudeville, in contrast, our presence is repeatedly acknowledged. And if we are acknowledged as viewers,

Figure 4.22 Vaudeville performers often spoke directly to the audience, as illustrated by this silent film of the Gonzalez Brothers.

then the entire illusion of the fiction is undermined. The naturalistic concept of the believable character becomes immaterial to the vaudevillian.

Much of early television bore the legacy of vaudeville. Musical variety programs—mixing vaudevillesque music, acrobatics, ventriloquism, and comic skits—dominated early television. *The Milton Berle Show* (1948–67), *The Ed Sullivan Show* (1948–71), and *The Jackie Gleason Show* (1952–70) are just three of the long-running variety programs that were popular during that time. In each, a host spoke directly to the viewer, introducing the short performances that constituted the weekly show (tvcrit.com/find/variety). And the performances themselves were also directly presented to the viewer. Even the comic narrative pieces featured the performer looking directly at the camera (a taboo in dramatic television) and implicitly or explicitly addressing the viewer. An example of explicit address of the audience in a narrative program comes from *The George Burns and Gracie Allen Show* (1950–58), one of television's early successes. Before the story begins, Burns comes out and, speaking in front of a curtain as if in a theater, talks to the in-studio audience and, by extension, to the audience viewing at home (Figure 4.23; tvcrit.com/find/burns). He shatters the suspension of disbelief and the fourth wall by explaining, "For the benefit for those who have never seen me before, I am what is known in show business as a straight man. Know what a straight man is? I'll tell you. After the comedian gets through with a joke, I look at the comedian and then I look at the audience. Like this. [He demonstrates.]" Then, later in the show, we can see this vaudevillian technique in action during the narrative (Figure 4.24).

In the 1970s, the musical variety program fell from favor with the U.S. audience, but vaudeville-style performance continues in programs such as *Saturday Night Live* (1975–) and in comic monologues such as those that begin late-night talk shows and are presented in stand-up comic programs on cable television. And Burns's mix of vaudeville with the sitcom can still be found in comic remarks made directly to the viewer by characters on *Malcolm in the Middle* (Figure 4.25, [2000–06]; tvcrit.com/find/malcolm), *The Bernie Mac Show* (Figure 12.6, [2001–06]; tvcrit.com/find/mac), and *The Middle* (2009–), and in the voiceover narration of *My Name Is Earl* (2005–09).

Figure 4.23 George Burns simultaneously addresses a studio audience and the viewer of *The George Burns and Gracie Allen Show*. He comments on the episode's story...

Figure 4.24 ... sometimes breaking character in the middle of the show to acknowledge the audience.

Figure 4.25 Malcolm speaks directly to the *Malcolm in the Middle* viewer, while his brother sleeps behind him.

Brechtian Performance

German playwright and theorist Bertolt Brecht once posed rhetorically, "What ought acting to be like?" He then answered:

> Witty. Ceremonious. Ritual. Spectator and actor ought not to approach one another but to move apart. Each ought to move away from himself. Otherwise the element of terror necessary to all recognition is lacking.[7]

Brecht's theories, as exemplified by his plays, abandon the naturalistic ideal of a believable character with whom we can identify. In his so-called **epic theater** (which has little to do with the traditional epic), we are alienated from the characters rather than identifying with or "approaching" them. Actors do not relive characters as in the Method, but rather quote the characters to the viewer, always retaining a sense of themselves as actors, as separate from the characters. In other words, the actor presents the character to the viewer without pretending to actually be the character. Viewer and actor alike are distanced from the character; hence the term Brechtian **distanciation**.

What is the purpose of this distanciation? Brecht argues that conventional dramatic theater narcotizes the spectator. We immerse ourselves in a story for two hours and then emerge from the theater as if waking from a drug-induced nap. Brecht contends instead that we should be confronted, alienated. His is a Marxist perspective that believes that the theater should be used to point out social ills and prompt spectators to take action about them. He advocates nothing less than a revolutionary theater. Brechtian performance theory has found fertile soil in the cinema of filmmakers such as Jean-Luc Godard, whose 1960s work aspired to transpose the epic theater to the cinema (see the trailer for his 1962 film *Vivre sa Vie* for a taste of his take on Brecht; tvcrit.com/find/vivre). But its significance to broadcast television is, admittedly, marginal. However, Brecht has influenced avant-garde video production of the past 20 years, including works done in that medium by Godard and video artists such as Nam June Paik.

We can find small instances of Brecht skulking about the edges of commercial television, if we look hard enough. In two music videos for the Replacements' *Tim* album for instance, all that is seen is a black-and-white shot of an audio speaker in a room (tvcrit.com/find/replacements). The videos open with a tight close-up of it; then it starts to vibrate as the music begins. The camera pulls back to reveal a record player, a few albums, nothing spectacular. A person walks in front of the speaker and we see his out-of-focus arm while he smokes a cigarette, but his face is never in frame (Figure 4.26). The video ends without the band ever appearing, as is the convention in, say, 90 percent of music videos. So, to start with, there's really no one to identify with. Beyond that, however, *Left of the Dial* breaks some of music video's other conventions by refusing to create a spectacle. Nothing really happens. We are left to amuse ourselves, to think about the video and the conventions it's breaking. There's nothing for us to identify with: no spectacle, no characters (that is, band members). This, we would argue, could be considered Brechtian television. Thus, even though there is actually little Brechtian television to be found, we should be still aware that alternatives to naturalism do exist and, in film and theater, are actively investigated.

Figure 4.26 A music video by The Replacements defeats viewer expectations by refusing to show the faces of band members.

The Star System?

Not everyone who appears on television is a television star. Stars, as we will be using the term, are actors or personalities whose significance extends beyond the television program in which they appear. If actors' images do not range beyond their programs, then they are just actors trapped within the characters they've created—as are many of the younger actors in, say, *Game of Thrones*, whose names are barely known to viewers. A true **star image**, in contrast, circulates through the culture in a variety of media—Instagram, Facebook, print publications, other television programs—and has culturally delimited meanings associated with it. Sean Bean was one of the few true stars cast in the first season of *Game of Thrones* (as Eddard "Ned" Stark), having established his image on British television and film. His stature as an actor made it particularly surprising when his character was summarily executed and eliminated from the show.

Of Texts and Intertextuality

Often it seems as if we know stars personally and intimately. We see them weekly (or daily) on our television screens, read their Twitter feed, and hear them discuss themselves on talk shows. A large part of our conversation about television focuses on the personal lives of the stars. Wherever TV viewers congregate—social-media sites like Facebook, the office water cooler, or the high school lunch table—stars are a topic of conversation: "Do you think Jennifer Aniston is still in love with Brad Pitt?" or "Do you think Kim Kardashian is really as vain as she appears to be?" This illusion of intimacy is encouraged by television and other media, but it should not be confused with actual knowledge of someone's personality. We can never know stars' authentic natures because our knowledge of them is always filtered through the media.

Magazine articles, social media, and even celebrities' own Twitter feeds often claim to present genuine knowledge about the star's inner self, but we should take them all with a healthy dose of skepticism. Media-produced information about stars is like the layers of an onion. One article will discuss the "truth" about Pamela Anderson's feelings regarding her break-up with Tommy Lee and the circulation on the Web of their sexually explicit videotape; and then, inevitably, another comes along and undercuts that particular "truth" and proposes its own "truth," which is then countered by another article with its version of Anderson's emotions. We viewers can never cut through all of the layers of the onion and have direct knowledge of the star's psyche. But, for our purposes, the "true personality" of a star is a moot point. What we are concerned with here is how a star's image is built and how it fits into television's narratives.

In this regard, it is helpful to think of a star as a "text," as a collection of signifiers that hold meaning for the viewer. Various meanings cluster around stars. Their polysemy (literally: "many meanings") is generated by their presence in several media texts: television programs, commercials, social-media posts, Web search engines, and the like.

Taylor Swift, for example, is a formidable star text. In 2017, she was ranked by *Forbes* magazine as the highest paid celebrity in the United States.[8] Its ranking system is "a measure of entertainment-related earnings and media visibility (exposure in print, television, radio and online)" and in recent years has included a social-media ranking based on celebrities' presence on YouTube, Instagram, Facebook, and so on. Swift's star text, an image of how she lives and what she thinks, is constructed from the representation of her in all of these media texts. Thus, she has an **intertextual** presence in U.S. culture that creates a sense of her publicly available private life. Her **intertextuality** separates her from other actors and establishes her as a star. For our purposes, intertextuality is the main component distinguishing a star from an actor. Without intertextuality, an actor is "just" an actor. *Forbes'* list, then, functions as a gauge of an actor's intertextuality.[9]

The different types of media texts in which stars appear may be clustered into four sometimes overlapping groups:

1. promotion
2. publicity
3. television programs (and films)
4. criticism of those programs/films.[10]

By examining the stars' appearance in these media texts, we may better understand their intertextuality and how their polysemy evolves.

Promotion

Promotional texts are generated by stars and their representatives: agents, public relations firms, studios, networks, and so on. Principal among promotional texts are press releases containing information in the star's best interests, advertisements placed online and in television listings such as *TV Guide*, promotional announcements on television (whether created by a network or a local station), appearances on talk shows and news/informational programs (for example, *Entertainment Tonight* and the E! cable channel), and official, star-controlled social-media outlets (Facebook, Twitter, YouTube, and so on). Promotional materials represent the deliberate attempt to shape our perception of a star.

The majority of promotional texts place stars in the contexts of their television characters. Promotional announcements on television especially focus on the character and the program in which a star appears—sometimes excluding the star's name altogether. The strength of the star's influence determines whether star or character will be emphasized. Genie Francis, probably the biggest soap-opera star of the late 1970s and 1980s, left her role of Laura on *General Hospital* and began appearing on other, competing soap operas. The new networks then promoted her character as "Genie Francis in. . . ." This was extremely unusual for soap operas and indicated just how major a star image Francis was. Prime-time programs' promotional material stresses stars more than does daytime drama's, but the star's character always governs how the star will be presented.

Publicity

We will here separate publicity from promotion, although the two are often indistinguishably intertwined. For our purposes, publicity will be used to designate information beyond the control of stars and their entourages: news reports about scandalous events in the star's life, unauthorized biographies, interviews in which the star is embarrassed or confronted with some unsavory aspect of their life, mug shots posted on the *Smoking Gun* website and TMZ.com, and so on.[11]

There have been many instances in the history of celebrity where promotion posed as publicity. Indeed, the career of the very first film star, Florence Lawrence, was launched by her producer spreading a false rumor that she had been killed in a streetcar accident. He then took out an advertisement declaring, "We Nail a Lie," in which he vigorously denied the rumor (Figure 4.27). On a more mundane, day-to-day level, blogs, newspapers, and magazines often publish verbatim the promotional press releases sent to them by the networks. Thus, often what appears to be a news story (that is, "publicity") is actually the work of a star's publicist ("promotion").

Figure 4.27 The promotion of film actors as stars begins with Florence Lawrence and deceptive rumors of her death.

The distinction between publicity and promotion is not always clear, but there are some instances when it is quite obvious. When a tabloid magazine learned that Roseanne Barr had had a child before she was married, had put her up for adoption, and hadn't seen her in years, it published the story even before Barr could speak directly with her daughter. The articles about this event in Barr's publicly available private life constituted information beyond her influence. Publicity such as this raises interesting questions about the tensions and conflicts within stars' images—aspects that contrast with the official narratives of their lives. In the instance of Barr's child, the publicity related to her on-screen image as a sitcom mother. In her television program she was represented as a tough but ultimately loving mother. In contrast, the publicity represented her as a woman who abandoned her child. The tension between these two representations of Barr, and her bringing them together in a single person, illustrates how a star may reconcile a variety of sometimes conflicting meanings.

Television Programs

As we have noted above, the characters stars play in television programs determine much of how stars are perceived. However, to qualify as stars within our definition, they must first of all have images that go beyond that of their characters. Swift, Francis, and Barr are obviously stars. Their cultural currency extends beyond the texts of music videos, *General Hospital*, and *Roseanne*. But an actor such as Jon Hensley—who played the *As the World Turns* character of Holden Snyder off and on for 25 years—is not a star because he is not recognized outside of his long-running role.

When stars play roles, their polysemy may fit characters in a variety of ways.[12] Often, as in the case of **typecasting**, the star image perfectly fits the character. For example, Charlie Sheen's abuse of drugs and alcohol, encounters with prostitutes, combative marriages, and generally dissipated life, and the meanings associated with that, made for a perfect fit with his womanizing, dissolute character, also named Charlie, on *Two and a Half Men* (2003–15). Actor Sheen's publicly available private life and character Charlie's licentious behavior greatly resemble one another. Critics of television often presume that this **perfect fit** is the only way that stars are used in television. However, such is not the case.

Often there is a **problematic fit** between stars' polysemy and the attributes of the characters they are playing. When a character is cast against type, the star image contrasts with the character. When Farrah Fawcett, whose image centered around her physical attractiveness and implied a certain empty-headedness, was cast as the abused wife in the ambitious made-for-TV film *The Burning Bed* (1984), there was a problematic fit between her image and the character portrayed. Similarly, during the 1970s, soap-opera star Susan Lucci was represented in the press as a loving, devoted mother at the same time that her character, Erica on *All My Children*, was a manipulative woman who secretly took birth control pills to prevent conception.

Perfect and problematic fits of star image to role are less common than the **selective use** of the star's polysemy in the character's attributes. Larry Hagman, for example, has been represented in the press as an unpredictable man with a strong interest in spirituality and Eastern religions. His character of evil, manipulative oilman J. R. Ewing in *Dallas* (1978–91) selects Hagman's unpredictability but ignores or represses his spirituality. In this fashion, Hagman's star image is partially utilized in the construction of his character. This is probably the most frequent use of star image in characterization.

Criticism

The final media text contributing to a star's image is the commentary on stars and their programs that appears online, in print, and on television itself. Fans who post comments online and professional television critics are presumed to operate independently of studios, networks, and other promotion-generating organizations. And, although many a review has been written out of a network's press kit, critics write about stars from a viewer's point-of-view, evaluating their images and their use in television programs. Thus, fan-generated online texts and professional television criticism often share in the dissemination of a star image or help to change it.

Today, the critical writing by professional critics about stars in programs (e.g., Jeff Jensen in *Entertainment Weekly*) has virtually been eclipsed by the amount of material produced by fans and self-styled media critics and distributed through Facebook, Twitter, YouTube, blogs, Wikipedia, and other online social media. When a star appears in a new program, for example, the online texts about their presence in it will begin appearing before the program's pilot episode has a chance to conclude. The precise impact of all this online chatter on a star's image is difficult to assess—although **social listening** services such as ListenFirst, CrowdTangle, and Nielsen Social attempt to do so with companies' brands and celebrities' images. Clearly, the legitimacy and influence of some online texts is much greater than others. An article on Wikipedia that has been written and checked by dozens of contributors is generally going to have more weight and be read by more people than an entry in someone's self-created WordPress blog. And the opinion of Facebook friends that you know and trust will sway you more than a television commercial. Despite the ambiguity of social-media's part in the star-text process, it cannot be denied that we have entered an era when publishing television criticism is no longer limited to professional TV critics. And there can be no doubt that such social-media texts help to construct stars' images. Stars themselves have taken advantage of this and use services such as Twitter to communicate directly with fans, often bypassing the publicity departments of studios and networks. Ashton Kutcher is one example of a television star who shapes his image through his Twitter feed (aplusk) and its 18 million followers (as of April 14, 2017). And, of course, former reality-TV star Donald Trump's Twitter activity has had an enormous impact—factoring heavily into his election as president.

Intertextuality and Polysemy: Tina Fey

To illustrate how stars' images (or texts) and their polysemy develop through intertextuality, we will focus on Tina Fey—one of the most notable television stars of the early twenty-first century. Her image is particularly instructive because the connection between her publicly available private life and her on-screen character is so strong. After all, Fey's *30 Rock* (2006–13) character, Liz Lemon, is the head writer of a sketch comedy show on NBC and Fey herself was the head writer for *Saturday Night Live* on NBC. And yet, there are still important divergences between Fey and Liz that illuminate the function of star texts within television texts.

Fey's image has developed principally through three sources: her television work, her theatrical film work, and the discourse or talk surrounding her (specifically, television, print, and online publicity that circulates about her—material that she does not control). In Richard Dyer's terms, these TV programs, films, and popular-culture materials are texts that function together to construct our image of Fey. They all work together and play off one another, thus generating intertextuality—the identifying mark of a true star. In this brief analysis, we'll examine these texts, recognizing that everything we know about Elizabeth Stamatina "Tina" Fey has been filtered through some media form.

Fey's intertextuality began, in a small way, after she graduated from the University of Virginia as a drama major in 1992 and moved to Chicago to become a part of the Second City, a theatrical improvisation group that has catalyzed the careers of many comedians/actors. Robert Klein, Joan Rivers, John Belushi, Bill Murray, Dan Aykroyd, Gilda Radner, Chris Farley, Steve Carell, Amy Sedaris, and Stephen Colbert all passed through the Second City—many of them on their way to NBC's *Saturday Night Live* (*SNL*). The Second City is sometimes even viewed as a farm team for *SNL*, but it has little national television presence on its own. Fey did not do much television work during this era, but she did appear in her first commercial in 1995—a regional one for Mutual Savings Bank (Figure 4.28; tvcrit.com/find/feymutual). So it wasn't until Fey parlayed her work at the Second City into an *SNL* spot in 1997 that she began to become a national public persona. But it's important to note that Fey did not go directly from the Second City to appearing on camera, co-hosting *SNL*'s "Weekend Update" segment. Instead, she was hired as a behind-the-scenes comedy writer for *SNL* and, as is inevitably noted in every overview of her career, she became the program's first female head writer in 1999. It wasn't until 2000, however, that she would get significant time on camera. Her well-received "Weekend Update" appearances, where she tartly skewered current events, brought her into the public eye and established her as a celebrity (Figure 4.29, from February 23, 2008; tvcrit.com/find/feywu2008).

Figure 4.28 Tina Fey appears in a 1995 Mutual Savings Bank commercial.

Figure 4.29 Fey's work on *Saturday Night Live*'s "Weekend Update" helped to establish her television credentials.

Fey's work both in front of and behind the camera were seen to be part of *SNL*'s resurgence in the 2000s. The program, which has been on the air since 1975, was said to have been reinvigorated by Fey's presence, and she won her first Emmy Award in 2001 in recognition of this. To capitalize on the renewed interest in *SNL*, NBC accepted Fey's pitch to create a scripted program about life behind-the-scenes at a sketch comedy show—with her playing the part of the fictional show's head writer and also functioning as one of *30 Rock*'s showrunners. In numerous ways, *30 Rock* playfully blurs the distinction between fiction and reality, starting with using the nickname for NBC's corporate headquarters at 30 Rockefeller Plaza as its title. Much of *30 Rock*'s humor is itself intertextual. It refers to all manner of popular-culture texts (songs, films, comic books, and many TV programs) and tweaks NBC's corporate culture. Even Comcast's takeover of NBC in real life is satirized on *30 Rock*, where an entity called Kabletown is angling to buy NBC. Thus, the program encourages us to blend reality and see Fey and her character, Liz, as a perfect fit (in Dyer's words).

30 Rock's ratings were never impressive, but its critical reputation was quite high and it garnered numerous awards—setting a record for Emmy nominations in 2008, with Emmys awarded to Fey for her acting, writing, and producing. The success of her *30 Rock* and *SNL* television work opened doors for her in theatrical film. Two years after the debut of *30 Rock*, Fey performed in her first starring role in a feature film. In *Baby Mama* she continued her *30 Rock* persona as an uptight, successful business woman with an unsatisfactory, childless personal life. In the film, Fey's character hires a surrogate mother to provide her with a child, although, naturally, complications ensue. The year that *Baby Mama* was released, 2008, saw Fey's image catapulted onto the national scene, but it was due less to this film or *30 Rock* than to her unnerving resemblance to Republican vice-presidential candidate Sarah Palin (Figure 4.30, with Fey on the right).

Fey's impersonation of Palin on five *SNL* shows is an essential part of her intertextuality.[13] (For her September 27, 2008, appearance as Palin, see Figure 4.31, tvcrit.com/find/feypalin.) It raised her national visibility well beyond that of the star of a well-reviewed, but low-rated, television program and overshadowed the modest success of *Baby Mama*. Fey as Palin has been described as "remarkable, dead-on, spot-on, fantastic, pitch-perfect, striking, spooky, transcendent, already legendary, and a bull's eye" (as summarized by strategic communication scholars Arhlene A. Flowers and Cory L. Young).[14] Fey was reportedly reluctant to take on the impersonation of Palin as she had not done much impersonation comedy before: "I was very

Figure 4.30 Sarah Palin and Tina Fey have an uncanny resemblance to one another.

Figure 4.31 Fey's impersonation of Palin on *SNL* brought her national attention during the 2008 election.

resistant to acknowledge that there was a resemblance. Then my kid saw Sarah Palin on TV and said, 'There's Mommy.'"[15] Fey's impersonation drew so much press that Palin herself agreed to appear on *SNL*. And there was considerable online chatter about how Fey's characterization of Palin as a witless dolt may have influenced the election.

Fey's turn as Palin made her (Fey) one of the most talked-about television stars of 2008, but, in general, she has mostly kept her private life out of the mainstream press. And she is seldom mentioned in the tabloid press. In contrast to, for example, Lindsay Lohan (who starred in a film that Fey wrote: *Mean Girls* [2004]), Fey has had remarkably little written about her publicly available private life. And what has surfaced has mostly appeared in nontabloid publications such as *The New Yorker*, *Harper's Bazaar*, and *Vanity Fair* (which has twice featured her on the cover). If we used Dyer's sense of the term publicity to refer to published texts about stars that are beyond their control, then Fey's publicity has stressed how stable and ordinary her life is. Articles about her emphasize her career as a writer first and actor second; her stable marriage to the *30 Rock* music composer, Jeff Richmond (whom she dated for years before marrying in a Greek Orthodox ceremony); and, since 2005, her struggle to be both a mother to her daughter and a successful television showrunner. Even the mystery of the scar on her left cheek did not entice tabloid writers to investigate her past. It wasn't until the January 2009 *Vanity Fair* piece that it was fully revealed she had been slashed by a stranger when she was five. Previously, she had demurred from discussing it: "It's a childhood injury that was kind of grim.... And it kind of bums my parents out for me to talk about it."[16]

What is the ideological function of a star? How do stars embody taken-for-granted assumptions about how the world works? We can begin to answer these questions as we examine Fey's polysemy, the meanings that constellate around her image. We may identify at least three central themes running through Fey's image: intellect, third-wave feminism, and the ordinariness-versus-glamour opposition (conjoined with her "metamorphosis" into a "sex symbol"). These themes have been constructed through her media texts—TV programs, films, the analysis of those programs/films, and the discourse surrounding her publicly available private life.

The most obvious marker of Fey's intellect is her glasses, which frequently have been described as her trademark and signature. On television and, in Hollywood in general, glasses are an unmistakable objective correlative of intelligence. Fey herself has often joked about their significance, remarking in 2003, "Glasses would make anyone look smarter. You put glasses on Woody Harrelson in *Indecent Proposal* and he's an architect. You put a pair of glasses on Denise Richards and she's a paleontologist." When the interviewer followed up her comment by asking, "Do you feel trapped by your glasses? Are they your Samson's locks? Take them off and the career comes crashing down around you?" Fey responded, "Definitely. I'm not that famous with the glasses, but I'm really not famous without them."[17]

Fey's intelligence, however, is constructed through more than just this obvious prop. Publicity texts feed the sense of her as an intellectual by stressing her work as a television and film scriptwriter. She doesn't just mindlessly recite dialogue, as a presumably less-than-intelligent actor does, she also creates it. As she said in a 2000 interview, before she got the "Weekend Update" job, "Writers have more power and control [than actors]."[18] Combine that with her showrunning work on *30 Rock* and, more recently, *Unbreakable Kimmy Schmidt* (2015-), and you have no less than a television auteur. Further, her scriptwriting ties in with her time spent as a Second City improv comic. Just like a scriptwriter, a comic/actor who can improvise creates their own dialogue. Thus, an improv comic is represented as smarter than a performer who numbly runs through memorized jokes. Other biographical elements—such as her college degree—help construct her image as an intellectual, but the principal ones are her writing and improvisation skills, in concert with her famous horn-rimmed glasses.

The feminist element of Fey's polysemy originates in her promotion to *SNL* head writer. News reports about her promotion invariably identify her as the first female head writer for a program that had been criticized for its male bias. A *Writer's Digest* author refers to *SNL* as a "bastion of testosterone" in an interview with Fey, who responds, "There are a lot of boys [at *SNL*].... We'll order food and I'll look around at a sea of boys eating steaks. I'm like, 'I gotta go.' It's like being in a cave full of bears."[19] Although Fey, in other quotations, downplays her role as a trailblazer, the publicity about the promotion overwhelmingly portrays it as a breakthrough for women comedy writers. In addition to this publicly available aspect of her offscreen life, Fey's feminism is also constructed through the television/film texts she has written, performed in, and produced. Specifically, feminist critiques of gender roles may be found in many of her *SNL* sketches, "Weekend Update" reports, and *30 Rock* episodes and, to a lesser extent, her theatrical film work.

Of course, feminism is a broad category, but we may be able to narrow it down. Ashley Barkman argues that Liz Lemon, Fey's character on *30 Rock*, is best positioned within third-wave feminism (a post-1992 women's movement discussed further in Chapter 14).[20] Barkman notes that Liz takes for granted the gains for equality won by second-wave feminism in the 1970s (especially equal job opportunity), and embodies the third wave's inclusive attitude that suggests that women may define themselves in a broad variety of ways, some of which would rankle second-wave feminists. According to third-wave feminism, women need not present themselves as anti-men or anti-sex or even as opposed to traditional female roles such as child-rearing. And third-wave feminists have, perhaps unfairly, accused second-wave feminists of doing just that.

We can extend Barkman's argument by noting that third-wave feminists have also defended "girlie" culture, and it is probably no coincidence that Liz's program is titled *The Girlie Show*—although in *30 Rock*'s pilot episode it is changed to *TGS with Tracy Jordan*. Looking to other characters that Fey has played, we can see more evidence of third-wave feminism. In her role doing a segment titled "Women's News" on "Weekend Update," Fey proclaims, "It's a great time to be a lady in America!" (tvcrit.com/find/feywu2008). She then launches into an editorial advocating Hillary Clinton over Barack Obama during the 2008 primary campaign:

> Maybe what bothers me the most is that people say that Hillary is a bitch. Let me say something about that: Yeah, she is. So am I.... You know what, bitches get stuff done.... So, I'm saying it's not too late Texas and Ohio, bitch is the new black!

As evidenced by Elizabeth Wurtzel's book *Bitch: In Praise of Difficult Women* (1998), "bitch" is among the derogatory terms for women that have been recuperated by third-wave feminists.[21] Amy Richards explains:

> For so long those words were used against women. Now using them is women's attempt to reclaim them and to say, "Yes, I am difficult. I am a bitch. Call me a bitch. I'm going to reclaim bitch and make it my own word, because the word has more hostility when it's being used against me than when it's being used by me."[22]

Like many third-wave feminists, Fey's television roles present her as the difficult, unruly woman, one who disrupts the patriarchal order, although often in ambivalent fashion. Her influence can be seen in the wide-ranging impact of the phrase "bitch is the new black."[23]

In Fey's publicly available private life, however, we can observe contradictions to this representation of her. Where Liz is comically inept at maintaining a boyfriend, Fey has been with the same man since 1994. Where Liz spends several episodes desperately and futilely trying to obtain a child, Fey is presented as a happy, if over-extended, mother of her two daughters. Where the "Tina Fey" on "Weekend Update" is sassy and irrelevant, articles about the offscreen Tina Fey describe her as bookish and monastic. The contradictory elements within Fey's star text illustrate how celebrities are often able to hold opposites together in the same physical human body. The combining of opposites is also evident in the final theme found in Fey's star image: the transformation of the ordinary into the glamorous or sexual.

In virtually every overview of Fey's career trajectory, the author notes that Fey transformed from a plain, virginal, "mousy" woman, during her Second City days, into a glamorous figure, sparkling with sexual allure. Her metamorphosis is evident if we contrast her rather unexceptional image in the 1995 Mutual Savings Bank commercial with her glamorous appearance on *Late Show With David Letterman* in 2010 (Figures 4.28 and 4.32; tvcrit.com/find/feymutual and

Figure 4.32 Fey shows a more glamorous image on *Late Show With David Letterman*.

tvcrit.com/find/feylateshow). She's been dubbed a "geek goddess," and "the sex symbol for every man who reads without moving his lips."[24]

Thus, her sexuality is most often paired with her intellect, which is very rare in American popular culture, where sexual potency and intellectual ability are portrayed as mutually exclusive. Maureen Dowd, in *Vanity Fair*, summarizes Fey's metamorphosis in typical fashion:

> Elizabeth Stamatina Fey started as a writer and performer with a bad short haircut in Chicago improv. Then she retreated backstage at *SNL*, wore a ski hat, and gained weight writing sharp, funny jokes and eating junk food. Then she lost 30 pounds, fixed her hair, put on a pair of hot-teacher glasses, and made her name throwing lightning-bolt zingers on "Weekend Update."[25]

This narrative of the ugly duckling turning into a swan is repeated in much of the publicity about Fey, and the exact amount of weight she lost is repeatedly noted. An inherent, and usually unexamined, double standard threads through this narrative. The male comics—most notoriously John Belushi and Chris Farley—who made the transition from the Second City to *SNL* certainly weren't expected to lose weight in order to make it into the cast. And yet, this was demanded of Fey. When Lorne Michaels asked legendary agent Sue Mengers if he should put Fey on air, she replied flatly, "She doesn't have the looks."[26]

Fey's success story relies upon a very common star narrative: the transformation of the ordinary into the extraordinarily glamorous. It's a story at least as old as MGM turning Julia Jean Turner into Lana Turner in the 1930s. But, on *30 Rock*, Fey was in a tricky position where she could not appear too glamorous in her main role as Liz—a character drawn from Fey's life before she was transformed. Thus, when she was selected in 2007 as one of *People* magazine's most beautiful people, she was placed in the "Not So Ugly Betties" category: "They Play Meek, Geeky or Fashionably Challenged on TV, but Off-Screen These Sexy Stars Shine." When she constructed the character of Liz, therefore, she had to repress her image's glamorous side. As she has commented, "It takes about an hour just for hair and makeup. It's weird how much thought goes into a look that's supposed to look like I didn't do very much." Or, in other words, Liz's look is a constructed one, but it must look like it is not.

In sum, *30 Rock* and *SNL* encourage us to think of Liz Lemon, "Weekend Update's" Tina Fey, and Tina Fey (the living, breathing human) as the same entity, as Dyer's "perfect fit," but it's more accurate to understand how her on-screen roles make "selective use" of her overarching star text. That is, the on-screen roles pick bits and pieces out of the polysemy that is the Tina Fey star text. In contrast, Fey as Palin is a "problematic fit." Despite their superficial physical resemblance, the "role" of Palin is a complete mismatch with Fey's star image. Palin is a proud anti-intellectual and commonly mangles words (e.g., she called for peaceful Muslims to "refudiate" the community center near the September 11th attack site), while Fey is an intellectual whose skills with dialogue have won awards. Palin promotes "family values" and conservatism, while Fey is associated with feminism and liberalism. But, of course, it is this mismatch of role and star image that allows for satiric humor at Palin's expense. Had a comic with conservative values played Palin, it would not have had near the impact.

Summary

Our relationship to the human figure on the television screen is a complicated and conflicted one, and we may never completely decipher its intricacies. However, it is possible to break down character, performance, and star images into their building blocks. Characters in narrative, actors acting, and star images lure us to the television set. The analyst must step back from that lure and ask how character, performance, and star image are constructed, how they function in narratives.

We have adopted a semiotic approach in this endeavor. Characters are made up of character signs—a variety of signifiers that communicate the character to the viewer. Acting is a matter of performance signs—facial, gestural, corporeal, and vocal signifiers that contribute to the development of character. And star images have been presented as texts fabricated through the media texts of promotion, publicity, television programs, and criticism. The existence of stars as real persons has been de-emphasized in favor of their signifying presences within U.S. culture, as is exemplified in the case of Tina Fey.

We have also briefly explored two different schools of performance construction: naturalistic and anti-naturalistic. The former dominates television, film, and theater—relying upon the principles of repertory performance and the Method. The latter is less well known, but we can still see the influence of vaudeville and Brecht upon television programs.

Notes

1. Richard Dyer, *Stars* (London: British Film Institute, 1998), 106–17.
2. Ibid.
3. John Ellis, *Visible Fictions: Cinema: Television: Video*, rev. ed. (Boston: Routledge, 1992).
4. Dyer, 134–36.
5. Several authors have discussed performance signs. The terms here are Barry King's, as quoted in Andrew Higson, "Film Acting and Independent Cinema," *Screen* 27, nos. 3–4 (May–August 1986), 112.
6. Delsarte himself did not record his method in book form. These images are from Genevieve Stebbins's description of the Delsarte method. She learned it from Steele MacKaye, one of Delsarte's students. See Genevieve Stebbins, *Delsarte System of Expression*, 6th ed. (New York: Edgard S. Werner Publishing, 1902); available online at tvcrit.com/find/delsarte. These images are excerpted from Google Book Search's scan of this public-domain work: books.google.com. Other images related to Delsarte's method are also reproduced in Dyer, 138.
7. Bertolt Brecht, *Brecht on Theatre: The Development of an Aesthetic*, edited and translated by John Willett (New York: Hill and Wang, 1964), 26.
8. "The Celebrity 100," *Forbes.com*, accessed March 30, 2017, tvcrit.com/find/celebrity100.
9. Interestingly, Dr. Phil McGraw (4), Howard Stern (7), Rush Limbaugh (10), and Ellen DeGeneres (13) were the only television-based celebrities to rank in the top 20 of *Forbes'* 2016 list. However, if we include music-video stars as "television" stars, then eight more could be added: Taylor Swift (1), One Direction (2), Adele (9), Madonna (12), Rihanna (13), Garth Brooks (15), AC/DC (17), and the Rolling Stones (18).

10 See Richard Dyer's classification of film stars' media texts. Dyer, 60–63.
11 *The Smoking Gun* website specializes in publicizing materials that celebrities cannot control—such as mug shots and court documents. It is owned by a cable-TV network, Court TV. *The Smoking Gun*, December 8, 2005, tvcrit.com/find/smoking.
12 See Dyer, 126–31.
13 Fey appeared as Palin on September 13 and 27, and October 4, 18, and 23, 2008. On the October 18 show, Palin herself appeared. She and Fey are seen passing in a backstage hallway but don't speak to one another.
14 Arhlene A. Flowers and Cory L. Young, "Parodying Palin: How Tina Fey's Visual and Verbal Impersonations Revived a Comedy Show and Impacted the 2008 Election," *Journal of Visual Literacy* 47, no. 21 (2010), 62.
15 "Tina Fey Wants to 'Be Done' With Palin After November," *Reuters*, September 22, 2008, tvcrit.com/find/feypalindone, accessed March 30, 2017.
16 Alex Witchel, "Counterintelligence; 'Update' Anchor: The Brains Behind Herself," *The New York Times*, November 25, 2001, tvcrit.com/find/anchor, accessed December 20, 2010.
17 Eric Spitznagel, "Tina Fey," *The Believer*, November 2003, tvcrit.com/find/feybeliever, accessed March 30, 2017.
18 Julianne Hill, "Tina Fey: Head Writer for *SNL*," *Writer's Digest* 80, no. 8 (August 2000), 53.
19 Ibid., 40.
20 Ashley Barkman, "And the Followship Award Goes to . . . Third-Wave Feminism?" in *30 Rock and Philosophy: We Want to Go There*, J. Jeremy Wisnewski, ed. (Hoboken, NJ: Wiley & Sons, 2010).
21 Elizabeth Wurtzel, *Bitch: In Praise of Difficult Women* (New York: Doubleday, 1998).
22 Tamara Straus, "A Manifesto for Third Wave Feminism," *AlterNet*, October 24, 2000, tvcrit.com/find/manifesto, accessed March 30, 2017.
23 It was even chosen by author Helena Andrews as the title for her memoir. Helena Andrews, *Bitch Is the New Black: A Memoir* (New York: Harper, 2010).
24 Maureen Dowd, "What Tina Wants," *Vanity Fair*, January 2009, tvcrit.com/find/feyvf, accessed March 30, 2017.
25 Ibid.
26 Ibid.

Further Readings

The significance of characters to the television text is explained in John Fiske, "Cagney and Lacey: Reading Character Structurally and Politically," *Communication* 9 (1987), 399–426. Fiske continues and enlarges upon this discussion in *Television Culture*, Second Edition (London: Routledge, 2011; originally published in 1987). Len Masterman, ed., *Television Mythologies: Stars, Shows and Signs* (New York: Routledge, 1987) draws upon the writings of semiotician Roland Barthes to explain aspects of television stardom—focusing mainly on British television.

Many substantive writings on television actors as stars have focused on female performers. Patricia Mellencamp, "Situation Comedy, Feminism and Freud: Discourses of Gracie and Lucy," in *Studies in Entertainment: Critical Approaches to Mass Culture*, Tania Modleski, ed. (Bloomington, IN: Indiana University Press, 1986) applies Freudian psychology to Gracie Allen's and Lucille Ball's television performances. Roseanne Barr has been discussed in several essays, most notably in a chapter from Kathleen K. Rowe, *The Unruly Woman: Gender and the Genres of Laughter* (Austin, TX: University of Texas Press, 1995). An earlier version of Rowe's work, along with Gloria-Jean Masciarotte's analysis of Oprah Winfrey, is included in Lucy Fischer and Marcia Landy, eds., *Stars: The Film Reader* (London: Routledge, 2004).

The impact of television stardom on early television has been assayed in several articles and books. Susan Murray, *Hitch Your Antenna to the Stars: Early Television and Broadcast Stardom* (New York: Routledge, 2005) chronicles the development of an early TV star system, one that differed considerably from the model used in the classical film. Denise Mann, "The Spectacularization of Everyday Life: Recycling Hollywood Stars and Fans in Early Television Variety Shows,"

Camera Obscura, no. 16 (January 1988), 49–77, explores the significance of performers like Martha Raye to television in the decade after World War II. Similar to Mann's approach, but in much more detail, two books dissect the phenomenon of movie stars on early television: Christine Becker, *It's the Pictures That Got Small: Hollywood Film Stars on 1950s Television* (Middletown, CT: Wesleyan University Press, 2008); and Mary R. Desjardins, *Recycled Stars: Female Film Stardom in the Age of Television and Video* (Durham, NC: Duke University Press, 2015).

The specifics of Tina Fey's star image and its use in her impersonation of Sarah Palin are exhaustively illuminated in Arhlene A. Flowers and Cory L. Young, "Parodying Palin: How Tina Fey's Visual and Verbal Impersonations Revived a Comedy Show and Impacted the 2008 Election," *Journal of Visual Literacy* 47, no. 21 (2010), 62. J. Jeremy Wisnewski, *30 Rock and Philosophy: We Want to Go There* (Hoboken, NJ: Wiley & Sons, 2010) is concerned more with *30 Rock* than Fey's star image, but its implications still underpin several of its essays. Profiles of Fey in popular magazines also offer clues as to the elements of her star image, especially Maureen Dowd, "What Tina Wants," *Vanity Fair*, January 2009, tvcrit.com/find/feyvf. As might be expected, Fey's own autobiography is quite conscious of her constructed image: *Tina Fey, Bossypants* (New York: Reagan Arthur Books/Little, Brown and Company, 2011).

Discussion of women performers in music videos can be found in E. Ann Kaplan, *Rocking Around the Clock: Music Television, Postmodernism and Consumer Culture* (New York: Methuen, 1987); and Lisa A. Lewis, *Gender Politics and MTV: Voicing the Difference* (Philadelphia: Temple University Press, 1990). Kaplan is most interested in Madonna as a figure who blends aspects of popular culture into a postmodern puree. Lewis examines Madonna, Pat Benatar, Cyndi Lauper, and Tina Turner principally in terms of their fans and the relationships between the fans and the stars. Madonna has been discussed in numerous critical essays and empirical studies—including Jane D. Brown and Laurie Schultze, "The Effects of Race, Gender and Fandom on Audience Interpretations of Madonna's Music Video," *Journal of Communication* 2 (1990), 88–102. In many respects, Lady Gaga continues Madonna's disruption of gender politics—as is argued by Rebecca M. Lush in "The Appropriation of the Madonna Aesthetic." Lush's chapter is from an anthology devoted entirely to Lady Gaga analysis: Richard J. Gray II, ed., *The Performance Identities of Lady Gaga: Critical Essays* (Jefferson, NC: McFarland, 2012). And Beyoncé has also attracted academic analysis in an anthology: Adrienne Trier-Bieniek, ed., *The Beyoncé Effect: Essays on Sexuality, Race and Feminism* (Jefferson, NC: McFarland, 2016); Daphne A. Brooks, "'All That You Can't Leave Behind' Black Female Soul Singing and the Politics of Surrogation in the Age of Catastrophe," isites.harvard.edu/fs/docs/icb.topic1292676.files/BrooksBeyonceSoul singin.pdf.

The student of television who is interested in the star phenomenon should also investigate the body of literature on cinema stars that has been developing since the late 1970s—especially since many television stars cross over into other media (for example, Tina Fey, George Clooney, Tom Hanks, Madonna). Some of the work done on the cinema may be transferred, with caution, to television studies. Richard Dyer, *Stars* (London: British Film Institute, 1998), remains the best introduction to the study of stars and characters. Originally published in 1979, it laid the groundwork for most star discussion since then. He has augmented that book with *Heavenly Bodies: Film Stars and Society* (New York: St. Martin's Press, 1986), which approaches Marilyn Monroe in terms of sexual discourse, Paul Robeson in terms of racial discourse, and Judy Garland in terms of her reception by gay viewers.

Although not an actor per se, Princess Diana has been called the "first icon of the new age of the electronic image and the instantaneous distribution of images" by Nicholas Mirzoeff.

His essay "Diana's Death: Gender, Photography and the Inauguration of Global Visual Culture" addresses many of the issues of stardom and performance (in *An Introduction to Visual Culture* [London: Routledge, 1999], 231–54).

A variety of key essays on performance and star image may be found in two anthologies: Jeremy G. Butler, ed., *Star Texts: Image and Performance in Film and Television* (Detroit: Wayne State University Press, 1991); and Christine Gledhill, ed., *Stardom: Industry of Desire* (New York: Routledge, 1991).

5 Beyond and Beside Narrative Structure

Sometimes it seems as if everything on television tells a story. Commercials are filled with miniature narratives. Nightly newscasts and news magazine programs such as *60 Minutes* (1968–) contain segments called "stories," which should, according to one news executive, "display the attributes of fiction, of drama. [They] should have structure and conflict, problem and denouement, rising and falling action, a beginning, a middle, and an end."[1] *Survivor* (2000–), *The Bachelor* (2002–), *The Real Housewives of Atlanta* (2008–), and other **reality-TV** series are sold like soap operas—emphasizing dramatic conflict. As the executive vice president of programming at the Fox network said about one reality program, "We need to market the characters and the stories like you would market a good quality drama."[2] All these stories, all this narrative, cannot help but make us wonder if there truly is anything real on TV or if it is just one big fiction.

The simple response would be, no, there is nothing real on TV. The makers of television programs do not and cannot present a portion of reality (a car wreck, a football game, an earthquake) without first recasting it in the language of television and thereby modifying or "fictionalizing" it to some extent. They will necessarily present it from a certain camera angle and within a certain context of other shots. It will be accompanied by certain sound effects or music and perhaps even narrated in a certain fashion. In their transition from reality to television, images and sounds are massaged, manipulated, and placed in new contexts. They are transformed into television material, cut to the measure of television.

But television's relationship to reality is not that simple. Many programs would not exist if we did not believe they were presenting some form of reality. The quiz shows of the 1950s, for example, based their enormous success on the believable illusion that ordinary people were competing in an impartial, improvised contest, in real time, with an outcome that was not predetermined by a scriptwriter. When it was revealed that the contests were rigged—staged to maximize dramatic impact—viewers were appalled and congressional investigations were begun. Similarly, but on a smaller scale, accusations of biased judging by Paula Abdul on *American Idol* led to outrage and investigations in 2005.[3] Obviously, the illusion of reality was paramount to quiz shows in the 1950s and continues to be a fundamental component of today's televised competitions, as well as news and sports programs and some commercials. Although all of these programs are fictionalized and manipulated on some level, each is also a "fiction (un)like any other"—as Bill Nichols has suggested, using a tricky bit of punctuation.[4] They may not be pure reality, as they sometimes advertise themselves, but they are still distinct from standard, scripted television fiction (the TV industry has taken to labeling fiction programs as "scripted" to distinguish them from reality programs, even though all programs have some form of written preparation).

It begs the issue, therefore, to say that all television is fiction or that every program tells stories. What is crucial is an understanding of how TV constructs its illusions of reality, its representations of the real; in other words, how some of its fictions are unlike other fictions. This chapter treads that slippery slope, suggesting some of the ways that **non-narrative television** represents reality. We discuss the aesthetic principles that undergird that representation, the economic choices that are made in the process, and the technological limitations to television showing reality "as it really is." Moreover, we need to remain mindful of television's basic structure of flow, interruption, and segmentation and the restrictions it places upon representing the real.

To accomplish these goals, we begin this chapter with some global considerations of television's reality—of reality as it is represented on TV. We then address the modes of non-narrative television and some of its particular genres: news, sports, game shows, and what has come to be called reality TV. Non-narrative commercials are considered in Chapter 6, in the context of commercials in general.

Television's Reality

Everyone has his or her own commonsensical understanding of "reality." Most of us think of it as the world in which all people exist, where events—some caused by other events, some seemingly random—occur all the time, everywhere. Reality has no inherent meaning; or perhaps its meanings are so varied that they are virtually limitless. Things just keep happening, regardless of our attention or inattention to them: a woman drives to work, moss grows on a tree, a political prisoner is killed in a jail, a cat naps, a war begins (or ends), two men play checkers, a president is elected. The real is "polymorphous," as John Fiske suggests.[5] By that, he means it assumes many shapes and styles and is open to many interpretations.

Most important for our study, reality does not itself suggest interpretations or emphasize one event over another. A spotlight did not suddenly appear on the voting booth of the person who cast the deciding vote in the last presidential election. A stirring musical crescendo did not accompany the beginning of the war in Iraq. The meaning, the importance, the cultural significance, the appropriateness for television of reality's events are determined by the makers of non-narrative television—in conjunction with historians, newspaper columnists, textbook writers, and other cultural workers and industrial gatekeepers. These persons represent a global reality back to all of us living in one small portion of it. Since we cannot experience all of reality directly, we must rely on television, the Internet, magazines, newspapers, books, and movies to represent it to us. Thus, our knowledge of the reality beyond our own personal sphere is always filtered through the mass media. In a very substantial sense, the media determine what is real and what is not, emphasizing certain events and ignoring others.

Equally important, the media manipulate and process those events that they have selected for us. Reality is mediated according to technological abilities (cameras cannot capture what occurs in darkness) and economic imperatives (footage of moss growing will not earn advertising dollars). It is also mediated according to ideological, institutionalized parameters such as the Radio-Television News Directors Association's (RTNDA) code of ethics. From where we viewers sit it is often difficult, if not impossible, to isolate the actual events from their processed version. We are often unable to "separate reality from reality-as-described" because we have no direct knowledge of that reality.[6] We are only exposed to its description, to reality-as-described. That is, the only alternatives to one medium's description of reality are other descriptions generated by other media.

One need only look at coverage of any armed conflict to see how the media provide selective, competing understandings of reality. Our knowledge of the war in Iraq, for example, is entirely based on media news reports, which have been tightly controlled by government censors. One battle in the Iraqi city of Falluja yielded conflicting news reports. A documentary titled *Falluja: The Hidden Massacre*, which aired on Italian television (RAI) in 2005, claims that U.S. forces used incendiary white phosphorous, a chemical weapon, against Iraqi civilians in the November 2004 attack—a violation of the Geneva Convention.[7] But these charges were not included in U.S. media coverage of the assault on Falluja. The Italian television account spins the story in one direction, while the U.S. military reports and other media spin it in another; and viewers are left to sort through conflicting accounts. The point is not so much which spin a reporter chooses to present as more real, but that *any* account is going to be an incomplete description of reality—emphasizing some events and ignoring others. We viewers have no direct access to a war's reality and so we must counterbalance one reality-as-described with another—as we constantly do when watching nonfiction television. Short of traveling to Iraq, observing combat, and interviewing soldiers and civilians, we viewers will never be able to generate our own description of wartime activities. We have no choice but to rely upon their varying and incomplete representations in the media.

This chapter does not offer analytic methods that will allow the reader to glean reality or truth from media representations of the real world. But it does examine the structure of those representations, allowing the reader to better understand them as such rather than as reality itself. It encourages skepticism when viewing television's reality and explains the factors that allow, encourage, and, in some cases, force television to manipulate the reality it presents to us.

Before we start, however, it may be helpful to adopt two of Bill Nichols's terms for discussing the reality depicted by television.

First, Nichols prefers the phrase **historical world** or **historical reality** over the term "reality." This distinction helps him stress that nonfiction television is not able to represent an *unmediated* reality. Instead, nonfiction television is always signifying a processed, selected, ordered, interpreted, and incomplete reality. Just as historians fashion a narrative out of reality's jumble of events, so do nonfiction television texts denote a particular reading of reality. The terms "historical world" and "historical reality" do not refer solely to events of major significance, as when a sports reporter announces that the breaking of a record is a "historical event." Rather, historical in our sense of the term refers globally to all the events that could be represented on television—that is, to those aspects of the real world that may be used to tell stories.

Second, Nichols introduces the term **social actor** into the debate on nonfiction television and film. As he explains,

> This term stands for "individuals" or "people." . . . I use "social actor" to stress the degree to which individuals represent themselves to others; this can be construed as a performance. The term is also meant to remind us that social actors, people, retain the capacity to act within the historical arena where they perform.[8]

When we see people in nonfiction television programs, we see them as social beings, as individuals functioning within a society of other individuals. Whether the individuals on TV are anonymous persons describing car accidents or Brad Pitt and Angelina Jolie announcing their divorce, their appearances on television are warranted by their social significance, their significance to society. And, as Nichols implies, persons on television act according to social codes of behavior to represent themselves to others. In a sense, we all perform according to certain conventions in public; we all act conventionalized social roles. When we go to a restaurant we wait to be seated; eat food in a certain prescribed order (salad, entree, dessert); and pay in response to the presentation of the bill. Each of these actions is part of a learned behavior, a role, that we perform in a particular social setting. Persons who deviate too greatly from these socially approved roles are removed from society and placed in prisons or psychiatric hospitals.

In sum, then, nonfiction television presents to the viewer the interaction of social actors in the historical world. In parallel fashion, fiction television presents the interaction of constructed characters, portrayed by professional actors, in a narrative world. It's easy to see how the two might become blurred—as is illustrated by actors in political office, such as Ronald Reagan and Arnold Schwarzenegger. Moreover, television frequently encourages the confusion of social actors and professional actors, as in commercials where actors wear lab coats and imitate scientists, or professional wrestling, where scripted storylines take precedence over uncontrolled competition. Despite television's common meshing of historical world and narrative world, much programming still depends upon distinguishing between the two. News and sports programs would be disdained and ignored if they lost contact with the historical world. Our goal is to better understand how the contact between the historical world and the narrative world of television is depicted.

Television's Reality: Forms and Modes

The defining characteristic of nonfiction television is its apparent relationship to the historical world. Unfortunately, there is not much agreement among television theorists regarding this fundamental relationship. This causes much confusion, as you can imagine. For our purposes, it is best to rely upon a strategy devised by Nichols and elaborated upon by Julianne Burton.[9] Modifying slightly their approach, we may distinguish nonfiction television's four principal **modes of representation**—the ways that it depicts historical reality and addresses itself to the viewer about that version of reality:

1. expository (or rhetorical)
2. participatory (formerly "interactive")
3. observational
4. reflexive.

As we consider each mode we will examine how the television text corresponds to the historical world it appears to represent. Individual nonfiction genres (news, sports, game shows, reality TV) are not limited to one single mode but instead draw upon each as needed. We will particularize some of these genres and their uses of these modes below.

Expository Mode

The essential component of an **expository** television text is that it presents an argument about the historical world. It assertively or even aggressively selects and organizes the "facts" of that world and presents them to the viewer in a direct address. For example, a commercial for an exercise device, the Bowflex Max Trainer, presents a shot of a woman's taut abdominal muscles (Figure 5.1), and then a graph illustrates how its scientific, computer-programmed system maximizes the time you spend on it. Later, a presumed Max Trainer user says, "Max Trainer is a great

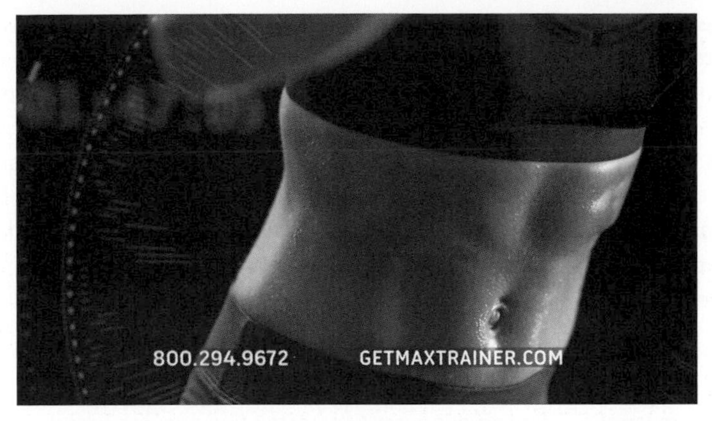

Figure 5.1 Abdominal muscles offer "evidence" of the effectiveness of the Bowflex Max Trainer exercise device.

full-body work-out. It got me shredded in my arms, legs, my abs; it makes my butt look so good!" The commercial is choosing evidence from the historical world to give credence to its argument. And it also represses counter-evidence: "Individual results may vary," the ad disclaims in a minuscule font. In this case, the evidence for the device's effectiveness is both visual (the image of a muscular abdomen), graphical (the work-out graph), and verbal (the testimonials)—and is emphasized through the conjunction of the three.

Note that even though this exercise commercial is manipulating material from the historical world, it is not relying upon narrative form to guide its manipulation. The logic, the organizing principle, of this commercial is rhetorical rather than narrative. There are many ways that rhetoric, arguments, may be structured. In this case, evidence (a series of images and words) is presented and then a call-to-action conclusion is propounded ("To learn about special financing for 18 months and how you can save up to 350 dollars, *call* or go to GetMaxTrainer.com!"). In other expository texts the conclusion may come first, or a question will be rhetorically posed ("Should you buy this device?") so that the argument may answer it ("Yes, you should!"); or perhaps emotional appeals will be made rather than evidence cited. Even narrative may be put in the service of rhetoric. A commercial may tell a story to illustrate a point, for instance. But narrative is not absolutely necessary for expository texts; plenty of them argue a position without telling a story. Thus, even though the Max Trainer commercial is not an unvarnished, unmediated chunk of the historical world, it is still not narrative and not fiction, in the narrow sense of the words.

Note also that this commercial, as in many expository texts, addresses its argument directly to us. In effect, it is saying, "Hey *you*! Here is the proof for my argument. Now, *you* come buy this device!" This contrasts sharply with the form of address in narrative television, which speaks to us indirectly, obliquely. Most narrative television programs do not acknowledge the viewer (excepting shows such as *Malcolm in the Middle* [2000–06] and *The George Burns and Gracie Allen Show* [1950–58] where characters speak to the camera). Instead, the characters interact as if there were no one watching. This is a charade, of course. There are millions watching. But the point is that the characters do not speak directly to us, as they often do in expository texts. Characters in narrative TV address one another. They are sealed within their narrative worlds. Thus, we are not the direct target of the dialogue, as we are in many rhetorical texts.

There is little doubt that commercials are based on rhetoric, argument, and persuasion; but what of other nonfiction television such as network news? Nichols contends that television news also falls within the expository mode. His point is that reporters and anchorpersons make sense of a chaotic historical world that is overloaded with meaning. They select facts from that world and organize them into a coherent presentation. This has become increasingly important during the so-called information age. As Jamie McIntyre, CNN's senior correspondent at the Pentagon, notes,

> With the Internet, with blogs, with text messages, with soldiers writing their own accounts from the front lines, so many people are trying to shape things into their own reality. I don't worry so much anymore about finding out every little detail five minutes before someone else. It's more important that *we take that information and tell you what it means* [emphasis added].[10]

By "telling you what it means," reporters are arguing implicitly for the validity of their specific selections and their organization of reality; often they are even arguing explicitly for a specific interpretation of these facts. The news anchor, for Nichols, is the ultimate structuring authority in the expository mode. Walter Cronkite, who anchored CBS's evening newscasts for nearly two decades (1962–81), proclaimed, "And that's the way it is" at the end of each program. He was certifying the truth value of CBS News's selection and arrangement of the material (its evidence) drawn from historical reality.

One other aspect that establishes the news as an expository text is its use of direct address. In television news, the anchors and reporters face the cameras directly (discussed further below, Figure 5.19) and present their argument to us—just as an advertisement presents its claims. Their gaze at the camera is facilitated by the TelePrompTer, an inventive bit of technology that is placed directly in front of the lens, seemingly blocking it (Figure 5.2). The copy is displayed on a video monitor pointed upwards, which is reflected in an angled, two-way mirror. The camera shoots right through it. This renders the copy invisible to the camera and us but allows the anchor to see it (Figure 5.3). As Mike Budd, Steve Craig, and Clay Steinman contend, the TelePrompTer "makes it possible for anchors and others to appear to be telling us things that come from them rather than from something they are reading."[11] It thereby lends authority to the claims they make about historical reality. (Politicians commonly use similar devices when making speeches to heighten their contact with the audience.)

Anchors also introduce us to field reporters, who then present their reports directly to us. At the beginning and end of reporters' stories, or "packages," as they are sometimes called, they may speak to the anchor (and not to us); but the majority of the newscast is addressed directly to the viewer. Thus, news does not use the form of address most common to TV narrative but rather shares its mode of address with the commercial.

Participatory Mode

A **participatory** text represents the interaction of the historical world with the realm of the video/filmmaker. (Note: Previous editions of *Television*, as well as Nichols's early work, referred to this mode as "interactive." However, in the digital age "interactive" has come to mean something quite specific, and Nichols's most recent work has adjusted to the new meaning by renaming this mode "participatory."[12]) This interaction occurs in one of two ways: The social actor is brought into a television studio (for example, talk shows, game shows); or a representative of

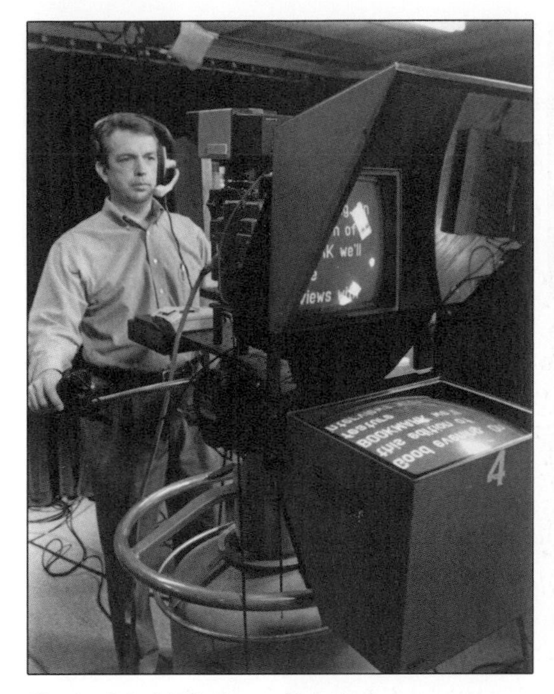

Figure 5.2 A TelePrompTer displays news copy directly in front of the lens.

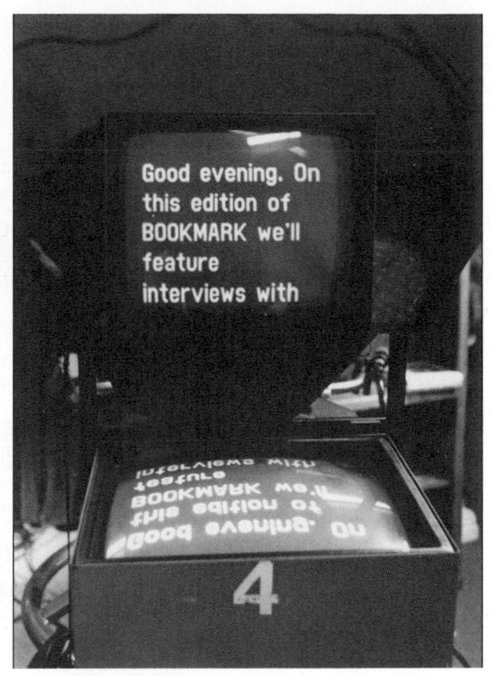

Figure 5.3 What newscasters see when they look into a TelePrompTer.

television goes out into the historical world to provoke a response from social actors (for example, Mike Rowe, the host of *Dirty Jobs* [2005–12], trying to do the job of a social actor). In either case, social actors knowingly participate in the creation of these television products.

The participatory mode differs significantly from the expository mode in terms of how it addresses the viewer. Like narrative television, the address of participatory texts is not aimed at the viewer. The social actors within the text speak with the television producers and not directly to us. When an investigative reporter confronts a corrupt politician and the politician argues with the reporter, the two are addressing each other, not us. We may identify with the reporter (or with the politician, depending upon our sympathies) and thus feel that the politician's responses are indirectly aimed at us. But the politician is not speaking directly to us. They indirectly address us through our emissary, the TV reporter.

In other cases, the social actor can become our textual representative—as in reality TV and game shows such as the long-running *The Price Is Right* (1956–65, 1972–), where participants are chosen from the studio audience (Figure 5.4). We presumably identify with the participants, who are, like us, members of the historical world. Through the contestants we interact vicariously with the host, Drew Carey (formerly Bob Barker). Thus, when Carey addresses participants at their podiums (Figure 5.5) and asks them to guess the price of a toaster, he is indirectly addressing us (Figure 5.6). Regardless of whether we identify with a social actor or a television producer in a participatory text, we are still not placed in the same viewer position as in the expository text. In participatory texts, the address is always indirect; in expository texts, it's quite often direct.

When social actors enter the realm of television, they are representatives of "our" world, of historical reality, but it would be naive to suppose that social actors are not affected by their contact with television. Any social actor appearing on TV is subjected immediately to the

Figure 5.4 An audience member enters the world of television in *The Price Is Right*.

Figure 5.5 A social actor competes on *The Price Is Right*.

Figure 5.6 Drew Carey indirectly addresses the television viewer when he speaks to a contestant on *The Price Is Right*.

medium's rules and conventions. Contestants on game shows or guests appearing on interview programs (whether *The Oprah Winfrey Show* [1984–2011] or *The O'Reilly Factor* [1996–2017])[13] are screened before the show; those unsuited for television's needs (based on visual interest, verbal skill, suitability to a particular topic) are filtered out early. Once the cameras are on, these social actors are permitted to speak "in their own words." However, the framing questions are Carey's, Winfrey's, and O'Reilly's; the rhythm of the show is strictly controlled by the hosts; and the final edit belongs to the producer. Even more than talk shows, game shows rigidly limit improvisation by situating the social actor within a tightly structured competition.

Hypothetically, there are many ways that television people could interact with social actors. They could touch one another or write letters or gesture with their hands. But, of course, the principal form this interaction takes is speech, dialogue, conversation—in short, interviewing. And it is in the interview that we may locate the rudimentary logic of the participatory text. Where the expository text is governed by the logic of the argument and gathering evidence, the participatory text's logic is largely shaped by how the interview is structured. Even game shows, which adhere to a logic of competition and the format of the specific game, also contain instances of interviewing between the host and the social actors—though obviously they are much less central than interviews in talk shows and the like.

We particularize two basic types of interviews: the dialogue and the pseudomonologue.[14] They are distinguished by the degree to which the interviewer is present—on camera and on microphone—within the text.

In a **dialogue**, the voices of the interviewer and the interviewee are both heard, and both persons may be visible on camera—as in Ellen DeGeneres's interviews of celebrities. The participants exchange comments, speaking "freely" to one another. Of course, interviewers are always in positions of relative power, since they determine which questions to ask and how to frame them. The interviewers, or their bosses, also decide who shall be interviewed to begin with and thus who has the television clout to warrant an invitation. A television dialogue doesn't begin unless the interviewer chooses to point the cameras in the direction of a particular social actor. Because of this unequal power relationship, the dialogue can never be truly free. It always fits within the constraints of television.

In a **pseudomonologue**, a similar interchange occurs between a social actor and a television representative, but it is presented differently. Interviewers and their questions are not evident in the text. Only the interviewee's answers are included. Thus, it makes it appear as if social actors are speaking directly about their experiences or opinions, even though they have been prompted by the interviewers' questions. This approach is frequently used in *The Deadliest Catch*, a documentary series about crab fishermen (2005-). Numerous shots from interviews in Captain Keith Colburn's wheelhouse (Figure 5.7) are interspersed with footage of the workers on the deck. The interviewer remains a mysterious figure. We rarely see him, although in some episodes the interviewer and video crew appear on camera and help out in a crisis—as when another captain, Phil Harris, suffered a stroke. Significantly, we don't hear the questions the interviewer puts to Colburn; we only hear Colburn's responses, as if he were speaking without prompting—in his own voice. In a pseudointerview, the reporter remains invisible and unheard, thus making it seem as if social actors like Colburn or a hurricane victim were performing unrestrained monologues or soliloquies in a play.

The pseudomonologue blurs the line between expository and participatory nonfiction modes. What is presented to us as monologues of interviewees' comments, an unmediated expression of their thoughts, is actually the result of participatory dialogues between the interviewers and the interviewees. That is, the pseudomonologue often appears as if the social actor were speaking directly to the viewer, as in exposition; but most viewers know pseudomonologues were originally addressed to reporters constructing their stories. The news reporter will tell us that the hurricane has wrought devastation. The story will then cut to pseudomonologues of hurricane victims describing their plight—seemingly to us directly. Hence, the pseudomonologue is often used as evidence in the journalist's ordering of "reality" into a comprehensible logic

Figure 5.7 Captain Keith Colburn speaks in a pseudomonologue in *The Deadliest Catch*.

and the development of a television argument about the historical world. It is not surprising, therefore, that numerous commercials have used pseudomonologues as testimonials for their products' superiority.

Even though the interviewer's absence encourages viewers to presume the pseudomonologue is addressed directly to them and not to someone else present at the scene, the social actor's eyes often undercut this illusion of direct address. If you look closely, for example, at Figure 5.7 and follow the direction of Colburn's eyes, you can clearly see that they are not looking at the camera. Instead of engaging viewers by looking directly at them (through the camera lens), his eyes are looking just off camera, to where the interviewer is located. If this were a true monologue, presented by Colburn with no coaching from an interviewer, then he would look directly at the lens/viewers. Contrast his "look" with that of the news anchors discussed below (Figure 5.19). The anchors' looks are aimed straight at the camera and exemplify true direct address. Thus, although the pseudomonologue shares some characteristics with a genuine monologue, the look of the pseudomonologue betrays its true nature as a dialogue between a television interviewer and one or more participatory social actors.

Observational Mode

Expository and participatory modes dominate non-narrative television, but there are occasions when a television producer's presence becomes nearly invisible and their manipulation of the historical world is relatively minimal. In **observational mode** the producer observes rather than argues about (exposition) or engages with social actors (participation). Of course, this is always something of a sham. The moment a camera is pointed at a social actor and selects one view, and consequently neglects another, manipulation and argument begin. And just by being in the same room with social actors, videographers will begin to interact with them, influencing behavior—even if they don't speak with each other. Still, there are nonfiction programs that invite us to suspend our distrust of television's "devious" ways. For their impact these programs depend upon our belief in the television producer's nonintervention.

The most famous television experiment along these lines is *An American Family* (1973), a 12-part PBS series that observed the family of Pat and Bill Loud. Cameras recorded more than 300 hours of the day-to-day life of what was supposed to be a stable, average U.S. family. Direct interaction between the filmmakers and the family members was minimized. Over the course of the filming, however, the family fell apart and the parents decided to divorce. Rather than organize this raw material into a treatise on the decay of the U.S. family, however, the producers presented it mostly without explicit commentary in the form of voiceovers. Notably, the program also avoided interviews with the family members or video diaries when they spoke directly to the camera. It is as close to pure observation as television ever gets.

More recently, other programs have toyed with this concept. *Cops* (1989–) is presented as if we were riding American streets with police officers, observing their daily experiences. The show does include some pseudomonologues of officers explaining (to us) what is occurring—monologues that have been prompted by the producers even though their questions are always edited out (Figure 5.8). But the bulk of the program is video of police in action, social actors interacting with other social actors (lawbreakers) rather than with the camera. Significantly, there is no narrator providing an overall continuity to the program. The social actors speak for themselves.

MTV has had great success with the observational mode in its long-running *The Real World* (1992–). Its premise is announced at the start of each episode: "This is the true story of seven

Figure 5.8 A police officer drives and narrates events in *Cops*.

Figure 5.9 Behind the scenes in *The Real World*, a camera operator "observes" his "subjects."

strangers, picked to live in a house, and have their lives taped, to find out what happens when people stop being polite and start getting real." The situation is clearly contrived by Bunim/Murray Productions for MTV, but the video recording is mostly done in observational mode: no narrator, few interviews (pseudomonologues), little interaction between the videographers and the "subjects" (Figure 5.9).

Furthermore, one episode of *The Real World* illustrates just how fragile the division between videographers and a cast of social actors can be. During a Jamaica segment in the first season, producer Bill Richmond and cast member Becky Blasband crossed the line and became romantically involved. MTV handled it by removing Richmond from the project—and putting him in front of the camera, videotaping him socializing with her and the other cast members. He wasn't permitted to be both part of the television world (as a producer) and part of the historical world (as a cast member). One cannot observe and participate at the same time, according to the logic of the observational mode. The blurry division between observation and participation or influence is also illustrated in a behind-the-scenes episode of *American Chopper* (2003–10), a documentary program that observes the motorcycle-building work of the Teutul family. The episode shows the Teutul crew going out for ice cream on their choppers. In one scene, we see an interview with Paul Teutul, Sr., from his perspective (Figure 5.10), and hear one of the program's

Figure 5.10 A scene from *American Chopper* is recorded...

Figure 5.11 ... resulting in this shot when the episode is broadcast.

Figure 5.12 Tiny cameras record a conversation in *Taxicab Confessions*. The driver knows they're there, but the passenger does not.

producers say, "So, ah, hotter than a son-of-a-bitch, but you decide to take the guys out for a little ice cream and ride some bikes." Responding to this cue, Teutul says, on camera (Figure 5.11):

> You build so many bikes.... I like to start 'em up. Get everybody on 'em. Ride 'em. See what they look like going down the road. It's about 105 degrees. Good ice cream day. We're on our way back. That's how I roll.

Although Teutul isn't reading a script, it's obvious that his dialogue has been influenced by the producer. Clearly, the "rules" of the observational mode are seldom strictly adhered to.

The observational mode was influenced in the 1990s by the ever-shrinking technology of surveillance cameras and microphones. Their inconspicuous size has enabled TV producers to observe human behavior without betraying the presence of the camera—unlike *Cops* and *The Real World*, where the cameras are never totally invisible. Programs such as *Punk'd* (2003–09, 2012, 2015) and *Taxicab Confessions* (1995–2003, 2005–06, 2008, 2010) rely on such technology. The former uses actual surveillance videotape of employee misbehavior. The latter places lipstick-sized cameras in a taxicab where the drivers encourage their passengers to talk intimately about their lives (Figure 5.12). In both situations, the persons on tape do not realize they are being recorded, which is the ultimate goal of the observational mode. However, *Taxicab Confessions* is not purely observational, since it places an undercover TV "host" in the cab with the unsuspecting passengers. By provoking the passengers, these hosts violate the principle of the observers not affecting the observed.

Reflexive Mode

Certain non-narrative programs invite the viewer to examine the techniques of television production and the conventions of non-narrative programs themselves. These texts could be said to reflect back on their own devices. Hence, they may be called **reflexive** programs.

Reflexive texts differ from other modes of non-narrative television in their relationship to the historical world and its representation. A reflexive text does not just depict that world—making an argument about it or interacting with it or observing it—as most non-narrative TV does. Rather, it draws our attention to the process of depiction itself, shifting the focus away from historical reality proper to the relationship between that reality and television. In Errol Morris's *The Thin Blue Line* (1988), for example, some facts are presented about the murder conviction of Randall Adams, a social actor in the historical world. But the essence of the program is the different narratives surrounding the murder, which Morris presents to us in ambiguous, stylized recreations. Morris does not advocate a single truth as much as he critiques the idea of finding truth and implicitly breaks down the mechanisms that are used to tell stories about historical reality. It is a film both about truth and about the tendency of TV and film to represent reality by transforming it into narrative.

Not surprisingly, *The Thin Blue Line*, which was shown on PBS after an initial theatrical run, belongs to a rare breed of documentary television. Not many programs are willing to call into question their basic assumptions, as *The Thin Blue Line* does. To do so often raises doubt about a program's truthfulness, which is dangerous to any documentary. So the reflexive mode remains on the edges of documentary television, the result of somewhat avant-garde experimentations with the medium.

Reflexivity is less menacing to the foundations of commercials and non-narrative comedy programs, where it is often found in the skits parodying TV on *Saturday Night Live* (1975–) and *Key and Peele* (2012–15). And *The Daily Show* (1996–) reflects back on the conventions and devices of news shows for most of its humor. In typical reflexive fashion, it is both a news show and a parody of one. Its hosts report actual news events (although sometimes the events are totally fabricated), but they also ridicule the process of news reporting itself. For example, in *The Daily Show*'s coverage of the 2004 Democratic National Convention, reporter Stephen Colbert recorded a fake live report from the convention floor. Host Jon Stewart called him on the deception and Colbert then admitted his fakery, walking into a freeze frame of his fake report (Figure 5.13). Consequently, viewers saw a "real" Colbert standing in front of a "fake" Colbert—practically a literal reflection of himself. The two Colberts illustrate how easily comedy programs can reflect back on the conventions of television—in this case, on how live reports are presented.

After leaving *The Daily Show*, Colbert created an entire show based on self-parody, *The Colbert Report* (2005–14). He literally flies through *The Colbert Report*'s opening credits, firmly grasping an American flag, while hyperbolic terms—"star-spangled," "powerful," "chiseled," "passionate," "all-beef," "national treasure," "tallish," "high-fructose"—float past (Figure 5.14). Clearly, the Colbert character on the program is not the "real" Stephen Colbert but rather a caricature of right-wing political pundits such as Bill O'Reilly. His advocacy of "truthiness" epitomizes the notion of reflexivity as it lays claims to be the truth at the same time as it satirizes the often dubious form of truth presented on television. Truthiness is truth as "truth"—undercut by ironic quotation marks. Colbert left *The Colbert Report* behind for *The Late Show With Stephen Colbert* in 2015, and in moments of reflexivity he's occasionally referred to his former "Stephen Colbert" character. He's mostly left that character behind, but one time he did introduce a recording of himself as "his identical cousin, Stephen Colbert" (see the video at tvcrit.com/find/colbert).

Figure 5.13 The Daily Show pokes fun at the conventions of news reporting, with Stephen Colbert standing in front of a video image of himself.

Figure 5.14 The Colbert Report satirizes news reporting.

Television comedy's self-parody and reflexivity are parts of a long-standing tradition, one that is essential to television's evolution. As a television device or convention ages, it is ridiculed through parody and then replaced with a modification of it. Thus, while reflexivity is relatively rare in non-narrative documentary works and can endanger basic assumptions about truth and historical reality, it is quite common in non-narrative comedy—refreshing the form and rejuvenating stale conventions.

Television's Reality: Genres

These non-narrative modes—expository, participatory, observational, reflexive—find expression in a broad variety of television programs. We may make some sense out of the chaos of non-narrative programs by categorizing them into specific **genres**. Much as we might categorize narrative programs into such genres as the soap opera and the sitcom, we will specify four types of non-narrative material:

1. newscasts
2. sports programs
3. game shows
4. reality television.

This is not a comprehensive list. There are other non-narrative genres (for example, talk shows and science programs such as *Nova* [1973–]), but these four will serve to illustrate the diversity in non-narrative television. Furthermore, we will return to non-narrative genres when we discuss genre study in Chapter 13 on textual analysis.

Some of the categories above are echoed by economically based divisions within the TV industry. Completely separate staffs at the networks and the syndication studios are assigned to handle news, sports, and "entertainment" (as if news and sports weren't entertaining). Beyond the industry's view of itself, however, the viewer/critic can make important distinctions among these genres based on the non-narrative texts themselves and their relationship to the viewer.

Network and Local Newscasts

The newscasts produced on national networks and on local stations all share a common assumption about historical reality: An event is not significant, is not newsworthy, unless it disrupts the ordinary, day-to-day functioning of life on earth. Presumptions of newsworthiness immediately divert TV news away from the common incidents in reality and direct it toward the odd, the unusual, and the unsettling. Once an incident ceases to disrupt the norm, it stops being "news" and disappears from the television screen. We are not likely to see a newscast begin, "Gravity: It's still holding things down!"

Typically, network news producers select the following types of events from the enormous miscellany of the historical world:

- catastrophes: natural and otherwise;
- international relations: political and armed conflicts;
- national politics: legal and judicial activities, election campaigns, politicians' other enterprises;
- law and order: crime and the activities of criminals;
- economics: financial trends;
- celebrities: marriages, scandals, deaths.

Local newscasts deal with many of the same subjects but on a smaller scale. The catastrophes are car accidents and house fires rather than earthquakes, and the politicians are governors and mayors rather than presidents, but the approach is modeled on the national newscasts. Local newscasts also incorporate sports and weather information that the national networks do not address.

Newscasts largely use an expository mode to present information collected from the historical world. That is, evidence is displayed to support a reporter's or editor's particular interpretation of events. Inevitably this evidence is arranged, ordered, into some form of conflict: Democrat versus Republican, individual versus institution, police versus killer. The basic logic of most news stories is an argument where the historical world is explained as a series of conflicts between two opposing forces.

Conflict is normally most obvious and deadly in the case of international warfare—pitting one nation against another. NBC's and CBS's coverage of a particular international incident may illustrate the expository nature of TV news. The Balkan War of 1991–95 was a particularly difficult one for TV news to fit into a simple structure of "A versus B." Battles raged among Serb, Croat, and Muslim factions in the Federation of Bosnia and Herzegovina (parts of the former Yugoslavia). Moreover, peacekeeping forces from NATO and the UN were thrown into the middle of this complicated situation. In September 1992 a UN plane flying relief supplies was shot down in Bosnia. CBS and NBC both featured Bosnian relief efforts in their nightly newscast—highlighting attempts to bring food and medicine to the town of Goražde.

As in most incidents outside North America, CBS and NBC relied on exactly the same video footage from Bosnia. The only differences in the two stories were the editing and the voiceover added by CBS's and NBC's reporters based in London: Tom Fenton and Keith Miller, respectively. The CBS story includes footage of decaying Serb bodies that are excluded from the NBC story (Figure 5.15). And the CBS story ends with shots of Muslim fighters on a hilltop (which are also excluded from the NBC story), with Fenton commenting, "Now the main concern will be to keep a lifeline open for the newly liberated town. That will depend on if the Muslims can continue to

Figure 5.15 CBS's coverage of a Balkan War incident includes decaying corpses that are not shown in NBC's reporting of the same incident.

Figure 5.16 CBS's story ends with Muslim fighters on the literal high ground...

Figure 5.17 ... while NBC's coverage concludes with birds on a nonfunctional runway.

hold on to the high ground around them" (Figure 5.16). In contrast, NBC chose to end with a shot of the deserted airport runway and the remark, "If the plane was shot down, then the UN will somehow have to eliminate the threat" (Figure 5.17). (See tvcrit.com/find/bosnia for a shot-by-shot comparison of the videos.)

Remembering that reporters Fenton (CBS) and Miller (NBC) worked from the same video (identical images of historical reality), what differences can we observe in the "arguments" they present about that reality? NBC's story argues that the main conflict in this incident is between UN relief workers and the forces that shot down the plane—forces that were not yet determined. CBS includes that conflict as a major part of the story, but Miller's editing and voiceover add a different perspective. Miller argues that the Muslims are valiant freedom fighters by placing them literally and figuratively on the "high ground" (Figure 5.16). They are "liberating" the town, forcefully pushing back the Serb paramilitary forces (resulting in decomposing bodies in the road [Figure 5.15]). This incident occurred nine years before the World Trade Center attacks by radical Muslims on September 11, 2001. One wonders if CBS would represent Bosnian Muslims as freedom fighters today. Would CBS's expository argument about Muslim social actors in the historical world be quite different now?

Since none of CBS's or NBC's viewers were actually in Goražde that day, they have no way to authenticate either of these reports through personal experience. They have only these "stories," told in an expository mode, upon which to make their judgments. However, by remaining alert to the connotations of terms like "liberated" and "high ground," viewers may better understand how news organizations are constructing their arguments about the historical world.

Reporters are encouraged to view the historical world in terms of conflicts and not cooperation or collaboration. They are trained to present an issue "in a way that is balanced, accurate and fair"—as it is stated in the RTNDA code of ethics. We can see a similar principle in Fox News' rather disingenuous "Fair & Balanced" trademark.[15] Let's examine for a moment what it means to be "balanced." A balanced presentation presumes two equally valid sides that are in conflict. It is the reporter's job to argue each side without prejudice. Consequently, reporters seek the core conflict of an issue and then use the expository mode to articulate each side of that conflict, assuming that they are equivalent.

The 2016 election of Donald Trump threw the principle of balance into crisis as reporters struggled to present two sides to claims he made that were certified as false by fact-checking organizations. For instance, at a November 21, 2015, rally in Birmingham, Alabama, Trump stated that Muslims in the U.S. had celebrated the 9/11 attack: On television, "I watched in Jersey City, New Jersey, where thousands and thousands of people were cheering as that building was coming down." The nonpartisan site PolitiFact investigated his claim and declared it "pants on fire" false, that there was no record of celebrations and no broadcast of such images on television.[16] Moreover, PolitiFact keeps a running "scorecard" on Trump's utterances and, as of May 18, 2017, found that 68 percent of his statements that they checked fell into its categories of "mostly false," "false," and "pants on fire."[17] Traditional journalists would take claims such as Trump's statement about celebrating Muslims and attempt to present both sides of the issue—perhaps interviewing people who believe the incident happened and those who believe it did not. However, Trump's avalanche of baseless assertions led venerable, established news organizations like *The New York Times* to begin to present single, and thus unbalanced, accounts of claims that were verifiably false. Instead of presenting both "sides" of the Muslims celebrating claim, many news organizations reported the story as a conflict between Trump's reality and the truth. Whether seeking balance between equivalent claims or recognizing a disjunction between a public figure's statements and the truth, the result is conflict, which has certainly been a hallmark of Trump's campaign and presidency. And just as television narrative is fueled by conflict, so is television news. It's no coincidence that all major TV news organizations have seen an increase in viewership since Trump's arrival on the political scene.

Conflict in news stories must be explained to viewers in terms of its impact upon particular individuals—regardless of how abstract and general the topic may be. Complicated economic developments are illustrated by the inability of a specific person to find work. Airplane crashes are related in the words of the individual survivor—or dramatized in the fate of the specific victim. Reporters "cast" social actors in roles that illustrate abstract topics.

Despite the development of 24-hour-per-day cable news channels during the 1980s and the rapid circulation of news on social media today, the format of American newscasts still follows a model developed in the 1960s on the major broadcast networks. We'll here look mostly at the self-contained newscast presented on general interest networks such as ABC, CBS, NBC, and Fox; but many of these generalizations also apply to full-time news networks such as Fox News, CNN, and MSNBC.

At the center of the broadcast-network newscast's format is the news anchor (or anchors; many newscasts use two). The anchors serve several purposes. Principally, they maintain the television flow, introducing **packages** (news stories), as well as weather and sports components, and guiding the viewer into commercial breaks with **teasers** (brief announcements of upcoming stories). Because anchors frame every element of the newscast (setting them up beforehand and often commenting afterwards), they are also represented as authenticating and authorizing the views of the historical world that the reporters and meteorologists deliver—regardless of whether the stories were actually chosen by them or the newscast's producers. As the newscast's authority figures, the anchors offer to make ideological sense out of the day's random events, as Cronkite's "And that's the way it is" suggests. They serve as the central spokespersons for the newscast's exposition. Reporters out in the field create expository packages about the historical world, and the anchors stamp them with their approval.

Television newscasts differ in form depending upon when they are telecast during the day—where they fit into linear television's daily flow. Morning newscasts emphasize the weather and the time of day; late-night newscasts summarize the day's events. The preeminent network newscast is broadcast in the evening at 5:30 or 6:30, depending upon the viewer's time zone. Local news usually follows, and often precedes, this newscast. These network and local newscasts share the basic organizing principle of anchors providing continuity to a program, but their form differs in its structure because the local newscast is designed to complement the national newscast, to fill in regional information not pertaining to national interests. It's as if the network and local evening newscasts must be taken together to provide the "total" picture of the historical world. We may make some generalizations about how each evening newscast organizes the material it presents.

In day-to-day news production, it is the producer, not the anchor, who establishes the structure of a newscast by setting the order of the stories. (Some anchors also hold the title of executive producer.) This order is mostly determined by three factors: journalistic principles, aesthetics, and economic determinants. The basic journalistic guidelines, which television shares with print journalism, are:

- timeliness (How recently did the event occur?);
- prominence (How famous are the participants?);
- proximity (Did it occur close to the viewers?);
- pertinence (Will it affect viewers' lives? Sometimes abbreviated as WIIFM impact. There should be a clear answer when viewers ask, "What's in it for me?");
- unusualness (Is it a common event or something unique?);
- conflict (Will it lend itself to the news' structure of "pro versus con"?).

Other practical and logistical factors that also influence TV-news priorities include:

- visual impact (Are there strong, affective video images available?);
- cost (For example, was a video truck rented to do a live, remote broadcast?);
- promotional value (Does the story boost the station's/network's prestige? For example, is it an exclusive interview that illustrates the superior news-gathering ability of the station or network?).

If all of these factors are equal, network news programs tend to move from the general to the specific, from the international to the national to the regional—including editorial material toward the end of the newscast.

Also, network news tends to begin with **hard news** and move toward **soft news** at program's end. Although these terms are not very well defined, hard news is generally thought of as stories addressing the *social*—examining events that affect U.S. society as a whole (for example, national and international relations). Soft news deals with the *personal*—gossip, scandal, murder, mayhem, and so-called human interest stories (which is something of a misnomer since all news stories interest some humans). Hard news, it is presumed, appeals to viewers' intellect; soft news attracts the emotions. Soft news also includes weather and sports.

Significantly, soft news often does not fit the journalistic criteria of timeliness, prominence, proximity, or pertinence that is applied to "real," hard news. A soft news story about a gourd the shape of Taylor Swift's head, for instance, is neither timely, prominent (it doesn't involve Swift directly), nearby, nor pertinent to most viewers. Because it lacks these qualities, it often is placed at the newscast's conclusion. It serves as filler and may be cut if other packages run long.

Television inherited this hard/soft notion from the print media, where we find hard news on the front page of *The New York Times* and soft news in *Us Weekly* magazine. Hard news is the better respected of the two, which is indicative of journalism's trivialization and neglect of the personal. There may also be some sexism lurking in this distinction, as women's issues often exist within the realm of the personal.

The mixture of material in local newscasts and its categorization are different from the national newscasts. On a local level, the newscast is categorized into segments of news, sports, and weather (see Table 5.1). This division is somewhat artificial, however, for all three segments are, in a sense, "news." Each represents aspects from the historical world to the viewer. Thus, "sports" is more accurately "news about sports events"; and "weather" is "news about weather events." And when the "news value" of a weather or sports event becomes significant the story will easily cross over into the news portion of a newscast—as in the case of a hurricane. This arbitrary categorization of the news is not limited to television, of course. It can be traced back through radio to the newspaper (for example, its separate sports section). Though it is not unique to television, it is particularly well suited to television's need for segmentation.

Typically, a local newscast is segmented—interrupted—by three or four commercial breaks. The division of a newscast into news, sports, and weather helps to justify those breaks. It provides a rationale for suspending the program flow at a particular point to begin the flow of commercials. And, since weather and sports are two popular elements of the newscast, their position late in the program may be used to "tease" us into continued viewing.

In many local newscasts, the structure of flow and interruption results in the following segmentation:

- news block
- commercial break
- weather
- commercial break
- sports
- commercial break
- news block.

This structure is typical of many local newscasts: news first, then weather and sports, followed by a final news update (or soft news feature)—all interspersed with commercials. We can see this structure in action and better understand newscasts' organizing principles if we select a newscast and list each of its elements along with their durations, as we have done for a randomly chosen, 6:00 p.m. newscast that aired on WVTM (NBC affiliate, Birmingham, Alabama) on December 5, 2016, a typical late-autumn day leading up to the holiday season (for details, go to tvcrit.com/find/newscast). Figures 5.18 and 5.19 are screen shots of the newscast's opening, and Table 5.1 contains a summary of the durations of various categories of the newscast's components and sorts them based on length.

Examining our newscast dissection, we find that the first news block was mostly devoted to stories of local crime and low-level disasters: shootings, a carjacking and police chase, a pipeline explosion, and similar mayhem. As they say in the local news business, "if it bleeds, it leads." The longest stories in this block were soft, "human-interest" packages about a teenager who saved a woman and her baby from being hit by a train and donation requests for a boy found locked in a basement by abusive adoptive parents. Weather and sports appeared, as is conventional, after the news blocks and each took up approximately two-and-a-half minutes of the time slot—longer than any individual news story. Commercials, teasers, and promotions (which are just commercials for the station itself) occupied a significant amount of time in this local newscast. As seen in Table 5.1, about 23 percent of the total newscast time was devoted to commercials, teasers, and promotions—6 minutes and 25 seconds out of the 28-minute newscast. In comparison, about 50 percent of the total time was allocated to news—13 minutes, 53 seconds. Thus, although the lion's share of this newscast was dedicated to communicating information about the historical world, almost a quarter of its time was consumed with advertising and another quarter was devoted to weather and sports.

From one perspective, the difference between the news and the commercial is blurry, more so than the difference between the narrative program and the commercial. Recall that both

Figure 5.18 Opening credits for an evening newscast on WVTM, an NBC affiliate in Birmingham, Alabama, which leads to...

Figure 5.19 ... a shot of the anchors, Brittany Decker and Lisa Crane, in a split screen with meteorologist Harmony Mendoza.

Table 5.1 Local Newscast Timings, 6:00 p.m. newscast on WVTM (NBC affiliate, Birmingham, Alabama), December 5, 2016

Component	*Duration*		*Percentage*
	Sec	*Min:Sec*	
News Stories	833	13:53	49.7%
Commercials	304	5:04	18.1%
Sports	162	2:42	9.7%
Weather	149	2:29	8.9%
Opening/Closing	146	2:26	8.7%
News Teasers	50	:50	3.0%
Promos	31	:31	1.9%
Totals	1,675	27:55	100.0%

news and commercials, in Nichols's terms, are expository forms. Both present evidence to the viewer that is designed to support an argument about the historical world. In this regard, then, commercials could be considered "news" about products and services. Television journalists would dispute this interpretation, asserting that anchors and reporters are not trying to sell the viewer anything. It could be argued, however, that to be profitable a newscast must market its interpretation of the historical world as accurate and true—as in Fox News' "Fair & Balanced" claim.[18] A newscast's vision of the world is sold directly through its promotional spots and indirectly through the arguments about the world that it expresses in its news reports. In this regard, television news differs from fiction programming, whose structure is narrative rather than expository and thus does not share this kinship with commercials.

Sports Programs

Sports events differ from the events shown on newscasts that we have discussed so far, even though both originate in the historical world. Sports activities, particularly those at the professional and college levels, are products or commodities designed for spectators. Spectators are seated in a stadium designed for their comfort and the optimum display of the playing field. The stadiums themselves frequently bear the names of sponsoring corporations. For example, in 2016 a residential mortgage company bought the naming rights to the Chicago White Sox ballpark and renamed it Guaranteed Rate Field. The game is organized according to rules that maximize its entertainment value for the spectator. Spectator sports such as professional baseball do not occur randomly, for free, in uncomfortable, inconvenient, unsponsored locations, with unsuspecting, disorganized participants—as do most other historical world events that are deemed newsworthy (earthquakes, traffic accidents, wars, and so on). Significantly, the commodification of sports occurred before television entered the equation. Well before TV began subsidizing sports events, spectators were buying the opportunity to attend them. Professional baseball in the U.S., for instance, was a financially successful enterprise for decades before televised sports were popularized in the 1950s.

Sports programs, thus, are very different from other news incidents because they present a commercial event, a spectacle really, that has already been contrived to please spectators and marketed to attract an audience. This has obvious economic implications for television sports, but it also affects the form of the programs in less obvious ways.

First, economically speaking, the right to broadcast sports events must be purchased from sports leagues and team owners, unlike the right to broadcast the sort of historical world events we have been discussing so far. These rights do not come cheap. CBS, Fox, NBC, and ESPN inked a deal with the National Football League covering seasons from 2014 to 2022 at a combined cost of $4.5 billion per year.[19] These numbers do not include local stations or cable networks other than ESPN that have cut their own deals and Twitter, Amazon, and other digital services that are eager to stream NFL games live. These expensive contracts mean, plainly enough, that networks and individual stations have a vested interest in promoting—in emphasizing the importance and entertainment value of—the sports events they've purchased. Moreover, some stations have more than just a passing financial interest in professional sports because many media corporations wholly own sports teams. The Atlanta Braves, for example, used to be one of the holdings of media conglomerate Time Warner, which also owned Atlanta TV station WTBS. Not surprisingly, WTBS featured all of the Braves games.

As you might expect in such a financial situation, journalistic notions of objectivity become a little twisted. Network coverage of sports tries to maintain a distance between the commentators and the teams, but the former still need to emphasize the significance of the event and try to maintain our interest during the game. Local coverage need not even preserve that level of objectivity. Often the commentators will be employed by the team itself—common practice in professional baseball since radio days. These announcers do not just offer expert commentary; they also boost fan support for the sponsored team. When a commentator such as the Chicago Cubs' Harry Caray exclaimed "Holy cow!" at a Cubs home run, he was supporting the team that paid his salary. It's hard to imagine a news anchor making a similar remark.

The expense of televising sports has also led networks to develop innovative ways of integrating advertisements into the game itself. In the 2005 World Series, the Chicago White Sox played the Houston Astros in a park named for beverage producer Minute Maid. On the wall behind the home-plate umpire an ad for Sprint was displayed (Figure 5.20). However, as we can see in Figure 5.21, which shows a replay of the action in Figure 5.20, Fox used green-screen technology to insert the Sprint ad into the ballpark's architecture (each inning a different sponsor was inserted). Even the seemingly dry area of sports statistics has become commercialized. State Farm Insurance, for example, sponsored a statistic about the Astros' fielding ability in this same World Series (Figure 5.22). Again, the difference between sports and so-called hard news

Figure 5.20 A telecast of a World Series game features an ad for Sprint behind home plate...

Figure 5.21 . . . that does not appear in the replay of the same pitch. It was added using green-screen technology.

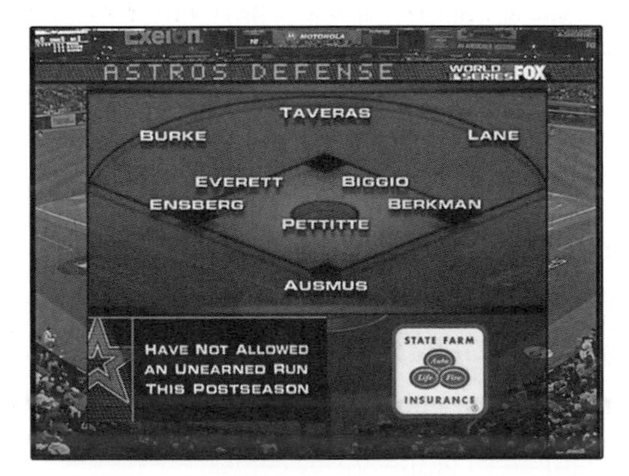

Figure 5.22 World Series statistics sponsored by State Farm Insurance.

about historical reality is obvious. In sports, corporations are permitted to affect the look and sound of television in ways that would not be allowed in news. (For more examples of products digitally placed into sports events, see tvcrit.com/find/pvi.)

In an era of cord-cutting and viewers moving away from linear TV, television networks have come to rely heavily upon the ratings success of live sports events. Correspondingly, professional and college sports associations have come to depend upon television money to survive. TV and sports have thus become mutually dependent and have fashioned various financial liaisons. They have formed into what Sut Jhally calls a sports/media complex.[20] His point is that spectator sports and the electronic media, especially television, have become so enmeshed that it's becoming impossible to separate the two. Only a small percentage of the viewers of professional football and baseball, for example, actually see games in arenas or stadiums. For the vast majority of sports fans, pro sports are mostly experienced through television. This has resulted in certain aesthetic adjustments to spectator sports.

The aesthetic structure of television sports is best seen as the blending of television form with the preexisting form of the particular sport. Most sports on television existed long before TV was invented and had already evolved rules to govern a game's fundamentals:

- time (for example, four 15-minute quarters in football);
- space (for example, the layout of a baseball diamond and players' movements around it); and
- scoring/competition (that is, how one wins).

These rules/structures presumed, of course, that the sport would be viewed in an arena or stadium.

When television began broadcasting sports events it soon adapted itself to shooting games in their natural settings. Multiple-camera shooting styles—using powerful telephoto lenses—quickly developed to capture a sport's essential action. But this adaptation process was not one-sided. If a sport was to successfully attract a large television audience, it too had to adapt. As a result, all of the major television sports in the United States, especially football, baseball, and basketball, have adjusted their rules to accommodate television's form. In particular, these sports have found ways to adjust to the medium's organization of time and space.

Let's take professional football as an example. During the 1970s, pro football turned into a major force on U.S. television. As of 2017, the NFL Super Bowl programs accounted for nine of the ten most watched programs in the entire history of the medium. And the 2010 telecast eclipsed the long-standing number held by the final episode of *M*A*S*H* for the first time; subsequent Super Bowls have often set new records.[21] The immense popularity of pro football on television is obviously due to many different factors, but what concerns us here is how football and television accommodate each other structurally.

The Organization of Time

The rhythms of football are inherently well suited to linear television's flow and interruption. The lull after each play while the offensive team huddles provides the opportunity for television to insert itself, "interrupt" the game, and present slow-motion replays, accompanied by commentary.

The "instant replay" was introduced in the 1963 Army-Navy football game and quickly gained popularity.[22] By repeating plays and slowing down the action, the technique feeds television's need for redundancy and repetition and helps combat the viewer's distraction and inattention. Repeating parts of a game—replaying portions of television time—helps to pull the viewer's attention back to the game. And an instant replay rehashes the most interesting parts of a game—repeating them for announcers to analyze and for inattentive viewers to catch up. In effect, the instant replay is the equivalent of a narrative flashback and is the most common and significant way that television manipulates the time of a game.

Television not only repeats segments of a game's flow, it also requires breaks in game play. Football's many time-outs provide convenient stoppages in action for television to cut to commercials. These time-outs were not frequent or long enough for television's needs, however, and the NFL accommodated TV by adding "television time-outs." Charged to neither team, they may be called by officials during the first and third quarters if there has been nine minutes of play without interruption.[23] In addition, all time-outs have been lengthened to ensure enough time for commercials. Other sports, such as soccer, suffer because their constant play minimizes the opportunity for replays and commercial breaks.

There are other ways that football time has been manipulated to serve the needs of television. The starting time of games depends nowadays on where they will fit into the television schedule. The most radical shifting of game time was when games were moved from the weekend to Monday evening solely for the benefit of ABC's prime-time schedule (with *Monday Night Football* [1970–], which was later picked up by ESPN). The introduction of sudden-death overtime to the NFL (1974) was also a concession to television time, providing a quicker ending to drawn-out games (as with the tiebreaker in professional tennis). Time is a commodity on television; it's what is sold to advertisers. A sport must adjust to the restrictions of television time if it is to flourish on the medium.

This manipulation of time is modulated by the announcers. Most television sports use two types of announcers: **color** and **play-by-play**.

Color announcers such as Cris Collinsworth, John Madden, and Terry Bradshaw are often former athletes and/or coaches, with firsthand expertise. Their analysis serves both expository and narrative functions. First, in the expository mode, they are arguing for a specific interpretation of the action. A basketball team, it might be suggested, is losing a game because its passing has broken down. Announcers back up their arguments with evidence for their specific interpretation: replays, statistics, electronic "chalkboards" that allow them to draw right on images of the players. Statistics are an interesting aspect of sports in this regard. They legitimize a particular event as part of the history of sport by comparing or contrasting a current game with games past, and they provide seemingly objective evidence of the game's significance, or lack thereof. Every year there seem to be more and more types of statistics to absorb. They can be commonplace (for example, football's rushing yardage) or more and more specialized (for example, the number of games in a row that a batter has gotten a hit in the baseball games after the regular season has ended).

Color announcers add quasi-narrative elements to a game, helping to convert athletes—who are social actors—into characters that television can better utilize. Announcers dispense details about the athletes that serve to "characterize" them, to turn them into recognizable sports character types—stereotypes, really. For example, baseball's Nolan Ryan (a record-setter for longevity) was characterized as the crafty, battle-scarred veteran at the end of his career. His experience was counterposed against more agile but inexperienced rookies—another familiar character type. Sometimes it seems as if each sport on television has only six or seven character types into which each athlete is fit. The game thus becomes, in one sense, a narrative of stock characters constructed by, among other things, the comments of the color announcer.

Play-by-play announcers function similarly to news anchors. They serve as the program's apparent authority figure and guiding force—even though a producer or director back in the satellite truck is really in control. Play-by-play announcers narrate the events of the game, prompt the comments of the color announcers, and reiterate (over and over and over) the score and the play-by-play passage of time. Compared to color announcers, play-by-play announcers are slightly distanced from the athletes. Color announcers were athletes and as such possess special experiential knowledge, born of their locker-room camaraderie. They are in essence part of the sport that is being covered (often their past exploits will be referred to). In contrast, play-by-play announcers are seldom former players or coaches. Instead, they are usually professional broadcasters such as Chris Berman, Al Michaels, or Michele Tafoya. Since they are not actually part of the athletes' world, they may operate as an intermediary between that world and ours. Like the news anchor, they place historical reality into context for the viewer and regulate reality's flow so that it matches the flow of television.

The Organization of Space

The space of any sport is strictly delineated on its playing field or court. In sports such as football, basketball, and hockey, this space is premised on notions of territory, where one team invades the other's turf and attains a goal of some sort. Television has had to find ways to represent this territorial dispute clearly and dynamically. One recent addition to televised football that illustrates this is the computer-generated first-down marker—seen in Figure 5.23 at the 13 yard line—along with the line-of-scrimmage marker and the down-and-yardage label ("2nd & 8"). This digital effect visualizes the territory necessary for a first down in a fashion that's much more TV-friendly than an announcer telling you they have eight yards to go. Football has always been a game of territory won and lost, and the digitally generated first-down marker

Figure 5.23 A computer-generated graphic visualizes the territory needed for a first down.

emphasizes that. To facilitate the heightened visualization of sports events, stadiums and arenas that have been built since the advent of television have made provisions for cameras and announcers: announcers' booths, special camera platforms at particular vantage points, supports for Skycam systems (where cables support a camera over the field), and the like.

The playing field or court itself is not often changed for television presentation.[24] But there have been television-accommodating rule changes that affect the players' appearance and their movement around these fields or courts. Names on football uniforms, a relatively recent addition to the NFL, do not make much impact on viewers in the stands. But they are significant in television coverage—making it easier for announcers to identify individual athletes as part of the process of turning them into character types. The NBA's rules permitting three-point shots and encouraging teams to play man-to-man alter the way that the space of basketball is utilized.[25] Man-to-man defense speeds the pace of the game (as does the 24-second clock)[26] and highlights the confrontations between individual players, making it easier for TV to transform the game's team conflict into a conflict between individuals. For example, NBA games between the Los Angeles Lakers and the Chicago Bulls during the 1980s were often described largely in terms of a battle between individual stars Magic Johnson and Michael Jordan. Television coverage reduces sports, even *team* sports, to the conflict among individuals.[27] Viewing from a distance in arenas and stadiums, in contrast, emphasizes team play and de-emphasizes the importance of the individual.

Those individuals highlighted by television are not necessarily the ones who are athletically superior. As Jimmie Reeves has noted, "personality, character, and color are as interesting to [television] audiences and as crucial to media stardom as run-of-the-mill competitive superiority."[28] Television needs distinctive individuals, not just athletically capable ones. In the 1992 Olympics, for example, U.S. volleyball player Bob Samuelson became a major television figure not so much because of his athletic ability but because he had overcome a childhood illness (which left him bald) and because of his feisty arguments with officials. When one such argument cost the team a game, every member of the U.S. volleyball squad shaved their heads in a show of support for Samuelson's actions. This group shearing brought the team even more television attention, and their distinctive appearance became as significant as their playing ability. Similarly, Anna Kournikova was a Russian tennis player of modest skills in the 1990s, but television (and other media, too) assigned her the role of glamorous ingenue. Her popularity was so great that, by 2001, she ranked eighth on Google's list of top searches for women that year—right behind celebrities such as Madonna, Kylie Minogue, and Shakira. Consequently, she received considerable TV coverage despite her inability to win major tournaments—leading ESPN to include her among the "25 Biggest Sports Flops of the Past 25 Years" in 2005.[29]

The Organization of the Scoring/Competition

In football's sudden-death overtime and tennis' tiebreaker we can see instances in which the structure of a sport's scoring has been modified to suit television's structure. In more general terms, a sport's scoring, the structure of its competition, suits television best when it echoes the conflicts of narrative (individual protagonist vs. individual antagonist) and poses enigmas as television narratives do. The most important sports enigma is, naturally, "Who will win?" If a game becomes so lopsided that the outcome is obvious, then the game runs the risk of television death—either from our switching channels or the network turning to a concurrent, more suspenseful game. Sports programs must maintain that quasi-narrative enigma if they are to succeed on television.

The conclusion of each game determines the winner for that day. But, like serial fiction programs, the closure is incomplete. Most professional sports on U.S. television are predicated on a season that leads to a championship: for example, the Super Bowl, the World Series, or the NBA finals. The weekly games resolve the question of athletic superiority for a particular day, but they leave open the larger question of who will triumph over the course of the season. This season-long conflict is a significant part of what draws us back each week. It also contributes to the high ratings that championships such as the Super Bowl earn as they bring to a climax months of conflict. (The lack of a definite season and a final championship may contribute to the comparatively modest draw of sports such as tennis and golf.) Thus TV sports share a fundamental structural principle with other TV series: each individual program offers a small amount of closure within the ongoing TV schedule. Full closure would mean the death of the series. Sports championships provide that closure and effectively kill off the sport for that specific year—only to be regenerated the following year.

Game Shows

Game shows, like sports programs, are based on competition, on winning a contest. But from there the two program types mostly part ways. College and professional sports, though heavily dependent upon TV money, do still have an existence outside of television. They preserve a presence in historical reality. Game shows do not. Furthermore, most televised sports existed before television came into being and thus evolved their structure before being telecast. Television has had to adapt to their structure more than they have had to adapt to TV. Game shows do not possess this pre-television history, even though they do draw on previous gaming traditions. *Who Wants to Be a Millionaire*, for instance, did not exist before it appeared on TV. It was designed for television and could not survive without it.

In sum, the game show does not re-present a preexisting historical reality to us. It does not originate in the historical world. Rather, it originates in television. It constructs a television reality and brings social actors, representatives from the historical world, into it. The television world is clearly interacting with the historical one here (as in the participatory mode), rather than constructing an argument about it (as in the expository mode) or observing it from a distance. The announcer on *The Price Is Right* urges contestants to "Come on down!" As they do, they travel from the historical world of the audience/viewers to the television world of the podiums (Figure 5.4), and, if they are lucky, they get to share the stage itself with Drew Carey, a typical game show host. Once they leave the audience and participate in the game, their movement and speech are shaped by the rules of the game, which of course are administered by the host. It is indicative of the game show's control over social actors that they must come to a television sound stage, the space of a television reality, rather than television going into historical reality to interact with social actors.

The host is comparable in function to the news anchor and the sports play-by-play announcer. All three are authorized by TV to place some order on the chaos of historical reality. In this regard, the host is a much more powerful figure than either the anchor or the sports announcer. For hosts can totally and directly control the behavior of social actors participating in the game (stand here, answer this question, leave the stage), while anchors and sports announcers can only interpret and partially shape (through interviewing techniques, editing, etc.) that behavior in the historical world. The hosts, moreover, know *all* of the answers to the questions they pose—whether it's the price of a toaster oven or the 14th president of the U.S. Even the most skillful news interviewer is not as all-knowing.

Game shows bring together components from reality with those of television, but it is clear which is the dominant force. They also borrow elements from other aspects of television to create their basic structure. As in television fiction, game shows rely upon a narrative-like enigma to provide the engine that drives the show forward. "Who will win this game?" is the central question, which obviously links game shows with sports programs. Even though the game show is something of a hybrid genre, drawing on narrative and sports conventions, it is important to seek the ways that it is unique, to distinguish its form from other television programs. This should become evident as we consider its address, textual organization (of time and space), and competition.

Semidirect Address

There are parts of any game show where the host speaks and looks directly at us. Like a news anchor or sports play-by-play announcer, the game show host welcomes us at the start of the show, guides us in and out of commercial breaks, and bids us farewell at the end. The address of the game show becomes more complicated than that of the news program, however. During most of the game show, the host does not speak directly to us, but instead addresses directly the contestants—as when Alex Trebek poses an "answer" to contestants on *Jeopardy!* (1964–75, 1978–79, 1984–). At this point, the game show's address resembles that of narrative, where we are generally not acknowledged. It's thus unlike news or sports, which acknowledge and speak toward the viewer. In game shows, host and contestants speak to one another without noticing us; in narrative programs, characters do the same thing. But contestants and narrative characters do not bear the same relationship to the viewer. Game show contestants are drawn from the ranks of TV viewers. They are social actors. Characters are not.

This crucial distinction changes the address of the game show. In a somewhat schizophrenic manner, we are invited to see ourselves *as contestants*, but at the same time we are also invited to *compete with the contestant*. The connection between contestants and viewers is most evident when contestants are stumped by a question in *Who Wants to Be a Millionaire*. At that point they may poll the audience or call a friend for help. Additional social actors (the audience members, the friend) are drawn into the game and encouraged to try to answer the question—just as, implicitly, the viewer at home is. The alliance between spectators and participants is here affirmed, even though the contestant does not look directly at us—that is, at the camera (Figure 5.24). The connection is implicit rather than explicit direct address. We not only root for the contestants, we also assist them, and the host's questions are implicitly addressed toward us as much as toward the contestants.

However, the majority of game shows do not permit this collaboration between contestants and other social actors. Instead, most programs present the questions to the contestants and the television viewer in a timed fashion that encourages us to try to beat the contestant to the answer. While contestants are positioned as identification figures for the viewers, they are also presented as our antagonists, competitors for prizes. The address of game shows is thus direct (the host's greeting of the viewer), indirect (the host's conversation with the contestants), and a blurry mixture of the two (the host's posing questions to the contestants to which we viewers may also respond).

The Organization of Time and Space

Unlike sports and news, which must adapt historical world time and space to the demands of television, game shows create their own time and space from scratch and thus are specially designed to suit television's time/space structures.

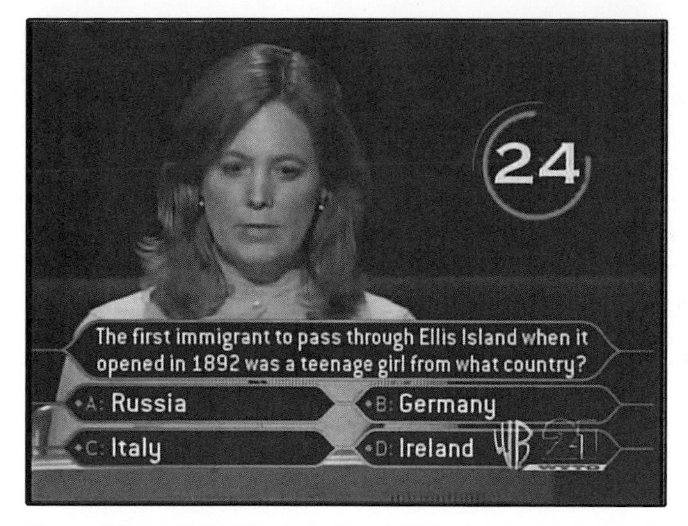

Figure 5.24 A *Who Wants to Be a Millionaire* contestant calls her husband for help with a question. The graphic shows they have 24 seconds remaining.

The time of a game show divides the contest into increasingly intense segments—thereby managing the flow and interruption of television time. On *Jeopardy!*, for instance, the competition is split roughly into regular jeopardy, double jeopardy, and final jeopardy. Each segment is separated by commercial breaks. The competition escalates until the climactic final moment, when the outcome is decided. Time is strictly regimented. Game shows, unlike sports programs, never run overtime. Interestingly, game shows also differ from sports programs in that they rarely repeat segments of themselves—through instant replays or other forms of flashbacks. In a game show, the competition always pulls us forward in time.

The space of a game show is determined by its set, which is wholly designed for television and has no historical world counterpart. It exists completely within television's rarefied realm. The implications of this style of set design are discussed later (see Chapter 8).

Competition

The main thing separating game shows from sports programs is the form of their competition. In sports it takes the form of physical prowess; in game shows it is different types of knowledge. Certainly, professional sports require a knowledge of the game and the ability to implement successful strategies, but these qualities would mean little if the players were not athletically superior. Most game shows involve little physical ability (exceptions include *Wipeout* [2008–14] and *American Ninja Warrior* [2009–]). Instead, they rely upon their contestants' knowledge of the world and human nature.

According to John Fiske, the knowledge tested in game shows may be grouped by type:

- Factual knowledge
  - "Academic" knowledge
    - *Mastermind*
    - *The $64,000 Question*
    - *Sale of the Century*
    - *Jeopardy!*

'"Everyday" knowledge
The Price Is Right
Wheel of Fortune
Human knowledge
Knowledge of people in general
Family Feud
Play Your Cards Right
Knowledge of a specific individual
The Newlywed Game
Mr. and Mrs.
Perfect Match.[30]

As Fiske proposes with his "factual knowledge" category, the type of knowledge that is most prized on game shows is a warehousing of facts, of individual bits of information. Even "intelligent" game shows such as *Jeopardy!* and *The $64,000 Question* do not require contestants to synthesize, analyze, interpret, or otherwise *process* information. What is required instead is a lightning-fast retrieval of data. These data may be obscure "academic" information taught in school, such as this *Jeopardy!* answer: "The first of these Roman waterways was the Aqua Appia, built about 312 B.C. by Appius Claudius." (The question was, "What is an aqueduct?") Or they may be more common, everyday data learned through interaction with other humans in social situations. Familiar phrases (for example, "Don't put your foot in your mouth," as on *Wheel of Fortune* [1975–]) and the prices of household appliances (as on *The Price Is Right*) are part of our everyday knowledge about the world.

Fiske's "human knowledge" category pertains to less clear areas of human behavior. As Fiske comments,

> This is a knowledge that resides in the human or social rather than in the factual. It has no absolute right and wrong answers and thus cannot be possessed or guarded by an elite [as teachers guard academic knowledge]. It depends instead upon the ability to understand or "see into" people, either in general or as specific individuals.[31]

In *Family Feud* (1976–85, 1988–95, 1999–), for example, family groups answer questions hoping to match their responses with those of a surveyed audience. The family that best approximates the survey results—in other words, the contestants with the greatest knowledge of the average—are the winners. Other programs in the human knowledge category include ones that demand detailed knowledge of one person: a spouse or a lover or even just a date. On *The Newlywed Game* (1966–74, 1977–80, 1984–89, 1996–2000), husbands and wives compete through their knowledge of each other. In *The Dating Game* (1965–73, 1986–88, 1996–2000) and other programs related to dating and romance, the contestants display their knowledge of each other's emotional-sexual experiences.

The competition on many game shows is not entirely based on any particular type of knowledge. Much of the contestant's success in programs such as *Wheel of Fortune* depends upon luck or good fortune—the spin of the wheel. The element of chance is foregrounded in game shows. It serves to further complicate the show's progression. Each spin of the wheel raises new enigmas. Chance also serves as a leveling agent. All contestants are equal when they grab onto the wheel. Consequently, the most knowledgeable contestant is not necessarily the one who will march straight to victory. Basically, devices that bring chance into the game show function to delay the game's outcome and to keep it from becoming too obvious. As in sports and narrative programs, the conclusion must be kept in doubt as long as possible. Otherwise, the program ends prematurely.

In summary, the game show is a non-narrative program supremely suited to the demands of linear television. Its rhythms are television rhythms. Its space is television space. And its form of address is uniquely designed to captivate the television viewer. It is a genre that interacts with the historical world but does so on its own terms.

Reality Television

All of the forms of television discussed in this chapter could conceivably be labeled with the phrase "reality television." They are all television texts that pull their substance—actors, settings, situations—from reality, or what we have here called the historical world. However, the "reality television" category has its own particular meaning these days. That meaning is very difficult to pin down, but it's clear that the term started popping up in the talk surrounding TV during the 1990s when programs like *Cops* (1989–) and *The Real World* (1992–) adapted and revitalized the form of observational-style documentaries. But *Cops* aired on the fledgling Fox network, which was not yet considered a viable competitor to ABC, CBS, and NBC; and *The Real World* was on MTV, an influential cable channel, but in 1990 cable was in only 56 percent of the homes with television and MTV wasn't carried on every cable system.[32] Reality TV didn't become a full-fledged cultural phenomenon until the turn of the century and the nearly simultaneous appearance of *Who Wants to Be a Millionaire*, *Big Brother*, and *Survivor* on international, prime-time, major-network television.[33] *Millionaire* is a conventional game show, but its enormous popularity in England led ABC to pull the U.S. version out of the ghetto of daytime television—where game shows normally languish—and push it into prime time, making it one of the very few non-narrative programs during that era. *Big Brother* and *Survivor*, which had their starts outside the U.S., draw upon conventions of the game show, too, but they reworked the genre in ways that started water-cooler conversations and inspired doctoral dissertations. Reality TV had arrived. Now the arguments about what it was could begin.

Many have criticized reality television as being neither authentic reality nor well-made television. Or, as the website *Reality Blurred* more colorfully puts it, the form is "TV's bastard child"—implying perhaps that it's born of the unhealthy union of "reality" and "television."[34] In the 2000s, it became a critical cliché to dismiss the form with irony-indicating quotation marks—as in "reality" TV—or chide it as a "phrase that shows no embarrassment at its oxymoronic ring."[35] But, as we argued at the very beginning of this chapter, criticizing non-narrative television for not being real enough is too easy, and it condescendingly presumes an extremely naive, and probably nonexistent, viewer who does not know that television's reality has been manipulated. What's significant about reality television, then, is "primarily its discursive, visual and technological claim to 'the real,'" as Su Holmes, Deborah Jermyn, and other scholars contend.[36] This claim to the real allows us to conveniently lump together some very different programs, but it also provokes a variety of questions. How does reality TV make a claim to the real, and what is meant by "the real"? What realist discourse does it engage? That is, how does it talk about reality, about authenticity? How does it present reality through specific styles of sound and image? What new technologies (the Internet, text messaging, and so on) does it use to present the historical world?

The woefully short consideration of reality television that follows cannot answer all these questions. For that, we suggest you investigate the Further Readings listed at the end of the chapter. What we can do here is provide two analytical contexts for understanding reality TV.

First, we address how reality TV might be considered a genre. This in itself may be contested. Some critics maintain that reality television is not merely a "genre" but instead that it fundamentally disturbs the aesthetics of American television and the political economy of its industry. Television, some scholars say, has entered an era of "post-documentary culture."[37] Our rationale for calling reality television a genre arises from the discussion of genre study in Chapter 13, Textual Analysis. Genre definition, we contend, is often based on cultural consensus, on what most people believe a genre is. And this consensus of viewers' beliefs is also shared with the television industry. In that context, it seems clear that a majority of television viewers and producers accept a category labeled "reality TV." Even if it's a fuzzy or self-contradictory category, it still exists in the discourse surrounding television. That makes it a genre. Moreover, quite a bit of critical work has already been done on this "unabashedly commercial genre."[38]

Our second approach to reality TV explores the new meanings it brings to non-narrative television's modes of representation. Reality TV employs all of the modes we have discussed in this chapter: expository, participatory, observational, and reflexive. It is here, perhaps, that we may see a substantial disturbance of television's conventional forms. For reality TV may well be at the forefront of the convergence of linear television and networking technologies—from the Internet to text messaging. We may well find the future of television is hidden in this genre.

Reality TV and Genre

If we tentatively propose generic boundaries around reality television that include programs with (1) a minimum of scripted dialogue and action, (2) a cast of social actors drawn from the historical world, and (3) a style of sound and image drawn from the documentary and/or the game show, then the first task at hand is to delineate the many, many *sub*genres that these boundaries contain. Looking at *TV.com*; *Wikipedia*, the consensus-built encyclopedia; and recent writings on the genre, we have derived the list in Table 5.2 (in chronological order).[39] In the case of each subgenre we note one of the antecedents that have paved the way for reality television.

As one attempts to define the reality-television genre it quickly becomes clear that it is fundamentally a hybrid form that cobbles together aspects of both narrative (the soap opera, the sitcom, the adventure film, the mystery) and non-narrative genres (*cinéma-vérité* documentary, sports, the talk show, and, especially, the game show) that have come before it. This "hybridity," as Holmes and Jermyn term it, is not surprising from a genre whose own name purports to blend the seemingly disparate phenomena of "reality" and "television."[40] Some critics delight in calling the genre an oxymoron, a contradiction in terms. And some are appalled by the mixture of fact and fiction—regarding it as a "violation of treasured fundamentals of the documentary genre."[41] To its opponents, reality television contributes to the descent into a postmodern world where it's impossible to tell what is real and what is a simulation. Reality TV is the triumph of what Jean Baudrillard has called "hyperreality," a world dominated by simulations, by simulacra.[42]

For the student of television genre who is unafraid of simulacra, however, hybrid forms are particularly fascinating. Jennifer Gillan, for example, contends that the best way to understand *The Osbournes* (2002–05)—MTV's program about musician Ozzy Osbourne's family—is to situate it on a "continuum of television genres."[43] This "reality star sitcom," as she calls it, bears the legacy of programs from 50 years ago—such as *I Love Lucy* (1951–57), *The George Burns and Gracie Allen Show* (1950–58), and *The Adventures of Ozzie and Harriet* (1952–66). To her, "the appeal of MTV's reality star sitcom lies in its continuities with traditional forms, not in its groundbreaking originality."[44] She proves her point by tracking the similarities and differences in these programs according to conventions of narrative (e.g., the stereotype of the bumbling father) and celebrity images

Table 5.2 Reality-TV Subgenres

Courtroom and Law Enforcement
– Antecedent: *Divorce Court* (original version: 1957–69) – *America's Most Wanted* (1981–2012) – *The People's Court* (1981–93, 1997–) – *Cops* (1989–) – *Judge Judy* (1996–)
Dating
– Antecedent: *The Dating Game* (original version: 1965–73) – *The Bachelor* (2002–) – *Flavor of Love* (2006–08) – *Dating Naked* (2014–16)
Courtroom and Law Enforcement
– Antecedent: *An American Family* (1973) – *The Real World* (1992–) – *Newlyweds: Nick and Jessica* (2003–05) – *The Jersey Shore* (2009–12)
Gamedoc (i.e., competition or group-challenge shows)
– Antecedents: sports, hundreds of game shows – *Big Brother* (2000–)* – *Survivor* (2000–) – *The Amazing Race* (2001–) – *Fear Factor* (2001–06)
Hidden Camera (i.e., surveillance [CCTV] and pranks)
– Antecedents: *Candid Camera* (original version on radio [1948] and network TV [1953–]); George Orwell's book, *1984* – *Taxicab Confessions* (1995–2003, 2005–06, 2008, 2010) – *Busted on the Job: Caught on Tape* (1996) – *Punk'd* (2003–07)
Makeover/Self-Improvement
– Antecedent: *Queen for a Day* (original version on radio [1945–57] and network TV [1956–64]) – *Extreme Makeover* (2002–07) – *Queer Eye for the Straight Guy* (a.k.a. *Queer Eye* [2003–07]) – *Biggest Loser* (2004–)
Reality Sitcoms
– Antecedents: hundreds of sitcoms, *The George Burns and Gracie Allen Show* (1950–58) – *The Osbournes* (2002–05) – *The Simple Life* (2003–07) – *Here Comes Honey Boo Boo* (2012–14)
Renovation
– Antecedent: *This Old House* (1979–) – *Extreme Makeover: Home Edition* (2003–12) – *Pimp My Ride* (2004–07) – *Fixer Upper* (2013–18)
Talent Contests/Searches
– Antecedents: *Ted Mack and the Original Amateur Hour* (original version on radio [1934–46] and network TV [1948–70]), *Star Search* (1983–95) – *Pop Idol* (2001–03) – *American Idol* (2002–) – *The Apprentice* (2004–)
Daytime Talk Shows (known as "chat shows" in the UK)
– Antecedent: *Person to Person* (1953–61) – *The Oprah Winfrey Show* (1985–2011) – *The Jerry Springer Show* (1991–) – *The Ellen DeGeneres Show* (2003–)

* The U.S. and UK versions started in 2000, but other international versions precede and succeed it.

(e.g., blurring the on-screen and offscreen lives of show-business figures). Derek Kompare also addresses the generic conventions of *The Osbournes* and does so by setting it alongside one of the most famous early attempts at reality TV, *An American Family* (1973).[45] Unlike Gillan, he's less interested in the celebrity component of the programs than in how family is constructed and how that construction functions through television genres. "The key question for reality TV," writes Kompare, "is not *whether* its reality is produced but *how* it is articulated with existing codes and expectations."[46] Obviously, this process of genre articulation is not limited to sitcoms. One could, for example, debate how reality TV has taken the codes and expectations of the game show and re-articulated them, in *Survivor* and *The Amazing Race*, outside of the television studio.

Thus, studying reality television from a generic perspective goes beyond the rather bureaucratic task of naming categories and populating them with programs. It allows the critic to investigate issues of narrative form and its evolution, the significance of generic codes, the interplay of viewer expectation and experience, and the relationship between documentary and fictional conventions or codes.

Reality TV and Modes of Representation

Much of the discussion that reality television has provoked centers on its modes of representation—on the way that it represents reality to the viewer, on the uses it makes of the historical world. Although we have previously discussed reality television's importance to the observational, fly-on-the-wall mode, we can also see the impact of reality TV on the expository, participatory, and reflexive modes.

For the most part, reality television conceals its use of the expository mode. Programs like *The Amazing Race*, *The Apprentice*, and *Survivor* are based on the premise that they accurately and fairly represent what occurred during the competitions. Consequently, their producers hope to make invisible the post-production process whereby hours of video are compressed into just a few minutes of air time. Their selections are expository in nature as they hope to convince us that their narratives of historical-world events are accurate and true. As is obvious to all but the most naive viewers, narrative tension and conflict are carefully constructed through the addition of music and through shot selection and ordering—even if that means changing the original chronological order. We viewers know this and yet we are discouraged from thinking about it by the power of the narrative engine. The constructed story pulls us along, regardless of the story's origin in "reality." It's all part of the suspension of disbelief.

One significant exception to this repression of the expository is *Big Brother*. It has become a regular feature of that program for its companion website to include 24-hour-a-day video feeds from the house. This unblinking surveillance has the important side effect of foregrounding the program's expository choices.[47] Viewers could potentially watch the unedited online streams, contrast them with the edited programs (with their accompanying music), and analyze the editing and sound work done by the program's editors and producers. As one of the creators of *Big Brother* bragged, "It's the first time the public have been able to form a view about how a programme is edited. It's the first time they've seen the rushes."[48] No previous program in the history of television has offered such access to what is essentially its raw footage. Imagine if a narrative program—say, *Stranger Things*—were to regularly show you its outtakes. It might radically alter the viewing experience.

Big Brother, along with competitions such as *Dancing with the Stars* and *American Idol*, also raises interesting issues for the participatory mode of representation. These three reality-TV programs provoke interaction between the world of television and the world of the viewer in ways that only became possible in the twenty-first century. This participatory interaction requires further clarification. In conventional game shows such as *Wheel of Fortune* and *The Price Is Right*, representatives of the viewers' world (that is, of "reality") are presented in television contexts and, as previously discussed, they act as our emissary when they play the game (see Figures 5.4–5.6 [*The Price Is Right*]). Or, in other words, historical-world contestants stand in for us viewers as they *interact* with television-world hosts like Pat Sajak and Drew Carey and *participate* in a game. The interaction of viewers with the programs, however, is limited to a competition by proxy where our participation (guessing at phrases or prices in *Wheel of Fortune* and *The Price Is Right*) has no real effect on the program. *Big Brother*, *Dancing with the Stars*, and *American Idol* change that, however. Through polls conducted via online surveys, instant and text messaging, Twitter hashtags, and special phone numbers, viewers actually determine the winners. This gives viewers a way of participating in determining the outcome of the game that is not available to viewers of conventional game shows.

Online and telephone voting by viewers is rooted in radio and television competitions from the media's early days when in-studio audiences voted for participants—as in *Queen for a Day*—but its significance goes beyond that. This voting changes the viewer-text relationship, bringing it closer to the relationship viewers have with their computers. When computer users move cursors and click on web pages' hypertext links or press controllers' buttons to play video games, they have a direct and immediate impact on what they see on the screen. Aside from our use of the remote control and a digital video recorder (DVR), we television viewers do not usually have that power. Reality television's voting process offers viewers, as a group, a small taste of that power and a stronger sense of interactivity, community, and agency—according to Misha Kavka and Amy West.[49] It fits in with a more general "interactive revolution," in Mark Andrejevic's words, that one sees embodied in devices such as DVRs, video-on-demand, and downloadable movies.[50]

The final mode of representation introduced above is reflexivity. In brief, does reality TV call attention to its own conventions? Many of the early attempts in the genre did not. *Cops*, for example, strictly avoids showing its camera and sound operators on-screen and never lets its producers be heard asking the police questions—with the rare exception of the episode in which two police cars collided and a videographer and sound man were slightly injured (Figure 5.25).

Recently, however, there has been a change in the genre's attitude toward itself. John Corner contends that post-documentary culture—of which reality TV is a major component—is marked by "new levels of representational play and reflexivity."[51] One can observe this most blatantly in the numerous mockumentaries that use documentary conventions to create humor—as in *This Is Spinal Tap* (1984) and, more pertinently to television, *The Office* (2001–03, UK version; 2005–13, U.S. version). In *The Office*, for example, the actor Steve Carell "performs" an interview as if he were a social actor drawn from reality and being interviewed by a film crew. And this performance is presented to us in documentary style—a medium close-up of Carell as he looks just off the lens where the (fictional) interviewer is located (Figure 5.26). The program's directors imitate what we term a pseudointerview above by choosing this framing and editing out the supposed interviewer's questions. They further play with documentary style by framing other shots as if the camera operator were sneaking up on individuals and filming them surreptitiously from behind plants and books (Figure 5.27).

Corner maintains that a "performative, playful element has developed strongly within new kinds of factual production," resulting in a "degree of self-consciousness now often displayed by

Figure 5.25 A sound man is injured on *Cops*.

Figure 5.26 *The Office* mimics a documentary style by "interviewing" actor Steve Carell...

Figure 5.27 ... and shooting as if they were spying on the actors.

the participants in observational sequences."[52] Corner is speaking specifically about *Big Brother*, which principally uses the observational mode of representation but breaks that mode when its participants refer to the apparatus of the program itself. He cites the example of "Nasty Nick" in the first British season, who attempted to subvert the voting system and was caught. This led to self-reflexive discussion by the participants of the way the competition is structured and the program is being recorded. Contrast this with *Cops*, where there are remarkably few references to the camera by either the police or the people with whom they deal.

Big Brother is not the only reality-TV program with strikingly reflexive aspects. Several critics have pointed out how the genre has foregrounded what it means to be a celebrity in the early twenty-first century. Programs such as *The Osbournes*, *The Simple Life*, and *The Surreal Life* (2003–) not only feature celebrities, they also ridicule their celebrity casts and call into question the talent upon which their fame was built. In *The Osbournes*, heavy-metal musician Ozzy Osbourne is turned into a stuttering, faltering, ineffectual father. In *The Simple Life*, two women who are famous solely for being famous—Paris Hilton and Nicole Richie—try to live as "ordinary" people do and fail miserably. And *The Surreal Life* places has-been celebrities in a *Big Brother*-style house, reveling in the misery of fallen stars.[53] The reflexivity of *The Surreal Life* was further enhanced in its debut season by the casting of a celebrity from another reality-TV program: Jerri Manthey from *Survivor: The Australian Outback* (2001).

In addition to feeding on celebrity, reality television can also participate in the creation and construction of celebrity—as can be seen in talent search programs such as *Pop Idol*, *American Idol*, and *America's Next Top Model* (2003-). These shows are reflexive in that they not only create celebrities, they also self-consciously expose the creation process. *American Idol*'s selection system serves as part of the program itself. It includes video of failed applicants and showcases the singing of successful competitors. Indeed, the failure to become a celebrity is as much a part of the program as winning is. Thus, talent-search programs are reflexive to the extent that they provide what Andrejevic calls a "demystifying, behind-the-scenes glimpse of the spectacle as the *latest spectacle*."[54] In paradoxical manner, they may undercut the celebrity-construction process at the same time that they promote it—"simultaneously debunking celebrity and creating new stars."[55]

The peak of reality television's reflexivity, however, must be the short-lived MTV production titled simply *The Reality Show* (2005). It didn't last long, but, in essence, it was a reality show about creating a reality show. A panel of former reality-show participants judged proposals for new reality shows sent in by contestants.[56] The prize was to be participation in that reality show. It was quite a reflexive hall of mirrors but failed to find an audience.

Viewing reality TV through the lens of representational modes—observational, expository, participatory, and reflexive—brings into sharp focus its relationship to the real, to the historical world. It also provides a method for investigating the claims to reality offered by all reality shows. Since this claim is all that holds together an extremely fragmented genre, the analysis of modes helps the critic come to terms with its generic structure. One aspect of reality television we have neglected is its political economy. Industry deregulation, increased competition from cable and satellite services, and the general decline of television viewing along with a threatened decrease in ad revenue created a climate the 1990s in which inexpensive reality programming was very attractive to the networks. However, due to space limitations we have slighted political economy and mostly limited our discussion to reality-TV's generic structure, the mode of its address of the viewer, and its purported relationship to the real world. For considerations of political economy we refer you to the Further Readings section, where you will find discussions of the impact of 1990s economy and public policy upon television programming and their consequences for reality television.

Summary

This chapter seeks to make sense out of television's perplexing and contradictory relationship to reality. To this end we have incorporated the terms *historical world* (or *historical reality*) and *social actor* to describe that reality more accurately. Non-narrative television, in this terminology, draws upon the actions of social actors in the historical world. It depicts those actions through four principal modes of representation: expository (argumentation), participatory (interaction between the historical world and that of television), observational (TV watching historical reality and minimizing its intrusive effect), and reflexive (emphasizing self-reference and intertextuality).

To see these modes in action, we considered four types of non-narrative material: newscasts, sports programs, game shows, and reality television. As we have dealt with each, we have considered four aspects:

1. *The realm of historical reality it depicts*: Since TV cannot present everything, it must select certain aspects of historical reality and neglect others. Which technological, economic, and aesthetic reasons explain why one incident is chosen and another is not?

2. *The implied relationship between the television world and the historical world*: Do they appear to interact? Do the TV producers appear to influence the social actors? Does the television world affect the historical world?
3. *The implied relationship between the text and the viewer*: Is the viewer addressed directly or through a representative in the text?
4. *The textual organization (or logic)*: What principles dictate how the information will be presented? For example, is it organized according to the principles of argumentation or does it hijack narrative conventions?

Our consideration of non-narrative genres is necessarily incomplete. A comprehensive study would need to be another full book, at the very least. However, the preceding discussion does lay the groundwork for analyzing non-narrative television.

Notes

1 Reuven Frank was an executive producer at NBC News when, in 1963, he made these comments in a memo to his staff. Quoted in "Frank Reuven," *The Museum of Broadcast Communications*, November 10, 2005, tvcrit.com/find/reuven, accessed July 13, 2017. For a content analysis that explores the validity of Frank's principle, see Maria Elizabeth Grabe and Shuhua Zhou, "News as Aristotelian Drama: The Case of *60 Minutes*," *Mass Communication and Society* 6, no. 3 (2003): 313–36.

2 David Nevins was speaking about *American High* (2000). Considering that the program was canceled after only four airings, it appears that they did not find the drama they wanted. It was subsequently picked up by PBS and won an Emmy Award for "Outstanding Non-Fiction Program (Reality)." Dan Snierson, "Taking the High Road," *Entertainment Weekly* 553 (August 4, 2000), 43.

3 Contestant Corey Clark alleged that he had a sexual relationship with Abdul and that she was not an impartial judge, but this was never proven and she remained on the program.

4 Bill Nichols, *Representing Reality: Issues and Concepts in Documentary* (Bloomington, IN: Indiana University Press, 1991), 105–98.

5 John Fiske, *Television Culture*, Second Edition (London: Routledge, 2011; originally published in 1987), 285.

6 Dennis K. Mumby and Carole Spitzack, "Ideology and Television News: A Metaphoric Analysis of Political Stories," in *Television Criticism: Approaches and Applications*, Leah R. Vande Berg and Lawrence A. Wenner, eds. (New York: Longman, 1991), 316.

7 Phil Stewart, "US Denies Using White Phosphorus on Iraqi Civilians," November 8, 2005, tvcrit.com/find/iraq. The original Italian report was available at Sigfrido Ranucci, "La strage nascosta," *RAI News*, November 25, 2005.

8 Nichols, 42. Nichols adapts the concept from its introduction by Erving Goffman in *The Presentation of Self in Everyday Life* (Edinburgh: University of Edinburgh Social Sciences Research Centre, 1956; reprinted in the US in 1959); see tvcrit.com/find/goffman.

9 These modes draw upon the "documentary modes of representation" developed in the work of Bill Nichols and Julianne Burton. See Nichols, *Ideology and the Image: Social Representation in the Cinema and Other Media* (Bloomington, IN: Indiana University Press, 1981); Julianne Burton, "Toward a History of Social Documentary in Latin America," in *The Social Documentary in Latin America*, Julianne Burton, ed. (Pittsburgh: University of Pittsburgh Press, 1990), 3–6; and Nichols, *Representing Reality*.

10 Katharine Q. Seelye, "Answering Back to the News Media, Using the Internet," *The New York Times*, January 2, 2006, tvcrit.com/find/seelye, accessed July 13, 2017.

11 Mike Budd, Steve Craig, and Clay Steinman, *Consuming Environments: Television and Commercial Culture* (New Brunswick, NJ: Rutgers University Press, 1999), 126.

12 As Nichols writes in 2017, "*Interactive mode*: permits viewers of interactive or web-based documentaries to make choices that alter what they see and hear." Bill Nichols, *Introduction to Documentary*, 3rd ed. (Bloomington, IN: Indiana University Press, 2017), 23.

13 The premiere dates for these two programs are for their original versions. *The Oprah Winfrey Show* began as a regional program (in Chicago) in 1984 and was nationally syndicated in 1986. *The O'Reilly Factor* started out as *The O'Reilly Report* in 1996 on the Fox News Channel.

14 These categories derive from ones developed by Nichols, but they modify his concepts. Nichols, *Representing Reality*, 51–54.

15 Parodied in Al Franken, *Lies and the Lying Liars Who Tell Them: A Fair and Balanced Look at the Right* (New York: Dutton, 2003).

16 Lauren Carroll, "Fact-Checking Trump's Claim That Thousands in New Jersey Cheered When World Trade Center Tumbled," *PolitiFact*, November 22, 2015, tvcrit.com/find/trump911.

17 "Donald Trump's File," *PolitiFact*, May 18, 2017, tvcrit.com/find/politifact.

18 The website *Media Matters for America* is one that contests Fox News' claims of being fair and balanced. It presents counterarguments to Fox's—trying to persuade readers of its own interpretation of the historical world.

19 "Top 10 Biggest TV Rights Deals in Sports (Currently Active)," *Total Sportek*, tvcrit.com/find/nfldeal, accessed May 12, 2017.

20 Sut Jhally, "Cultural Studies and the Sports/Media Complex," in *Media, Sports, and Society*, Lawrence A. Wenner, ed. (Newbury, CA: Sage, 1989), 77.

21 Sources: "TV Basics: Top 50 Specials of All Time," *TV Basics: A Report on the Growth and Scope of Television*, Television Bureau of Advertising, tvcrit.com/find/basics. TBA is using data from Nielsen Media Research covering January 1964-February 2010. More recent data are available here: tvcrit.com/find/super and tvcrit.com/find/super17.

22 John R. Hitchcock, *Sports and Media* (Terre Haute, IN: ML Express, 1989), 2.

23 The television time-out was instituted on a trial basis in 1955 and adopted permanently in 1958. Steven Barnett, *Games and Sets: The Changing Face of Sport on Television* (London: British Film Institute, 1990), 122.

24 There have been exceptions to this. In 1969, for instance, the pitching mound in professional baseball was lowered in order to make it tougher for pitchers to strike out batters. The goal was fewer defensive battles, which are not visually interesting. Barnett, 124.

25 Until the 2001-02 season, the NBA banned zone defenses and thus forced teams to play man-to-man. In that season it rescinded the ban but instituted a new rule called the "defensive three-second rule." The new rule discourages zone defenses without explicitly banning them. "NBA Rules History," NBA, May 2, 2008, tvcrit.com/find/nba.

26 A team must make a shot at the basket within 24 seconds of receiving the ball. This rule was instituted in 1954.

27 As noted by Margaret Morse. Margaret Morse, "Sport on Television: Replay and Display," in *Regarding Television: Critical Approaches—an Anthology*, E. Ann Kaplan, ed. (Frederick, MD: University Publications of America, 1983), 47-48.

28 Jimmie L. Reeves, "TV's World of Sports: Presenting and Playing the Game," in *Television Studies: Textual Analysis*, Gary Burns and Robert J. Thompson, eds. (New York: Praeger, 1989), 214.

29 "ESPN25: The 25 Biggest Sports Flops," *ESPN*, October 19, 2005, sports.espn.go.com/espn/espn25/story?page=listranker/25biggestflops.

30 Fiske, *Television Culture*, 271.

31 Ibid., 268.

32 Interestingly, despite MTV's presumed influence, it only reaches about one-fourth of the households with television—according to 2004 data. Sources: "Cable & VCR Households," *Media Info Center*, November 1, 2005, tvcrit.com/find/cablehh; and "Television Reach: Broadcast vs. Cable," *Media Info Center*, November 1, 2005, tvcrit.com/find/tvreach.

33 *Who Wants to Be a Millionaire* was initially developed in the UK in 1998 and in the U.S. in 1999. *Big Brother* originated in the Netherlands in 1999, followed by releases in the U.S. in 2000 and in the UK in 2001. And the U.S. program *Survivor* (2000) was inspired by the Swedish program *Expedition Robinson* (1997).

34 Andy Dehnart, *Reality Blurred*, October 31, 2005, tvcrit.com/find/realityblurred.

35 Bill Nichols, *Blurred Boundaries: Questions of Meaning in Contemporary Culture* (Bloomington, IN: Indiana University Press, 1994), 60.

36 Su Holmes and Deborah Jermyn, "Introduction: Understanding Reality TV," *Understanding Reality Television* (New York: Routledge, 2004), 5. Laurie Ouellette and Susan Murray make a very similar point when they maintain that reality TV is a "fusion of popular entertainment with a self-conscious claim to the discourse of the real." Laurie Ouellette and Susan Murray, "Introduction," in *Reality TV: Remaking Television Culture*, Susan Murray and Laurie Ouellette, eds. (New York: New York University Press, 2004), 2.

37 John Corner, "Performing the Real: Documentary Diversions," *Television and New Media* 3, no. 3 (August 2002), 257. This piece is a revision of John Corner, "Documentary in a Post-Documentary Culture? A Note on Forms and Their Functions," *Changing Media—Changing Europe*, November 3, 2005, tvcrit.com/find/postdoc.

38 Ouellette and Murray, 2.
39 Sources: "List of Reality Television Programs," *Wikipedia*, May 18, 2017, tvcrit.com/find/realitytv; "Reality," *TV.com*, May 18, 2017, tvcrit.com/find/realitytvtvg; Laurie Ouellette and Susan Murray, eds., *Reality TV: Remaking Television Culture* (New York: New York University Press, 2004), 3–4.
40 Holmes and Jermyn, 2. Craig Hight, in an essay included in this volume, notes, "The term 'hybrid form' is increasingly used to suggest the manner in which these texts deliberately play with the lines between fact and fiction genres." "It Isn't Always Shakespeare, But It's Genuine: Cinema's Commentary on Documentary Hybrids," in Holmes and Jermyn, 249. Further, Anita Biressi and Heather Nunn note that reality TV "is usually taken to refer to the surge in a variety of 'new' or more often hybrid genres which were launched in the later 1990s." *Reality TV: Realism and Revelation* (London: Wallflower Press, 2005), 10. Yet another reality-TV analysis that emphasizes the hybrid nature of the genre is Toni Johnson-Woods, *Big Brother* (St. Lucia, Queensland: University of Queensland Press, 2002), 50–68.
41 Ibid., 248.
42 Jean Baudrillard, "Simulacra and Simulations," in *Jean Baudrillard, Selected Writings*, Mark Poster, ed. (Stanford: Stanford University Press, 1998), 166–84.
43 Jennifer Gillan, "From Ozzie Nelson to Ozzy Osbourne: The Genesis and Development of the Reality (Star) Sitcom," in Holmes and Jermyn, 55.
44 Ibid., 56.
45 Derek Kompare, "Extraordinary Ordinary: *The Osbournes* as 'An American Family,'" in Murray and Ouellette, 97–116.
46 Ibid., 112.
47 It also makes the program even more like *1984*, George Orwell's prescient novel in which citizens are constantly watched by Big Brother.
48 Peter Bazalgette, Creative Director at Endemol, as quoted by Holmes and Jermyn, 12.
49 See Misha Kavka, Amy West, "Temporalities of the Real: Conceptualising Time in Reality TV," in *Understanding Reality Television*, Su Holmes and Deborah Jermyn, eds. (New York: Routledge, 2004), 138.
50 Mark Andrejevic, *Reality TV: The Work of Being Watched* (Lanham, MD: Rowman & Littlefield, 2004), 12. As early as 1977 and the Qube service in Columbus, Ohio, there have been attempts to make television more interactive. See Ken Freed, "When Cable Went Qubist," *Media Visions*, January 30, 2009, tvcrit.com/find/qubist.
51 Corner, 246.
52 Ibid., 263.
53 The first, 2003 season also featured faded actors (Gabrielle Carteris, Corey Feldman, Emmanuel Lewis), musicians (MC Hammer, Vince Neil), and a *Playboy* model (Brande Roderick).
54 Andrejevic, 16.
55 Ibid.
56 The host was Andy Dick and the judges were Steve-O (*Jackass*), Veronica Portillo (*The Real World*), Austin Scarlett (*Project Runway*), Trishelle Cannatella (*The Real World*), Omarosa Manigault-Stallworth (*The Apprentice*).

Further Readings

The most comprehensive attempt to theorize non-narrative television, and the book that has guided our analysis here, is Bill Nichols, *Representing Reality: Issues and Concepts in Documentary* (Bloomington: Indiana University Press, 1991). He revised his approach in *Introduction to Documentary*, 3rd ed. (Bloomington, IN: Indiana University Press, 2017) and extended his commentary on television in *Blurred Boundaries: Questions of Meaning in Contemporary Culture* (Bloomington, IN: Indiana University Press, 1994)—discussing the permeable boundary between narrative and non-narrative TV and the implications of reality-television programs such as *Cops*. The standard historical/critical study of the documentary is Erik Barnouw, *Documentary: A History of the Non-Fiction Film*, 2nd ed. (New York: Oxford University Press, 1993), which places the television documentary in the context of film documentaries made for theatrical distribution. Barnouw's book, however, came out well before the current reality-TV phenomenon and thus could use some updating. One such updated study is Betsy A. McLane, *A New History of Documentary Film*, 2nd ed. (New York: Continuum, 2012).

Television news is often studied separately from the fully developed documentary. Fred Shook, John Larson, and John DeTarsio, *Television Field Production and Reporting*, 5th ed. (Boston: Pearson Education, 2008) provides practical instruction on creating news stories. Short summaries of the evolution and the structure of television news can be found in Raymond Carroll, "Television News," in *TV Genres: A Handbook and Reference Guide*, Brian G. Rose, ed. (Westport, CT: Greenwood Press, 1985); and Stuart Kaminsky, *American Television Genres* (Chicago: Nelson-Hall, 1985). The Radio-Television News Directors Association's "Code of Ethics and Standards" (tvcrit.com/find/rtnda) has itself evolved over the decades.

Television news is presumed by many to be a major purveyor of ideology. Not surprisingly, several authors analyze the ideological function of the news: Charlotte Brunsdon and David Morley, *Everyday Television: "Nationwide"* (London: British Film Institute, 1978); William Gibson, "Network News: Elements of a Theory," *Social Text* 3 (Fall 1980), 88–111; Andrew Goodwin, "TV News: Striking the Right Balance," in *Understanding Television*, Andrew Goodwin and Garry Whannel, eds. (New York: Routledge, 1990); John Hartley, *Understanding News* (London: Methuen, 1982); Patricia Holland, "When a Woman Reads the News," in *Boxed In: Women and Television*, Helen Baehr and Gillian Dyer, eds. (New York: Pandora, 1987); Margaret Morse, "The Television News Personality and Credibility: Reflections on the News in Transition," in *Studies in Entertainment: Critical Approaches to Mass Culture*, Tania Modleski, ed. (Bloomington, IN: Indiana University Press, 1986); Gaye Tuchman, "Representation and the News Narrative: The Web of Facticity," in *American Media and Mass Culture: Left Perspectives*, Donald Lazere, ed. (Berkeley: University of California Press, 1987).

Interviews and talk on television are obviously not limited to newscasts and news magazines. The daytime talk show ("chat show," in the UK) has developed its own interview format, which is discussed at length in Wayne Munson, *All Talk: The Talkshow in Media Culture* (Philadelphia: Temple University Press, 1993).

The significance of television sports is the topic of several essays in Lawrence A. Wenner, ed., *Media, Sports, and Society* (Newbury Park, CA: Sage, 1989); and Arthur Raney and Jennings Bryant, eds., *Handbook of Sports and Media* (Mahwah, NJ: Lawrence Erlbaum Associates, 2006). Steven Barnett, *Games and Sets: The Changing Face of Sport on Television* (London: British Film Institute, 1990); and Alvin H. Marill, *Sports on Television* (Westport, CT: Praeger, 2009) offer mostly historical considerations of TV sports, focusing on the UK and the U.S., respectively. Analyses of how television represents sports include John Hoberman, *Sport and Political Ideology* (Austin: University of Texas Press, 1984); Margaret Morse, "Sport on Television: Replay and Display," in *Regarding Television: Critical Approaches*, E. Ann Kaplan, ed. (Frederick, MD: University Publications of America, 1983); Geoffrey Nowell-Smith, "Television–Football–The World," *Screen* 19, no. 4 (Winter 1978–79), 45–59; and Jimmie L. Reeves, "TV's World of Sports: Presenting and Playing the Game," in *Television Studies: Textual Analysis*, Gary Burns and Robert J. Thompson, eds. (New York: Praeger, 1989). Recent scholarship on sports in a variety of media is collected in Andrew C. Billings, ed., *Sports Media: Transformation, Integration, Consumption* (New York: Routledge, 2011).

The critical analyses of the game shows are not nearly as numerous as those of documentary/news and sports. There have, however, been some attempts to deal with these issues. The cultural significance of the quiz show, one prominent genre of game shows, is examined in Olaf Hoerschelmann, *Rules of the Game: Quiz Shows and American Culture* (Albany, NY: State University of New York Press, 2006); and Su Holmes, *The Quiz Show* (Edinburgh: Edinburgh University Press, 2008). The game show of the 1950s is the subject of William Boddy, "The Seven

Dwarfs and the Money Grubbers," in *Logics of Television: Essays in Cultural Criticism*, Patricia Mellencamp, ed. (Bloomington, IN: Indiana University Press, 1990). Michael Skovmand uses four different international versions of *Wheel of Fortune* to investigate how the game show functions as a "cultural practice"—"Barbarous TV International: Syndicated *Wheels of Fortune*," in *Television: The Critical View*, Horace Newcomb, ed. (New York: Oxford University Press, 2000). John Fiske's short chapter on game shows, "Quizzical Pleasures," in *Television Culture* is cited in the chapter above. Morris B. Holbrook takes issue with Fiske's approach and provides his own interpretation of *The Price Is Right* in *Daytime Television Game Shows and the Celebration of Merchandise:* "The Price Is Right" (Bowling Green, OH: Bowling Green State University Popular Press, 1993).

The predominance of reality television in the 2000s and its enormous popularity have inspired a wealth of academic analyses: Mark Andrejevic, *Reality TV: The Work of Being Watched* (Lanham, MD: Rowman and Littlefield, 2004); Anita Biressi and Heather Nunn, *Reality TV: Realism and Revelation* (New York: Wallflower, 2005); David S. Escoffery, ed., *How Real Is Reality TV? Essays on Representation and Truth* (Jefferson, NC: McFarland, 2006; James Friedman, *Reality Squared: Television Discourse on the Real* (New Brunswick, NJ: Rutgers University Press, 2002); Annette Hill, *Reality TV: Audiences and Popular Factual Television* (New York: Routledge, 2005); Su Holmes and Deborah Jermyn, eds., *Understanding Reality Television* (New York: Routledge, 2004); Susan Murray and Laurie Ouellette, eds., *Reality TV: Remaking Television Culture* (New York: New York University Press, 2009); and Matthew J. Smith and Andrew F. Wood, eds., *Survivor Lessons: Essays on Communication and Reality Television* (Jefferson, NC: McFarland, 2003).

The various subgenres of reality TV are elucidated in Annette Hill, *Restyling Factual TV: Audiences and News, Documentary and Reality Genres* (New York: Routledge, 2007). The specific genres of makeover and dating reality-TV shows have attracted enough analytical attention to fill two anthologies: Dana Heller, ed., *Makeover Television: Realities Remodelled* (London: I. B. Tauris, 2007); and Judith Lancioni, ed., *Fix Me Up: Essays on Television Dating and Makeover Shows* (Jefferson, NC: McFarland, 2010). Race and the conflict among races have often provided fodder for reality TV. A special issue of *Critical Studies in Media Communication* (25, no. 4 [October 2008]) is devoted to unpacking the layers of racism overlaid on many reality-TV genres. Finally, the impact and structure of one of the first reality-television programs, *An American Family*, are discussed in detail in Jeffrey K. Ruoff, *Family Programming: The Televisual Life of an American Family* (Minneapolis: University of Minnesota Press, 2001).

6 The Television Commercial

Most television commercials are not bashful about their economic function. They exist to sell products and services. And they do so quite effectively. Huge corporations would not be spending the largest chunk of their American media-advertising budget on linear television if their market research did not show that viewers are positively affected by this avalanche of ads.[1] Corporations still depend heavily upon conventional, linear-television networks and such networks in the U.S. rely solely upon advertising for their economic sustenance—unlike VOD portals such as Netflix that are funded through subscriptions or television in many other countries that is government supported. Just as with radio before it, U.S. television's economic structure is undergirded by commercials, as are online video services such as YouTube that do not require users to buy subscriptions.

To us viewers, commercials are annoying, interruptive reminders of our economic bargain with corporate culture. Linear television has been "free" since the network era, if we were willing to "pay" for it with our viewing time and our buying behavior when we visit the store. And so we invite advertisers into our homes to repetitively hammer away at us about the tastiness of Pepsi over Coke or the efficacy of the latest exercise machine or the sublime pleasure of Taco Bell's newest recombination of beef, cheese, and flour tortilla. But not all advertising is alike.

Not all television advertising seeks to persuade us through repetition and sledgehammer exhortations to buy, buy, buy! Not every ad uses the mind-numbingly blunt approach of a Shake Weight spot. Many advertisers understand what Paul Messaris calls the "value of indirectness."[2] They use humor and evocative imagery to persuade without attacking or numbing the viewer's sensibilities. And yet, they *all* still seek to persuade us in some fashion.

This chapter explores the form that that persuasion takes. It views commercials as television texts that have developed particular techniques of persuasion in order to serve the economic needs of the industry. We know that ads must sell us products in order to survive, but what the television analyst needs to understand is *how* that selling is accomplished. What ideologically loaded imagery do commercials use and how do they deploy it? How are commodities associated with particular lifestyles, values, and presumptions about the world? How are we encouraged to consume conspicuously? What visual and sound techniques are used to sell? In short, how do economics, ideology, aesthetics, and technology come together in the rhetorical form of the television commercial?

U.S. Linear-TV's Economic Structure

More than any other television texts, commercials are shaped by their economic context. Commercials are produced in a certain way due both to the current state of corporate, transnational economics and to specific aspects of the television economy. Thus, a basic understanding of television's economic structure is one key to understanding the commercial. Unfortunately, U.S. television's economic system in the 2010s is in a state of flux that is unparalleled since the rise to dominance of the major broadcast networks in the 1950s. Huge chunks of the audience that the so-called Big Three (ABC, CBS, NBC) commanded have been lost to VOD portals, the Internet, DVD/Blu-ray disc viewing, video games, cable networks, newer broadcast networks (Fox, WB, UPN, Univision), and a multitude of cable networks. The older broadcast networks have seen their advertising dollars shrink as online industries have relentlessly stolen advertising income from them. It seems clear that the economic models of the past 70 years are fast changing under the impact of the convergence of broadcast (over-the-air) television, theatrical film, cable and satellite services, and digital technologies. No one truly knows where it will all lead, although venture capitalists are betting on the outcome with enormous sums of money. The next few years are going to be very interesting ones for the television industry.

Before we begin discussing commercials we must make one additional caveat. Due to space limitations, we will focus on linear-television advertising as it has functioned in the United States since the network era and not take on the vast expanse of nonlinear, online advertising. Such digital advertising is, of course, a massive business, and it is currently dominated by industry giant Google (a.k.a. Alphabet), which inserts so-called pre-roll commercials before YouTube videos, weaves ads into web pages and Gmail, and interpolates sponsored content within results during Google searches, among other ad placements. Although much of this commercial material borrows persuasive techniques and content from the traditions of linear-TV commercials, digital advertising facilitates forms of interaction that are impossible on linear television. Simply put, the diversity of online commercial texts is too great for us to account for here. Also, we focus our attention on American TV's use of the commercial. Many countries have commercial-free television, while others blend commercially supported programs with noncommercial fare—resulting in distinctly different persuasive strategies. Still, the generalizations we make here about U.S. commercials may find application in other countries' attempts to sell products through video.

In the complicated and quickly changing economic model of advertising-supported linear television, there are five principal players:

1. production companies—who actually create TV programs;
2. wholesalers—networks and syndicators;
3. retailers—local over-the-air stations, cable systems, and DBS (direct broadcast satellite) systems;
4. advertisers—targeting national, regional, and local audiences;
5. consumers—that is, viewers.

We'll begin our consideration of commercials by outlining the basic structure of U.S. linear broadcasting. We'll then explain how advertising fits into this structure.

Diverging Channels and Converging Corporations: Narrowcasting and Media Mergers

In the earliest years of U.S. television broadcasting, corporations produced and sponsored programs such as the enormously popular *Texaco Star Theatre* (1948–55). However, direct sponsorship of individual programs did not last long. An advertising model began to dominate in the

1950s in which production companies, advertisers, and wholesale/retail broadcasters were quite distinct and separate. Production companies were either independent producers or subsidiaries of large motion-picture companies and were not owned by advertisers or broadcast networks. In the 1950s and 1960s, independent studio Desilu Productions, for instance, produced *I Love Lucy* and *Star Trek* (1966–69), among others. It rented these programs' broadcast rights—for a specified length of time—to wholesalers such as CBS and NBC (in the cases of *I Love Lucy* and *Star Trek*, respectively), which provided them to their affiliated stations. The affiliates, most of whom were not actually owned by the networks, were the retail outlets that "sold" their wares to the consumers/viewers. (Certain key stations in large cities were owned and operated by the networks and known as O&Os.) After the initial broadcast run, the studios—not the networks—syndicated programs directly to local stations or rented broadcast rights to wholesale syndicators, which handled distribution. From the 1950s to the 1980s, U.S. governmental regulation and economic tradition separated production companies, wholesalers, and retailers.

Synergy Within Transnational Corporations

In the 1980s, the loosening of governmental regulation coincided with significant technological changes and colossal corporate mergers. At a time when the federal government was permitting large, merged, **transnational corporations (TNCs)** to stake a claim on more and more of the media terrain, there were also new technologies for delivering programming to television sets—principally, cable, DBS, and videocassette (see Chapter 14 for a discussion of the political economy of TNCs). The number of television channels received in the average U.S. home increased from fewer than ten to dozens. In 2008, for instance, the average household could receive 118 diverse channels (ironically, the average viewer watched no more than 16 of those on a regular basis).[3] And, to complicate matters further, we've also seen the explosion of competing types of video screens—cell phone, computer, and handheld video game screens—that are delivering images/sounds that may include conventional TV programming content but also feature applications for a vast variety of information and entertainment.

This divergence of programming and technology, however, has been matched by a convergence of media corporations. One recent significant example of such convergence is Comcast Corporation's acquisition of a majority of stock (51 percent) in NBC Universal. This deal, approved early in 2011, means that a company that is already the largest cable operator and the largest Internet service provider now controls a major broadcast network. Another massive merger is in its final stages as of this writing (summer 2017), assuming the deal between media giants AT&T and Time Warner clears antitrust hurdles. And so, fewer and fewer corporations are responsible for more and more programming. The largest corporations have their fingers in numerous media pies.

From the industry perspective, a diversity of holdings encourages a certain synergy among them. One unit within a conglomerate should be able to help out another. For example, NBC Universal and its subsidiaries—the NBC network, individual television stations, Universal Pictures (theatrical film production), and Universal Parks & Resorts—can nurture one another (see Table 6.1). NBC-affiliated stations might run commercials and other spots to help support the release of the latest Universal movie, which may then even wind up as the basis for a ride in a theme park. In fact, one of the factors that delayed Comcast's acquisition of NBC was that it might permit a bit too much synergy—if Comcast were to privilege NBC affiliates on its cable service and block NBC's competitors. Consequently, government regulators looked very closely at the Comcast-NBC

Table 6.1 Select NBC Universal and Comcast Media Assets

Television Networks	NBC, Telemundo, USA Network, Syfy, Chiller, CNBC, MSNBC, NBCSN, Bravo, Golf, The Weather Channel, NBC Universo, and Oxygen
Television Production and Distribution	NBC Entertainment, NBC Universal Sports & Olympics, Telemundo Television Studios
Television Stations	28 NBC and Telemundo O&O stations
Radio	NBC News Radio (on iHeartRadio)
Film Production and Distribution	Universal Pictures, Focus Features, Universal Pictures Home Entertainment
Online Entities	Hulu, Fandango, Seeso
Theme Parks	Universal Parks & Resorts
Notable Comcast Media Assets	E! Entertainment, Golf and G4 channels

Source: "Company Overview," *Comcast*, tvcrit.com/find/comcast.

merger, the first of its kind between a major cable provider and a major broadcast network. And they have been similarly concerned about the AT&T-Time Warner merger.

Synergy can be quite complicated and contradictory, however. Mike Budd, Steve Craig, and Clay Steinman discuss an example of failed synergy within the Disney corporation:

> In 1997, Wind Dancer Production Group, a partner in *Home Improvement*, sued Disney, claiming that the company allowed ABC (its newly acquired network) to renew the show's contract for a smaller licensing fee than the program was worth, effectively cutting into Wind Dancer's profits. As the *Wall Street Journal* put it, "Call it the dark side of synergy: the not-unanticipated consequence of having both the suppliers and the distributors of TV programs and movies under one single roof. In today's Hollywood, deal-makers are increasingly wrestling with a tricky question: 'How hard a bargain can you drive when, in essence, you're negotiating with yourself?'"[4]

Moreover, synergy is undercut by long-standing contracts that predate corporate mergers and splits. Consider the example of *Frasier*. Even though Viacom owned both CBS and Paramount, which produced *Frasier* during its first run, the program was not broadcast on the CBS network. Rather, it appeared on NBC, where it began airing well before Viacom acquired CBS. (And, subsequently, Viacom and CBS have split, making the whole issue moot!)

TV Ratings: Coin of the Realm

Production companies, networks, syndicators, local stations—all of these entities rely on sponsors to make money. Some do so directly and others indirectly, but the ultimate source of most money in the linear-television economic system is advertisers. Broadcasters ostensibly sell broadcast time to advertisers, but, of course, what they are really selling is TV viewers and *their* time. Consequently, the value of broadcast time is determined by its **ratings**—by estimates of the number of viewers and, equally importantly, the types of viewers who are watching. On a regular basis, the one TV program that typically commands the highest price for its ads is the NFL Super Bowl, which is also the program that usually carries the highest ratings for the year. In fact, the 2015 Super Bowl between the New England Patriots and the Seattle Seahawks set a new record as the most watched U.S. television program of all time—bringing in some 114.4 million viewers to the NBC telecast.[5] Presumably, this justified NBC's asking fee of approximately $4.5 million for each 30-second spot—compared to under $500,000 for spots on the most expensive contemporary, nonfootball show, *Empire*.[6]

Super Bowl commercials are not just the most expensive. The Super Bowl has come to attract television's most innovative and prestigious commercials as well—beginning with a strikingly Orwellian commercial that heralded Apple's introduction of the Macintosh computer in 1984 (see description on p. 152–53). The commercials have come to be as much a part of the Super Bowl spectacle as the game itself, especially considering the frequently lopsided scores. It's not surprising, therefore, that broadcast, print, and online news media give substantial coverage to the commercials themselves. Each year, for instance, *USA Today* invites its readers to view and vote for their favorites on the "Super Bowl Ad Meter" on its website.

In contemporary television, the size of the audience is not the only determining economic factor. Lower ratings do not automatically mean less revenue. Many advertisers are looking for very specific audiences, for a particular **demographic** group. The explosion in the number of linear-TV channels in the 1980s has resulted in a phenomenon known within the industry as narrowcasting. Instead of *broad*casting to a large but mixed audience, these channels narrowly define their viewing audience and hope to find a limited, but homogenous, demographic population for advertisers. MTV made its fortune on this premise—delivering a much smaller audience than broadcast networks but filling its audience with a young crowd with disposable income. It's easy to see how advertisers for music, cosmetics, hygiene products, and the like would be attracted to MTV. Indeed, the 18-to-49-year-old demographic is the most highly prized age group for most advertisers. A similar narrowcasting strategy is customary in other specialized channels: Food Network, Court TV, Syfy, Cartoon, Golf, and so on. Moreover, the Internet is the ultimate in narrowcasting, with entire sites devoted to topics as particular as *The Dictionary of Obscure Sorrows*, *The Gallery of Ill-Fitting Pants*, *Modern Moist Towelette Collecting*, and *The Sheep Brain Dissection Guide*.[7]

As one might imagine, these narrowly defined channels necessitate advertising techniques that are distinctly designed for that limited slice of the audience pie. What persuades viewers of MTV is not the same as what persuades viewers of the Golf channel or of general interest networks such as ABC, CBS, and NBC. Since ratings and demographics define these narrowcasters, it is essential to understand how ratings function during this era of increasing specialization.

Nielsen Media Research has long dominated TV audience measurement in the U.S. Arthur C. Nielsen began developing methods for measuring radio listeners in 1923. These methods were modified for use on television in 1950 and have been the ratings standard ever since. Although Nielsen's supremacy has been challenged in recent years by new audience-ratings services that specialize in measuring viewers' engagement on social media, Nielsen ratings remain a powerful force in the U.S. television economy. Networks use them to determine whether programs will live or die and what their advertising rates will be.

Anyone with a casual interest in the TV industry is familiar with the term "Nielsen ratings," but it's worth noting that these "ratings" are not ratings in the sense that they evaluate or rate programs, as a TV critic might. They do not analyze the program's characteristics, but, rather, they are solely concerned with the behavior of the audience. Additionally, Nielsen ratings do not indicate how much or how little viewers enjoy a program or even whether viewers might dislike a program that they watch regularly. They also do not explain what meanings viewers construct from TV. The Nielsen ratings data are quantitative measurements, indicating how many viewers watch and who they are by aggregating them into demographic groups. Nielsen Media Research itself clarifies its perspective: "Our ratings aren't qualitative evaluations of how much a program is 'liked.' Instead, they're the simplest, most democratic measurement: how many people watched."[8]

Nielsen compiles its ratings by tracking television use in a limited sample of U.S. homes. Obviously, it doesn't ask each of the over 300 million U.S. residents what they watch on TV. Instead, Nielsen records viewing behavior through People Meters it installs in approximately 20,000 households, which is less than two-*hundredths* of one percent of the 118.4 million households in the U.S. that have television sets (numbers based on the 2016–17 TV season).[9] People Meters are brick-sized devices that sit near the television set and automatically record that it is on and that it is tuned to a specific channel. The people in the vicinity of the TV are equipped with a remote control device with a button assigned to each of them. They push their assigned buttons to indicate when they start/stop watching TV.

People Meters are not the only method Nielsen uses to measure the audience. Four times a year, during periods known as **sweeps**, Nielsen selects viewers in **designated market areas (DMAs)**—cohesive metropolitan zones—to fill in diaries accounting for a week's worth of TV watching. The origin of the term "sweeps" is rather obscure, but Nielsen provides the following explanation:

> These measurement periods are called "sweeps" because Nielsen Media Research... collects and processes the diaries in a specific order. The diaries from the Northeast regions are processed first and then swept up around the country, from the South, to the Midwest and finally ending with the West.[10]

In addition to diaries and People Meters, Nielsen uses special types of television set meters in the largest DMAs. These meters gather information only about the set's off/on status and its tuning, not who is in the room watching. Nielsen also monitors the use of DVRs, factoring in programs that were recorded, but only if they are watched within a short period of time.

Through these processes, Nielsen is able, in theory, to measure who is viewing what. There are significant problems with these systems. As noted above, they do not gauge viewers' feelings about programs and commercials. The Nielsen numbers tell us nothing about how viewers interpret the programs they watch. They tell us only where viewers are bobbing along in the television flow. And there is some controversy about how effectively Nielsen measures that. In order for People Meters and diaries to be accurate, viewers must be both honest and diligent in recording their viewing habits. But there's little in the TV-viewing experience that encourages diligence. How do we know that a viewer hasn't left the TV on while she takes a nap or he changes the baby's diaper? Or perhaps a viewer might listen to a soap opera playing in the living room while he is in the kitchen, washing dishes, and can't be bothered to push his button on the People Meter's remote control.

One may think of circumstances that might degrade the accuracy of the Nielsen ratings, but this has little impact on the television industry's acceptance of their validity when it comes time to determine advertising rates. As Nielsen explains, "ratings are used like currency in the marketplace of advertiser-supported TV."[11] Despite the Nielsen ratings' inadequacies and problems, they are still the coin of the realm. Networks sell viewers to advertisers based upon the Nielsen numbers. The Nielsen ratings thus establish the exchange rate under which advertisers purchase broadcast time. Using these numbers, broadcasters promise to deliver a certain number of viewers at a specific cost to the advertiser. Viewers are usually measured in thousands, but, oddly, this rate is not known in the business as "CPT," as in "cost per thousand." Instead, it takes the acronym **CPM** or **cost per mil**—which stems from *mille*, the Latin word for thousand.

As you can see in Table 6.2, which shows the top ten programs for the week ending March 19, 2017, the Nielsen numbers actually consist of two components: the **rating** and the **share**. Both are calculated as percentages of viewers.

Table 6.2 Top Ten Network Primetime Series: Total Households week ending March 19, 2017

Rank	*Program Name*	*Households*			*Viewers*
		Rating	*Share*	*Audience*	
1	NCIS	8.7	15	10.3	14.2
2	THIS IS US	7.9	13	9.3	12.8
3	VOICE	7.3	12	8.6	12.2
4	VOICE-TUE	7.1	12	8.4	11.7
5	60 MINUTES	6.7	12	7.9	10.9
6	NCIS: NEW ORLEANS	6.6	12	7.8	10.0
7	LITTLE BIG SHOTS	5.7	10	6.7	9.6
7	NCIS: LOS ANGELES	5.7	10	6.7	9.0
9	GREY'S ANATOMY	5.3	10	6.2	8.0
9	BACHELOR, THE	5.3	9	6.3	8.4

All numbers are based on viewing plus same-day DVR playback. Audience and Viewers numbers are in millions. Copyright 2017 Nielsen Media Research.

The rating indicates the percentage of households with TV sets that are tuned into a specific program. Or, Nielsen explains it this way:

> The estimate of the size of television audience relative to the total universe [the total persons or homes in a given population], expressed as a percentage. [The rating is] the estimated percent of all TV households or persons tuned to a specific station.[12]

Since Nielsen estimates that TV households number 118.4 million in the U.S., the rating percentage shows how many households out of that 118.4 million were actually tuned in to a specific program.[13] *NCIS* scored an 8.7 rating in our sample week, which made it the top-rated show. This rating indicates that 8.7 percent of TV households watched the program. We are then able to figure the actual number of tuned-in households by calculating 8.7 percent of 118.4 million. That result would be 10.3 million households. And, based on additional data from its People Meters and other sources, Nielsen estimated that 14.2 million individual viewers in those households were actually watching. However, as far as the key "adults 18–49" demographic is concerned, *NCIS* was rated much lower that week—coming in at number 15 for this highly prized age group. When children under 18 and adults over 49 are excluded from the numbers, the top-rated program that week was *This Is Us* (2016–).

The share is different from the rating. The share measures the percentage of households with TV sets *turned on at that particular time* that tuned into a specific program. Nielsen refers to this as the **HUT—"households using television**." In our *NCIS* example, the program earned a 15 share—meaning that 15 percent of the households watching TV at 8:00 p.m. Eastern Time, March 14, 2017, tuned in to *NCIS*. Thus, while the *rating* marks the percentage of a relatively stable number (total households with TV), the *share* is the percentage of a constantly fluctuating number since the HUT varies throughout the day and the year—with summertime being the season with the least viewing.

If you find all these rating/share numbers confusing, consider this simplified example. In a ten-home universe, six households have their TVs turned on, and three are tuned into channel 5 to watch *NCIS*:

- Rating = 30
  3 (sets tuned to channel 5) divided by 10 (total homes) = 30%

- Share = 50
  3 (sets tuned to channel 5) divided by 6 (turned-on sets) = 50%

In light of the calculation of rating and share, it is interesting to consider how viewing of the major broadcast networks has precipitously declined. In the 1952–53 season (the first one for which Nielsen ratings are available), ABC, CBS, and NBC had a combined average rating of 74.8. In other words, three-quarters of the TV households in the U.S. watched these three networks all the time. By the 2000s, that number had fallen to less than one-quarter of the TV households. Even if we include newer broadcast networks (Fox, CW, Univision, and so on), that rating is still not even half of what the big three used to command. Additionally, the top program in that first ratings season was CBS's *I Love Lucy*, with a hefty 67.3 rating. Two-thirds of the TV nation regularly watched it each week. In contrast, the top show from the week discussed above, *NCIS*, commanded a comparatively meager 8.7 rating—approximately one-eighth of *I Love Lucy*'s. Broadcast networks and their programs clearly no longer command the enormous audiences they once did. The dispersion of the audience is obvious. Advertisers have had to adapt their commercials to this new world of increasingly narrow, but more homogenous, audiences.

Paying for "Free" TV

Every time you visit the store and buy, say, one of Procter & Gamble's many products that you saw advertised on television, you are paying for "free" TV. Portions of those products' purchase prices were added to the products to ameliorate P&G's advertising budget, which can top $2 billion per year for television alone.[14] How do P&G and other multinational corporations pay for linear television? For the most part, there is no direct contact between TV's sponsors and the companies that actually create TV programs—although there are significant exceptions to this, such as P&G's production of soap operas. Also, many advertisers pay production companies and networks to insert their products directly into programs. This **product integration** (a.k.a. **product placement)** is an increasingly common strategy for brands to cope with the demise of the commercial break in the video-on-demand era. If a house flipper is driving a prominently displayed GMC truck to the job site on a home-improvement show, then the viewer won't be able to skip past the product as they might a 30-second commercial. Nielsen tracks the impact of product integration so that sponsors have a better sense of its value. For instance, during April 2010, Nielsen found that the top three most recalled product placements were:

1. Victoria's Secret in *The Office*: "Michael interrupts meeting to offer Donna a retail store's catalog";
2. Ford in *Cold Case*: "Cole Austin points to his Mustang and says he still owns it";
3. Skype in *Law & Order: SVU*: "Joyce tells Benson and Stabler that she talks to Andrew online."[15]

Product integration can be rather deviously added during post-production, too—as when digital trickery was used to place a box of Club Crackers on a coffee table in a *Yes, Dear* (2000–06) scene where it didn't physically exist.[16] Product integration is thus more common than a sponsor producing a program itself, but most advertisers do neither and have little influence over programs during their actual production. Instead, they must deal with the sales departments of TV's wholesalers and retailers.

The TV and advertising industries classify advertising expenditures in five categories: network, cable, local, syndication, and national spot. "Network" refers to time bought on the major broadcast networks, which, as of 2018, are ABC, CBS, NBC, Fox, CW, and Ion. The term may also include Spanish-language broadcast networks: Univision, Telemundo, UniMás (formerly Telefutura and now owned by Univision), and TV Azteca. These broadcast networks are also sometimes called "terrestrial networks" because they transmit through earthbound local stations. "Cable" designates commercials on more specialized networks such as ESPN, MTV, and CNN that are delivered through a system of satellites to cable providers or directly to viewers through services such as DirecTV. "Local" advertising is time bought on individual broadcast stations and cable services by local merchants. Network and cable purchases are not the only way advertisers reach a national audience. Advertisers may also buy time on syndicated programs that are aired nationwide on local stations and cable networks. Or they may place their ads directly on numerous local stations and cable services through "national spot" advertising. With spot commercials the advertiser may promote its products in specific regions without going to the expense of a full national or network campaign. Katz Television Group, for example, represents nearly 800 television stations in DMAs across the U.S. Using Katz or another national representative, a manufacturer of air conditioners based in Phoenix could buy air time throughout the Southwest and South while minimizing its expenditures in New England.

Despite declining ratings, the general-interest broadcast networks still command a large portion of television advertisers' dollars. Even in 2009, during a continuing worldwide recession, U.S. advertisers still bought over $25 billion worth of time on network television, or approximately 41 percent of all television advertising expenditures.[17] However, one recent trend in TV advertising has been to seek smaller, but more cohesive, audiences. This is reflected in the amount of money spent on cable networks, which occupy specialized niches. During television's boom years, the percentage increases for cable networks have vastly outpaced those of the traditional broadcast networks, and during the current bust years, broadcast networks have lost advertising more quickly than cable has.

Which companies buy this time, buy these audiences? As you might well imagine, TV ad purchases are dominated by huge transnational corporations. In particular, the top five advertisers on network television as the 2010s began were, in order, Verizon Communications, AT&T, Ford Motor Company, Chrysler Group, and Honda Motor Company.[18] More interesting, perhaps, are the types of goods that are sold on television—as shown in Table 6.3, the Television Bureau of Advertising's classification of the top categories of network-TV advertising in 2009. In the U.S. at least, these are the products and services one sees most on network television. In the following section, we'll explore the meanings commonly associated with these commodities.

Table 6.3 Top Categories of Network-TV Advertising (2009)

	Category	*Spending (millions)*
1	Automotive	$2,433,283,100
2	Communications/Telecommunications	$2,198,044,800
3	Prescription Medication & Pharmaceutical Houses	$1,683,099,800
4	Restaurants	$1,421,493,800
5	Motion Pictures	$1,283,609,800
6	Financial	$1,079,157,400
7	Toiletries & Cosmetics	$1,078,929,400
8	Food and Food Products	$868,933,700
9	Medicines and Remedies (excluding Rx)	$700,744,300
10	Insurance	$653,697,300

Source: *TV Basics: A Report on the Growth and Scope of Television*, Television Bureau of Advertising, www.tvb.org/media/file/TVB_FF_TV_Basics.pdf, accessed November 29, 2010.

The Polysemy of Commodities

Television advertising presents a discourse on modern life in a culture based on buying and selling. It tells us what it means to be a consumer and suggests activities we should pursue as consumers. Principally, it is telling us to buy commodities and services, but often it does so in quite an indirect manner. Many ads conceal their function as advertising and simply appear to be short stories or evocative vignettes about the human condition. All ads—regardless of their bluntness or subtlety—are inscribed with packets of meanings for viewers to decode. All ads contain the fundamental meaning "Buy this product," but they also suggest various other meanings that range from "Buy this product *and* you will become beautiful" to "Buy this product *and* you will be well liked" to "Buy this product *and* your dog's fur will really shine."

In this section we consider what comes after "buy this product." We look at the socially defined meanings, values, and illusions—the polysemy—that are commonly employed in the service of selling products. TV commercials present an ongoing discourse about objects and attempt to connect them to a range of meanings. We may identify eight broad categories of such meanings:

1. luxury, leisure, and conspicuous consumption;
2. individualism;
3. the natural;
4. folk culture and tradition;
5. novelty and progress;
6. sexuality and romance;
7. alleviation of pain, fear/anxiety, and guilt;
8. utopia and escape from dystopia.

Although this list does not exhaust all of the meanings that commercials invoke, it does contain the principal values that advertisers use to entice consumers.

Luxury, Leisure, and Conspicuous Consumption

The end graphic in an ad for the Lincoln LS sedan reads simply, "Lincoln. American luxury." Car companies such as Lincoln, Cadillac, and Mercedes have long traded on their value as luxury goods. The same could be said of Rolex watches, De Beers diamonds, *haute couture* fashion, and high-end electronics. When ads draw upon the notion of luxury, they imply that the goods advertised go beyond filling basic human needs for food, clothing, and shelter. Luxury items, by definition, are ones that are not necessities, that one could do without and still subsist. In addition to providing material comfort and utility, luxurious cars, jewelry, clothing, and electronics serve a significant social function. Such goods offer a way for the consumer to resemble or emulate members of an elevated social class.

The emulation of higher classes was initially conceptualized by Thorstein Veblen as the nineteenth century came to a close. Veblen also coined the term "conspicuous consumption" to refer to the showy, excessive purchase of nonessential, luxury goods. In his book *The Theory of the Leisure Class* (1899), he argues that members of the leisure class (persons who need not work for a living) must buy expensive commodities in a conspicuous manner in order to maintain their social status. Conspicuous consumption becomes an emblem, a sign, of their wealth and power. Individuals who are not quite that wealthy, but aspire to be so, *emulate* the leisure class by consuming conspicuously.

Emulation need not just be about wealth. When consumers buy name-brand clothing in order to adopt a certain style of dress, for instance, they seek to belong to a specific social group. Balmain jackets are no better at keeping one's body warm than generic garments, but they serve an important function nonetheless. They allow the wearer to emulate members of a social group (urban, hip hop). Emulation is also the central strategy at work in all celebrity endorsements of products. Why would Nike have paid Michael Jordan huge sums of money and created a shoe line bearing his name (the Air Jordan) if it didn't think that viewers, especially young viewers, would want to emulate him and wear the same shoes as he did? As the Gatorade campaign of the late 1990s suggested, many advertisers banked on teenage boys' desire to "be like Mike."

It's easy to dismiss such emulation and conspicuous consumption of luxury goods as crass social climbing and superficial status seeking, but, as Ellen Seiter writes (paraphrasing anthropologist Mary Douglas),

> any distinction between necessary and unnecessary goods fails to account for the crucial importance of consumption for ceremonial purposes, for social cohesion, and for the maintenance of networks of support.... To condemn people to a level of mere subsistence consumption is to exclude them from the basis for success and security within a social network.[19]

In modern societies, what we own shapes where we fit into societies' networks of work and play. Moreover, as Seiter discusses, children acquire crucial social skills through "consumption events": "birthday parties, holiday celebrations, visits at friends' houses, and so on."[20] TV commercials thrive upon and exploit the central function that consumption has come to have in social networking.

Individualism

One long-standing conflict in U.S. ideology is the rights of the individual versus those of the community. We enter into a social contract with the government and other citizens that holds that we will limit certain freedoms in exchange for a civil, well-ordered society. For instance, we have the capability of driving through the center of town at 80 m.p.h., but we don't. We observe traffic rules because we know that they serve the overall good of the community. Advertising, however, need not follow these rules as strictly. Many ads tacitly override the social contract in favor of individualist values—both good and bad. These individualist values are often based in the self: self-fulfillment, self-reliance, self-expression, self-absorption, even simple selfishness.

The U.S. Army entreats young men and women to "Be all you can be," to fulfill themselves and learn self-reliance through the military service—thereby repressing the discipline and obedience that attend that experience. Nike's "Just do it" campaign intimates that determination and self-expression will come to all who wear its shoes. And McDonald's has sold billions of Big Macs by telling viewers that it's okay to be a little self-absorbed and selfish: "You deserve a break today. So get up and get away to McDonald's." Leave behind your responsibilities to others, it implies, and escape to the comfort of a fast-food restaurant.

Pitching individualism in a mass medium such as television is a tricky business. Consider the tag line of a Burger King campaign begun in 1973. "Have it your way" implies that the individual is unique and uniquely deserving of special privileges—a hamburger prepared a certain way. By boasting that "Special orders don't upset *us*," Burger King's jingle taunted McDonald's for its assembly-line approach. But there is a fundamental problem when uniqueness is marketed by mass media. Burger King cannot provide hamburgers uniquely prepared a hundred million different ways. Rather, "your way" must be restricted to a fairly limited number of options within a very controlled environment. You can get your hamburger with or without tomatoes, but you cannot get it marinated overnight in an assortment of seasonings and broiled over dampened mesquite chips. Thus, the individualism that Burger King is selling is not unique. As it turns out, "your way" is the same way as millions of others'. Similarly, Budweiser commercials may declare, "This Bud's for you," but the TV viewer knows that this is not literally true, that Anheuser-Busch didn't brew that bottle of beer to the viewer's own specifications.

"Advertising shepherds herds of individuals," notes Leslie Savan.[21] By this she means that television addresses viewers as individuals, not as a group. It invites them to experience life as individuals, to break away from conformity and establish their own identity. This leads to what she identifies as mass media advertising's "most basic paradox": "Join us and become unique."[22] Clothing and other fashion products often appeal to individualist values and suggest to viewers that they will stand out from the crowd if they purchase these products, but since commercials are simultaneously encouraging millions of other viewers to purchase those same products they are perpetually creating or reinforcing fashion-based crowds of individuals. Thus, at the same time that commercials encourage viewers to be self-reliant individuals, they also entreat them to emulate others and join certain groups, enter certain networks.

An ad campaign of Gap commercials from 1999 illustrated this paradoxical "herd of individuals" appeal. In one of these spots, a group of models in their twenties stands in front of a white background, faces the camera directly, and lip syncs to Depeche Mode's "Just Can't Get Enough" (Figure 6.1; tvcrit.com/find/cantgetenough). It concludes with the Gap's logo and the tagline, "Everybody in leather." Other commercials in the series ended with "Everybody in cords" and "Everybody in vests." By suggesting (commanding?) "Everybody in..." the Gap uses the appeal of networking and emulation—hoping the viewer will think, "I want to *be like* these models," which included Aaron Lohr, Alex Greenwald, and Monet Mazur before they each hit peak popularity. Significantly, these models do not interact with one another—in stark contrast to a contemporary series of Gap khaki ads in which dancers gleefully perform swing dances

Figure 6.1 Depeche Mode's "Just Can't Get Enough" accompanies a Gap commercial: "Everybody in leather."

with each other (Figure 6.2; tvcrit.com/find/gapswing). The khaki dancers function as a joyous, well-coordinated group, but the "Everybody in..." ads present a crowd of isolated individuals. They're all wearing leather/cords/vests, but in different ways. Their dress and body language (they all strike different poses) set them up as individuals even as the framing and song pull them together as a group. Hence, they are paradoxically alone together—much like the millions of viewers simultaneously watching TV from their separate homes.

The Natural

Commodities may be associated with nature and aspects of the natural—wholesomeness, healthfulness, purity. Medical, food, and beverage products often emphasize their natural ingredients and thereby suggest that the products are wholesome, healthy, and pure. Pertussin cough syrup was promoted in the 1960s as a "safe *natural* way to relieve night cough." Its ads resemble those of homeopathic medicine, claiming it is "made from nature's healing medicinals." The ads don't specify which medicinals, but they do stress that Pertussin does not contain "codeine, antihistamines, and nerve-dulling drugs." Post Grape-Nuts cereal was similarly advertised as the "Back-to-nature cereal" in TV commercials from the early 1970s featuring naturalist Euell Gibbons (tvcrit.com/find/grapenuts). He claims, "Its *natural*, sweet taste reminds me of *wild* hickory nuts" (emphasis added). Gibbons's comment is a bit disingenuous because Grape-Nuts contains no nuts—hickory or otherwise—but rather is manufactured from wheat and barley (which, granted, are natural ingredients).

In similar fashion, commercials for Coors Light beer make obvious connections between the natural qualities of the Rocky Mountains and Coors beer by suggesting that you "Tap the Rockies" (tvcrit.com/find/coorslight). Coors emphasizes its beer contains "Rocky Mountain water" and no additives or preservatives—alluding to nature's purity and repressing the company's exploitation of natural resources in order to make beverages. There have, however, been attacks on its use of the majestic images of the Rockies. In 1997, "Tap the Rockies" billboards in upstate New York were vandalized with the accusation, "Rape the Rockies, racist scum, toxic polluters."[23]

Another sense of naturalness is that which is opposed to the technological or artificial. Makeup products commonly present this illusion of the natural. An ad for CoverGirl Clean Sheer Stick, for example, promises, "It doesn't look like makeup—just great skin." As with many "beauty" products,

Figure 6.2 Dancers dressed in khaki pants gleefully connect with one another in a Gap commercial.

the appeal of Clean Sheer Stick is its ability to conceal its artifice and appear natural. Makeup such as this promises to transform a person's natural face (just as certain bras and other undergarments promise to transform the body) while hiding the artificiality of that transformation.

It should be noted that the natural is not always viewed in a positive light. Advertising often qualifies its use of the natural world. Post's Grape-Nuts commercial extolled its "back-to-nature" virtues at a time (1960s to 1970s) when this phrase signified a new environmental consciousness, but in the early part of the twentieth century Post seemed just as proud of the scientific processing of the natural world as it was of its naturalness. Text on Grape-Nuts boxes from that time proclaims that Grape-Nuts is "a food containing the natural nutritive elements of these field grains *thoroughly and scientifically baked*" (emphasis added).[24] Nature is all well and good, apparently, but only if science is baked into it. Even natural beauty, as alluded to in the CoverGirl commercial, has not always been universally admired. In some circles, it is associated with coarseness and vulgarity or seen as a trait of the presumably inferior working class. The royal French court during Louis XVI's and Marie Antoinette's reign (1774–93), for instance, preferred ostentatious powdered wigs and a blatantly artificial style of makeup and clothing. A more recent example is Goth fashion—including dyed hair, extremely pale complexions (often achieved through makeup), black lipstick, and nail polish colors that are "not-seen-in-nature."[25] The Goths and the Louis XVI court have little interest in looking "natural." Instead of valuing the natural, cultures such as these emphasize otherworldliness, a certain sense of sophistication, refinement, and connoisseurship.

Folk Culture and Tradition

Closely allied to the imagery of naturalness is folk culture. Advertising calls upon folk culture to represent traditional principles such as trustworthiness, simplicity, authenticity, and raw patriotism. "We make money the old-fashioned way," intones John Houseman in the Smith-Barney ad, "We earn it." Chevrolet's television commercials have long rested on folk associations—especially in its truck ads. From 1986 to 1993, the "Heartbeat of America" campaign presented numerous images of folk life in the rural United States and thereby evoked the virtues of small-town life. Earlier, during the contentious 1970s, its ads sang the virtues of "baseball, hot dogs, apple pie, and Chevrolet" (tvcrit.com/find/chevbaseball). In this instance, small-town, folk values are blended with patriotism and nostalgia for a bygone era. Baseball ("America's pastime") and hot dogs connote the positive values of team sport (athletic prowess, cooperation, loyalty, courage in the face of adversity), while apple pie carries implications of motherly nurturing and down-home nutrition.

The Chevrolet truck ad goes like this:

> In the years that I been livin' lots of things have surely changed. Lots of things have come and gone, some even came back again. But through all the many changes, some things are for sure. And you know that's a mighty fine feelin', kinda makes you feel secure. 'Cause I love baseball, hot dogs, apple pie, and Chevrolet.[26]

Irony is not normally associated with folk discourse, but Gallo Winery's Bartles & Jaymes wine cooler ads playfully parody folk narratives. They present the ostensible owners of the company as a couple of genial old codgers—Frank Bartles and Ed Jaymes. Actually, it is pure fiction, invented by Gallo's advertising agency, Ogilvy & Mather, in order to sell a new alcoholic beverage to young professionals. Over the course of seven years (1985–92) and some 230 commercials, Bartles (played by David Rufkaur) chronicled their marketing endeavors (Figure 6.3).

Figure 6.3 David Rufkaur (right) and Dick Maugg perform as Frank Bartles and Ed Jaymes, respectively, the fictional creators of Bartles & Jaymes wine coolers.

The first Bartles & Jaymes wine cooler ad's text is as follows (tvcrit.com/find/bartles):

> Hello there. My name is Fred Bartles and this is Ed Jaymes. You know, it occurred to Ed the other day that between his fruit orchard and my premium grade wine vineyard, we could make a truly superior premium-grade wine cooler. It sounded good to me. So Ed took out a second on his house, and wrote to Harvard for an MBA, and now we're preparing to enter the wine cooler business. We will try to keep you posted on how it's going. And thank you very much for your support.

The folk values incarnated in the Bartles character included guilelessness, simplicity, and honest directness. Much like the Chevrolet spots that revel in the past as a gentler, "simpler" time, Bartles appears to be from another era where selling products is a direct, honorable process. Sitting on his front porch with a wooden screen door behind him, he seems out of touch with the principles of slick contemporary marketing campaigns. There is considerable irony here, of course, since all of Bartles's guilelessness is a sham, and the ad's honest directness was fabricated by a high-powered advertising agency.

Unlike many commercials that rely upon folk culture, however, the Bartles & Jaymes series presumes that viewers are themselves wary of appeals based on baseball, hot dogs, and apple pie. The wine cooler was designed for sophisticated young professionals who might be skeptical of small-town values and bald-faced sentiment. The ads subtly play to that urban audience by softly parodying small-town perspectives—as when the first ad suggests Jaymes would write to Harvard for a Master's in business. The humor of many of the spots relies upon the viewer's awareness of marketing jargon and strategies. "Thank you for your support" is a hollow phrase commonly used in marketing, advertising, and PR. When we hear it coming sincerely from the mouth of a country bumpkin, we laugh at the incongruity.

In a sense, the Bartles & Jaymes ads have it both ways: they appeal to viewers' desires for a simpler era at the same time they chide the simplicity of that era—inviting the viewers in on the joke by alluding to the complicated machinations of modern marketing.

Novelty and Progress

The flip side of advertising's appeal to folk culture and tradition is its incessant hawking of the new and the merits of progress. Long-standing marketing research shows that consumers are drawn to packaging with the words "new" and "improved" prominent on it. To capitalize on this tendency, advertisers subject us consumers to product improvements which are dubious at best. One commercial for "new mild, new formula" Zest soap promises "new lather," but it's hard to imagine what could be strikingly new about bubbles of soap. And the 2001 model of the Dodge Caravan closely resembled other minivans, but nonetheless a spot for it starts with a shot of tulips blooming, the title "Different," and the claim "We began anew." It then lists several minor changes. "New, new, new! Dodge Grand Caravan, the best minivan ever." It concludes with the self-mocking question and a graphic: "And did we mention it's new? [pause] The All-new Dodge Caravan. Different." There is nothing that is literally "all-new" or completely different in the world of merchandise. If you changed everything in the design of a minivan, it would no longer be a "minivan." It'd be something completely new and different. Manufacturers and advertising agencies are not prepared to risk all-out newness.

Part of the appeal of newness and novelty stems from a positive attitude toward progress. Americans are accustomed to regular reports of scientific advances in medicine, physics, and other technological fields where the work of researchers builds upon previous efforts and moves toward particular goals: a cure for cancer, sending a human to the moon, a car that will get 1,000 miles per gallon. Applying the notion of scientific progress to soap, automobiles, or fashion is usually just hyperbole. Zest's new lather might well be different from its old lather (although even that is debatable), but that doesn't necessarily mean that it is an advance over the older lather. The new lather is different from—rather than an advance over—the old.

Coca-Cola's executives learned this lesson the hard way. New Coke received an enormous publicity campaign in 1985, but it turned into one of the biggest marketing fiascos of the century. Most Coke drinkers found the new, sweeter taste (designed to be closer to Pepsi's formula) was not to their liking. This led Coca-Cola executives to hurriedly reissue Coke's old formula under the name "Coke Classic"—a name that evokes images of a traditional soda fountain and all its folk associations. It's interesting to note that Coca-Cola's marketers changed the position of the word "Coke" in the name when they released Coke Classic. That is, with "*New* Coke" they emphasized the newness of the product, but with "*Coke* Classic"—and not "Classic Coke"—they stressed its Coke-ness. There are no casual decisions in the naming of products. Deciding to put the word "Coke" first probably arose from hours of brainstorming and focus groups. Later, in 1992, "New Coke" became "Coke II." After seven years on the market it was presumably no longer new, although it was still being presented as a successor ("II") to standard Coca-Cola. Subsequently, Coke Classic has returned to being the one "true" Coca-Cola and New Coke/Coke II has been phased out altogether.

Sexuality and Romance

It's no secret that sexuality and romance have been associated with thousands of products over the decades of TV's short history. "Sex sells," it has often been said in the advertising industry. One need not look far to find overt references to sex and sexual allure in television commercials—although, of course, U.S. network standards still prohibit nudity (which is quite common in European commercials) or graphic representation of sexual intercourse. Indeed, most of the broadcast networks continue to reject condom commercials. Still, ads for perfume or cologne, lingerie, bathing suits, shampoos, and cosmetics—which often feature women and men in revealing, tight-fitting clothing—are clearly banking on associating sex with their products.

The two most obvious ways that sexual imagery sells are (1) implying that the product will make the viewer more sexually appealing, and (2) associating the product itself with sexuality and thereby stimulating a hormonal rush in order to draw the viewer's attention to it. The first type of appeal is evident in products such as perfumes and shampoos. The second comes into play in ads for beer and cars that have been designed for heterosexual men and have attractive women posing by the products.

Victoria's Secret manages to incorporate *both* of these appeals in its commercials. During the 1999 Super Bowl between the Denver Broncos and the Atlanta Falcons, it advertised a Web-based fashion show by addressing itself principally to male viewers: "The Broncos won't be there. The Falcons won't be there. You won't care." The bulk of the ad consists of images of its minimally dressed models (tvcrit.com/find/vssuperbowl). The "you" in this instance is the male viewer who might be sexually attracted to the women of Victoria's Secret. *Entertainment Weekly* attacked the ad as the "Worst Blatant Exploitation of T&A ['tits-and-ass']" of the Super Bowl ads: "The plot: Jiggle, jiggle, jiggle, Web address. This embarrassingly unsubtle spot announces an upcoming Internet fashion show for the lingerie catalog—because God knows we need more soft-core cyberporn."[27]

Evidently, the Super Bowl spot hopes to entice men to purchase lingerie for the women in their lives, but, in a commercial for its "Body by Victoria" collection, Victoria's Secret mainly speaks to female viewers. It posted a video to its official YouTube channel with the caption, "Got Spring Fever? Check out the new Body by Victoria collection . . . bras you'll want to live in every day, all season long" (Figure 6.4; tvcrit.com/find/vsbody). The target viewers and the implicit "you" of this ad's text are certainly not men. This bra is plainly marketed to women themselves and, perhaps secondarily, to men who might buy lingerie for them. The heterosexual

Figure 6.4 Victoria's Secret addresses its female viewers, claiming this is a bra "you'll want to live in every day, all season long."

male viewer is not excluded from the appeal of this ad, however, as it features conventionally attractive women wearing lingerie and posing provocatively, presumably inciting his libido. In true polysemic fashion, this commercial has room for several sexual interpretations: both, "buy this product and you will become sexier" for women viewers and "this product is itself sexually enticing" for heterosexual male viewers.

Paul Messaris contends that not all appeals to sexual themes are blatant. Subtle, even covert or hidden, presentations of sexuality occur in "at least three types of situations":

> [F]irst, when sex is being used metaphorically and what the ad is really promising is something else; second, when the link between the product and sex is frowned upon; and, third, when the type of sex is socially unacceptable.[28]

One famous instance of metaphoric sex is a 1960s commercial for Noxzema shaving cream. In tight close-up, Gunilla Knutson, a former Miss Sweden, suggestively runs her lips across a string of pearls (Figure 6.5; tvcrit.com/find/noxzema). With her distinctly Swedish accent, she breathlessly intones, "Men, nothing takes it off like Noxzema Medicated Shave." A brass band then begins to blare "The Stripper," which accompanies close-ups of a man shaving his face (Figure 6.6). "Take it off," Knutson commands, "Take it *all* off."

What is the source of the enduring appeal of this ad? Much like Victoria Secret's bra ad, this product ostensibly improves the sexual desirability of its user, but the strategy used in its pitch is a metaphoric one. The act of a man removing shaving cream is metaphorically linked to the act of a woman removing clothing: shaving = stripping. The phrase "Take it off" contains the literal meaning of shaving cream removal and the metaphoric meaning of clothing removal. In the 1960s, this was seen to be quite risqué. Messaris argues that metaphoric sex and double entendres continue to be widely used in contemporary advertising as well—especially in commercials associating sex and food. One unlikely example of a recent sex-food association may be found in a Carl's Jr. commercial promoting its premium salads and featuring Kim Kardashian (tvcrit.com/find/carls). One typically doesn't think of a salad as sexy, but that's exactly the metaphoric point of this commercial. As the narrator asks, "Who says salads can't be hot?" we get a variety of shots of Kardashian sensually eating salad—shot in the manner of a soft-core porn film (Figure 6.7). The meaning is far from subtle.

Messaris's second category of covert sexuality in commercials contains ads in which "the link between the product and sex is disparaged or condemned by public opinion. Cars, liquor, and

Figure 6.5 Noxzema Medicated Shave relies on metaphoric sex for its impact.

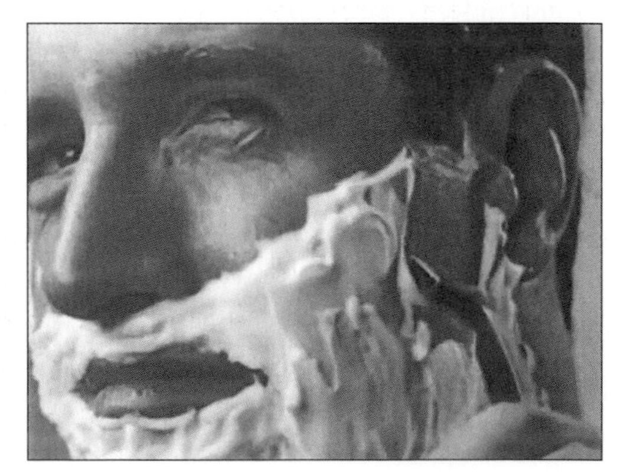

Figure 6.6 "Take it off. Take it all off."

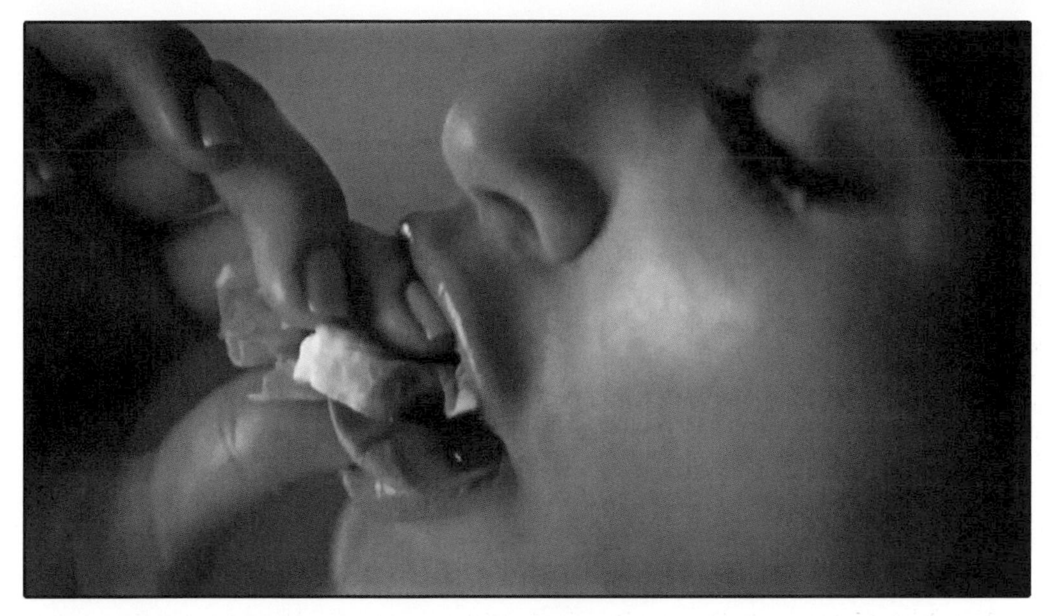

Figure 6.7 Kim Kardashian sensually eats a Carl's Jr. salad.

cigarettes are among the most prominent examples of products in this category."[29] If advertisers were to state seriously that their cars, liquor, or tobacco products (which have been banned from U.S. TV ads since 1971) will enable men to attract women for the purpose of sexual activity, viewers would scoff or laugh at the ads. And yet that is exactly the implicit message of many commercials—especially local car commercials—in which conventionally attractive women pose beside various products. Messaris's point is that sexual associations with cars, beer, and other products have not disappeared from U.S. television. Rather, they have just been displaced from unabashed verbal statements to the more subtle language of the visuals.

Messaris's third category of implicit sexuality contains forbidden sexual themes. What qualifies as a sexual taboo on broadcast television advertising is, of course, quite tame and circumscribed when compared to online videos, premium channels (e.g., HBO or Showtime), or theatrical films. For instance, bondage and homosexuality are never unabashedly represented in U.S. commercials. They find their way into television commercials mostly through covert allusion—often cloaked in comedy or self-parody. In a Heineken Light commercial from 2016 (tvcrit.com/find/heineken), Neil Patrick Harris, who identifies as gay, extols the virtues of the beer to the "Grill Master," as he's named on Heineken's YouTube channel—a bearded man tending burgers on a grill (Figure 6.8). Harris's dialogue alludes to gay sex in heavily coded terms.

Neil Patrick Harris:	"Heineken Light makes it okay to flip another man's meat."
Grill Master:	"No, no, no. You never flip another man's meat."
NPH:	"Award-winning Heineken Light is the best light beer you've ever tasted."
GM:	"That's true. Can I have one?"
NPH:	"Can I flip your meat?"
	(beat)
GM:	"No."
NPH:	"Suit yourself."

Figure 6.8 Neil Patrick Harris offers to "flip the meat" of the Grill Master, toying with a gay subtext without making it explicit.

The innuendo of this spot could easily be missed or ignored, but it did stir some controversy. *LGBTQ Nation* reported that "Homophobes freak out over new Neil Patrick Harris Heineken Light ad" and an *AdLand* author was perplexed: "I have no idea what the innuendo is because I am not a gay man but I am pretty sure there's some innuendo here. I feel like a kid watching my parents verbally flirt, I know something is going on but I'm not getting it."[30] From Messaris's perspective, this commercial has skillfully employed a taboo (in terms of broadcast TV) sexual activity to heighten viewers' interest in a product. And it has done so without explicitly mentioned gay sex.

Child and teenage sexuality is similarly avoided in the manifest content of TV commercials. Messaris discusses what happened when an advertiser violated this particular taboo in the 1995 Calvin Klein jeans campaign.[31] The print and TV ads from that campaign feature very young, barely pubescent, models in revealing poses. Many critics of the ads argued that they appealed to the prurient interest of adult male viewers and thus qualified as child pornography. After considerable public protest, Calvin Klein withdrew the ads. Evidently, the commercials were not covert enough for the U.S. media audience.

Alleviation of Pain, Fear/Anxiety, and Guilt

Numerous commercials use a simple narrative formula: Someone is in pain or feeling anxious and the ad's product alleviates that pain or anxiety. Case closed. All medicinal ads are based on this premise, as are those for many hygiene (e.g., deodorants, mouth washes, feminine douches) and food products. The Alka-Seltzer jingle "Plop, plop, fizz, fizz. Oh, what a relief it is!" unmistakably exemplifies this approach.

Soap operas, several of which used to be produced by hygiene and food giant Procter & Gamble, and other serial narratives are awash with this sort of commercial. It's interesting to consider how the serial narrative structure is the exact opposite of the narrative in its commercials.

Serial stories never reach a definitive ending. Each small conclusion is the basis for a new enigma and further questions. But in commercials presented during serial programs, crises are quickly solved in 30 seconds. A child's cough is soothed. A woman's dandruff is controlled. A "tension headache" is eased. Hunger is satisfied. Commercials are small bits of closure inserted into the serial's vast sea of open-ended narrative.

Guilt is often attached to issues of pain and suffering. Mike Budd, et al. explain how advertisers mount a "guilt campaign":

> This involves airing commercials that imply that the viewer is not really a loving mother and homemaker unless she uses Downey to make her towels soft, Pampers to keep her baby dry, and Duncan Hines to bake cakes for her husband and children.[32]

Often the guilt is heaped upon the woman by someone observing her not using the sponsor's product. A classic in this vein is the Wisk detergent commercials produced by the BBDO agency and begun in 1968. In this series, a wife and mother is repeatedly shamed for being unable to deal with the "ring around the collar" problem—until, that is, she learns to apply Wisk directly to the offending stains (tvcrit.com/find/wisk). Such ads encourage the viewer to seek alleviation of guilt through the purchase of commodities.

Utopia and Escape From Dystopia

In her consideration of children's advertising and consumer culture, Seiter argues, "Like most popular entertainments, commercials are utopian in many respects—portraying a childhood world more exciting, intense, and exhilarating than everyday life."[33] In Seiter's study, she found that child-centered commercials often counterpose this utopian childhood world to the adult world of restraint and boring responsibilities. Of course, utopianism is not limited to children's commercials. Numerous commercials invite the adult viewer into a utopia of intensity of experience, exhilaration of emotion, and unbridled hedonism (a total lack of responsibility).

Seiter draws upon Richard Dyer's more general discussion of utopianism in film, television, and other mass entertainments. Dyer characterizes utopia as "the image of 'something better' to escape into, or something we want deeply that our day-to-day lives don't provide."[34] In contrast to the tensions and inadequacies of contemporary life, Dyer argues, utopia offers:

- abundance (elimination of poverty for self and others; equal distribution of wealth);
- energy (work and play synonymous);
- intensity (excitement, drama, affectivity of living);
- transparency (open, spontaneous, honest communications and relationships);
- community (all together in one place, communal interests, collective activity).[35]

Each of these traits can be found in television commercials.

An ad for the MCI Network explicitly alludes to utopia (tvcrit.com/find/mci). It begins by explaining, "People here communicate mind to mind." Then it continues:

> Not black to white. There are no genders. Not man to woman. There is no age. Not young to old. There are no infirmities. Not short to tall. Or handsome to homely. Just thought to thought. Idea to idea. Uninfluenced by the rest of it. There are only minds. Only minds. What is this place? This place? Utopia? No. No. The Internet. The Internet. The Internet.[36]

MCI represents utopia as a community fostering the unfettered interchange of ideas; a place where nothing will constrict its citizens. Its ad insinuates that the Internet might be mistaken for utopia and that its networking can thus convey the customer to a utopian realm.

A commercial for a Mercedes-Benz roadster is less high-minded in its presentation of a utopian experience. In the ad, Peter Pan and Tinkerbell float into the bedroom of Michael, a middle-aged man. Michael is sleeping in respectable-looking pajamas next to a woman who is presumably his respectable spouse. Peter entices him, "Do you remember when we were eight and we went flying?" When he protests that he can't fly any more, Peter corrects him, "It's never too late to fly!" We then cut to Michael, still in his pajamas, driving a roadster and shouting, "Woooohooo!" Notably, Peter and Tinkerbell are beside him, but his spouse is not. The spot fades to black as Michael shifts into high gear. Then the only text in the ad fades in: "Exhilaration" (followed by the Mercedes-Benz logo). With its allusions to Neverland and the boy who won't grow up, this commercial associates its product with a utopian view of childhood pleasures and passions.

A dystopia is the exact opposite of a utopia. It's a land where freedoms are restricted and life is oppressive and colorless. Advertisers' products frequently promise to liberate consumers from such oppression. McDonald's modest suggestion that "You deserve a break today" could be viewed as an inducement to flee the dystopian home—soiled laundry, dirty bathrooms, and unfed children—and enter a world of culinary surplus and happy circus characters (Ronald McDonald).

The most unequivocal TV-commercial attack on dystopia is the Apple Computer spot which announced the release of the Macintosh computer in 1984. Apple drew heavily upon George Orwell's *1984* (originally published in 1949), which contains the best-known dystopia in twentieth-century fiction. In it, Big Brother rules a harshly repressive totalitarian state where the Ministry of Truth rewrites history and the Thought Police arrest anyone who dares resist. The Apple "1984" commercial shrewdly transforms its archrival, IBM, into Orwell's Big Brother—without ever mentioning IBM by name. IBM tyrannized the computer world at that time and its corporate culture was a very conservative, contained one. Chiat/Day, Apple's advertising agency, chose to present the Mac as a liberating force, hoping to challenge IBM's monopolistic control of the computer industry. They hired feature film director Ridley Scott, who'd recently shot the dystopian *Blade Runner* (1982), to direct it. And they paid $500,000 for a one-time broadcast during the 1984 Super Bowl. (No other national broadcast time was purchased, although the ad was screened repeatedly on news programs.)

In the ad, an audience of ashen-faced, shaved-head drones watch a large screen where their ruler harangues them about the "Information Purification Directives" and "Unification of Thought" (Figures 6.9–6.11; tvcrit.com/find/1984):

> For today, we celebrate the first glorious anniversary of the Information Purification Directives. We have created, for the first time in all history, a garden of pure ideology. Where each worker may bloom secure from the pests of contradictory and confusing truths. Our Unification of Thought is more powerful a weapon than any fleet or army on earth. We are one people. With one will. One resolve. One cause. Our enemies shall talk themselves to death. And we will bury them with their own confusion. We shall prevail!

A young woman wearing a runner's outfit and wielding a sledgehammer sprints into the room, pursued by armed soldiers (Figure 6.11). Her red shorts and vigorous skin tone contrast sharply with the colorless minions. She flings the sledgehammer at the screen, which causes it

Figure 6.9 Apple Computer's introduction of the Mac in 1984 relied on imagery drawn from the novel *1984*: enslaved workers...

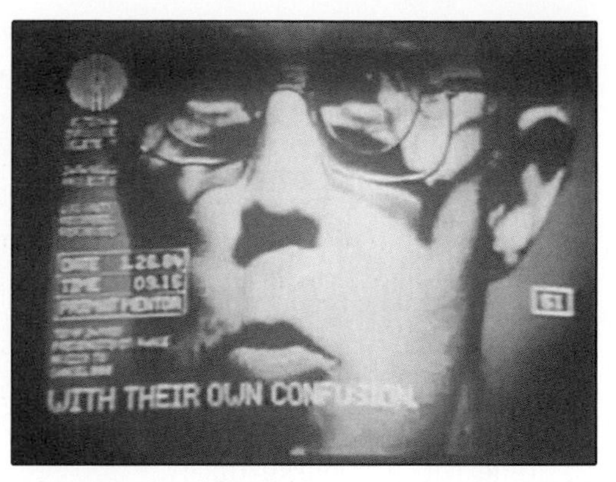

Figure 6.10 ... and a Big Brother figure on a video screen (meant to represent Apple's rival, IBM)...

Figure 6.11 ... which is smashed by a young woman wielding a sledgehammer.

to explode. Text scrolls over the image as the voiceover begins: "On January 24th, Apple Computer will introduce Macintosh. And you'll see why 1984 won't be like '1984.'"

When this ad ran, viewers had never seen Macintosh computers. The Mac is not shown in the commercial and no features of it are described. Viewers could have had no tangible sense of how Macs might differ from other manufacturers' computers. Instead, Apple relied entirely on the theme of liberation from dystopia to sell its new machine.

The Persuasive Style of Commercials

As we have seen above, commercials rely on a fairly predictable polysemy to persuade consumers to buy products. One clear persuasive strategy, then, is to build an argument that a particular product is associated with positive meanings and images or eliminates negative ones. But so far we have not concentrated on *how* that argument is built. What sound/image techniques and rhetorical strategies do commercials use to make products seem desirable? What, one might say, is the persuasive style of the TV commercial?

Some commercials persuade with a jackhammer-blunt style, while others so carefully hide their persuasion that viewers are left wondering just what was being advertised. As we examine the techniques used to persuade us, we'll find that they can be grouped into the following general categories. The list is not an exhaustive one and new persuasive styles will doubtlessly evolve in the future, but the majority of TV commercials rely on one or more of these persuasive devices:

1. metaphor;
2. utopian style;
3. product differentiation and superiority;
4. repetition and redundancy;
5. extraordinary and excessive style: "televisuality" and counter television;
6. graphics and animation;
7. violating reality (visual effects);
8. reflexivity and intertextuality.

Let's examine how these tactics are employed in specific commercials.

Metaphor

Perhaps the most common way that advertisers assert the desirability of their products is to associate them with activities, objects, or people that are themselves desirable. Essentially, such association constructs a metaphor between the product and that desirable activity, object, or person. These metaphors often link products with unexpected or incongruous things or activities. For example, Noxzema implies that shaving is metaphorically equivalent to stripping in the ad discussed on p. 148, in which "The Stripper" plays and a seductive woman urges men to "take it all off." The metaphor in this case is created through the commercial's sound mix (the woman's dialogue and the music). By bringing together sound and image that are normally not connected, Noxzema creates the metaphoric meaning. That is, the commercial's meaning is not a literal one ("The man is stripping") but rather a metaphorical one ("Shaving is like stripping in that something is removed in both cases"). It sounds bland and boring when summarized so simply, but to suggest that removing shaving cream is similar to removing clothing fastens a sexually provocative connotation to a normally routine activity.

Another method for generating metaphors is through a sequence of images—much as Russian filmmaker Sergei Eisenstein theorized 90 years ago. By bringing two or more images together in sequence, a filmmaker can imply that one image should be compared with the other and that there are similarities between them. A staunch socialist and revolutionary, Eisenstein advocated the use of visual metaphor or, as he called it, intellectual montage, for political causes. In the instance of his film *Strike*, he intercut shots of heroic striking workers being beaten by police with shots of a bull being slaughtered (Figures 6.12 and 6.13; tvcrit.com/find/strike). The metaphoric meaning is clear: strikers are cattle. And, further, it graphically argues that a gross injustice is being done.

Advertisers have usurped Eisenstein's principle to sell commodities. For instance, a commercial for the Audi 55 Sportback car constructs a metaphor that associates the car with the famous racehorse Secretariat (tvcrit.com/find/audi). It begins with shots of a horse and jockey making their way onto a racetrack and into a starting gate. When the gate opens, however, the Audi accelerates down the track (Figure 6.14). With a quick cut to the horse, the narrator intones, "What made Secretariat the greatest racehorse who ever lived? Of course he was strong. Intelligent. Explosive" (Figure 6.15). The editor cuts back and forth between the car and the horse—suggesting, obviously, that the car is strong, intelligent, explosive, but never saying that plainly. Viewers must draw that conclusion on their own.

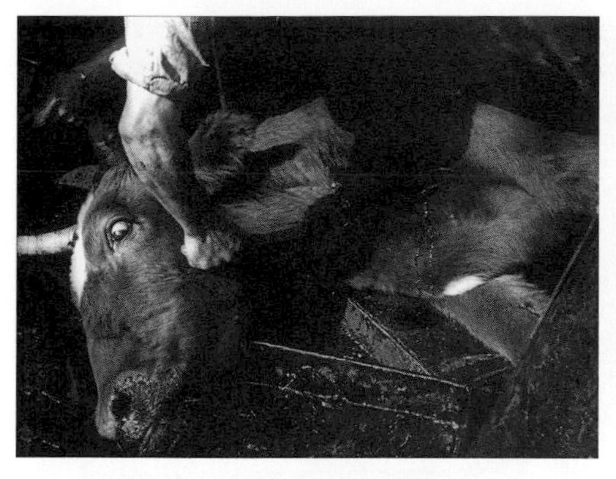

Figure 6.12 Strike: Sergei Eisenstein intercuts a bull being slaughtered with...

Figure 6.13 . . . workers being attacked by police–generating a visual metaphor of workers = cattle.

Figure 6.14 An Audi S5 Sportback accelerates down a horse racetrack, intercut with shots of...

Figure 6.15 ... a horse on the same track as the narrator talks about the strengths of the famous racehorse Secretariat.

Then the narrator answers his rhetorical question about what made Secretariat the greatest: "The true secret in his perfection was a heart twice the size of an average horse." This is reinforced with shots of veterinarians looking at an x-ray of some random horse with a large heart (Figure 6.16)! Are we to think that this Audi automobile has a large "heart" in some sense? The intended meaning is not nailed down and the narrator provides no further clues, but an evocative graphic of a black frame with white text follows the x-ray shots: "The all-new, 354 hp Audi S5 Sportback is here." Then, "Progress is powered from within." Thus, Audi is emphasizing the 354 horsepower of this machine by metaphorically linking it to the literal power of a horse, Secretariat. Just as an oversized heart powered Secretariat, the ad implies, so does an oversized engine power the S5 Sportback. But, again, this is never clearly stated by the narrator or the text.[37]

The sequentiality of the images, aided by the narration and the music, carries the commercial's meaning *indirectly*. As Messaris argues, indirectness is commonly used in advertising. He maintains that it has two advantages over direct approaches. First, an indirect, visual argument such as the Audi ad elicits a "greater degree of mental participation" from viewers.[38] It requires viewers themselves to make the semantic connection between the product and the other objects (e.g., between the Audi S5 Sportback and Secretariat). Messaris contends that viewers are more likely to retain the commercial's message because they themselves have helped to generate it. Second, Messaris contends, "the [explicit] verbal claims made in advertisements

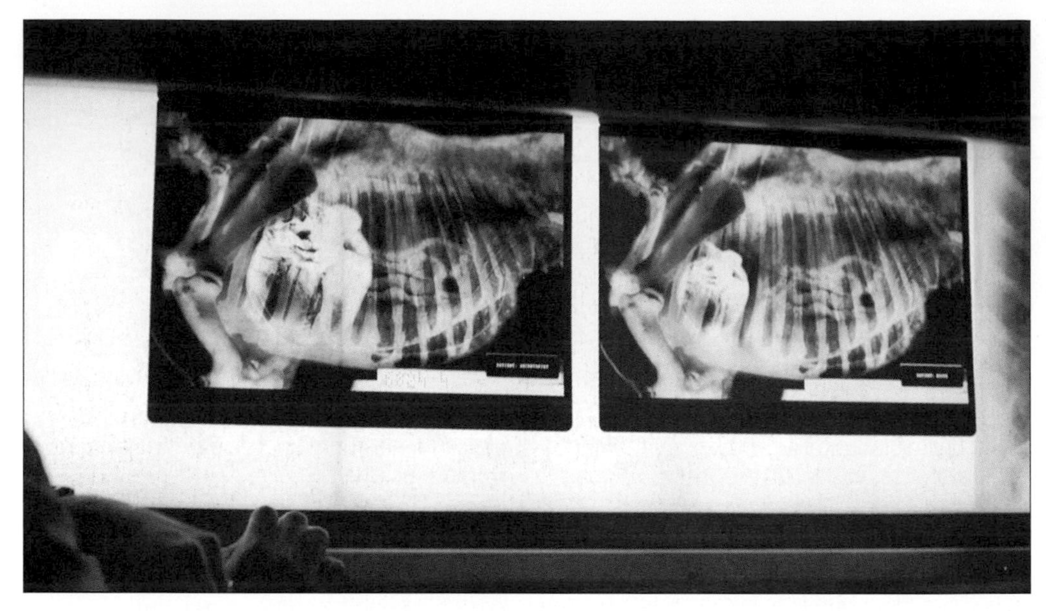

Figure 6.16 X-ray technicians examine film of a horse with a large heart, illustrating what Secretariat's might have looked like.

tend to be held to much stricter standards of accountability than whatever claims are implicit in the ads' pictures."[39] His illustration of this is ads for cigarettes, which show happy, healthy-looking people smoking—thus making the indirect, implicit claim that smoking is a healthy activity when, of course, we know it is not. Commercials can metaphorically suggest many things in the visuals that they would be prohibited from stating explicitly in the dialogue.

Utopian Style

We discussed above how commercials promise admission to utopia through the purchase of commodities—as when Michael escapes with Peter Pan to the utopia of a Mercedes-Benz roadster. Dyer contends that utopianism in mass entertainment is not just evident in the worlds it portrays. He takes the principle of utopianism a step further and finds it in the *style* of presentation, in aspects of mise-en-scene, cinematography, and, crucially, music.[40] That is, he argues that qualities of utopia (abundance, energy, intensity, transparency, and community) may be found in a medium's style. For Dyer, this is most evident in the film musical. Since music is fundamental to most, if not all, commercials, it seems reasonable that we might look for this utopian style in the television commercial.

Many commercials that emphasize music and dance offer clear examples of utopianism's embodiment in style. Consider a Carvana spot from 2017 (tvcrit.com/find/carvana). It begins with two short shots of people leaving car dealerships and declaring, "That sucked!" Then we cut to the commercial's protagonist as he buys a car online via Carvana and says, in disbelief, "That didn't suck!" He launches into a victory song and dance, the chorus of which is "That didn't suck!" He's suddenly joined by a troupe of dancers in his living room and on the street who share his celebration, as the camera tracks in and out (Figure 6.17). From Dyer's position, the commercial quickly establishes the dystopia that is car purchasing and then offers us the utopia of obtaining a car from Carvana—which, coincidentally (?), rhymes with "nirvana," the

Figure 6.17 A Carvana customer enters a utopia of song and dance.

Buddhist state of ultimate peace and happiness. As Dyer might point out, the protagonist's experience of utopia/nirvana is expressed less through words than through movement and music. The lyrics of his victory song are bland and repetitive, but its lively, percussive beat and the gyrations of the dancers convey exuberance through style of sound and image. Energy and intensity—in Dyer's sense of these terms—are embodied in the commercial's style by *how* the movement and sound are presented rather than *what* the actors are saying.

Product Differentiation and Superiority

To survive in the marketplace, every product must distinguish itself from others in the same category. Coke must be perceived as different from Pepsi, Tide from Cheer, Ford from Toyota, Levi from Wrangler, Apple from Microsoft, and on and on. At the core of all advertising is the establishment and maintenance of a product's identity, its brand. The key to brand identity is a product's **unique selling proposition** (**USP**), as advertising standard-bearer Rosser Reeves termed that certain something that separates a product from the rest of the field.[41] Even when there is very little actual difference between commodities, the USP principle holds that the advertiser must find or even fabricate one. Reeves is often quoted as explaining the USP this way: "Our problem is—a client comes into my office and throws down two newly minted half-dollars onto my desk and says, 'Mine is the one on the left. You prove it's better.'"[42] This lack of difference between products is called **brand parity**.

Reeves faced the challenge of brand parity in 1952 while developing an advertising campaign for Anacin, a pain reliever whose active ingredients consisted solely of aspirin and caffeine. How was he to differentiate Anacin from regular aspirin? His solution was a series of cleverly worded commercials that feature a fanciful animated representation of an ailment he dubbed the "tension headache" (Figure 6.18; tvcrit. com/find/anacin). A compressed spring and a jagged electrical spark metaphorically represent the overwrought human nervous system (several ads in the series include a small hammer pounding away, too). The ads' catchphrase of "fast, fast,

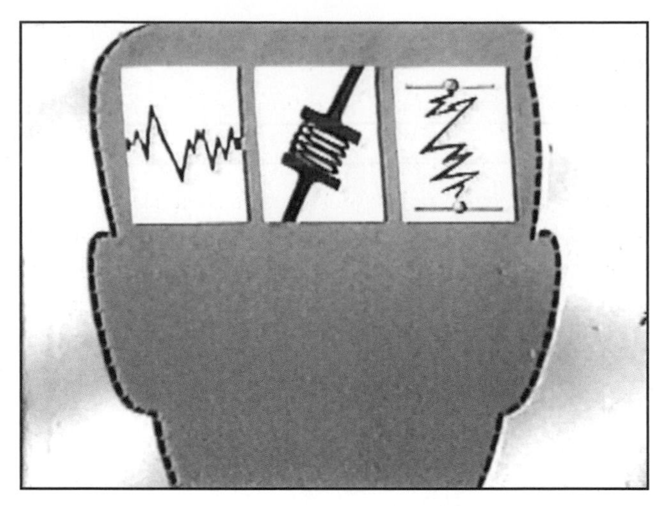

Figure 6.18 Ad man Rosser Reeves invented the "tension headache" . . .

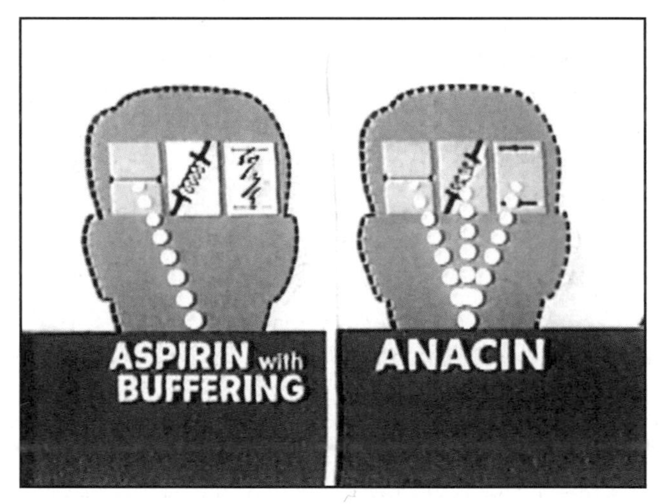

Figure 6.19 . . . which his client Anacin—and only Anacin—could remedy.

fast relief" became part of the 1950s popular culture lexicon. But it wasn't enough for Reeves to explain how Anacin relieved pain. He also needed to "prove" that it lessened discomfort in a *different* manner from aspirin—even though aspirin was its main pain-relieving agent. He needed to find Anacin's USP.

In one commercial from this long-running campaign, the announcer explains, "Aspirin has just one pain reliever. Add buffering, you still get just one. Only Anacin of the four leading headache remedies has special ingredients to relieve pain *fast*, help overcome depression *fast*, relax tension *fast*." Anacin's combination of ingredients comprises its unique selling proposition, according to Reeves, because only Anacin has that particular recipe. To emphasize this point, side-by-side animation shows Anacin relieving headache pain that aspirin cannot alleviate (Figure 6.19). Nowhere in this ad does the announcer reveal that the principal "special ingredient" in Anacin is aspirin itself. Instead, we're allowed to imagine that its ingredients are wholly different from aspirin. If we examine the text of the ad carefully, we find that the announcer does not deny that Anacin contains aspirin. He is just, let us say, less than forthcoming about the nature of its ingredients. In fact, one premise of the commercial is that "Three out of four doctors recommend the ingredients in Anacin." He doesn't specify what those ingredients are, but we may well suppose that the primary one is aspirin. Note also that the copy does not say that the doctors specifically recommend Anacin but just that they recommend the ingredients Anacin contains.

If we were to rewrite this commercial without the need to create a unique selling proposition and in a more forthcoming, purely informational manner, it might go something like this: "Three out of four doctors recommend aspirin for headache pain. Anacin contains 325 mg of aspirin and is also laced with 32 mg of caffeine, which may speed the alleviation of your pain or may just give you the jitters." To be fair to Reeves, we should note that in his book *Reality in Advertising* he contests the suggestion that Anacin's USP is a made-up one. He argues that the difference between Anacin and aspirin is not "minuscule." He claims that distinguishing Anacin from aspirin is not based on a "deceptive differential" but rather is "the stuff and substance of good advertising."[43]

Advertisers currently express disdain for Reeves's hard-sell approach. It's said to be too simplistic for today's "sophisticated" consumers, and yet television commercials continue to wage battles against brand parity. From the Apple commercials entreating computer users to "Think different" to the taste tests of the "Pepsi Challenge" to the Dodge ads beginning and ending with the word "Different" to Aleve claiming just two of its pills are superior to six Tylenol tablets (discussed below, p. 172), we see the persistent influence of Reeves's unique selling proposition and the need for advertisers to differentiate their products from those of their competitors.

Repetition and Redundancy

In addition to the USP, Reeves was also known as an advocate of blunt-force repetition in television commercials. The Anacin spot above exemplifies this in its use of the word "fast." It appears eight times in the 30-second spot and three times in the tagline alone: "Anacin—for fast, fast, incredibly fast relief." Not only did Anacin's slogan contain repetition, but it was itself reiterated thousands of times in repeated airings of this commercial and in numerous different Anacin ads, which were themselves also frequently aired. All successful advertising campaigns use repetition within ads, in repeated airings of ads, and across numerous other ads in the same campaign.

Repetition in advertising serves one major, obvious function: reinforcement. The first time you hear a word or see an image, you may not remember it. Each repetition of it makes recall more likely. But what, in general terms, are TV commercials reinforcing? They're doubtlessly reinforcing particular qualities of particular commodities, but in a more general sense they're reinforcing brand identity. If advertisers can get you to remember the names of their products when you visit a store, they feel they've achieved 75 percent of their goal. If they can get you to remember the superiority of their brands and subsequently purchase their products, they've achieved the remaining 25 percent.

SIDEBAR 6.1 Ten Slogans of Modern Brands

How many can you match with their products? (Answers below.)

1. American by birth. Rebel by choice.
2. Think small.

3. There is no substitute.
4. Power, beauty and soul.
5. Save money. Live better.
6. I am what I am.
7. Just do it.
8. Impossible is nothing.
9. Between love and madness lies obsession.
10. Quality never goes out of style.

Answers: 1. Harley Davidson, 2. Volkswagen, 3. Porsche, 4. Aston Martin, 5. Walmart, 6. Reebok, 7. Nike, 8. Adidas, 9. Calvin Klein, 10. Levis. Excerpted from Sarosh Waiz, "40+ Best Advertising Slogans of Modern Brands," *Advergize*, tvcrit.com/find/slogans.

Another technique that is closely related to repetition is redundancy. Most of the information that we hear and see repeated in TV commercials is redundant information. It exceeds what is necessary to make the point. Sound and image often redundantly convey identical information in commercials. For instance, in Apple's groundbreaking "1984" commercial (discussed on p. 152–53) the narrator speaks the same words that we see crawl up the screen at the end. This is quite typical of the ends of commercials, where ads make their final bids to remain in the viewer's consciousness. Redundancy is common in much television, but it exists at a much higher level and is absolutely crucial to the commercial.

Extraordinary and Excessive Style: "Televisuality" and Counter Television

Generally speaking, viewers do not seek commercials. They do not tune into television for the commercials themselves (with the significant exception of shopping channels). Indeed, they commonly use remote controls, DVRs, and channel browsing or direct their attention to their cell phones to avoid watching commercial breaks. Or they avoid commercials altogether by obtaining TV through subscription-based video-on-demand portals. And so, advertisers are continuously challenged to develop mechanisms for snaring viewers' attention, for hailing them, one might say, as one hails a cab. In other words, commercials must use techniques that say, "Hey, *you*! Watch me! Watch me *now*!" One way that hailing is achieved is through what John Caldwell terms "televisuality"—"defined by excessive stylization and visual exhibitionism."[44] He believes that much of 1980s television, and not just commercials, is marked by televisuality, but we will limit our application of it to TV ads.

In order to understand excessive or exhibitionistic television, we must recall its stylistic norm. By the 1970s, television had found its own "classical" style, much like the cinema developed its classical style in the 1930s. Part II describes this conventional television style in terms of mise-en-scene, videography, editing, and sound as they may be observed in sitcoms, soap operas, prime-time dramas, and other narrative and non-narrative programs. Central to this approach is that style should not draw attention to itself, that it should in a sense be invisible. What's meant by this is that style should support the narrative so effectively that the viewer may submerge into the story without being distracted by the style.

One of the quintessential principles of television commercials is that television classicism may be exceeded—and even violated—in order to attract the viewer's attention. Stylistic excesses and violations are used by commercials to snap viewers out of their dreamlike connection with television narrative, to shock them out of their television lethargy and make them sit up and take notice of the advertised products. Following Bertolt Brecht's "epic theater" and Peter Wollen's claims for a Brechtian "counter cinema" in radical films of the 1960s and 1970s, we might think of this disruptive stylistic approach as "counter television."[45] Although epic theater and counter cinema were both Marxist attempts to combat capitalism and consumerism and although the notion of Brechtian commercials may make Brecht spin like a top in his grave, it is impossible to deny that techniques once associated with experimental theater and film are now routinely used in television commercials.

Since we divide our consideration below of television's classical style into chapters on mise-en-scene, videography, editing, and sound, let us illustrate the commercial's use of counter television with examples from each of these areas.

Mise-en-Scene

We will explain in more detail in Chapter 8 that mise-en-scene is made up of set and costume design, lighting, and the performance of actors. Here, we'll look primarily at the impact of performance in the commercial and how it may be used to capture the viewer's attention. First and most significantly, actors in commercials hail viewers by directly addressing the camera. As discussed in Chapter 5, news anchors and game show hosts typically address viewers directly by looking straight into the camera lens, but actors in fictional, narrative programs do not. Instead, actors in narrative programs look only at one another and *indirectly* address the viewer. Interestingly, commercials incorporate direct address in *both* non-narrative and narrative instances. In a non-narrative commercial for Rogaine, a client looks straight at the camera and details the benefits of the product (Figure 6.20). It's evident that he's addressing viewers directly—specifically hailing men who feel anxious about hair loss. We find a more unconventional use of direct address in the narrative commercials for Bartles & Jaymes wine coolers. In this case we have fictional characters looking into the camera and speaking their lines (Figure 6.3, above). These actors thus violate the taboo against direct-camera gazes, and they do so in a fashion that implores the viewer's return gaze.

Commercials' performance style is commonly pitched a notch or two higher than the acting in narrative programs and the behavior of individuals in non-narrative programs. The goal of performers in many commercials is not so much plausibility or realism as it is noticeability. An excessive performance style can get commercials noticed during their 15- or 30-second bid for

Figure 6.20 A Rogaine user looks directly at the camera as he presents his testimonial.

our attention. In the 1980s, Federal Express featured fast-talker John Moschitta, Jr., in a series of successful ads (tvcrit.com/find/fedex). Moschitta's ability to speak at the rate of 530 words per minute served a dual purpose for FedEx: to capture viewers' attention and to make a metaphoric connection between their delivery service's rapidity and Moschitta's speech. Excessive speed is also used in the selling of automobiles—where vehicles frequently careen recklessly around race tracks (even horse race tracks!), desert trails, and mountain passes. A notice on ads such as the Audi one discussed above tells us that these are "professional drivers on a closed course" and that we shouldn't attempt such stunts ourselves, but if risky driving draws viewers' attention then its persuasive function has been served.

Nonhuman figures also perform in unconventional ways in commercials. Animals frequently talk, sing, and dance. And objects that usually cannot move on their own commonly violate the laws of physics in commercial performances. We've seen singing raisins and talkative M&M candies, and we've been introduced to the Pillsbury Doughboy and Speedy Alka-Seltzer (Figures 6.21 and 6.22). By giving animals the human property of speech and by animating normally inanimate objects, commercials violate the behavioral rules of the real world.

Direct gazes at the camera, the excessive performance of actors, and the unconventional behavior of nonhuman "actors" all hail viewers—entreating them to pay attention and to be persuaded by commercials.

Videography and Cinematography

Despite the televisual exhibitionism Caldwell has found in several 1980s and 1990s programs, most television since the 1970s has adhered to television's classical conventions in terms of videography or cinematography. Music television, however, is a significant exception. When it arrived in the early 1980s, its stylistic flourishes and visualization of music had a major impact upon the videography/cinematography of programs such as *Miami Vice* (1984–89) and the short-lived *Cop Rock* (1990). More importantly, it inspired a small revolution in the videography of commercials, which use music-video style to distinguish themselves from the program material they are interrupting. For commercial directors, counter-television videography is yet another way to draw the viewer's attention.

Table 6.4 counterposes the principal videographic elements of TV classicism with counter-television techniques commercials use to catch our eye. Let us consider examples of each of these elements.

Figure 6.21 Nonhuman figures such as the Pillsbury Doughboy...

Figure 6.22 ... and Speedy Alka-Seltzer often pitch products.

First, multiple, vertical frames-within-the-frame are used to maximum effect in an Acura TLX car ad (Figure 6.23; tvcrit.com/find/acura). The spot combines live-action shots of the car with animation and a variety of visual effects. At one point, two frames are divided by a jagged, lightning-like line and the car pushes beyond one frame into the second. The overall effect is to reshape the size of the images within the frame—forcing one's eye to adjust to the odd shape of the frame and the multiplicity of images. The commercial constantly reshapes the frames-within-the-frames and makes the image size unpredictable.

A second manipulation of the image within the frame occurs when the composition is imbalanced. Classical television favors compositions that are balanced—that is, where the main point of interest is right in the middle of the frame, as can be seen in many of the previous examples in this chapter (e.g., Figures 6.1, 6.3, 6.5, 6.6, 6.11). If more than one point of interest exists within the frame, then they are placed in such a way as to balance one another visually. For instance, the dancing customer of Carvana (Figure 6.17) has dancers equally spaced around him in a visually balanced fashion. A counter-television commercial breaks this convention by locating points of interest near the edge of the frame—as in a Marshall's/T.J. Maxx commercial where a woman is placed on the left of the frame, looking to the left (Figure 6.24; tvcrit.com/find/imbalanced).

Table 6.4 Commercial Videography: Classicism vs. Counter Television

Classical Videography	*Counter-Television Videography*
Image fills the frame	Black areas or multiple images within the frame
Balanced composition	Imbalanced composition
(Objects centered)	(Objects at the frame's edges)
In-focus main figure	Out-of-focus main figure
Regular speed action	Variable speed action (slow motion and fast motion)
Color	Black-and-white
Limited camera movement	Extremely active camera movement
Eye-level camera angle	Extreme low and high angles
"Normal" focal length	Extreme wide angle and telephoto

Figure 6.23 An Acura commercial breaks up the composition with frames within the television frame.

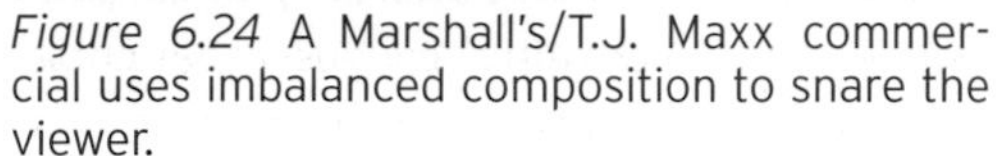

Figure 6.24 A Marshall's/T.J. Maxx commercial uses imbalanced composition to snare the viewer.

Figure 6.25 Lyrica's logo and warning statement are the only parts of the image in focus.

This image would be more conventional if she were looking to the right, into the center of the frame, but she is not. Instead, she's looking to the left and out of the frame. The result is a strikingly imbalanced composition. Also notable is the fact that two-thirds of this shot is markedly out-of-focus and remains that way for the duration of the shot. That is, we do not shift focus to the background. Similarly, a Lyrica drug ad superimposes its logo and a side-effect warning over an out-of-focus image of women in a garden (Figure 6.25; tvcrit.com/find/outoffocus). With virtually the entire image out of focus, we can do nothing but read the warning, but the lack of focus also catches our eye as we try to make sense of the blurry image.

Although the next counter-television technique, variable speed action, was partially inspired by music videos, television sports was more significant to its popularization. Ever since the 1960s–when advances in videotape technology enabled TV to replay action at variable speeds—slow motion has been an integral part of televised sports. As we have seen with excesses in mise-en-scene and videography, variable speed action is an attention grabber. Because narrative programs don't normally use variable speeds, slow motion and fast action make us attentive. They may also be used, as they are in sports programs, to emphasize strength and majesty and to show viewers actions that normally occur too quickly for the human eye to comprehend.

Consider the Mountain Dew commercial in which a cyclist chases a cheetah and pulls a can of soda from its throat (tvcrit.com/find/slomo). Both fast and slow motion are used in this spot. The cyclist's pedaling as he gains on the cheetah is shown in speeded-up action—making it seem faster than is humanly possible. Slow motion is used in several shots: the cheetah running, the bicyclist leaping on it, and the bicyclist's friends pouring Mountain Dew down their throats. By using slow motion, we are able to see details in the cheetah's running and the bicyclist's leap that we wouldn't discern at regular speed. And the slow-motion pouring enhances the appearance of the Mountain Dew—in theory making it more appealing.

Color came to television through a complicated and circuitous route. Once it was established in the 1960s, however, narrative programs discontinued use of black-and-white—with only very rare exceptions. Color was the last major technological component of TV classicism to evolve. Its arrival signaled the beginning of black-and-white as a counter-television component. Before color became the norm, it itself was capable of hailing viewers. Imagine how striking a color commercial must have seemed to viewers who were accustomed to black-and-white imagery.

Most frequently, commercials have used black-and-white or sepia-toned images to allude to the past—as can be seen in a Winn Dixie grocery store commercial that starts with black-and-white shots of a mother and daughter in 1960s attire and then transforms them into color consumers when they enter the store (tvcrit.com/find/winndixie). However, the significance of black-and-white imagery is not always so clear. Take, for example, a spot about estrogen loss during menopause that was sponsored by the pharmaceutical company American Home Products and broadcast, among other places, during the sitcom *Everybody Loves Raymond* (1996–2005), which, not surprisingly, is in color (tvcrit.com/find/bw). Actress Lauren Hutton is shown cooking vegetables, running along the beach, and talking about menopause. Half of the shots are in color and half are in black-and-white. The black-and-white images are not supposed to be from the past and, indeed, there is no obvious meaning one can glean from the black-and-white cinematography—aside from the counter-television function of differentiating this commercial from the color programs during which it appears. Further, the Victoria's Secret spot discussed above (Figure 6.4; tvcrit.com/find/vsbody) is entirely in black-and-white. Obviously that choice does not signify "the past," but what purpose does it serve? One possible answer would be to link the imagery with the aesthetics of black-and-white erotic photography.

A Reebok ad for EasyTone shoes is also in black-and-white, until it actually presents the shoes to the viewer (tvcrit.com/find/easytone). It begins with black-and-white imagery of a nearly nude woman on a bed, viewed from behind. The narrator addresses the viewer directly, claiming that EasyTone shoes will improve the shape of her body. The camera moves suggestively down the woman's body, and when it reaches her shoes they are presented in color, within a mostly black-and-white image (Figure 6.26). This precisely lit, black-and-white imagery emphasizes the tone and shape of the woman's body and also differentiates the commercial from the color imagery in the television texts that precede and follow it. The subtle touch of color (the silver shoes with blue stripes) mildly startles the viewer and draws her attention from the sensual legs to the product she must buy to acquire those legs herself.

Extreme camera movement, angle, and focal length—the final three videographic elements in Table 6.4—are not as distinct as the other videographic techniques. Instead of being unambiguous violations of classical TV style, they are more exaggerations of techniques ordinarily used in conventional narrative programs. Where classical programs often include some camera

Figure 6.26 A predominantly black-and-white Reebok commercial presents the shoes in color

movement (to follow action), slightly low/high angles, and various focal lengths (wide angle to telephoto), commercials incorporate camera gyrations, odd low/high angles, and focal lengths that are so extreme the optical distortion is evident. Strange angles and focal lengths may be observed in an extreme low-angle shot of a guitar player in a Smirnoff vodka commercial (Figure 6.27; tvcrit.com/find/smirnoff) and the exceptionally wide-angle shot of a Chevrolet car commercial (Figure 6.28). When distortion is this exaggerated it draws attention to itself and violates the principal classical tenet of invisible, unobtrusive style. This, then, is the definition of Caldwell's televisual exhibitionism.

The SMIRNOFF word and associated logos are trademarks ©The Smirnoff Co 2013

Figure 6.27 Smirnoff vodka: An excessively low-angle shot of a guitar player.

Figure 6.28 A wide-angle lens distorts the hood of a Chevrolet car, making it appear wider than in reality.

Editing

The first thing one notices about the editing of many commercials is its speed. The editing in commercials is typically paced faster than that in soap operas, sitcoms, and prime-time dramas. Rapid editing serves as a hailing device because each shot quickly presents new information for viewers to absorb. Additionally, viewers are constantly adjusting to different framing, composition, and camera angles. Each cut is a potential disruption as we instantaneously move from one camera position to another and new visuals are thrown before our eyes. This visual disorientation is used by commercials to jolt us into gazing at the advertised product.

Commercials, even narrative-based ones, are also not bound by the rules of classical film editing and its pursuit of an invisible, seamless style (discussed at length in Chapter 10). Breaches of that style's conventions abound in TV ads. A 2008 commercial for Taco Bell illustrates the commercial's flexible use of classical editing (tvcrit.com/find/tacobellad). Without any dialogue, it tells the story of a group of individuals buying inexpensive food and ecstatically consuming it. In 15 seconds, the commercial presents 24 shots—most less than one second long and three only 10 frames long (one-third of a second). Its first five shots and two later shots are shown in Table 6.5. It begins with a fairly conventional establishing long shot of a Taco Bell restaurant taken from a moving car, a portion of which is barely visible in the frame (Figure 6.29). The camera cuts to a

Table 6.5 Taco Bell Commercial

Shot Number, Scale, & Length	*Figure*
1 long shot 11 frames	 *Figure 6.29*
2 close-up 20 frames	 *Figure 6.30*

(continued)

Table 6.5 Taco Bell Commercial (continued)

Shot Number, Scale, & Length	*Figure*
3 close-up 33 frames	 *Figure 6.31*
Pull focus to...	 *Figure 6.32*
4 medium close-up 19 frames	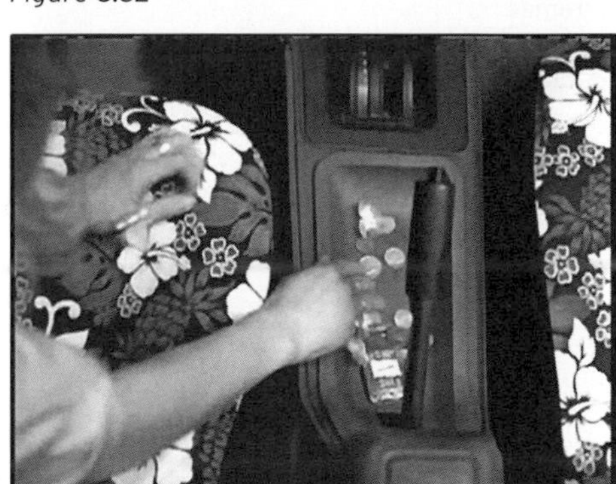 *Figure 6.33*
5 medium shot 24 frames	 *Figure 6.34*

Table 6.5 Taco Bell Commercial (continued)

Shot Number, Scale, & Length	*Figure*
15 close-up 13 frames	 *Figure 6.35*
20 long shot 29 frames	 *Figure 6.36*

close-up of the driver of a convertible—a conventional cut from long shot to close-up to show us a detail of the scene (Figure 6.30). But then the classical editing goes haywire.

The driver begins to point with her left hand, but we cut to another passenger, from an indeterminate position, pointing with her (presumably a woman's) right hand in shot 3 (Figure 6.31). This violates classical stylistic conventions because it does not match the action of the first shot and does not clearly establish the space of the scene; in fact, it confounds it. This third shot rapidly pulls focus to an illuminated menu (Figure 6.32), showcasing Taco Bell's inexpensive offerings. "Why pay more!"—which is the main point of the commercial—is visible at the top of the menu. A grammatically correct question mark has been replaced by the more emphatic exclamation point. The commercial's on-screen text later reinforces this thrifty message (again without a question mark): "More stuff. Less cash. Why pay more."

The fourth, following shot is an overhead medium close-up of the driver picking through change (Figure 6.33)—an acceptable classical cut showing us a detail from the scene. Close examination of Figure 6.34 reveals that the driver's seat is mostly empty, as if the driver is now out of the car; but this would probably not be perceived by the television viewer since the shot is only 19 frames long (about two-thirds of a second). The next cut, however, violates classical principles as we jerkily cut from the driver's hands to a man who has not previously appeared, giving the change to a mostly offscreen Taco Bell employee (Figure 6.34). The rest of the commercial contains seemingly random images of people eating—including the driver (Figure 6.35)—interspersed with shots of menu prices. One individual is so overcome with Taco Bell joy that he leaps on to the top of a car and throws his arms in the air (Figure 6.36). The camera hops from one person to the next, with little regard for classical-film conventions.

If this editing were used in a conventional segment from a narrative program, it would break numerous "rules" of contemporary TV production, but it works effectively in this commercial because (1) it uses utopian style to strongly convey the celebratory response provoked by Taco Bell's menu choices (as imagined by Taco Bell's advertising team), and (2) its editing style differentiates it from the narrative program it interrupted. Jerky, discontinuous editing is not unheard of in narrative programs, but a series of shots such as those in Table 6.5 would commonly be relegated to Eisensteinian montage sequences, where time and information are compressed. Such montages are relatively rare in narrative programs and so their frequent use in commercials helps distinguish them from the program they're interrupting.

Sound

As with mise-en-scene and videography, the sound of commercials is quite different from the sound of the programs surrounding them—especially when contrasted with the sound of scripted, storytelling programs. We can observe this in terms of both the speech of commercials and the music of commercials. The speech/music of television programs is extensively considered in Chapter 11.

The style of speech in commercials has been discussed at numerous points above—including its importance to hailing and direct address. Unlike dialogue in scripted, narrative programs, commercial speech must be persuasive in some fashion and it must be succinct because it doesn't have much time to persuade us. Also, the presence of an announcer's voice distinguishes commercial speech from narrative programs and aligns it with news and sports programs. As in news and sports, a voice that is not part of the commercial's diegetic world talks over it. It's a voice of authority—speaking directly to viewers and urging them to be convinced by the commercial's rhetoric.

The music of commercials is yet another rhetorical device that has less in common with narrative programs than with another television genre—specifically, the music video. This is not surprising since music videos are essentially commercials for music and musicians. The principal similarity between commercial music and music videos and the crucial difference between it and nondiegetic music in narrative programs is a seemingly simple one: both commercials and music videos use songs with lyrics, while nondiegetic music normally does not (excepting nondiegetic music where it is clearly commenting on the action—as when a popular love song plays while lovers walk beside a river).

Why is this apparently modest distinction so important? Because the use of lyrics—jingles in the case of commercials—draws one's attention to the music itself and classical, nondiegetic music isn't devised for that. Nondiegetic music strives for invisibility, hoping to shape the emotions of viewers without being noticed. Jingles, in contrast, are designed to be noticed and, of course, to be remembered. Many viewers recall commercial jingles decades later, but how many of them can say they remember the nondiegetic music of old programs? The jingle has faded in prominence in the twenty-first century partially because conventional broadcast radio, for which many jingles were originally created, is in decline. The jingle has not been entirely replaced by pop songs and other nondiegetic music, of course. For an overview of the top jingles from the twentieth century, see Sidebar 6.2, where advertising-industry magazine *Advertising Age* counts down its ten favorites.

SIDEBAR 6.2 Top Ten Jingles of the Twentieth Century

How many can you match with their products? (Answers below.)

1. You deserve a break today.
2. Be all that you can be.
3. ______________________hits the spot.
4. M'm, m'm good.
5. See the USA in your______________________.
6. I wish I was an______________________wiener.
7. Double your pleasure, double your fun.
8. ______________________tastes good like a cigarette should.
9. It's the real thing.
10. A little dab'll do ya.

1. McDonald's, 2. U.S. Army, 3. Pepsi Cola, 4. Campbell's, 5. Chevrolet (GM), 6. Oscar Meyer, 7. Wrigley's Doublemint gum, 8. Winston, 9. Coca-Cola, 10. Brylcreem hair cream. *AdAge.com*, 2000, November 7, 2000, tvcrit.com/find/jingles.

Graphics and Animation

Almost every commercial on television contains some graphics (letters, numbers, cartoon characters, and corporate logos) on the screen. As we have seen exemplified in Apple's "1984" spot, the most common use of text is a redundant reinforcement of speech. Announcers speak their scripts and the same or similar words crawl up the screen—frequently at the conclusion of the spot and usually accompanied by the product's visual emblem, its brand identity further reinforced by its logo. In the case of "1984," the distinctive Apple logo (a rainbow-colored apple with a bite taken out) follows the concluding text.

Text is not limited to this redundant function, however. It may also supplement, clarify, and disclaim the explicit meanings of the dialogue and the implicit meanings of the images. The supplementing role of text is best exemplified in the nearly illegible legal qualifications included at the end of commercials for contests, car dealerships, pharmaceuticals, and the like. Tiny on-screen text provides warnings, disclaimers, and clarifications that the advertisers wish to downplay—as in the Lyrica ad discussed on p. 164 (Figure 6.25) that warns of "swelling of the face, mouth, lips, gums, tongue, throat or neck." Since the 1960s, the U.S. Federal Trade Commission (FTC) has cracked down on misleading claims in medicinal and food advertising—leading to more and more disclaimers. Consequently, many ads now contain seemingly unnecessary warnings, such as "Use only as directed," in order to avoid legal liability. A Crest toothpaste commercial's spoken dialogue entreats us to "Get ready for a whole new level of clean. Introducing advanced cleaning from Crest Multi-Care." The dialogue implies that Multi-Care is measurably superior to other brands. However, in small text the ad clarifies that Multi-Care is only advanced "VS. CREST CAVITY PROTECTION"—that is, in comparison to other Crest products. It might well lag behind other brands in terms of toothpaste technology. The ad only certifies that it's advanced beyond Crest's previous level of cavity protection, just in case the FTC or the lawyers for Colgate may be watching.

One final example of textual disclaimers is found in the case of dramatizations, where actors portray real people. For instance, an Aleve ad visually presents what appears to be a documentary—an unmanipulated record—of an interview with a woman about her use of the drug. "This is Joanne," the narrator begins, "Her long day as a hair stylist starts with shoulder pain. Hey, Joanne, want to trade the all-day relief with two Aleve for six Tylenol?" A hand offers an out-of-focus bottle of Tylenol to her. "Give up my two Aleve for six Tylenol? No, thanks!" Then she looks directly at the camera and testifies, "For me, it's Aleve!" But it's actually all a fiction, a dramatization. We must read the "fine print" to realize this. Only there does text stating "actor portrayal" disclaim what the images proclaim—that, despite appearances, this is an actor pretending to be devoted to Aleve (Figure 6.37; tvcrit.com/find/aleve).

Redundant, reinforcing text and small-print disclaimers are important functions of TV graphics, but equally significant is the ability of graphics to catch viewers' eyes, to hail or entreat them to look at the screen. The most important device for graphical hailing is the ability of text and cartoon elements to be animated, for moving graphics are enormously more attention-grabbing than static ones. Animation in commercials arrived with television's growth in the 1940s and early 1950s, but it was initially limited to techniques borrowed from the cinema. For example, a 1950s commercial for Philco refrigerators has a cartoon pixie flitting about the crisper and ends with text fading in over a seal of quality: "Philco famous for quality the world over" (Figures 6.38, 6.39; tvcrit.com/find/philco). The animated pixie and the simple fading in of the characters were created on film, using an analog process called optical printing. On most commercials, the graphical elements are sliding or floating or otherwise moving. Further, commercial graphics use an illusion of three-dimensionality to make letters and numbers appear to rise toward the viewer. Even in this 60-year-old spot, the 3-D shading on the "Philco quality" letters gives them a more dynamic aspect.

As Margaret Morse explains in her overview of the history of TV graphics, the movement and three-dimensionality of graphic elements accelerated phenomenally with the development of digital technology in the late 1970s and 1980s. Hyperactive letters and logos could then seem to be flying past us or us toward them. Examine the opening credits for *As the World Turns*—a program not known for its visual flourishes (August 15, 2000; tvcrit.com/find/atwt). The title

Figure 6.37 Aleve: The fine print disclaims what the image proclaims. What appears to be the testimonial of a real person is actually an "actor portrayal."

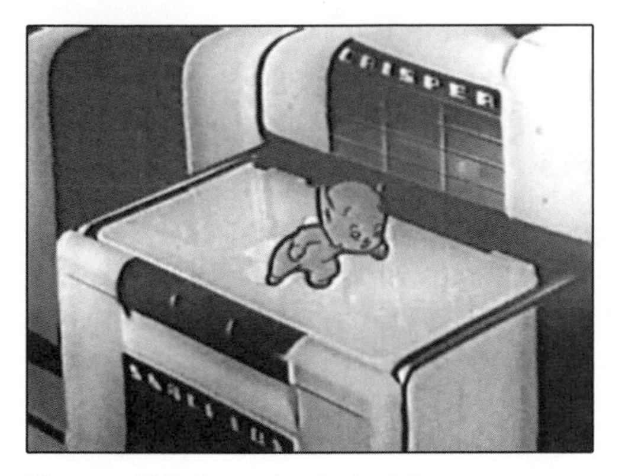

Figure 6.38 An animated pixie appears on top of a photograph of a Philco refrigerator.

Figure 6.39 Shading creates a primitive three-dimensional effect...

Figure 6.40 . . . which became much more elaborate in the era of computer-generated graphics. Even soap operas such as *As the World Turns* feature text virtually flying through space...

Figure 6.41 ... nearly colliding with this world of images...

Figure 6.42 ... and seeming to careen toward the viewer, as if the camera could move into the letters.

comes from a virtual space *behind* us (Figure 6.40), rotating and swooping toward a globe constructed out of images from the program (Figure 6.41). The title then comes back toward us and we ostensibly pass *through* the "o" of "World" (Figure 6.42). "The viewer ... seems to be freed from gravity in a virtual experience of giddy speed through a symbolic universe of abc's,"[46] notes Morse regarding similar sequences. In such a universe, the letters are far from flat or two-dimensional. The movement of the *As the World Turns* letters and their design make them look like thick pieces of glass, with a sense of density and smooth texture.

Graphics flying toward the viewer are the visual equivalent of verbal direct address. Remember that in narrative programs the visuals are designed much like the theater—as if a fourth wall has been removed and you are peering into a room. This is particularly true in sitcoms and soap operas because their sets are constructed with a missing fourth wall, but it also holds true for prime-time dramas shot on location. Consequently, there is limited actor movement in depth—toward or away from the camera. The action mostly occurs on a plane perpendicular to the camera's; thus there is more left-and-right movement and less back-and-forth. Actors do not enter sitcom/soap-opera sets from behind the camera the way the letters in the *As the World Turns* title sequence do. And actors do not exit by walking toward and past the camera the way the *As the World Turns* title does. When graphic elements behave this way, they, in a sense, say to viewers, "Pay attention! Here we come—right towards you. Duck!" As you can see, in commercials animated graphics serve a similar purpose to announcers speaking directly to the viewers. Both hail viewers—one through visually moving words and the other through verbally spoken ones. As Morse argues, these graphics are predecessors of increasingly interactive computer environments, from first-person games (e.g., *Call of Duty* and *Overwatch*) to virtual reality worlds.

A final and obvious form of animation in TV commercials is the use of cartoon characters. The Pillsbury Doughboy and Speedy Alka-Seltzer, discussed on p. 162, are just two of the non-human entities called upon to pitch products on television. The function of these characters (differentiating products) has not changed much over the past 70-odd years of television commercials. However, it should be mentioned that computer animation has had a major impact upon the technology used to create these characters. Up until the 1990s, animated characters were either drawn or were created through stop-action animation (the frame-by-frame movement of dolls), as in the case of Speedy Alka-Seltzer. Now, however, animated characters are usually computer generated—as in the current incarnation of the Pillsbury Doughboy, the Coca-Cola polar bears, or the very photo-realistic rattlesnake and rabbits in a Travelers Insurance spot (Figure 6.43; tvcrit.com/find/travelers).

Figure 6.43 A CGI rabbit is almost indistinguishable from a photograph of one in this Travelers commercial.

Violating Reality (Visual Effects)

"In a medium whose very essence is the ability to reproduce the look of everyday reality, one of the surest ways of attracting the viewer's attention is to violate that reality,"[47] contends Paul Messaris. What intrigues him is advertising's use of distorted imagery to make a viewer notice a product. Studies in cognitive psychology show that this distortion is most effective when it varies only slightly from a familiar object. As Messaris explains, "if the discrepancy between the unfamiliar shape and some preexisting one is only partial, the mental task of fitting in the new shape becomes more complicated. As a result, such partially strange shapes can cause us to pay closer attention."[48] If an object is wholly different from what you are familiar with, you may ignore it completely or place it in a new visual category; but if it is partially similar, then your cognitive processes work overtime trying to figure out whether or not it is a familiar object.

Messaris cites digital morphing as a prime example of this principle. A morph takes two dissimilar objects and creates a seamless transition from one to the other. In so doing, it creates a strange, reality-violating hybrid of two familiar objects. Morphing first came to viewers' attention in the films *Willow* (1988) and *Terminator 2: Judgment Day* (1991), where humans morph into various shapes (tvcrit.com/find/willow, tvcrit.com/find/terminator), but it found its widest exposure in Michael Jackson's *Black or White* music video and television commercials in the 1990s (tvcrit.com/find/blackorwhite).[49] Notably, a Schick Tracer razor commercial morphs between a variety of faces—effectively communicating the idea that the Tracer will fit any shaped face and simultaneously getting viewers to concentrate on the ad by violating the reality of human physiognomy—as when a white man transforms into a black one (Figures 6.44 and 6.45; tvcrit.com/find/schick). Morphing remains a common part of the CGI toolbox. There's even a quick morph in the Winn-Dixie commercial (2010) discussed on p. 164, when the mother and daughter transition from black-and-white to color (tvcrit.com/find/winndixie).

Morphing is just one example of violating reality through visual effects. By the 2000s morphing was already being surpassed by new advances in digital graphics—leading to widespread incorporation of visual effects in commercials. What makes digital visual effects particularly successful is their uncanny resemblance to historical reality. Consider a DirecTV ad where a man uses a TV remote control to pause and restart futuristic robots battling in his house—moving from the kitchen to the dining room to the bedroom (tvcrit.com/find/vfx). The setting is a familiar home scene, but an incongruous and fantastic element intrudes into that reality. A similar approach is taken in an Ikea

Figure 6.44 Schick Tracer razor: A man shaving his face morphs into...

Figure 6.45 ... a man of a different race shaving his face.

spot where a "flock" of T-shirts migrates across great distances before flying into a boy's room and neatly folding themselves inside Ikea furniture (Figure 6.46; tvcrit.com/find/ikea). The incongruity of T-shirts behaving like birds "gives us a jolt, and it gets us to look," as Messaris says about similar commercials.[50]

Reflexivity and Intertextuality

In Chapter 5 we introduced the notion of reflexivity in non-narrative television. Commercials thrive on the television cannibalism that is reflexivity. TV commercials frequently parody films, television programs, other commercials, and even themselves in their efforts to market a product. Energizer batteries were featured in a series of advertisements where a plausible but sham commercial (usually a sly spoof of a familiar one) is interrupted by a battery-powered toy rabbit intruding into the frame. In one, Ted Nugent is singing the praises of "Mi Cucaracha" ("my cockroach") restaurant when a drum-beating bunny interrupts him (tvcrit.com/find/energizer2). In another, a commercial for the nonexistent Nasatine sinus medicine is suspended when the Energizer rabbit appears (Figure 6.47; tvcrit.com/find/energizer). In essence, these spots are commercials consuming other commercials. The Energizer ad campaign is particularly remarkable for the accuracy of its parodies. The Nasatine spot includes Anacin-style animation and a copyright notice for a fake pharmaceutical company, Clow Laboratories! Reflexive commercials refer first of all to other television material, rather than referring directly to historical reality, where their products actually reside. In essence, an extra layer of television has been added.

A close relation to parody is pastiche, the use of fragments of previous texts. Popular songs, for example, are regularly put to new uses by advertisers. The Knack's "My Sharona" was turned into "My Chalupa" by Taco Bell, and Nick Drake's "Pink Moon" sells Volkswagen cars. Even the Beatles' "Revolution" has been used in a Nike shoe commercial (though it did result in a lawsuit against Nike). Pastiche in television commercials has reached new heights of technological sophistication since the advent of digital visual effects. One Diet Coke ad, for instance, has

Figure 6.46 Ikea: Digitally generated T-shirts behave like birds and fly home to a boy's bedroom.

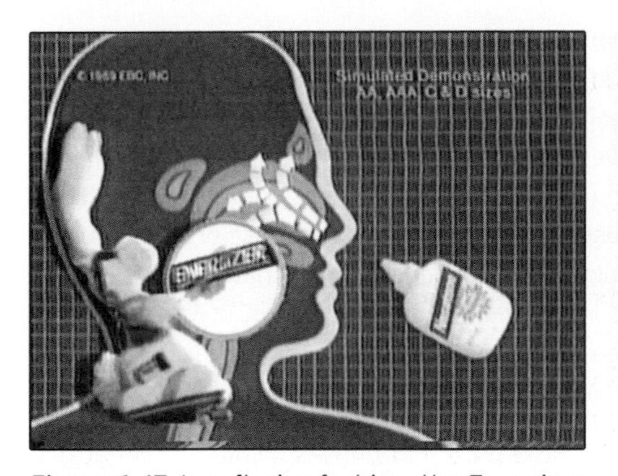

Figure 6.47 In reflexive fashion, the Energizer Bunny spoofs a commercial for a nonexistent nose-spray product.

Figure 6.48 A Dior J'adore perfume commercial features a digitally re-animated celebrity, Marilyn Monroe, who died over 50 years ago.

Paula Abdul dancing with and talking to long-dead film actors: Gene Kelly, Cary Grant, and Groucho Marx (tvcrit.com/find/reflexivity). And a spot for Dior's J'adore perfume features Charlize Theron backstage at a fashion show (tvcrit.com/find/dior), where she encounters digitally re-animated versions of iconic movie stars Grace Kelly and Marilyn Monroe (Figure 6.48). Monroe lovingly caresses a bottle of the Dior fragrance even though she was famously associated with rival perfume Chanel No. 5 during her lifetime.

Parody and pastiche are two examples of TV's high degree of intertextuality, drawing it away from historical reality and reflecting it back on itself (see the discussion of intertextuality in the context of TV stars in Chapter 4). One television text (a commercial) refers to another (a program or previous commercial), which may well refer to another and another. Commercials are an integral part of this network of meanings and allusions. Familiar songs and images provide a shorthand for developing the persuasive argument for a product. Why write a new jingle when an old tune is already inscribed on our minds? Why refer to historical reality when we are more comfortable with television reality? Commercials are nourished by intertextuality and reflexivity.

Summary: "Capitalism in Action"

At the start of a commercial break on ABC one evening in fall 2000, a self-mocking title came up: "And now capitalism in action." On U.S. linear television, commercials are the most visible effect of the medium's underlying economic system. Multinational corporations strike deals with wholesalers (networks, syndicators, and national spot representatives) when they wish to buy TV time for national exposure. And local merchants buy TV time from individual stations and cable systems when they are shopping for exposure in a specific DMA. These purchases of time are essentially purchases of viewers' attention as it has been calculated by Nielsen Media Research and other audience-measurement services. TV's wholesalers and retailers use the money they have exchanged for their viewers' time to rent programming materials from production companies, with the goal of attracting more viewers and/or viewers of a more desirable demographic (specifically, adults 18 to 49). And that is capitalism in action on American TV of the network era and in linear television today. Online portals such as Netflix engage capitalism in different ways, relying on subscriptions instead of selling advertising time. However, video advertisements still thrive on other online services such as YouTube and the bulk of commercial websites. There are some differences between network-era TV commercials and those we see online, but they share many of the same meanings and persuasive strategies we have detailed in this chapter.

Although it is evident that commercials signify the positive side of consuming, it would be wrong to say that that is their only meaning. Despite their often naked intent to sell, commercials also play host to a diverse polysemy. We have here outlined eight components of commercial discourse and examined how they are used to persuade us to purchase products. These include luxury, leisure, and conspicuous consumption; individualism; the natural; folk culture and tradition; novelty and progress; sexuality and romance; the alleviation of various forms of distress; and utopianism. Commercials endeavor to figuratively and literally associate their products with these values and/or they make claims that their products will transform consumers if they buy them.

Commercials' styles may be rude and obvious or entertaining and obscure, but in some fashion they must always attempt to convince the viewer. We have identified eight persuasive strategies employed by commercials: metaphor, utopian style, product differentiation and superiority, repetition and redundancy, extraordinary and excessive style, graphics and animation, violating reality (visual effects), and reflexivity and intertextuality. In many instances, we have seen that the style of commercials is excessive and exhibitionistic and that it falls within John Caldwell's notion of televisuality. Commercial style, unlike classical narrative television and film, doesn't need to be invisible. Indeed, its forthright visibility may well help draw viewers' interest to the product.

Notes

1 In 2015, advertising spending in the U.S. was largely split between television (37.7%) and digital media (32.6%), with radio, print publications, and directories accounting for the rest. Industry analysts expect television's share to decrease in the next five years as digital media command more ad dollars. eMarketer, "Distribution of Advertising Spending in the United States From 2010 to 2020, by Media," *Statista—the Statistics Portal*, Statista, tvcrit.com/find/tvads, accessed June 13, 2017.

2 Paul Messaris, *Visual Persuasion: The Role of Images in Advertising* (Thousand Oaks, CA: Sage, 1997), 164.

3 Nielsen Media Research, "Average U.S. Home Now Receives a Record 118.6 TV Channels, According to Nielsen," *Nielsen.com*, June 6, 2008, tvcrit.com/find/nielsenchannels, accessed November 29, 2010.

4 Mike Budd, Steve Craig, and Clay Steinman, *Consuming Environments: Television and Consumer Culture* (New Brunswick, NJ: Rutgers, 1999), 30.

5 John Breech, "Super Bowl 49 Watched by 114.4M, Sets U.S. TV Viewership Record," *CBSSports*, February 2, 2015, tvcrit.com/find/superbowl49, accessed June 13, 2017.

6 Lindsay Kramer, "Super Bowl 2015: How Much Does a 30-Second Television Commercial Cost?," *Syracuse*, tvcrit.com/find/syracuse, accessed June 13, 2017. Jeanine Poggi, "TV Ad Pricing Chart: A Show in Its 13th Season Returns to the Top 10 Most Expensive Buys," *AdvertisingAge*, June 13, 2017, tvcrit.com/find/tvadprices.

7 John Koenig, *The Dictionary of Obscure Sorrows*, tvcrit.com/find/sorrow, accessed July 14, 2017; Laurie Ann Franks, *The Gallery of Ill-Fitting Pants*, 1999, accessed November 7, 2000, tvcrit.com/find/pants; Michael Lewis, *Modern Moist Towelette Collecting*, accessed December 1, 2005, tvcrit.com/find/moist; and *The Sheep Brain Dissection Guide*, December 1, 2005, University of Scranton, accessed November 7, 2005, tvcrit.com/find/sheep.

8 "Inside TV Ratings," *Nielsen Media Research*, December 5, 2005, tvcrit.com/find/nielsonratings.

9 Twenty thousand is an approximate number that Nielsen released in 2012. See "Celebrating 25 Years of the Nielsen People Meter," *Nielsen*, August 30, 2012, tvcrit.com/find/peoplemeters, accessed June 14, 2017. Nielsen announced its estimate of American TV households in "Nielsen Estimates 118.4 Million TV Homes in The U.S. for the 2016–17 TV Season," *Nielsen*, August 26, 2016, tvcrit.com/find/nielsen2016, accessed June 14, 2017.

10 "'The Sweeps'—Local Market Measurement," 2000, *Nielsen Media Research*, November 7, 2000, tvcrit.com/find/sweeps.

11 "What TV Ratings Really Mean . . . and Other Frequently-Asked Questions," 2000, *Nielsen Media Research*, December 20, 2005, tvcrit.com/find/mean.

12 "Television Audience Measurement Terms," *Nielsen Media Research*, December 1, 2005, tvcrit.com/find/nielsenterms.
13 This number of households (118.4 million) represents 96 percent of all households in the U.S.
14 For instance, in 2007 P&G spent $2.4 billion on television. "National Advertisers Ranked 1 to 50," *Advertising Age* 79, no. 25 (2008), S-6. However, P&G, like many advertisers after the 2008 recession, reduced that spending to $1.6 billion in 2009. Bradley Johnson, "Top Outlays Plunge 10% but Defying Spend Trend Can Pay Off," *Advertising Age* 81, no. 25 (2010), 1, 10-11.
15 "Nielsen IAG Top Ten Most-Recalled In-Program Placements: Dramas/Comedies," *Advertising Age*, May 12, 2010, tvcrit.com/find/product, accessed December 6, 2010.
16 The Club Crackers incident is an example of "digital brand integration," where products are inserted during post-production. See Sam Lubell, "Advertising's Twilight Zone: That Signpost Up Ahead May Be a Virtual Product," *The New York Times*, January 2, 2006, tvcrit.com/find/twilight. As viewers' ability to skip commercials increases through on-demand portals, TiVo, and other devices, so does the pressure to use skip-proof product placements. This trend has reached the point where marketing research firms have had to develop methods to measure viewers' recall of "in-program placements."
17 *TV Basics*.
18 Ibid.
19 Ellen Seiter, *Sold Separately: Children and Parents in Consumer Culture* (New Brunswick, NJ: Rutgers University Press, 1993), 43-44.
20 Ibid., 44.
21 Leslie Savan, *The Sponsored Life: Ads, TV, and American Culture* (Philadelphia: Temple University Press, 1994), 8.
22 Ibid., 9.
23 "World Wide Diary of Actions: United States 1997," *Animal Liberation Frontline*, 1997, November 7, 2000, tvcrit.com/find/actions.
24 "Post Grape-Nuts and Grape-Nuts Flakes," *Kraft Foods*, 2000, November 7, 2000, tvcrit.com/find/grape.
25 Elisabeth Van Every, "Goth Style," *Academia Gothica*, 2000, November 7, 2000, tvcrit.com/find/goth.
26 Quoted in Bernice Kanner, *The 100 Best TV Commercials–and Why They Worked* (New York: Random House, 1999), 17.
27 A. J. Jacobs, "Remote Patrol," *Entertainment Weekly*, February 7, 1999, 66.
28 Messaris, 246.
29 Ibid., 249.
30 Bil Browning, "Homophobes Freak Out Over New Neil Patrick Harris Heineken Light ad," *LGBTQ Nation*, September 6, 2016, tvcrit.com/find/lgbtqnation; Dabitch, "Heineken Light–Neil Patrick Harris & the Grill Master 'Flip Your Meat,'" *Adland*, September 1, 2016, tvcrit.com/find/adland, accessed June 16, 2017.
31 Messaris, 255-57.
32 Budd, 79-80.
33 Seiter, 115. Furthermore, she discusses the racism inherent in advertising's utopia: "access to this child-centered utopia is restricted; full citizenship is denied to girls of all races and to boys of color" (Seiter, 115-16).
34 Richard Dyer, "Entertainment and Utopia," in *Movies and Methods*, vol. 2, Bill Nichols, ed. (Berkeley: University of California Press, 1985), 222.
35 Ibid., 228.
36 As quoted in Bob Garfield, "Is Internet Utopia? Good Heavens, No," *AdAge.com*, January 20, 1997, tvcrit.com/find/utopia, accessed August 17, 2011.
37 See Messaris, 196-203, for further discussion of generalization in ads.
38 Messaris, xviii.
39 Ibid., xix.
40 Dyer in Nichols, 222-26.
41 Rosser Reeves, *Reality in Advertising* (New York: Alfred A. Knopf, 1961), 46-49. Moreover, he defined advertising as "the art of getting a unique selling proposition into the heads of the most people at the lowest possible cost" (121).
42 Sut Jhally, *The Codes of Advertising: Fetishism and the Political Economy of Meaning in the Consumer Society* (New York: Routledge, 1987), 127; quoting D. Pope, *The Making of Modern Advertising* (New York: Basic Books, 1982), 287.
43 Reeves, 62.
44 John Thornton Caldwell, *Televisuality: Style, Crisis, and Authority in American Television* (New Brunswick, NJ: Rutgers University Press, 1995), 352.

45 Bertolt Brecht, "The Modern Theatre Is the Epic Theatre," in *Brecht on Theatre*, John Willett, ed. (New York: Hill and Wang, 1964), 33–42; Peter Wollen, "Godard and Counter Cinema: *Vent d'Est*," in *Readings and Writings: Semiotic Counter-Strategies* (London: Verso, 1982), 79–91.
46 Margaret Morse, *Virtualities: Television, Media Art, and Cyberculture* (Bloomington, IN: Indiana University Press, 1998), 72.
47 Messaris, 5.
48 Ibid., 7.
49 An ABC News story in 1991 revealed the behind-the-scenes work that went into morphing at that time (tvcrit.com/find/morphing).
50 Messaris, 7.

Further Readings

There are many books analyzing advertising and its discourse, but only a few target television commercials specifically. The most comprehensive of such TV-commercial books is Mike Budd, Steve Craig, and Clay Steinman, *Consuming Environments: Television and Commercial Culture* (New Brunswick, NJ: Rutgers University Press, 1999), which details the structure of the network-era TV industry and investigates the style and structure of commercials. Ellen Seiter, *Sold Separately: Children and Parents in Consumer Culture* (New Brunswick, NJ: Rutgers University Press, 1993), is more narrowly defined, but in its analysis of the discourses of commercials for children she provides many insights that may be applied to all commercials. The history and significance of the Super Bowl to advertising is chronicled in Bernice Kanner, *The Super Bowl of Advertising: How the Commercials Won the Game* (Princeton, NJ: Bloomberg Press, 2004). The ideological analysis of commercials is undertaken in Sut Jhally, *The Codes of Advertising: Fetishism and the Political Economy of Meaning in the Consumer Society* (New York: Routledge, 1987), which views television through the lens of political economy. And the cultural impact of popular music upon commercials is examined in Bethany Klein, *As Heard on TV: Popular Music in Advertising* (Burlington, VT: Ashgate, 2009); Nicolai Graakjær and Christian Jantzen, eds., *Music in Advertising: Commercial Sounds in Media Communication and Other Settings* (Aalborg, Denmark: Aalborg University Press, 2009); and Nicolai Graakjær, *Analyzing Music in Advertising: Television Commercials and Consumer Choice* (New York: Routledge, 2015).

Of the general books on advertising, the most useful to television students are Paul Messaris, *Visual Persuasion: The Role of Images in Advertising* (Thousand Oaks, CA: Sage, 1997); and Arthur Asa Berger, *Ads, Fads, and Consumer Culture: Advertising's Impact on American Character*, 5th ed. (Lanham, MD: Rowman & Littlefield, 2015). Messaris considers the impact of images in both print and television advertising and has useful insights into the function of visual style in the advertising process. Berger has an extended analysis of Apple's "1984" commercial. The specific significance of words in advertising is assayed by Michael L. Geis, *The Language of Television Advertising* (New York: Academic Press, 1982) and Greg Myers, *Words in Ads* (London: Edward Arnold, 1994). The semiotic perspective of Robert Goldman and Stephen Papson, *Sign Wars: The Cluttered Landscape of Advertising* (New York: Guilford Press, 1996), applies to both images and words as signs. Their analysis includes discussions of intertextuality, reflexivity, and the process of hailing. Mary Cross, ed., *Advertising and Culture: Theoretical Perspectives* (Westport, CT: Praeger, 1996), brings together a myriad of viewpoints—with writers from literary criticism, communication, and the social sciences.

Another general book on advertising is Jean Kilbourne, *Deadly Persuasion: Why Women and Girls Must Fight the Addictive Power of Advertising* (New York: The Free Press, 1999). As is evident from the title, Kilbourne's book is a strong polemic against the influence of advertising and its discursive world. The analyses of Leslie Savan, the advertising columnist for the *Village Voice*, are often perceptive and entertaining although seldom fortified by academic research. They have been collected in *The Sponsored Life: Ads, TV, and American Culture* (Philadelphia: Temple University Press, 1994).

Access to commercials for research purposes can readily be found on YouTube.com, where many advertisers maintain their own channels (e.g., Old Spice and DirecTV); Archive.org (tvcrit.com/find/archive); and Duke University's AdViews: A Digital Archive of Vintage Television Commercials (tvcrit.com/find/adviews). Commercials are also regularly reviewed by *Advertising Age* (adage.com), ispot.tv, and Shots.net.

Part II

Television Style

Image and Sound

7 An Introduction to Television Style

Modes of Production

In order to investigate why television programs look and sound the way they do, we must understand the process by which they are made. Throughout this book, we emphasize the close analysis of the television text. We use detailed descriptions of plot points, camera angles, dialogue, lighting, set design, and so on to argue for certain interpretations of that text. And when talking about elements of visual and sound style we must often, one might say, *reverse engineer* the text.[1] We must make assumptions about how a text was assembled in order to better disassemble it. You may notice that we don't often guess at the intentions of the people who made a television text while we do this disassembly. We avoid those guesses on purpose because it is extremely difficult to know with any certainty, for example, what director Pamela Fryman was thinking on the set on the day she decided to zoom out to capture some action instead of cutting to a wider shot.[2] And yet, we must know some fundamental things about the production practices of the television industry in order to know that camera zooming is even possible. (It was not possible when television first began to flourish in the 1940s.) If we see objects within the camera frame begin to shrink in size, we "reverse engineer" what we see on the screen and identify it as the camera zooming out.

Fundamental to understanding the TV industry's production practices is the concept of **mode of production**. A mode of television production is an *aesthetic* style of shooting that often relies upon a particular *technology* and is governed by certain *economic* systems. Television production forever blends aesthetics, technology, and economics—resulting in conventionalized practices for the actual making of TV. Television's mode of production is influenced by standards of "good" television (aesthetics); by the available camera, sound, and editing equipment (technology); and by budgets (economics)—along with other factors such as governmental policies and laws and network standards.

In the U.S., television programs are created according to the "rules" of two predominant modes of production: **single-camera** and **multiple-camera** (also known as **multi-camera** and **multicam**). In its purest form, a single-camera production is filmed with just one camera operating at a time. The shots are not recorded in the order in which they will appear in the final product but instead are shot in the sequence that will most efficiently get the production done on time and under budget. Consider, for example, a scene composed of shots alternating between two characters named Eugene and Lydia. Shots 1, 3, 5, 7, and 9 are of Eugene and shots 2, 4, 6, 8, and 10 are of Lydia. The single-camera approach to this scene would be to set up the lighting on Eugene, get the camera positioned, and then shoot the odd-numbered shots one after another. Then Lydia's lighting would be set up and the camera would shoot all the even-numbered shots of her. Later, the shots would be edited into their proper order.

Multiple-camera productions have two or more cameras trained on the set while the scene is acted out. In our hypothetical ten-shot scene, one camera would be pointed at Eugene while the other would simultaneously be pointed at Lydia. The scene could be edited while it transpires or it could be cut later, depending on time constraints. Sequences in soap operas, talk shows, and game shows that air daily—in addition to live programming such as sports and special events—may be edited while they are recorded or broadcast, but weekly multiple-camera sitcoms tend to take more time with their editing process. The latter generally assemble the recordings of the multiple cameras after the shooting is completed.

These modes of production are more than just a matter of how many cameras the videographer/cinematographer brings to the set. They define two distinct approaches, whose differences cut through

- **pre-production**: the written planning for the shoot;
- **production**: the shoot itself;
- **post-production** (often simply called "post"): everything afterward, including editing and sound design.

In this chapter, we will briefly cover these three phases and detail significant aspects of pre-production. Elements of production and post-production will be examined in subsequent chapters.

Historically, the single-camera mode of production came first. It developed initially in the cinema and has remained the preeminent way of making theatrical motion pictures. On television, it is the main mode used to create prime-time and SVOD dramas, music videos, and nationally telecast commercials. As it is also the foundation of most production practices, we will begin our discussion there. Subsequently we will consider the multiple-camera mode of production, which dominated television production when it first evolved as a mass medium in the 1940s. Sitcoms, soap operas, game shows, sports programs, and newscasts are shot using several cameras at once. Although multiple-camera shooting has developed its own conventions, its underlying premises are still rooted in certain single-camera concepts.

Before discussing the particulars of these modes of production, it should be noted that the choice of single-camera or multiple-camera mode is separate from that of the recording medium (film or video). Up until the 2000s, most single-camera productions were shot on film and not on video, but high-definition, digital video (DV) has since come to replace film on single-camera productions—with a few significant exceptions. An early, notable convert to DV was George Lucas, who shot *Star Wars: Episode II—Attack of the Clones* (2002) in that format while most of Hollywood was still committed to shooting on film. Multiple-camera productions are also not tied to one specific format. They have a long history of being shot on both film and video. Today, virtually all single-camera and multiple-camera productions originate on digital video, which facilitates post-production digital editing as well. As we shall see, these modes of production are not determined by their technological underpinning and the availability of film, analog-video, or digital-video formats—although that is certainly a consideration. Rather, they depend as much on certain economic and aesthetic principles as they do on technology.

Single-Camera Mode of Production

Initially it might seem that single-camera production is a cumbersome, lengthy, and expensive way to create television images and that television producers would shy away from it for those reasons. But television is not a machine driven solely by the profit motive. When analyzing television, we must be wary of slipping into an economic determinism. We must avoid the mistaken belief that television producers' aesthetic decisions and technological choices will always be determined by economic imperatives, that it's always "all about the money." In a study of how and why the Hollywood film industry adopted the single-camera mode of production, David Bordwell, Janet Staiger, and Kristin Thompson contend that technological change has three basic explanations:

1. Production efficiency: Does this innovation allow films to be made more quickly or more cheaply?
2. Product differentiation: Does this innovation help distinguish this film from other, similar films and thus make it more attractive to the consumer?
3. Standards of quality: Does this innovation fit a conventionalized aesthetic sense of how the medium should "evolve"? Does it adhere to a specific sense of "progress" or improvement?[3]

Although single-camera production is more expensive and less efficient than multiple-camera, it compensates for its inefficiency by providing greater product differentiation and adhering to conventionalized aesthetic standards of high quality. Because single-camera mode offers more control over the image and the editing, it allows the **director**, the person in charge on the set, to maximize the impact of every single image. Consequently, it is the mode of choice for short television pieces such as commercials and music videos, which rely upon their visuals to communicate as powerfully as possible. Commercials in particular need a distinctive style to distinguish them from surrounding messages that compete for our attention.

Stages of Production

Pre-Production

To make single-camera production economically feasible, there must be extensive pre-production planning. Chance events and improvisation would be expensive distractions. The organization of any single-camera production—whether an NBC sitcom episode or a Pepsi commercial—begins with a **script** or **screenplay**. Preparation of single-camera television typically evolves through four revisions or drafts of the script: the writer's draft, table draft, network draft, and production draft. Examining each stage of the revision process illuminates how much of the work done in pre-production determines what happens during shooting and post-production. In other words, *pre-production* scripting is where the *production* work and the *post-production* editing of scenes are originally conceptualized. If writers, directors, and producers don't plan to shoot a specific shot, there will be nothing for the camera operator to shoot or the editor to cut! Moreover, a consideration of script revision also shows the fundamentally collaborative nature of television production.

The writer's draft is the initial version of the script, prepared by a scriptwriter or, as is the case in many comedy shows, assembled by a team of scriptwriters. This rough draft is worked over by the director and producers in order to prepare the table draft. In comedies, a "table reading" is conducted where the cast and key creative members of the crew, along with network executives, literally sit around a table and read through the table draft. (Dramas often skip this step.) From this quasi-performance, the creative personnel get a sense of what will get laughs and what won't. And the network executives are introduced to the material so that they can then give their "notes" to the writers and director. The notes are incorporated by the writers into a network draft, which the executives approve. Finally, the writers and director do yet another tweak of the script to prepare it for actual shooting—resulting in the production draft or **shooting script**. Further revisions might yet be made during shooting, with additional pages (in different colors) inserted into the production draft. In order to ensure consistency through all these drafts, each step of the revision process is overseen by the **showrunner**, the producer responsible for the actual creation of individual episodes. In television, showrunning producers wield much more clout than directors. In fact, many showrunners come to producing through writing and not directing—although they may wind up directing eventually. Some examples of showrunners who established themselves as scriptwriters first include Shonda Rhimes (*Grey's Anatomy*), Vince Gilligan (*Breaking Bad*), Amy Sherman-Palladino (*Gilmore Girls*), Christopher Lloyd and Steven Levitan (*Modern Family*), and Joss Whedon (*Buffy the Vampire Slayer*).

Each episode goes through this four-script process, with the significant exception of a series' debut episode or **pilot**. Broadcast and cable networks, as well as streaming services, generally do not develop pilots with their own production personnel. Previously, in the old days of the Hollywood studio system, writers were on staff to a studio like Warner Brothers and cranked out movie ideas all day long. Today's network environment is more complicated. Each of the major networks is affiliated with a studio that feeds shows to that network. On rare occasions, an affiliated studio might produce a show for a network to which it is not attached. Producer/director Ken Kwapis provides the example of 20th Century Fox Television (the studio) producing *My Name Is Earl* (2005–09) for NBC instead of Fox Network. He explains further:

> Many writers and producers have overall deals at television studios. Some are "first look" deals, which means that a given studio (Universal, for instance) gets first crack at a writer's idea. If the studio passes on the idea, that writer can pitch it elsewhere. Some writers have "exclusive" deals at a particular studio, which is not dissimilar to being "under contract" in the classic sense. As a freelance writer/producer, you pitch your idea to network executives (NBC, for instance); if the network buys it, you develop the pilot script with studio executives (Universal Television, in this case).[4]

In other words, writers and producers with a commitment to a studio may verbally present or **pitch** their series ideas to networks. If a network is sold on a pitch, it authorizes its affiliated studio to produce it.

Individuals without a studio commitment must find ways to entice network executives to hear their pitch. Commonly this is done via a **logline**, a one-sentence synopsis of the program's premise, which an agent or manager brings to a network to try to earn a meeting for a pitch session. Industry publication *Variety* maintains a "TV Pilots/Development Scorecard" of potential new shows and suggests a logline for each one—though not necessarily a logline created by the show's producers (see tvcrit.com/find/logline). In spring of 2017, *The Mayor* was picked up for series development by ABC; *Variety*'s logline for it was "A single-camera comedy about an outspoken, idealistic rapper who runs for office as a publicity stunt and actually gets elected." And NBC picked up a pilot for *The Assignment*, whose logline was:

> Based on short stories by best-selling author Charlaine Harris comes a high-octane series that mixes humor, romance and espionage centering on a pair of former operatives who get reactivated and drawn into a larger conspiracy while attempting to maintain their undercover lives.

A network pitch meeting centers around the concept for the pilot episode and the character arcs that will develop out of that pilot—leading to subsequent episodes. Network executives must be convinced that the show can evolve over episodes and seasons. If the pitch is bought by the network, the writer/producer will then submit a **pilot outline**. If the outline is approved, the series can "go to script." From there, many impediments might block the writer/producer from ever getting to create a pilot. Casting is a key step, naturally, and many projects collapse at this stage. Presuming the pilot is "green lit" and actually gets shot, then it must survive various forms of market testing before the network offers the writer/producer a series commitment. Even then, the network might not order an entire season of shows. For example, NBC initially ordered only five episodes of *The Office* at the start of what turned out to be a nine-season run. Figure 7.1 shows an excerpt of the pilot script that Marc Cherry wrote for *Desperate Housewives* (aired on October 3, 2004), which led to ABC shooting the pilot and ordering episodes from his production company. Thus, pitches, outlines, and pilot scripts are part of what one might call the *pre*-pre-production phase of a television program's life.

Commercials, animation, music videos, and other visually complicated, single-camera television productions will take the pre-production planning one step further and create **storyboards**, which consist of drawings of images for each shot or of several images for complicated shots (Figure 7.2). Storyboards indicate the precision with which some directors conceptualize their visual design ahead of time. Alfred Hitchcock, for example, was well known for devising elaborate storyboards. For him, the filmmaking process itself was simply a matter of creating those images on film. Similarly, when director Ken Kwapis was preparing to shoot *ER* (1994–2009) episodes, he created shot lists to account for each shot in every scene:

1. EXTREME LOW ANGLE/WIDE on Benton & Carter (in wheelchair). CAMERA LEADS them down the hall. O.S. wheel gets stuck in door.
2. REVERSE CLOSE on Carter/OTS Benton. Conversation about Benton's dating m.o.
3. INSERT Wheel jammed in door.
4. WIDE on Carter & Benton, from inside Recovery Room. Carter snaps. Benton frees the wheelchair, pulls him into the room and sits on the bed. ARC to MEDIUM WIDE 50/50 Carter & Benton.

Storyboards and shot lists show how single-camera productions are, in a sense, pre-edited during the pre-production stage. Even before a single shot is captured, the basic editing of the episode has been conceived.

```
EXT. SUBURBAN STREET—DAY

We're DRIVING down a tree-lined suburban street. We finally stop at a
well-kept UPPER MIDDLE CLASS house complete with white picket fence.

                          MARY ALICE (V.O.)
              My name is Mary Alice Scott. When you
              read this morning's paper you may
              come across an article about the
              unusual day I had last week.

CLOSE-UP—MARY ALICE SCOTT

The camera pulls back to reveal an ATTRACTIVE WOMAN IN HER EARLY 30'S
wearing gardening gloves, emerging from the house. She crosses to the
flower bed and begins pruning.
```

Figure 7.1 Mark Cherry's script for the *Desperate Housewives* pilot indicates setting and dialogue in a strict format.

1. Car speeds recklessly down a tree-lined road.

2. Woman and man in front seat. He drives.

3. The road; his point of view.

4. Front seat, same scene as in #2.

5. Woman looks toward man.

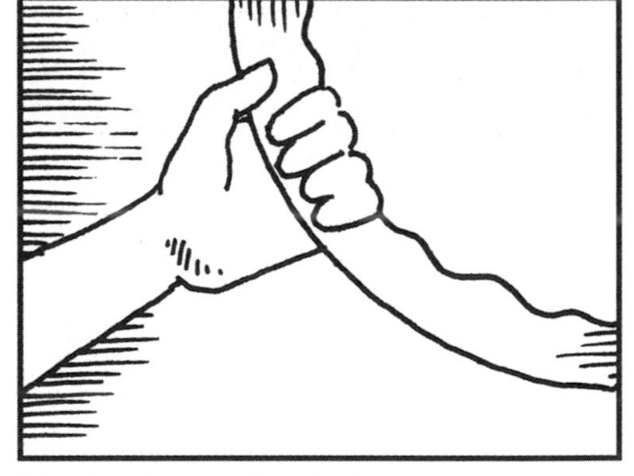
6. Her hand reaches for wheel.

Figure 7.2 During the planning of a television program, a storyboard may indicate the framing and composition of individual shots.

Production

In this mode of production, a single camera is typically used on the set and the shots are done out of order (although there are exceptions to this; see the section below on hybrid modes of production, pp. 278–80). Actors typically rehearse their scenes in entirety, but the filming is disjointed and filled with stops and starts. Because the final product is assembled from all these fragments, a **continuity person** must keep track of all the details from one shot to the next—for example, in which hand the actor was holding a cigarette and how far down the cigarette had burned. Nonetheless, small errors do sneak through, illustrating just how disjointed the whole process is. For instance, in Figure 7.3, a frame enlargement from a *Northern Exposure* (1990–95) scene, there is a dishrag on actor Janine Turner's shoulder. At the very beginning of the next shot, Figures 7.4 and 7.5, the dishrag has disappeared.

The "production" stage of making television is under the immediate control of directors. They approve the lighting and set design, coach the actors, and choose the camera angles—as we will discuss in Chapters 8 and 9. Most television directors do not create the scripts they direct (which is done in pre-production), and most do not have total control over the editing (post-production). However, the actual recording process (the production phase) is their specific responsibility.

Post-Production

The task of the technicians in post-production is to form the disjointed fragments into a unified whole. Ideally the parts will fit together so well that we will not even notice the seams joining them. The editor consults with the director and producers to cut the shots together.

Figure 7.3 Northern Exposure: A match cut starts with Maggie beginning to sit down...

Figure 7.4 ... and then continuing to sit (due to a continuity error, she has lost the dishrag that was on her shoulder)...

Figure 7.5 ... settling into a medium close-up. The change in camera angle helps to make the continuity error less noticeable to the viewer.

Once the editing of the image has been finalized or "locked" in narrative production, the **sound editor** and **musical director** are called upon to further smooth over the cuts between shots with music, dubbed-in dialogue, and sound effects. Of course, in music videos and many commercials, the music provides the piece's main unifying force and is developed well before the visuals. Indeed, the music determines the visuals in those cases, not vice versa, and becomes part of the pre-production planning. The specifics of this post-production process are discussed in Chapters 10 and 11.

Multiple-Camera Mode of Production

Although a good deal of what we see on television has been produced using single-camera production, it would be wrong to assume that this mode dominates TV in the same way that it dominates theatrical film. The opposite is true. Although prime time is currently divided equally between single-camera and multiple-camera, programs outside of prime time—daytime soap operas, syndicated game shows, weekend sports coverage, and late-night talk shows—are almost all multiple-camera productions. Obviously, multiple-camera production is the norm on broadcast television, as it has been since the days of television's live broadcasts—virtually all of which were also multiple-camera productions (Table 7.1).

It is tempting to assume that since multiple-camera shooting is less expensive and faster to produce than single-camera, it must therefore be a cheap, slipshod imitation of single-camera shooting. This is the aesthetic hierarchy of style that television producers, critics, and even some viewers themselves presume. In this view, multiple-camera is an inferior mode, a necessary evil. However, ranking modes of production is essentially a futile exercise. One mode is not so much better or worse than another as it is just different. Clearly, there have been outstanding, even "artistic," achievements in both modes. Instead of getting snarled in aesthetic snobbery, it is more important to discuss the differences between the two and understand how those differences may affect television's production of meaning. In short, how do the different modes of production influence the meanings that TV conveys to the viewer? And what aesthetic principles do they share?

Stages of Production

Pre-Production

Narrative programs such as soap operas and sitcoms that utilize multiple-camera production start from scripts much as single-camera productions do, but these scripts are less image oriented and initially indicate no camera directions at all. Sitcom and soap-opera scripts consist almost

Table 7.1 Top Ten Prime-Time Shows: 1950–51

Of the following, all but the Westerns (*The Lone Ranger* and *Hopalong Cassidy*) and *Fireside Theatre* were telecast live using multiple camera technology. (The first season during which the A.C. Nielsen Company [which became Nielsen Media Research] rated programs was 1950–51.)

1.	*Texaco Star Theater*	6.	*Gillette Cavalcade of Sports*
2.	*Fireside Theatre*	7.	*The Lone Ranger*
3.	*Philco TV Playhouse*	8.	*Arthur Godfrey's Talent Scouts*
4.	*Your Show of Shows*	9.	*Hopalong Cassidy*
5.	*The Colgate Comedy Hour*	10.	*Mama*

entirely of dialogue, with wide margins so that the director may write in camera directions. The sort of detailed description of action we see in Cherry's script for the *Desperate Housewives* pilot (Figure 7.1) would seldom appear in a soap-opera script. Storyboards are rarely, if ever, created for these programs. Multiple-camera scripting is emblematic of the emphasis on dialogue in such programs. The words come first; the images are tailored to fit them.

Non-narrative programs (game shows, talk shows, reality TV, and so on) have even less written preparation. Instead, they rely upon a specific structure and a formalized opening and closing, which causes them to sometimes be inaccurately labeled "unscripted" television. Although the hosts may have written lists of questions or other prepared materials that can be somewhat script-like, they and the participants are presumed to be speaking in their own voices, rather than the voice of a scriptwriter. This adds to the program's impression of improvisation.

Production

A multiple-camera production is not dependent on a specific technological medium. That is, it may be shot on film or videotape (analog or digital), recorded **direct to disk** (i.e., the video is stored digitally on a hard disk), or even broadcast live. The sitcom *Two and a Half Men* (2003–15) was recorded on film, but the soap opera *Days of Our Lives* (1965–) was captured on high-definition, Digital Betacam videotape for many years. Non-narrative talk shows and game shows are recorded in various video formats. Some local news programs and *Saturday Night Live* are telecast live—as daytime soap operas used to be in the 1950s and 1960s.

If a program is shot on film, the editing and the addition of music and sound effects must necessarily come later, during post-production. If a program originates on video, however, there are the options of editing in post-production or while it is being recorded. (Obviously, a live program must be edited while it is telecast.) Time constraints play a factor here. Programs that are broadcast daily, such as soap operas and game shows, seldom have the time for extensive editing in post. Typically, the director will edit a version of the show during the production stage, while the feeds from all the cameras are being recorded. This **line cut**, as it is known, is created by the director switching among the three or more cameras while the show is going on. Later, the line cut is used by the show's editors as a rough guide while they cut the recorded camera feeds.

The choice of recording format is, once again, dependent in part on technology, economics, and aesthetics. Since the technology of videotape was not made available until 1956, there were originally only two technological choices for recording a multiple-camera program: either film live broadcasts on **kinescope** by pointing a motion-picture camera at a TV screen; or originally shoot the program on film (and then broadcast the edited film later). Early-1950s programs such as *Your Show of Shows* (1950–54) and *The Jack Benny Show* (1950–65, 1977) were recorded as kinescopes. In 1951, the producers of *I Love Lucy* (1951–59, 1961) made the technological choice to shoot on film instead of broadcasting live. Although this involved more expense up front than kinescopes did, it made economic sense when it came time to distribute the program in syndication to local stations. A filmed original has several benefits over kinescope in the syndication process. It looks appreciably better than a kinescope and is easier and quicker to prepare since all the shooting, processing, and editing of the film have already been done for the first broadcast. Figures 4.23 and 4.24, from an early 1950s kinescope of *The George Burns and Gracie Allen Show*, exemplify the inferior image quality of that process. An *I Love Lucy* episode from the same era would have looked much better, due to its relatively high resolution. Since producers make much more money from syndication than they do from a program's original run, it made good economic sense for *I Love Lucy* to choose film over live broadcasting and kinescope. Moreover, its enormous success in syndication encouraged other sitcoms in the 1950s to record on film.

After the introduction of videotape, the economic incentive for multiple-camera productions to shoot on film no longer held true. A videotape record of a live broadcast may be made and that videotape may be used in syndication. This videotape—unlike kinescopes—looks just as good as the original broadcast. Until recently, producers who shot film in a multiple-camera setup did so primarily for aesthetic reasons because film used to hold a slight edge over video in terms of visual quality. However, the introduction of high-definition digital video in the early 2000s spelled the end for film's visual superiority. Today it is nearly impossible to distinguish HD video from film when viewed on a television screen. And the same is also true in movie theaters. Only a few specialty movie theaters show film prints anymore; the industry essentially converted to digital recordings and screenings during the 2010s, once digital formats approximated the image resolution of analog-film formats. Similarly, "prestige" multiple-camera productions that would have been shot on film 20 years ago are now being shot digitally.

Multiple-camera narrative programs that are not broadcast live and thus must be edited in post-production follow a conventionalized production procedure. The actors rehearse individual scenes off the set, then continue rehearsing on the set, with the cameras. The director maps out the positions for the actors and the two to four cameras that will record a scene. The camera operators are often given lists of their positions relative to the scene's dialogue. Finally, an audience (if it is a comedy) is brought into the studio to record their responses to the scenes (for diagrams of TV studios, see Figures 8.7 and 8.8, below).

A multiple-camera episode is performed one scene at a time, with 15- to 20-minute breaks between the scenes—during which, at sitcom recording sessions, a comedian keeps the audience amused. One major difference between single-camera and multiple-camera shooting is that in multiple-camera the actors always perform the scenes straight through, without interruption, unless a mistake is made. Their performance is not fragmented, as it is in single-camera production. Each scene is recorded at least twice, and if one or two lines or camera positions are missed, individual shots may be shot in isolation afterwards.

Further, in multiple-camera sitcoms, the scenes are normally recorded in the order in which they will appear in the finished program—in contrast, once again, to single-camera productions, which are frequently shot out of story order. This is done largely to help the studio audience follow the story and respond to it appropriately. The audience's laughter and applause are recorded by placing microphones above them. Their applause is manipulated through flashing "applause" signs that trigger their response, which is recorded for the program's **laugh track**. The laugh track is augmented in post-production with additional recorded laughter and applause, a process known as **sweetening** in the industry. The entire process of recording one episode of a half-hour sitcom takes about three to four hours—if all goes as planned.

Live-on-tape productions—such as game and talk shows—are similar in their preparation to those edited in post-production, but the recording process differs in a few ways. (The phrase "live-on-tape" has persisted, even in productions that record to disk instead of actual tape cassettes.) Once the video starts recording on a live-on-tape production, it seldom stops. Directors use a **switcher** to change between cameras as the scene is performed—creating their line cut. The shots are all planned in advance, but the practice of switching shots is a bit loose. The cuts don't always occur at the conventionally appropriate moment. In addition to the switching/cutting executed concurrently with the actors' performance, the scene's music and sound effects are often laid on at the same time, though they may be fine-tuned later. Sound technicians prepare the appropriate door bells and phone rings and thunderclaps and then insert them when called for by the director. All of this heightens the impression that the scene presented is occurring "live" before the cameras, that the cameras just happened to be there to capture this event—hence the term live-on-tape. The resulting performance is quite similar to that in live theater.

In soap operas and comedies shot without a studio audience, individual scenes need not be shot in the order of appearance in the final program. Since they do not have to worry about confusing a studio audience, their scenes are shot in the fashion most efficient for the production. Normally this means that the order is determined by which sets are being used on a particular day. First, all the scenes that appear on one set will be shot—regardless of where they appear in the final program. Next, all the scenes on another set will be done, and so on. This allows the technicians to light and prepare one set at a time, which is faster and cheaper than going back and forth between sets.

As we have seen, narrative, scripted programs made with multiple cameras may be either recorded or broadcast live and, if recorded, may either be switched during the production or edited afterward, in post-production. Non-narrative, unscripted programs, however, have fewer production options. Studio news programs, game shows, and talk shows are always broadcast live or shot live-on-tape. This is because of their need for immediacy (in the news) and/or economic efficiency (in game and talk shows). Participants in the latter do not speak from scripts, they extemporize. And, since these "actors" in non-narrative programs are improvising, the director must also improvise, editing on the fly. This further heightens the illusion of being broadcast live, even though most, if not all, such programs are on videotape or disk.

Post-Production

In multiple-camera programs, post-production varies from minimal touch-ups to full-scale assembly. Live-on-tape productions are virtually completed before they get to the post-production stage. Their final cuts are often quite close to their line cuts, and most of their music and sound effects have already been added. But similar programs that have been recorded live but *not* switched at the time of recording must be compiled shot by shot. For instance, sitcoms often record whatever the three or four cameras are aimed at without editing it during the actual shoot. The editor of these programs, like the editor of single-camera productions, must create a continuity out of various discontinuous fragments. (Multiple-camera post-production is discussed further in Chapters 10 and 11.)

Hybrid Modes of Production

Single-camera and multiple-camera modes of production have become less and less distinct over the years. Or, to put it another way, they have become more and more like one another. We have emphasized their differences here to help the reader understand the particulars of each approach, but the day-to-day practices of television production in the U.S. blur the distinction between them. There are "single-camera" shows that sometimes use more than one camera on the set and there are "multiple-camera" shows that sometimes use just one. We'll conclude our consideration of modes of production, then, by recognizing their increasingly hybrid nature.

First, there are several instances when single-camera productions bring a second (or third or fourth) camera onto the set. The most common is for scenes using explosions, car crashes, or other practical effects on the set. If a building can only be set on fire once, then the director is sure to use numerous cameras to capture it from a variety of angles (and as a backup in case one camera has a technical issue). But another, somewhat surprising use of two cameras on single-camera productions is for simple conversation scenes. Some directors on single-camera productions prefer to bring in a second camera to capture additional angles during the simplest of scenes and to allow actors to play through a scene with fewer interruptions.

The hybrid quality of single- and multiple-camera modes of production is not a one-way street. Just as some single-camera productions make use of multiple cameras, so some multiple-camera productions incorporate single-camera techniques. This is most evident in sitcoms. When Tom Cherones directed episodes of the multiple-camera show *Seinfeld*, he often filmed shots after the studio audience departed, bringing a single camera into the set, moving walls around, and capturing images from angles not possible during the multiple-camera shooting process. And *How I Met Your Mother* (2005–14) developed its own, virtually unique, hybrid mode of production. It mostly looks like a conventional, multiple-camera, laugh track-accompanied production recorded on a studio set with a live audience, but it was actually shot without an audience. Its directors used three (or more) cameras while shooting, but the lack of an audience and a longer-than-usual shooting schedule (three days instead of one) allowed them to move the cameras into the set in order to create shots that would normally be impossible in a multiple-camera shoot.

Thus, we can find single-camera programs borrowing techniques from the multiple-camera mode of production and vice versa. Does this crossover negate the division we have made between the two modes? No, but it does mean that the number of cameras on a set is not the ultimate determinant of which mode a program employs. Instead, the principal difference between the two modes stems from their underlying aesthetic. Multiple-camera mode of production borrows its aesthetic from the theater. It is *as if* the actors were up on a vaudeville stage and the cameras were in the audience recording their performance as it occurs live, without retakes (see Chapter 4 for more on vaudeville). It is *as if* the cameras do not control their movements and speech, but just capture them as they happen. We viewers know some of this is untrue, but liveness and this sense of live performance are central to the illusion of multiple-camera productions. In fact, the multiple-camera show *Cheers* (1982–93) asserted its liveness each week by proclaiming that "*Cheers* was filmed before a live studio audience." In contrast, single-camera mode of production borrows its aesthetic from the cinema, from films made for release to theaters. In this case, it is *as if* the actors' performances had been broken into small pieces. It is *as if* the camera controlled their every movement and speech. It is *as if* these fragments were then assembled in an editing room, which is where the performance is finally constructed. The performance does not exist in the real world in order to be recorded. Instead, the performance is fabricated out of these fragments.

In the everyday world of television production, these aesthetics seldom exist in pure form, but the choice of one approach over another has a major effect on a television program's technological needs (types of cameras, editing equipment, etc.) and economic requirements (single-camera is more expensive than multiple-camera). Moreover, it determines many elements of the program's pre-production, production, and post-production phases.

Summary

To analyze television style, we must have a fundamental understanding of its two principal modes of production: single-camera and multiple-camera. Single-camera mode of production came first, originating in the cinema; but multiple-camera has been central to television since the 1940s. The single-camera mode typically uses one camera on the set to record fragments of a scene, which must be assembled later. The multiple-camera mode aims several cameras at the actors and the set in order to simultaneously capture their performances as they occur.

These modes of production influence the three principal stages of TV making: pre-production, production, and post-production. In this chapter, we comment on several aspects of these stages, but we will return to them in more detail in the other chapters in this part of the book. In anticipation of the discussion of production and post-production work, we do here specify the scripting that goes on during pre-production: the writer's draft, table draft, network draft, and production draft. A program's showrunner oversees all stages of pre-production scripting and may request detailed storyboards to augment the script if visual design is particularly important.

Pure forms of these modes of production seldom exist in the contemporary television industry. Rather, hybrid modes of production are becoming more and more common. "Single-camera" productions will bring extra cameras on set to capture explosions or additional camera angles of a conversation scene, and "multiple-camera" productions will rely on single-camera techniques to shoot on the set after the audience has left. The hybrid nature of the modes of production illustrates that economics, the bottom line, does not entirely determine how a television program will be shot. As always, the creation of television blends economic concerns with aesthetic principles and technological resources.

Notes

1 Film theorist and historian David Bordwell uses this specific phrase in *Figures Traced in Light: On Cinematic Staging* (Berkeley: University of California Press, 2005), 250.
2 Bordwell responds to the intentional fallacy issue: "This framework does not claim access to intentions as mental episodes, only to intentions as posited sources of patterns of action. Again, we reverse-engineer" (Bordwell, 257).
3 David Bordwell, Janet Staiger, and Kristin Thompson, *The Classical Hollywood Cinema: Film Style and Mode of Production to 1960* (New York: Columbia University Press, 1985), 243–44.
4 Ken Kwapis, e-mail message to the author, June 6, 2017.

Further Readings

U.S. television production modes in the twenty-first century and the culture surrounding them are assayed in John Thornton Caldwell, *Production Culture: Industrial Reflexivity in Film and Television* (Durham, NC: Duke University Press, 2008). Production studies is also advocated in Jennifer Holt and Alisa Perren, eds., *Media Industries: History, Theory and Method* (Malden, MA: Blackwell, 2009); and Vicki Mayer, Miranda J. Banks, and John T. Caldwell, eds., *Production Studies: Cultural Studies of Media Industries* (New York: Routledge, 2009). The latter was followed by a book by two of the same authors with a more international focus: Miranda Banks, Bridget Conor, Vicki Mayer, *Production Studies, The Sequel!: Cultural Studies of Global Media Industries* (New York: Routledge, 2015). Timothy Havens and Amanda Lotz, *Understanding Media Industries*, 2nd ed. (New York: Oxford University Press, 2016), positions production culture within modern Internet distribution of media.

For readers curious about the early days of American television, Edward Stasheff and Rudy Bretz, *The Television Program: Its Writing, Direction and Production* (New York: Hill and Wang, 1956), offers an interesting perspective on how TV was made in the mid-1950s.

The specific evolution of single-camera production is comprehensively described in David Bordwell, Janet Staiger, and Kristin Thompson, *The Classical Hollywood Cinema: Film Style and Mode of Production to 1960* (New York: Columbia University Press, 1985). John Ellis, *Visible*

Fictions: Cinema: Television: Video (Boston: Routledge, 1992), is not as exhaustive, but it does begin the work of analyzing the multiple-camera mode of production.

The scripting process is the subject of numerous books—many of which are "how to" books providing advice on breaking into the television business. Although such books can be revealing in their presumptions about how the TV industry works, they often are written like advice columns and thus are little help to the analyst who wants to reverse engineer television style. A few books that are useful to the TV critic are: Pamela Douglas, *Writing the TV Drama Series: How to Succeed as a Professional Writer in TV* (Studio City, CA: Michael Wiese Productions, 2005); Alan Schroeder, *Writing and Producing Television News: From Newsroom to Air* (New York: Oxford University Press, 2009); and Evan S. Smith, *Writing Television Sitcoms* (New York: Perigee Books, 1999). If you are interested in experimenting with scriptwriting yourself but are confused about the format required, you should try some of the free scriptwriting software available online. Several are listed at tvcrit.com/find/screenwriting.

Handbooks for television production provide many insights into the conventions of television's visual and sound style. Two foundational texts are Gerald Millerson, *Television Production*, 15th ed. (Boston: Focal Press, 2012); and Herbert Zettl, *Television Production Handbook*, 12th ed. (Belmont, CA: Wadsworth, 2014). A more ambitiously theoretical approach is taken in Gorham Kindem, *The Moving Image: Production Principles and Practices* (Glenview, IL: Scott, Foresman, 1987). Kindem endeavors not just to describe television's common practices but also to articulate the aesthetic rationales of those practices. Kindem's book is currently out of print, but Gorham Kindham and Robert B. Musburger, *Introduction to Media Production: The Path to Digital Media Production*, 4th ed. (Boston: Focal, 2009), covers many of the same aesthetic concerns in addition to offering practical instruction in video production. And Musberger, more recently, has co-authored with Michael R. Ogden, *Single-Camera Video Production*, 6th ed. (Boston: Focal, 2014).

The sole attempt to create an entire stylistics of television production is Herbert Zettl, *Sight Sound Motion: Applied Media Aesthetics*, 7th ed. (Belmont, CA: Wadsworth, 2013). Zettl's ambitious undertaking is occasionally idiosyncratic and quirky—and also quite provocative. The most thorough guide to interpreting television's visual style, however, is not a TV book at all: David Bordwell and Kristin Thompson, *Film Art: An Introduction*, 11th ed. (New York: McGraw-Hill, 2016). Although Bordwell and Thompson have nothing to offer on some crucial aspects of television (e.g., multiple-camera editing), they provide an extensive introduction to understanding cinema production.

8 Style and Setting

Mise-en-Scene

In the theater, the director positions actors on a carefully designed set, organizing the on-stage space. This staging of the action was dubbed, in French, **mise-en-scene**. The mise-en-scene of a play, then, is all the physical objects on the stage (props, furniture, walls, actors) and the arrangement of those objects to present effectively the play's narrative and themes. "Mise-en-scene," the phrase, was adapted by film studies in the 1960s and broadly used and sometimes misused. For some film critics the term carried almost mystical connotations, while for others it vaguely described any component of visual style. For our purposes, we will adopt a much narrower understanding of the term. Mise-en-scene will here refer to the staging of the action for the camera. Mise-en-scene thus includes all the objects in front of the camera and their arrangement by directors and their minions. In short, mise-en-scene is the organization of *setting*, *costuming*, *lighting*, and *actor movement*.

Mise-en-scene is a powerful component of the television apparatus. It forms the basic building block of narrative in fiction programs, influencing our perception of characters before the first line of dialogue is spoken. It directs and shapes our understanding of information in news, game shows, and sports programs. And it forcefully channels our perception in advertisements and other didactic TV material. To understand these narrative, informational, and persuasive uses of mise-en-scene, we need to consider its basic materials.

Set Design

The walls of a room, the concrete and asphalt of a city street, the trees of a tropical rain forest, the stylized desk of a TV newsroom; all are elements of a setting that must be either built or selected by the **production designer**, subject to the approval of the director or producer. In a sense, the production designer is the architect of a television program—creating a physical space for the actors, news anchors, game show hosts, and so on to inhabit.

One initial distinction that may be made in television set design is between **studio sets** (constructed) and **location settings** (selected). Newscasts, game shows, talk shows, multiple-camera sitcoms, and soap operas all rely upon sets erected on television **sound stages**. Prime-time dramas and single-camera sitcoms shoot on studio sets, too, but they also make extensive use of location shooting.

The decision to stage a program on a studio set or on location is in equal parts economic, technological, and aesthetic. In-studio shooting is more economically efficient because the production resources are centralized. Equipment, actors, and technicians are all conveniently close at hand. For programs such as game shows and sitcoms that incorporate a studio audience, it would obviously be impractical to bus the entire group to a distant location. Technologically speaking, it is certainly possible to set up cameras in a remote location (sports programs do it every day), but the equipment cannot be as easily controlled and manipulated when it is out of the studio. This leads to slower production time and increased costs. Aesthetic convention also encourages indoor, studio-based set design for some genres. Soap operas, for example, tend to tell "indoor" stories. Their aesthetic emphasis on tales of emotion necessitates indoor scenes: hospital rooms, restaurants, bedrooms, and so on. And even when soap-opera narratives do go outdoors, such as the exterior scenes at Miller's Falls in *All My Children*, they are still mostly shot on studio sets—as is also true of sitcoms (see *That 70's Show*, Figures 10.33 and 10.34). In contrast, the aesthetics of crime dramas and other action genres demand exterior shooting to facilitate the fast-paced movement of people and cars around city streets. Moreover, location shooting adds a certain patina of "realism" to these programs, which is another aesthetic concern.

Studio Set Design

Studio sets fall into two broad categories: narrative and non-narrative.

Narrative Studio Set Design

The main function of narrative sets is, obviously enough, to house characters engaged in a story. But sets in fiction television are not just neutral backgrounds to the action; they also signify narrative meaning to the viewer. Bada Bing!, the bar in *The Sopranos*, for instance, conveys meaning about the characters who socialize and work there, especially Tony Soprano, the bar's owner (Figure 8.1). Its decor (a stage for nude dancers, boxing mementos on the walls, a salacious sign) helps characterize Soprano as a very masculine character and suggests a sexist male camaraderie associated with an unsavory strip club. (Contrast its negative associations with the positive ones attached to the neighborhood bar in *Cheers*, "where everybody knows your name.") Thus, these sets and props serve as objective correlatives, or symbols, of the characters who inhabit and use them. Or, to put it in different terms, they are narrative **icons**—objects that represent aspects of character. Remaining sensitive to the **iconography** of television programs can help the analyst understand just how characterizations are created.

Figure 8.1 The setting of Bada Bing! signifies the unsavory, hyper-masculine nature of characters in *The Sopranos*.

Narrative significance is not the only thing governing the look of studio sets. Overriding economic, technological, and aesthetic considerations combine to determine how those sets will be designed.

There are no ceilings on most studio sets, for the simple technological/aesthetic reason that lighting is done from above (more on this later). The lights are hung on a grid where the ceiling would normally be. This lack of ceilings limits the shots that may be done with the camera down low, looking upward at the characters; such an angle might reveal the tops of the sets and the lights. It also means that ceilings cannot be used within the frame to enclose the characters, creating a slightly claustrophobic sensation—as was popular in 1940s films following the lead of *Citizen Kane* (1941; Figure 8.2). One exception to this is *Mad Men* (2007-15), which, especially in its first season, does indeed reveal the ceilings in its sets (Figure 8.3). By so doing,

Figure 8.2 A scene from *Citizen Kane* reveals the set's ceiling, which was quite unusual in 1941...

Figure 8.3 ... and in 2007 *Mad Men* used the same technique to highlight its fluorescent light grid.

it traps its characters within a visual maze that echoes the rat-race world of 1960s advertising. Additionally, it emulates a prestigious style of shooting not normally associated with cable television—helping AMC distinguish its brand from those of its cable-network competitors. *Mad Men*'s sophisticated visual style doubtlessly helped it earn its Emmy Awards.

Studio sets are normally wider than they are deep, rectangular rather than square. Generally speaking, studio sets are shallow. And, of course, they are constructed of three walls rather than four, with the side walls occasionally splayed outward. The lack of a fourth wall, an aesthetic holdover from the theater, is further necessitated by the technological need to position two or three (or more) bulky cameras in front of the actors. The added width gives the camera operators room to maneuver sideways, allowing them to vary their camera positions, mostly along a line that, in a sense, forms the invisible fourth wall. In multiple-camera studio production, the cameras do not move forward or backwards very much because the closer they get to the actors, the more likely they will be within range of another camera behind them. As with the cameras, the actors also tend to move side-to-side, rather than up-and-back, because of the limited depth of the sets.

Figure 8.4 diagrams the main apartment in the sitcom *Frasier* (1993–2004)—as is shown in Figures 8.5 and 8.6.[1] The lateral orientation of the set for this multiple-camera production is quite evident. To the left is the door through which family and friends enter. From there we encounter the living room furniture (Figure 8.5). The dining table, kitchen, and a hallway are on the right (Figure 8.6). The function of this set is to permit free interaction among the main characters—three of whom live together. Although the movement on this set is predominantly side-to-side, there is a hallway to the bedroom on the left and a balcony in the back of the set that are occasionally incorporated.

The positioning of doors on the sides facilitates actors entering and exiting the room without obstructing or being obstructed by other actors. Aesthetic convention also holds that doors not be located "behind" the cameras on the invisible fourth wall. On television, characters never exit toward the cameras or enter from behind them. This shows, once again, the aesthetic influence of the theater, where such an entrance or exit would mean walking into or out of the audience. Television maintains the sense of our being behind the cameras and does not want to draw attention to us by having the characters walk directly toward us.

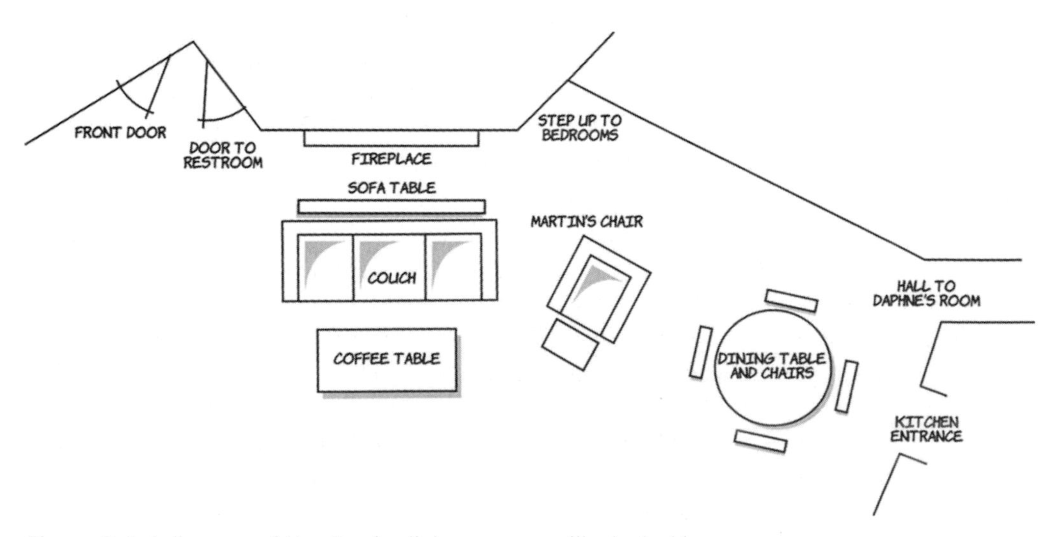

Figure 8.4 A diagram of the *Frasier* living room, as illustrated by…

Figure 8.5 ... a view toward the front door...

Figure 8.6 . . . and a view toward Daphne's bedroom.

The quick and easy entering/exiting of characters is important to all narrative programs, but it is especially significant to ones in which the narrative is segmented and interruptible. Soap opera is the pinnacle of this trend. Soap-opera characters are constantly coming, going, and being interrupted by other characters' entrances and exits. This is necessitated by the genre's frequently interrupted narrative structure. (Just when the two young lovers are about to consummate their romance, someone knocks on the door or the phone rings; more instances of coitus interruptus have appeared on soap opera than any other genre in narrative history.) Thus, a seemingly small detail like the position of the doors in a set's design fits into the overall narrative scheme of a genre. Set design follows narrative function.

These three-sided rectangular boxes are arrayed in specific fashion in television sound stages, depending on whether an audience is present while it is recorded. This economic/technological concern influences the size and shape of the sets, as well as the number of settings an episode will have. Narrative multiple-camera programs with studio audiences, such as *Frasier* or *The Big Bang Theory*, typically have room for only three (or at most four) sets, which are arranged next to one another, facing the audience (Figure 8.7). The program's main location, such as the *Frasier* living room, is usually placed in the center, so that most of the audience can see it well. In contrast, multiple-camera narrative programs *without* audiences are produced on sets parallel to one another, leaving the middle space open for cameras and other equipment. In the CBS studios in New York, two separate studios were dedicated to videotaping *As the World Turns* (1956–2010). Six to ten sets were put together every single day, although some of the more elaborate sets were left standing from one day to the next. They were positioned against the walls (Figure 8.8), with the video control room located right next door.

As you can readily see, multiple-camera programs would have great difficulty shooting on a set with a fourth wall, but single-camera programs have more flexibility in this regard. The single-camera show *ER* (1994–2009) was shot on highly elaborate four-wall sets that spanned two normally separate sound stages (see diagram at tvcrit.com/find/er).[2] Its spinning camera movements frequently revealed the presence of all four walls, and the camera would often travel through the corridors of the emergency room (see tvcrit.com/find/ermovement). In this case, as in most four-wall television sets, a set's walls could easily be removed to provide more room for cameras, lights, or cast or crew members. In industry parlance, directors ask grips to "wild out" walls when they need more space. And, of course, single-camera productions also have the option of shooting on locations in real, four-wall hospitals, homes, offices, and so on.

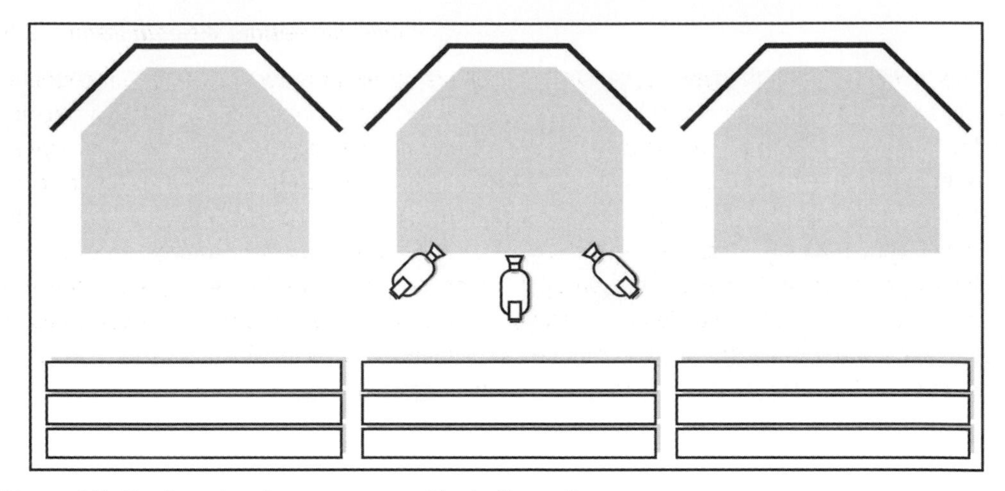

Figure 8.7 Studio setup for programs with studio audiences.

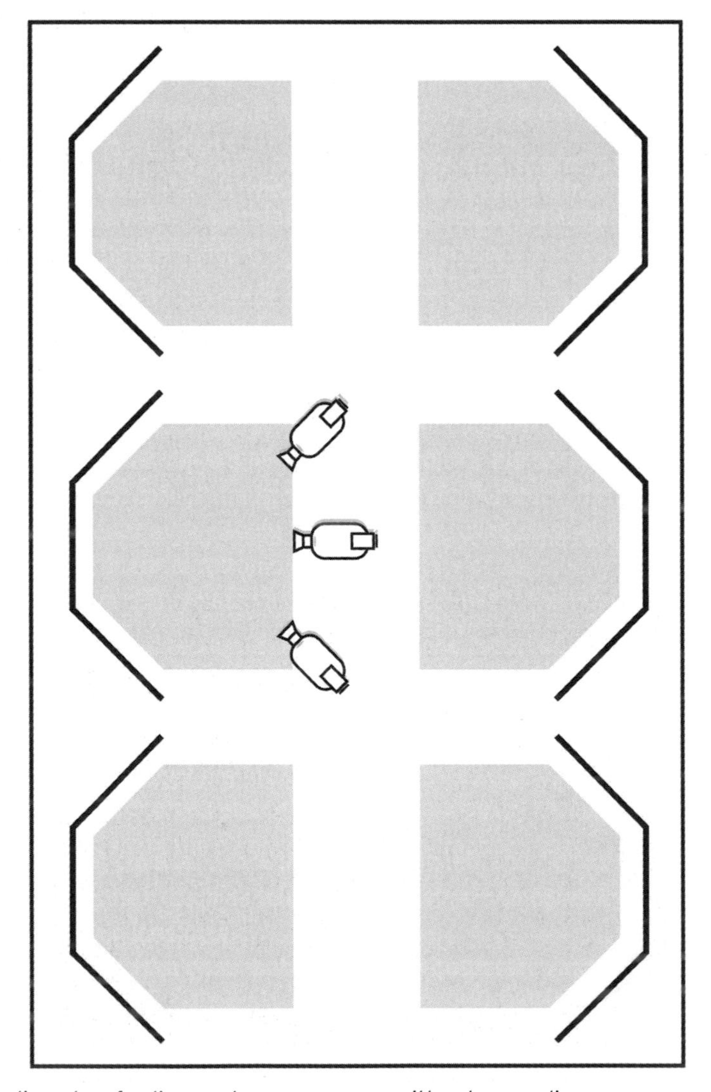

Figure 8.8 Studio setup for live-on-tape programs without an audience.

The economic reliance upon studio sets in multiple-camera productions has the aesthetic repercussion of limiting the stories to a very few locations: just three or four in a weekly sitcom, and seven or eight in the more narratively complicated daily soap opera. In a sense, stories must be written for the sets. Characters must be brought together in locations that are as much economically required as they are aesthetically determined. (This is also why when characters die or leave soap operas other characters often move into their homes.) And a large part of what they may do and what themes are presented is determined by where they are. Hospital sets are used to deal with issues of life, death, paternity, and maternity. Courtrooms house questions of justice. Private homes are the sites of intense personal and interpersonal emotions. In television programs, setting often determines story and theme, rather than vice versa.

Non-Narrative Studio Sets

Most non-narrative genres (e.g., news, sports programs, and game shows—discussed in Chapter 5) make a very different use of space than narrative programs do. This use of space aligns with a different way of addressing the viewer. Non-narrative programs seldom create the illusion of an everyday room, preferring instead to construct a space that more resembles that of non-narrative theater (that is, music and dance performances): a stylized presentational space that *directly* addresses the performance to us. Non-narrative programs do not create the illusion that we do not exist, but instead acknowledge us by performing toward us. The direct address of non-narrative television is evident in the way that the set design positions the spectacle for our entertainment. News desks and anchors face the cameras straight on (Figure 5.19). Game show hosts stand behind podiums that are aimed at the cameras (Figure 8.9). The furniture on talk show sets positions guest and host at approximately 30-degree angles to one another so they face the camera as much as each other—as in *The Late Show With Stephen Colbert* set (Figure 8.10). In short, the set design of non-narrative programs is emblematic of the form of address they use.

The studio sets we see on newscasts, game shows, talk shows, musical variety programs, and the like follow different conventions than those of narrative television. Within each non-narrative genre, the conventions of set design are often quite rigid. What follows is a sampling of the various non-narrative set designs and is not meant to be exhaustive.

Figure 8.9 Bob Eubanks at the podium of *The New Newlywed Game*.

Figure 8.10 Stephen Colbert, behind a conventional desk, interviews Kumail Nanjiani on *The Late Show*.

Figure 8.11 On the set of the *CBS Evening News*, anchor Anthony Mason is dwarfed by enormous video displays, one of which purports to show a newsroom.

The sets of most local news and many network/cable news broadcasts include some form of desk behind which the anchors sit. The desk implies that these are busy, working journalists, pausing briefly from tracking down leads to pass a few tidbits on to the viewer. Behind them, on many news sets, is a newsroom (actual or digital) that re-emphasizes the earnestness of their journalistic mission (Figure 8.11). These newsroom sets stress the up-to-the-minute nature of TV news, as if one of the worker drones in the background might hand the anchor a news flash at any moment. Adding to the illusion of immediacy are video screens into which reporters on location may insert remote segments at that moment.

The mise-en-scene of game shows is one of the few that regularly incorporates members of the audience, social actors, into it (see Chapter 5). Consequently, the sets of many game shows play up the audience's presence by incorporating the audience area into what still might be called the performance area. As the difference between spectator and performer blurs, so does the demarcation between audience space and performance space. This is particularly evident in *The Price Is Right*, where host Drew Carey draws the competitors from the audience (Figures 4.4-4.6). These competitors function as our surrogates, pulling us into the action in a way that is possible in few other television genres. The program's set design confirms this alliance.

Other conventions of the game show set include some form of scoreboard, a space for contestants, and a podium for the host. Beyond that, each program must develop some distinctive contest, which may be represented in visual terms: for example, *Wheel of Fortune* (1975-) contestants spin an oversized roulette wheel and a woman in evening wear reveals letters forming a phrase by touching blocks in a frame (Figures 8.12 and 8.13). Surrounding the game itself may be a visible studio audience and a broad assortment of neon-bright colors and on-stage lights—unlike most other genres, where the audience and studio lights are hidden from view. In Figure 8.14, from *The Price Is Right*, we see the audience from the host's perspective and the camera is pointed directly at the lights. In this shot, the lights cause a distortion, known as a lens flare—drawing attention to themselves. Similarly, the set design of *Who Wants to Be a Millionaire* emphasizes lights above and below the host and the contestants and even reveals part of the structure that appears to support the lights (Figure 8.15). Obviously, these swirls of light and color signify excitement and heighten competitive tension. They also re-emphasize the value of winning and the glamorous validity of competition.

Many talk show sets have inherited the desk from television news—as we can see in Figure 8.10 from *The Late Show* (tvcrit.com/find/nanjiani). In this instance the desk provides a boundary between guest and host and further establishes the authority of the host over the guests, who do not get their own desks and, on *The Tonight Show*, must eventually share a couch with other guests. Additional areas of the set establish separate, *theatrical* spaces for performances by the hosts and visiting musicians and comics (Figure 8.16; tvcrit.com/find/monologue). Thus, set design facilitates the talk show's two main functions: conversation and performance.

Location Set Selection

Most sports programs and news events (or **actualities**) are recorded on location. The reason for this is obvious enough: sports and news activities occur out in historical reality, where the newscasters "capture" them for us (see Chapter 5). Not all parts of historical reality are equally

Figure 8.12 Contestants and the host stand behind the iconic wheel on the set of *Wheel of Fortune*.

Figure 8.13 Letters are revealed as part of the game play on *Wheel of Fortune*.

Figure 8.14 The lighting grid above the set is revealed in *The Price Is Right*...

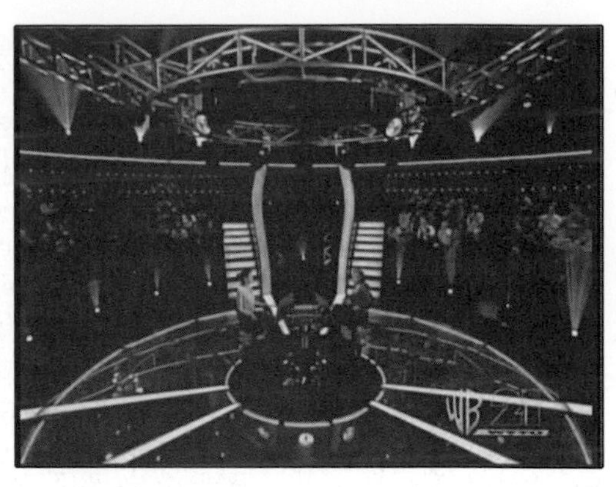

Figure 8.15 . . . and *Who Wants to Be a Millionaire*.

Figure 8.16 Stephen Colbert emerges from behind the desk to perform the monologue on *The Late Show*.

significant, however. Some settings are invisible to television. Why? Either they are taken for granted and are not considered important enough for TV (e.g., the inside of a factory, unless there's a strike or an industrial accident); or they are officially banned by the government (e.g., battlefields during wartime); or they are censored by television itself (e.g., a gay bar). Missing from television's location settings are the ideologically safe (that which is so "normal" it has no meaning) and the ideologically dangerous (that which is so "abnormal" or threatening it must be contained and censored).

There are certain television sports and news settings, or types of settings, that recur over and over again and acquire meaning from this repetition. In sports, for example, the center court stadium at Wimbledon carries specific connotations of British royalty, wealth, and class status, in addition to the tennis competition. The mud-and-crushed-cars setting of a monster truck competition carries a whole separate set of connotations.

Television news also makes pointed use of iconography. Figure 8.17 is a shot of reporter Kris van Cleave standing before a significant news scene, the Phoenix airport during a heat wave so intense that planes were grounded. This denotes, first, that "he is really there," and, second, that the information he is giving us must be true because he is at the scene and has witnessed something personally. Thus, setting is typically used in TV news to validate the authenticity of the report. Further, when local newscasters present themselves standing on the site of a murder or car crash or the like, it is usually hours after the event has taken place. The event itself

Figure 8.17 Noticeably sweaty reporter Kris van Cleave's position at the site of a news event lends credibility to his report about a heat wave in Phoenix. His attire is notably less formal than the anchor's.

cannot be shown, so its setting is used to stand in for it, to certify that it really took place and that it really happened as the reporter is telling us it happened. Setting thus becomes a guarantor of television's **verisimilitude**–its illusion of truth and reality–and it helps authenticate the reporter's interpretation of the event.

Sports and news programs are not the only television shows that shoot on location, however. Many narrative programs also use location settings. Although most multiple-camera sitcoms and soap operas do not usually record shows on location (except during "sweeps weeks," when ratings are taken), single-camera dramas and comedies frequently shoot outside the studio walls. Mostly, this location shooting is used for outdoor, **exterior** scenes. Indoor, **interior** scenes are still shot on studio sets, except in rare circumstances. Location setting in narrative programs is used, as in news, to heighten television's sense of verisimilitude, of being "true to reality." Police and crime programs, for instance, are prone to location shooting to authenticate the realism of the show. *Law & Order* (1990-2010) would strike us as "phony" if the exterior scenes were shot on a studio lot. However, verisimilitude isn't the only motivating factor in the use of location settings in narrative programs. Narrative, like the news, makes extensive use of the preestablished iconography of the real world. *Miami Vice* is a particularly good example of this. The program's opening credits consist of a collage of Miami sights (and sites) and thus play on our associations with the city: Cuban culture, money, power, overheated sexuality, potential violence, and so on (Figures 8.18-8.20). *Ironside* (1967-75); *Hawaii Five-O* (1968-80; 2010-); *The Streets of San Francisco* (1972-77); and *Magnum, P.I.* (1980-88) are among the other police/detective programs that draw upon the iconography of a particular location. And, since 2002, the potency of the Miami milieu has been exploited once again in *CSI: Miami* (2002-12). Thus, setting–whether constructed or selected–is not iconographically neutral. It always has the potential to contribute meaning to the narrative or the program's theme.

Figure 8.18 The imagery of *Miami Vice*'s opening credits draws on the city's reputation for exoticism...

Figure 8.19 ... sexuality...

Figure 8.20 ... and wealth.

Costume Design

In narrative television, costume design is closely allied with set design. Just as props and backgrounds are objective correlatives or icons designed to establish character, so are the clothes a character wears. Sonny Crockett's Armani suit, pastel T-shirt, Aviator sunglasses (*Miami Vice*), Columbo's distinctively rumpled trench coat (Peter Falk on *Columbo* [1971–77]), B.A.'s copious jewelry (Mr. T on *The A-Team* [1983–87]), and even Eric's hat and Kenny's snow parka (*South Park* [1997–]) help construct the characters who wear them (Figures 8.21, 8.22, 8.23, 8.24, respectively). Costume is one of the first aspects of a character that we notice and upon which we build expectations. It is a significant part of the program's narrative system. Detective Columbo was so clearly identified by his iconography that ads for a Columbo made-for-TV movie needed only ask rhetorically: "How many detectives can catch a killer with nothing but a trench coat and a cigar? Only one. Peter Falk in the role he made famous... *Columbo: Ashes to Ashes* [2000] on ABC."

Costume design is not limited to narrative television. News and sports have their own coded conventions of appropriate dress. Sports teams are the most regimented, with their uniforms identifying both which side of the conflict they are on and what their position within that conflict is (e.g., football players' uniforms are numbered according to the positions they play). The dress of sportscasters is practically as regimented as the players', with men wearing the inevitable

Figure 8.21 The nature of a character can be conveyed through an Armani suit (Sonny Crockett on *Miami Vice*)...

Figure 8.22 . . . a trench coat (Columbo on *Columbo: Ashes to Ashes*)...

Figure 8.23 ...jewelry (Mr. T on *The A-Team*)...

Figure 8.24 . . . or a snow parka (Kenny on *South Park*).

blazer and women dressed in modified blazers or some variation on the businesswoman's suit. In news there is a sharp demarcation between the formal business dresses and suits of the anchorwomen and men and the less formal dress of the reporters in the field (Figure 8.17). The studied "informality" of the field reporters (appearing without ties, in casual attire, sometimes with a reporter's notebook in hand; or wearing fatigues while covering international incidents) signifies that they are the ones in the trenches, digging stories out by any means necessary.

Lighting Design

In the early years of television, camera technology dictated that sets be broadly and brightly lit. Because the early TV cameras were not very sensitive to light, a huge amount of illumination was necessary to transmit the simplest image. Consequently, TV cameras could only broadcast images of outdoor scenes in direct sunlight or indoor scenes under powerful studio lights. Today, however, cameras are much more sensitive, which presents videographers with the ability to manipulate lighting to serve a variety of functions. No longer is it a matter of simply getting enough light on the set; now lighting may be used to develop mood or tone and contribute to the telling of a story. In some instances, the videographer/cinematographer may even "paint with light" and create an image of pictorial beauty for its own sake.[3]

The Characteristics of Light

There are four basic characteristics or properties of light in television: *direction*, *intensity*, *color*, and *diffusion* (or *dispersion*).

Lighting Direction and Intensity

Probably the most significant lighting characteristic is the direction in which the light is shining. Lighting direction has long been used to imply aspects of a character. Underlighting (the light source below the subject) has suggested a rather sinister character in hundreds of horror and suspense television programs. In Figure 8.25, from *Buffy the Vampire Slayer* (1997–2003), the innocent schoolgirl appearance of Darla (Julie Benz) is undermined by eerie lighting. She is, of course, a vampire. Backlighting may be used to mask a killer's identity or imply a generally enigmatic situation. In the case of *CSI: Miami*, backlighting is just one of several visual techniques utilized by its directors and cinematographers to construct a mysterious atmosphere where even the motives of its crime scene investigators are sometimes obscure (Figure 8.26). The variation of lighting position derives much of its significance from its deviation from a conventional norm of lighting known as **three-point lighting**.

Figure 8.25 Eerie underlighting of Darla in *Buffy the Vampire Slayer*.

Figure 8.26 Backlighting silhouettes the actors and adds to the mystery of *CSI: Miami*.

Three-point lighting is yet another part of the legacy that television inherited from the cinema. According to this aesthetic convention, an actor (or object) should be lit from three points or sources of light of varying intensity: the **key light**, the **fill light**, and the **back light** (Figure 8.27). Steven DiCasa, co-founder of Rethink Films, offers a *Three Point Lighting Tutorial* that usefully illustrates these three "points" of light (tvcrit.com/find/3point and www.Rethink-Films.com). The key light is the main source of illumination, the most intense light on the set. Normally, it is positioned at an oblique angle to the actor's face—not directly in front or directly to the side. And, as in all three points of light, it is above the actor's head and several feet in front. When DiCasa lights himself with a single source—as in Figure 8.28—there are deep shadows on the right side of his face; and these, in conventional television, are thought to be unsightly. Consequently, he adds a second source of illumination to fill the shadows (Figure 8.29). This fill light

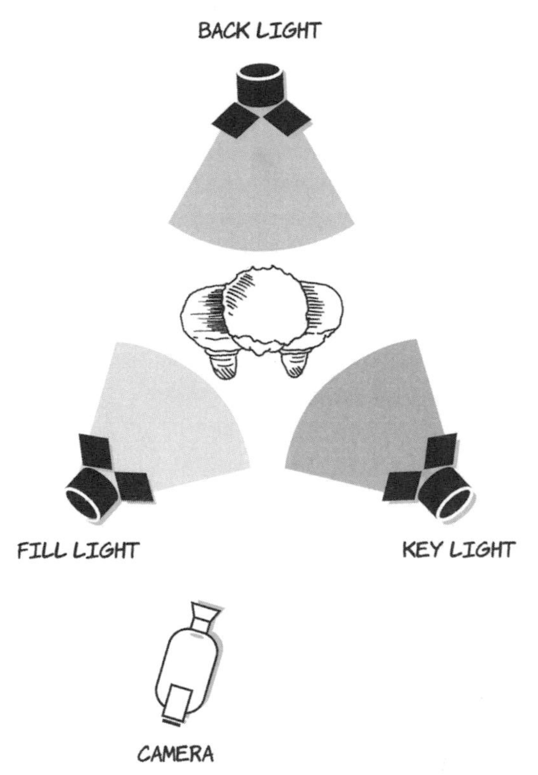

Figure 8.27 Three-point lighting: key light, fill light, and back light.

Figure 8.28 Steven DiCasa, co-founder of Rethink Films, is illuminated with a key light only—no fill or back lights. (Used with permission.)

Figure 8.29 A second light fills in most, but not all, of the shadows cast by the key light. (Used with permission.)

Figure 8.30 DiCasa is illuminated with all three lights. (Used with permission.)

is directed obliquely toward DiCasa from the opposite side of the key light, at approximately the same height (or a little lower), and is roughly half as bright as the key light. Ideally, this light fills in some, but not all of the shadows cast by the key light. When key and fill lights are equal in intensity, a bland, washed-out image is the result. To complete the three-point set-up, DiCasa places one more light, the back or rim light, behind and above himself (Figure 8.30). Its main function is to illuminate his head and shoulders, creating an outline of light around him. This outline helps to distinguish him from the background. With key, fill, and back lights in place, the three-point set-up is complete.

On any particular studio set, three-point lighting is achieved with more than just three lights. A **lighting plot** (a diagram of the position of lights on a set) for *Mad Men* reveals that cinematographer Chris Manley used at least ten different types of lights and arrayed dozens of them over the space of the Drapers' home (see tvcrit.com/find/mmlighting). Still, the basic principle of one main source of illumination, one source filling in shadows, and one source backlighting the actors dominates *Mad Men* and all television production. For example, Joan (Christina Hendricks), in our example of a studio set with a ceiling, is presented in three-point lighting (Figure 8.3). Indeed, this lighting principle exists in programs as diverse as prime-time dramas, multiple-camera sitcoms, and local news broadcasts. This norm is so accepted, so taken for granted, that any deviation from it—such as underlighting or sidelighting—seems odd and, more important, communicates meaning to us about the characters.

Two related lighting styles earn their names from the key light: **high-key lighting** and **low-key lighting**.

High-key lighting means that the set is very evenly lit, as in most scenes from 1960s sitcoms such as *The Dick Van Dyke Show* (1961–66). Even though Figure 8.31 is from a shot that occurs at night, the lighting is still bright and even. In other words, the difference between the bright areas of the set and the dark areas is very little; there is a low contrast between bright and dark. High-key lighting is achieved by pumping up the fill light(s) so that the key light is comparatively weaker. Consequently, none of the shadows cast by the key light are very dark. One odd example of this in Figure 8.33 is the shadow cast by the table lamp in the scene. Clearly, this lamp is providing very little of the illumination on the set! It even blocks a bit of a key light, but the shadow it casts is not pitch black because the fill lights are so strong.

Figure 8.31 High-key lighting in a nighttime scene in *The Dick Van Dyke Show*. Note the shadow cast by the lamp shade.

Figure 8.32 Low-key lighting in the music video *Only You*.

Figure 8.33 The lighting in Rembrandt van Rijn's *The Nightwatch* is a prime example of chiaroscuro.

Most talk shows, game shows, soap operas, and sitcoms use high-key lighting (examples include Figures 8.5, 8.6, 8.9, 8.10, 8.12, 8.13). The economic decision to shoot these programs in the multiple-camera mode of production (which, remember, is cheaper than film-style single-camera shooting) leads to the technological necessity of high-key lighting. When several cameras are shooting at the same time, the lighting needs to be fairly even so that different camera angles are fully illuminated. In addition, such programs as sports and game shows, which allow for unpredictable figure movements by social actors, need a broadly lit stage so that people do not disappear into the darkness.

These economic and technological imperatives result in an aesthetics of high-key. As the norm, high-key lighting comes to signify normalcy, stasis, equilibrium. Variations on high-key lighting—specifically, low-key lighting—result in alternative meanings: abnormalcy, dynamism, disequilibrium.

Low-key lighting means that there is a high contrast between bright and dark areas, that the bright areas are very bright and the dark areas are very dark. In Figure 8.32, from the music video *Only You*—performed by Portishead and directed by Chris Cunningham—the image has brightly lit areas (the boy's face) that contrast strongly with very dark areas (the shadows on his neck and behind him). To achieve low-key lighting such as this, the key light must be comparatively stronger than the fill light, so that the bright areas are especially bright. As you can see in Figure 8.34, Cunningham has chosen not to fill in the shadows at all; they remain pitch black. However, the key light is still intense. Low-key lighting style often has shafts of light cutting through dark backgrounds—a style that also goes by the name of **chiaroscuro** when applied to theatrical productions or Rembrandt van Rijn's dark paintings (e.g., *The Nightwatch*, 1642; Figure 8.33).[4]

If high-key lighting is associated with normalcy, then low-key represents oppositional values: deviance, even social rupture. On TV, it is linked to criminal elements or the supernatural and is commonly used in enigmatic music videos like *Only You*, as well as detective, suspense, and mystery programs. You can see low-key lighting at work in numerous episodes of *Buffy the Vampire Slayer*—including the one noted on p. 212. Director Scott Brazil selects low-key lighting and a light source splintered by Venetian blinds to illuminate a scene in which Buffy (Sarah Michelle Gellar) speaks with Angel (David Boreanaz), not yet knowing that he is a (redeemed) vampire (Figure 8.34 and 8.35).

Lighting Color

Light may be colored by placing a **filter** or **gel** (short for "gelatin") in front of a light source. Colored light is used to convey different moods (say, blue light for sorrow) and times of day (orange tints for morning, blue for twilight) in narrative television, but principally it is used in

Figure 8.34 Buffy the Vampire Slayer: Buffy's face is half in darkness, and shadows from Venetian blinds cross her chest as she talks to Angel...

Figure 8.35 ... who is similarly lit.

stylized set designs for game shows and music videos. Otherwise, colored light is too great a deviation from the norm for use in conventional programs.

Lighting Diffusion

On an overcast day, when the sun's rays are diffused through the clouds, the shadows that are cast have indistinct, blurred outlines. In television, this form of illumination is called **soft light**. It is often used to make actors look younger or more vulnerable. Figure 8.32, used previously to exemplify low-key lighting, is also an example of soft light. Note how the bright areas of the boy's face blend into the dark areas. This blending or blurring is typical of soft light. **Hard light**, in contrast, is illustrated by direct, undiffused sunlight and the harsh, distinct shadows it casts. You may see this exemplified in outdoor scenes, such as those on *American Chopper* (see Figures 5.10 and 5.11). Figure 5.11 further emphasizes the harshness of sunlight because it lacks any fill light. Also, shots that are illuminated by a single light mounted on the camera itself, as is common in the nighttime footage on *Cops* (Figure 8.36), can be very hard. Hard light's use is not limited to non-narrative television, however. Narrative TV commonly uses hard light to emphasize characters' toughness and invulnerability—turning their faces into impenetrable masks. Returning to the episode from *Buffy the Vampire Slayer* mentioned above, we find an evil demon named the Master (Mark Metcalf) plotting to destroy Buffy. A hard, harsh light emphasizes every wrinkle and pock mark in his face and makes his eyes appear to be hollow sockets (Figure 8.37).

Actor Movement

Chapter 5 discussed the basics of performance in television. Now let's add a few thoughts about how actors are incorporated as part of the mise-en-scene, how they are moved around the set by the director. In the theater this pattern of movement around a set is known as **blocking**.

In blocking a scene, the director must first take into consideration the position of the cameras and the layout of the set. How can the actors be positioned in such a fashion as to best reveal them to the camera(s) recording them?

Since the sets are typically fairly shallow in most multiple-camera studio productions, the actors usually move side-to-side, rather than up-and-back (see Figure 8.4, from *Frasier*.). The cameras are positioned where the fourth wall would be, pointed obliquely at the set, in indoor

Figure 8.36 Hard light may illuminate scenes in both non-narrative (*Cops*)...

Figure 8.37 ... and narrative (*Buffy the Vampire Slayer*) programs.

Figure 8.38 A scene from *Young Sheldon* is blocked in deep space, but shallow focus. Tam (foreground) tries to convince Sheldon to come to a party while behind him, out of focus, his sister, Missy, eagerly agrees.

Figure 8.39 When Sheldon exits the frame, the focus shifts, or pulls, from him back to her.

scenes. Consequently, actors' movements tend to be at angles to the cameras as they move laterally side-to-side—in this **shallow space**.

Deep space blocking, in contrast, is not commonly used on multiple-camera shows such as *Frasier*, with their shallow studio sets. However, single-camera programs shot without studio audiences have much more flexibility in both set design and blocking and may, at times, emphasize the depth of a set by positioning actors in front of one another. Consider a scene from *Young Sheldon* (2017–), which is a single-camera production that was spun off a multiple-camera show, *The Big Bang Theory* (Figure 8.38). In this scene, director Chris Koch placed the camera behind Tam (Ryan Phuong), looking over his shoulder through the bedroom window of Sheldon (Iain Armitage) and his sister, Missy (Raegan Revord). We see Tam and Sheldon standing at the window in the foreground, with Missy several feet behind them, in her bed in the background. Tam wants Sheldon to sneak out of his house and join him at a party. Sheldon hesitates, but his sister enthusiastically agrees. Once Sheldon is convinced to go and exits the frame, the focus shifts back to Missy as she excitedly exclaims, "I need a minute to change" (Figure 8.39). Thus, the director has used deep-space blocking to counterpoint the moods of the characters in the foreground and background.

Deep space blocking normally uses **deep focus**, where the entire image is in focus (see Figure 9.12, discussed in the next chapter). However, deep space will occasionally be used without deep focus, rendering one or more of the actors out of focus—as in Figure 8.38, where both Tam and Missy are blurry. As you can see, deep space and deep focus, though often confused, are independent of one another. It is entirely possible for directors to position actors in depth on a set, but still throw some elements out-of-focus.

Summary

Every television program has a mise-en-scene that communicates meaning to the viewer—meaning that may be understood before a single line of dialogue or news copy is spoken. Mise-en-scene contributes to the narrative system of fiction programs, the informational system of news and sports programs, and the persuasive system of commercials. It is shaped by the needs of these systems and by other economic, technological, and aesthetic concerns.

The frugality of studio shooting has led to a specific style of setting that caters to the technological demands of multiple-camera production. Three-walled, ceilingless studio sets form the backdrop for game shows, soap operas, news programs, sitcoms, and the like. In each of these types of programs, the studio setting performs a slightly different function—heightening competition in game shows, signifying journalistic ethics in news programs, and helping construct characters in narrative programs. Location settings play the additional role of signifying verisimilitude—the illusion of reality—in both news and narrative programs.

Costuming is closely linked with set design. Both are aspects of the program's iconography—the objects that signify character and theme.

Most of television's settings and costumes are illuminated in high-key, three-point lighting. But there are important deviations from that style. Each of the main properties of light (its direction, intensity, color, and diffusion) can be manipulated in order to contribute to the narrative or the mood of a program. In low-key or chiaroscuro lighting, for instance, the relative intensities of the light sources are varied to create a high-contrast image of bright light and dark shadow.

Mise-en-scene was originally a theatrical term. Converting it for use in television studies, we must keep in mind that the mise-en-scene of TV is experienced only through the camera; hence it must be designed explicitly for that purpose. This technological parameter thus governs all aesthetic designs of setting, costuming, lighting, and actor movement. The particulars of the camera's recording and transformation of mise-en-scene are detailed in Chapter 9.

Notes

1 The DVD of *Frasier*'s first season includes photographs of the apartment set.
2 Carly Reichert, "TV's Hit ER: Learning How It's Made," *TCNJ Magazine*, Spring 2004, tvcrit.com/find/er, accessed June 21, 2017.
3 Patrick Keating argues that classical film lighting can be categorized into four, sometimes overlapping, functions: "storytelling, realism, pictorial quality, and glamour." *Hollywood Lighting: From the Silent Era to Film Noir* (New York: Columbia University Press, 2010), 6.
4 Public domain image acquired from Wikimedia Commons, tvcrit.com/find/nightwatch, Provided by user Alonso de Mendoza, February 27, 2016, accessed June 22, 2017.

Further Readings

Mise-en-scene is discussed in many of the handbooks for television production suggested at the end of Chapter 6. In addition, Karen Lury, *Interpreting Television* (London: Hodder Arnold, 2005) makes interesting points about mise-en-scene as she distinguishes between "space" and "place." John Gibbs, *Mise-en-Scène: Film Style and Interpretation* (London: Wallflower, 2002) argues for the significance of mise-en-scene, but his definition of the term is considerably broader than ours—including, as it does, aspects of the camera.

Jane Barnwell, *Production Design: Architects of the Screen* (London: Wallflower, 2004) provides a useful overview of the work of the production designer and the power of sets to communicate meaning. Terry Byrne, *Production Design for Television* (Boston: Focal Press, 1993) is more of a how-to book, but it does specify many of the conventions of set and lighting design in TV. Several books deal exclusively with lighting, including Blain Brown, *Motion Picture and Video Lighting*, 2nd ed. (Boston: Focal Press, 2007); and Dave Viera and Maria Viera, *Lighting for Film and Digital Cinematography*, 2nd ed. (Belmont, CA: Wadsworth, 2005). The specifics of lighting during the classical cinema are assayed in Patrick Keating, *Hollywood Lighting: From the Silent Era to Film Noir* (New York: Columbia University Press, 2010). Keating examines the conventions of classical lighting and how they were established, but he goes beyond description to discuss the functions these conventions served and the discourse, the talk, about them in trade publications and elsewhere.

9 Style and the Camera

Videography and Cinematography

When we look at television, our gaze is controlled by the "look" of the camera. What the camera "saw" on the set or on location during a production, we now see on our television screens. The camera's distance from the scene and the direction in which it is pointed, among other factors, determine what we will see in a television image. In essence, our look becomes the camera's look and is confined by the frame around the image. To understand the camera's look, it becomes necessary to understand the aesthetic, economic, and technological factors that underpin the camera's perfunctory gaze.

The camera, although a mechanical reproducing device, does not neutrally reproduce images. The camera fundamentally changes the objects it reproduces: three dimensions become two; the colors of nature become the colors of video or film; the perimeter of the camera frame delimits the view. The reproduction process of film and video could more accurately be thought of as one of translation, where the three-dimensional physical world is translated into the two-dimensional "language" of television images. This camera language is a major part of the visual style of a television program. It works in conjunction with mise-en-scene (Chapter 8) and editing (Chapter 10) to create a program's overall visual design.

This chapter concerns the components of camera style, the elements of **videography** and **cinematography** that record an image and affect our understanding of it. In simplest terms, videography designates the characteristics of the video camera, while cinematography refers to those of the film camera. The person overseeing the video camera is the **videographer**; the corresponding person in charge of the film camera is the **cinematographer**. However, in these days of digital recording of the moving image, the distinction between videography/videographer and cinematography/cinematographer has become blurred. In any event, in a television production the videographer/cinematographer in charge of visual design is generally referred to and credited as the **director of photography** (**DP**). In years past, the distinction between the visual quality of videography and cinematography was quite obvious, and video was a visually inferior format. But advances in digital video technology in the twenty-first century have erased this distinction. Ever since George Lucas's decision to shoot *Star Wars Episode II: Attack of the Clones* (2002) in digital video, the film and TV industries have evolved toward all-digital processes for recording, editing, and presenting moving images—whether viewed in a movie theater, on a home TV screen, or on a cell phone. Today, a few diehard film devotees do persist in shooting on film, but, essentially, the digital-video revolution has arrived.

DPs typically leave the actual handling of the camera to the **camera operator**, who is not credited as a full-fledged DP. We will here use the abbreviation "DP" to refer to the person most responsible for designing a program's camera style, while "camera operator" will denote the work of the person handling the camera. In any event, both operate under the guidance of the program's **director**. The director is the architect of the program's overall style of image and sound, with the DP working within the specific province of camera style.

On the most basic level, camera-style characteristics are shaped by technological considerations. For instance, one could not have recorded videographic images in the 1890s, before video was invented. But we should be wary of overemphasizing the importance of technology. As we have seen in our discussion of mise-en-scene in Chapter 8, the ways that camera technologies have been used are always shaped by aesthetic convention and economic determinants. The aesthetic conventions of composition in European oil painting, for example, greatly influence the composition of TV images. And economics often determines the resolution at which video will be recorded, since higher resolution cameras are more expensive. Thus, technology, aesthetics, and economics merge together in determining camera style. To fully understand camera style we must remain alert to each of these three counterbalancing elements.

Basic Optics: The Camera Lens

The earliest "camera," the **camera obscura** as it was named in the seventeenth century, had no lens at all. It was merely a large, darkened room with a hole in one wall. ("Camera" is Latin for chamber or room.) Light entered through that hole and created an image of the outdoors on the wall opposite the hole. Very little could be done by way of manipulating that image. Today's camera lens, the descendant of the camera obscura's hole-in-a-wall, permits a variety of manipulations—a catalog of optical controls that the camera operator may exercise.

Chief among these optical controls is **focal length**. One need not be a physicist to understand focal length, although sometimes it seems like it. The focal length of a lens, usually measured in millimeters, is the distance from the lens's optical center to its **focal point**, which is that spot where the light rays bent by the lens converge before expanding again and striking the film or electronic pickup at the **focal plane** (Figure 9.1). This definition, however, tells us very little about the images that result from lenses of different focal lengths. In more familiar terms, the three conventional types of focal length are:

1. wide angle (or short)
2. "normal" (or medium)
3. telephoto (or long or narrow).

The reader may already know these terms, but it is important to recognize the different and sometimes subtle effects these focal lengths have on the image.

The **wide-angle lens** gives the viewer a wide view of the scene, and it also heightens the **illusion of depth** in the image. All television images are two-dimensional, of course; there is no true depth to them. They have dimensions along only two axes: horizontal and vertical (left and right, up and down). Using principles of visual perspective, however, the television image creates an illusion of depth (back and forth). Because of this illusion, some objects seem to be in front of other objects; the space seems to recede into the image. A wide-angle lens increases that illusion of depth. Objects filmed with a wide-angle lens seem to be farther apart from one another than they do with normal or telephoto lenses. In Figure 9.2, which was shot with a wide-angle lens, the distance between the two arms of the park bench is stretched, giving the image an illusion of great depth—as if the arm in the rear of the image is far away from the one in the

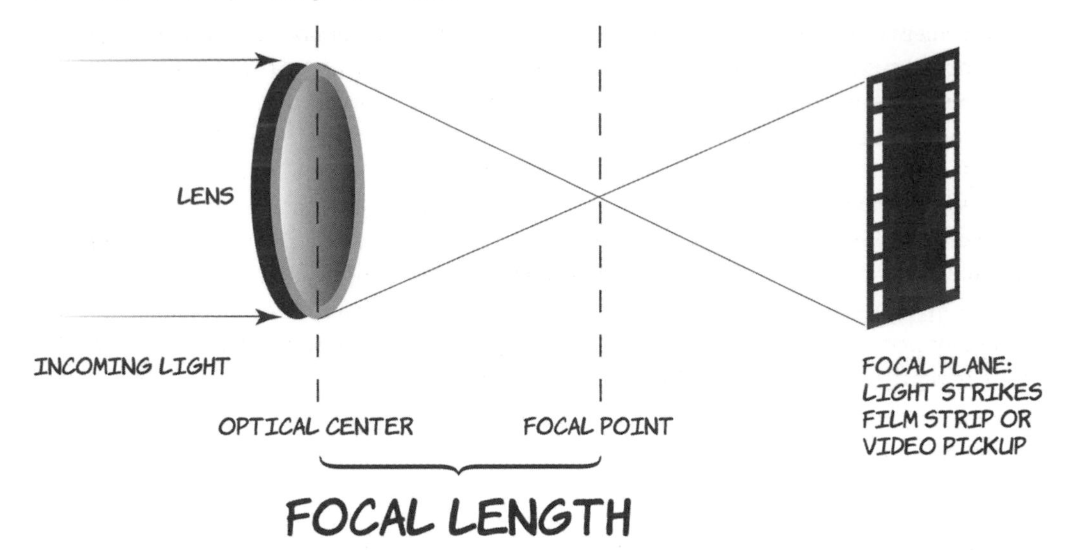

Figure 9.1 The physics of focal length.

Figure 9.2 A wide-angle focal length emphasizes the distance between the bench's armrests...

Figure 9.3 ... as can be seen when contrasted with a telephoto shot of the same scene. Now the armrests appear closer together.

foreground. Similarly, in Figure 5.12, from *Taxicab Confessions*, there appears to be a large space between the taxi driver in the front seat and her fare in the back seat.

The **telephoto lens** gives a narrower view of the scene than a wide-angle lens but magnifies the scene (brings it "closer"). In Figure 9.3 the same park bench as in Figure 9.2 has been shot with a telephoto lens. Compare how the distance between the arms of the bench appears. Just as the wide-angle lens heightens the illusion of depth, the telephoto lens diminishes it. Thus, the illusion of depth appears to be compressed in telephoto shots, and the arms of the bench seem to be much closer than in the wide-angle image. Telephoto lenses are widely used in sports coverage, to get a "closer" view of the action (see the baseball shot in Figures 5.20 and 5.21). The pitcher in Figures 5.20 and 5.21 appears to be much closer to the batter than he would to someone sitting in the bleachers because of the compression of depth by the telephoto lens. The longer the lens, the more compressed the depth will appear.

The so-called *normal* focal length lens is medium-sized in comparison to both wide angle and telephoto. This is the lens that has come to be accepted as "natural." However, the normal focal length does not actually approximate the human eye's range of vision (it's narrower) or illusion of depth (it's shallower). Rather, it creates an image that, to the Western world, seems correct because it duplicates that style of perspective developed during the Renaissance of the 1400s and 1500s. For instance, the courtyard rectangles receding into the distance in *Christ Handing the Keys to St. Peter*, a Sistine Chapel fresco created by Pietro Perugino 1481–82 (Figure 9.4), illustrate how Renaissance artists portrayed linear perspective—which differed markedly from previous methods of rendering depth in two-dimensional art.[1] Camera lenses that approximate Renaissance perspective have come to be accepted as the norm, while wide-angle and telephoto lenses are defined as deviations from that norm.

Film and video cameras may be supplied with individual lenses of different focal lengths. In the early years of television, three or four lenses were attached to the cameras in a turret mount that could be turned around (Figure 9.5). More commonly today, cameras come equipped with a **zoom lens**, which in optical terms is a *variable focal length* lens. With a zoom, one can shift immediately and continuously from wide angle to telephoto without switching lenses. To **zoom in** is to vary the focal length from wide angle to telephoto, getting increasingly "closer" to the object and narrowing your angle of view (Figures 9.6 and 9.7). To **zoom out**, in contrast, is to vary the focal length from telephoto to wide angle—thereby getting "farther" from the object as the angle of view widens. *Closer* and *farther* are misleading terms when referring to the zoom lens, however, because the camera does not get physically closer to or farther from the object it is recording. Thus, to be accurate, the zoom really just magnifies and de-magnifies the object. The point-of-view from which we see the object does not change.

A characteristic of the camera lens even more fundamental than focal length is its **focus**. On television, the image is nearly always in focus. Only perhaps in sports events do we see occasional out-of-focus images as the camera operator struggles to follow a fast-moving athlete. However, in most television images there are areas of the image that are not in focus, parts that have been left out of focus to de-emphasize them. Camera operators can selectively focus parts of the image and unfocus other parts. In other words, they can use focus for specific effect.

Figure 9.4 Linear perspective in Renaissance paintings such as *Christ Handing the Keys to St. Peter* became the basis for the modern norm of camera lenses.

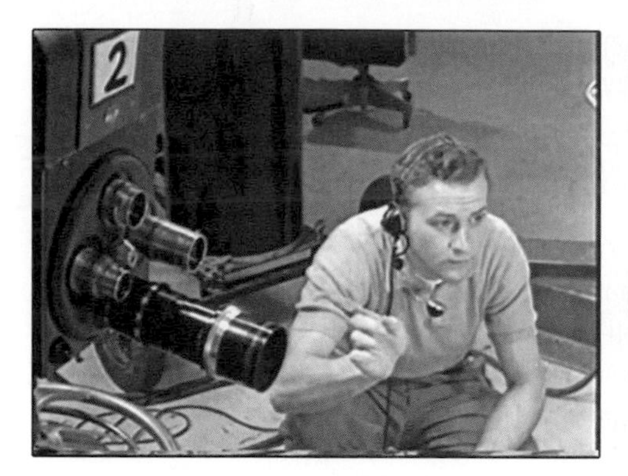

Figure 9.5 To achieve multiple focal lengths, early television cameras were equipped with several nonzooming lenses on a turret.

Figure 9.6 A wide-angle shot of a sculpture of a dove stands outside a blacksmith's shop.

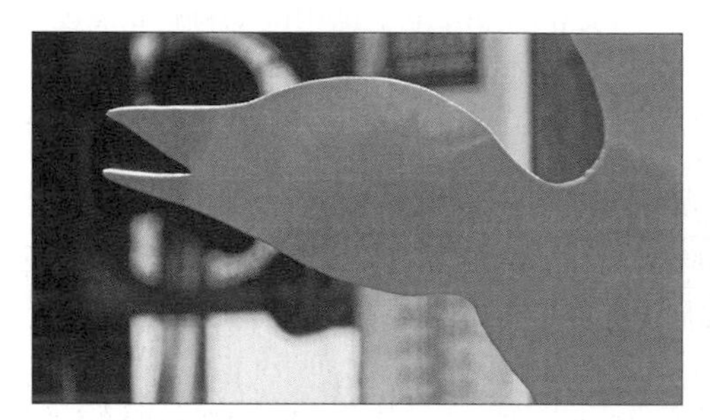

Figure 9.7 The difference between zooming in...

Figure 9.8 ... and tracking in can be seen by looking for the thermometer behind the sculpture. In the tracking shot, the bird's head conceals more of the thermometer, but we see more above and below it than in the zoom-in shot.

The selective use of focus is facilitated by the photographic phenomenon of **depth of field** (Figure 9.9). (Care should be taken not to confuse depth of field with the *illusion* of depth discussed on p. 221–23.) Depth of field is the distance in front and behind the **focus distance** that is also in focus (the focus distance being the distance from the camera to the object being focused on). If a lens is focused at 10 feet, as in Figure 9.9, some objects nearer to and farther from the camera will also be in focus. This range (say, 8 to 14 feet in this instance) is the depth of field. Typically, the range is approximately one-third in front of the focus distance and two-thirds behind it. The camera operator can manipulate depth of field to influence our perception of an image—decreasing the visual impact of parts of the frame by rendering them out of focus and indistinct. A small depth of field—so that *only* the foreground, middle ground, *or* background is sharply focused—is termed **shallow focus**. Moreover, camera operators can even control how the out-of-focus regions of images appear. For instance, are the fuzzy elements circular, with smooth edges; or angular, with harshly defined edges? The aesthetic look of these out-of-focus areas is referred to as the image's **bokeh** (pronounced "bow-keh," rhyming with "meh"), a term coined from the Japanese word for blur, *boke*.[2] Bokeh is perhaps more important for still images, where one might leisurely examine the quality of a picture's out-of-focus zones, than it is for motion images, where bokeh is typically viewed only briefly and in passing. And yet when a large portion of a TV image is out-of-focus (e.g., Figure 9.10), viewers cannot help but

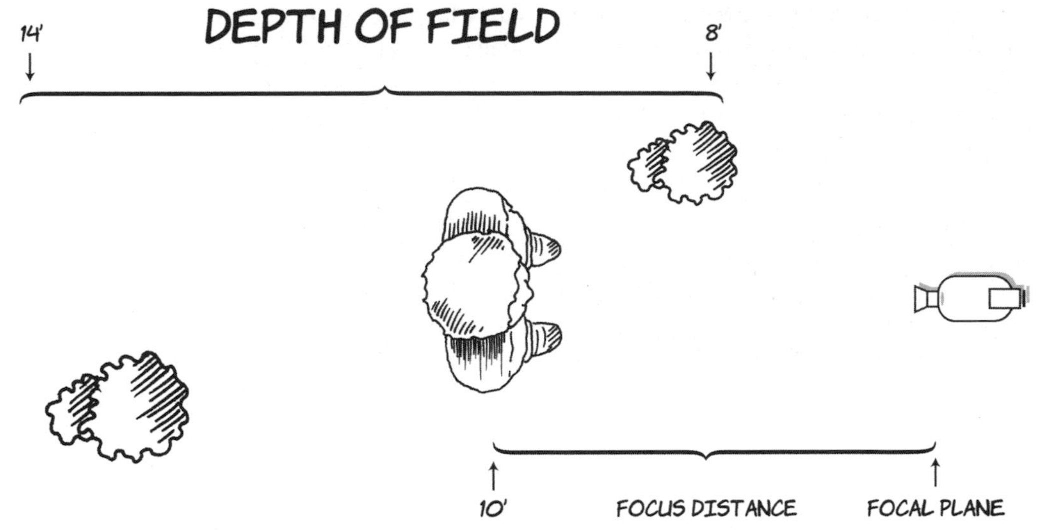

Figure 9.9 Depth of field is the range in front of and behind the distance at which the lens is focused. In this diagram, the focus is set at 10 feet, and the depth of field extends from 8 to 14 feet.

Figure 9.10 CSI: Crime Scene Investigation: A reassembled vase is sharply in focus and a book and lab technician (Wendy) behind it are out of focus until...

Figure 9.11 ... director Nathan Hope pulls focus past the book to Wendy, leaving the vase out of focus in the foreground.

be viscerally affected by the quality of its bokeh—although maybe only subconsciously or on an emotional level. (Further, cell phones have recently introduced bokeh effects into the portrait modes of their cameras.)

In Figure 9.10, from *CSI: Crime Scene Investigation* (2000–10), director Nathan Hope has placed a reconstructed vase in the foreground of the image (tvcrit.com/find/csifocus). Lab technician Wendy Glenn (Darcy Farrell) and a book behind the vase are illegibly out-of-focus. The shallow focus of this shot is then manipulated by shifting the focus from foreground to background, from the vase to the book to Wendy. This change of focus is known as **racking** or **pulling focus** (Figures 9.10 and 9.11), and in this case it is cued by Wendy's comments about a missing vase piece. As the shot develops, Hope uses even more rack focusing and some subtle camera movement to bring another character into the scene. As in this instance, rack focus is frequently used to conceal and reveal diegetic information and to add some visual interest to a shot without changing to a new camera position and revising the lighting setup (and costing the producers money).

Shallow focus sounds confusingly similar to **soft focus**. However, in a soft focus shot the entire image, not just a single plane within it, is slightly out of focus. Soft focus is often used in conjunction with special filters and lighting—and even Vaseline on the lens—to create an image that conventionally signifies romantic attraction, vulnerability, sweetness, or youthfulness (concealing wrinkles in an actor's face) in a character.

Focus does not have to be shallow or soft, however. In **deep focus** shots, all planes of the image are in focus—as in one shot from a *Mad Men* episode where deep focus enables the viewer to see Peggy (Elisabeth Moss) peeking in a window in the background while Don (Jon Hamm) has a moment of crisis in the foreground (Figure 9.12). The background establishes Peggy's spying on Don and her concern about him. Deep focus is often used in conjunction with deep space blocking, where background and foreground interact with one another—illustrated, also, by the shot from *Citizen Kane* discussed in Chapter 8 (Figure 8.2), where, as with this *Mad Men* shot, one character is visible outside a window in the background.[3] It's important to recognize, however, that deep *focus* is not absolutely necessary for deep *space*. In Chapter 8's *Young Sheldon* example, where a sister is in bed behind her brother, the space is deep, but the focus is shallow (Figures 8.38 and 8.39).

Deep focus has been heralded by film critic André Bazin as a major advance in the realism of the cinema. He argues that:

- deep focus is more like the human perception of reality (we mostly see the world in deep focus); and
- deep focus preserves the continuity of space by maintaining the visual connections between objects in their environments.

His principles are further explained and illustrated in an amusing online video essay by Majestic Micro Movies: tvcrit.com/find/deepfocus. Bazinian realism could also be applied to television (although his theories have had minimal impact on television aesthetics), but with caution. The smaller size of the television screen is a major impediment to deep-focus staging of action.

Figure 9.12 In deep focus and deep space, Peggy spies on Don in *Mad Men*.

The background actors/objects can become so small as to have negligible impact on the shot's meaning.

Image Definition and Resolution

The more clearly objects in an image appear and the more details one can discern in it, the higher that image's **definition** or resolution is said to be. **Film stocks**, **standard-definition** (**SD**) video, **high-definition** (**HD**) video, and various digital-video formats have different levels of clarity, and this clarity/definition/resolution can be manipulated for narrative, informational, or rhetorical effect. *The Blair Witch Project* (1999) and the *Paranormal Activity* film series (2007–15) are two examples from recent years of a filmmaker's decision to use low-resolution recording technologies (Hi8 digital video and black-and-white 16mm film in *The Blair Witch Project*; and degraded, "surveillance" digital video in *Paranormal Activity*) both to set a tone and to signify aspects of narrative. Digital video and 16mm film—along with underexposed shots, jittery, handheld camerawork, and surveillance angles—set the tone of these horror films by echoing the disturbing events in ragged, sometimes obscured imagery (Figure 9.13). And in *The Blair Witch Project* the technology signifies elements of the narrative by reinforcing the claims of the dialogue that this is the work of student filmmakers. In other words, the film's dialogue (falsely) tells us that students shot this footage and the degraded quality of the image itself confirms that. If the footage featured high-definition images and a slick, professional style, then it would contradict the dialogue. Similarly, in *Paranormal Activity* the low-quality, surveillance-style shooting tries to persuade us that this is "found" footage.

These two films use an intentionally low-quality image to mark the films as documentaries, but that is only one use to which image degradation can be put. To understand how variation in image quality can be manipulated and incorporated in television material, we must first consider some of the technological bases of both film and video. This gets us into a very complicated and highly technical area—one that is rapidly changing. We'll skim the surface here, but the reader should recognize that we've had to simplify the topic for the sake of readability. Still, we do offer a basic understanding of, first, how image quality can be manipulated by television

Figure 9.13 The Blair Witch Project uses low-quality images to suggest that this fiction film is a documentary—as is indicated by the washed-out facial features.

DPs and, second, how image quality is greatly affected by the transmission of television and the viewer's reception of it on some type of screen.

Nowadays, a television screen—if we define "television" loosely—could be just a few inches wide (a cell phone or tablet) or several feet wide (projected video in a theater), which obviously is going to have a major impact on the quality of the image. Thus, our discussion of image definition/resolution must account for both the *recorded* film/video image and the *transmission* and *reception* of that image. One thing that will become clear in our discussion is that video producers are in a difficult spot these days. They must record images that will be received on both small and large screens and need to look good on both—a seemingly impossible task. This contradictory impulse is certain to have an impact on twenty-first century television imagery, but no one yet knows what it will be.

Definition/Resolution of the Film Image

Although hardly any television is shot on actual film stock (the specific type of film) today, it's still useful to understand film resolution because so many network-era shows were shot on film (and still appear on TV) and because DPs sometimes manipulate digital video to give it a "film look." Film stock's resolution is primarily determined by the size of the **grain** on which the image is recorded. The grains are the silver halide crystals that swim around in the chemical soup, or emulsion, that is attached to the celluloid backing, or base, of a piece of film. In **fine-grain** film stocks the grain is smaller, less noticeable, and the definition is higher. Just how noticeable a film stock's grain is depends principally upon the width of the recording medium.

In general, smaller **format** film stocks are grainier than larger format stocks. (Format here refers to film width and is measured in millimeters.) Thus, of the three most common film formats—super-8, 16mm, and 35mm—the largest also has the finest grain, the highest definition. One might think therefore that 35mm's high definition would mean that it is the only film stock used in production for television. This is not the case. Both economic and aesthetic factors created specific niches for each of the formats. Inexpensive super-8 (and its immediate predecessor, "regular" 8mm) was the size of choice for home movie makers for over three decades—until the 1980s, when low-cost video cameras virtually destroyed the super-8 market. Documentary work, low-budget films, and some TV programs used 16mm film, although it has generally been replaced by digital-video formats of equivalent quality. And 35mm film long dominated filmmaking for theatrical movies, prime-time television programs, and national commercials, but its supremacy has been eclipsed by high-definition video formats. Super-8 and 16mm—with their noticeably higher grain levels—are still used to achieve particular effects. For example, the fuzzy, high-grain images of a 1960s family that are used in the credit sequence for *The Wonder Years* (1988–93) denote "home movies" and connote nostalgia for a bygone era. (Those scenes were shot in super-8 or 16mm, while the rest of the program was shot in 35mm.) Blurry, high-grain images—particularly black-and-white images—are also used to connote "documentariness" in *The Blair Witch Project* and fiction television programs. Further, they have appeared in many music videos and commercials to convey a raw or unpolished look.

Definition/Resolution of the Video Image

High-definition video was part of a massive overhaul of the technology underpinning the entire U.S. broadcasting system in the early twenty-first century. In 2009, high-definition television (HDTV) was bundled into the conversion of the analog television system to an all-digital process (**digital television**, or **DTV**). This required television stations and networks to convert millions of dollars of equipment, and it forced viewers either to replace their old, analog TV sets or to add a device to them that receives digital transmissions (which few consumers did). With so much at stake, it is not surprising that the conversion was marked with legal wrangling and discord and reluctance on the part of both television stations and consumers. After many delays, the digital switch was finally flipped on June 12, 2009.

It is important to recognize that digital television and high-definition television are not the same thing. One must have a digital television set to receive high-definition images, but not all digital transmissions are in high definition. Thus, one may watch *standard*-definition programming on a digital television monitor. Confusion between digital television and HDTV standards left consumers baffled. One study found that nearly half of the early owners of HDTV sets never watched high-definition programming on them.[4] Indeed, 14 percent of the HDTV consumers thought they were watching high-definition television when they were not! Now, after a decade of over-the-air digital-television broadcasting, the conversion of satellite and cable system to digital technologies, and viewers' reliance on streaming systems (Netflix, Hulu, etc.) that were "born digital," digital imagery has become the norm. Still, not everything we see is "full high definition" and, to confuse matters further, TV manufacturers have thrown an even higher-definition standard at consumers: **4K video** (with 8K video lurking on the horizon).

To clarify this very murky situation we need to examine some technical aspects of the television image and understand how **scan lines** and **pixels** work. The video image is made up of glowing, phosphorescent dots. These dots are arranged in horizontal scan lines crossing the TV screen. To be precise, these "dots" are really three, tiny, colored *rectangles*—one red, one green, and one blue—clustered together to form a single "picture element," or pixel. Definition in video is not a factor of graininess, since video images are not composed of chemical grains. However, much as in film grain, the number of pixels packed into an image determines the definition of that image. A clear, highly detailed video image—like a fine-grain film—has a lot of very small pixels. And to accommodate these large numbers of pixels you need a large number of scan lines to hold them. Hence, one measure of video image definition is the number of scan lines—the higher the number, the higher the definition.

In the U.S., the resolution of standard-definition television was established decades ago by the **National Television System Committee** (**NTSC**) as 486 visible scan lines. (The actual number of scan lines in the NTSC standard is 525, but some of them are reserved for use by the system itself and are not meant to be seen. Consequently, the number of lines that actively present images to the viewer is reduced to 486.) Outside the U.S., different systems are used with different numbers of scan lines; but in the U.S., the NTSC standard dominated until the conversion to digital television. To set the new standards for digital television, the **Advanced Television Systems Committee** (**ATSC**) was formed in 1982 by various broadcast, cable, and consumer-electronics groups as a nonprofit and nongovernmental organization. It recommended 480 scan lines for standard definition and 720 or 1,080 scan lines for high definition.[5] Subsequently, the ATSC and other industry players settled on 3,840 scan lines for **ultra high definition** (a.k.a. 4K) televisions. Even though "4K" projectors have 4,096 lines and are precisely 4K, ultra HD television monitors are not. We are simplifying here and leaving out some technical details. What's most important to recognize when analyzing TV is that there are different levels of resolution and that they may be manipulated for artistic, emotional, and/or informational effect. Further, it's not just standard-definition and high-definition images that one sees on one's TV screen. DPs also make use of **low-definition** images in many situations. The number of scan lines in

Table 9.1 Level of Definition of Various Video Modes

Video Mode	*Width (pixels per line)*	*Height (visible scan lines)*	*Total Megapixels*	*Aspect Ratio (visible image)*	*Common Uses*
Early cell-phone cameras	320	240	76.8	1.33	Recording/playback of home movies
VHS	486	220	106.9	1.33	Recording/playback of home movies & recorded movies
NTSC Broadcast SD	486	330	160.4	1.33	Playback of analog broadcast TV
DVD	540	486	262.4	1.33	Playback of movies, pre-recorded TV shows
ATSC Broadcast SD	640	480	307.2	1.33	Playback of digital broadcast TV
ATSC Broadcast HD (720)	1280	720	921.6	1.78	Playback of digital broadcast TV
ATSC Broadcast HD (1080)	1920	1080	2,073.6	1.78	Playback of digital broadcast TV
Blu-ray disc	1920	1080	2,073.6	1.78	Playback of movies, recorded TV shows
Super 16mm film	2058	1237	2,545.7	1.66	Recording of network-era prime-time TV shows, commercials
DCI* 2K digital-cinema projection	2048	1080	2,211.8	1.9	Playback of movies in theaters
4K Broadcast UHD	3840	2160	8,294.4	1.78	Playback of digital video
DCI* 4K digital-cinema projection	4096	2160	8,847.4	1.9	Playback of movies in theaters
4K recording	4096	3112	12,746.8	1.32	Recording of movies, prime-time TV shows, commercials
Super 35mm film	4153	3112	12,924.1	1.33	Recording/playback of movies, network-era prime-time TV shows, commercials
8K Broadcast	7680	4320	33,177.6	1.78	Playback of digital video

* Digital Cinema Initiatives (DCI) is an industry consortium that established a standard for 2K and 4K movie projection in theaters.

low-definition video has not been specified by the ATSC and thus it's broadly categorized as any video with fewer scan lines than standard definition has.

Table 9.1 tries to sort out all this confusion by counting the number of pixels in standard-definition television and establishing that as the dividing line between low(er) definition and high(er) definition (the tint in the Table 9.1 indicates this dividing line). Remember, there are 480 scan lines running horizontally across the standard-definition, digital television image, and there are 640 pixels in each scan line. Thus, the SD image is 480×640, or a total of 307,200 pixels. A low-definition image such as something shot with an early cell-phone camera might have half as many scan lines—say, 320—with half as many pixels in each line—say, 240. And in a 320×240 image there will be only 76,800 pixels, which is why such video results in some very blurry, blocky, distorted images. On the other, high-definition extreme of the definition spectrum, a 35mm film frame can be up to 4,153 points wide by 3,112 points high, for a total of 12,924,136 points (since it's an analog medium it has "points" instead of "pixels" and does not have actual scan lines).[6]

The pixels in low- and standard-definition television are so large that the scan lines are visible to the naked eye—if one should care to sit so close to the TV. Current state-of-the-art high-definition formats cannot make scan lines disappear altogether, but they almost seem to. Contrast the high-definition image taken from a broadcast of *Bones* (2005–17) with a simulated standard-definition image (Figures 9.14 and 9.15). In the originally broadcast, high-definition, 1,920×1,080-pixels image, you can make out the time on the clock tower (11:45) and the letters on the coffee truck ("Baristas"), but in the standard-definition, 640×480-pixels image, both the clock and the letters are illegible. Further, since standard definition is not as wide as HD, we've also lost some of the image from the edges (more about widescreen on p. 245–46) and can no longer see all of the people in line for coffee. *Bones* was shot on 35mm film, which, as you can see in Table 9.1, is even higher resolution than the high-definition video broadcast. The image you watch on your HD monitor thus began at an even higher resolution and was reduced for broadcast purposes.

Historically, original HD recording was done on film, but newer, 4K resolution video recording is quickly approaching the resolution of 35mm film, and the upcoming 8K standard may even surpass it. The standard width of 4K recording is 4,096 pixels (or 4K, in binary counting) and it can generate up to 12,746,752 pixels—virtually the equivalent of 35mm film's 12,924,136 points of data. At this time, film recording has not been entirely eliminated (see, for example, *Mad Men*), but most prime-time productions that would have been shot on film ten years ago are now being recorded on video. For example, *Arrested Development* (2003–06) and *Fargo*, the TV series (2014, 2015, 2017), have a film look to them, but both were shot in video formats. And some programs that began on film are now switching to video, as did the *CSI* programs.[7] Moreover, most movie theaters have been converted to digital-video projection—usually referred to as **digital cinema**, with U.S. standards set by Digital Cinema Initiatives (DCI). Since the mid-2010s, when you go to the movie theater, you're seeing projected video up on the screen.

In the world of television production and transmission, standard-definition video is the minimum required for what is called broadcast-quality work. SD video was, for decades, used to record sitcoms, talk shows, and soap operas but was disdained by higher prestige, and visually more elaborate, prime-time dramas such as *Bones* and *Fargo*—which are typically recorded in high definition. Low-definition recording modes are designed for circumstances like surveillance and police dashboard cameras, where image quality is less important than other factors such as the ability to conceal the camera and to record hours or entire days at a time.

Figure 9.14 The viewer can see many details in this high-definition image from *Bones*...

Figure 9.15 ... that are lost in this (simulated) standard-definition version of the same image.

As you may have gathered already, the quality of a TV image gets worse and worse as it travels from a studio set to your living room. The image gets squeezed over and over again as it is sent from a production company to a network to a broadcasting station or online portal to your television screen. The image size must be reduced at many stages in the process. **Data compression**—the reduction in size of any digital source—is a complicated topic and space does not permit an extended discussion of it here, but it does have a major impact on the look of television in the twenty-first century and so a few comments are in order. When a cable is attached to a **digital video** (**DV**) camera, massive amounts of sound-and-image data can be pumped out of it—regardless of whether it's standard-definition or high-definition video. When it comes time to transmit that video over the air, through a satellite/cable-TV system or via the Internet, it must be shrunk so that the transmission system will not be overloaded. The compression process inevitably degrades the image and sound that we receive in our homes. And, once again, this is true of both standard-definition and high-definition transmissions.

The negative effects of compression are sometimes visible when you watch video on an online portal. Let's focus on Netflix as our compression example, because it dominates the SVOD market and accounts for a massive amount of *all* data traveling across the Internet. In fact, Netflix alone represented over one-third of traffic on North American networks in 2016.[8] When Netflix launched on April14, 1998, as a DVD-by-mail service, the distribution of video over the Internet was still in its infancy—mostly because Internet speeds were too slow to support large video files. It would be nine years before Netflix felt confident that it could deliver an acceptable product online, rolling out its streaming service to customers in 2007. Even then, the resolution of the video was highly compressed and barely standard-definition quality—not to mention plagued by frequent signal buffering.

Over the years, of course, Internet speeds have increased exponentially, Netflix's crafty use of the Internet has gotten more efficient, and video compression has become almost imperceptible. Almost. We've all had the experience of a Netflix stream trying to lock into a high-definition video and appearing rather blocky and blurry for a few seconds. In Figure 9.16, we've simulated (and exaggerated) **compression artifacts** in a screen shot of Joyce Byers (Winona Ryder) from

Figure 9.16 A Netflix-delivered image from *Stranger Things* is heavily compressed, which causes it to degrade into small blocks (simulated).

Stranger Things (2016–), which was originally released in compressed, digital streaming format on Netflix. When pixels are evident like this, it is sometimes known as "checker boarding." Other compression artifacts include "mosquito noise" (small dots appearing around the edges of people and things) and "stair-stepping" of curves (curved lines that resemble steps of stairs—such as Joyce's shoulder in Figure 9.16). Compression artifacts are not limited to streaming portals. Live sports events sometimes suffer from image degradation if a signal has been compressed in order to bounce it off a satellite from a distant location. And satellite-TV services must compress their signal—even if it's touted as "HD" or "4K"—in order to deliver it from a satellite to a small dish on your roof. Regardless of whether the TV signal is coming through your Internet service provider, down a cable, or via satellite transmission, it is going to be compressed to some degree or another. Only when you experience moving images in a theater are you seeing digital video at close to full, uncompressed resolution.

The Economics and Aesthetics of Lower Definition

If you've priced a 4K television set, then you know that flavors of HD are considerably more expensive than SD. What's true for us consumers is also true for the producers and transmitters of television: HD is not cheap. But it's not just economics that lead the directors and DPs of television to choose low- and standard-definition formats. Like super-8 film, low-definition video is sometimes used in HD narrative programs to denote "home movie" or "surveillance" style. In one episode of *CSI* shot on film (before the series converted to video), a woman points a video camera at the investigators (Figure 9.17, looking over her shoulder; see tvcrit.com/find/csivideo). When she does we cut to what the video camera is supposedly recording and we also change from 35mm film, on which this episode originated, to video—allowing us to compare/contrast the two formats (Figure 9.18). In the video shot, not only is the resolution reduced, but the colors shift and the contrast is higher. And, similar to this use of low-definition video, the SD video formats used in television news and reality-TV programs are sometimes used in fiction programs to signify "news" or "reality TV" style—much as the *Blair Witch Project* filmmakers used Hi8 and 16mm film. Moreover, SD video is sometimes incorporated into parodies of TV programs that are conventionally shot in that format. *Reno 911* (2003–09), for example, pokes fun at *Cops* and, like that reality program, it's shot in SD video. The incorporation of low- and standard-definition video into television material is not limited to parodies, however. These formats appear when directors want images that look rough and raw. Commercials and music videos, for example, sometimes incorporate such degraded imagery.

Figure 9.17 *CSI* shifts from an image recorded on high-quality 35mm film to . . .

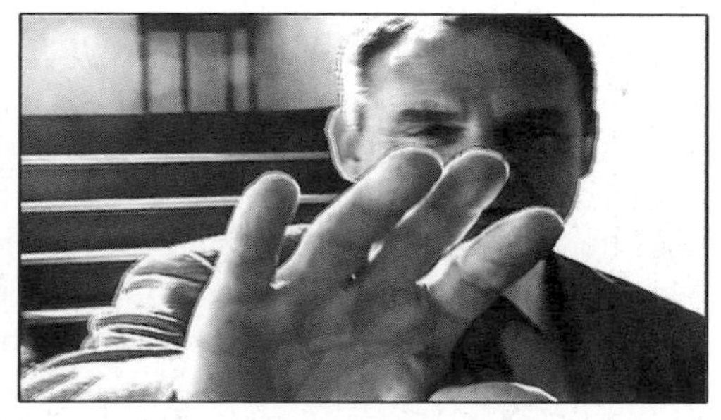

Figure 9.18 . . . low-quality video, suggesting that we are seeing what a character is recording.

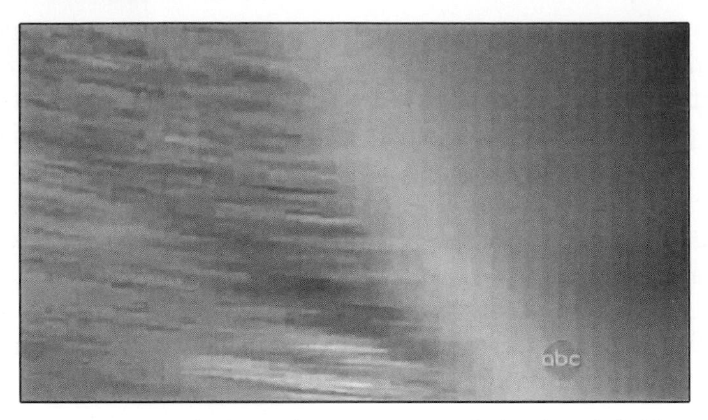

Figure 9.19 The abstract appearance of the low-definition image from *AFV* authenticates it as a home video.

Television news and shows like *America's Funniest Home Videos* (abbreviated as *AFV*; 1989–) may also make use of low-definition formats. Home-video and camera-phone formats appear when "amateur" recordings of news events (tornadoes, earthquakes, police brutality) or surveillance recordings of crimes are broadcast. The poorer resolution of these recordings—their difference from SD or HD formats—becomes significant in these instances. It marks the recordings as "authentic," as unposed and spontaneous and supposedly a pure piece of the historical world. In an *AFV* clip where a man is run over by a small motorbike, we can see how style guarantees its authenticity (tvcrit.com/find/afvclip)—something the *AFV* producers are constantly concerned about. (Obviously, they don't want to run faked or posed clips.) In the clip, the camera is shaking and the image is not "properly" framed. After the motorbike hits the man, the person holding the camera swings it around wildly and the motion of the image makes the low definition more obvious. As in our *Stranger Things* example, checker boarding is clearly visible here (Figure 9.19). In fact, the motion is so violent and the visual distortion is so great that Figure 9.19 resembles abstract art! Of course, we can't know for sure that this clip wasn't faked, that it wasn't professionally shot with a high-definition camera and then digitally manipulated. But regardless of how that clip was obtained, it *appears* to be an authentic part of reality because we consciously or unconsciously link it with other amateur video we have seen. Thus, the technology (in this case, video from a phone) creates a visual style (low-definition images) that carries certain significations based on our association with other video-recorded images.

Color and Black-and-White

The most basic color characteristics are **hue**, **saturation**, and **brightness**. Hue designates a specific color from within the visible spectrum of white light: for example, red, green, blue. The level of saturation defines a color's purity—how much or little grayness is mixed with the color. Deep, rich, vibrant colors such as those in a brand-new U.S. flag are said to be heavily saturated. They become less saturated as the weather-beaten flag's colors fade. Saturation is also termed **chroma** or **chrominance** in video color. Brightness or **luminance** in video indicates how bright or dark a color is.

Over the history of video and film there have been different approaches to creating color images. Video constructs colors by adding them together (**additive color**; see online illustration in color, tvcrit.com/find/additivecolor). A single phosphor on the TV screen is colored red, green, or blue. When three nearby phosphors are ignited on the screen they combine their individual colors, thus generating a broad variety of colors. Film, in contrast, was always a **subtractive color** process. As white light from a projector lamp passes through a piece of motion-picture film, yellow, magenta (reddish), and cyan (bluish) colors are filtered out of the light (see online illustration in color, tvcrit.com/find/subtractivecolor). The colors that are not filtered out form the many colors of the spectrum.

Thus, both video and film rely upon three-color systems to generate color images. Different video systems and film stocks **balance** these three colors in different ways. Some are more sensitive to red, others to blue; some appear more naturalistic under sunlight, others under tungsten light (as in household light bulbs). No video system or film stock captures color exactly as it exists in nature, but this is not necessarily a drawback. Rather, it presents a wide range of color options to the DP. Color may be manipulated through the choice of video system and film stock, as well as through lens filters and colored gels on the lights. And, of course, colors are also tweaked during post-production in a process known as color correction or color grading.

In the 1980s, long after television had been a strictly color medium, black-and-white video and film began to be reintroduced. Although black-and-white images are uncommon in narrative programs, they have been used to indicate dream sequences or events that occurred in the past. In these cases, black-and-white's contrast to color has been used to communicate narrative information. It becomes **diegetically** significant—significant in the world the characters inhabit. Black-and-white is also used in non-narrative television such as commercials and music videos. In these situations the colorless images cannot always be anchored in specific meanings beyond product differentiation. Yes, there have been several commercials in which everything is black-and-white except for the product advertised (Figure 6.26); but there are also black-and-white music videos in which the significance of the lack of color is ephemeral, elusive, or somehow "artistic," as in the Victoria's Secret commercial discussed in Chapter 6 (Figure 6.4). In any event, black-and-white recording is still another option that the camera operator may use to affect the viewer.

Framing

Basic Aesthetic Conventions

The **framing** of a shot, at a most rudimentary level, determines what we can and cannot see. In the early years of television (the 1940s), camera operators tended to choose a distant view of the action, which showed the entire setting. This framing was based on an aesthetic assumption (inherited from the theater) that the "best seat in the house" would be in the center, about seven or eight rows back, where one could see all of the action at once. Also, early television cameras were large and cumbersome, which made it difficult to move them around a set to achieve a variety of camera positions. Soon, however, camera technology improved. Television directors discovered the impact of a variety of framing and began incorporating the **close-up** in their programs.

Since the "invention" of the close-up, television directors have developed several conventions of framing. It is possible to chart television's conventional framing with the human body as a standard, since that is the most common object before the camera. Each of the following examples is from the first season of *Weeds* (2005–06) (the conventional abbreviation of each framing is included in parentheses):

1. **extreme long shot** (**XLS**): the human form is small, perhaps barely visible—the point-of-view is extremely distant, as in aerial shots or other distant views (Figure 9.20);
2. **long shot** (**LS**): the actor's entire body is visible, as is some of the surrounding space (Figure 9.21);
3. **medium long shot** (**MLS**): most, but not all, of the actor's body is included, but less of the surrounding space is visible than in the LS (Figure 9.22);
4. **medium shot** (**MS**): the actor is framed from the thigh or waist up (Figure 9.23);

5. **medium close-up** (**MCU**): the lower chest of the actor is still visible (Figure 9.24);
6. **close-up** (**CU**): the actor is framed from his or her chest to just above his or her head (Figure 9.25)—commonly referred to as a **single**;
7. **extreme close-up** (**XCU**): any framing closer than a close-up is considered an XCU (Figure 9.26).

Figure 9.20 Weeds contains examples of extreme long shots (XLS)...

Figure 9.21 ... long shots (LS)...

Figure 9.22 ... medium long shots (MLS)...

Figure 9.23 ... medium shots (MS)—as in this two shot...

Figure 9.24 ... medium close-ups (MCU)...

Figure 9.25 ... close-ups (CU)...

Figure 9.26 ... and extreme close-ups (XCU).

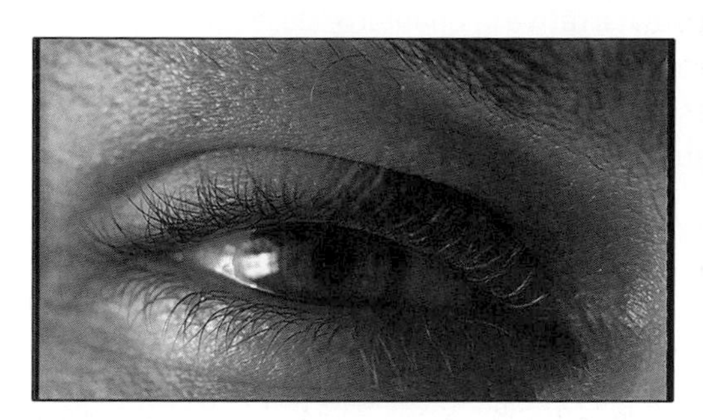

Figure 9.27 Extreme close-ups from *The Sopranos*...

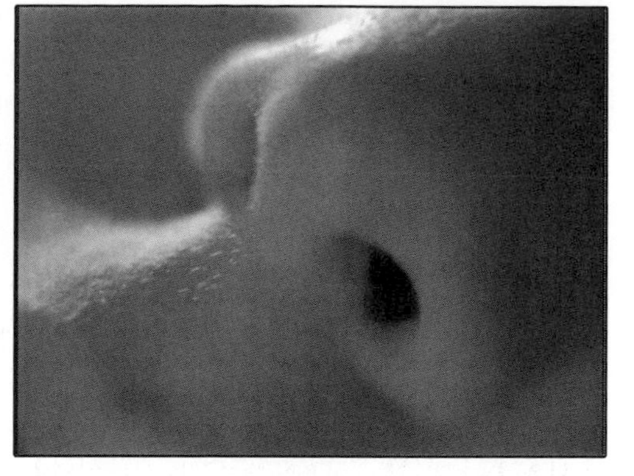

Figure 9.28 ... and *Malcolm in the Middle*.

In actual video production, these terms are imprecise. What one director considers a medium close-up, another might term a close-up. And there is some variation between shooting for television and theatrical film shooting, with the former tending toward closer framing to compensate for the smaller screen. A "TV close-up" thus might be slightly more tightly framed than a "theatrical-film close-up." Despite this imprecision, the above terminology does provide some guidelines for discussing framing.

In fiction television, the long shot is—among other things—used for positioning characters within their environment and can thereby construct aspects of those characters. A long shot of a woman in a newspaper office, a prison cell, or a convent could establish her as a journalist, a convict, or a nun, respectively. The *Weeds* long shot of the James family kitchen in Figure 9.21 sets a domestic scene of Heylia (Tonye Patano) and her daughter, Vaneeta (Indigo), being told a story by Nancy Botwin (Mary-Louise Parker). This homey environment contrasts with their profession as drug dealers. Environment feeds our understanding of character, and the long shot facilitates that understanding. A long shot that specifically helps to establish character or setting is known as an **establishing shot**. It often starts a scene.

The medium shot is frequently used for conversation scenes. The framing of two characters from the waist or knees up as they converse is so often used that it has been designated with the term **two shot** (Figure 9.23). (Similarly, a **three shot** frames three characters). The medium shot can establish relationships between characters by bringing them into fairly close proximity.

For some, the close-up provides the "window to the soul" of the actors/characters, a gateway to their innermost emotions. Romantic hyperbole such as this aside, the close-up functions both to emphasize details and to exclude surrounding actions, channeling viewer perception. It thus exercises the most extreme control over the viewer's gaze, as when we are invited to examine Andy Botwin's (Justin Kirk) reaction to a situation (Figure 9.25). This is particularly true of extreme close-ups, the tightness of which can range from a shot of a hand (*Weeds*, Figure 9.26) to an eye (*The Sopranos*, Figure 9.27) or a nose (*Malcolm in the Middle*, Figure 9.28).

The aesthetics of framing follows certain conventions of function. The close-up is the dominant framing in television programs such as the soap opera, where the emotional states signified by the actors' faces are stressed. Television soap opera's reliance upon the close-up has coincided with the evolution of its acting style, which favors the human face over larger gestures. As we saw in our discussion of soap-opera narrative in Chapter 3, close-ups often mark the end of a segment and suggest a moment of intensity just before the commercials begin (Figure 3.13). Television sports and action genres, in contrast, place more emphasis on medium and long shots—to facilitate the movement of automobiles, planes, and human bodies through space (Figure 5.20).

Camera Height and Angle

In most television shots the height of the camera matches that of the actors' faces. This camera height is so ingrained in our understanding of camera style that eye level has become synonymous with "normal" height. It becomes transparent to the viewer, taken for granted. Variations on this height consequently become important, apparently signifying something about the characters. The two principal variations on eye-level camera height are:

1. **low angle:** in which the camera is lower than the filmed object (*Fargo*, Figure 9.29);
2. **high angle**: in which the camera is higher than the filmed object (*Fargo*, Figure 9.30).

The low-angle shot of IRS agent Larue Dollard (Hamish Linklater)—at his desk examining key documents that will lead to the unraveling of a vast network of criminal activity—implies that he might just have the moral strength to confront the show's evil figures.

We should be careful about generalizing the effect of low and high angles. It has become a truism in television production manuals to observe that a low angle—as when we look up at Agent Dollard—makes a character appear stronger and more powerful, while a high angle—looking down on an actor—weakens the character's impact. We can see the commonsensical basis for this assumption: when looking up at an object, it tends to appear large; and when looking down at it, small. But in actual television programs this use of low and high angles is much less systematic and predictable. The extremely high-angle shot from *Fargo* in Figure 9.30 is of an unknown man, Donald Woo (Virgil Chow), walking past gas pumps to his car. Director Keith Gordon's choice of angle functionally conceals Woo's identity from us as we hear police sirens approaching and assume that they are going to arrest a murderer. But it doesn't make him look

Figure 9.29 A low-angle shot of IRS Agent Dollard in *Fargo* positions him as a strong figure. (Note slight letterboxing—discussed later—here and in figure 9.30.)

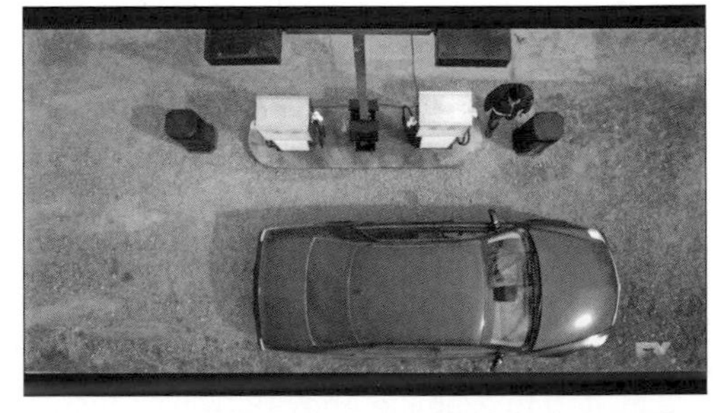

Figure 9.30 Fargo: An extreme high-angle, overhead shot of a man makes him look small and obscures his identity from the viewer.

small or weak and, besides, it's all a ruse. He's been hired to confess to murders he did not commit. Viewing nothing but the top of his head delays our understanding that he is a narrative misdirection, but it doesn't make him look small and vulnerable. Consider one other example. In Figure 9.31, from *Breaking Bad* (2008–2013), Walter (Bryan Cranston) and Todd (Jesse Plemons) are shot from a low, supposedly empowering angle; yet the mood of the scene is one of regret and melancholy, with Walter telling Todd, "I don't want to talk about it." (In addition, the frame formed by the trunk visually traps them.) Obviously, the low camera angle is not enough to turn this into a triumphant moment.

Stylistic elements such as camera angle do communicate meanings and concepts to viewers, but those meanings are always set within the context of the program and general aesthetic practice. Consequently, it's impossible to generalize about the "vocabulary" of television technique, where technique A = meaning B. Technique A does indeed have meanings, but only when considered within the entire textual system of a program.

The Moving Frame

Film cameras had been around for 20 years or more before tripods and dollies and other mechanical devices were developed that permitted the movement of the camera. Early films initially had little or no camera movement because of this technological limitation and because camera operators had to hand crank the cameras, thus making their turning or movement awkward. When cameras finally did begin to move, they were limited by the practical aesthetics of early directors. Little use was seen for camera movement beyond following character action and panoramic views. Filmmakers gradually expanded the functions of camera movement, and, by the time television arrived, film camera movement was smooth and relatively frequent. Early television cameras, because of their enormous bulk, were as stationary as the first film cameras. Also, initial studio-based television was constricted in its camera movement by lack of space—as can be seen in the overview of the *I Love Lucy* set (Figure 9.32). Before long, however, television developed its own uses for the moving camera.

Figure 9.31 Low angles do not always make characters look large and powerful. Walter and Todd are seen from the inside of a car trunk, staring down at a corpse, in a low-angle shot from *Breaking Bad*.

Figure 9.32 Desi Arnaz talks to the audience on the original set of *I Love Lucy*.

Principal among the functions of the moving camera are:

- to establish a space, a particular area;
- to establish a relationship between objects/actors in a certain space;
- to follow action;
- to emphasize/de-emphasize one portion of a space, or an object/actor within that portion.

To achieve these functions, a variety of camera movements have evolved.

Panning and Tilting

The most rudimentary camera movement derives its name from the affection for broad, "panoramic" views in early motion pictures. The **pan** is when the camera twists left and right, on an imaginary axis stuck vertically through the camera (tvcrit.com/pan). The camera support—the legs of the tripod—does not move in a pan; only the tripod head turns. Similarly, in a **tilt**, the camera twists up and down on an axis stuck horizontally through the camera (tvcrit.com/tilt). The camera height does not change; only its angle of vision.

Several other camera movements depend upon the movement of the *entire* camera support rather than just the tripod head: dollying/tracking/trucking; craning/pedestaling; handheld; and Steadicam. Camera technology provides the names for these movements, rather than the actual direction of the movement (as in "tilting") or what is represented (as in "panning" over panoramic views). Thus, the conventionalized method for viewers to describe these movements is to refer to presumptions of the technology used to create them.

Dollying, Tracking, and Trucking

In television there are several terms used to describe the sideways and backward/forward movement of the camera. Principal among these are **dollying**, **tracking**, and **trucking**. Each of these differs from the pan in that the entire camera support moves, rather than just the tripod head. It's like the difference between twisting one's head left and right—the human equivalent of panning—and walking in one direction or the other—human dollying.

The dolly shot is named for the device that creates it, the camera dolly—a wheeled camera support that can be rolled left and right or forward and backward. In a behind-the-scenes video of *Grey's Anatomy* (2006–), one can see the camera operator seated on the dolly, with a grip pushing him and a focus puller adjusting the focus as Meredith (Ellen Pompeo) and Derek (Patrick Dempsey) talk in a hallway (tvcrit.com/find/dolly). The operator pans as the dolly moves past the actors. The resulting shot, as it appears in the episode, is only eight seconds long and combines a pan with the dolly shot (the difference in Meredith's wardrobe suggests that the behind-the-scenes shot is of a rehearsal or alternative take; see tvcrit.com/find/dollyresult).

Similar to the dolly shot, the tracking shot earns its name from small tracks that are laid over rough surfaces, along which the dolly then rolls. In practice, "tracking" is such a broadly applied term that it may be used to refer to any sideways or backward/forward movement, even if actual dolly tracks are not involved. In addition, in television studio production sideways movement is sometimes called trucking or crabbing, and a semicircular sideways movement is usually called **arcing**. Many of these terms are used interchangeably. Also, dollying need not be in straight lines that are either perpendicular or parallel to the action; dolly shots may move in curves, figure eights, and any other direction a dolly can be pushed or pulled.

To most viewers, dollying in or out is indistinguishable from zooming in or out. There are, however, important visual differences between the two techniques. Even though it takes a practiced eye to recognize them, the differences may generate disparate perceptions of the objects and humans that are presented.

When camera operators zoom in or out, they change the focal length of the camera and magnify or de-magnify the object, but the position from which the object is viewed remains the same. The point-of-view of the camera is thus constant. In contrast, when camera operators dolly forward or backward, the position from which the object is viewed shifts. And because the point-of-view changes in the dolly shot, we see the object from a different angle. Parts of it are revealed that were previously concealed, and vice versa (see Figure 9.8, taken from the ending of a dolly-in shot that begins at the same position as the zoom-in of Figure 9.6). If we compare the end of the dolly shot (Figure 9.8) with its beginning (Figure 9.6), we can note that the bird's beak and head are now covering part of the door and a large amount of the thermometer, where they were not before, and begin to see around the post to which the thermometer is attached. At the end of the zoom shot (Figure 9.7), in contrast, we see as much of the thermometer as we did at the beginning; it's just been enlarged (and is out of focus). Even though the subject matter is enlarged in the zoom-in, it is still seen from the same point-of-view; the camera is still in the same position as at the start of the zoom. Moreover, because we have changed the focal length, we also changed the image's illusion of depth. Everything looks flatter, more compressed as we zoom in. Disregarding the change in depth of field for the moment, we can observe that, at the end of the zoom-in shot (Figure 9.7), the sculpture looks very close to the thermometer behind it, while at the end of the dolly-in shot (Figure 9.8) the thermometer looks far behind the dove's head.

Are you wondering why the thermometer is out-of-focus at the end of the zoom-in when it wasn't at the start of the shot? The explanation comes from the impact a lens's focal length has on depth of field. Essentially, the more telephoto the focal length is, the smaller the depth of field will be. In the zoom-in, we shifted the focal length from wide angle to telephoto and thereby caused the depth of field to shrink from about 15 feet to perhaps one foot. Other factors affecting depth of field include distance from the camera to an object and the amount of light hitting that object.

Thus, although the zoom and the dolly share the quality of enlarging or reducing an object before our eyes, they differ in how they represent point-of-view and the illusion of depth. Consequently, they serve different functions on television. For example, camera movement—not zooming—is conventionally used when the viewer is supposed to be seeing through the eyes of characters as they move through space—say, as killers approach their prey. Zoom shots do not conventionally serve this function because they do not mimic human movement as convincingly as dollying does. Zooming, in turn, is more common in contemporary television production as a punctuation for extreme emotion. In soap operas, camera movement is fairly limited and zoom-ins function to underline character emotions. In this case economics blends with aesthetics. Zoom shots are less time-consuming to set up than dolly shots and thus less expensive. Consequently, the modestly budgeted soap operas favor the zoom.

Craning, Pedestaling, and Aerial Cinematography

A traditional camera crane or boom looks just like a crane on a construction site, except that there is a camera mounted on one end (see tvcrit.com/find/cranes for examples). In television studios today, a variety of smaller devices—most of which are remotely controlled—are used to achieve similar effects. A pedestal is another device that supports a camera. It is the vertical post of a camera dolly. Cranes and pedestals are the technology that permits the upward/downward movement of the camera, and those movements—**craning** and **pedestaling**—take their names from that technology. Thus, in a crane shot the camera is swept upward or downward. In one shot from the studio portion of *America's Funniest Home Videos*, for example, the camera moves from near the studio floor, up and over the heads of the audience, and finds host Tom Bergeron in their midst (Figures 9.33 and 9.34; tvcrit.com/find/afvcrane). Additionally, since the crane is mounted on wheels or suspended from a wire grid above the set, it can also be moved in all the directions a dolly can—as in the forward movement of the *AFV* shot. A pedestal shot is one in which the camera is raised or lowered straight up or down. The crane or pedestal movement is different from the tilt: in a tilt, the tripod head is twisted up or down—as if the camera were nodding—while in craning and pedestaling the entire camera body is moved higher or lower.

Crane shots serve a variety of functions. Typically, a crane down may be used first to establish a location with a wide-angle shot from up high and then particularize one element of that location by craning down to it (or up to it, as in our *AFV* example). And cranes up and back are often used to end sequences or programs. Craning up and away from characters at the end of a program, we are literally distanced from them at a point when we are about to leave the characters' story.

Figure 9.33 The *AFV* camera begins craning up from the floor...

Figure 9.34 . . . coming to rest on host Tom Bergeron.

Aerial cinematography has been revolutionized in recent years with the development of lightweight, high-definition cameras and affordable, remote-controlled **drones** to carry them. Shots that used to require expensive, difficult-to-operate cranes can now be quickly done with drones. For example, Todd Media created a promotional video for a shopping center that begins with a shot of its sign (Figure 9.35) and then performs a "pedestal" type movement straight up until it's perhaps 50 feet above the center's roofs (Figure 9.36)—a shot that would be extremely difficult or even impossible to achieve with a conventional crane or a helicopter. The small size of drones allows them the flexibility of capturing angles that are relatively close to the actors, gliding along beside or just above them, in additional to striking aerial angles. Drones are not without controversy, however. Various laws and regulations about serious drone-related matters have yet to be fully worked out—such as how close drones will be permitted to airports and the licensing of drone operators—and yet it appears that drones have become an essential part of production for television.

Handheld and Steadicam

A **handheld** shot is one that was filmed just as the name implies: with the camera held in the operator's hands instead of being placed on a camera mount. As a consequence, the handheld shot is noticeably unsteady—especially during quick movements when the camera operator is running. A large percentage of news and sports shooting is done with handheld cameras: shots from the field of play in sports shows (for example, courtside shots at basketball games); documentary footage of automobile crashes; murder suspects leaving a courtroom; and so on.

We might think that handheld shots would be avoided entirely in the more controlled camera style of fiction television. Even though the majority of camera movements in fictional programs are not handheld, handheld shots do serve several narrative functions. First, handheld work is used to create a documentary feel, to signify "documentary-ness," within works of fiction. Many episodes of *NYPD Blue* (1993-2005), *Homicide: Life on the Streets* (1993-99), and *24* (2001-10) include noticeable handheld camerawork—signifying the program's "realism" (for example, tvcrit.com/find/homicide). Second, handheld movement is often used when we are seeing through a character's eyes—as was mentioned above regarding dolly shots (tvcrit.com/find/subjectivehandheld). Indeed, handheld camera is more frequently used in this situation than dollying because handheld is thought to more closely approximate human movement. After all, we all have legs like a camera operator, not wheels like a dolly. Third, handheld movement can convey a sense of disturbance, even violence. In the pilot episode of *The Sopranos* (1999-2007),

Figure 9.35 A drone shot begins on a shopping center sign...

Figure 9.36 ...and then pedestals straight into the sky, hovering 50 feet above the ground.

for example, mob boss Tony Soprano (James Gandolfini) drives his car into a man fleeing him. After Soprano gets out of the car, director David Chase shoots him with a handheld camera as he further assaults his victim (tvcrit.com/find/sopranos). The unsteady camera movement mirrors Soprano's malevolent actions.

Steadicam is a registered trademark for a piece of technology that has come to identify a style of camera movement. Shots generated with a Steadicam closely resemble those of a handheld camera, but are substantially less jittery. The Steadicam is a gyroscopically balanced device that is strapped to the operator's body (Figure 9.37). The resulting motion is virtually as smooth as that produced with a dolly. It is conventionally used in situations where stability is desired but economic and technical practicalities dictate that dolly tracks cannot be laid. *ER* (1994–2009) was among the first TV programs to use a Steadicam on a daily basis. Its camera operators move through the sets in ways previously reserved for feature films. Subsequent hospital shows have also relied on a Steadicam, as can be seen in another behind-the-scenes video from *Grey's Anatomy*—with a Steadicam operator following Meredith and Derek down the hall (tvcrit. com/find/steadicam). In the resulting scene, the long take of them walking and turning the corner has been cut into several Steadicam shots, ranging from an establishing long shot to medium close-ups (tvcrit.com/find/steadicamshot).

Figure 9.37 An operator readies his Steadicam.

Aspect Ratio

Aspect ratio, in simplest terms, is a comparison of the width of an image with its height. Most TV monitors manufactured today are in a ratio of 16 units wide by 9 units high, but this was not always the case. TV and movie theater screens have come in a range of shapes during the decades since the invention of motion pictures in the 1890s. These differing shapes were motivated by aesthetic, technological, and industrial forces, as is always the case with TV stylistic elements. Consequently, even though we mostly watch TV on monitors, tablets, and phones with shapes clustering around 16:9, the programs and movies we watch may not have been originally designed for that shape, and they may have been heavily modified to conform to it. Since the shape of the frame can have a substantial impact on our viewing experience, it's instructive to learn a bit about the history of film and television's various rectangles and consider how TV has sometimes damaged the original shapes of TV programs and movies when it forced them into its dimensions. (All of the major TV and film aspect ratios discussed below are diagramed in Figure 9.38.)

A Brief History of TV and Film Aspect Ratios

During the first TV boom, after World War II ended in 1945, the TV frame stabilized at a size of 4 units wide by 3 units high—the same dimensions as movie screens of the time. That is to say, a screen 4 feet wide would be 3 feet high; a screen 16 inches wide would be 12 inches high; a screen 40 feet wide would be 30 feet high; and so on. Standard-definition TV's width compared to its height is thus 4:3, which may be reduced to 1.33:1 or simply 1.33. After remaining stable for decades, television's aspect ratio began changing in the 2000s. The new, high-definition television demanded a wider image—with an aspect ratio of 1.78 to 1, although it is normally identified as 16 to 9.

Film producers perceived television as a threat to their livelihood and reasoned that theatrical films must provide viewers with something they cannot get from television. How else could they coax customers away from their television sets? Thus, in the 1950s film studios attempted

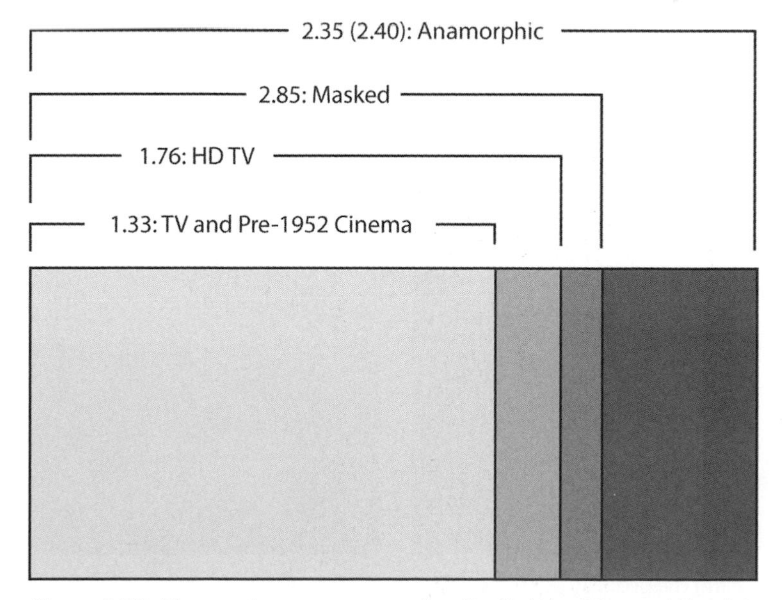

Figure 9.38 The most common aspect ratios in television and theatrical film.

a variety of technological enticements: color, 3D, stereo sound, and wider screens. Widescreen, its advocates maintained, presented the viewer with a larger and grander image—one in which they could immerse themselves fully. (Its detractors claimed that it was only suitable for filming snakes and dachshunds.) These new, wider screens had aspect ratios of 2.35:1 and 2.55:1, almost twice as wide as the standard ratio of 1.33:1.[9] At first, widescreen was used principally for travelogues such as *This Is Cinerama* (1952) and lavish productions on the order of *The Robe* (1953). But by the 1960s widescreen films had become quite commonplace.

The first commonly used widescreen process was based on an **anamorphic** lens and is best known by its trademark labels: **CinemaScope** and Panavision. During the shooting of the film, the anamorphic process uses a special lens that squeezes the image. If we were to look at a frame of the film itself, everyone and everything would appear skinny (Figure 9.39). When this film is projected the process is reversed; it is projected through an anamorphic lens, which unsqueezes the image and presents a broad, wide view (Figure 9.40). The 'Scope frame thus achieves an expanded aspect ratio. Originally, that ratio was 2.35:1, but subsequent developments in the anamorphic process have settled on a current ratio of 2.40:1.

The second, more common, widescreen process is created through **masking** and does not involve the use of a special lens while shooting or projecting. Masked widescreen is created during the projection of the film, not the actual filming. A regular 1.33 frame is used, but horizontal bands across the top and the bottom of the frame are "masked" or matted out (blackened). As is evident in Figure 9.41, the frame *within* the frame is wider than the old 1.33 ratio. This widescreen frame-within-the-frame—with a ratio of 1.85:1—is enlarged to fill the screen. This shape dominates theatrical film presentation, with perhaps 90 percent of contemporary films being presented in the 1.85 aspect ratio.

Aspect Ratios on TV Today

All these numbers can be quite bewildering. To summarize, we offer an explanatory diagram in Figure 9.38, an extensive inventory of resolutions in Table 9.1, and the following abbreviated list of the most significant screen shapes, from narrowest to widest:

1. Pre-1952 film and standard-definition TV (1.33)
2. High-definition TV (1.78)

Figure 9.39 During the process of shooting *He Said, She Said*, an anamorphic lens squeezed Kevin Bacon and Elizabeth Perkins...

Figure 9.40 . . . but when the film was projected in a theater they were expanded to their normal widths.

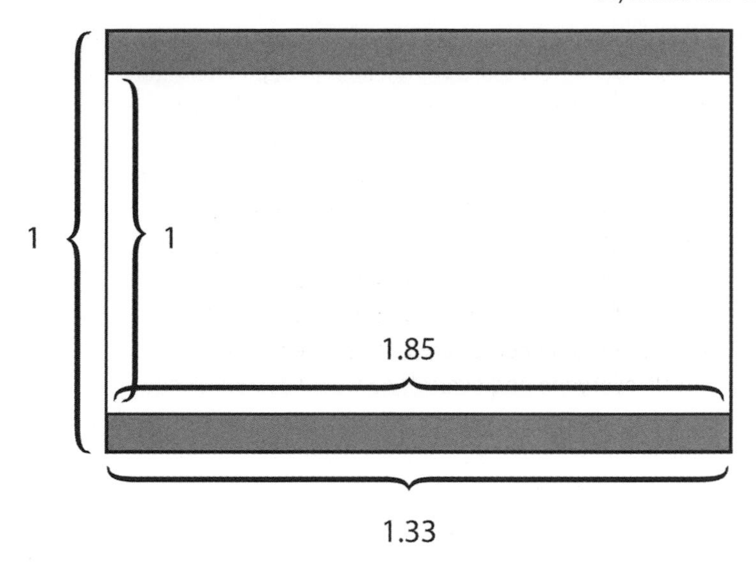

Figure 9.41 Masked widescreen (1.85:1) achieves a wider frame by embedding itself within the older ratio of 1.33:1.

3. Masked widescreen film (1.85)
4. Anamorphic film (2.35 or 2.40).

As mentioned above, digital-cinema standards for projection in the U.S. have been set by Digital Cinema Initiatives (DCI). Although digital-cinema projectors don't rely on the same technology as masked and anamorphic film do, they continue to present films in the same aspect ratios. The projectors in theaters changed from analog to digital in the 2010s, but the screen shapes stayed the same.

As a glance at this list illuminates, the programming we watch on our 1.78 screens may have been originally designed for that shape, or it may have been narrower or wider. Thus, television devices have had to develop methods for coping with source material that could go either way.

When Source Material Is Too Wide

Television has adopted a variety of strategies to present widescreen theatrical movies with a minimum of viewer annoyance. The greatest widescreen challenge to TV's ratio is the anamorphic frame's 2.40 width. In other words, television has had to find a way to fit an anamorphic film's extra-wide image into the skinnier television screen. Two processes have emerged to deal with the conversion from 2.40 to 1.33 (or 1.78): **letterbox** and **pan-and-scan**.

Letterboxing preserves most of the original image but shrinks it. This process closely resembles widescreen masking for the theater, in that the tops and bottoms of the video frame are blackened. In letterboxing, the anamorphic film frame is reduced and fit into the frame-within-the-television-frame. In Figure 9.42, from a letterboxed DVD release of *He Said, She Said* (1991), the reader may see how the anamorphic frame from the original film has been shrunk and placed within the television frame. Most of the width of the original composition has been maintained. We can see both Kevin Bacon and Elizabeth Perkins on opposite sides of the frame as she bounces a coffee mug off his head.

The pan-and-scan process was mostly necessary during the network-era days of standard-definition television and has become less common as consumers have made the transition to

Figure 9.42 Using letterboxing, all of the wide, anamorphic image of *He Said, She Said* is preserved but shrunk to fit a narrower frame—resulting in black masking at the top and bottom.

widescreen TVs, tablets, and phones. Pan-and-scan reduces the 2.40 anamorphic frame to SD television's 1.33 by selecting the most "significant" part of the frame and eliminating the rest. There are no black bars over parts of the screen and the entire SD frame is filled. In addition to destroying the visual composition of the source material, pan-and-scan can affect both camera movement and editing. The pan-and-scan frame need not remain fixed on one portion of the original frame. It can slide or "scan" left or right across the original. And, in terms of editing, the pan-and-scan version can alter the rhythms of the original edit by cutting between portions of a shot—even if there had been no cutting in the film version. Thus, a pan-and-scan version could alter the composition, camera movement, and editing of widescreen films.

The damage done to anamorphic, 2.40, widescreen films by pan-and-scan processes was largely associated with videocassettes and standard-definition, network-era broadcasts, but it has not disappeared entirely in the era of high-definition digital TV. An anamorphic image with its 2.40 image is still significantly wider than HD television's 1.78 aspect ratio. Some TV presentations of such wide images will simply trim a bit from the sides in order to fill the 1.78 frame, a less drastic form of pan-and-scan. However, the current fashion is to letterbox wide images when shown on TV. In fact, the screen shots from *Fargo* in Figures 9.29 and 9.30 were letterboxed when originally broadcast on FX. The *Fargo* frame was composed at a rather odd aspect ratio of 2:1—perhaps with the thought of an international theatrical release—and needed a bit of letterboxing to fit into HD TV's 1.78 frame. This sort of letterboxing of "prestige" programs has become more and more common—even with shows like *Fargo* that were not shown in theaters before their TV presentations. Back in the days of network-era television, there was an overriding compulsion to fill the image, to leave nothing blank. The visual voids at the top and bottom of letterboxed films thus did not suit the medium at that time, but aesthetic norms have shifted and viewers are perhaps more willing to accept letterboxed presentations today.

Aesthetically Reshaping the Frame

On occasion, television texts reshape the frame from within the standard rectangle for aesthetic purposes—although these reshapings are mostly limited to commercials and music videos. In the Acura car ad discussed in Chapter 6 (Figure 6.23, tvcrit.com/find/frames) multiple frames disrupt the image. Letterboxing may also be used to reshape the image, as can also be observed in the *Fargo* example and quite a few music videos (for example, *Lean On* by Major Lazer and DJ Snake, featuring MØ; tvcrit.com/find/lean; Figure 9.43). Both of these examples alter the image's aspect ratio without actually changing the dimensions of the picture frame. Commercials and music videos can also be found that blacken all but a small rectangular or circular portion of the image. Each of these manipulations of the frame leaves blank areas in the image that would not be tolerated in network-era television. The result is an image that looks oddly distinct, that distinguishes itself from "normal" television and thereby captures our attention—which is precisely the effect needed in prestigious shows, commercials, and music videos.

When Source Material Is Too Narrow

The introduction of widescreen HDTV has created a new issue for television programmers: What can you do when the original source you're presenting is too *narrow* for the television monitor? It's the exact opposite problem of widescreen movies on a skinny, network-era TV set. Essentially, there are three options: (1) cropping off the top and bottom, (2) stretching the image sideways and thereby distorting it, or (3) **pillar boxing**.

FXX network ran into the problem of narrow source material in 2014 when it featured a *Simpsons* marathon that included every single episode aired over dozens of seasons. The aspect-ratio problem was that *The Simpsons* had been originally broadcast in the narrower and thus *taller* standard-definition aspect ratio of 1.33 for some 20 seasons before converting to HD production. FXX wanted to broadcast all the episodes in 1.78, high definition, and it decided to crop off the top and bottom of the SD image. Of course, this infuriated *Simpsons* fans, who anticipated the ruining of many visual gags. The criticism may have chastened FXX, because once the marathon event concluded, it and Hulu (which owns the streaming rights to some older *Simpsons* material) began presenting episodes in the original shape in order to placate the fans. Further, the *FX Now* application for phones, tablets, and Apple TV offers users the option of watching *Simpsons* episodes in 1.33 or 1.78. The HD version takes the standard-definition original, zooms into the center of the frame, and then trims the top and the bottom. In the original broadcast of the "Mom and Pop Art" episode, Homer dreams he is in Salvador Dalí's painting *The Persistence of Memory* (1931), and a shot shows two melting clocks and cliffs in the background (Figure 9.44). In the high-definition

Figure 9.43 Letterboxing is used to alter the shape of the frame in the music video *Lean On* by Major Lazer and DJ Snake, featuring MØ.

Figure 9.44 The original, SD composition of a *Simpsons'* gag based on Dalí's painting *The Persistence of Memory* retains many of the visual elements of the original.

Figure 9.45 The HD composition of the same shot zooms in to the center of the image and chops off parts of the top and bottom.

Figure 9.46 Showrunner David Simon demanded that *The Wire* be shown on HBO in the SD, 1.33 aspect ratio.

Figure 9.47 When *The Wire* was remastered, it was widened to the HD, 1:78 aspect ratio by adding visual elements to the sides—such as the face of the man talking to Wallace.

rendering of it, we zoom in on Homer to the extent that the cliffs are hidden, the second clock is partially missing, and the image overall looks less like the Dalí original, which diminishes the impact of the gag (Figure 9.45). The only advantage to the HD version is that the animation has been re-rendered at a higher resolution than the original was; consequently the new version is clearer and sharper than the old, even if it does mess with the original version's composition.

Interestingly, the remastering of some standard-definition TV shows for high-definition presentation has been able to avoid cropping by going back to the original film on which the episodes were shot and including new visual elements that had previously been cropped out to fit the standard-definition frame. *Seinfeld*, *Friends*, and *The Wire*, for instance, are programs that have "benefitted" from this treatment. TV producers are not always in agreement with network decisions to add these elements. Showrunner David Simon, of *The Wire*, had been quite intentional in his selection of the 1.33 ratio for his program and was notably ambivalent when HBO decided to remaster it with extra material. Some shots were improved by the remastering, he explained, while others suffered.[10] Figures 9.46 and 9.47 show the original SD version and the new HD version, respectively, of a shot from *The Wire* to allow you to compare the two (see also, tvcrit.com/find/wirecomparison). The SD screen shot visually isolates Wallace (Michael B. Jordan), a young drug dealer who has not yet been completely hardened by his occupation. The HD screen shot incorporates more of the projects behind him, and the face of the person to whom he's talking intrudes into the frame, in a potentially menacing composition.

Image-stretching can be a part of the expensive process of remastering SD shows for HD presentation, but it is a more commonly a simple by-product of watching an SD program on an HD television monitor or an SD network transmitting a show to an HD system. Figure 9.48 shows the result of widening *Dawson's Creek*—which was originally shot in the standard 1.33 aspect ratio—to fit a widescreen television monitor. You can see that James Van Der Beek's head appears slightly too wide because the screen is being expanded from a 1.33 format to a 1.78 one. If you look carefully, you'll often observe this sort of image-stretching in publicly displayed HD televisions in restaurants and airports. This distortion is what happens when a standard-definition source is displayed on a widescreen TV.

Pillar boxing manages to avoid the image distortions of cropping and stretching the original by putting a standard-definition image in the middle of a widescreen frame—as in this pillar-boxed version of *Dawson's Creek* (Figure 9.49). Black masking fills in the missing width, effectively creating a sideways "letterbox." The original image now looks like a "pillar" in the middle of the widescreen frame. Pillar boxing "wastes" part of the widescreen frame, but it preserves the original aspect ratio of a 1.33 program. Now Van Der Beek appears in his authentic proportions.

A Note About Aspect Ratio and Cell Phones

More and more of our video viewing is done on cell phones these days. This is, obviously, a less engaging, more distracted experience than seeing TV on a large HD monitor or a movie in a theater, but what the experience lacks in intensity, it makes up for in convenience—allowing us to watch television and movies virtually anywhere. Cell phone TV viewing raises potential issues involving aspect ratio. Most modern cell phones (and many tablets) rely on the same aspect ratio as HD television, but they're rotated 90 degrees into a vertical or "portrait" orientation. So, instead of being 16 units wide by 9 units tall, cell phones are typically 9 units wide by 16 units tall. These matching aspect ratios—albeit rotated 90 degrees—are why *Game of Thrones* looks like a postage stamp when you view it vertically, but conveniently fills the entire screen when you rotate your cell phone to a horizontal or "landscape" position.

Figure 9.48 Viewing *Dawson's Creek* on an incorrectly set widescreen television monitor can lead to distortion—making actor James Van Der Beek appear too wide.

Figure 9.49 A pillar-boxed view of *Dawson's Creek* inserts black bars on the sides and returns the actor to his normal size, even on a widescreen monitor.

Thus, if we focus on aspect ratios and set aside the matter of increased distraction, using a cell phone to watch HD TV has only minor implications. A simple twist of the wrist can set things right. But what about video recorded by a cell phone in vertical orientation? To many videographers and others accustomed to horizontal aspect ratios, vertical videos are a detestable abomination. A humorous, widely viewed video on the Glove and Boots YouTube channel purported to be a public service announcement addressing the disease of "Vertical Video Syndrome" (2012, tvcrit.com/find/vvs). The puppets in it advise, "Say *no* to vertical videos. Vertical videos happen when you hold your camera the wrong way. Your video will wind up looking like crap! Vertical Video Syndrome is *dangerous*!" Although the PSA is satiric, it does raise reasonable questions about the aesthetics of aspect ratios. Is there something inherently "wrong" about shooting a video vertically? Not really. There are some events that might profit from a vertical frame—a pole vaulter's jump or a skyscraper on fire, perhaps. And there are others that won't—like a Monument Valley vista or a slithering snake. As a *New York Times* article put it, "Vertical video on a small screen? Not a crime."[11] And since we're all watching more video on our phones, skinny videos fit better on those vertically held screens—especially when viewed within social-media apps such as the highly influential Snapchat, which is natively vertical in its layout and requires traditional media partners such as CNN and *Wired* to reformat their videos into portrait mode if they want to appear on its platform.[12]

Vertical video must often be converted into horizontal formats, too, if it's to be presented on YouTube—the video player for which remains steadfastly horizontal—or an HD television set. The long-running amateur movie show *America's Funniest Home Videos* was a pioneer in this regard as it needed to figure out how to present early cell-phone videos of babies taking pratfalls and grooms fainting at the altar. Beginning in the 2000s, a large portion of *AFV*'s "home videos" were shot on cell phones, in vertical orientation. *AFV* chose to pillar box its vertical videos, but the result was more drastic than the *Dawson's Creek* pillar-box example discussed above (Figure 9.49). Why? Because when a cell phone's *vertical* aspect ratio appears in a *horizontal* format, it leaves much more blank space on either side of the image. Or, in technical terms, pillar boxing has to fit cell phone's 9-by-16 ratio inside HD's 16-by-9 HD ratio. (The cell-phone and HD ratios can also be expressed as .56 to 1 and 1.78 to 1, respectively.) *AFV*'s solution was to put abstract patterns on either side of the skinny video, after zooming in slightly. That approach is employed by many video editors today—sometimes branding the space with a network logo. Other editors incorporate a blurring technique by which the original video is enlarged and used to fill in the pillar-box spaces but is blurred out so that it's not recognizable (Figure 9.50, tvcrit.com/find/blur).

Regardless of the pillar-boxing technique chosen, vertical video's aspect ratio has come to signify "authenticity," "social media," and "nonprofessional" recording, much like the degraded image quality in the *CSI* clip discussed above. We've come to expect vertical video in social-media movies, but, more seriously, it is also associated with amateur video of police violence or natural disasters. Because of these associations with breaking news, TV producers will sometimes insert vertical videos into fictional, narrative programs as a stylistic signifier for raw, unmediated video shot by amateurs. Imagine, for example, a murder mystery in which the victim secretly video recorded the killer on his phone, which the detectives then discover after the crime. An editor could cut fabricated, vertical footage into the episode to suggest what the victim saw in the moments before his death. Vertical aspect ratios, thus, may carry signifiers of verisimilitude, of unvarnished and unmanipulated truth—even if they're incorporated into a fictional TV episode.

As viewers, we need to be aware of film and television's differing aspect ratios to understand the implications they may carry and anomalies such as the horizontally stretched actors in

Figure 9.50 Home video that was shot in vertical orientation by a cell phone is inserted into a wider, high-definition frame via a pillar box with blurred images on each side.

Dawson's Landing. These anomalies are becoming less and less frequent, however, as the social-media, television, and film industries become more and more intertwined. HDTV's ratio of 1.78 is not all that different from masked widescreen's 1.85—making it easier to fit theatrical films into HD frames. And many widescreen films—both anamorphic and masked—are now composed with television's aspect ratio in mind. For this reason, even widescreen films tend to position the actors in the center of the frame—for fear of losing them when displayed on narrower screens. And the lowly, initially despised vertical video of the cell phone can have purposeful framing effects as well. Thus, the technological and economic necessities of converting differing aspect ratios generate aesthetic results in the way the image finally appears on the various screens we use to experience television.

In-Camera Visual Effects

Visual effects are not, strictly speaking, part of the style of the camera. Very few visual effects are achieved solely by using a camera. Rather, most are accomplished by computers transforming the video images acquired by the camera or by originating images in the computer—a process called **computer-generated imagery** (**CGI**). Still, a few comments on visual effects seem in order at this point, because some visual effects can be created in-camera—that is, just by using the camera itself. Also, by way of clarification, in the U.S. television and film industries, "visual" effects are commonly separated from **mechanical effects**. The latter are created on set through machinery, make-up, pyrotechnics (explosives), and the like. The former exist in the digital, not physical, realm.

Among the first visual effects to be developed for television was **keying**, which is an electronic process but not necessarily a digital one. That is, a computer is not required. In keying, a portion of a video image is cut out and another image is placed in that video "hole." The simplest form of keying is the insertion of letters and numbers into an image, as can be seen in Figure 8.17, discussed above in terms of mise-en-scene. The text—"Kris van Cleave—Phoenix"—has been keyed into the image using a visual effects generator. The process is instantaneous and can be done while a program is broadcast live.

Chroma key is a special type of keying in which a particular color (blue or green, usually) is subtracted from an image and a new image is inserted in its place. Weather forecasters, for example, stand in front of a blue screen, which is transformed into map or radar images. The Weather Channel forecaster in the background of Figure 9.51 is in a studio gesturing toward a blue screen. As can be seen in the monitors on the lower left and far right, a map has been created by a computer and inserted into the image behind him, taking the place of the blue screen.[13]

One final visual effect that can be created either in-camera or after shooting, through digital effects processing, is the speed of motion. The most common way speed is manipulated in television is slow motion, which is of inestimable importance to sports television (see the discussion if it in Chapter 5). But speed of motion may also be sped up, as in time-lapse photography that shows a sunrise in a matter of seconds; or motion may even be stopped entirely, as in a freeze frame.

Manipulating the speed of motion goes beyond the instant replay. In a narrative context, slow motion can suggest the power of an action or emphasize the violence of a gun battle. In *The Six Million Dollar Man* (1973–78), Steve Austin (Lee Majors) is part human and part machine. When he kicks into cybernetic overdrive—running really, really fast or lifting a car—the program slows the motion down to signify strength and speed. The irony of slowing the motion in order to signify a character's quick movement went unnoticed. Slow motion can also represent a dreamlike state or a fantasy situation—as when a boy harbors a crush on a girl and, from his perspective, we see the girl shake her hair in slow motion. Freeze frames—motion that is slowed so much that it stops completely—appear in dozens of TV programs from the 1970s and 1980s and are often used to signal the end of the narrative. *Moonlighting* (1985–89) episodes, to pick one program among many, conclude with a freeze frame over which the end credits display. The practice was so widespread that it became a cliché and isn't seen much in current programs. Fast motion turns up in credit sequences such as the one for MTV's *Viva la Bam* (2003–05), but

Figure 9.51 Via blue-screen chroma key technology, the Weather Channel inserts a forecaster (rear) into a weather map (foreground monitor).

it is used much less frequently than slow motion or freeze frames. Still, it can serve expressive purposes in television narrative segments. For instance, slightly speeded-up motion can show that a character is harried or anxious. In their deviation from normal speed, both fast and slow motion generally express a deviation from characters' normal states—whether shifting into a dream or realizing superhuman strength. Both are techniques that may be put to aesthetic use.

Summary

This chapter has been filled with more technological information—mechanical, chemical, electronic, and digital—than the other chapters. This is because camera style is inevitably described in technological terms—words borrowing from technological roots for their meanings: *dolly shot, anamorphic framing, telephoto shot*. To discuss television style, then, it becomes necessary to understand television technology. Technology does not exist in a vacuum, however. The use of specific technological inventions—high-definition video, camera drones, and so on—depends upon the TV program's budget and the aesthetic conventions of the time. Moreover, many elements of camera style are not at all determined by technology. Framing and camera-height decisions, for example, do not depend upon specific technological devices. Instead, they result from shifting aesthetic conventions.

Technology, economics, and aesthetic convention blend together in the director of photography's and/or director's manipulation of camera style. Today, the persons responsible for visual style choose initially between digital-video formats and thereby determine much about the look of the final product. But—regardless of the originating medium—focal lengths, depths of field, framings, camera heights, and movements will be selected to maximize narrative, informational, or commercial effect. Each of these camera-style aspects serve many functions on television, affecting our understanding of a program. As critical viewers, we need to remain alert to the significance of camera-style techniques. We can then understand their function within television and their impact on television's construction of meaning.

Notes

1 Public domain image acquired from Wikimedia Commons, tvcrit.com/find/keys. Provided by user Zetelakiapu, March 12, 2013, accessed June 28, 2017.
2 Mike Johnston, "Bokeh in Pictures," *The Luminous Landscape*, January 13, 2009, tvcrit.com/find/bokeh, accessed August 25, 2017.
3 In the cinema, deep focus was not used much until the 1940s, when directors such as Orson Welles and cinematographers such as Gregg Toland began incorporating it. In *Citizen Kane* (1941) and *The Magnificent Ambersons* (1942), Welles uses deep focus to coordinate simultaneous action on several planes: for example, while a young boy's mother and father discuss the boy's future, he (the boy) is visible through a window, playing in the snow in the far background (*Citizen Kane*).
4 "The True-Def of Hi-Def," *Scientific-Atlanta*, December 6, 2005, tvcrit.com/find/hidef.
5 The two principal HD formats are defined by 1,080 and 720 horizontal lines of resolution, but there are others with different standards. Moreover, the scanning system—progressive or interlaced—and the number of frames per second are two other significant factors in HD video's resolution level.
6 Many experts argue over the number of points in a film image. We have taken our figures from a publication by Arri, a major film-equipment company. Hans Kiening, *4K+ Systems: Theory Basics for Motion Picture Imaging* (Munich, Germany: Arnold & Richter Cine Technik, 2008).
7 Simon Wakelin, "CSI: Miami Transitions to HD With the Addition of the Panavision Genesis," *HDVideoPro*, April 1, 2010, tvcrit.com/find/miami, accessed October 22, 2010.
8 Netflix itself is notoriously closedmouthed about such statistics, but a company specializing in network analysis, Sandvine, came up with an estimate of 35.2 percent of downstream traffic in North America. "Global Internet Phenomena Report," *Sandvine*, June 21, 2016, tvcrit.com/find/netflixuse, accessed June 26, 2017.

9 Although these are the numbers generally used in discussions of aspect ratios, some qualifications could be made. The 1.33 standard typically wound up closer to 1.37 on actual film prints made for projection.
10 Russ Fischer, "See 'The Wire' HD Remaster Compared to Original Presentation," *Slash Film*, December 5, 2014, Russ Fischer, accessed June 28, 2017.
11 Farhad Manjoo, "Vertical Video on the Small Screen? Not a Crime," *The New York Times*, August 12, 2015, tvcrit.com/find/crime.
12 Clive Thompson, "Vertical Reality: Phones Have Tilted Our Worldview," *Wired*, September 2017, 40.
13 On the issue of whether to use blue or green for chroma key, Greg Stroud, former senior brand manager, comments, "Most places switched to green walls long ago because talent kept complaining that they couldn't wear blue in their wardrobe. A legit complaint, since blue is a very common wardrobe element. However, the green used in a green wall is very reflective. Because of that, the talent cannot stand very close to the wall or the green reflects back on them, not only giving them an odd skin tone but then keying them out. So to use green, you have to have a very deep studio with proper lighting." Greg Stroud, phone conversation with the author, 2011.

Further Readings

Camera style is discussed in many of the handbooks for television production suggested at the end of Chapter 8. In addition, Peter Ward, *Picture Composition for Film and Television*, 2nd ed. (Woburn, MA: Focal Press, 2002); and Roy Thompson and Christopher J. Bowen, *Grammar of the Shot*, 2nd ed. (Woburn, MA: Focal Press, 2009), address the specific principles behind the framing of images with the camera and the positioning of objects and humans within that frame. And Leo Enticknap, *Moving Image Technology: From Zoetrope to Digital* (New York: Wallflower Press, 2005), focuses mainly on the camera and its technology in this historical overview, which includes a chapter on television and video.

The nuts-and-bolts of digital video production are well covered in Ben Long and Sonja Schenk, *The Digital Filmmaking Handbook*, 5th ed. (Independence, KY: Cengage, 2014); and Michael Rubin, *Nonlinear 4: A Field Guide to Digital Video and Film Editing* (Gainesville, FL: Triad, 2000). The convoluted story behind the evolution of digital TV is chronicled in entertaining fashion in Joel Brinkley, *Defining Vision: The Battle for the Future of Television* (New York: Harcourt Brace, 1997). Readers interested in the specifics of *film* camera technology should consult Kris Malkiewicz and M. David Mullen, *Cinematography*, 3rd ed. (New York: Fireside/Simon & Schuster, 2005).

10 Style and Editing

Editing is at once the most frequently overlooked and the most powerful component of television style. We are seldom conscious of a program's arrangement of shots, and yet it is through editing that television producers most directly control our sense of space and time, the medium's building blocks. For many theorists of television, editing is the engine that powers the medium.

At its most basic, editing is deceptively simple. Shot one ends. Cut. Shot two begins. But in that instantaneous shot-to-shot transition, we make a rather radical shift. We go from looking at one piece of space from one point-of-view to looking at another piece of space from a different perspective. Perspective and the representation of space suddenly become totally malleable. Time, too, can be equally malleable. Shot two need not be from a time following shot one; it could be from hours or years before. The potential for creative manipulation is obvious.

Within the U.S. television industry, however, editing is not completely free of conventions—far from it. Many "rules" or standard craft practices, one might say, govern how one shot is connected to the next. These editing practices initially developed in the silent cinema of the 1910s and 1920s and were codified as a fundamental part of the single-camera mode of production. When sound arrived in 1927, the film industry tweaked that mode of production to incorporate this new technology into its editing practices. Thus, by the early 1930s, the single-camera editing rules were well established, and they have persisted, with little change, to the present day. When television's multiple-camera mode of production arrived in the 1940s, it adopted many of these editing practices but had to modify them to suit its simultaneous use of several cameras. To understand how editing works in television we must therefore start with the single-camera mode of production before moving on to multiple-camera.

The Single-Camera Mode of Production

In the single-camera mode of production, editing is largely determined during the pre-production and production stages. As discussed in Chapter 7, storyboards and shot lists are created during pre-production, and the director decides which shots to record during the actual production. The actual assembly of shots occurs during the post-production stage.

The post-production process was revolutionized in the 1990s by computer-based **nonlinear editing** (**NLE**) on systems such as Adobe Premiere, Apple's Final Cut Pro, and the Avid Media Composer. Virtually all post-production editing in television and film today is accomplished on NLE systems. To understand what makes these systems "nonlinear" and why that is significant, a bit of history is required (see tvcrit.com/find/history for further details).

Early video editing systems were strictly *linear*. To assemble shots A, B, and C, you first put shot A on the master tape and then shot B and then shot C. If you decided later that you wanted to insert shot X in between A and B, you were out of luck. You had to start all over and put down shot A, followed by X, and then B and so on. One shot had to follow the other (there were exceptions to this, but we are simplifying for clarity). In contrast to this linear system for video, film editing was always *nonlinear*. If film editors wish to insert shot X between shots A and B, they just pull strips of film apart and tape them together again. Digital editors changed video's reliance on linear systems and made video editing more like film editing.

An NLE system typically uses a widescreen monitor or two monitors placed side-by-side—as can be seen in the center of Figure 10.1. This particular editing suite also has a larger monitor above the NLE screens so that shots can be examined in detail or shown to clients seated behind the editor. Figure 10.2 illustrates the Adobe Premiere layout chosen by an editor of a TV cooking show being developed at the Center for Public Television and Radio, the University of Alabama. Adobe refers to each rectangle within the layout as a "panel," which can be moved and resized as the editor prefers. In our layout, two panels next to each other show the finished project on the right (the "program monitor") and a preview of a clip that might be added to the video on the left (the "source monitor"). In the lower left corner, you see a list (a "bin") of available video and sound source clips (indicated with thumbnails), which is enlarged in Figure 10.3. The key to any NLE editor's layout is a video project's timeline, which appears in the lower right panel of Figure 10.2 and is enlarged in Figure 10.4.

NLE systems use timelines to structure the editing. In our sample timeline, each shot is signified by a rectangle, marked with a thumbnail and a label. Unlike *linear* video editing, the editor may place any shot anywhere on the timeline, inserting shots between other shots if they wish. In a Premiere timeline, the editor may create fairly sophisticated visual effects in between shots—as is exemplified by the truncated "Cross Dissolve" rectangle on the track labeled "V3,"

Figure 10.1 A nonlinear editing suite at the Center for Public Television and Radio, the University of Alabama.

Figure 10.2 A cooking show is edited in Adobe Premiere, a widely used nonlinear editor. The screen is divided into four "panels": the source monitor (upper left), the program monitor (upper right), the bin (lower left), and the timeline (lower right).

Figure 10.3 A listing of a film's resources—principally, video and audio clips—is displayed in Premiere's bin.

which indicates a dissolve from a shot on the V3 track to one on the V2 track. The editor may work on several simultaneous video tracks (labeled "V1" through "V5" in Figure 10.4) and build visual effects among them all. In this manner, the editor may create fades, dissolves, and more elaborate

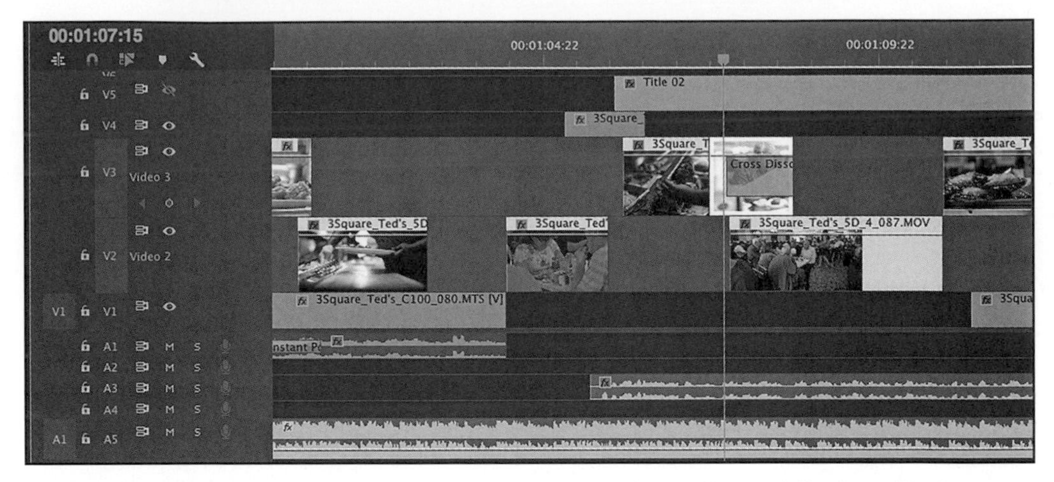

Figure 10.4 The order of shots and audio segments, their lengths, and the transitions among them are set in Premiere's timeline.

transitions. Also visible in the enlarged timeline in Figure 10.4 are audio tracks (labeled "A1" through "A5"), with the relative loudness of the audio indicated by the jagged lines. Several other overlapping audio tracks can also be added—allowing editors to create complicated sound mixes.

NLE is a big part of the digital overhaul of the television industry. NLE systems are cheaper than old-fashioned video editing equipment, and NLE provides television editors with much greater aesthetic flexibility. Moreover, NLE is part of the motivation behind the move to digital video (DV). Analog video and film must be converted to a digital format before they can be sucked into an NLE computer, but DV can skip this process since it is already digital. The ease and relative lack of expense of DV and NLE have changed the face of post-production and facilitated work by low-budget independent video producers—such as the people behind *The Blair Witch Project* (1999), *Napoleon Dynamite* (2004), *Super Size Me* (2004), and *Paranormal Activity* (2009).

The Continuity Editing System

We've seen how the editing of a television program is conceptualized and then implemented by scriptwriters, directors, and editors during pre-production, production, and post-production, respectively. They are able to function well together within the single-camera mode of production because they all share a particular approach to editing that has come to be known as **continuity editing**. This editing approach operates to create a continuity of space and time out of the fragments of scenes that are contained in individual shots. It is also known as invisible editing because it does not call attention to itself. Cuts are not noticeable because the shots are arranged in an order that effectively supports the progression of the story. If the editing functions correctly, we concentrate on the story and don't notice the technique that is used to construct it. Thus, the editing is done according to the logic of the narrative. Scriptwriters, directors, and editors work together to facilitate this narrative logic.

There are many ways to edit a story, but Hollywood classicism evolved a set of conventions, of craft practices, that constitute the continuity system. The continuity editing system matches classicism's narrative coherence with continuities of space and time. Shots are arranged so that the spectator always has a clear sense of where the characters are (space) and when the shot is happening (time)—excepting narratives that begin ambiguously and clarify the "where" and "when" later (for example, murder mysteries). This spatial and temporal coherence is particularly crucial in individual **scenes** of a movie.

A scene is the smallest piece of the narrative action. Usually it takes place in one location (continuous space), at one particular time (continuous time). When the location and/or time frame change, the scene is customarily over and a new one begins. To best understand the continuity system, we will examine how it constructs spatial and temporal continuity within individual scenes. How these scenes then fit together with one another in a narrative structure is discussed in Chapter 3.

Spatial Continuity

In the classical scene, the space is oriented around an **axis of action**. To understand how this axis functions, consider Figure 10.5, an overhead view of a rudimentary two-character scene. Let's say that the action of this scene is Brent and Lilly talking to one another in a cafeteria. The axis, or line of action, then, runs through the two of them. The continuity system dictates that cameras remain on one side of that axis. Note the arc in Figure 10.5 that defines the area in which the camera may be placed. If you recall your high school geometry, you'll recognize

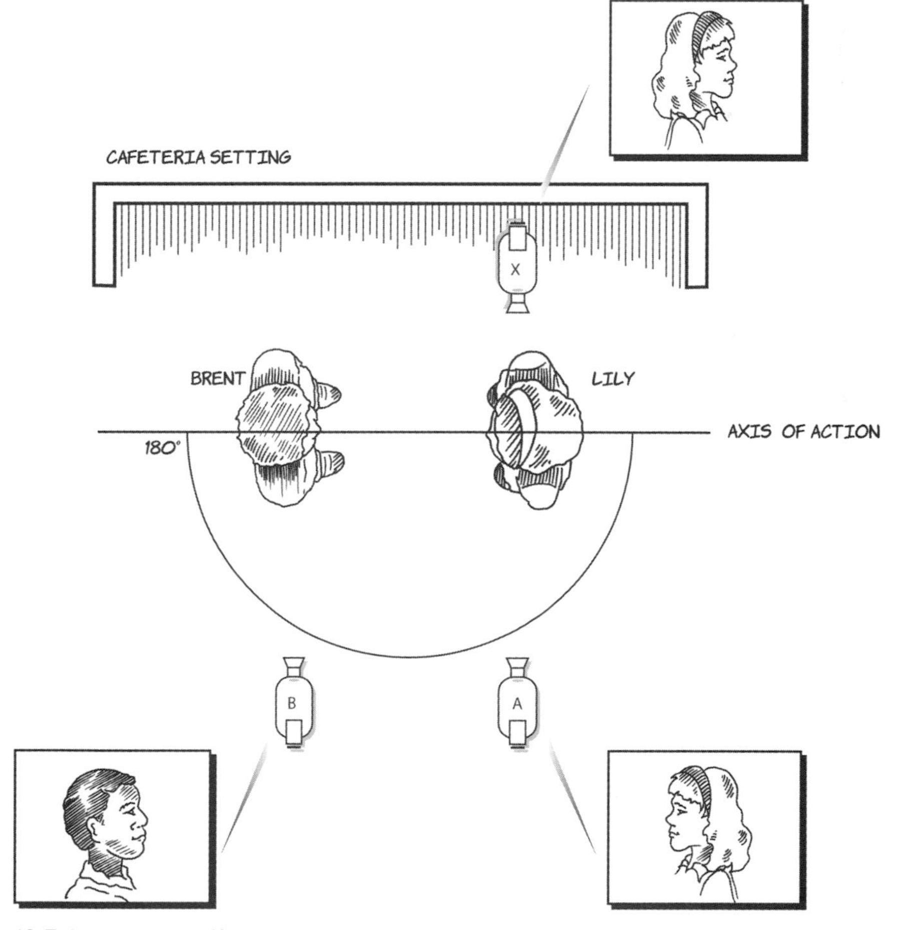

Figure 10.5 In a conversation scene, cameras A and B remain on one side of the axis of action in order to preserve the 180° rule. Camera X breaks the rule.

that this arc describes 180°. Since the cameras may be positioned only within the 180° arc, this editing principle has come to be known as the **180° rule**.

The 180° rule helps preserve spatial continuity because it ensures that there will be a similar background behind the actors while cutting from one to the other. The cafeteria setting that is behind Brent and Lilly recurs from shot to shot and helps confirm our sense of the space of the room. A shot from the other side of the axis (position X) would reveal a portion of the cafeteria that had not been seen before and thus might contain spatial surprises or cause disorientation.

More important than similar backgrounds, however, is the way in which the 180° rule maintains **screen direction**. In the classical system, the conventional wisdom is that if characters are looking or moving to the right of the screen in shot one, then they should be looking or moving in the same direction in shot two. To cut from camera A to camera X (Figure 10.5) would break the 180° rule and violate screen direction. In a shot from camera A, Lilly is looking screen left. If the director had cut to a shot of her from position X, Lilly would suddenly be looking screen *right*. Even though the actor herself had not changed position, the change in camera angle would make her *seem* to have changed direction. This is further illustrated by camera position B. A cut from Brent (camera B) to Lilly from the hypothetical X position would make it appear as if they were both looking to the right, instead of toward one another. Breaking the 180° rule would confuse the spatial relationship between these two characters.

Peter John Ross's instructional video *Moviemaking Techniques and Other Indie Film Tips* offers a real-life example in which a cut across the 180° line violates screen direction (tvcrit.com/find/180degreerule). A man and a woman are seated at a table (Figure 10.6). If we shoot the man from one side of the axis of action (Figure 10.7) and then cut to the woman from a camera on the other side (Figure 10.8), then they are both looking screen right—thus violating screen direction and confusing the viewer, who expects them to be looking toward one another.

Maintaining screen direction is also important to action scenes filmed outdoors. If the directors are not careful about screen direction, they will wind up with car chases where the vehicles appear to be moving *toward* each other rather than following. In such chases, the axis of action runs down the middle of the road and cameras stay on one side or the other. And, similarly, if screen direction is muddled, then antagonists in confrontational scenes might appear to be running in the same direction rather than challenging one another.

There are, of course, ways of bending or getting around the 180° rule, but the basic principle of preserving screen direction remains fundamental to the classical construction of space. For this reason, the **continuity system** is also known as the 180° system.

Built upon the 180° rule is a set of conventions governing the editing of a scene. Although these conventions were more strictly adhered to in theatrical film during the 1930s and 1940s than they are on television today, there are several that still persist. Some of the most prevalent include:

- the **establishing shot**;
- the **shot-counter shot** editing pattern;
- the **re-establishing shot**;
- the **match cut**—including the **match-on-action** and the **eyeline match**;
- the prohibition against the **jump cut**.

This may best be illustrated by breaking down a simple scene into individual shots. Table 10.1 analyzes a *Grey's Anatomy* scene shot-by-shot. Each shot is described in terms of its dialogue, music, action, framing, and shot length—with at least one frame capture from each shot (Figures 10.9

Figure 10.6 A long shot establishes a scene's axis of action for the 180° rule. The man looks right and the woman looks left.

Figure 10.7 The camera observes the 180° rule when closing in on the man.

Figure 10.8 The 180° rule is broken in the woman's close-up and thus confuses screen direction (she looks to the right when she previously looked left).

Table 10.1 *Grey's Anatomy* Scene Découpage

Shot Number, Scale & Length	*Figure*	*Action,* ***Dialogue and Music***
1 long shot to medium shot 10 secs.	 *Figure 10.9*	[*Dissolve in* from a transitional shot of the Seattle skyline.] *Nondiegetic music*: Trent Dabbs's "Your Side Now" slowly fades out. Meredith (in VO): It feels cruel…
	 *Figure 10.10*	[The actors walk toward the camera, into a medium close-up.] Lexie: Hey. Mark: Hey. Lexie: How did…
2 medium close-up 2 secs.	 *Figure 10.11*	Lexie:… Sloane's surgery go? Mark: I slept with Addison.
3 close-up 4 secs. 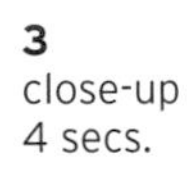	 *Figure 10.12*	Lexie: Oh, thank God…

Table 10.1 Grey's Anatomy Scene Découpage (continued)

Shot Number, Scale & Length	*Figure*	*Action,* ***Dialogue and Music***
4 close-up 8 secs.	 *Figure 10.13*	Mark: ... because I slept with Alex. I was feeling so... well...
5 close-up 3 secs.	 *Figure 10.14*	Lexie: ... you know how I was feeling. Which is why this is great. You know, we're even. We kind of canceled each other out.
6 close-up 6 secs.	 *Figure 10.15*	Mark: You slept with [Alex] Karev?
7 close-up 2 secs.	 *Figure 10.16*	Lexie: Yeah. Mark: While I was dealing with my sick daughter...

(*continued*)

Table 10.1 Grey's Anatomy Scene Découpage (continued)

Shot Number, Scale & Length	*Figure*	*Action,* ***Dialogue and Music***
8 close-up 5 secs.	 *Figure 10.17*	*Nondiegetic music*: Matthew Mayfield's "Better" starts to fade in. Mark: . . . while I was hurting. Lexie: Ah . . .
9 medium close-up 3 secs.	 *Figure 10.18*	Lexie: You weren't hurting. You were sleeping with Addison. Mark: You . . .
10 medium close-up 6 secs.	 *Figure 10.19*	Mark: . . . broke up with me. Left me . . .
11 close-up 6 secs.	 *Figure 10.20*	Mark: . . . and just . . . wow.

Table 10.1 *Grey's Anatomy* Scene Découpage (continued)

Shot Number, Scale & Length	*Figure*	*Action,* ***Dialogue and Music***
12 close-up 7 secs.	 Figure 10.21	Mark: I can't even look at you right now. *Nondiegetic music*: Lyrics begin, "Two fires, they're breathing..."
13 medium shot 7 secs.	 Figure 10.22	*Nondiegetic music*: Lyrics rise "... running out of air." Meredith (VO): ... and against common sense. *Nondiegetic music*: Lyrics continue, "Two hearts, they are beating..." [Mark exits the frame.]
	 Figure 10.23	[*Cut to* the first shot of the following scene.]

through 10.23; see also tvcrit.com/find/greysanatomy). And in Figure 10.24, the scene's basic camera positions are diagramed. While examining the frame captures from this scene, keep in mind that *Grey's Anatomy* is a single-camera production (initially recorded on film, and later on HD video). That is, a standard multiple-camera set-up is typically not used. Just one camera is on the set at the time of filming—with the occasional exception. In the behind-the-scenes *Grey's Anatomy* video cited in the Chapter 9 discussion of camera movement (tvcrit.com/find/greysanatomy2), we can see this reliance on a single camera.

The first shot of a classical scene is typically a long shot that shows the entire area and the characters in it, as in the long shot of Mark and Lexie exiting the hospital in Figure 10.9 (camera position A in the diagram). The shot starts as a long shot and then the characters walk toward

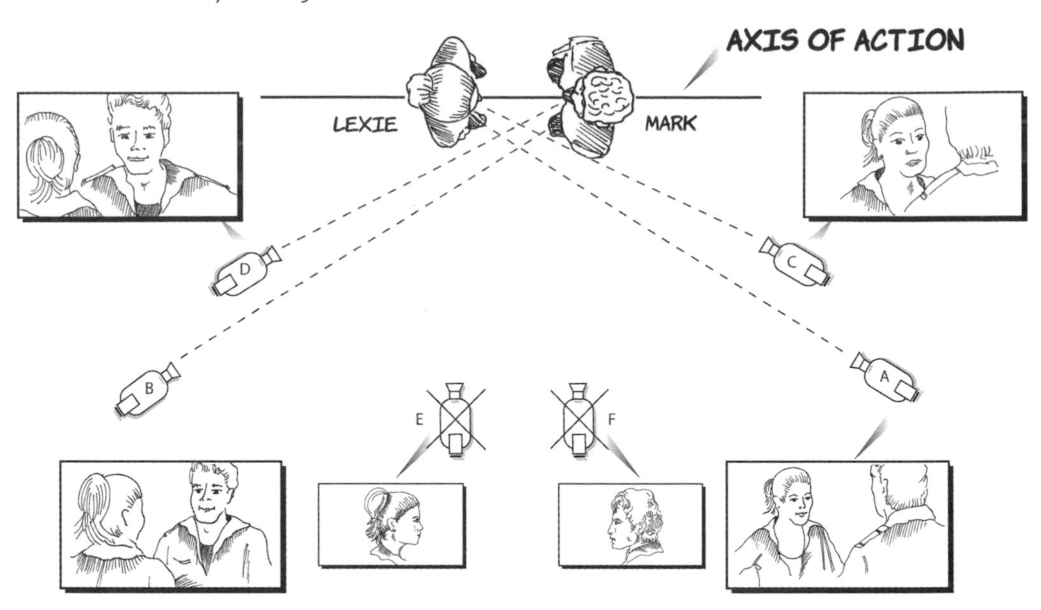

Figure 10.24 In a two-person scene from *Grey's Anatomy*, the cameras are placed in positions A, B, C, and D—using shot-reverse shot to acquire close-ups and medium close-ups. Camera positions E and F are not used.

the camera, into a medium close-up (Figure 10.10). This **establishing shot** introduces the space and the narrative components of the scene: Mark, Lexie, and the semi-private space of the hospital entrance, away from all the other characters. In a sense, the establishing shot repeats the exposition of the narrative, presenting specific characters to us once again. If the establishing shot in a scene is from a very great distance, it may be followed by another establishing shot that shows the characters clearly in a medium shot or medium long shot.

From there most scenes typically develop some sort of alternating pattern, especially if it is a conversation scene between two persons. Thus, shots of Mark are alternated with shots of Lexie, depending on who is speaking or what their narrative importance is at a particular point. The first two shots in this alternation are medium close-ups (camera positions A and B, Figures 10.10 and 10.11). These are followed by six alternating shots in a tighter framing, a close-up (camera positions C and D; for example, Figures 10.12 and 10.13). Note that once again the 180° rule is adhered to, as the cameras remain on one side of the axis of action—that imaginary line between Mark and Lexie. Note also that the camera angles crisscross each other, rather than being aimed at Mark's or Lexie's profile from positions E or F. That is, camera B's angle crosses camera A's; and camera D's angle crosses camera C's. The "prohibited" camera positions (E and F) do not violate the 180° rule, but positions A through D are preferred in the continuity system for two reasons. First, these angles show more of the characters' faces, giving us three-quarter views rather than profiles. We observe their faces without gazing directly into their eyes, which would break the taboo against actors looking into the camera lens (and at the viewer). Second, since we see Mark's shoulder in Lexie's shot (Figure 10.12) and vice versa (Figure 10.13), the space that the two share is reconfirmed. We know where Mark is in relationship to Lexie and where she is in relationship to him.

Since shots such as B and D in our diagram (Figure 10.24) are said to be the counter or reverse angle of shots such as A and C, this editing convention goes by the name **shot-counter shot** or **shot-reverse shot**. Shot-counter shot is probably the most common editing pattern in both single-camera (such as *Grey's Anatomy*) and multiple-camera productions (for example, soap operas).

Once shot-counter shot has been used to detail the action of a scene, there is often a cut back to a longer view of the space. This **re-establishing shot** shows us once again which characters are involved and where they are located. It may also be used as a transitional device, showing us a broader area so that the characters may move into it or another character may join them. Often it is immediately followed by another series of shot-reverse shots.

The *Grey's Anatomy* scene does not contain this type of re-establishing shot but provides a variation of it. After a series of six shots in fairly tight close-up (Figures 10.12–10.17), the camera cuts back to a *medium* close-up of Lexie (Figure 10.18), thus signifying a shift in tone. The scene is then played at medium close-up for just two shots (Figures 10.18 and 10.19), as Mark and Lexie drift apart emotionally. Then we return to a close-up of Lexie as her shame mounts. The emotional peak of the scene is reached in shot 12, where Mark declares, in close-up, "I can't even look at you right now" (Figure 10.21). Lexie is struck silent and the scene resolves with a final close-up of her crestfallen face as Mark exits the frame and the music mounts: "Two fires, they're breathing, running out of air" (Figures 10.22 and 10.23). The scene ends inconclusively, as is essential to the serial narrative form. The last line of dialogue in the scene is Mark saying, "I can't even look at you *right now*," which leaves open the possibility that he might forgive her in the future. Indeed, during season six of *Grey's Anatomy*, episodes often returned to this on-again, off-again relationship.

Thus this scene's framing has gone from long shot to medium close-up to close-up, coming closer to the characters as the scene intensifies. But it does not remain at close-up. The camera cuts back to medium close-up and then returns to close-up at the scene's end. The key to any classically edited scene is variation—closer and farther as the narrative logic dictates.

Two other editing devices are among those used to maintain space in the continuity system: the **match cut** and the **point-of-view** or **subjective shot**.

In a match cut, the space and time of one shot fit that of the preceding shot. One shot "matches" the next and thereby makes the editing less noticeable. Matching may be achieved in several ways. Two of the most common are the **match-on-action** and the **eyeline match**.

In a match-on-action cut, an activity is continued from one shot to the next. At the end of a shot in a *Northern Exposure* scene, Maggie begins to sit down (Figure 7.3); at the start of the next shot she continues that movement (Figures 7.4 and 7.5). The editor matches the action from one shot to the next, placing the cut in the midst of it. This, in effect, conceals the cut because we are drawn from one shot to the next by the action. We concentrate on Maggie's movement, and the cut becomes "invisible." In fact, the action matches so strongly that we probably don't even notice the continuity error (the disappearing dishrag).

An eyeline match begins with a character looking in a direction that is motivated by the narrative. For instance, in *Black-ish* (2014–) dining room/kitchen scenes are sometimes edited based on the looks and glances of the characters. Jack (Miles Brown) and Diane Johnson (Marsai Martin) look in a specific direction in one shot (Figure 10.25), and editor Jamie Pedroza uses that look as a signal to cut to their mother, Rainbow Johnson (Tracee Ellis Ross; Figure 10.26), toward whom the kids had glanced. The kids' *eyeline* provides the motivation for the cut and impels the viewer toward the new space. In an eyeline match such as this, the second shot is *not* from the perspective of the person who is looking but rather shows the area of the room in the eyeline's general direction. Even though the kids' glance cued the shot of Rainbow, the camera angle is not from anywhere close to the kids' perspective.

A shot made when the camera "looks" from a character's perspective is known as a point-of-view shot. A point-of-view shot is a type of framing in which the camera is positioned physically close to a character's point-of-view. The shots of Mark and Lexie in Figures 10.9–10.23, for

Figure 10.25 Black-ish: An objective, eyeline, match cut uses Jack and Diane's glance as a cue to cut to the person they are looking at...

Figure 10.26 ... which is Rainbow. The camera is not placed where the kids are sitting, which would have created a subjective shot.

Figure 10.27 Black-ish: Dre angrily looks toward...

Figure 10.28 . . . a woman who has stolen a parking space from him. The camera "looks" from Dre's perspective as she returns his gaze and makes an obscene gesture.

example, are all point-of-view shots. In each, we can see from Mark's or Lexie's point-of-view. If the camera were positioned as if it were inside the character's head, looking out his or her eyes, then it would be known as a subjective shot.[1] Frequently, point-of-view and subjective shots are incorporated in a simple editing pattern: in shot one someone looks and in shot two we see what they are looking at from their perspective. In Figure 10.27, from another *Black-ish* scene, Dre (Anthony Anderson) is annoyed by a woman who has stolen his parking space and angrily looks at her. The camera cuts to a medium close-up of the woman as she returns his gaze and makes an obscene gesture, which the ABC censors have pixillated (Figure 10.28). Subjective shots such as this are very similar to objective eyeline matches, but the latter does not go to a shot that is exactly the character's perspective. To observe the difference, contrast the objective eyeline match from Figures 10.25 to 10.26 with the subjective eyeline match from Figures 10.27 and 10.28. Also, if you carefully examine the glances of the actors in the analyzed *Grey's Anatomy* scene, you'll find that they are not looking directly at the camera but, rather, are locking onto the eyes of the other actor. In this *Black-ish* subjective shot, however, the parking-lot woman looks directly into the camera lens because the lens has become a surrogate for Dre's eyes.

The opposite of a match cut is a **jump cut**, which results in a disruptive gap in space and/or time so that something seems to be missing. Jump cuts were regarded as mistakes in classical editing, but they were made fashionable in the 1960s films of Jean-Luc Godard and other European directors. Godard's first feature film, *Breathless* (1960), features numerous jump cuts, as is illustrated in Figures 10.29 and 10.30. The camera maintains similar framing while the woman's position shifts abruptly and a mirror appears in her hand. Today, jump cuts similar to this are quite common in music videos and commercials and even find their way into more mainstream narrative productions. *Homicide: Life on the Street* (1993–99) is peppered with them, although some are rather subtle. For example, in Figure 10.31 Detective Frank Pembleton (Andre Braugher) lectures his rookie partner, Tim Bayliss (Kyle Secor), about interrogating witnesses (see tvcrit.com/find/homicide). The camera cuts in the middle of this lecture to a slightly different angle of Pembleton and Bayliss, as one can see from the amount of Bayliss's shoulder that suddenly intrudes into the frame in Figure 10.32. The jump cuts in *Homicide* keep viewers on edge, jerking them around unexpectedly with these visual discontinuities. It is not a conventionally edited show. In most narrative television programs, match cuts still remain the norm and jump cuts are generally avoided.

Sample Découpage

The best way to understand editing is to take a scene and work backward toward the shooting script, thereby reverse engineering the scene. The process of breaking down a scene into its constituent parts is known as découpage, the French word for cutting things apart.

Figure 10.29 Breathless: A jump cut is created by cutting from Patricia riding in a car with her hands in her lap to...

Figure 10.30 ... her looking in a mirror, from the same camera position. There is a noticeable gap in the action as we do not see her raise the mirror.

Figure 10.31 Homicide: Detective Frank Pembleton chews out a rookie. His tirade is interrupted with a jump cut to...

Figure 10.32 ... a similarly framed shot, which emphasizes the gap in action.

In our discussion of *Grey's Anatomy* we have created a sample découpage in Table 10.1 (Figures 10.9 through 10.23). You may want to perform a similar exercise with a short scene of your own choosing. Watch the video several times with the sound turned off. Try to diagram the set and each of the camera positions from a bird's-eye view, as in Figure 10.24. Draw a shot-by-shot storyboard of the scene. Or, if you're watching the video on a computer, make screen shots from each shot. Ask yourself these questions:

1. How is the scene's space, the area in which the action takes place, introduced to the viewer? Does an establishing shot occur at the start of the scene (or later in it)?
2. What is the narrative purpose or function of each shot? What does each shot communicate to the viewer about the story?
3. Why was each shot taken from the camera position that it was? Do these angles adhere to the 180° rule? Is screen direction maintained? If not, why is the viewer not disoriented? Or if the space is ambiguous, what narrative purpose does that serve?
4. If the characters move around, how does the editing (or camera movement) create transitions from one area to another?
5. Is an alternating editing pattern used? Is shot-reverse shot used?
6. How does the camera relate to the character's perspective? Are there point-of-view or subjective shots? If so, how are those shots cued or marked? That is, what tells us that they are subjective or point-of-view shots?
7. Is match-on-action used? Are there jump cuts?
8. How does the last shot of the scene bring it to a conclusion?
9. In sum, how does the organization of space by editing support the narrative?

Temporal Continuity

To understand editing's impact on time, on the temporal qualities of a TV show, we need to return to the concepts of story time and screen time introduced in Chapter 3—with story time being the amount of time represented in the story (a day, a month, a year in the characters' "lives") and screen time being the amount of time it takes to watch a program. Within individual scenes, story time and screen time are often the same. Five minutes of story usually takes five minutes on-screen. Time is continuous. Shot two is presumed to instantaneously follow shot one. Transitions from one scene to the next, however, need not be continuous. If the story time of one scene always immediately followed that of another's, then screen time would always be exactly the same as story time. A story that lasted two days would take two days to watch on the screen. Obviously, story time and screen time are seldom equivalent on television. The latter is most commonly much shorter than the former. There are many gaps, or ellipses, in screen time. In addition, screen time may not be in the same chronological order as story time. Through flashbacks, for example, an action from the story past is presented in the screen present. So, both time's *duration* and its *order* may be manipulated in the transition from one scene to the next.

To shorten story time or change its order without confusing the viewer, classical editing has developed a collection of scene-to-scene transitions that break the continuity of time in conventionalized ways, thus avoiding viewer disorientation. These transitions are marked by simple visual effects that are used instead of a regular cut:

1. The **fade**: a **fade out** gradually darkens the image until the screen is black; a **fade in** starts in black and gradually illuminates the image. The fade out of one scene and fade in to the next are often used to mark a substantial change in time.

2. The **dissolve**: when one shot **dissolves** into the next, it means that one shot fades out at the same time the next shot fades in, so that the two images overlap one another briefly. Dissolves are more conventionally used to signal a passage in time; and the slower the dissolve, the more time has passed.

In addition to these transitional devices, classical editors also use sound and visual effects to indicate flashbacks. In films of the 1930s and 1940s, the image may become blurry or wavy as the story slips into the past (or into a dream). The visual effect signals to the viewer, "We're moving into the past now." During the prime of the classical era, changes in time were inevitably clearly marked.

Fades and dissolves were part of the stock-in-trade of the film editor during the cinema's classical era, and they are still evident in today's single-camera productions. Historically, however, narrative filmmakers have used these devices less and less. Initially, this was due in large part to the influence of 1960s European filmmakers, who accelerated the pace of their films through jump cuts and ambiguous straight cuts (no visual effects) when shifting into the past or into dream states. The jump cuts in Godard's *Breathless* revolutionized classical editing (Figures 10.29 and 10.30), breaking many of its most fundamental "rules." And Luis Buñuel's and David Lynch's films enter and exit dream states and flashbacks without signaling them to the viewer in any way, creating a bizarre, unstable world.

Classical editing is not a static phenomenon. It changes according to technological developments, aesthetic fashions, and economic imperatives. Current fashion favors straight cuts in narrative, single-camera productions, but fades and dissolves are still in evidence. Indeed, the fade out and fade in are television's favorite transition from narrative segment to commercial break and back. In this case, the fade out and fade in signal the transition from one type of television material (fiction) to another (commercial).

Single-Camera Editing for the News

Not all television material that is shot with one camera tells a story. There are single-camera commercials, music videos, and news segments that do not present a narrative in the conventional sense of the term. They have developed different editing systems for their particular functions. Some bear the legacy of continuity editing, while others depart from it. The specifics of editing for commercials are discussed in Chapter 6, but we will here consider some aspects of editing for television news.

Although the in-studio portion of the nightly newscast is shot using multiple cameras, most stories filed by individual reporters are shot in the field with a single video camera. The editing of these stories, or **packages** (ranging in length from 80 to 105 seconds), follows conventions particular to the way that the news translates events from reality into television material (see Chapter 5). The conventional news story contains:

- the reporter's opening **lead** (sometimes spelled "lede");
- a first **sound bite**, consisting of a short piece of audio, usually synced to image, that was recorded on the scene: for example, the mayor's comment on a new zoning regulation, or a bereaved father's sobbing;
- the reporter's transition or bridge between story elements;
- a second sound bite, often one that presents an opinion contrasting with that in the first sound bite;
- the reporter's concluding **stand-up**, where they stand before a site significant to the story and summarize it.

This editing scheme was inherited, with variations, from print journalism and a specific concept of how information from reality should be organized. The reporter typically begins by piquing our interest, implicitly posing questions about a topic or event. The sound bites provide answers and fill in information. And, to comply with conventional structures of journalistic "balance" (inscribed in official codes of ethics), two sound bites are usually provided. One argues pro, the other con, especially on controversial issues. The news often structures information in this binary fashion: us/them, pro/con, yes/no, left/right, on/off. The reporters then come to represent the middle ground, with their concluding stand-ups serving to synthesize the opposing perspectives. Thus, the editing pattern reflects the ideological structure of news reporting.

The Multiple-Camera Mode of Production

As explained in Chapter 7, multiple-camera shows can be cut during the actual shooting of the program—especially in live-on-tape and necessarily in live broadcasts. In programs produced daily, the final edit and the director's line cut (created while shooting the scenes) might be quite similar, as the editing is very functional and seldom stylized. Soap-opera editor Lugh Powers explains, "Dialogue is driving the show so we stay on the actor speaking."[2] That is, the editing follows the strict pattern of: one actor speaks, cut, another actor speaks. No fancy stuff allowed. On weekly programs, however, editors have the luxury of a bit more time to experiment with the editing.

It might appear that soap operas, sitcoms, and the like would have a ready-made continuity, since the scenes were performed without interruption (except to correct mistakes) and the cameras rolled throughout. What we must recall, however, is that there are always several takes of each scene. The editor must choose the best version of each individual shot when assembling the final episode. Thus, shot one might be from the first take and shot two from the second or third. The dialogue is usually the same from one take to the next, but actors' positions and expressions are not. Inevitably, this results in small discontinuities. In one *That 70's Show* scene, for instance, three characters are talking outdoors: Steven Hyde (Danny Masterson), Michael Kelso (Ashton Kutcher), and Suzy Simpson (Alyson Hannigan). In one shot, Hyde, on the left of the frame, stands with his right hand outside his sweatshirt (Figure 10.33). The camera cuts to a reverse angle and instantaneously his hand is in the sweatshirt's pocket (Figure 10.34). Evidently, the editor selected these two shots from alternative takes of the same scene. (Another example of a continuity error in a multiple-camera sitcom is evident in Figures 4.18 and 4.19

Figure 10.33 A continuity error in the multiple-camera production *That 70's Show*. The actor on the left's hand is at his side...

Figure 10.34 ... and is suddenly in his pocket in the next shot.

from *The Big Bang Theory*. Note the position of Sheldon's arms in these images taken from two successive shots.)

To hide continuity errors from the viewer, the editor of a multiple-camera production relies on editing principles derived from the single-camera 180° editing system (for example, shot-counter shot, match cuts, eyeline matches, and so on). Also, the soundtrack that is created in post-production incorporates music, dubbed-in dialogue, sound effects, and laugh tracks to further smooth over discontinuities and channel our attention.

The Legacy of the Continuity System

It is striking how much multiple-camera editing of narrative scenes resembles that of single-camera editing. In particular, the 180° principle has always dominated the multiple-camera editing of fiction television. This is true in part because of the aesthetic precedent of the theatrical film. But it is also true for the simple, technologically based reason that to break the 180° rule and place the camera on the "wrong" side of the axis of action would reveal the other cameras, the technicians, and the bare studio walls (position X in Figure 10.5). Obviously, violating this aspect of the 180° system is not even an option in television studio production.

However, acceptance of the continuity editing system in multiple-camera production goes beyond maintaining screen direction due to an ad hoc adherence to the 180° rule. It extends to the single-camera mode's organization of screen space. As you read through the following description of a typical scene development you might refer back to the description of single-camera space on pp. 260–71.

A scene commonly begins by introducing the space and the characters through an establishing shot that is either a long shot of the entire set and actors or a camera movement that reveals them. See, for example, the opening shots for the first two scenes in the *Friends* episode analyzed in Chapter 3 (Figures 3.6 and 3.7). On weekly or daily programs, however, establishing shots may be minimized or even eliminated because of the repetitive use of sets and our established familiarity with them. In any event, after an opening shot a conventionalized alternating pattern begins—back and forth between two characters. In conversation scenes—the foundation of narrative television—directors rely upon close-ups in shot-reverse shot to develop the main narrative action of a scene. After a shot-reverse shot series, the scene often cuts to a slightly longer view as a transition to another space or to allow for the entrance of another character. Standard, single-camera devices for motivating space (match-on-action, eyeline matches, point-of-view shots, etc.) are included in the multiple-camera spatial orientation. Try watching a scene from a multiple-camera sitcom with the sound turned off and see if it doesn't adhere to these conventions.

The differences between multiple-camera and single-camera editing are very subtle and may not be immediately noticeable to viewers. But these differences do occur, and they do inform our experience of television. The main difference between the two modes is how action is represented. Although multiple-camera shooting arranges space similarly to the space of single-camera productions, the action within that space—the physical movement of the actors—is presented somewhat differently. In multiple-camera shooting, some action may be missed by the camera and wind up occurring out-of-sight, off-frame, because the camera cannot control the action to the degree that it does in single-camera shooting. For example, in one scene from the multiple-camera production *Days of Our Lives*, the following three shots occur (see tvcrit.com/find/dool):

1. Medium shot of Will (Chandler Massey) and Susan (Eileen Davidson) as her deception regarding him is revealed by (Figure 10.35). He is overwhelmed and she is upset and denies her crimes.

Figure 10.35 Days of Our Lives: Will hides his face in disbelief, having just learned that Susan is not his real mother. She continues to deny the deception and is clearly delusional.

Figure 10.36 Susan's boyfriend, Roger, confirms the deception to Will and tries unsuccessfully to reason with her.

Figure 10.37 While Roger was speaking, Susan has covered her ears and Will has removed his hand from his face.

2. Medium shot of Susan's boyfriend, Roger (John Enos), as he tries to reason with her and break through her confusion (Figure 10.36).
3. Medium shot from the same camera angle as before. Susan's hands cover her ears and Will's hand is no longer in front of his face (Figure 10.37).

Here, the camera operators had trouble keeping up with the actors' hand movements and key aspects of their performances occur off-screen. Specifically, we do not see Eileen Davidson raise her hands to her ears.

Not only is action missing from multiple-camera programs, but the framing of action is also less well controlled and somewhat haphazard. For instance, in a scene from *As the World Turns*, Brad (Austin Peck) has hidden a diamond ring next to a piece of cheesecake that Katie (Terri Colombino) is about to eat (see tvcrit.com/find/atwtediting). The camera cuts to a tight close-up of the cheesecake as she puts her fork into it (Figure 10.38). The framing is unusually tight for a soap opera and a distracting glass is in the foreground. Then, as she moves the fork toward her mouth, the camera operator has trouble keeping up with her gesture and loses the action for a moment. In addition, Brad's shoulder partially blocks the shot (Figure 10.39). Finally, Katie takes a bite of the cheesecake and the camera reframes her in close-up (Figure 10.40).

If these two multiple-camera, soap-opera scenes had been shot in single-camera mode, these actions would have been carefully staged and tightly controlled so that all the significant action was on-screen and "properly" framed—with no distracting or obscuring foreground objects. In other words, multiple-camera editing frequently leaves out "significant" action that single-camera

Figure 10.38 *As the World Turns*: A shot begins with a tight framing of a fork cutting into a piece of cheesecake.

Figure 10.39 The camera operator loses the fork as Katie raises it to her lips...

Figure 10.40 ... and catches up with her as she eats.

editing would include. Had single-camera editing been used in the *Days of Our Lives* scene, the editor could have cut back to Davidson before she put her hands over her ears—better emphasizing her character's distress. And a single-camera production would have allowed the camera operator to perfectly frame Katie's fork as it traveled to her mouth in *As the World Turns*.

Small visual gaps and inaccurate framing such as these examples, along with other departures from the continuity editing system, occur frequently in multiple-camera editing. What significance do they have? They contribute to the programs' illusion of "liveness." They make it seem as if the actors were making it up as they went along and the camera operators were struggling to keep up with their movements, as if the camera operators didn't know where the actors were going to go next. Of course, in reality they do know the actors' planned positions, and yet they cannot know exactly where the actors will move. In single-camera shooting the action is controlled precisely by the camera, bound by the limits of the frame. In multiple-camera shooting that control is subtly undermined. As a result, in their editing, multiple-camera narrative programs (soap operas and sitcoms, principally) come to resemble talk shows and game shows. The visual "looseness" of multiple-camera editing comes to signify "liveness" when compared to the controlled imagery of single-camera productions. The spatial orientation of the two modes is quite similar, but the movement of actors through that space is presented a bit differently.

Non-Narrative Editing: Functional Principles

The non-narrative programs that are shot with several cameras in a television studio include, principally, game shows, talk shows, and the portions of news programs shot in the studio. (Sports programs, reality TV, and other outdoor events such as parades also use several cameras at once, but that is a specialized use of multiple-camera production.) These programs do not share the need of narrative programs to tell a story, but their approach to space is remarkably similar to that of narrative programs. Typically, their sets are introduced with establishing long shots, which are followed by closer framings and inevitably (in conversation-oriented genres such as talk shows) result in shot-reverse shot patterns. Game shows also follow this pattern of alternation, crosscutting between the space of the contestants and that of the host (Figures 5.4–5.6). The mise-en-scene of non-narrative programs is quite distinct from narrative settings (see Chapter 8), but the shot-to-shot organization of that mise-en-scene follows principles grounded in the continuity editing system.

Continuity Editing and Hybrid Modes of Production

In Chapter 7 we explained how the distinction between modes of production is blurred during the actual shooting of television episodes. More than one camera is used on the set of a "single-camera" shoot, or a single-camera approach is used on the set of a "multiple-camera" shoot. The hybrid nature of the production process has ramifications for continuity editing, too.

For example, it's become quite common for directors of single-camera productions to employ two cameras to "cover" simple conversation scenes. The **A camera** (the main camera on the set) will be pointed at a specific actor, and a supplemental **B camera** will also be pointed at them from the same side of the set, but at a slightly different angle. We're not referring to shot-reverse shot here. In that case one camera would be pointed at each of two actors. Rather, two cameras are shooting one actor. To see how this works, examine our *Grey's Anatomy* découpage in Table 10.1 (Figures 10.9–10.23). It is entirely possible that director Randy Zisk and director of photography Herbert Davis had both A and B cameras trained on Chyler Leigh while she said her lines. The A and B cameras are set to capture different shot scales: perhaps a medium close-up in the A camera and a tighter close-up in the B camera. If you compare her medium close-ups with her close-ups (Figure 10.18 and Figure 10.20, respectively) you can see that they're on similar, but slightly different, angles—as we've indicated in the diagram of the scene (Figure 10.24). Note, in particular, the relative positions of the two actors' bodies. In the tight close-up Eric Dane is blocking her more than in the medium close-up—suggesting that two different camera positions were used.

This two-camera method of shooting is used to save time and give the editors a greater variety of angles and framings. However, it is disdained by many directors and DPs. *Mad Men*'s cinematographer, Chris Manley, is highly critical of two-camera shooting: "I've used two cameras on most of my TV shows in order to keep on schedule, but that requires some compromises with position and focal lengths. You are usually further away with longer lenses, which affect everything from lighting to sound and performances. We use a single camera most of the time [on *Mad Men*], and a B camera when it doesn't compromise how we cover scenes."[3] In this instance we can see how a DP's aesthetic sense comes into conflict with the economics of television production.

Continuity editing is also affected when multiple-camera and single-camera modes are blurred together—as can be seen in three shots from *How I Met Your Mother* (Figures 10.41,

10.42, and 10.43; see tvcrit. com/find/howimet). First, a long shot (Figure 10.41) establishes the main characters sitting in a bar booth—a frequently used setting in the program—and director Pamela Fryman has positioned Lily (Alyson Hannigan) and Ted (Josh Radnor) on the left and Barney (Neil Patrick Harris) and Marshall (Jason Segel) on the right, with Marshall closest to the camera. In a sitcom with an audience, the camera would stay on Lily's and Marshall's side of the booth, shooting shots of her from over his left shoulder, as, indeed, Fryman does in several shots (Figure 10.42). However, she also cuts to a camera on the other side of the booth—a camera position that would have been visible in the long shot—and shoots Lily over *Barney's* right shoulder (Figure 10.43). She thus breaks the 180° rule. Note the differences in the backgrounds of the two shots of Lily. In the conventional medium close-up recorded from the same side of the booth as the long shot, we see an adjoining booth in the background; but in the medium close-up from the other side we see a wall. And that wall is where a camera would conventionally be positioned when shooting in a studio with an audience! Clearly, Fryman did multiple takes of this scene and, for some of them, positioned the camera inside the set—as one could only do in the single-camera mode of production. (For more on the show's hybrid mode of production, see p. 196.)

Figure 10.41 A long shot establishes the characters of *How I Met Your Mother* in their favorite bar and sets up an axis of action.

Figure 10.42 A close-up of Lily preserves the 180° rule.

Figure 10.43 A later close-up breaks the 180° rule by crossing the axis of action established in the long shot.

Thus, continuity editing is modified in hybrid programs, where a "pure" implementation of single-camera or multiple-camera modes of production does not exist. The 180° system still dominates the editing room, but today's standard craft practices have considerably more wiggle room than editors in 1930s Hollywood had.

Summary

In our consideration of editing on television, we have witnessed the pervasiveness of the continuity system. Although originally a method for editing theatrical films, its principles also underpin both of the major modes of production for television: single-camera and multiple-camera.

The continuity system functions, in a sense, to deceive us—to make us believe that the images passing before us comprise one continuous flow—when actually they consist of many disruptions. Or, in other terms, one could say this system constructs a continuity of space and time. Many techniques are used to construct this continuity. The 180° rule maintains our sense of space and screen direction by keeping cameras on one side of an axis of action. Shot-reverse shot conventionally develops the action of a scene in alternating close-ups. Match cuts (especially matches-on-action and eyeline matches) and the basic point-of-view editing pattern motivate cuts and help prevent viewer disorientation.

Time on television is not always continuous. Indeed, gaps and ellipses are essential to narrative television if stories that take place over days or months are to be presented in half-hour or hour time slots. Through editing, the duration and order of time may be manipulated. Within the continuity system, however, our understanding of time must always be consistent. We must be guided through any alteration of chronological order. Fades, for instance, are used to signal the passage of time from one scene to the next.

These principles and techniques of the continuity system are created in both single-camera and multiple-camera modes of production. The key distinction is that single-camera productions shoot scenes in discontinuous chunks, while multiple-camera ones (especially live productions) allow scenes to be played out in entirety while the cameras "capture" them. Even so, both modes of production must find ways to cope with discontinuity and disruption, and it is here that the continuity system's principles come into play, regardless of the actual production method used to create the images.

Non-narrative television is not as closely tied to the continuity system as narrative programs are, yet it does bear the legacy of continuity-style editing. Establishing shots, shot-reverse shot editing patterns, and the like are as evident on talk shows and game shows as they are on narrative programs.

The power of editing, the ability to alter and rearrange space and time, is a component of television that is taken for granted. Its "invisibility" should not blind us, however, to its potency.

Notes

1 Many people use "point-of-view" and "subjective" interchangeably. Here, however, we will distinguish between subjective shots from within the head of the character and point-of-view shots that are nearby, but not through the character's eyes.
2 "Soap Editor Lugh Powers," *The Joy of Editing*, September 10, 2010, tvcrit.com/find/joy.
3 Bob Fisher, "A Conversation With Chris Manley, ASC," *Kodak OnFilm*, motion.kodak.com/US/en/motion/Publications/On_Film_Interviews/manley.htm, accessed October 1, 2010.

Further Readings

Editing style and mode of production are discussed in many of the handbooks for television production suggested at the end of Chapter 8.

The evolution of single-camera production is comprehensively described in David Bordwell, Janet Staiger, and Kristin Thompson, *The Classical Hollywood Cinema: Film Style and Mode of Production to 1960* (New York: Columbia University Press, 1985). John Ellis, *Visible Fictions: Cinema, Television, Video* (New York: Routledge, 1992) is not as exhaustive, but it does begin the work of analyzing the multiple-camera mode of production. Few other sources make such an attempt.

In the cinema, the principles of editing have long been argued. This stems from the desire to define film in terms of editing, which was at the heart of the very first theories of the cinema. These initial forays into film theory were carried out in the 1920s by Soviet filmmakers Sergei Eisenstein, Lev Kuleshov, and V. I. Pudovkin. See, for example, Sergei Eisenstein, *Film Form: Essays in Film Theory*, edited and translated by Jay Leyda (New York: Harcourt, Brace & World, 1949); Lev Kuleshov, *Kuleshov on Film*, edited and translated by Ronald Levaco (Berkeley: University of California Press, 1974); and V. I. Pudovkin, *Film Technique and Film Acting*, translated by Ivor Montagu (New York: Bonanza, 1949).

Editing has also been a central component of debates within film studies over the position of the spectator, as can be seen in Jean-Louis Baudry, "Ideological Effects of the Basic Cinematographic Apparatus," in *Narrative, Apparatus, Ideology*, Philip Rosen, ed. (New York: Columbia University Press, 1986), 286–98; Nick Browne, "The Spectator-in-the-Text: The Rhetoric of *Stagecoach*," in Rosen, 102–19; and Daniel Dayan, "The Tutor-Code of Classical Cinema," in *Movies and Methods*, Bill Nichols, ed. (Berkeley: University of California Press, 1976). Kaja Silverman, *The Subject of Semiotics* (New York: Oxford University Press, 1983), reviews this debate.

Chris Wadsworth, *The Editor's Toolkit: A Hands-On Guide to the Craft of Film and TV Editing* (Boston: Focal Press, 2016); and Christopher J. Bowen and Roy Thompson, *Grammar of the Edit*, 4th ed. (Boston: Focal Press, 2018), approach editing from a hands-on perspective—explaining editing principles and the operation of editing systems. Karen Pearlman, *Cutting Rhythms: Intuitive Film Editing*, 2nd ed. (Boston: Focal Press, 2016), dives into editing's creative process. A course on Lynda.com explains the specifics of "Multi-Camera Video Production and Post," tvcrit.com/find/lynda. Ken Dancyger, *The Technique of Film and Video Editing: History, Theory, and Practice*, 5th ed. (Boston: Focal Press, 2010), offers a broad historical and critical overview of film editing that includes a limited section on editing for television. The scripting process and its impact on modes of production are detailed in Chad Gervich, *Small Screen, Big Picture: A Writer's Guide to the TV Business* (New York: Three Rivers Press, 2008).

Despite the obvious impact of editing on television style, television studies has been slow to articulate its significance. However, this work has begun, as noted in the previously cited Jeremy G. Butler, *Television Style* (New York: Routledge, 2010); and Herbert Zettl, *Sight Sound Motion: Applied Media Aesthetics*, 8th ed. (Boston, MA: Cengage, 2017). Also, the statistical analysis of television editing is included in ShotLogger.org and CineMetrics (www.cinemetrics.lv). These online applications calculate editing aspects such as the average length of shots.

11 Style and Sound

Up to this point our discussion of television style has dealt primarily with visual elements: mise-en-scene, the camera, and editing. But television is not solely a visual medium. Sound has always been a crucial component of television's style. This is not surprising when one remembers that, in economic and technological terms, television's predecessor and closest relation is *radio*—not film, literature, or the theater. Economically, television networks replicated and often grew out of radio networks. Technologically, TV broadcasting has always relied on much of the same equipment as radio broadcasting (microphones, transmitters, and so on). With these close economic and technological ties to radio—a *sound-only* medium—it is almost inevitable that television's aesthetics would rely heavily on sound. The experience of *watching* television is equally an experience of *listening* to television.

Sound's importance to the medium becomes obvious if one performs a simple experiment. Turn the sound off and watch 15 minutes of a program. Then "watch" the next 15 minutes with the sound on, but do not look at the picture. Which 15-minute segment made more sense? Which communicated the most narrative (or other) information? Which had the greatest impact? Typically, sound without image is more self-sufficient than image without sound. Sound affects the viewer and conveys television meaning just as much, and possibly more, than the image does. Indeed, so little is communicated in the visuals of some genres—talk shows, game shows, soap operas—that they would cease to exist without sound. Consider how different this is from, say, the screens you view while engaged in online activities. When reading Twitter or browsing most web pages, you do so in silence until you intentionally seek out audio-rich sites such as YouTube or a favorite podcast. The Web is silent by default, while television is noisy by default.

In approaching television sound, we need to understand:

- the different types of television sound and how they are produced through a conventionalized mode of production;
- the purposes that sound serves on television;
- sound's basic acoustic properties and how they are rendered through television sound technology; and
- the significance of sound to television's structuring of space, time, and narrative.

Types of Television Sound

The types of sound that are heard on television can be divided into three main categories:

1. speech (principally, **dialogue**)
2. music
3. **sound effects** (**SFX**).

Sound editors bring these three aspects together into a program's **sound mix**. In less complicated, smaller-budget productions, all audio might be recorded on a single **digital audio workstation** (**DAW**). In such situations, the **sound mixer** separates the three categories into different **tracks** of the DAW. In television's higher-budget productions, separate sound mixers individually create and shape speech, music, and sound effects on three (or more) DAWs, with numerous tracks on each—generating individual sub-mixes for dialogue, music, and sound effects.

DAWs are the audio-only version of nonlinear digital video editing (NLE) and are configured much like the Adobe Premiere editor discussed in Chapter 10. Figure 11.1 shows a detail of a representative set-up in Pro Tools, the preeminent DAW software in Hollywood today (for the full screen shot, see tvcrit.com/find/protools). In a single-mixer set-up the sound editor would typically divide the audio into numerous discrete tracks—labeled "Speech," "Music," and "Sound FX," or something similar. However, Figure 11.1 is a Pro Tools screen shot from an editing session for *Ugly Betty* (2006–10) where editor Craig Pettigrew is mixing nothing but music. Each track indicates the relative volume of a music element with jagged lines known as **waveforms**, which visually represent the shape of a sound wave occurring over time. In Figure 11.1 you can see that Pettigrew has stacked waveforms for percussion ("perc"), violin and cello ("Vln-Cello"), and piano and harp ("Piano-Hp") that have been prepared by composer Jeff Beal. We are looking at a small part of the music mix prepared for 13 minutes, 24 seconds, and 8 frames into the series finale. The track labeled "UB 420 LOCKED VAM-04.L" shows the dialogue under which the music is laid. *Ugly Betty* has a music score that is fuller than most TV programs, thus necessitating a separate music editor.

As you might expect, the taller a waveform is, the louder the sound element is—as can be seen in Figure 11.2, an enlargement of one waveform that shows human speech. A discrete sound, such as a gunshot, a person talking, or a music element, can be placed in each of these tracks and is thereby separated from the other sounds. This allows the sound editor to manipulate individual sound components before assembling them into the finished, composite mix. The use

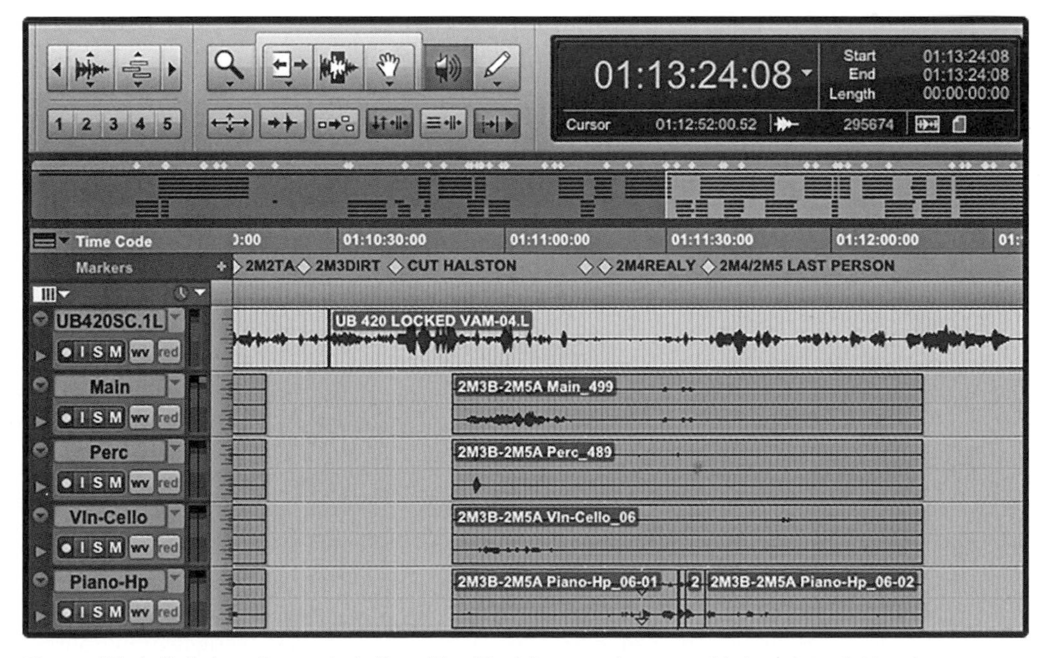

Figure 11.1 A digital audio workstation (Pro Tools) separates sound into separate tracks.

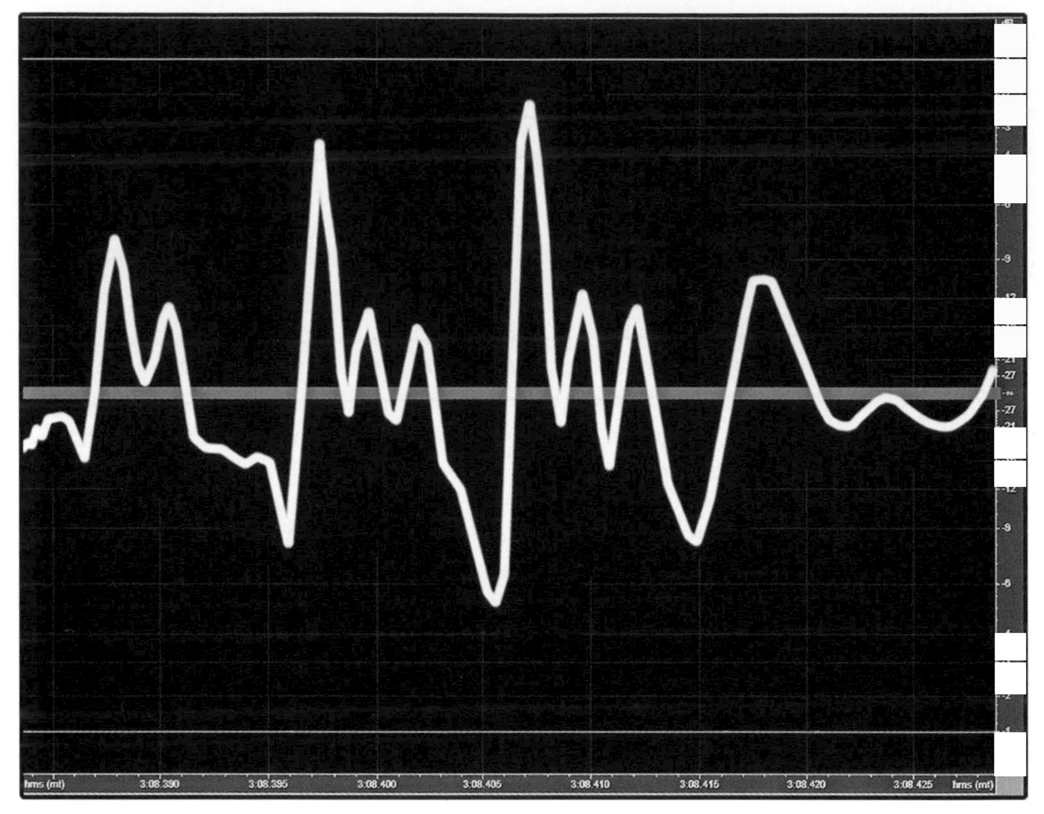

Figure 11.2 An enlarged waveform shows the changing volume of human speech.

of multi-track technology and the assignment of labor to the sound mixers indicates how the industry categorizes sound. That is, the industry's mode of production mirrors the categories of television sound. These categories will underpin our investigation of sound in television.

Speech

Without doubt, talk is the most conspicuous aspect of television sound. Soap operas thrive on it and the talk show takes its name from it. Even sports programs, which one would think would provide enough visual interest to get along without commentary, rely heavily upon discussion of the game. Once in the early 1980s, NBC experimented with broadcasting a football game without announcers, providing only the sights and sounds of the game and on-screen statistics.[1] Sports fans were not comfortable with this and it hasn't been tried since. Apparently, television visuals are lost without speech. Sometimes it appears as if the images were superfluous, as if TV were, as one critic put it, a "lava lamp" with sound.

Speech in narrative television most commonly takes the form of **dialogue** among characters. Dialogue does not typically address viewers. It is as if they were eavesdropping on a conversation. Characters speak to each other as if we were not listening. In some comic situations, however, a character will break this convention of the "fourth wall" and speak directly to the camera. It was done as early as *The George Burns and Gracie Allen Show* (1950–58) and continues into twenty-first-century television with *Malcolm in the Middle* (2000–06) and *The Bernie Mac Show* (2001–06)—see Figures 4.24, 4.25, 13.6, respectively; and see tvcrit.com/find/burns, tvcrit.com/find/malcolm, and tvcrit.com/find/mac, respectively, too. These direct addresses of the viewer are from an intriguing, narratively ambiguous space. When Malcolm talks to us, he clearly does so from within the diegetic space—as a character, not the actor, Frankie Muniz. But when George Burns and Bernie Mac speak to us, it is as the actors, Burns and Mac, but they're still embedded in the fiction, in the diegetic space. Although Burns was actually married to Gracie Allen, he wasn't really friends with the characters in the show. And Mac was a comic in real life and on the show, but he wasn't actually married to Kellita Smith, the actress who played his wife. When Burns and Mac look us in the "eye" and talk to us, they are doing so *both* as actors and as characters. The programs deliberately blur the distinction for humorous effect. Other programs do not put the character on-screen when he or she addresses us. Through **narration** or **voiceover**, in which a character's or omniscient narrator's voice is heard over an image, a character can speak directly to the viewer. For example, the adult Kevin Arnold talks to the viewer about his younger self in *The Wonder Years* (1988-93), and an unidentified narrator (Ron Howard) comments on the hapless Bluth family in *Arrested Development* (2003-06; see tvcrit.com/find/arresteddevelopment).[2] (Note the difference between "narra*tion*," which refers to a voice speaking over an image, and "narra*tive*," which we use more generally to refer to some sort of story or fiction.)

Speech in non-narrative television, in contrast, is frequently directly addressed to the viewer (see Chapters 5 and 8). News anchors and reporters look at and speak toward the viewer (Figures 5.19, 8.17). Stephen Colbert directs his monologue right at the camera. The announcers in advertisements cajole viewers directly, imploring them to try their products (Figures 6.3, 6.20). Other programs are more ambiguous in the way they address the viewer. Some fiction shows (e.g., *The Office* [U.S. version, 2005-13] and *Modern Family* [2009-]), employ the conventions of TV news and "interview" the characters, having them look directly at the camera as if they were nonfiction (see tvcrit.com/find/office and tvcrit.com/find/modernfamily). The "target" of address in game shows is ambiguous, too. They pose questions to the social actors on-screen, but these questions are also meant for the viewer so that he or she can play along (Figures 5.5 and 5.6). Needless to say, the way that speech is addressed can be quite complicated, and even contradictory.

In terms of standard production practice, speech is most often recorded live on the set during the "production" phase, rather than during pre-production or post-production (see Chapter 7). This means that speech is usually recorded at the same time that the image is, but not always. Post-production sound work can modify the dialogue or, indeed, can even add to it or replace it altogether—as occurs when sound is **dubbed** or dialogue is changed using **automatic dialogue replacement** (**ADR**, also known as automated dialogue replacement or looping).

In dubbing and ADR, one voice is substituted for another, as is illustrated in the backstage film *Singin' in the Rain* (1952), where one woman's voice is dubbed in for another's in the movie within that movie. ADR is conventionally used in several instances in television. First, when an actor's reading of a line is not considered satisfactory it may be replaced with an alternative reading by that same actor. Second, if an actor's voice is not considered appropriate to the character it may be replaced by a different actor's. For example, when Andie McDowell played Jane, a British character, in *Greystoke: The Legend of Tarzan, Lord of the Apes* (1984), the producers felt that her natural Louisiana dialect did not suit the role. Subsequently, Glenn Close's voice was dubbed in for all of McDowell's dialogue (see tvcrit.com/find/greystoke). Third, dubbing is used in animation, as when Nancy Cartwright "voices" Bart Simpson. Fourth, and finally, in the instances in which foreign-language films or television programs are shown on U.S. television they are frequently dubbed into English, although on movie-oriented channels such as TCM, Sundance, and IFC, they are more often **subtitled** or captioned instead of dubbed. (In subtitling/captioning, the English translation is printed on the bottom of the screen and the original dialogue is retained.)

Music

Music and speech go hand-in-hand on television. In many programs, dialogue will always be accompanied by music. It is a rare line of dialogue in *Ugly Betty*, for example, that has no music beneath it. And portions of programs that have no dialogue—say, a car chase—will almost always increase the presence of the music. In any event, television is seldom devoid of both music and speech. It is not a quiet medium, which is why the awkward silences in *The Office* are so effective in emphasizing the characters' embarrassing situations (see tvcrit.com/find/office).

Television music comes in many different genres—from the rock soundtrack of *That 70's Show* (1998-2006), to the country tunes of *The Dukes of Hazzard* (1979-85), to the rap music of *In Living Color* (1990-94). Television absorbs a fairly broad spectrum of popular music, although it seldom presents avant-garde performances, and classical music appears infrequently (and is relegated to its own "highbrow" ghetto on PBS). In the 1980s, music videos enjoyed broad popularity on television, providing the basis for MTV—literally, "music television." Currently, however, their presence on linear television has diminished. Even though they now flourish online, there are very few music videos on television anymore. (For more information on music videos, please see the music television chapter from previous editions of *Television*, which is available online: tvcrit.com/find/musictv.) Since they are promotional materials created by the music labels, music videos feature recognizable popular artists, as you would expect. In contrast, narrative television programs long avoided using popular tunes. From the 1950s through the 1970s, studio musicians were commonly used to create any necessary rock music, instead of licensing a well-known performer's work. When *WKRP in Cincinnati* premiered in 1978, it was thought to be ground-breaking because it featured music by original performers rather than sound-alikes.

Television's reticence about using popular music in narrative programs is partially an economic decision and partially an aesthetic one. As far as economics goes, if a program's **music supervisor** chooses a song that has been **copyrighted**, then licensing fees must be paid. Music licensors or **performing rights organizations** (**PROs**) negotiate payment for broadcast rights, and particularly popular musical artists can command tens of thousands of dollars. **Music clearance**, as this process of obtaining licenses is called, can be a very tricky business because there are often two separate licensing components of a song: the license for its composition and the license for a particular recording of that composition. For instance, Tom Waits composed "Way Down in the Hole," but different recordings of it were used as the theme song for *The Wire*'s different seasons: The Blind Boys of Alabama (season one), Tom Waits himself (season two, see tvcrit.com/find/tomwaits), the Neville Brothers (season three), DoMaJe (season four), and Steve Earle (season five). *The Wire*'s music supervisor had to clear a **synchronization license** from Waits for the composition and a **master use license** from each of the musicians for their recording of it. More accurately, *The Wire*'s producers had to pay PROs for these licenses and the PROs then distributed the money to the song's publishing companies and artists. If there is no current copyright on a piece of music, then it is said to be in the **public domain** and may be used without charge.

These licensing fees may surprise you. You might think that the recording industry would be the one paying TV producers to include its music as a form of advertising, of product placement.[3]

Even recording executives such as Gillian Morris, of Wind-Up Records, acknowledge, "What we've found is that, especially when TV shows announce what music is used, if it's an established act it really does spur their catalog sales."[4] For instance, after a Tegan and Sara song was incorporated in *Grey's Anatomy* (2005–), its digital downloads skyrocketed from 59 to 1,200 per week.[5] And, indeed, there are some deals struck between music supervisors and music licensors. Sometimes a license fee will be reduced or eliminated if credit for the music is provided via an **ad card** at a show's conclusion—as illustrated by the promotional announcement for Jimmy Eat World in the end credits of a *One Tree Hill* (2003–12) episode, shown in Figure 11.3. However, ad cards only occur in exceptional shows—often ones like *One Tree Hill* and *The O.C.* (2003–07), which target young viewers and rely on indie rock performers such as Jimmy Eat World and Beck, respectively, for part of their allure.[6] More typically, record labels see television programs as a source of revenue, not costly advertising, in times when their income is dropping precipitously. Copyright is a form of property, which is why copyright law is known as **intellectual property (IP)** law. Thus, for the foreseeable future record labels will be charging television producers to use their property. This provides an obvious economic incentive to avoid copyrighted music and encourages producers to either use public domain music or generate new, original music.

One annoying development in licensing in the digital era is that streaming, DVD, and Blu-ray releases of television programs frequently do not include the music that was originally used when they were broadcast. The master rights paid for broadcast specifically exclude the rights for subsequent distribution on DVD, BD, or online, which often cost as much as or more than the original licensing fee. For instance, *Dawson's Creek* (1998–2003) was a program that relied heavily upon copyrighted, licensed music. Its producers claimed that paying licensing fees would make the DVD releases prohibitively expensive and chose to replace most of the original music on the DVD releases. The *Dawson's Creek Music Guide* website tracks all of these replacements, as is represented in Table 11.1 for the "Like a Virgin" episode (September 29, 1999). Even its theme song, Paula Cole's "I Don't Want to Wait," has been replaced on several of the DVD releases. As you can see, music licensing provides a complicated disincentive for television producers to use copyrighted music.

One other, principally aesthetic, reason that some TV genres have shied away from popular music in the past is because rock music during the 1950s and 1960s was associated with

Figure 11.3 An ad card promotes music used in an episode of *One Tree Hill*.

Table 11.1 Music in *Dawson's Creek* DVD release: Season 3, Episode #301 "Like a Virgin"

Original Song	*Replacement Song*
"Old Time Rock & Roll," Bob Seger	"Urge," Supersparkle
"Who's Who," The Pretenders	"Love Goes Down," Annie Minogue
"Sleep Together," Garbage	"Emma Peel," Bionica
"Dead Again," Buckcherry	"Turn It Up," Squad Five-Oh
"Let Us Sing," Tricky Woo	(original song)
"Push It," Garbage	"So High," Motorbaby
"Hold On," Mary Beth Maziarz	(original song)

Source: tvcrit.com/find/dawsonscreek.

subversive or counter-cultural elements. Soap operas and sports programs, for instance, avoided rock music until the 1980s because it was perceived as too decadent for those historically conservative genres. The fact that both sports and soaps now regularly incorporate rock tunes indicates both a change in rock's position in U.S. culture (it has now become mainstream) and a change in these genres themselves, an attempt on their part to attract younger viewers.

Music fits into television's mode of production slightly differently than speech does. Unlike speech, very little music is recorded live on the set during the production phase—excepting, of course, video recording/broadcasting of live musical performances (for example, the musical segments of *Saturday Night Live* [1975–], late-night talk shows, the Boston Pops Orchestra broadcasts). Instead, most music is prepared either before the production or after. In music videos and performances in programs such as *Glee* (2009–15), the music is recorded ahead of time (with a few, very rare exceptions). The performers then mouth the words to the song while they are filmed or videotaped. This form of synchronization of image to music is known as **lip sync**.

Aside from musical productions, however, it is more common to add music to the image later, in post-production, than before shooting begins. Most scenes are shot without music, even ones in which music is supposed to be in the background—for example, a nightclub or dance. Music is laid on later so that the sound technician can get a clear recording of the dialogue and the director can tightly control the music's impact. Further, programs that are designed to be distributed internationally, in foreign languages, need to keep music and sound effects separate from dialogue so that the dialogue alone may be replaced on the soundtrack. This dialogue-free version of the sound track is typically referred to as the **M and E track** (music and effects).

Live-on-tape productions have a fairly unique approach to music. In both narrative (principally, soap operas) and non-narrative programs (talk shows and game shows) that are recorded live-on-tape, the music is inserted while the program is being videotaped rather than during post-production. In narrative programs that are edited while being shot, short bits of music, known as **cues**, are prepared in advance and inserted when called for by the director, while the program is recording. **Production sound**—the sound recorded on the set by the production sound mixer—is thus enhanced by these cues. During 2003, for example, Deborah N. Hurwitz composed cues for *Guiding Light* with titles such as "positive romance," "relentless," and "pulse sustained v1." Non-narrative programs follow the same procedure for their theme music. On *Who Wants to Be a Millionaire* (debuting in the U.S. in 1999) there are dozens of music cues for various expected events—from the host's and guest's entrances to questions asked at various money amounts. Other non-narrative programs such as late-night talk shows include a live band (for example, Reggie Watts's on *The Late Late Show with James Corden* [2015–]) and live performances by guests. The principle remains the same, however. The music is inserted while the program is being recorded—the only difference being that the music is performed rather than played back on an audio device.

Sound Effects (SFX)

All the elements of television's sound that are not speech or music fall into the catch-all category of sound effects (SFX). This includes gunshots, doorbell rings, footsteps on the pavement, the crunch of a fist into a jaw, and so on. It also includes the background sound of a particular room or other space—in other words, the room's **ambient sound**. In live-on-tape productions, most of these sound effects are whatever is picked up on the set or inserted by the sound editor during the original recording of the image, but in programs that are edited in post-production, sound effects can be fabricated and manipulated in seemingly infinite ways.

During the actual recording of the program, sound technicians will capture the background noise and various other sound effects elements, but they will try, as much as possible, to isolate those sounds from the dialogue. This gives them the greatest flexibility in post-production sound editing and facilitates the creation of an M and E track, if it's required. Footsteps may be heightened to increase suspense, or the background sound of a jet chancing to pass by during program recording may be eliminated. Sound effects, like speech and music, are endlessly malleable—especially through the use of digital audio workstations.

Commonly, sound effects are created in post-production work using the **Foley** process. Foley artists view a segment of video in a sound studio, a Foley stage, that is equipped with different floor surfaces (rug, tile, wood, etc.), a variety of doors (car doors, screen doors, house doors, etc.), and many other sound effects contraptions. While the segment is projected on a screen, the Foley artists recreate the appropriate sounds. When a character walks up to a door, the Foley artist is recorded walking along the studio floor. When the character opens the door, the Foley artist is recorded opening a door in the studio, and so on. Some programs have only occasional Foley work in them, but others, especially high-budget single-camera productions, might create all of the sound effects in this manner.

Audio's Mode of Production

Before we move on, it is worth assembling the details of audio work we have described in this section into a general understanding of U.S. television audio's mode of production. As with the single-camera and multiple-camera modes of editing discussed in Chapter 7, there is a conventional mode of audio editing and production in the U.S. television industry. We have already alluded to some of the elements of this mode, but it might not yet be clear how they all fit together. Let's walk through that process now, generalizing as much as possible, but recognizing that this mode does not apply to all TV programs.

Audio production for a TV program may begin at the pre-production phase. Producers, directors, music supervisors, and, occasionally, scriptwriters may note specific copyrighted songs or music cues that should accompany certain lines of dialogue. And, obviously, the dialogue for narrative, "scripted" programs is developed through a collaboration among the scriptwriter, director, and producer. In contrast, "nonscripted" shows (e.g., reality programs, game shows, and so on) focus less on dialogue and more on creating certain situations where improvisation may occur. Still, to call reality programs and their brethren "un-scripted" is a little misleading as they all have some form of pre-production dialogue preparation—even if it's just introductory material such as the monologue of a late-night talk show host.

During the production phase, the production sound mixer records dialogue as cleanly as possible, trying to separate the actors' words from any background sound effects—to facilitate ADR later. In multiple-camera, live-on-tape productions, music cues are mixed in at this time.

Otherwise, all sound mixing is done during post-production. **Audio post**, as it's known in the industry, begins after the visual editing has been finalized and the episode is "locked."

During audio post, any additional sound effects are created, often through the Foley process, and ADR is used to correct or supplement dialogue. Then, all elements from the three sound categories—speech, music, and sound effects—are brought together into a final soundtrack. Depending on the program's budget and audio complexity, mixers construct the audio on a single DAW or on individual DAWs devoted to each category. In either case, multiple waveform tracks are assembled to build the program's audio. Also during audio post, the music supervisor and his or her staff confer with the producers and directors to decide on any copyrighted songs that the episode will include.

Purposes of Sound on Television

Among the many purposes that sound serves on television, four will concern us here:

1. capturing viewer attention;
2. manipulating viewer understanding of the image;
3. maintaining television flow;
4. maintaining continuity within individual scenes.

The production techniques used to create sound function together to support these purposes.

Capturing Viewer Attention

The first and perhaps most significant purpose of television sound is to snare the attention of the viewer. Television, unlike cinema and the theater, exists in an environment of competing distractions. Most people watch television in a brightly lit living room or a public space like a bar or doctor's office, with the TV set positioned amid a variety of visual and sound stimuli (unlike the darkened, sound-insulated room of a theater). While the television is on, conversations continue, Snapchat and other apps' alerts vibrate/sound, a tea kettle may start boiling, the cat may rub against a viewer's leg. In sum, television viewing is an inattentive pastime. The viewer's gaze may be riveted to the set for brief, intense intervals, but the overall experience is one of the distracted glance.

In this setting, visuals alone are not captivating enough to grab the viewer's attention. Sound is a much more effective stimulus in this regard. This is not just the case of the loud, abrasive commercial demanding your attention. It's also the sports announcer's excited comments and the cheers of the crowd that cause one to look up from folding laundry to see an instant replay; or the soap-opera character posing the question, "So, April, are you ready to reveal the true father of your child?" that brings one running back from the kitchen. Sound invokes viewers' attention, cuing them to significant visual action or a major narrative twist. In other words, sound may be used to hail viewers—much as one hails a cab or as a phone's ringtone impels us to answer.

Manipulating Viewer Understanding

The second purpose sound serves is to shape our understanding of the image. The sound-image relationship is a complex one that we will return to several times in this chapter. In the most general terms, this relationship manifests itself in three ways:

1. Sound and image support one another.
2. Sound and image contradict one another.
3. Sound helps to emphasize select elements within the image.

Sound and image can support each other in a variety of fashions. In Figure 10.18, from our discussion of editing in *Grey's Anatomy*, we see a medium close-up of Lexie, over Mark's shoulder (see tvcrit.com/find/greysanatomy). Her lips are moving. On the soundtrack is the sound of a woman's voice, coordinated with the moving lips, and, in the background, we can barely hear Matthew Mayfield's song "Better." The viewer presumes that that voice originates from those lips; the acoustic properties (discussed on pp. 295–96) of the voice help characterize Lexie's mounting distress during her confession to Mark about her infidelity. The background music builds as the scene progresses and then bridges to the next scene. Its chorus, "Make me a better man," suits the theme of flawed characters struggling to do the best they can. In this example, sound supports and heightens the impact of the image.

One of the most blunt ways in which television sound underscores the image and directly attempts to affect viewer response is the **laugh track**. The laugh track constructs a virtual audience from recordings of real audiences. That is, all laugh tracks, even for shows recorded before studio audiences, are a mixture of sound from various sources. If the actual audience does not provide enough laughter, the sound editor can easily add more, in a process often called **sweetening**. This is particularly important toward the end of sitcoms' recording sessions, when, typically, much of the audience has become bored and left the studio and, thus, the level of real laughter is diminished. And, obviously, if a program was recorded without a studio audience (for example, *Gilligan's Island* [1964–67] or *The Andy Griffith Show* [1960–68]), the entire laugh track has been fabricated. The purpose of a laugh track is simple enough. It inveigles the viewer into responding as the synthetic audience is responding. Similarly, crowd noise from sports events encourages viewers to respond as the crowd is responding. The inclusion of crowd noise in television is as much of a conscious decision as that of the laugh track. Why, for example, are football and baseball commentators forced to yell over the noise of the crowd when they could just as easily offer their commentaries from a soundproofed booth? The answer is that TV producers believe crowd noise pulls viewers into the action and immerses them in the excitement of the game. And that noise suggests a preferred response to the game. Television is one of the few media, if not the only one, that includes its implied audience response within texts themselves. Imagine a book, for example, telling you to laugh on page 32. In many cases in TV, sound is the vehicle by which response is both presented and elicited.

Sound does not always reinforce the image, however. Contrasting sound-image would be exemplified if in the scene between Lexie and Mark above Mark's voice accompanied the image of Lexie's moving lips, or peppy music were played under the anxious dialogue. Obviously this stark contradiction between sound and image occurs infrequently on television. When sound does contrast with image it's normally to make some sort of narrative or editorial point.

For instance, tvcrit.com contains an audio experiment featuring a Dodge commercial from the 1950s that illustrates how contrasting sound can make an argument about the image (see tvcrit.com/find/audioexperiment). In the original commercial, shots of happy, productive workers are accompanied by a song about the joys of car assembly. The narrator sings/shouts, "Turn her out, Henry! Turn her out, Joe! We'll put her together and watch her go!" The images show "Henry" and "Joe" "turning her out" (Figures 11.4 and 11.5). And the music punctuates the narrator's exhortations with brass fanfares (there is no sound directly from the presumably deafening factory floor). It's a clear, rhetorical, supportive use of song and music.

The tvcrit.com experiment, however, shows what happens if we change the music to make an editorial point. First, we replace the original audio with a slow, sorrowful classical piece: Erik Satie's Gymnopedie No. 1. Now the images of work on the assembly line no longer seem joyful

Figure 11.4 Workers in a Dodge commercial from the 1950s are urged by a narrator to "Turn her out, Henry!..."

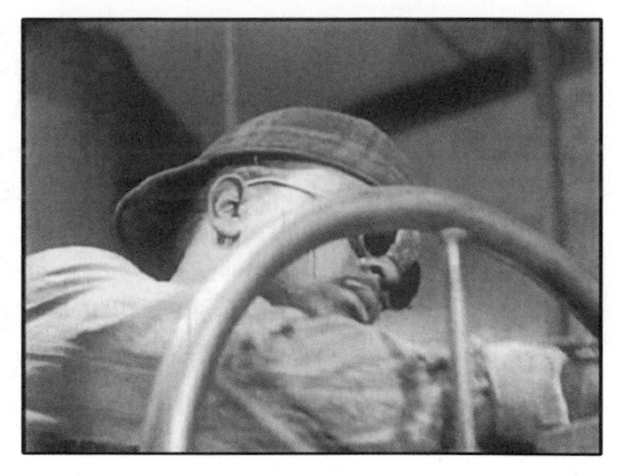

Figure 11.5 "... Turn her out, Joe! We'll put her together and watch her go!"

and productive. The grin of Henry is contradicted by the plaintive music and perhaps even made grotesque. A second audio replacement is even more pointed. If we replace the song written by Dodge's advertising team with Ralph Chaplin's "Solidarity Forever," the commercial becomes an argument for unions and workers' power:

> When the union's inspiration through the workers' blood shall run,
> There can be no power created anywhere beneath the sun.
> Yet what force on earth is weaker than the feeble strength of one?
> But the union makes us strong.
> Solidarity forever! Solidarity forever!

Propagandists of every political stripe have long understood the ability of sound to alter images' impact or contrast with images' original meanings.

The sound-image relationship need not simply be one of either support or contrast. Often sound emphasizes part of the image while negating or de-emphasizing other parts. In Figure 11.6, a scene from the series finale of *Ugly Betty*, we see a long shot of Betty's (America Ferrera) neighborhood where her father Ignacio (Tony Plana) is cooking on a grill (see tvcrit.com/find/uglybetty). Ignacio is small in this extreme long shot, the beginning of a crane down to street level, but his voice is relatively loud. It sounds as if we are standing right next to him. Sound is used in this shot to draw our attention to him in the back of the image. (See the discussion of sound perspective on pp. 299–302.) Even though this use of sound is implausible, it would likely not be noticed by most viewers. Why? Because this use of sound fits the narrative logic of the scene; it helps to emphasize the importance of Ignacio in this scene.

One could imagine other expressive, selective uses of sound in Figure 11.6. The sizzling of food on the grill could be heard above everything else, suggesting how good the food is or how hungry the characters are. The sound of characters eating might dominant the soundtrack, signifying they are gluttons. Or, in contrast, an eerie foreboding could be represented by the street being totally, unnaturally silent. Or, further, if the soundtrack were filled with sounds of marching bands (off camera), it could suggest a parade is about to come down the street. Each of these uses of sound and silence would move the story in a different direction. Each is an example of how, in subtle or not-so-subtle ways, the viewer's attention and comprehension may be channeled by the sounds accompanying the image.

Figure 11.6 A mismatch of sound and image perspective in *Ugly Betty*: We hear Ignacio as if he were close to us, but the camera views him from far away.

Maintaining Television Flow

The third purpose sound serves on television is the maintenance of television's pulsion, its forward drive. As is discussed in Chapter 1, television struggles to pull the viewer along in a flow of segments leading from one to the next. Sound plays a major role in this segment-to-segment flow.

Audio transitions between scenes parallel the visual transitions described in Chapter 11. One may **fade out** or **fade in** sound just as one may fade out/in image—although the two fades are often not quite simultaneous. Image frequently fades out just a bit earlier than sound. Additionally, the sound equivalent of a dissolve is the **cross-fade**, in which one sound fades out while the other fades in and the two overlap briefly. Another term for the transition from one sound to another—especially one song to another in music presentations—is **segue** ("seg-way"), which may be a cross-fade or a fade out/in.

There are several ways in which sound aids television flow, working to keep the viewer watching. First, the speech of television announcers and the dialogue of characters are frequently used to pose questions and enigmas in order to lure the viewer into staying around to see what happens next. Station and network promotional announcements promise uncommon sights to come, and narrative dialogue frames questions that the viewer may hope to see answered—as we saw in our discussion of serial narrative on p. 45. You may recall the example we cited: just before a commercial break, *All My Children*'s Ryan says to Kendall, "You are carrying my child. So, what the hell are we going to do about that?" And in our *Grey's Anatomy* scene, Meredith's voiceover elliptically refers to the action. That is, in the scene prior to the analyzed one, in which a couple reunites, we hear her say, "We have to damage the healthy flesh, in order to expose the unhealthy," but she has not completed her thought. She pauses as that scene dissolves to a Seattle skyline shot, which dissolves to the first shot of the analyzed scene, where she continues to muse ("It feels cruel...") and trails off so the scene's dialogue can begin. Regular viewers are familiar with Meredith's voiceovers linking disparate scenes together and enticing the viewer to stay tuned to find out how she'll complete her thoughts. In these nondiegetic and diegetic examples, speech plays on our curiosity to pull us into the television flow.

But speech is not the only sound device that pulls the viewer into the flow. Music is another common hook. Within programs it is especially common that the music does not end at the same time as the scene. Rather, the music continues–if only for just a few seconds. *Grey's Anatomy* frequently employs this technique. Trent Dabbs's "Your Side Now" continues from the previous scene to the analyzed one, and then "Better" slowly starts in the analyzed scene and then peaks in the following scenes.

This continuity of music helps to soften the disruption inherent in the transition from one scene to the next. It is seldom used, however, between one program and the next or between one commercial and the next. Here it is more important for linear television to differentiate slightly between the shows/commercials, to signal that one segment is ending but that another follows immediately. Many programs also develop very distinctive musical themes–think of *Seinfeld*'s slapping bass–to serve as interludes between scenes and between scenes and commercial breaks. For regular viewers, hearing that theme prompts their attention because they know something new is about to appear. Further, Karen Lury points out that these themes, in addition to the music used during programs' credits, are "often quite complex audio signifiers of the style, pace and structuring narrative of the programmes they identify."[7] This can be as straightforward as choices for theme songs such as *Gilmore Girls*' "Where You Lead," *Married... With Children*'s (1987–97) "Love and Marriage," and *The Wire*'s "Way Down in the Hole." Or they can be more evocative–as in the hospital-inspired sounds of *ER*'s lyric-less theme music.

Audience applause is one final aspect of sound that plays an important role in television transitions. Applause is commonly used as the marker of the end or beginning of a segment. However, in contrast to its traditional meaning as a sign of audience respect or appreciation or enjoyment, television applause more often simply means: "This is the beginning" or "This is the end." As everyone knows, studio audiences of sitcoms and talk shows are *told* when to applaud–often through "applause" signs that blink on and off. Also, sitcoms usually splice together alternative takes of scenes. Artificially induced applause and laughter help to conceal the transition between the shots.

Maintaining Continuity Within Scenes

A fourth and final use of sound is within each individual scene to help construct the continuity of space and time. As explained in Chapter 10, each television scene is made up of a variety of shots that are strung together according to the continuity editing system. The main purpose of this continuity system is to smooth over the potential disruptions that are caused by cutting from one shot to another. In this way the space and time of a particular setting and scene are made to appear continuous, even though they may have been recorded out of order. Dialogue, music, and ambient sound all play parts in maintaining this continuity.

Dialogue scenes, especially in the single-camera mode of production, are edited so that the cuts do not coincide with vocal pauses or the ends of sentences. (This is less true in live-on-tape productions, which are switched much more approximately.) Instead, the dialogue usually continues across a cut, helping to ease the transition from one shot to the next. In the scene from the single-camera production *Grey's Anatomy* analyzed in Chapter 10 (see Figures 10.9–10.23), most cuts come in the middle of a phrase–creating, in a sense, a verbal match cut as the words continue across the cut. At its most basic, shot-reverse shot editing does tend to show the person speaking while they speak, but editors don't cut at the end of each line. They allow lines to bleed over the cuts in the image. At the very end of shot 9 of Lexie, Mark begins to say, "You broke up with me." The cut to the following shot happens during, "You broke..." The mid-phrase edit serves as the glue holding the cut together.

Similarly, music and ambient sound unify the shots. The forward movement of a melody such as "Better" in *Grey's Anatomy* helps to propel the story onward. The temporal continuum of the music, its ability to flow through time, overrides the discontinuous time of the editing. Music helps to draw the viewer's attention from jump cuts, continuity errors, or other disruptions in the visuals. Ambient sound serves the same purpose, though even less noticeably. Ambient sound signifies a specific space and time to the viewer. A particular room, for example, has a particular sound associated with it at a particular time. Even slight shifts in that ambient sound can disrupt the viewer by making it appear that the space and/or time has changed. This is why sound technicians will record ambient or wild sound to lay down over shots that were originally done silent or to make consistent the sound behind dialogue that was shot at different times or locations. Consistent background sound, in a sense, certifies that the action took place in the same location at the same time, even though the shots are from different angles and may have been taken hours or days or weeks apart.

Laugh tracks also function in the background to underscore the continuity of a scene. As mentioned above, *The Andy Griffith Show*, a single-camera sitcom, incorporated a laugh track even though there was no studio audience. In each episode, the laughter continues across the cuts within a scene and thereby diminishes their disruptive potential. Viewers, in theory, don't notice the cut because they are too busy laughing along with the laugh track. In addition, multiple-camera programs such as *Rowan & Martin's Laugh-In* (1968–73) are recorded in short segments, with a laugh track tying all the segments together in post-production.

Acoustic Properties and Sound Technology

Sound on television appears deceptively simple. This is largely due to the fact that the sounds emanating from the TV speaker closely resemble the sounds that surround us in our everyday lives—unlike television's two-dimensional images, which are fundamentally dissimilar from our visual experience of the three-dimensional world. A person's voice on TV is not that different from a voice coming from someone sharing the living room with you. In contrast, a person's image on TV is flat and two-dimensional compared to the 3D person sitting next to you on the couch. The aesthetic techniques and digital/mechanical technology that are used to create sound are much less intrusive than those used to create image. It sometimes seems as if television sounds are merely an exact copy of the sounds of reality. This makes television's manipulation of sound even more difficult to detect than its manipulation of image. One aim of this chapter is to alert the reader to the ways that the makers of television shape our perception and our understanding by controlling acoustic properties and sound technology.

General Acoustic Properties

Even though we are mostly concerned here with the differences between television sound and real-life sound, it would be foolish to presume that there are not rudimentary similarities between the two. Any television sound shares three basic characteristics with the sounds we hear in reality:

1. **loudness**, or **volume**
2. **pitch**
3. **timbre** (pronounced "tam-burr"), or **tone**.

Loudness

How loud or soft a sound is plays an obvious role in our perception of it. The more amplified a sound is, the greater its impact. Loudness is used for more than just emphasis in television, however. It can also, among other things, signify distance. The louder a sound is, the closer we assume the person or thing causing the sound must be—an assumption that is toyed with in Figure 11.6. Further, the variation of loudness can be used for different effects. A sudden loud noise after a quiet segment, needless to say, causes shock or surprise. In contrast, soft sounds after a loud segment can force viewers to focus their attention in order to hear what's going on.

Pitch

Pitch is how high or low a sound is. On television, pitch is especially important to the meanings that voices convey (see Chapter 4). For example, higher-pitched voices carry conventionalized connotations of femininity and lower ones of masculinity. Pitch is significant to the impact of television music as well as its speech. In narrative scenes, higher notes are often used to accompany suspenseful situations, while lower notes can imply an ominous presence. These examples should not be taken proscriptively (high notes don't *always* mean suspense), but they do indicate how television conventionalizes pitch to signify meanings and establish atmosphere. As with all stylistic conventions, the meanings associated with pitch shift over time and from culture to culture.

Timbre

Timbre is a term borrowed from music theory. It signifies the particular harmonic mix that gives a note its "color" or tonal quality. A violin has a different tone than a cello. A saxophone's tone can be distinguished from a piano's, even when both play the same note.

The human voice also has timbre, and that tonal quality can be used by actors and directors to convey meaning. A nasal timbre can make a character into an annoying toady. A throaty timbre in a woman can signify a certain androgynous sexuality. In particular contexts, timbre communicates particular meanings.

TV-Specific Acoustic Properties

The sounds that the viewer hears on television are altered as they journey from sound stage to living room. The technology of various audio machines affects those sounds and provides the sound technicians with opportunities to manipulate volume, pitch, and timbre. Their use of this technology is guided by aesthetic conventions, by "rules" regulating the function of sound on television.

Digital Versus Analog

Before **digital** technology changed our concept of sound recording in the 1980s, audio and video tapes were based on **analog** principles. Analog sound (and image, too) has mostly disappeared from the consumer marketplace. Analog vinyl recordings and audio cassettes have been replaced by digital MP3s and CDs. However, it is still important to understand how digital recording works because sound in the real world is, of course, an analog phenomenon and must be *converted* to a digital format. That conversion holds the potential for changing sound. And, besides, the remnants of analog technology will be with us for some time to come. There has even recently been a resurgence in the sales of vinyl records, one of the first analog recording technologies!

First, let's consider the basic difference between all analog or digital phenomena. Anything labeled "digital" is rooted in digits or, put more simply, in numbers. An analog replica of something, in contrast, is a model that reproduces that thing in a different form from the original. The concept is a slippery one but may become clearer if we consider the differences between analog and digital representations of temperature. An analog thermometer is one in which the mercury appears as a line within a tube. When the line goes up to a certain area it signifies "warm," when it goes farther it signifies "hot." There are numbers calibrating the heat, but they aren't entirely necessary because the length of the line represents, in analog fashion, the amount of heat. The line's length is, in a sense, a model of the amount of heat. When it's long, it's hot. A digital thermometer, one that just displays numbers (for example, 32°), converts the amount of heat into digits. It doesn't tell us "warm" or "hot" or show us a model of the heat; it only gives us numbers. Further, as you can see in this example, all digital information is packaged in discrete units (for example, a single degree), while analog models are unbroken continua (for example, the continuous length of a mercury line in a tube).

We can apply this principle to sound recording. To begin, let's go a bit deeper into the basic, physical nature of sound. "Sound waves involve tiny disturbances or changes in the pressure of the air," Charles Taylor explains. "Each disturbance... then travels out through the surrounding air creating spherical wave surfaces round the origin of the sound—a three-dimensional counterpart of the circular ripples produced by a pebble striking the surface of a pond."[8] Analog sound technology creates replicas of these ripples or waves on audio tape (or, earlier, on vinyl records and wax cylinders). That is, the sound wave is converted into an electronic replica that is recorded on a piece of **magnetic tape**—a ribbon of plastic with a coating on it that is sensitive to magnetic impulses created by electricity. These magnetic impulses are modulated on the tape in a fashion that parallels the sound wave's modulation (that is, the way the sound vibrates through the air or other substance, like water). Visually, sound waves are commonly shown as waveforms of curving or jagged horizontal lines, indicating the up and down modulation—the vibration—of air pressure over time. This is evident in the digital audio workstation waveforms in Figures 11.1 and 11.2.

In contrast to analog recording, digital technology transforms the sound wave into numbers through a process called **sampling**. To clarify, this is not the same process, also called "sampling," in which a short piece of music is reproduced in a new recording. For example, Joni Mitchell singing "You don't know what you've got till it's gone" is sampled, in this sense, in Janet Jackson's "Got Till It's Gone" (see tvcrit.com/find/gottillitsgone).[9] In contrast, the sampling of a sound wave is when a digital recorder takes a tiny snippet from a sound—a fraction of a second—and measures the characteristics of the sound at that very instant. To illustrate this, imagine slicing the enlarged waveform in Figure 11.2 into very small pieces or what might look like the waveform of dots in Figure 11.7. The characteristics of each dot or sample are then converted into a set of binary numbers—just strings of zeros and ones—and recorded on a magnetic surface (a tape, flash drive, or hard drive). Thousands of samples are taken each second and then combined to create a digital representation of the sound. Much like our digital thermometer, this digital recording contains no information other than groups of digits—lots and lots of zeros and ones.

That, then, is the difference between analog and digital recording. But what is the significance of digital recording to television sound as it is played back on various electronic devices?

For years, the sound (and image) technology of our television sets was analog, but in 2009 that changed. For the home user, the digital audio revolution began in the 1980s with CDs, which are little more than a collection of numbers that have been pressed into aluminum (or

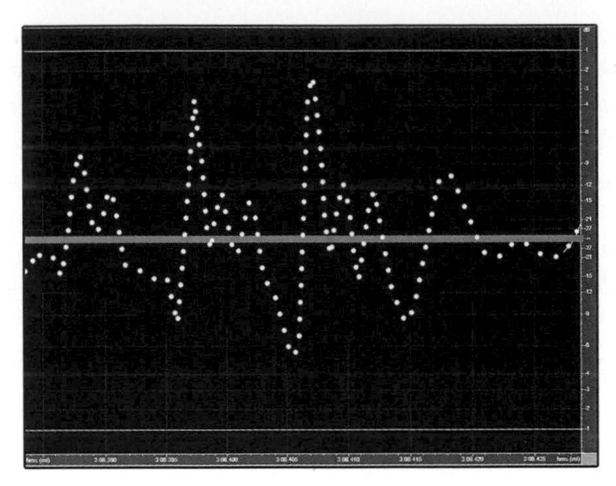

Figure 11.7 A waveform is broken into individual samples (shown as dots here) in the digitizing process.

occasionally gold) and coated with plastic. MP3s and other audio-file formats took that revolution to the extreme, with consumers replacing their physical disks with digital files. And on June 12, 2009, U.S. broadcasters finalized the switch to **digital television** (**DTV**). Now, sounds emanating from our phone and TV screens are fully digital—excepting those old audio/video cassettes and vinyl LPs we refuse to part with!

What does the difference between analog and digital really mean to the listener? If you compare the sound of a digital recording with that of a comparable analog one you'll notice three aspects of the digital recording: (1) less background noise (hiss and the like caused by analog recording), (2) a larger **dynamic range** (reproducing softer sounds without noise obscuring them and louder sounds without distortion), and (3) a greater **frequency response** (reproducing a wider range of low-to-high tones). It's hard to hear these advantages if you're listening to television through your phone's ear buds, but today's home-theater audio systems are taking greater advantage of the digital enhancement of audio.

Perhaps more significant than the digital recording process and its high quality are the abilities of digital technology to both process existing sounds and manufacture new sounds. A broad variety of sound effects (SFX) are now achieved using digital audio workstations, which may significantly alter the volume, pitch, and timbre of any recorded sound. There is virtually no way for the viewer to be able to tell when this sort of subtle manipulation has taken place. It is equally difficult to discern when sound, especially music, has been totally synthesized. This manufactured music has become popular in live-on-tape productions where a variety of music is needed, particularly for game shows, sports programs, and narrative programs such as soap operas.

Just about any type of instrumentation—from lush orchestral sounds to jazz and rock quartets—can be digitally created, instantaneously and inexpensively. This has greatly changed the musical sound of many genres. Productions that previously could not afford a full orchestra may now synthesize that sound cheaply. Soap operas, for instance, always used to be accompanied by a lone organ. That organ sound was so identified with the genre that it was a prominent part of soap-opera parodies such as "As the Stomach Turns" on *The Carol Burnett Show* (1967–79). Nowadays, however, the soaps have a wide-ranging variety of music, most of which is synthesized digitally. For examples, listen to the background music used in the *General Hospital* episodes at tvcrit.com/find/generalhospital. In contemporary television music, economic limitations and technological advances work together to change television's aesthetics.

Sound Perspective and Directionality

The position of a microphone, like the position of a camera, sets up a relationship between the recording device and the person or object creating the sound. The point-of-view that this relationship implies is its **sound perspective.** If a mike is placed close to someone's lips, then the sound recorded will be an intimate, "close-up" perspective. And if the mike is positioned far away, then the sound perspective will be distant, similar to a long shot. In a sense, then, mike position "frames" the sound for viewers, signaling to them how "close" they are to the sound-producing person or object. Mike placement and the division of sound into different, discrete channels (left, right, and so on) permit the manipulation of sound perspective—thus influencing the viewer's understanding of a scene.

In terms of distance from the mike to the recorded object or person, there are four conventional positions:

1. overhead boom (which can also be beneath the actors)
2. lavaliere
3. handheld
4. close-miking.

These positions incorporate different types of microphone technology based largely on the direction in which the mike is capable of picking up sound. That is, some mikes pick up sound from all directions *equally* and are thus **omnidirectional** (Figure 11.8). Other mikes are more sensitive to sound coming from certain directions. These **unidirectional** mikes usually have somewhat heart-shaped pickup patterns, which have come to be labeled **cardioid** and **hypercardioid** (from the Greek word for "heart"; Figure 11.8). A cardioid mike's pickup pattern looks like an inverted heart, with most of its sensitivity aimed toward the front. Similarly, hypercardioid mikes emphasize sound from the front, but they also allow sound from the rear to be recorded as well. The aesthetics of microphone positioning works with the technology of microphone directionality to determine how sound is picked up.

The overhead boom mike is held on a long arm that enables the **boom operator** to position it above or below the actors, just out of the view of the camera (see Figure 5.10, a boom operator

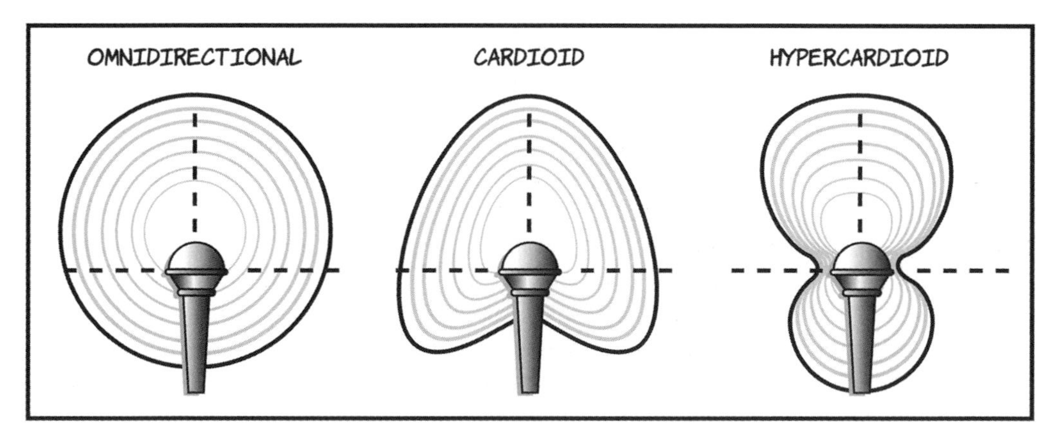

Figure 11.8 A microphone's pickup pattern indicates where it is most sensitive to sound.

miking Paul Teutul, from *American Chopper*). It uses a hypercardioid, shotgun mike so that the operator may aim it directly at a specific person and minimize the surrounding ambient sound. Since the mike is three or four feet away from the actors' mouths, the sound perspective is roughly equivalent to the sound one hears when standing near a group of people and engaging in conversation. Boom miking helps position the viewer vis-à-vis the characters or performers. This particular position implies an objective point-of-view, of being slightly distanced from the characters—or, at least, of not hearing subjectively through a character's mind.

The boom mike position has become the conventionalized norm for most narrative programs, whether using the single-camera or multiple-camera mode of production. Moreover, it is the only way that multiple-camera sitcoms and soap operas may be produced. They are recorded straight through, and consequently the mikes must record several persons from one mike position. Thus the economic imperative of shooting these programs live-on-tape results in the technological necessity of using boom mikes, causing the aesthetic consequence of a certain "objective" sound perspective.

The omnidirectional lavaliere mike is attached to actors' chests, clipped to their clothing, under which the microphone wire is concealed. Lavaliere miking is the norm for news broadcasters in the studio, though not for those out in the field, who use a more directional mike to filter competing, incidental sounds. It's also commonly used on talk shows. In Figure 11.9 a lavaliere mike is attached inconspicuously to Jimmy Fallon's tie, and another large, but nonfunctional mike sits on this desk—a holdover from when Johnny Carson hosted *The Tonight Show* and actually used a similar mike. Although closer than boom miking, the lavaliere mike is still about one foot from the broadcaster's mouth. The sound that it picks up is the audio equivalent to the medium close-up and close-up perspectives that typify framing in contemporary news practice.

The handheld mike sounds much like the lavaliere mike because it is also positioned around chest height, although it may also be held higher than that. Handheld mikes are used in news and sports field production (for example, in interviews with athletes and social actors) and in some talk shows and game shows (Figure 5.6, from *The Price Is Right*). These cardioid or hypercardioid mikes yield a sound perspective quite similar to the lavaliere mike, but, because they are directional microphones, the pickup may be aimed in one direction or another.

Handheld mikes are never utilized in narrative programs. Unlike boom and lavaliere mikes, the handheld mike is both visible and obvious to the viewer (the lavaliere mike is so small it can be overlooked or mistaken for a broach or a tie-clip). To use it in narrative programs would make

Figure 11.9 A lavaliere mike is barely noticeable on Jimmy Fallon's tie.

evident the technology involved in creating television; it would be like having a camera appear on-screen. This violates conventions of repressing television devices in narrative programs; to see a mike would make the viewer conscious of the whole production apparatus, which is taboo unless you are avant-garde playwright Bertolt Brecht or comedian Garry Shandling (in *It's Garry Shandling's Show* [1988–90] and *The Larry Sanders Show* [1992–98]). Even mockumentary programs like *The Office* seldom show the mikes or cameras recording the program.

In news reporting, the handheld mike is sometimes wielded like a club, intruding into the personal space of interviewees whether or not they wish to be spoken to. Thus, the handheld mike has come to signify broadcast journalism in certain contexts. Occasionally, it means overly aggressive reporting.

In **close-miking**, the mike is positioned right next to a person's mouth—the "extreme close-up" of miking. Its main use in narrative programs is to record subjective narration, such as Meredith's in *Grey's Anatomy*. More common, however, is the close-miking of radio and television announcers—the ones who read promotional announcements and advertisements. *The Breakfast Club* radio program—which also appears on YouTube—close-mikes its hosts and their guests, often with large microphones such as those that are favored in sound studios (Figure 11.10). This type of miking creates sound that has a full, rich timbre, a wide frequency response (often emphasizing bass pitch for male studio announcers), and very little ambient noise. Viewers have come to expect the close-miked sound in television announcements and music videos. For these elements of television, close-miking is the norm. However, close-miking can also prove to be disruptive when used in narrative programs. Dubbing and other ADR in narrative programs are often recorded in close-miking. This can clash with the viewer's expectations of the sound perspective created with boom-miking. To cut from a boom-miked piece of dialogue to one that is close-miked makes it sound as if the characters were suddenly right on top of you. To avoid this, sound technicians position the mike away from the ADR actors.

Sound perspective is not limited to a sense of closeness, of near or far. The widespread acceptance of stereo-TV sets and programs in the 1990s afforded sound editors another tool for representing perspective. By altering the relative loudness of sounds in the right and left channels, they give us a sense of the lateral (that is, sideways) position of a person or object. For example, a gun appears on the right side of the frame, and when it is fired the gunshot principally emanates from the right-hand speaker. This sound cue confirms our spatial sense of the position of the gun.

Figure 11.10 Kevin Hart is close-miked on *The Breakfast Club*, a radio show originating on WWPR-FM—as can be seen when the show appears on its YouTube channel.

Sound mixing in theatrical films, DVDs, BDs, and DTV has seen the number of channels multiply in recent years. Dolby Digital, for instance, was introduced in film theaters in 1992 and DTV in 1998. It boasts 5.1 channels. The Dolby website explains their arrangement:

> Dolby Digital programs can deliver surround sound with five discrete full-range channels–left, center, right, left surround, and right surround–plus a sixth channel for those powerful low-frequency effects (LFE) that are felt more than heard in movie theaters. As it needs only about one-tenth the bandwidth of the others, the LFE channel is referred to as a '.1' channel (and sometimes erroneously as the "subwoofer" channel).[10]

Thus, Dolby Digital 5.1 is actually created with six speakers: four speakers for the left, right, center, and LFE channels in front of the viewer. The two so-called "surround" channels emanate from speakers placed *behind* the viewer. By literally surrounding viewers with six speakers, Dolby Digital creates a sound space in which sounds may come from behind and in front, and to the left and right–unlike the sound in original monaural TVs, which only came from a single point in front of the viewer.

Dolby Digital and other multi-channel sound systems greatly enhance the potential for sound-perspective manipulation on TV, but the placement of sounds in particular channels is not without its "rules" and conventions. Almost all dialogue is placed in the center channel–even if actors are positioned to the far left or right of the frame. Left/right channels are reserved for music and sound effects only. The rear left/right ("surround") and the LFE channels contain only sound effects, no dialogue or music. Aside from the LFE channel, there is no technical reason for this assignment of channels to certain types of sound. Thus, the seemingly endless variety of sound perspective is constrained by aesthetic convention–with sound again being largely divided into speech, music, and effects.

To this point, we have suggested ways in which sound perspective may be roughly equivalent to image perspective. But directors and sound editors, especially in narrative programs, need not rely upon that equivalence. Indeed, they may try to subvert it for specific narrative effect. In the scene from *Ugly Betty* discussed on pp. 292-93 (Figure 11.6), for instance, Ignacio is shown in the background in long shot, perhaps too distant for the viewer to hear clearly, but his voice is presented at "normal," boom-miked level. Sound perspective contrasts with image perspective in order to achieve a specific narrative effect–in this case, the importance of Ignacio's emotional state as Betty is leaving home. This is a major plot point in the narrative, and sound design helps to emphasize it. Further, it is likely that the dialogue for this scene was done using ADR during audio post, since the sound perspective is close but no microphones are positioned close to the actor (as would be revealed in the long shot).

Space, Time, and Narrative

Much of what we hear on TV comes from a source that we can see on TV at the very same time. In other words, much TV sound originates in on-screen space and is synchronized with the time of the image. But this is not true of all sound on television. Sound is often significantly disconnected from the image it accompanies. If sound does not match the image's space or time, then what effect does this disjuncture cause? What does it signify?

Sound and Space

In Chapter 9 we discussed how the aesthetic/technological fact of the camera frame can be used by the director and videographer/cinematographer to achieve a variety of framing effects.

The frame is also important to our consideration of sound. It forms the boundary between offscreen space and on-screen space, between what is within the frame and what is presumed to be outside it. Often the source of a sound will be situated offscreen. This is quite common in non-narrative, live-on-tape productions when a voice is heard from an actor who is not currently on-screen—for example, band leader Reggie Watts's chortle following one of James Corden's jokes. And, of course, the laughter and applause of the studio audience normally come from offscreen, too.

Our commonsensical understanding of offscreen space is also used in narrative programs. A voice or sound from offscreen helps to create the illusion that life is going on all around the characters that we see on-screen. Offscreen space thus aids the construction of the continuity of space—that is, it enhances the sense that the on-screen space *continues* out beyond the camera frame. This can be as simple as the sound of traffic inserted in the background of the *Grey's Anatomy* scene discussed on pp. 262–69, or it can involve the more complicated manipulation of sounds and framing that create the illusion of a killer following a victim in a shadowy alley. In short, sound draws the viewer's mind out past the frame into a fictional world that has been created for this narrative.

Sound and Time

The time of a sound, in relation to the image it accompanies, can be:

1. earlier than the image;
2. simultaneous with the image; or
3. later than the image.

Obviously, the vast majority of sound falls into the second category, but there are also many instances of sound being displaced from the time of the image.

In a sound flashback we hear speech, music, or sound effects from an earlier time than the image currently on the screen. This occurs frequently in narrative programs. We can see this technique in the August 14, 2007 episode of *Damages* (2007–), a program known for complicated flashbacks (see tvcrit.com/find/damages). The episode flashes back to an incident in 2002. In the story's present time, two attorneys are interviewing Katie (Anastasia Griffith) about her past encounters with Gregory (Peter Facinelli). We cut back and forth between 2007 and 2002. As a bridge to those 2002 images, the sound editor laid dialogue from the past over an image of Katie in the present (Figure 11.11). Specifically, as we see 2007 Katie, we hear 2002 Gregory say, "Holy shit, you live in Brooklyn, too?" The reverse—that is, sound later than the image—can also occur. When a sound flashforward is used, the viewer hears sound from a future part of the story. The same *Damages* episode actually begins in the past, in a flashback from 2002. In the flashback, Katie's image freezes and we hear dialogue from the present day spoken over it (Figure 11.12). The interview in the present is already in progress and one lawyer's (Felicia Marquand [Marlyne Afflack]) instruction to Katie to "Wait, wait, wait" seems to interrupt the flashback. In this case, 2007 sound is heard over a 2002 image. The same sort of image-sound displacement happens in *The Wonder Years* when we see an image from the 1970s and hear the voice of Kevin in the 1990s commenting on it.

Sound and Narrative: Diegetic and Nondiegetic Sound

The Greek word **diegesis** has been used in media studies to refer to the story itself, the narrative action. The physical world in which this narrative action takes place is the **diegetic space**.

Figure 11.11 Damages: We see Katie in the present day, but we hear dialogue from five years prior.

Figure 11.12 We see Katie in a flashback to the past, but we hear dialogue from the present day.

Seinfeld's (1990–98) diegetic space, for example, is Jerry's apartment and the New York City locations he and his friends frequent (for example, Monk's Cafe). Diegetic sound, then, consists of speech, music, and sound effects whose source is in the world of the story: the dialogue of Jerry, Elaine, George, and Kramer; the noises and ambient sound in the apartment; and so on.

Diegetic sound may be either objective or subjective. Objective diegetic sound originates in the external world of the narrative and would include, for example, Jerry and George's conversations. Subjective diegetic sound comes from inside a character's head and cannot be heard by other characters at the same location—as often occurs in *Grey's Anatomy* with Meredith's thoughts (but usually not the other characters' thoughts). When characters' voiceovers are used to signify their thoughts, then diegetic sound is being used subjectively.

Not all of the sound on narrative TV programs, however, originates in the diegesis. The so-called mood music or **underscore** that accompanies each scene is heard by the viewer but not by the characters because it is not part of their world. Sound-studies scholars such as Ron Rodman call this **intradiegetic** audio.[11] It is connected to the construction of the story for the viewer, but it is not embedded in the diegetic world of the characters. Lexie and Mark do not hear Matthew Mayfield singing, for example. Characters also do not acknowledge the narration of an omniscient announcer (one who is not a character)—as in *Arrested Development* (tvcrit.com/find/arresteddevelopment). Intradiegetic music and narration are commonly used to guide the viewer's perception of the narrative, but they have no impact on the characters in the stories.

Rodman's study of television music extends to audio that is not in service to the narrative. Consider the station announcements for upcoming shows or weather alerts, programs' theme music, commercials' jingles, and all the other audio material that is squeezed in between narrative segments. All of this audio is fundamental to television's flow, but it is disconnected from a program's diegesis. Rodman therefore labels the music in these TV elements **extradiegetic**. This sort of audio has long been a part of linear television's attempts to hail viewers and hold onto them for hours of continuous watching. It is a part of linear TV that has to be rethought in the new era of on-demand streaming services, however. When a service inserts a **pre-roll** commercial before a video we are attempting to stream, then we are experiencing extradiegetic audio/video. But that extradiegetic commercial has not hailed us, pulling us in to watch a video, the way that linear TV functions. Rather, we have requested to have a video shown to us. In short, there is extradiegetic material involved in our on-demand viewing experiences, but it would be inaccurate to assume it functions exactly as extradiegetic audio/video do in linear television of the network era and today.

Summary

The importance of sound to television is easy to overlook because it is often difficult to detect how sound has been manipulated by the makers of television programs. When watching television, however, it is important to recognize how the different types of sound (speech, music, and sound effects), have been molded in order to achieve particular purposes. As always, these manipulations, these purposes, are ruled by television's aesthetics, economics, and technology.

The essential purpose of sound on TV is to hail the viewer to watch TV. This purpose cannot be overestimated. The producers of commercials have long understood the significance of sound in capturing viewer interest. Once we have been hooked, sound channels our perception of an image by either reinforcing the meaning of that image or directing us toward select elements of the image. In less common instances, it may subvert what the image seems to be saying.

Sound also functions to propel television forward. Within individual scenes, the illusion of continuity is preserved through the mix of music, speech, and sound effects. Sound thus becomes an integral part of the continuity editing system. On a larger scale, sound also helps maintain the flow between one television segment and the next. Speech is especially significant in its construction of enigmas to pull the viewer into the television current.

Sound on television is in some ways identical to the sounds of life. In both, sound may be characterized in terms of its volume, pitch, and timbre, but it would be wrong to assume that TV sound is not manipulated in its transition from historical world to TV speaker. Digital and analog technologies present sound editors with a broad audio palette from which to choose. They may orchestrate preexisting sounds or even create them, synthesize them, from scratch. One of the simplest components of sound technology is the positioning of the microphone and the effect that this has on sound perspective. Different types of microphone technology, in different locations, give the viewer an audio point-of-view from which to hear the action.

Most of the sound we hear on television is synchronized with the space and time of the images we are watching, but it need not always be so. Sounds can be offscreen as easily as they are on-screen. Offscreen sound draws the viewer out beyond the frame, further constructing spatial continuity. And the time of a sound may be displaced from that of the image. Sound of an earlier or later time can be laid over an image to various effects.

Thus television sound, which so often appears to be the "simple" recording of life's speech, music, and sound effects, is actually another manipulated and/or fabricated component of the television medium. The majority of this manipulation occurs during audio post—the post-production phase of a program's creation—where an efficient mode of production has evolved. Sound editors and music supervisors and composers blend various sound elements into a final soundtrack that works hand-in-hand with the image to tell stories, inform, and persuade the viewer.

Notes

1 It was NBC's broadcast of a game between the New York Jets and the Miami Dolphins on December 20, 1980.

2 Kevin, as a youth, was played by Fred Savage, but the voice of the adult narrator Kevin belonged to Daniel Stern.

3 When MTV first began, record labels provided music videos for free, as advertising for the music, but subsequently began charging for them.

4 Bryan Reesman, "DVD A Boon for Music via Licensing," *GRAMMY*, August 3, 2005, www.grammy.com/features/2005/0803_tvdvd.aspx, accessed December 28, 2005.

5 Ibid.
6 For example, *The O.C.* executive producer Josh Schwartz chose five Beck songs, including "E-Pro" and "Girl," for the "The Mallpisode" episode (March 10, 2005). An ad card credited Beck at the end of the program. He commented, "Usually I'm a little bit wary of TV shows or licensing songs. I didn't know much about the show, but there were all these bands whose music was on the show who I never thought would be on the show and apparently, the gentleman who puts the music together has excellent taste." Melinda Newman, "Beck's Back," AZCentral.com, March 21, 2005, www.azcentral.com/ent/music/articles/0322beck.html, accessed December 28, 2005.
7 Karen Lury, *Interpreting Television* (London: Hodder Arnold, 2005), 75.
8 Charles Taylor, With Murray Campbell, "The Nature of Sound," *Grove Music Online*, January 4, 2006, grovemusic.com.
9 Joni Mitchell's line is from the song "Big Yellow Taxi."
10 "Dolby Digital FAQ," *Dolby Laboratories, Inc.*, December 29, 2005, tvcrit.com/find/dolby.
11 Ron Rodman, *Tuning In: American Narrative Television Music* (Oxford: Oxford University Press, 2010), 53–54. For a concise discussion of Rodman's terms, see tvcrit.com/find/rodman.

Further Readings

Sound style is discussed in many of the readings suggested at the end of chapters in Part II.

"Sound studies," the critical study of sound in media, has recently begun to gain traction—after having been overshadowed by work on the visual for many years. In terms of television sound, much of this activity focuses on the use of music in the medium. And early effort in this regard was Philip Tagg's 1979 dissertation, titled, "*Kojak*—50 Seconds of Television Music (Towards the Analysis of Affect in Popular Music)" (e-book edition, New York: Mass Media Music Scholars' Press, 2000). More recently, significant studies on TV music have been published in the twenty-first century: Paul Attinello, Janet K. Halfyard, and Vanessa Knights, eds., *Music, Sound and Silence in* Buffy the Vampire Slayer (Burlington, VT: Ashgate, 2010); James Deaville, *Music in Television: Channels of Listening* (New York: Routledge, 2011); K. J. Donnelly, *The Spectre of Sound: Music in Film and Television* (London: BFI, 2005); and Ron Rodman, *Tuning In: American Narrative Television Music* (New York: Oxford University Press, 2010). These sources emphasize music in narrative television, spending little time on television's other musical forms. Specifically, music videos are not addressed.

We have also slighted music videos in this chapter and, indeed, have eliminated a music-television chapter that was included in previous editions of *Television*. The reason is simple: very few music videos are shown on linear TV these days. The bulk of them have migrated to YouTube and the like. However, the *Television* chapter on music television remains available online: tvcrit.com/find/musictv. And in it its author, Blaine Allan, glosses significant readings in this subject area, including: E. Ann Kaplan, *Rocking Around the Clock: Music Television, Postmoderism, and Consumer Culture* (New York: Methuen, 1987); Andrew Goodwin, *Dancing in the Distraction Factory: Music Television and Popular Culture* (Minneapolis: University of Minnesota Press, 1992); and Andrew Goodwin, Simon Frith, and Lawrence Grossberg, eds., *Sound and Vision: The Music Video Reader* (London: Routledge, 1993). More recent investigations of the topic are also available: Carol Vernallis, *Experiencing Music Video: Aesthetics and Cultural Context* (New York: Columbia University Press, 2004); and Kevin Williams, *Why I (Still) Want My MTV: Music Video and Aesthetic Communication* (Cresskill, NJ: Hampton Press, 2003).

Rick Altman, "Television/Sound," in *Studies in Entertainment: Critical Approaches to Mass Culture*, Tania Modleski, ed. (Bloomington: Indiana University Press, 1986), 39–54, builds on his pioneering work on sound in the neighboring medium of the cinema. Stephen Heath and Gillian Skirrow, "Television: A World in Action," *Screen* 18, no. 2 (Summer 1977), 7–59, is not wholly devoted to sound, but it does make some keen observations on the sound-image relationship.

Also important for their considerations of sound's significance are the previously cited John Ellis, *Visible Fictions* and Herbert Zettl, *Sight Sound Motion*. The latter's companion website (tvcrit.com/find/sightsoundmotion) contains sound files that help explain principles such as harmony, timbre, and so on.

The critical differences between sound for TV and sound for theatrical film are discussed in Michele Hilmes, "Television Sound: Why the Silence?" *Music, Sound and the Moving Image* 2, no. 2 (Autumn 2008), 153–61. Moreover, many interdisciplinary articles on music may be found in that journal, which published its first issue in 2007. Still, the study of sound in a single medium, the cinema, can also provide insights into television. Foundational essays on sound in film are collected in Elisabeth Weis and John Belton, *Film Sound: Theory and Practice* (New York: Columbia University Press, 1985), and two journal issues on the topic: *Yale French Studies* 60 (1980) and *Screen* 25, no. 3 (May–June 1984). Since then, Michel Chion has written two pertinent books that theorize about sound in film: *Audio-Vision: Sound on Screen* (New York: Columbia University Press, 1994); and *The Voice in the Cinema*, translated by Claudia Gorbman (New York: Columbia University Press, 1999). And George Burt, *The Art of Film Music* (Boston: Northeastern University Press, 1994); and Claudia Gorbman, *Unheard Melodies: Narrative Film Music* (Bloomington, IN: Indiana University Press, 1987), have detailed the interaction between sound and film narrative. Additionally, K. J. Donnelly, ed., *Film Music: Critical Approaches* (New York: Continuum, 2001), is particularly useful as it surveys different critical methods that have been applied to film music.

Finally, FilmSound.org presents a "learning space dedicated to the art and analyses of film sound design." Its "Post Audio FAQ's" (tvcrit.com/find/audiopost) offers valuable insights into sound's mode of production. Other online sound resources include, obviously, YouTube, Apple Music, and other online music providers, but also helpful are the "Glossary of Music Licensing Terms" (tvcrit.com/find/musiclicensing) and sound designer David Filskov's "Guide to Sound Effects" (tvcrit.com/find/soundeffects). Plus, *A Digital Media Primer for Geeks* (tvcrit.com/find/digitalmediaprimer) offers a wealth of information about sound fundamentals and the differences between analog and digital media.

Part III

Television Studies

12 An Introduction to Television Studies

This book offers the reader a set of tools for analyzing television. We hope anyone—even a casual viewer—might use them to better understand the medium. But perhaps you'd like to take your understanding of television beyond that of a casual viewer. Perhaps you'd like to study the medium in a more rigorous fashion. If this is your interest, then you'll need to understand some of the methods that have evolved in the study of television from a **critical studies** perspective—rooted in analytical methods applied to literature, art, history, economics, political science, the cinema, and the theater. These methods tend to be clustered together in a discipline known as **television studies**, which blossomed as the twentieth century ended and has continued into the 2010s, as can be seen from this flurry of book releases:

1998: *The Television Studies Book*
1999: *Critical Ideas in Television Studies*
2002: *Television Studies: The Key Concepts*
2002: *Television Studies*
2004: *The Television Studies Reader*
2004: *An Introduction to Television Studies*
2009: *Television Studies After TV*
2010: *Television Studies: The Basics*
2011: *Television Studies*
2012: *The Television Reader: Critical Perspective in Canadian and US Television Studies*
2014: *The SAGE Handbook of Television Studies*[1]

What interests us most are the critical methods underlying the different strains of television studies that first developed during the 1980s and 1990s and continue to this day. This part of the book will outline the most significant of those strains. We have divided them into approaches that focus mostly on TV programs "themselves," without theorizing extensively about the TV viewer or the TV industry; and approaches that examine how TV's meanings, its discourses, are received by viewers and produced by TV-industry workers. Chapter 13 addresses the former, examining authorship, stylistics, genre study, and semiotics. Chapter 14 summarizes the latter, considering ideological analysis, political economy, feminism, queer theory, and race and ethnic studies. As you'll see, our division quickly crumbles as textual analysis inevitably makes assumptions about the viewer/industry, and viewer/industry research has little relevance if it doesn't also talk about programs. Nonetheless, clustering these approaches into different chapters allows us to see certain common areas of interest in them.

The principles of the critical approach might not be immediately obvious, and so before getting into any specific research methods, we will examine the fundamental presumptions behind it. We should also acknowledge that television studies is not the only category of research methods/theories that has been applied to the medium. There is also a long-standing research tradition that operates under the umbrella term of **mass communication research**. While television studies employs critical methods, mass-comm research favors scientific research methods. Readers interested in the mass-comm approach may find a summary of it in Appendix II.

Critical Research and Television

Basic Principles and Presumptions

The critical approach rests on the fundamental principle of *interpretation*. To interpret a television program, the television industry's discourse about production, the publications of a TV fan community, or any other cultural object is to pursue its meaning or significance. Scholarly critics seek to understand their objects of study by:

- engaging with them intellectually (and perhaps even emotionally);
- closely examining their constituent parts;
- arguing for certain meanings and significance; and
- commonly, placing them within the analytical tradition of an interpretation-based theory and/or method.

For centuries, this approach has been employed to understand phenomena from the ancient theater to literature, painting, sculpture, the cinema, television, and all other arts and mass media.

Although there are numerous types of critical inquiry, we may still generalize about its underlying presumptions. This does some damage to the diversity among critical approaches, but it allows us to grasp their key elements. The following two chapters can then be spent discussing various flavors of critical work, of interpretive theories and methods. Those underlying presumptions include:

1. Knowledge about an object of study—its meaning—is not solely within it, waiting to be discovered. Rather, meaning is generated through the researchers' interpretive interaction with phenomena. The process of making meaning is always that of a human intellect reacting to some "text"—a TV program, an interview with a showrunner, a sample of fan fiction, and so on. Moreover, interpretation is usually based in a particular theory about the phenomenon's characteristics and essence.
2. Critical researchers do not lay claims to objectivity. The nature of their enterprise is subjective because meaning can only arise through the interaction of the phenomenon with the researcher's subjectivity—their psyche. Critical research acknowledges and even cherishes the researcher's unique mix of theoretical perspective, training, and even their psychological makeup.
3. Since critical approaches rely upon opinion, they are not replicable; i.e., if a study is repeated, it is not guaranteed that exactly the same results will occur.
4. Critical researchers do not collect facts for their own sake. Facts are only useful to the extent that they advance interpretation.
5. Critical research results are messy, ephemeral, and occasionally contradictory. Consequently, they do not lend themselves to being expressed in (reduced to) numbers.
6. Theory is used to speculate about the object of study and provides the basis for the evaluation of the critical work by other scholars. In a sense, the act of criticism is the process of putting theory to work, of *applied* theory.

These presumptions characterize the critical process as subjective, not replicable or verifiable, unconcerned with facts, speculative, and even self-contradictory. Dedicated social scientists reading this—and perhaps even skeptical students—might presume therefore that critical work has no basis in "reality" and that there are no criteria for evaluating critical work, that one opinion is just as valid as another. Such is not the case. To summarize the criteria used by many critical scholars, Leah R. Vande Berg, Lawrence A. Wenner, and Bruce E. Gronbeck pose four questions one may ask about a critical piece:

1. Does it possess internal consistency?
2. Does it provide sufficient, appropriate evidence for the claims implied by the thesis and advanced in the essay?
3. Does it offer a plausible rationale for its cultural, critical, theoretical, or practical significance?
4. Does it cause an astute reader to accept the critical interpretation or explanation argued for in the essay as a reasonable one?[2]

If we consider each of these criteria in more detail, we can come to a better understanding of what it is that critical researchers actually do and how they justify and evaluate their work.

If essays, articles, or books possess "internal consistency," their authors have presented their arguments in a logical fashion. They have proposed core concepts, built upon them with well-reasoned examples drawn from the objects of study, and then argued for the validity of certain conclusions regarding them. One step leads to the next and the next and the next; they do not ramble from one point to another, or contradict themselves, or get lost in unnecessary digressions. Thus, within the world of their interpretation (i.e., "internal" to it) they have coherently developed their theses (i.e., been "consistent" in their arguments). Or, in other words, the internal parts of their arguments fit together into consistent wholes.

"Evidence" that supports an interpretation is necessary in any critical enterprise. Moreover, some interpretations are more valid than others because of the strength of their evidence. The type of evidence needed depends largely upon the nature of the object of study. In the specific case of television studies, evidence is drawn from various sources:

1. *Television programs themselves*: narrative and non-narrative structures, styles of mise-en-scene, videography, editing, sound (dialogue and music), and so on.
2. *Other mass media related to TV and created by media industries*: publicity photographs; interviews; network-controlled websites; interviews, articles, and advertisements in popular and industry publications; memos stored in archives; the promotional material on streaming video services; and so on.
3. *Materials created by the audience*: statements in interviews with viewers, fan-created websites and blogs, fan fiction, and so on.

In short, evidence for one's critical analysis may be found on television and in all the ancillary material that surrounds the medium—whether generated by the industry itself or by members of the audience.

An essay may be internally consistent and offer a large bulk of evidence, but it still might not be "significant." It might still prompt the reader to ask, "So what?" Vande Berg, et al. answer the so-what question by scrutinizing the "cultural, critical, theoretical, or practical significance of the critic's analysis."[3] Following their lead, we might translate "So what?" into these questions that resonate more specifically with television studies:

1. *Cultural*: Does the analysis help us understand the shared values of our culture? Does it place television into the context of broader cultural concerns and thereby illuminate both TV and the culture to which it belongs? For example, cultural studies seek to articulate television's unstated meanings and examine how they support a society's power structure.
2. *Critical*: Does the analysis help us understand television's narrative and non-narrative structures and styles of mise-en-scene, videography, editing, and sound? Does it provide insights into how television constructs its meanings? For example, genre study seeks the narrative structures and visual styles common to groups of programs.
3. *Theoretical*: Does the analysis help us understand a theoretical perspective? Some work in television studies seeks to advance a particular theory—such as Marxism, political economy, or feminism. For example, analyses of Lady Gaga's image might illustrate the concerns of contemporary feminist theory and suggest new directions for feminists to take.
4. *Practical*: Does the analysis help us live our daily lives? Does it help us understand our relationships with family members and colleagues? For example, an analysis of an *Oprah* episode may give us a better understanding of our own relationships with family members.

The final criterion proposed by Vande Berg, et al. is reasonableness. For them, this is based on the critic's persuasive skills. An analysis is deemed reasonable if its arguments and evidence persuade us that it is "plausible, sufficiently well supported, and concerned with a socially, critically, or aesthetically important issue, construct, or text."[4] We don't have to accept an analysis as *the* one and only "truth" about a topic. We only have to judge that it is *a* credible truth. Remember, critical analyses are, by their nature, subjective. There can therefore be no claims for objective truth, but some claims are still more reasonable and compelling than others.

In gathering the material for the next two chapters, the author has repeatedly applied these criteria to and asked these questions of the critical theories and methods that follow. As you will see, I have found that they all pass the standards of internal consistency, appropriate evidence, significance, and reasonableness. I hope you agree, but I invite you to pose these same questions as you read these chapters and come to your own conclusions. In short, I ask you to do a critical analysis of these critical methods!

Notes

1 Robert C. Allen and Annette Hill, eds., *The Television Studies Reader* (New York: Routledge, 2004); Manuel Alvarado, Milly Buonanno, Herman Gray, and Toby Miller, eds., *The SAGE Handbook of Television Studies* (Thousand Oaks, CA: Sage, 2014); Jonathan Bignell, *An Introduction to Television Studies*, 3rd ed. (New York: Routledge, 2012); Bernadette Casey, Neil Casey, Ben Calvert, Liam French, and Justin Lewis, *Television Studies: The Key Concepts* (New York: Routledge, 2002); John Corner, *Critical Ideas in Television Studies* (Oxford: Clarendon Press, 1999); Christine Geraghty and David Lusted, eds., *The Television Studies Book* (New York: Arnold, 1998); Jonathan Gray and Amanda D. Lotz, *Television Studies* (Cambridge, UK: Polity, 2011); Tanner Mirrlees and Joseph Kispal-Kovacs, eds., *The Television Reader: Critical Perspective in Canadian and US Television Studies* (Oxford: Oxford University Press, 2012); Toby Miller, ed., *Television Studies* (London: BFI, 2002); Toby Miller, *Television Studies: The Basics* (New York: Routledge, 2010); Graeme Turner and Jinna Tay, eds., *Television Studies After TV: Understanding Television in the Post-Broadcast Era* (New York: Routledge, 2009).

2 Leah R. Vande Berg, Lawrence A. Wenner, and Bruce E. Gronbeck, *Critical Approaches to Television*, 2nd ed. (Boston: Houghton Mifflin, 2004), 30.

3 Ibid., 30.

4 Ibid., 31.

Further Readings

We began with a list of 11 "television studies" books. Of these, five are designed for students and attempt to summarize current concepts and research in the discipline: Jonathan Bignell, *An Introduction to Television Studies* (New York: Routledge, 2004); Bernadette Casey, Neil Casey, Ben Calvert, Liam French, and Justin Lewis, *Television Studies: The Key Concepts* (New York: Routledge, 2002); John Corner, *Critical Ideas in Television Studies* (Oxford: Clarendon Press, 1999); Jonathan Gray and Amanda D. Lotz, *Television Studies* (Cambridge, UK: Polity, 2011); and Toby Miller, *Television Studies: The Basics* (New York: Routledge, 2010). They all do a good job in this regard.

The other six television studies books in our list are anthologies: Robert C. Allen and Annette Hill, eds., *The Television Studies Reader* (New York: Routledge, 2004); Manuel Alvarado, Milly Buonanno, Herman Gray, and Toby Miller, eds., *The SAGE Handbook of Television Studies* (Thousand Oaks, CA: Sage, 2014); Christine Geraghty and David Lusted, eds., *The Television Studies Book* (New York: Arnold, 1998); Tanner Mirrlees and Joseph Kispal-Kovacs, eds., *The Television Reader: Critical Perspective in Canadian and US Television Studies* (Oxford: Oxford University Press, 2012); Toby Miller, ed., *Television Studies* (London: BFI, 2002); Graeme Turner and Jinna Tay, eds., *Television Studies After TV: Understanding Television in the Post-Broadcast Era* (New York: Routledge, 2009). *The Television Studies Reader* is particularly substantial, with over 38 essays arranged in seven parts.

Another useful anthology is Janet Wasko, ed., *A Companion to Television* (Malden, MA: Wiley-Blackwell, 2010), which includes an overview of the history of television studies by one of its long-standing proponents, Horace Newcomb.

In terms of placing television studies into the context of other theories and methods, the most ambitious book is Robert C. Allen, ed., *Channels of Discourse, Reassembled*, 2nd ed. (Chapel Hill: University of North Carolina Press, 1992). Separate chapters, with annotated bibliographies, cover semiotics, narrative theory, audience-oriented criticism, genre study, ideological analysis, psychoanalysis, feminism, and cultural studies. One chapter also outlines the debate over postmodernism and television. *Channels of Discourse* remains relevant to television studies despite being last revised nearly two decades ago. It provides a clear summary of the state of television studies in the 1980s, upon which current work builds.

Similarly, Leah R. Vande Berg, Lawrence A. Wenner, and Bruce E. Gronbeck, eds., *Critical Approaches to Television* (Boston: Houghton Mifflin, 1998) introduces the reader to numerous separate critical methods, some of which have been influenced by a communication studies perspective. Although it does touch upon several of the same topics as *Channels of Discourse*, it also provides space for hermeneutic, mythic, rhetorical, and sociological critical methods. *Critical Approaches to Television* furnishes applications of each method. Other books offering helpful overviews of television criticism include John Fiske, *Television Culture*, 2nd ed. (London: Routledge, 2011; originally published in 1987); and Paul Monaco, *Understanding Society, Culture and Television* (Westport, CT: Praeger, 2000).

Additional general anthologies are less explanatory in their presentation but do offer the reader a sampling of critical methods: Tony Bennett, Susan Boyd-Bowman, Colin Mercer, and Janet Woollacott, eds., *Popular Television and Film* (London: Open University Press, 1981); Todd Gitlin, ed., *Watching Television: A Pantheon Guide to Popular Culture* (New York: Pantheon, 1986); Andrew Goodwin and Garry Whannel, eds., *Understanding Television* (New York: Routledge, 1990); E. Ann Kaplan, ed., *Regarding Television: Critical Approaches* (Frederick, MD: University

Publications of America, 1983); Colin MacCabe, ed., *High Theory/Low Culture: Analysing Popular Television and Film* (New York: St. Martin's Press, 1986); Patricia Mellencamp, ed., *Logics of Television: Essays in Cultural Criticism* (Bloomington, IN: Indiana University Press, 1990); Horace Newcomb, ed., *Television: The Critical View*, 7th ed. (New York: Oxford University Press, 2006).

John Ellis, *Visible Fictions: Cinema: Television: Video*, 2nd ed. (Boston: Routledge, 1992), is particularly valuable for its correlation of television with the cinema. In 2000, he examined how television is changing during a time of major technological changes in *Seeing Things: Television in the Age of Uncertainty* (London: Tauris, 2000).

13 Textual Analysis

Within television studies, it is common to refer to TV as consisting of a variety of texts, which can include a program itself or a commercial or a newscast or any other television segment. Textual analysis, then, includes any research method that dissects those texts. Authorship studies, stylistics, genre study, and semiotics all endeavor to explain (1) the patterns one can see within TV texts, (2) the common elements there are among texts, and (3) how texts have changed over the years. In Part III of this book, we have separated these approaches from ones that focus on viewer response and industry production. However, that distinction is not a hard and fast one and we will find ourselves occasionally straying into considerations of viewer interpretation of the text and the text's creation by TV-industry practitioners. Our first approach below, authorship studies, illustrates this point as it links thematic, narrative, and stylistic patterns in the text with the work of specific practitioners—to varying degrees of success.

Television Authorship

Who is the author of a TV program? It seems like it ought to be an easy question to answer, but it is not. There are, of course, scriptwriters, who are the literal authors of episodes in the sense of generating words that an actor eventually speaks, but in a soap opera or a sitcom there may be a dozen or more scriptwriters working on dialogue as the months go by. Is any one of them truly responsible for the overall tenor of the show, or are they just following rigid guidelines set down by other scriptwriters ahead of them? And the script is just the blueprint of an episode anyway. Actors, production designers, directors, videographers, editors, and on and on, are all necessary to construct an episode from that blueprint. Should we call one of them the author? And, at a more basic level, should we even bother looking for authors in television? Do viewers need to know who created a program in order to enjoy it? What does it add to our appreciation or understanding of television if we assign authorship of a program to an individual?

In the closely related medium of the cinema, questions such as these have been answered by the **auteur theory**, which stems from the French word for "author," *auteur*. Its basic precept is that a single individual is, and should be, the "author" of a work in order for it to be a good, artistically valuable work. A book, poem, film, or television show should express this individual's personality, his "vision" (the masculine pronoun is significant; auteurist studies almost all focus on men). This notion stems from the nineteenth-century Romantic image of the author as a figure who sits alone in a dingy room, scratching out angst-ridden poems with a quill pen. The tormented, misunderstood author or artist is a cherished character type that can be traced back to the poet Lord Byron (1788–1824) and observed in numerous portrayals of demented painters, musicians, and writers in television programs and other media. Consider this: Have you ever seen or read a story about a creative person who wasn't somehow strange or crazy?

The auteur theory originated in French film criticism of the 1950s, where it was initially theorized that auteurs could be drawn from the ranks of producers, directors, scriptwriters, actors, and other filmmaking personnel.[1] However, the vast bulk of auteurist film criticism has been about directors: Alfred Hitchcock, John Ford, and Quentin Tarantino, among many others. In television, however, the director has much less influence than in film. Indeed, most series will employ several directors over the course of a season. Recognizing the diminished power of the director, television auteurism has taken a different tack and focused instead on the "vision" of producers and so-called **showrunners** (producers who are responsible for the ongoing production of a program). Television auteurist studies have been published, for example, on producers David Lynch (*Twin Peaks*), Paul Henning (*The Beverly Hillbillies*), Matthew Weiner (*Mad Men*), and Joss Whedon (*Buffy the Vampire Slayer*).[2] And a book of "conversations with creators of American TV" is tellingly titled *The Producer's Medium*.[3] To date, there has been no similarly comprehensive anthology of interviews with directors.

Whether they are discussing directors or producers, auteurist critics work along three interconnected lines. First, they discuss how an auteur's thematics, narrative structure, and stylistic techniques—the use of sound and image—are expressed in individual programs. Second, they articulate the entire career of the auteur, explaining how this particular program fits into the overall trajectory of the auteur's work. For the extreme auteurist critic, a bad program by an auteur is more significant than a good program by an undistinguished director or producer. Why? Because the auteur's mistakes may still tell you something about their thematics, narrative structures, and stylistic techniques. A good program by a nonauteur is just a curiosity, a critical dead end. Third, auteurist studies often position the auteur as a principled David up against the mercenary Goliaths of the studios or networks. Auteurs are often cast in industry myths where they must fight for "art" within an industry that cares only about money.

For the auteurist critic, the auteur's vision or presumed personality furnishes the context within which the meaning of a particular element in a particular program will be understood. In David Marc's analysis of the producer Paul Henning, Jed Clampett (*The Beverly Hillbillies*) becomes a go-between, a "moral interlocutor." He divides and judges the contrasting worlds of city and country, the banker Drysdale and Jed's Granny, "modern culture" and "folk culture." Auteur Henning develops this thematic clash between modern culture and folk culture *over the course of several programs*.[4] The meaning of this character is thus determined by Henning's other work, his other texts. Marc relies less on Henning's publicly available statements about his television texts than on the evidence from the texts themselves. This is the form of auteurism or authorship studies that qualifies principally as textual analysis. Other auteurist forms blend textual analysis with interviews and industry-based materials in order to interact more directly with industry practitioners. We will address those approaches in more depth in the section on production studies in Chapter 14.

There are many problems with the application of auteurism to TV. The key issue is that its Romantic notion of the artist does not suit the corporate and collaborative realities of contemporary television. Bankers, market researchers, scriptwriters, actors, set designers, and others contribute to the production of any TV show. To single out the showrunner ignores the work of many. Further, as John T. Caldwell contends, any individual having total "authorial control" is undercut by numerous established industrial mechanisms—including rampant idea stealing, "writing by committee," and production "notes" from network executives and departments of "standards and practices."[5] According to Caldwell, content creation in Hollywood "runs off the systematic cultivation of idea theft, primarily based on two factors: the excessive generation and overproduction of story ideas; and the porous, loose, and largely oral ways that ideas are broached and bartered in pitch sessions [meetings at which concepts are presented to executives] and in writers' rooms."[6] Contemporary Hollywood, he contends, depends on a system in which tons of story concepts are tossed into the open in hopes of one being bought. In that sort of environment, ideas are commonly stolen—sometimes intentionally, sometimes not—which makes it difficult to ascertain who created a specific idea. If an idea is green-lit by a studio or network, authorial control remains elusive during the program's production as scripts are often pounded out in group writing sessions and network executives monitor on-set activities and force changes to be made by "giving notes" to the creative personnel.

It's not just the structure of the industry that makes authorship difficult to ascertain. Equally important, all television programs employ the conventions of the medium; there is nothing totally new on TV nor anything totally unique to television auteurs. They do not work in an aesthetic vacuum, but, rather, they draw upon conventional characters and conventional plot lines and conventional uses of mise-en-scene and videography. (See previous chapters for the details of these conventions.) Certainly, some television "artists" do make unexpected uses of these conventions and do break the conventions in limited fashion. But television is perhaps 90 percent convention and 10 percent innovation. In general, the conventions of the medium tend to overshadow any television artist's individual creativity.

It is important to remember, however, that television's corporate/collaborative nature and its conventional structure do not necessarily make it mediocre. The fact that medieval cathedrals were constructed by hundreds of artisans, collaborating over decades and even centuries, does not make them less significant or less beautiful. The fact that a sonnet or haiku follows a very rigid, conventionalized verbal pattern does not make it uninteresting. Equating personal genius or the breaking of conventions with aesthetic quality is an outmoded concept that tells us little about television. Consequently, the auteur theory is not just wrong, it is also unnecessary when it comes to understanding television. Even the best TV programs are the result of behind-the-scenes negotiations in a collaborative work environment. Or, as Caldwell puts it, "negotiated and collective authorship is an almost unavoidable and determining reality in contemporary film/television."[7]

Style and Stylistics

In the context of auteurism, style has been used to refer to that mysterious, unknowable quality that auteurs possess that distinguishes them from merely competent directors and showrunners. In overheated prose, auteurist critics might gush about the style of Joss Whedon or J. J. Abrams. We can see this *evaluative* sense of stylistic analysis in Sue Turnbull's consideration of *CSI: Crime Scene Investigation*.[8] First, she notes that one of *CSI*'s creators/producers, Jerry Bruckheimer, worked with established film/TV auteur Michael Mann when he (Mann) was producing the visually audacious *Miami Vice* (1984–90). Then she relates the story of how Bruckheimer instructed a *CSI* director, Danny Cannon, to emulate Mann's style, his "cinematic look."[9] In this instance, "the cinematic" signifies a higher visual quality than that which is normally seen on television, and it is specifically anchored in an auteur's visual style. In Turnbull's attempt to evaluate style, we can see her engage with a taken-for-granted form of television aesthetics: specifically, that the cinematic equals the beautiful. She also presumes that good television is that which is the expression of an individual auteur. In Turnbull's analysis, therefore, we can pick out evaluative, aesthetic criteria that she applies to television style. We might therefore call her approach evaluative stylistics.

Stylistics is a term taken from linguistics and literary criticism to refer to the study of style, which in this context is the patterning of television techniques. A program's overall use of mise-en-scene, videography, editing, sound design, and so on is its style. Similarly, a stylistician is someone who specializes in stylistic analysis. Television stylistics may be divided into four overlapping categories:[10]

1. descriptive stylistics
2. evaluative stylistics (aesthetics)
3. analytic stylistics (interpretation)
4. historical stylistics.

Evaluative stylistics, as we've seen with Turnbull, seeks beauty in TV style and is indebted to the long history of aesthetics; but before she can pass judgment on style she must first describe it.

Descriptive stylistics, simply enough, includes methods by which style is described. It underpins the other stylistic categories as each of them must describe style before they can expound on its significance. Television stylisticians have struggled to find rigorously systematic words for describing a visual and sound medium that *moves* and occurs over time. Part II of this book exemplifies descriptive stylistics as we have presented tools for describing mise-en-scene, videography, editing, and sound—the building blocks of style. And we have included a wealth of screen shots to assist our descriptions. For some stylisticians, however, these terms are not precise enough. Consequently, some have adopted semiotics, which we will discuss on pp. 328–36, and some have embraced statistics. One example of the statistical description of style is the work that has been done on **average shot length** (**ASL**) by researchers Barry Salt, Yuri Tsivian, and Gunars Civjans, and online services CineMetrics and Shot Logger.[11] By counting the number of shots in a television episode or feature film and noting its length, one can calculate the average length of a shot. A rather crude description of a TV program's pacing may be gathered from these data. For example, the ASL of *Honeymooners* episodes from the 1950s is about 18 seconds, but ASLs from programs in the 2000s are usually 3 to 4 seconds—a notable increase in editing speed. Not all recent programs are cut so quickly, however. A 1997 episode of *ER* that was broadcast live had an ASL of a remarkably high 80 seconds. (See Table 13.1 for some characteristic ASLs.) Statistical style analysis can provide detailed numeric data such as these, but, on its own, it cannot interpret those data.

Table 13.1 Average Shot Lengths

Program	*Date*	*Length (secs.)*	*# of Shots*	*ASL*	*Max SL*	*Standard Deviation*
I Love Lucy	10/22/1951	1331	122	10.9	44	9.8
Honeymooners, The	10/1/1955	1505	85	17.7	90	16.0
Dick van Dyke Show, The	10/24/1962	1456	232	6.3	56	6.7
CHiPs	9/22/1977	2752	727	3.7	38	4.2
Cosby Show, The	1/10/1985	1221	227	5.3	64	6.5
NewsRadio	1/14/1996	1314	244	5.3	53	4.8
ER	9/25/1997	2567	32	80.2	206	41.3
CSI: Crime Scene Investigation	11/22/2001	2418	672	3.5	28	2.7
Office, The (U.S.)	4/12/2007	1257	253	5.0	47	5.1
Walking Dead	1/23/2014	2551	525	4.9	36	3.9

Any attempts to interpret stylistic descriptions fall into the general category of analytic stylistics. To analyze style, stylisticians must first figure out what purpose style serves in a TV program, or, to put it another way, they must first study how style functions in the television text. Does costume design further the story? Does lighting add to the beauty of a scene? Do music themes help convince us to buy Pepsi instead of Coke? What function does a stylistic element serve? Once stylisticians settle on style's function, they can then dissect how it serves that function. Thus, to comprehend analytic stylistics one must first identify style's functions in television as these functions determine how stylistic analysis proceeds. In *Television Style* I discuss eight stylistic functions, several of which were derived from the cinematic functions of style articulated by David Bordwell.[12] Here I will highlight five of those functions. In television, style can:

1. symbolize
2. decorate
3. persuade
4. hail or interpellate
5. differentiate.

Style functions symbolically when it suggests certain meanings, usually related to the narrative or the characters. For example, in Karen Lury's analysis of *CSI*'s set design, she argues that the crime lab's open layout and glass walls (Figure 13.1) symbolize one of the program's themes: "This sense of both depth and transparency at a visual level neatly echoes the push towards 'transparency' and truth in the crime-solving narrative."[13] The walls are literally transparent and the crime-solving activity is figuratively transparent. Thus, the open set design "symbolizes" the openness of the detection process.

Style functions as decoration when it exists only for its own sake. It does not support the narrative or symbolize the theme. It is so removed from the forward progression of the narrative that it entices the viewer to gaze upon it and ponder its beauty. There are shots from *House* (2004–12) that function in this manner, drawing our attention to the lighting or the camera angles without pushing the story forward. In Figure 13.2, for example, an artfully composed, high-angle, handheld, extreme long shot peeks over a balcony railing to find Dr. House (Hugh Laurie) and Dr. Foreman (Omar Epps) arguing—carefully framed to include a wall mural. An eye-level medium shot could have conveyed the same narrative information. The high-angle and handheld choices function as decoration, slightly obscuring our view of the action.

Figure 13.1 The openness of the *CSI* crime lab is suggested via its mise-en-scene.

Figure 13.2 A high-angle, handheld shot from *House* is more "artistic" than necessary to convey basic narrative information.

Some authors have made grand claims for style that is untethered from narrative or theme. John Fiske proclaims, "Images are neither the bearers of ideology, nor the representations of the real, but what [Jean] Baudrillard calls 'the hyperreal': the television image, the advertisement, the pop song becomes more 'real' than 'reality,' their sensuous imperative is so strong that they *are* our experience, they are our pleasure."[14] His point is perhaps a bit hyperbolic, but it is certainly true that highly stylized, detailed images can provide pleasure that has nothing to do with the plot. Some images are just fun to look at.

Style's persuasive and hailing functions are most obvious in commercials—as we discovered in Chapter 6—but they are part of any program that seeks to convince us of something. To review quickly, we can say that stylistic techniques such as utopian style and the violation of reality with visual effects subtly guide the viewer toward a certain attitude toward a product or idea. And that musical flourishes and other stylistic elements commonly demand the viewer's attention—hailing him or her. TV style, as with every other aspect of the medium, constantly works to pull you to the television set and keep you watching.

The final function of style we will consider here is product differentiation. As television has dispersed itself across many devices—from the living room high-definition monitor to the computer screen to the smartphone—it has been forced to develop new methods to differentiate its brand from other competing ones. Style is a major element of this differentiation. The distinctive visual style of the *CSI* franchise carries across many different screens and visual media (three TV programs, graphic novels, video games, and so on), making sure that viewers know what they are watching and hoping they will remain loyal to it.

Historical stylistics attempts to disentangle the varied histories of television's technological advances, economic development, and aesthetic conventions to account for the medium's style at any one particular point in time. These factors influence each other in order to determine stylistic standards. Consider the stylistic device of the zoom shot (see Chapter 9). The zoom lens was first used in cinema productions in the 1930s, before television existed as a mass medium. But the first TV cameras did not use this technology. Instead, early TV cameras had three nonzoom lenses mounted on them. So, obviously, programs of the 1940s to 1950s could not have this stylistic element because the technology was lacking. However, once zoom lenses were adapted for television cameras in the 1960s, the zoom became a popular stylistic device in soap operas, talk shows, and sports programs, in large part because zooms allowed for quicker shooting (less time was necessary to change lenses and set-ups) and thus cheaper productions. Hence, this stylistic choice was motivated by economic concerns. But not all stylistic choices are prompted by technological or economic limitations. Soap-opera scenes often end with a slow zoom-in on a character's face. These zooms are an aesthetic convention; they're part of the genre's conventionalized narrative form—unaffected by technology or economics. In this example, therefore, we can see the impact that technology, economics, and aesthetic conventions have on a stylistic element during certain periods of television history.

We discussed previously how "style" is, in auteurist circles, associated with the individual television auteur. Historical stylisticians are certainly interested in the way that specific showrunners, producers, scriptwriters, directors, and cinematographers, among others, have influenced television style. But many historians of style are less concerned with the work of specific individuals than they are with the standardized **craft practices** that dominate a particular time period or genre at a particular time, or, at least, that is the position of the best-known advocate of cinematic stylistics, David Bordwell. "Craft practices" refers to the various "crafts" of filmmaking—set design, cinematography, editing, sound design, and so on. During any particular era, the craftsmen and craftswomen of Hollywood tend to follow certain "rules" of their trades. (Many of these conventions and standards are covered in Part II.) In fact, according to Bordwell, we can bundle these rules or craft practices together into stylistic **schemas**, "bare-bone, routinized devices that solve perennial problems."[15] Schemas are typically common to a genre or a mode of production at a particular time. For example, if one were to list the elements common to the 1950s soap-opera schema, it would include things such as black-and-white video, in-studio shooting on basic sets, shot-reverse shot editing of conversation scenes, a reliance on medium close-ups (and few long shots), and so on. Gather all these stylistic features together and you have a schema. Individual soap-opera practitioners followed, modified, or rejected this schema of routinized devices, as Bordwell would say, but the schema still held dominant at that time within that segment of the television industry.

Descriptive, evaluative, analytic, and historical stylistics frequently blend together in research on style in a program or programs, but dividing them as we have done here helps to understand how stylisticians work. We have alluded here to how a genre can be characterized by its stylistic schema, but we have not yet explored what a genre is and what genre study involves. It is to that text-oriented method of criticism that we turn next.

Genre Study

Like the auteur theory, the term **genre** study is rooted in a French word. "Genre," meaning "type" or "kind," is probably the most common way that viewers themselves label television programs. One needn't know French or be a television scholar to call *The Big Bang Theory* (2007-) a situation comedy, *Game of Thrones* (2011-) a fantasy, and *NCIS* (2003-) a crime drama. And it is not just the viewers, obviously, who use these labels. The television industry also relies heavily upon the conventions of genres. In the formulaic world of TV production, the "rules" of a genre provide a foundation for developing new programs. Why reinvent the sitcom, for example, when you can simply inject the latest, hottest stand-up comic into its formula and thereby—the producers hope—rejuvenate it? Loglines are certainly filled with genre references. And genres are not just a factor in program development. Genre labels are commonly used by the industry to promote their latest products to the viewing public, too. They provide a convenient marketing shortcut. If we're told it's a sitcom, we will bring a set of expectations to it that we wouldn't bring to, say, a fantasy. The producers don't need to spend a lot of time explaining what a sitcom is since we all know already. Because genre formulas and conventions are employed by both the producers and the consumers of television, they can be said to be a common language or code shared by these two communities. And, some genre theorists maintain, this shared code and its implicit shared values make genres particularly important to the study of a society's belief systems at any one point in time. For in a popular genre we see formulas and values that an industry and a mass audience accept and with which they feel extremely comfortable. Genre-based television programs, some argue, operate as modern-day rituals that reinforce certain values and social beliefs. Just as the wedding ritual repeatedly confirms the validity of marriage, so does the sitcom "ritual" teach us over and over that husbands are bumblers who don't understand their wives.

Genre theorists begin from the assumption that television programs resemble one another and that grouping them together provides a context for understanding the meanings of a particular program (and possibly of the society for which it was designed). This would not seem controversial, but at a rudimentary level it becomes difficult to define what characterizes a specific genre. Here is the dilemma: To conceptualize what a particular genre is, researchers must watch TV programs and induce the genre's characteristic thematics, narrative structure, and/or stylistic techniques; but researchers do not know *which* programs to view until they have some idea of what the genre's characteristics are. It's a classic chicken-and-egg problem: one needs to know the genre's characteristics to pick which programs to consider, but before one can do that one needs to have looked at programs within the genre to define its characteristics, but before one can pick programs one needs to know the genre's characteristics, and around and around it goes.[16]

To escape this debilitating dilemma, genre critics have adopted two strategies, the first based in *theory* and the second in the *history* of television:[17]

1. *Theory*: define the genre's characteristics with criteria drawn from a preexisting theory or critical method; or
2. *History*: define the genre's characteristics with criteria based on what, over the years, the TV industry and most viewers have considered elements of that genre; the definition thus relies on a cultural consensus.

In practice, most genre critics combine these two strategies and create a genre's working definition *a priori*—that is, before viewing any programs—from what they presume to be a consensual definition of the genre. They may then measure programs by this standard to judge the applicability of the working definition. In other words, does this definition help us interpret the programs within this genre?

Determining historical, cultural consensus would appear to be a natural way that empirical methods (say, a survey research project) could be incorporated into the critical method. However, this is seldom, if ever, done in genre criticism. Instead, critics often depend on the slippery conception of the genre that derives from their own commonsensical understanding of it. More often than not, their definitions are based on the history of the genre to that point in time. As genre critic Jane Feuer argues, most television genres are thus historical ones and not ones wholly designed by a critic, fabricated only from preceding theories.[18]

If we survey both historical and theoretical definitions of genre, we'll find they fall into three categories:

1. definition by presumed audience response;
2. definition by stylistic schema—techniques of sound and/or image;

3. definition by subject matter—the structure and thematics of non-narrative and narrative programs.

These categories do not exist in isolation. They frequently overlap one another.

Audience Response

Several genres acquire their definitions from how the critic presumes the viewer will respond—usually without any empirical evidence as to how actual viewers responded. Comedy and horror are two such genres. Programs as different as *Saved by the Bell* (1989-93) and *Saturday Night Live* (1975-) have been labeled "comedies." What groups these programs together? The presumption that the viewer will laugh at them.

Television comedies are even more clearly marked as such than are theatrical film comedies because television often includes audience response in the text itself. The television laugh track signals to the viewer what the response to the program "should" be. TV comedies are distinctive in this regard. Theatrical film comedies never provide a laugh track, and television's noncomedy scripted programs are not normally accompanied by audience-response sound effects. Even television's horror programs, the flip side of comedies in terms of audience response, do not possess a "scream track" to cue the spectator when to respond in fear. The only other television programs that do include audience response within the text are non-narrative programs: game shows, talk shows, sports programs, and similar presentations. But as far as fictional programs go, the sitcom is the only genre that responds to itself.

Stylistic Schema

The stylistic definition of a genre is probably the least common. There are a few genres, however, that link programs based on *how* the material is presented. The techniques of sound and image that are used to construct the program—its schema—become critical to distinguishing it from other genres. Musicals tell stories through singing and dancing. For example, *Fame* (1982-87) and *Glee* (2009-15) tell high school stories through song and dance, while the short-lived *Cop Rock* (September-December 1990) uses the same technique to construct stories of police officers in action. The only thing linking these three programs generically is their musical stylistic schema. Or, to pick another example from a non-narrative genre, the type of documentary known as *cinéma vérité* often relies on the visual style of handheld camerawork.

Subject Matter

Most programs are joined into genres on the basis of their content: the narratives they tell or the non-narrative information they present and the thematic structure that underpins those stories and that information. Since the conventions of non-narrative television are detailed in Chapter 5, "Beyond and Beside Narrative Structure," we will here focus on how genre theorists have approached narrative television—recognizing that television often blends narrative and non-narrative elements in genres such as professional wrestling and the reality program.

In approaching the stories of a particular genre, the critic hypothesizes a narrative structure that is shared by the programs within the genre and the conventional characters that inhabit that narrative structure. The police show, for example, is populated by familiar figures: the police detectives, the uniformed officers, the victims, the criminals, and so on. These general types could be broken down even further. Television criminals, according to Stuart Kaminsky and Jeffrey Mahan, tend to be individual lunatics or organized crime figures.[19]

These character types are placed into action against one another in the police show narratives. Kaminsky and Mahan note that many police show narratives fit a common pattern or structure:

1. A crime is committed.
2. The police detective is assigned to the case by chance.
3. The destruction widens. The crime invades the detective's private world and he (usually a "he") becomes irrational.
4. The detective encounters the criminal but does not initially apprehend him or her.
5. The detective pursues the criminal, leading to a second confrontation.
6. "[T]he police destroy or capture the villain. The overwhelming tendency in television is not to destroy, but to capture, to contain and control the symbol of evil."[20]

Kaminsky and Mahan's narrative outline is general enough to provide for the variation within the genre, yet it provides specific information to distinguish the genre from others.

Genre analysis of narrative often relies on the concept of the narrative **function**, which was originally developed by Russian Formalists in the 1920s.[21] A function is a specific *action* or *attribute* of a character. In the Formalists' view, a story is best understood as a set of functions, as in the above list of police show actions. We can see in this list that most of these items are "actions"—things that happen to characters. However, when Kaminsky and Mahan describe the detective as irrational, they are referring to an "attribute" of the character. Formalist critics strive to establish the nature of these functions and their order, analyzing how they affect one another. The order of these functions defines the narrative structure of the genre.

Not all genre critics employ the term "function" in their narrative analyses, but narrative structure is the first, descriptive level of analysis for many genre critics. From there the process of interpretation begins. Geoffrey Hurd, for example, sees the following binary oppositions in the narratives of the British police series:

- police vs. crime;
- law vs. rule;
- professional vs. organization;
- authority vs. bureaucracy;
- intuition vs. technology;
- masses vs. intellectuals;
- comradeship vs. rank.[22]

For Hurd the critical process is one of looking for common threads in the plots of police programs. He then generalizes about how certain threads present values relating to obvious topics such as crime and policing but also broaching broader issues such as modern technology and bureaucracy. To best understand these issues, he argues, one can set up an array of oppositions through which you can categorize the characters and the actions they take. Once categorized, you can further argue about the values—positive and negative—associated with topics such as technology. Hurd thus illustrates one approach that interpretative analysis may take.

Hurd's approach does not exist in a theoretical vacuum. Like many genre critics, he relies upon analytical methods borrowed from disciplines outside television studies. Two such methods are **mythic analysis** and **ideological analysis**. Mythic analysis sees genres as contemporary myths, as stories shared by large segments of a culture, which offer the researcher evidence of that society's thought processes. The structural anthropology of Claude Lévi-Strauss—the basis of **structuralism**—is one form of mythic analysis. It stresses the importance of binary oppositions in the stories that societies tell themselves—much as Hurd does in the police show. Ideological analysis also sees genres as representative of society but differs from mythic analysis in that it defines society in terms of social forces. (As we'll discuss in detail on pp. 339-40, ideological analysis stems from Karl Marx's view of society and its classes.) Genre makes a particularly interesting case for mythic and ideological analyses because its codes, its conventions, are shared by the industry and the audience. The argument can thus be made that genres are clear examples of the belief systems pervading a culture at a particular time.

The definition categories of genres that we've outlined here—audience response, style, subject matter—often overlap one another. Their blending leads to hybrid genres or cycles within genres. The situation comedy, for example, is defined as a comedy based on the presumption of audience response (encoded directly in the laugh track), but the "situation" part of sitcoms is a matter of the genre's stories, its subject matter. The narrative dilemmas or situations in which the characters find themselves are the principal sources of humor in the genre—as opposed to comedies that generate their humor from physical pratfalls or verbal wit. Hence, its humor is predominantly situational, that is, a function of narrative. The point is that the sitcom is a genre that is defined not only by presumed audience response (laughter) but also by its content (narrative situations).

In addition to articulating genres' presumed audience response; narrative, non-narrative, and thematic structures; and sound/image style, the genre critic is also interested in tracing a genre's evolution. Indeed, genres must evolve to maintain their audiences' attention. A new program within a genre, if it is to succeed, must balance familiar genre elements with innovations that pique viewer interest. When the long-running *Law & Order* (1990–2010) premiered, for example, it was immediately evident that it fell within the parameters of the police show. It had various familiar character types—police detectives and criminals and the like—and familiar themes such as order versus chaos. But it also changed the genre by splitting the story into two parts: the work of the police and the work of the prosecutors. It succeeded—for over 20 years—largely because it blended the familiar and the unusual.

Many genres fall into an evolutionary pattern. Initially, the genre's tenets are established, often after a trial-and-error period where unpopular options are discarded. The genre thereupon enters into what might be called a **classical period**, during which thematics, narrative structure, and aural/visual style solidify into relatively firm conventions or rules—a **code** of the genre, one might say. At this point the genre becomes recognizable as a cohesive unit. After the classical period comes a time of **self-reflexivity** that is often accompanied by genre decay or even death, though not necessarily. In the self-reflexive period, the genre turns inward and uses its own conventions for subject matter. It becomes self-conscious, in a sense, and the result is often genre parodies.

These periods can be observed in the genre of the television soap opera. Initially, the soap opera made a rocky start on television. Although it had been immensely popular on radio, when it began its transition to television in the late 1940s it did not meet with immediate success. It wasn't until the 1950s that soap opera established a financially viable stylistic schema and narrative format that found a large daytime audience: unending stories of familial relationships, romance, birth, and death; live broadcasts; half-hour-long programs (originally they were 15 minutes long); and so on. Thus, the mid-1950s to mid-1960s would be the TV soap opera's classical era. Then, in the 1970s, the genre turned inward through parody. During this time, *Soap* (1977–81) and *Mary Hartman, Mary Hartman* (1975–78) made fun of the genre by exaggerating and perverting its conventions. As in any self-reflexive parody, the humor in these programs depended upon a prior knowledge of the genre. *Soap* and *Mary Hartman, Mary Hartman* could not have existed if there had not been a classical period of the soap opera. A genre's self-reflexivity often accompanies a period of decline and, indeed, the soap opera was suffering from a glut of programs and reduced viewership in the early 1970s. Rather than become moribund, however, the genre rebounded by incorporating new themes (birth control, abortion, interracial romance, etc.) and younger character types and enlivening its stylistic schema (faster editing and more elaborate sets, as exemplified by the innovative *The Young and the Restless* [1973–]). The consequence was a soap-opera revival that brought a large audience back to the genre and cleared the way for prime-time soaps such as *Dallas* (1978–91), *Dynasty* (1981–89), and *Knots Landing* (1979–93); as well as youth-oriented shows such as *Beverly Hills, 90210* (1990–2000), *Melrose Place* (1992–99), and *The O.C.* (2003–07); and recent medical dramas *ER* (1994–2009) and *Grey's Anatomy* (2005–). A variety of factors, including the rise of inexpensive talk and game shows and shifting audience viewing patterns, has brought the revival of daytime soap operas to an end in the twenty-first century. Even established programs such as *Guiding Light* (1952–2009), which was on radio and TV for 72 years, have been canceled and the genre's demise seems imminent. So, genre evolution is not necessarily limited to the pattern we have delineated, but one can often observe the pattern's cycles in television genres.

In sum, genre criticism is not without its weakness. Crucial to the study of any genre is its definition, and it is there that critics must be most wary. And yet, it seems clear that in viewing TV programs, we—critics, viewers, *and* television producers—do construct resemblances among programs, and in those resemblances is found meaning. Genre study can deepen our understanding of individual programs as it provides important contexts for the thematics, narratives, and sound/image styles we see in them. And it can provide clues to the fundamental values undergirding our society.

Semiotics

Semiotics is most briefly defined as the *science of signs*, but this does not tell us much about what semioticians actually do and what assumptions underpin their work. The basic premise of semiotics is that any object or sound that expresses a meaning to the person who sees or hears it may be thought of as a **sign**. Thus, the semiotician's "sign" includes:

- the everyday stop sign (Figure 13.3);
- the Nike "swoosh" logo (Figure 13.4);
- the word "kudzu," as written on paper and spoken aloud; and
- a photograph of a child standing on grass (Figure 13.5).

Each one of these examples expresses some meaning—whether it is the command to stop your car or the dynamic nature of a sports-shoe manufacturer or an invasive Southern vine or the existence of a particular child on particular grass. What interests semioticians, then, is figuring out *how* we come to know these meanings, or, to put it another way, *how* these meanings are signified. A stop sign (Figure 13.3), obviously, communicates its meaning through the letters printed on it, but, in the U.S., it is also identified by its characteristic shape (octagonal) and color (red). Even the dimensions, font, and size of its letters and its "reflectorization" (how it reflects headlights) are specified by the Federal Highway Administration (FHA)—as is illustrated in Figure 13.3, taken from an FHA manual and indicating the relative size of each component.[23] A semiotician analyzing

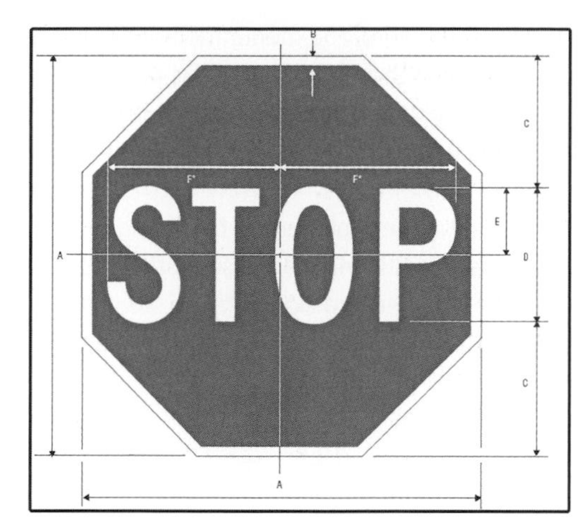

Figure 13.3 A stop sign, with dimensions marked on it that indicate Federal Highway Administration requirements.

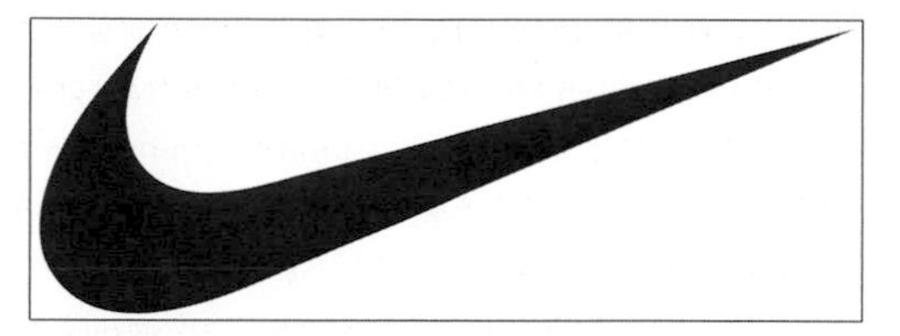

Figure 13.4 The Nike company's trademarked "swoosh."

Figure 13.5 A boy stands on the grass in a suburban backyard.

the stop sign would seek to break apart its signifying components (letters, shape, color, etc.) and understand how they fit together to get a certain meaning across to drivers. Thus, when we say that semiotics is the science of signs, we really mean that semiotics is the study of meaning and how it is signified through signs. In short, semiotics is the study of the *signification process*.

"Pure" semiotics tends to be text-oriented. That is, it does not deal with the intentions of the producer of that text or with its reception by the reader/viewer but rather focuses on the text "itself." In our case, that would mean television programs and commercials "themselves." Some film theorists have attempted to blend semiotics with Freudian psychology (i.e., psychoanalysis), theorizing the *relationship* between the reader/viewer and the text. The resulting analyses have been controversial. Psychoanalysis greatly influenced literary criticism and film studies in the 1970s but has yet to wield much influence over television studies. However, other approaches to studying actual viewers and their interpretations of texts have had considerable influence on television semiotics—as we will discuss on pp. 343–44 in our section on ethnographic research.

There has been a great deal of discussion (and argument) about the sign's basic characteristics, which is not surprising considering the sign is the fundamental concept upon which all semiotic study is based. Our short overview cannot hope to canvas all of the definitions of the sign in all their complexity, so we will consider just one to provide the reader with a sample of the semiotic method. However, it is important to recognize that not all semioticians subscribe to the following definition of the sign.

C. S. Peirce (pronounced "purse") was among the founders of semiotics around the turn of the twentieth century. He theorized that the sign consisted of two components: the **signifier** and the **signified**. The signifier is the physical aspect of the sign: a metal sign on a post or a blinking light (traffic signals), patterns of light and dark on a printed page or appearing on a screen (photographs, television, and film), ink on a page (written language), the modulation of air waves in sound (spoken language and music), and so on. The signified, then, is that which is represented by the signifier. The signified may be a concept, an object, a physical setting, or some other phenomenon. Our child image (Figure 13.5), as it appears on a page in this book, is thus a signifier; its immediate signified is the physical presence of that child on that grass. As always in the process of signification, the signified is not physically present and must be represented by the signifier to the reader/viewer through the process of signification. What most intrigues the semiotician is how that process works. How do humans manage to connect a signifier to a signified?

Peirce categorizes signs into three main types, depending upon the relationship of the signifier to the signified:

1. the indexical sign, or index;
2. the iconic sign, or icon;
3. the symbolic sign, or symbol.

In an **indexical sign** the signifier is physically caused by the signified. A footprint in the sand, for example, communicates the meaning "presence of a human." The footprint is the signifier and it is physically caused by its signified, the human foot.

In an **iconic** sign the signifier resembles the signified.[24] Photographs and most images on television are icons, in this sense of the term, because the light and shadow emanating from the television screen (signifier) resembles the visual field (signified; objects in a certain space) that was recorded by a camera. A filmed image of Bernie Mac sitting in an easy chair resembles the visual field of the real Mac in the real chair. That image is thus an iconic signifier of Mac's (and the chair's) appearance (Figure 13.6).

Finally, in a **symbolic sign** the signifier and the signified are linked solely through cultural convention, by the shared knowledge of a specific society. A corporate signifier such as the Nike swoosh logo is linked to the signified of the Nike corporation and its products by decades of cultural convention and high-powered marketing. If you don't belong to a society that shares the knowledge of Nike's meaning, then the swoosh is little more than a blob of ink on a page (or an expensive shoe). A symbolic sign such as this bears no meaning if you are outside its culture, if you have no socially produced context for it. Its meaning is solely cultural, a byproduct of ideology.

Figure 13.6 The Bernie Mac Show: Bernie addresses "America" from his easy chair.

But it's not just abstract corporate logos that qualify as symbolic signs. Most importantly, *all* written and spoken languages are composed entirely of symbolic signs. Cultural convention is all that ties ink on a page, formed into the letters *k-u-d-z-u*, to the concept of kudzu. There is no resemblance between these letters and their signified, a fast-growing vine that covers much of the U.S. South. If there were a resemblance, it would be an iconic sign. And kudzu's signified (the vine) doesn't physically cause the signifier, *k-u-d-z-u* (the word on a page). If it did it would be an indexical sign. Thus, the noun "kudzu" and all nouns are symbolic signs. If you don't belong to a culture that knows kudzu, then these letters on the page, *k-u-d-z-u*, mean nothing to you—which may well be the case if you didn't grow up in the South. It is the culturally based rules of English spelling and grammar that enable meaning to arise from black marks on paper.

Television consists of a variety of signs. Consider a simple shot from a 1958 Chevrolet commercial that begins with a close-up of a license plate and tracks back to show the girl in the car, who then looks off to the right (Figures 13.7 and 13.8; the entire commercial may be found at tvcrit.com/find/chevroletvideo).[25] That shot and, for that matter, the reproductions from it on this page qualify as iconic signs. Why? Because the two-dimensional, black-and-white pattern on the page visually resembles a three-dimensional girl in a station wagon. The original video image of her is also an indexical sign because, back in 1959, light bounced off her and struck a piece of motion-picture film in a camera, starting a chemical process that resulted in an image on celluloid. In this respect, then, the signified (a girl) caused the signifier (film image of the girl), as is the case in an index. So you can see that television is both iconic and indexical.

Can we also find symbolic signs in our Chevrolet commercial? Yes, the license plate—with its letters, numbers, and words—uses symbolic signs. And the Chevrolet emblem above the license plate is the same sort of corporate logo as the Nike swoosh discussed earlier. Although it sounds confusing and redundant to put it this way, we can see in this shot that a television image may *iconically* and *indexically* signify a *symbolic* signifier. All this means is that a video image (an iconic signifier) could record a symbolic sign—e.g., the Chevrolet logo—and represent it to the viewer. In this simple example we can see that all three of Peirce's types of signs are present in television.

Signs are always the starting point for semioticians' analyses as they are the building blocks from which meaning is assembled, but signs do not exist in isolation. They can only be understood in terms of how they interact with other signs. This brings us to the notions of **text** and **system**. In semiotics, a text is any combination of several signs into a discrete, finite entity. In television, the most limited sense of the term would apply to a single shot. The one shot from

Figure 13.7 The opening shot of a 1959 Chevrolet car commercial tracks back from a close-up of a license plate...

Figure 13.8 ... to reveal a girl looking out the rear window.

the Chevrolet commercial discussed above could be regarded as a text. It contains several signs within it (letters, a corporate logo, the image of a girl, etc.), and they have been combined to communicate meaning: "This is a girl in a Chevrolet station wagon. It is 1959. She is smiling and enjoying being in this company's product." This short visual text has already begun the process of signification contained in the 44-shot, 60-second car commercial. Even though one could describe this shot as a text, it would more typically be regarded as a text fragment since the following shots connect to it and give it additional meaning. But this example illustrates that the determination of where a television text ends can be quite arbitrary. Is one shot a text? Or is one commercial a text? Or is a half-hour time slot a text? Or is an evening of TV viewing a text? Or is one season of a program a text? Or are ten episodes of a program that are binge-watched on Netflix a text? These are questions that semioticians often have trouble answering.

Signs and their texts are governed by systems. The stop sign, for instance, only conveys meaning when placed into a strictly regulated system of traffic signs. It gathers significance when place in the context of that system and compared/contrasted with that system's other signs: yield, right-turn, merge, etc. A stop sign on its own would not communicate the same thing that it does when compared to yield signs and the rest. The meaning of television signs is also determined by systems. The conventions of television that we articulated in previous chapters are the "rules" of the television system. They determine how meaning will be expressed in TV.

Take the conventions of editing, camera movement and angle, and framing and blocking, and apply them to the first shot in the Chevrolet commercial. The camera moves from a close-up of the license plate to a medium shot of the girl in the back, who then looks off to the right (Figures 13.7 and 13.8). According to the framing system, close-ups emphasize an object's importance. The license plate shows us the year and identifies the brand of car that is going to be pitched to us. Within the system of camera movement, a backwards tracking shot is conventionally used to reveal additional information about a scene's space. In this case, it serves as exposition, revealing the body of the car and the girl, which we could not see previously. The fact that the girl is joking around establishes the mood of the commercial and encourages us to associate her mood with the pleasure of owning a Chevrolet. Finally, her look to the right fits into the system of point-of-view editing as it serves to signal what we will see next—the family toward whom she is looking. This short shot uses the conventions of television style to begin a narrative. The semiotician tries to understand the conventionalized systems controlling a text and postulates how those systems determine the meanings of its signs.

Semioticians stress that meaning, also known as signification, is achieved largely through the combination and contrast of signs. A word doesn't mean much, if anything, until it is placed in the context of a sentence. A single shot of a girl in a station wagon has little significance until it is combined with other shots (signs) into a sequence of images. This is especially true on a symbolic level. Recall Hurd's thematic oppositions within the police genre. Without criminals and evil, police and good would have no meaning. It is from opposition that meaning arises.

In semiotics there are two principal ways that signs are combined: the syntagmatic and the paradigmatic. (Beware of confusing the semiotician's "paradigmatic" with the more conventional sense of the term, "paradigm," which is a model or pattern.)

The **syntagmatic structure** is the way that signs are organized linearly or temporally (over time). Words in a sentence written on a piece of paper follow one another linearly, and their order shapes their meaning. Take the primitive sentence:

Dog bites boy.

If the linear order of the words is rearranged, the meaning is changed:

> Boy bites dog.

Or even:

> Boy dog bites.

Each of the three versions of this sentence expresses a different meaning even though the same words are used each time. The same holds true for the temporal order of shots on television, as can be illustrated by manipulating the order of the 44 shots in the Chevrolet commercial (see tvcrit.com/find/chevroletframes for frame grabs from each shot). The original commercial contains this sequence of shots (Figures 13.9–13.11):

1. The car salesman extols the virtues of the '59 Chevy's windows.
2. The father looks off-frame, to the left, with an amused expression while the mother looks skeptically at the father.
3. The boy rubs his nose.

Figure 13.9 The order of shots in a sequence greatly affects their meaning. In this commercial a shot of a salesman praising the car cuts to...

Figure 13.10 . . . a couple considering a car purchase, with the husband looking off to the left at the car and the wife looking at the husband...

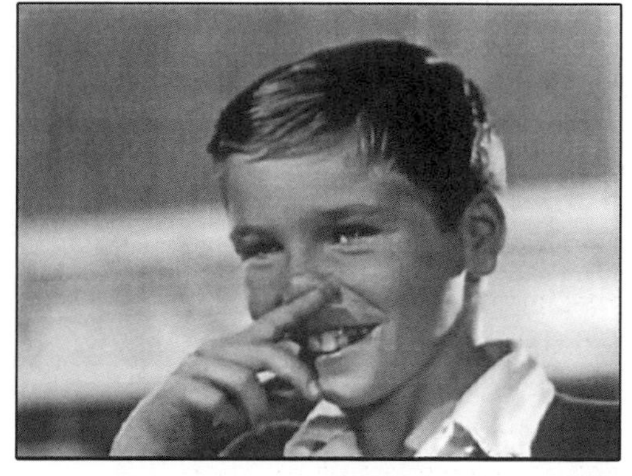

Figure 13.11 . . . followed by their son rubbing his nose impishly.

This sequence of shots suggests that the father is impressed by the car while the mother remains skeptical and the boy clowns around. These shots could be rearranged (Figures 13.12–13.14) so that the order is:

1. The car salesman extols the virtues of the '59 Chevy's windows.
2. The boy rubs his nose.
3. The father looks off-frame, to the left, with an amused expression while the mother looks skeptically at the father.

In this order, individual shots acquire new meanings. In shot 2, the boy's nose-rubbing appears to be in response to the sales pitch—suggesting he's making fun of it. And the father and mother appear to be reacting to the son's nose-rubbing instead of the car—the father approving and the mother disapproving. In television, the order of images can have powerful effects. This is particularly true in point-of-view sequences, where the order of the images determines what individuals seem to be looking at. The Chevrolet commercial strongly illustrates the power of shot order because its producers chose to emphasize the visuals and eliminate any dialogue between the characters. The entire small narrative is expressed through the order of the shots. To illustrate

Figure 13.12 Rearranging the order of the shots alters their meaning. If we start with the same shot of the salesman, but follow it with...

Figure 13.13 . . . the nose-rubbing boy and then...

Figure 13.14 ... the couple, it suggests that the father is looking at the boy instead of the car.

this, we have taken the commercial and rearranged the shots in six different ways—resulting in six different narratives—and posted the rearranged versions online at tvcrit.com/find/editingex.

In semiotics, the smallest chunk of story, the smallest narrative unit, is called a **syntagm**. (Usually this corresponds to a *scene* in television and film.) Just as the arrangement of individual shots can change a scene's meaning, so can the arrangement of individual syntagms/scenes change the meaning of the entire program. To take an extreme example, if the death of Malcolm Crowe (Bruce Willis) in *The Sixth Sense* (1999) were revealed at the start of the film, the entire narrative would be different. Or, less extreme, consider the narrative order of the *Friends'* episode "The One With Chandler's Work Laugh," analyzed in Chapter 3. The episode ends with Janice dumping Ross. If that scene were moved to the beginning of the episode and scenes of him dating her followed, as in a flashback, then he would seem doomed from the start to fail. It would make him a more pathetic figure.

The second way that signs are organized, according to semiotics, is via association, or paradigmatically. If the syntagmatic is linear or horizontal and existing over time, then the **paradigmatic structure** is vertical and has no specific time frame. The paradigmatic consists of the associations we make with a particular signifier that give meaning to that signifier. Let's return to our sentence from above and alter it slightly:

Pit bull bites boy.

The signifier "pit bull" holds certain meanings (aggression, violence) for readers because of the contrasting associations they make with potential substitutions for that breed of dog:

Chihuahua...
Terrier...
Collie...
Pit bull bites boy.

Pit bull carries its meaning partially because of the paradigm of "dog breeds" from which *pit bull* is chosen. Obviously, it has much different connotations from, say, *Chihuahua*.

There are many paradigms operating in television. All the elements of mise-en-scene, for instance, derive meaning paradigmatically. Consider the use of sets and props. When a man pulls out an Uzi and begins raking pedestrians with it, the viewer understands that this is an evil character even before he begins to shoot because of the paradigm of weapons. Because the character uses an Uzi, rather than a Magnum .45 or a Winchester rifle, or even a bow and arrow, the meaning "evil criminal" is signified. Where does this meaning come from? It comes from the gun's paradigmatic association with other weapons that could have been chosen.

It might appear that meanings generated from the syntagmatic and paradigmatic combinations of signs are limitless, open to infinite variation. This is where the semiotic concept of **codes** becomes significant. Codes consists of "rules," culturally based conventions, that govern signs and texts. These codes may be very precise, such as the grammatical rules that govern language. But more often the codes are ambiguous and changeable, delimited by history and cultural context. Fashion, for instance, has its own mercurial code. A black tuxedo signifies solemnity and is associated with major life events and upper-class characteristics. A lime-green, 100 percent polyester tuxedo with large lapels signifies 1970s garishness and perhaps a bit of sleaziness.

In television we can find both codes that are part of the general culture that television inhabits and those that are specific to the medium. The code of fashion exists in reality and also regulates the meaning signified by the clothing worn by actors on television. But the code of television and film editing, discussed in Chapter 10, is specific to these two media alone.

In sum, semiotics offers ways of talking about meaning production in television and aspires to a "science" of signs. It is not, however, a true science. Semiotic research seldom, if ever, employs the scientific method. The crucial component that semiotics lacks is the ability to repeat research projects and gather the same results each time. Without repeatability, conventional sciences will always view semiotics as an "impure," subjective science. What most prevents semiotics from confirming its interpretation through repeatable studies is an undeveloped theory of how viewers/readers understand the signs before them. Psychoanalysis and ethnography have offered some answers to this problem, but they are far from globally accepted.

Summary

The critical, television-studies methods surveyed in this chapter have historically focused their attention on the television text—its meanings and the construction of those meanings through specific narrative devices and sound/image techniques. These methods provide lenses through which to view television's polysemy and its signification process:

authorship studies → the producer/showrunner's career
stylistics → stylistic schema
genre study → films linked by similar audience response, style, or content

Semiotics attempts to account for *all* signification and representation processes and thus could be said to underpin every method above.

In each of these approaches to the text, we have seen presumptions about how the text is produced and how it's consumed. In Chapter 14, we'll consider approaches that examine these presumptions in more depth.

Notes

1 The term is based in the phrase *"la politique des auteurs"* ("the policy or polemic of the author") that first appeared in a 1955 *Cahiers du Cinéma* review of the film *Ali Baba and the Forty Thieves*, by François Truffaut. It was translated into "auteur theory" by American film critic Andrew Sarris in the early 1960s.
2 For example, Candace Havens, *Joss Whedon: The Genius Behind Buffy* (Dallas: BenBella, 2003), and Amy Pascale, *Joss Whedon: The Biography* (Chicago: Chicago Review Press, 2014; Kenneth C. Kaleta, *David Lynch* (New York: Twayne, 1995); David Marc, "The Situation Comedy of Paul Henning: Modernity and the American Folk Myth in *The Beverly Hillbillies*," in *Demographic Vistas: Television in American Culture*, rev. ed. (Philadelphia: University of Pennsylvania Press, 1996), 39-64. Also, Brett Martin, *Difficult Men: Behind the Scenes of a Creative Revolution* (New York: Penguin, 2013) centers on four TV auteurs: David Chase, David Simon, Matthew Weiner, and Vince Gilligan.
3 Horace Newcomb and Robert S. Alley, eds., *The Producer's Medium: Conversations With Creators of American TV* (New York: Oxford University Press, 1983).
4 Marc, 46, 62.
5 John Thornton Caldwell, *Production Culture: Industrial Reflexivity and Critical Practice in Film and Television* (Durham, NC: Duke University Press), 201.
6 Ibid., 210.
7 Ibid., 199.
8 Sue Turnbull, "The Hook and the Look: *CSI* and the Aesthetics of the Television Crime Series," in *Reading CSI: Crime TV Under the Microscope*, Michael Allen, ed. (New York: I. B. Tauris, 2007), 15-32.
9 Ibid., 27.
10 For more details, see Jeremy G. Butler, "Introduction," in *Television Style* (New York: Routledge, 2010), 1-25.

11 Barry Salt, "Practical Film Theory and Its Application to TV Series Dramas," *Journal of Media Practice* 2, no. 2 (2001), 98–114; "CineMetrics Database," *CineMetrics*, tvcrit.com/find/cinemetrics, accessed July 7, 2017; Jeremy Butler, "Shot Logger," tvcrit.com/find/shotlogger, accessed July 7, 2017.
12 Butler, *Television Style*, 11; David Bordwell, *Figures Traced in Light: On Cinematic Staging* (Berkeley: University of California Press, 2005), 33–34.
13 Karen Lury, *Interpreting Television* (London: Hodder Arnold, 2005), 47.
14 Fiske, *Television Culture*, 2nd ed. (London: Routledge, 2011, originally published in 1987), 262.
15 David Bordwell, *On the History of Film Style* (Cambridge, MA: Harvard University Press, 1997), 152.
16 Andrew Tudor terms this the "empiricist dilemma" because it is an observational question, a question of which programs to observe. And thus it's an empirical issue. See Andrew Tudor, *Theories of Film* (New York: Viking, 1973), 135–38.
17 Jane Feuer draws upon Tzvetan Todorov's distinction between historical and theoretical literary genres in her discussion of genre in television. Jane Feuer, "Genre Study," in *Channels of Discourse, Reassembled*, Robert C. Allen, ed. (Chapel Hill: University of North Carolina Press, 1992), 140.
18 Ibid.
19 Stuart M. Kaminsky and Jeffrey H. Mahan, *American Television Genres* (Chicago: Nelson-Hall, 1985), 56.
20 Ibid., 61–62.
21 Vladimir Propp, *Morphology of the Folktale*, translated by Laurence Scott, with an introduction by Svatava Pirkova-Jakobson (Austin: University of Texas Press, 1968).
22 Geoffrey Hurd, "The Television Presentation of the Police," in *Popular Television and Film*, Tony Bennett, Susan Boyd-Bowman, Colin Mercer, and Janet Woollacott, eds. (London: British Film Institute, 1981), 66.
23 *The Manual on Uniform Traffic Control Devices* (MUTCD) determines what these signs will look like. See U.S. Department of Transportation, May 2012, tvcrit.com/find/mutcd, accessed July 7, 2017.
24 Iconic signs are the most confusing and the most controversial within the study of semiotics. Some of the confusion stems from the use of the term "icon" or "ikon" in art history and religion to refer to an object with symbolic significance. The semiotic controversy revolves around the very question of iconicity. Many semioticians reject the notion of resemblance between signifier and real-world objects, contending that all signification is *constructed* by human interpretation and that "resemblance" implies an impossible, "natural," or necessary correspondence between signifier and signified. Ferdinand de Saussure, another one of semiotics' founders, is among those who reject the entire principle of iconicity.
25 "Brand New Door." General Motors Corporation, Chevrolet Division, Advertiser. Campbell-Ewald Co. Inc. (Detroit), Agency. Gerald Schnitzer, Inc. (L.A.), Producer. 1958.

Further Readings

There are a several books organized around specific critical methods within television studies.

Horace Newcomb and Robert S. Alley explore claims to television authorship in *The Producer's Medium: Conversations With Creators of American TV* (New York: Oxford University Press, 1983); as do Robert J. Thompson and Gary Burns in *Making Television: Authorship and the Production Process* (New York: Praeger, 1990); David Wild in *the Showrunners: A Season Inside the Billion-Dollar, Death-Defying, Madcap World of Television's Real Stars* (New York: HarperCollins, 1999); and Steven Priggé in *Created By—Inside the Minds of TV's Top Show Creators* (Los Angeles: Silman-James Press, 2005). Robert S. Alley and Irby B. Brown, *Women Television Producers: Transformation of the Male Medium* (Rochester, NY: University of Rochester Press, 2001) looks at specific challenges that women producers have faced. In contrast to these studies of producers as auteurs, the whole principle of individual authorship is brought into question at several points in John Thornton Caldwell, *Production Culture: Industrial Reflexivity and Critical Practice in Film and Television* (Durham, NC: Duke University Press).

Television stylistics is still establishing itself as a viable field of study—as is advocated in Jeremy G. Butler, *Television Style* (New York: Routledge, 2010). However, David Bordwell and others have already established the discipline in the closely related area of cinema studies. The best entry into his voluminous writings is via Bordwell and Kristin Thompson, *Film Art: An Introduction* (New York: McGraw-Hill, 2016), which is currently in its eleventh edition. More ambitious readers should seek out David Bordwell, *On the History of Film Style* (Cambridge, MA: Harvard University Press, 1997).

Glen Creeber, ed., *The Television Genre Book*, 3rd ed. (London: British Film Institute, 2015), anthologizes analyses of numerous genres, and Jason Mittell, *Genre and Television: From Cop Shows to Cartoons in American Culture* (New York: Routledge, 2004), summarizes the current state of TV genre study. Nick Lacey, *Narrative and Genre: Key Concepts in Media Studies* (New York: Palgrave Macmillan, 2000), makes an ambitious attempt to chronicle the history of all narrative theory and, specifically, of genre theory—providing examples from both film and television. Although long out of print, Horace Newcomb, *TV: The Most Popular Art* (Garden City, NY: Anchor Press, 1974), is a pioneering attempt to characterize television's genres.

One of the few book-length semiotic studies of television is Robert Hodge and David Tripp, *Children and Television: A Semiotic Approach* (Cambridge: Polity, 1986). Jonathan Bignell, *Media Semiotics: An Introduction*, 2nd ed. (Manchester: Manchester University Press, 2002), devotes three chapters to television semiotic analysis. And Arthur Asa Berger, *Making Sense of Media: Key Texts in Media and Cultural Studies* (Malden, MA: Blackwell, 2005), pulls apart 19 essays significant to semiotics and then explains their significance to contemporary media studies, including television. Sean Hall, *This Means This, This Means That: A User's Guide to Semiotics* (London: Laurence King Publishing, 2007), takes a very visual approach to semiotics, although it is not specifically focused on television. Robert Stam, Robert Burgoyne, and Sandy Flitterman-Lewis, *New Vocabularies in Film Semiotics: Structuralism, Post-Structuralism and Beyond* (London: Routledge, 1992), explain the central terms and concepts in semiotics—applying them to the cinema but in ways that are still pertinent to television studies.

14 Discourse and Identity

The television-studies methods and theories surveyed in this chapter go "beyond" the text in one way or another. Some investigate television's production and its implicit power structures, while others are more concerned with its consumption and the socially defined identities its consumers assume. Ideological criticism, cultural studies, fan studies, production studies, political economy, feminism, queer theory, race and ethnic studies all attempt to connect television research with broader social concerns such as homophobia, the exploitation of women, or the functioning of economic systems. They are not as text-centric, shall we say, as the methods and theories of the previous chapter, but they all still account for the television text and seek to illuminate its meanings.

Ideological Criticism and Cultural Studies

Ideology is an elusive term. In everyday use it has negative connotations. When politicians speak of "liberal ideology" or "conservative ideology" they usually imply brainwashing, suggesting that their opponents' political ideology clouds their views of the truth. Ideology, in this context, signifies a fraudulent and misguided image of reality. This sense of ideology stems from one of the original theorists of ideological criticism, Karl Marx.[1] It is with Marxism, therefore, that we need to begin our consideration of ideological criticism.

For Marx, writing in the mid-1800s, ideology is **false consciousness**. It is a counterfeit image of the world that is determined by social class: **aristocracy** (the class of kings and queens), **bourgeoisie** (middle class), or **proletariat** (working class). These social classes are grounded in economics and a person's relation to work, to labor. Aristocrats do not work; their power (what's left of it) is based in traditional laws of inheritance and ritual. Members of the bourgeoisie own the factories where goods are created and where men and women work. Bourgeois individuals therefore hold tremendous economic power. Proletarians must work to survive and thus must sell their labor power to the bourgeois. Labor—or its avoidance—defines each class. And it also defines the power that each class controls. The factories, which Marx calls the **means of production**, are controlled by bourgeois capitalists. They determine who shall work. The principal power the working class holds, as a group, is its ability to strike, to withhold the labor necessary for that production.

Marx sees history as a struggle among these classes to control the means of production. During any one particular era, one of these three classes will dominate a society. One class, thus, will be the **ruling class**. Since the Renaissance, according to Marx, the bourgeoisie has increased its power and the aristocracy has declined. Hence, over the centuries the bourgeoisie has become the ruling class as we know it today.

Marx's explanation of class is significant to his theory of ideology because he sees ideology as being delimited by class. A woman who owns a factory will interpret the world through bourgeois ideology. Workers in that factory will interpret the world through working-class ideology. However, Marx contends, individuals do not always believe the ideology associated with their class—especially if their class holds little power within a society. The class that controls a society's means of production and commands its economy also rules ideologically: "The ideas of the ruling class are in every epoch the ruling ideas, i.e., the class which is the ruling *material* force of society [that is, which controls the factories], is at the same time its ruling *intellectual* force."[2] This gives rise to the notion of a dominant ideology, a system of beliefs about the world that benefits and supports a society's ruling class. In most modern Western societies, the ruling class is the bourgeoisie; and its ideology, according to Marxists, is the dominant ideology. And the working class is subordinate to that ideology. Marx concludes that a class that is *not* dominant (currently, the working class) will accept a dominant (bourgeois) ideology because they have been intellectually bludgeoned into those beliefs by the agents of the ruling class: schools, the legal system, churches, the military, and so forth.

For example, one tenet of bourgeois ideology is that everybody may become financially successful if they work hard enough. This obviously benefits the capitalist system because it encourages proletarians to labor tirelessly—although economic success is more commonly based on the financial status of the family into which one is born than on an individual effort. As multimillionaire Malcom Forbes put it when asked by David Letterman how he earned his incredible fortune, "My father died."

Crucial to Marx's view is that ideology is shaped by economics. The class that controls a society's monetary system also controls its beliefs and values. Or, to put it in his terms, a society's economic **base** or **infrastructure** supports and *conditions* its ideology or **superstructure**. And, since the bourgeoisie wields power over the capitalist system, it also determines society's beliefs and values. The conventional base-superstructure model typically positions television within the superstructure, as an agent of the ruling class. The thinking is that, because huge multinational corporations own the television networks, all TV programs must toe the ideological line. In other words, television shows—both fiction and news—must necessarily support dominant ideology. Moreover, all viewers, whatever their class, are so inculcated with ruling-class ideology that they accept this capitalist version of reality as truth. If the ruling-class ideology becomes so pervasive that even people outside of the ruling class absorb its values as truth, then, contends Marxist theorist Antonio Gramsci, a state of **hegemony** has been achieved.[3] In a hegemony, people take ruling-class values for granted—even when they don't serve their own interests.

One need not be a Marxist or a socialist to hold this view of television's ideological function. Indeed, political and moral conservatives also see TV as an ideological demon, but from a different perspective. To them the values represented on television are decadent and immoral, ideologically offensive because they are too liberal. Conservative politicians such as Donald Trump rail against the "fake news" of the mainstream media that, they contend, has a liberal bias. And yet, such conservatives share the classical Marxist assumptions that

1. ideological apparatuses (such as television) contain a homogeneity of ideas; there are no contradictions within ideology;
2. the person exposed to the dominant ideology will necessarily accept it as truth.

The classical Marxist conception of ideology has been the topic of much debate over the past hundred years. During that time, a more subtle theory of ideology has evolved. As far as television studies is concerned, there are two central components of the current notion of ideology.

First, a society's ideology consists of many conflicting sets of meanings–**discourses**–struggling with one another. As John Fiske elaborates, a discourse is "a language or system of representation that has developed socially in order to make and circulate a coherent set of meanings about an important topic area."[4] Let's take a second to unpack the significant points he makes here:

- *A language or system of representation*: This phrase borrows from semiotics the idea that signs signify or represent meanings when they are organized into a system of other signs. Television relies on many systems of representation–from mise-en-scene and editing to narrative and non-narrative structure. So when Fiske talks about discourse and language he is not limiting himself to words and grammar and spoken language. Rather, he includes any meaning-generating system: spoken language, yes, but also television, websites, the cinema, newspapers, photography, and so on.
- *Developed socially*: Discourse is always grounded in the society that produced it. It fulfills a social purpose. A discourse can be blunt propaganda that serves one political party, such as the Nazi's condemnation of Jews, or it can be more subtle beliefs, such as the American notion that "hard work is rewarded" that benefits the bourgeois class (and not the working class). In each case, a specific social group profits from that discourse.
- *To make and circulate*: A discourse would mean nothing if it were not widely distributed within a society. It requires a mechanism for circulation, and that's where mass media come in. Television, the Internet, and other media circulate innumerable discourses–often conflicting with one another.
- *A coherent set of meanings*: Fiske's final, and perhaps most important, point is that a discourse is a set, a collection, of meanings. As in semiotics, meanings do not exist in isolation. They are clustered into sets that relate to one another. How does this work in practical terms? Let's take the discourse about the family that is produced socially by religious conservatives in the United States. There are several meanings that may be articulated in this discourse:
    - Men should work outside the house, earning money to support the family.
    - Women should work at home, taking care of children and the house.
    - Abortion is wrong.
    - Gay marriage is wrong.

These meanings cohere together into a discourse. That is, they support one another. One belief fits together with all the other beliefs into a set of meanings. For example, the belief that men should be the breadwinners connects to the belief that women should maintain the home. The two beliefs function together within this discourse. Thus, they have a discursive function.

We might add to Fiske's statement on discourse that he also endorses the concept of hegemony. In his terms, the dominant discourse is the one that is taken for granted, is seen as the commonsense explanation of the world within a particular society or within a social group inside a society. When persons of all social classes accept the dominant discourse as their own, a state of total hegemony has been achieved.

The second way in which theories of ideology have recently evolved is in the reexamination of an individual's position within ideology. Or, in other words, contemporary ideological theorists have dissected how individuals accept, reject, or negotiate ideology. This, for some, has involved the introduction of psychoanalytic theory into the discussion of ideology. In psychoanalytical Marxism, the individual in society is viewed as a **subject**, a psychological construct, who enters the meaning-filled world of ideology through certain Freudian mechanisms (specifically, the Oedipal complex). Other theorists eliminate Freud (and his major revisionist, Jacques Lacan) from their theory of the ideological subject, but they are still concerned with individuals' entries into the ideological world and their relationship to ideology. Regardless, contemporary ideological criticism contests the assumption that individuals are molded solely by the circumstances of their class and the influence of ruling-class ideology.

What impact does this recent work on discourse and the subject have on the study of television?

Under the banner of **cultural studies** or **reception studies,** a group of theorists has been attempting to analyze television in the context of contemporary ideological criticism. Stuart Hall, former director of the University of Birmingham (England) Centre for Contemporary Cultural Studies (CCCS), initially led this effort, and his work has been elaborated upon by Fiske, David Morley, Charlotte Brunsdon, and other scholars in England, the United States, Australia, and elsewhere.

Hall argues that television texts are **encoded** with many meanings—many discourses—by the **television apparatus**.[5]

Television as "apparatus" deserves further elaboration. It is useful to keep in mind that Hall was writing in the late 1970s and early 1980s, when television was exclusively a mass medium of three major broadcast networks that had not yet had their dominance challenged by VCRs and cable networks. Additionally, Internet delivery of video was still decades away. The network-era television apparatus consisted of bankers, media corporations, network executives, producers, directors, scriptwriters, and so on. They created TV according to unspoken "rules" of genre, narrative, technique, and so on, as well as economic limitations imposed by television's mode of production and political economy (see pp. 349–52). The network-era apparatus included all those factors—from flesh-and-blood bankers to ephemeral rules of editing—that constructed the medium as a pleasurable viewing experience, as something viewers enjoy doing. Today's media environment includes video distributed via YouTube that is produced by individuals who are not governed by profit margins and/or network executives, but the notion of an apparatus has not lost its usefulness. As a wide-ranging term to refer to the television experience and everything that goes into constructing it, it can encompass large-budget programs generated by major corporations and small-budget projects brought to YouTube or Vimeo by independent filmmakers.

Hall rejects the wholesale condemnation of the network-era television apparatus by certain Marxists who criticize TV as an ideological and hegemonic monolith, obeying ruling-class ideology. Hall contends instead that television texts are encoded with many meanings, a **polysemy**. Television's meanings may even contradict one another, as is the case when a program about a promiscuous playboy is interrupted by a public service announcement urging sexual restraint.

Television's polysemy, however, is not completely free-ranging, according to Hall. He writes, "Any society/culture tends, with varying degrees of closure, to impose its classifications of the social and cultural and political world. These constitute a *dominant cultural order*, though it is neither univocal nor uncontested."[6] Television—especially the programming generated by major networks—does not show us *everything*. It cannot signify *everything*. For years the life experiences of minorities were virtually invisible within network television. And gay characters and culture were also marginalized; their threat to the nuclear family was too great. Many subcultures were simply unspoken, unable to be classified, repressed from the television world by the dominant cultural order. With the rise of the Internet, those subcultures have been able to find a platform on which to communicate their own meanings, but they can remain marginalized nonetheless. Very few YouTube "stars" have been able to find success on major TV networks or streaming services, which still filter out messages from subcultures that might disrupt the dominant cultural order.

Despite these limitations, mass-media television does contain a surprisingly broad spectrum of discourses. And a large part of television's pleasure can be attributed to its polysemic nature. With so many meanings being transmitted, viewers can largely pick and choose those that adhere to their own ideology. As Hall suggests, TV does not univocally speak the dominant cultural order. This brings up another tenet of Hall's theory: **decoding**. Viewers decode television texts from three different ideological positions.[7]

1. *The dominant-hegemonic position*: Viewers who fully subscribe to ruling-class discourse interpret television from this perspective. Such viewers presumably include members of the class wielding economic control but also comprise working-class viewers who, in hegemonic fashion, value the dominant system. Hall and others often presume that the **preferred reading** encoded on the text by the television apparatus will be from this position.
2. *The oppositional position*: Viewers whose discourse is totally foreign to ruling-class discourse fully reject the dominant-hegemonic reading of the text, lending it their own interpretation. Individuals who are aggressively disenfranchised from the benefits of the ruling economic system decode television texts in unique ways. This includes immigrants who do not speak English, the poor, and so on.
3. *The negotiated position*: By far this is the most common decoding position. Most viewers are neither wholehearted supporters of dominant discourse nor wholly detached from it. The negotiated interpretation permits the dominant discourse to set the ideological ground rules, but it modifies those rules according to personal experience. Viewers select the meanings that apply to their personal situations.

Initially, Hall and other **ethnographic** researchers approached television from three directions. First, they sought to understand the ideological discourses in the text and the preferred readings that the television apparatus elects. They hoped to articulate television's polysemy and its limits. Second, crucially, they were also concerned with the ideological discourses *of the viewer*, of the *consumer* of television. They were fascinated with the text-as-decoded by actual human audiences. This marked a major departure from text-oriented methods such as those surveyed in Chapter 13 that would seldom, if ever, talk to actual viewers about their television consumption. More recently, a third ethnographic approach has evolved in which researchers explore television's production, analyzing the discourses of TV-industry workers, of television *producers* (in the broadest sense of the word) or practitioners. It is known as production studies (and discussed further on pp. 346–49), and its researchers analyze the production of the text. The basic premise of all these ethnographers, as Richard Johnson succinctly puts it, is that "[t]he text-as-produced is a different object from the text-as-read."[8] The TV program may have been produced, designed, to encourage a certain understanding by the television apparatus, but the viewers' discourses shape their decoding of the program so that the text-as-read never wholly aligns with the text-as-produced.

The process of ideological criticism for ethnographic researchers is to comprehend the following:

- How are these discourses produced?
- Which discourses are privileged over others in mass-media TV?

- Which social and economic interests are served by these discourses?
- How do the discourses of the text relate to the discourses of television's producers and consumers, workers and viewers?

Frequently, ethnographers employ a research method known as **participant observation** where they both participate with and observe TV workers/watchers as a significant part of their research. Such methods draw ethnographers closer to traditional social-science research, but ethnography still remains distinct from such empirical, positivist approaches. Where empiricism assumes that the answers to research questions lie in the acquisition of quantifiable numerical data, ethnographers see research as a more mercurial and less quantifiable *interaction* between the discourses of the text, the discourses of the producer/consumer, and even the discourses of researchers themselves. Knowledge about society is not pictured as being "out there," waiting to be dug up and reduced to a few "thin" equations, but in flux, in a process of signification—a system of counter-balancing or competing discourses that is best represented through **thick descriptions** of viewers' experiences and their viewing contexts.[9] As Mark Allen Peterson comments, "ethnographers seek to capture a sense of life as it actually happens, not just as people recount it in interviews, surveys, focus groups, or other quasi-experimental situations."[10]

Before leaving our consideration of reception studies, it is worth briefly exploring a subset that has come to prominence during the digital age: **fan studies**. This area within reception studies addresses viewers' **transformative** use of television texts.[11] In this context, a "fan" is not just a viewer who enjoys a particular program, but it is also a viewer who grabs something from television and puts it to his or her own use, transforms it into something else, and shares it with other fans. In Henry Jenkins's influential, discipline-establishing phrases, the fan is a viewer who engages in **textual poaching** and thus becomes part of a **participatory culture**.[12] Borrowing the poaching concept from Michel de Certeau, Jenkins first did ethnographic research on fans of *Star Trek* (1966–69, followed by TV sequels and feature films) and *Beauty and the Beast* (1987–90), among other popular culture phenomena, and found that they had created their own grassroots communities around these programs—dressing as favorite characters and attending conventions, creating their own texts (fiction and songs) based on the programs' characters, and, in short, making alternative use of television texts. Fans participate in these communities and generate the culture associated with them in a do-it-yourself fashion that goes beyond decoding/enjoying a television program in the privacy of one's own home.

At the time of Jenkins's initial studies (1992), fan cultures remained largely invisible outside of fandom universes. Of course, since then the Internet has revolutionized how individuals share material with one another. As the Internet became increasingly interactive and participatory, and as the tools for fans transforming TV's sounds and images became more easily accessible, the potential for textual poaching grew exponentially and the visibility and, notably, the *marketability* of fan communities/cultures did as well. Now, as Karen Hellekson explains, "Fans engage in a range of activities related to their passion: they write derivative literature called *fan fiction*, they create artworks, they write what's known as *meta* (analyses of fandom itself, or analysis of analysis), they play role-playing games, they blog, they make fan vids [videos], and they organize and attend conventions."[13] The Internet hosts massive amounts of user-generated content and online networking via **social media** that is carried on by fans. Some of this activity is encouraged and facilitated by television producers, studios, and networks—as when HBO, the network on which *Game of Thrones* runs, provided fans with a Snapchat lens to turn themselves into ghoulish White Walkers, with crystalline blue eyes and snow falling around them

Figure 14.1 The author as seen through the *Game of Thrones* Snapchat lens. HBO invited fans to create White Walker versions of themselves in anticipation of the eighth season premiere.

(Figure 14.1). Other activities are not so welcome and result in lawsuits and take-down notices. For instance, YouTube removes music videos made by **vidders**, who cut together scenes from TV shows and put them to copyrighted music (see tvcrit.com/find/fanvidding).[14]

Fan studies, then, seeks to describe how these fan activities and fan-created artifacts function and to comprehend what meaning and significance they hold. It is a branch of television ethnographic research that has become particularly important as participatory culture has exploded online. Any element of television that can be digitized is potential grist for fandom's online mill. Jenkins and other **aca-fans**—academic researchers who are also media fans themselves—are keenly interested in all aspects of fan culture, but they are particularly concerned with the building of fan culture/community, with its rituals, traditions, etiquette, and rules.[15] And, perhaps above all, they are intrigued by how fans share their knowledge of a television program—contributing to Pierre Lévy's **collective intelligence**.[16] Fans pool their opinions and knowledge about a show on fan discussion forums, websites, and social media, but also on general-interest sites such as Wikipedia, the encyclopedia that anyone may edit. This collective, participatory, group-authored intelligence and the user-generated content that is built upon it are manifestations of television consumers transforming themselves into television producers. Thus, fan studies is founded upon the axiom of the active viewer, a hybrid consumer-producer, and rejects the notion of the passive viewer/consumer common to many approaches to TV.

The Discourse of the Industry I: Production Studies

In twentieth-century television studies, ethnographic methods were almost exclusively applied to audience studies and attempts to understand viewers' decoding of the text. However, as the century turned, several scholars shifted the focus of ethnography from television reception to television production.[17] This growing field of media **production studies** looks at workers and workplaces to better understand the encoding of the text by the industry. The standard bearer for production studies has been John T. Caldwell, who has advocated for this approach since the early 1990s. His advocacy culminated in the 2008 book *Production Culture*, a virtual manifesto for a new way of thinking about the television and film industries.[18] As suggested by this title, Caldwell and like-minded researchers are less interested in the behavior of corporations than they are in the culture of the workers employed by those corporations. Instead of taking a top-down approach and analyzing phenomena such as the international spread of media corporations, their ceaseless mergers, and the global structure of media economics (see our discussion of political economy on pp. 349–52), Caldwell demands a bottom-up analysis of the texts and rituals associated with production work. He looks at how media practitioners (editors, production designers, costume designers, videographers, and so on) *talk* about their work. He examines how trade magazines/journals *write* about the various production crafts. He attends trade shows to see how production work is *represented* in convention-hall booths, panel discussions, and product demonstrations. And, using the ethnographic method of participant observation, he visits studio sets and *observes* worker interaction. In short, he asks, what is the social culture of media production? And how does the industry represent itself *to itself* and to the public?

To someone unfamiliar with television studies, it may seem surprising that so little research has been done on the industry itself and that, until recently, the vast majority of TV-studies work has ignored the television business in favor of the text and its reception by viewers. After all, an enormous amount of information about the industry is generated online, in print, and on television itself—as can be seen in industry publications such as *TVNewser*, *Cynopsis*, *Media Decoder*, *Deadline Hollywood*, and venerable *Variety*, which has been covering media industries since 1905 (Figure 14.2). But when ethnographers seek to rigorously and systematically study media industries, they run into two major problems: the limited access to significant industry insiders and the shaping of insiders' information into conventional stories.

The higher up the television food chain one goes—from camera operator to actor to writer to director to producer to studio head to network executive—the less likely a researcher is to be granted an interview. And the interviews that are permitted are themselves inevitably shaped by public relations puffery, standardized narratives of how the industry works. And, naturally, an interviewee does not wish to offend a future employer. Anyone who has ever heard an actor on a talk show extolling the virtues of their latest project and the brilliance of all the people who worked on it can sense the high level of fabrication and manipulation that goes into talk about behind-the-scenes activities. Plus, a dark veil of secrecy is intentionally drawn across many industry activities. Netflix, for example, is notorious for never revealing its inner workings; the audience size of its programs is always kept secret. Even low-level TV employees are required to sign nondisclosure statements prohibiting them from speaking on the record about television productions. And financial details are always held in strict secrecy so that studios/networks can manipulate the numbers to make every production appear to be a failure—thereby limiting the royalties due their employees. Thus, television-industry practitioners are limited in what they

Figure 14.2 *Variety* has covered show-business news since 1905, when the only entertainment industries were vaudeville, circuses, the stage, and a barely existing movie business.

can say by legal obligations, concerns over jeopardizing future employment, and conventionalized social discourses that shape lived experiences into cliched narratives.

Caldwell has directly addressed these issues and limitations. First, he contends that successful production-studies research must blend four different analytical methods: interviews with media professionals, analysis of corporate economic structure, participant observation of workers in the field (i.e., workers actually producing TV and also attending trade conventions and other professional meetings), and the interpretation of work-related texts.[19] However, he is not so naive as to accept interviews at face value.[20] Instead, he advocates a specific method for analyzing industry texts and practices that provides insight into the coded language practitioners use in interviews. He elaborates:

> My response to the coded and inflected nature of overt practitioner explanations [i.e. comments made in interviews and public statements] is to consider them alongside a more systematic study of what I term the *deep industrial practices* of film/video production.... I seek to describe the contexts in which embedded industrial sense making and trade theorizing occurs, and to do so I categorize artifacts and rituals into three registers: fully embedded, semi-embedded, and publicly disclosed "*deep texts*" [emphasis added].[21]

Caldwell contends that practitioners make sense of their industry and intuitively theorize their trade's significance through deep texts and repeated rituals. Some of these texts/rituals are available for the public to experience: e.g., the making of documentaries, network-controlled online material, and so on. Some are fully embedded within the industry and intended only for media practitioners themselves: e.g., individuals' demo reels, program pitch sessions, union newsletters, and so on. Lastly, some are designed for initial release to practitioners with the hope of having later impact on the public: e.g., **electronic press kits** (**EPKs**) sent to TV reviewers with the expectation that they'll be excerpted in reviews provided to the public; and advertiser "up-fronts" where networks preview programs to advertisers with the expectation that their ads will be embedded in programs for the public to view. All of these artifacts and rituals—from a private pitch session to a publicly released DVD/Blu-ray commentary—are meaning-producing, industry-generated phenomena that the researcher may deconstruct in order to grasp fully the production culture of that industry, the sense it makes of itself.

Caldwell's *Production Culture* has provided a systematic, methodological framework for doing production studies. Previous researchers have taken similar approaches in analyses of subjects ranging from the production of the police show *Cagney and Lacey* to the representation of Latino/as to the organization of public television in the U.S. and the BBC in the UK.[22] Elana Levine's look behind-the-scenes at *General Hospital* (*GH*) illuminates how research such as this might proceed, and, like Caldwell, she advocates new methods for media production research.[23] Her field work, conducted in 1997 and published in 2001, employed three of the methods proposed by Caldwell: interviews with key *GH* production personnel, an analysis of the program's ownership structure, and participant observation at *GH*'s studio, watching episodes being created. The only one of Caldwell's methods missing from Levine's study is an analysis of more than a few work-related texts—although one presumes she had access to scripts, production schedules, costume-design sketches, and the like, even though she does not discuss them in depth.

Levine divides the impact of *GH*'s production culture into five categories: "production constraints, the production environment, production routines and practices, the production of characters and stories, and the role of the audience in production."[24] She finds the production constrained in a variety of ways, some of which are due to its ownership by the network on which it's broadcast—ABC, which, in turn, is owned by the Walt Disney Company. Since ABC produces it outright, unlike other soaps that are produced by nonnetwork entities such as Procter & Gamble, it is directly involved in the production process. And ABC's standards and practices division has specific requirements such as a prohibition on guns aimed directly at characters' heads. However, on the positive side, during *GH*'s enormous popularity in the 1980s, ABC also provided financial security to the program and allowed it to build relatively elaborate sets and provide actors with long-term contracts. In Levine's discussion of *GH*'s production environment, she notes that its hectic five-episodes-per-week production schedule demands a highly efficient production flow and a fairly rigid organizational hierarchy where individuals' jobs are clearly defined. And she details the production routines and practices—down to daily work schedules—that evolve from that environment.

Central to *GH*'s organization is the production of characters and stories. Soap opera contains a level of narrative density unmatched by any other medium. When *Guiding Light* went off the air in 2009, it had created 72 years' worth of stories (including its time on radio)! In Levine's study, she dissects how writers, actors, and production departments must all function together to generate all this narrative. Finally, Levine accounts for the impact of the audience on *GH*'s production, but her consideration of "audiencehood" in the production process goes beyond *GH*'s handling of viewer response in letters and voice-mails. She contends that the cast and crew are also part of the audience, that they share viewers' interest in the stories and how they will turn out. And since most of them are not part of the long-term planning of narrative arcs, they don't know much more about *GH*'s narrative future than the viewers do. The final audience member that Levine considers is herself, a longtime *GH* viewer, and how her affection for the show influences her analysis of the production process. In so doing, Levine follows the cultural-studies principle of accounting for the impact of the researcher's interests on the study itself. She falls within Henry Jenkins's category of the aca-fan, the academic who is also a fan of what she studies.

As we have seen in Levine's study, in particular, and Caldwell's manifesto, in general, production studies is a burgeoning part of today's television studies. Both of these authors, as with most production-studies scholars, include the corporate structure of the industry as one part of their analyses. Indeed, one implicit axiom of U.S. production studies is that economics undergirds *everything* within the television industry. However, production studies sees economics as one part of a complicated social phenomenon and does not even consider it the most interesting part of the media industry. In contrast, scholars who do study political economy begin with the financially motivated behavior of corporations and work their way down to its impact on actual individuals—as we will see in the next section.

The Discourse of the Industry II: Political Economy

Political economists research how broader, even global, economic pressures shape studios' and networks' production of television—areas conventionally ignored by text-oriented analysts and most cultural-studies researchers. In 1996, broadcast historian and political economist Robert McChesney took audience-oriented and postmodern approaches to task, declaring that they were "politically timid and intellectually uninteresting and unimportant" and guilty of using "hepped up jargon."[25]

In some respects, McChesney and his colleagues advocate a return to classical Marxism. They, like Marx, contend that a society's economic system determines its ideology, but they recognize that contemporary economic systems are much different from the early capitalism that Marx knew in the nineteenth century. Indeed, there have been enormous economic changes since even the mid-twentieth century, when television began. Most significantly, **transnational corporations** (**TNC**s) now hold the purse strings of every media outlet except the Internet. In Marx's time (1818–83), the economic underpinnings of the mass media were quite different. There was little horizontal integration, as economists say. That is, newspaper publishers did not publish books, and vice versa. Each publication outlet stayed mostly within its own province and certainly did not extend into other nineteenth-century industries, such as railroads and textiles. Contrast that with the extreme horizontal integration of today's TNCs, where a company like Sony has investments in TV, film, music, video games, computer hardware, consumer electronics (e.g., Blu-ray players and TV monitors), and so on. And the mass media of Marx's time in England, where he wrote, or Germany, where he was born, were not owned by corporations in other countries. Publishers' reach did not extend far beyond national boundaries—mostly because international copyright and trademark law was virtually nonexistent and could not protect their products in other countries. Today, in contrast, it is commonplace for a Japanese or German or American company to operate in other countries; they are truly transnational.

Political economy examines television's economic institutions and their structure in this era of TNC dominance. It asks pragmatic questions such as:

- Who owns the networks and the production studios?
- What connections are there among television networks, Internet service providers, social media, film studios, music and video-game producers, print-media outlets, etc.? Does one

influence the other? Is there synergy among them? (See the discussion of synergy and commercials in Chapter 6.)

- How do these institutions generate revenue? Where does the money come from? How is it allocated?
- How do governmental agencies, policies, and laws affect the transaction of business? Importantly, in the U.S., how has deregulation in the 1990s changed the broadcasting landscape?

However, political economy is not solely concerned with writing histories of the media industries. Rather, its interest in economic institutions and infrastructure extends beyond industrial history to examine its impact on the discourses, narrative and non-narrative structures, and visual and sound styles of the media—specifically, in our case, of television. For instance, Edward S. Herman and Noam Chomsky argue that contemporary business models inevitably influence how news is reported in the mass media. In their view, news helps to "manufacture consent" to the dominant ideology.[26]

In the 1990s and since, political economy has focused on four aspects of the global economy and investigated how they have changed television:

1. the spread of transnational corporations' holdings and the subsequent concentration/consolidation of media ownership in a shrinking number of TNCs;
2. **globalization** and cultural imperialism;
3. television as an arena in which discourse and policy may be debated by the public (Jürgen Habermas's **public sphere**);
4. technological change and its effect on economics.

Although space does not permit a full exploration of each of these aspects, we can at least sketch their basic terms of engagement with television.

First, in McChesney's words, political economic analysis of television "needs to deal seriously with issues of ownership, subsidy, and control." He continues, "all broadcasting history must address the role and implications of the market for the nature of U.S. broadcasting, and for broadcasting's contribution to society at large."[27] In years past, this has led to studies of the formation of commercial broadcast networks in the U.S. and of the BBC in the UK. More recently, however, the most pressing issues of ownership stem from larger and larger corporations gobbling more and more television networks and stations and other media entities. (As of 2016, the five largest U.S.-based, media-oriented conglomerates are, in order of annual revenue, Alphabet [Google], The Walt Disney Company, Comcast, 21st Century Fox, National Amusements [which owns controlling stakes in Viacom and CBS].)[28] In the U.S., the Telecommunications Act of 1996 greatly loosened the regulation of radio and TV station, network, cable, and satellite ownership in the 1990s—leading to a consolidation of power in the hands of a very few. Political economists contend that this market-driven concentration of media ownership endangers the diversity of discourse available on our television screens. Smaller, independent, and/or alternative voices are often silenced in the consolidation process.

Second, globalization is rooted in some of the same economic changes that have nurtured media consolidation. As barriers to international trade have broken down, the influence of corporations has crossed national boundaries—leading to TNCs with a strong presence across the globe. But political economists are concerned with more than just the sale of television sets and smartphones across national borders and the outsourcing of jobs from the West to third-world countries. Equally important is the cultural component of globalization. It's not just money that travels across borders. It's also cultural products like movies and TV. When television programs and other cultural texts circulate from one country to another, they can sometimes replace or repress the culture of another country, which is referred to as cultural imperialism. If a U.S.-produced television program pushes locally produced programs off the air, then we are seeing cultural imperialism—the negative effect of globalization—in action. And if countries outside the U.S. adopt the dominant values of U.S. culture, then hegemony can be said to be spreading across the globe.

Third, McChesney demands that scholars commit "to finding an alternative, more democratic, system for both communication and society as a whole."[29] This concern for a fully democratic society often leads to Habermas's concept of the public sphere, which was developing in the early 1960s.[30] Peter Dahlgren summarizes the concept: the public sphere is "that realm of social life where the exchange of information and views on questions of common concern can take place so that public opinion can be formed."[31] Crucially, the public sphere is a conversational "space" that is *not* controlled by governmental bodies, by the state and its police force. One might imagine the public sphere as a figurative town square where citizens sit on park benches and talk about the issues of the day—rationally debating and exchanging views without the mayor or police chief or political party head dictating what can and cannot be said. Based on these discussions, citizens form beliefs and opinions about their society, how it should operate, and how its democratic system functions.

On a national or global level, this sort of direct interchange is obviously not possible, which is where the mass media—including television—enter the equation. Media, especially news media, constitute the twenty-first century's town square. And, like a huckster with a megaphone, they shout out views and beliefs that aim to convince passers-by. Perhaps they might pitch an opinion on abortion, a presidential nominee, or the validity of the war in Iraq—as can be heard on programs like Fox News' *Hannity*, CNN's *Inside Politics*, or even Comedy Central's *The Daily Show With Trevor Noah*. Habermas and scholars who have followed his lead are not so naive as to believe that what has been called the "mediasphere" gives equal and free access to ordinary citizens to express their divergent views.[32] Rather, they see the public sphere as essentially degraded and delimited, in the United States, by commercial interests. Television can be a forum for debate over ideas, but in the U.S. those ideas must be of interest and acceptable to advertisers who sell products to viewers. The main value discussed in television's corner of the public sphere is how best to consume products.

The mediasphere obviously perverts the pristine ideal of a democratic public sphere, but that does not render the concept useless. Numerous scholars have employed it as a way to chart the terrain of meaning-production that exists between state control (through laws and police forces) and person-to-person communication. On one extreme are the official, governmental forces of control and on the other is the private world of day-to-day human life. The public sphere exists in between the two, and scholars continue to be intrigued by how it influences—and is influenced by—pressures above and below it. It's the battleground upon which public opinion is fought.

The fourth and final aspect of the current global economy to interest political economists is the rise of digital technologies and networking and their impact upon media economics. As you read about the public sphere's exchange of views above, it may have occurred to you that the Internet provides many avenues for commonplace citizens to share their opinions with the world—much more so than television ever did. Are we on the verge of a democratic revolution heralded by inexpensively produced websites and blogs? Is the so-called **blogosphere** a latter-day realization of Habermas's ideal public sphere? And will television viewing continue to decline as broadband Internet use expands?[33] Perhaps. But political economists also warn that the convergence of the Internet with television (and other media) has not gone unnoticed by transnational corporations. It's too early to tell if television and other media from the twentieth century will find a way to adapt to and dominate new distribution models in the twenty-first century.

Discourse and Identity I: Gender

Ideological critics' key assumption is that U.S. culture as it appears on television is middle-class, male-dominated, white, and heterosexual—and that needs to change. Consequently, ideological criticism has opened the door for perspectives that exist on the margin, for individuals who reject hegemony, for voices that speak for repressed populations or cultures. These marginalized populations are typically defined by class, gender, sexual orientation, and race or ethnicity—ideologically charged categories. Over the past 20 years, the most powerful and fruitful ideological criticism of hegemony—as it expresses itself on TV—has been from under-represented and subordinated cultures. Can these cultures resist the allure of hegemonic television? And if hegemony is as all-encompassing as Gramsci claims, what form might resistance take? Mary Ellen Brown writes, "Resistance theory comprises a body of work which addresses the issue of how ordinary people and subcultural groups can resist hegemonic, or dominant pressures, and consequently obtain pleasure from what the political, social and/or cultural system offers, despite that system's contradictory position in their lives."[34] We continue this chapter with an examination of the most influential approaches to resisting television: **feminism**, **queer theory**, **race**, **and ethnic studies**.

"Image-of-Women" Feminist Criticism

The anti-hegemonic method with the longest history is **feminism**. In the U.S., the women's movement formally began in 1848 with the Seneca Falls Woman's Rights Convention and culminated in the 1910s during the fight for women's right to vote. When women's suffrage was granted in 1920, radio and the cinema were in their infancies and television did not even exist. Consequently, feminist criticism of broadcasting and film did not arise until the 1960s during the "second wave" of feminism.[35] At that time, women inspired by the anti-war movement began raising specific social and political concerns: equal job opportunity, combating violence against women, abortion rights, affordable day care for children, and so on. In other words, feminism has long battled in the arena of **sexual politics**—as Kate Millett refers to the power relationship between men and women.[36] But feminists have not been concerned solely with this political agenda, with marching in the streets to protest for abortion rights or suffrage, or against domestic violence. Intertwined with feminist political concerns is an interest in the representation of women in the mass media and the interpretation of those images by viewers, both women and men. How are women's images used in the media? What is the significance of those images in television? What ideas, concepts, and discourses are associated with or encoded on women as defined by television? How do viewers interpret or decode those images?

The simplest form of feminist television criticism presumes that television is a direct reflection of society. This approach searches television texts for women's **stereotypes**—that is, demeaning fictional character types that are based on ideologically defined social types. Stereotypes in television often represent society's exploited and subordinate groups in ways that keep them powerless. On *The Donna Reed Show* (1958–66), for instance, Donna Stone (Donna Reed) is said to embody the stereotype of the late 1950s–early 1960s American "housewife." Called into question by the women's movement of the late 1960s, the housewife is a social role for women that encourages their subservience to men. It suggests that they not consider their own needs and desires as they tirelessly care for their family. And on *The Donna Reed Show*, Donna is the "ideal wife"—as one episode is titled—selflessly preparing meals and vacuuming in high heels and pearls and never complaining about all the work she does for her husband and children.[37]

Analyzing TV characters as reflections or images of society's stereotypes has been criticized principally because it overly simplifies the television-to-society relationship. A mass medium such as TV has a very complex relationship with the society that produces it. Television stories, for instance, do not automatically or naturally "reflect" the ideology of the society that produces them. Rather, they emphasize some factors while repressing or even inverting other elements. A society's ideology is mediated by many factors—scriptwriters' and directors' aesthetic concerns, genre conventions, and the political economy of the industry among them—as it makes its way into a television program. If we, for example, accept that 1950s patriarchal ideology demanded women work only within the home—itself a huge, difficult-to-sustain generalization—then how do we account for the enormous popularity of unruly Lucy Ricardo (Lucille Ball) on *I Love Lucy* (1951–57)? The main premise of this program is that Lucy is constantly forsaking her duties at home in order to try to break into show business. Thus, the patriarchal containment of women in 1950s society is mitigated by sitcom genre conventions including trouble-making women and the behind-the-scenes fact that Lucille Ball wielded great power in Hollywood and co-owned the program's production company, Desilu Productions.

Transcending the "Image-of-Women"

Feminist television criticism since the 1980s has evolved in a variety of directions that transcend the image-of-women approach.[38] Feminist scholars still start from the common premise that a society run by men, a **patriarchy**, will encourage systems of beliefs that keep men in power, but they adopt different, more sophisticated methods for analyzing those systems than the relatively blunt approach of looking for stereotypes. Some researchers look at television texts and identify oppositional discourses in them. Others are more interested in the female viewer's experience of television and the contexts in which she watches it. Almost all believe that patriarchal discourses in television are not uncontested or monolithic even though feminists may not be optimistic about women's opportunities to overthrow them. And perhaps it goes without saying that most feminist scholars offer tactics for women to combat patriarchal power.

Soap opera, with its largely female audience, proved to be an early test case for the feminist analysis of television.[39] In a ground-breaking 1979 essay, Tania Modleski writes about the soap opera in terms of the narrative pleasure it affords the female viewer.[40] She is also interested in the ways that women are positioned within the narrative. The constant interruptions, the lack of a conclusion, and other soap-opera characteristics, she suggests, may qualify the genre as possessing a feminist narrative structure.[41] The rhythms of soap-opera storytelling match the rhythms of women's day-to-day experience. Her argument is typical of contemporary feminist criticism in that it articulates the ways that women are represented on television (specifically, through the narrative structure) and the position of the female spectator vis-à-vis the images that she sees on the screen. In so doing, Modleski is helping to define television viewing from a feminist perspective.

Modleski goes beyond textual interpretation (that is, interpreting a text's or program's themes, narrative structures, and visual style) and analyzes the viewing situation, but she does not do so by interviewing actual viewers. Rather, she analyzes the type of viewer for which the text is designed. This ideal viewing "position" is the target at which the text aims. A viewer occupying that position will enjoy a program to the maximum degree and will agree with all its underlying discourses. However, other strains of feminist television criticism look beyond the text and viewing positions to the experiences of actual women viewers and the social context of the viewing experience. This has taken feminist television criticism in two complementary directions:

1. ethnographic studies of television viewers;
2. analyses of the social situation in which viewing occurs.

Feminist ethnographers, as you might expect, are particularly interested in women viewers and how their television experiences are "gendered"—that is, how gender affects viewing. Or, in other words, do women experience television differently than men? Closely related to this are the feminist studies of gendered social situations. Television, especially when it first became popular in the 1950s, is a family experience and it reflects the gender dynamics of the family. In other words, the sexual politics of the family—who is in power, who is powerless—influences greatly how women experience television. For example, Lynn Spigel studies the "domestic architecture" surrounding television. In *Make Room for TV* she looks at popular media of the 1940s and 1950s (especially in women's magazines) for their representation of "television and the family ideal in postwar America."[42] What makes her research "feminist" is her emphasis on women's work—as wife, mother, and custodian of the home—and television's simultaneous disruption and confirmation of that work. For Spigel, family defines itself in terms of sexual politics.

Not all feminist television criticism since the 1980s has concentrated on the female viewer. Another strain within it centers on the complexities of **gender identity**. This notion resembles the much more limited concept of the stereotype but is founded on a nuanced understanding of how ideology works. A stereotype such as the housewife, the goth teenager, or the cheerleader is a relatively fixed image or role, to which, in this case, women in television conform. A gender identity, however, describes a container of society's discourse-based ideas of what it means to be a woman or a man. Identity may start with physical characteristics, but it's quickly buried beneath layers of cultural and social assumptions about masculinity and femininity: e.g., women are empathetic and intuitive while men are cold and analytical, and women should dress flamboyantly while men should not, and so on. In fact, these cultural assumptions, these layers of discourse, are a greater determinant of identity than "simple" anatomy, hormones, or DNA. Feminists that advocate this position turn their attention to the process by which identity is constructed.

As Judith Butler contends, one can see gender identity as something that is "performative"—suggesting that femininity is a performance or masquerade enacted by women (and some men).[43] While writing about female impersonators, she argues, "Consider gender . . . as *a corporeal style*, an 'act,' as it were, which is both intentional and performative, where '*performative*' suggests a dramatic and contingent construction of meaning."[44] Gender, in this sense, is defined as a constructed performance, act, or corporeal style—meaning a style of the body—and not dependent upon genitalia. For Butler, gender results from ideology, not biology. And consequently, one is feminine or masculine by culture more than by nature.

Butler's insights into gender identity arrived at a time (1990) when feminism had been stagnating, when some critics of feminism were declaring that we were moving into a "postfeminist" era as women had already achieved equality with men and no further struggle was necessary. Much of the debate about feminism's ostensible demise took place on television or revolved around television's characters and celebrities. Ally McBeal (Calista Flockhart), from later in the 1990s, was television's "postfeminist icon" for some (*Ally McBeal* [1997-2002]). A lawyer who wore impossibly short skirts to court, she pined for love and a baby (Figure 14.3)—leading *Time* magazine to put her on a 1998 cover with a provocative caption asking, "Is Feminism Dead?"[45]

Also, contentious "sex wars" had developed within feminist circles during the 1980s, where the representation of female sexuality and desire—particularly in film and television—was hotly argued, resulting in sharp divisions.[46] Then, in 1991, the televised Supreme Court confirmation hearings of Clarence Thomas foregrounded sexual and racial politics when he was accused of sexual harassment by law professor Anita Hill (Figure 14.4; for ABC news coverage of the

Figure 14.3 Ally McBeal's short skirts led *Time* magazine to ask, "Is Feminism Dead?"

Figure 14.4 Anita Hill testifies against Clarence Thomas in his Supreme Court confirmation hearings.

testimony, see tvcrit.com/find/thomasvshill). Her testimony was discredited and her accusations were dismissed. Hill's humiliation outraged many feminists and mobilized them to action—leading, for example, to a *Designing Women* (1986–93) episode directly critiquing the event.[47] And one college student, Rebecca Walker, expressed her anger and frustration by calling for a *third* wave of feminism in a 1992 article in *Ms.* magazine. "I am not a postfeminism feminist," she writes, "I am the Third Wave."[48] In the nearly two decades since her manifesto, the concept of "third-wave feminism" has been difficult to pin down, and some second-wave feminists have taken exception to it—asserting that third-wave feminism is less a break with second-wave feminism than it is a continuation of the latter's concerns. Nonetheless, as Merri Lisa Johnson's *Third Wave Feminism and Television* illustrates, third-wave feminism has had an impact on television studies, even if its boundaries are a bit difficult to specify.[49]

Johnson contends that she and other third-wave feminists take "for granted that all the shows on television today contain a mixture of feminist, postfeminist, antifeminist, and pseudofeminist motifs."[50] The role of the third-wave feminist viewer, then, is to take her television pleasures where she can without feeling guilty about doing so. She differs from the previous generation of feminists, who, in this view, were opposed to men, to visual pleasure, to women reveling in femininity and amusing themselves with it. In short, third-wavers chide second-wavers for not being able to have fun with their sexuality and their gender's conventional signifiers.[51] Third-wave feminists might become "riot grrrls," blending feminism with a punk-rock sensibility, or embrace "girlie" culture, where conventional notions of femininity are reclaimed by women and put to postmodern—or at least ironic—use. Girlies indulge in girl culture and might paint their fingernails, wear makeup, and learn knitting, but they also reject the patriarchal subjugation of women and the denial of female pleasure.[52] Third-wave feminism jettisons both the perceived seriousness of second-wave feminism and the restrictions of masculine discourse. Further, some third-wave feminists identify themselves as "pro-sex," "sex positive," or even "sex radical," leading to studies such as Carol Siegel's consideration of female heterosexual sadism in *Buffy the Vampire Slayer*.[53] As Johnson explains, "These media critics . . . import sex radical theories into television studies, valuing fantasy as a space of free play, advocating acceptance of our darker drives, and indulging in fascination with imagery that queers gender, decenters heterosexuality, and valorizes the erotic."[54]

Buffy is a seminal figure in third-wave feminist television criticism—appealing to such scholars as both a "girlie girl" and tough warrior battling an unending supply of vampires. But it is not just her image on the screen that interests third-wave feminists, it's also the uses viewers can make of that image. Third-wavers often focus on negotiated readings made by viewers themselves, where they derive pleasure from texts even though the texts' preferred readings might endorse patriarchal values. Third-wave feminists, for instance, might find virtues in a reality show such as *The Bachelorette* (2002), which would seem to advocate against feminism and for conventional heterosexual values. Nonetheless, it might be said that *The Bachelorette* "market[s] [itself] according to a postfeminist logic that embraces femininity and 'girliness' in the name of enlightenment and female empowerment."[55] Negotiating readings are not the only actions that may be performed on the texts by third-wave feminists. This generation of feminists matured at the same time as the Internet and have made notable use of blogs, social media, discussion forums, fan fiction, and mash-ups as ways to produce their own texts. Crucial to the notion of third-wave feminist media criticism is that the consumer is also a producer—as we have previously discussed in the context of fan studies. She is not the helpless victim of Big Media, but, rather, finds ways to accommodate television texts to her own pleasure.

In sum, as A. Susan Owen, Sarah R. Stein, and Leah R. Vande Berg contend, "Third Wave feminism defines itself through playful embrace of popular culture, exuberant expression of sexual identity and desire, rejection of a feminist/feminine binary, and an individualistic understanding of choice."[56] In practice, third-wave feminist television criticism is still centrally concerned with the construction and performance of gender identity, as was the previous generation of feminist television criticism. However, its advocates contend that it takes a more inclusive approach to feminine identity—celebrating aspects of women's experiences that were previously ignored or even condemned. Its advocates are also more flexible in their definition and celebration of female pleasure, risking the potential for patriarchal exploitation while reclaiming conventional feminine attractiveness and terms like "bitch" and "slut." Third-wave feminism had to learn how to adapt its advocacy to new, Internet-based social media—leading, some have said, from approximately 2008 onward to a *fourth* wave of feminists who are Internet natives and particularly adept at employing online media to advocate for reproductive justice and transgenderism and an end to slut-shaming and fat-shaming.[57] Regardless of the hazy distinctions between these successive waves, it is clearly evident that contemporary feminists are alert to the blurring of boundaries between gender identities and to the intersection of race with gender. It is to these two aspects of television criticism that we now turn.

Discourse and Identity II: Queer Theory

As discussed above, Judith Butler's work underpins many feminist analyses of gender in television. It also forms one of the foundations of **queer theory**—the study of discourse surrounding lesbian, gay, bisexual, transgender, and queer (LGBTQ) identities and their representation in our culture. When television studies was first developing, queer theory had minimal impact on it, even though queer theory was already well developed in film studies and literary criticism.[58] One reason for that is quite simple: until the late 1990s, there were precious few LGBTQ characters on television to be analyzed. As the twentieth century ended, that began to change (e.g., *Will and Grace* [1998–2006] and *Queer Eye* [2003–07], a.k.a. *Queer Eye for the Straight Guy*), and there has been a corresponding rise in queer theory-founded analyses of television. Queer theory shares with feminist theory a desire to examine how identity is built, but the identity it examines is based on sexual orientation in addition to gender. It also shares with feminism a concern for society's power structures. Categorizing LGBTQ individuals as outside of "normal" society creates an environment where gays can be excluded from the military and teaching school, banned from marrying, ridiculed through anti-gay jokes, and subjected to violent hate crimes. By labeling themselves as "queer," LGBTQ theorists capture a term that has been used to hurt gays and repurpose it—much as third-wave feminists did with derogatory words like "bitch." They revel in their "queerness," their otherness, their deviation from the heterosexual norm. In this context, television's relatively recent discovery of gay culture is not necessarily positive. Queer theory is therefore concerned with the manner in which that culture is absorbed or assimilated into mainstream or straight culture. How, for example, do recent shows such as *Modern Family* (2009–), *Orange Is the New Black* (2013–), and *Transparent* (2014–) use LGBTQ culture? What meanings do they attach to being LGBTQ and how do they do so? Is this representation empowering or degrading? These are the sort of questions that are asked about television by queer theorists.

One of the liveliest and most sustained examples of feminist/queer analysis of a gendered/sexualized television figure is the academic controversy swirling around the "Madonna phenomenon," as it was dubbed by Ann Kaplan.[59] (Of course, Madonna appears in many media, but

Figure 14.5 A woman in men's suspenders and cap...

Figure 14.6 ... and women with drawn-on mustaches in male attire transgress the boundaries between genders in Madonna's video for "Justify My Love."

she qualifies as a "television" star because of her work in music video.) At first, Madonna might seem like a trivial or sensational subject for academic analysis, but what intrigued feminists and queer theorists about Madonna was her ability to break through gender lines and, even more significantly, to focus on those very lines and how they're drawn. As Kaplan writes, the video for "Justify My Love" (1990) "forces the spectator to question the boundaries of gender constructs and the cultural constraints on sexual themes and sexual fantasies."[60] After showing images of Madonna making love with a man in a hotel room, the video ends with an intertitle suggesting how control and power are mixed into sexuality: "Poor is the man whose pleasures depend on the permission of another." And the boundaries that Kaplan discusses are clearly transgressed in shots of a topless woman wearing suspenders and one sexually ambiguous figure drawing a mustache on another (Figures 14.5 and 14.6).

Madonna and her critics push the deconstruction of gender identity to the limit, but one need not look to sexually charged music videos to analyze the construction of gender. Feminists and queer theorists have also addressed gender and sexual orientation in sitcoms (e.g., *Murphy Brown* and *Roseanne*), prime-time dramas (e.g., *L.A. Law*, *Buffy the Vampire Slayer*), and talk shows (e.g., *The Oprah Winfrey Show*).[61] What unites all these studies is their desire to investigate gender as an ideological construct. In sum, then, contemporary feminist and queer criticism of television transcends the image-of-women approach and deals with gendered and sexualized discourses. A feminist or queer critique of any television show must remain alert to the program's sexual politics at the same time that it dissects the positioning of women and gays within the text and the experience of female and/or gay viewers before the TV set.

Discourse and Identity III: Race and Ethnicity

In some respects, discussions of race and ethnicity have paralleled those of gender and sexual orientation. One can find, as in the early "image-of-women" studies, articles and books that describe and condemn racial stereotypes in television and other media. One such work, from 1983, is J. Fred MacDonald's *Blacks and White TV*, one of the few book-length studies of African Americans in television. Another is Darrell Y. Hamamoto's *Monitored Peril*, which considers television's "controlling images" of Asian Americans—by which he means the stereotypes that help to suppress subordinate groups.[62] And in the related field of cinema studies, the first overview of African-American representation even takes stereotyped labels as its title: *Toms, Coons, Mulattoes, Mammies, and Bucks* (1973).[63]

In the late 1980s and 1990s, however, television scholars studying race and ethnicity adopted new methodological tactics, drawing from political economy, cultural studies, and feminist theory. They turned their interest to the *discourses*, the sets of meanings, associated with racial and ethnic cultures—as is common in cultural studies. And they began to ask how these discourses *construct identities*—as is common in feminism. Many contemporary television scholars reject the idea of racial **essentialism**, which holds that a race is defined by a fixed, biological essence. Certain physical traits are said to always be associated with one race and, regardless of the context, these traits are what give that race its distinctiveness. Adolf Hitler, for example, believed that there were certain traits essential to the Aryan race—marking them as the "master race." Biologists and social scientists alike reject essentialism as deeply flawed. Instead of asking what the "essence" of a race is, they ask questions such as:

- What meanings are associated with being black or white or Asian?
- How do language and imagery build those meanings—on television and in society at large?
- Race categories depend overwhelmingly on cultural signifiers. Why, then, are they often represented as being essentially biologically determined, as being "natural"? Or, put another way, what is the politics of essentialism?
- How are ethnic-identity categories transgressed and blended—as in children of parents of different ethnicities, or hybrid cultural forms like rock music?

These questions underpin a **racial formation** approach, based on the work of sociologists Michael Omi and Howard Winant.[64] In short, the racial formation is the process by which bundles of social and political meanings are attached to persons of a certain skin color or language or dress or other physical signifier.[65] The racial formation is the ideological process by which those signifiers become **racialized** or **raced**. Much as a physical attribute such as eye makeup can become gendered (i.e., seen as specifically feminine or masculine), so can a signifier come to have racial significance.[66]

Consider how dreadlocks and cornrows have been racialized. Both are embedded in African and African-American culture through their social, political, and national histories. But they are not essentially, biologically, or naturally limited to a specific race—as is illustrated by the ability of individuals *not* of African descent to wear them.[67] One could make a similar point about the racialization of the Western European business suit. It's historically based in Western European culture and yet it's wearable by individuals not of Western European descent. Skin color and other bodily attributes are often racialized, but, from the racial formation perspective, they are *not* reliable, fixed, essential markers of race. For instance, the physical appearance of Latino/as in the U.S. is racialized; social institutions position them as nonwhite. However, as Mary Beltrán and Camilla Fojas point out in *Mixed Race Hollywood*, Latino/as are represented as white in Latin American countries.[68] Further, mixed-race television actors such as Benjamin Bratt, Lisa Bonet, Rashida Jones, Maya Rudolph, Rob Schneider, and Vin Diesel illustrate how unstable the boundaries between racial categories are. As we discussed previously in Madonna's blurring of masculine and feminine categories, figures that are in between socially defined categories can challenge the validity of those categories or indeed the entire process of categorization. What does it mean to be white, black, Latino/a, or Asian? How do we understand those categories and what race means?

Herman Gray's work on television examines racial categories and borrows from the racial formation perspective. He examines "television and the struggle for 'blackness'" in the book *Watching Race* and identifies three principal African-American discourses in television:

1. assimilationist (invisibility)—e.g., *I Spy* (1965–68), *Designing Women* (1986–93), *Grey's Anatomy* (2005–);
2. pluralist (separate but equal)—e.g., *Sanford and Son* (1972–77), *The Fresh Prince of Bel-Air* (1990–96), and *Girlfriends* (2000–08);
3. multiculturalist (diversity)—e.g., *Frank's Place* (1987–88), *In Living Color* (1990–94), and *The Wire* (2002–08).[69]

He maintains that these discourses "construct, frame, stage, and narrate general issues of race and, more specifically, black subjectivity and presence."[70] He is concerned less with identifying negative images or stereotypes of African Americans than with analyzing the social and political meanings associated with those images and the ways that television encourages or positions the viewer to understand them.

Briefly, assimilationist programs present a color-blind world, where the differences among the races are repressed in hopes of achieving "universal harmony."[71] Pluralist TV programs recognize "race (blackness) as the basis of cultural difference (expressed as separation) as a feature of U.S. society," and create a parallel world where races are separate, but equal.[72] Finally, multiculturalist programs recognize the socially constructed differences among races and examine "issues of racism, apartheid, discrimination, nationalism, masculinity, color coding, desegregation, and poverty from multiple and complex perspectives within blackness."[73]

This brief gloss of Gray's work should make evident that his method is clearly indebted to cultural studies but that his findings depend on the unique situation of African Americans in the U.S.—a situation very different from those of women or gays or even, for that matter, from persons who identify as Latino/a, Asian, or Native American.

In addition to the racial formation perspective, other strands of race studies have evolved recently. As has happened in cultural studies, contemporary race scholars have begun to extend their work beyond the discourse of the text itself to address concerns raised by political economy, the writing of history, and the positioning of the viewing subject.[74] The impact of race upon post-network television's changing economy has attracted the attention of several scholars. As the national audience has fragmented and narrowcasting cable networks (e.g., BET, Univision) and upstart broadcast networks (e.g., Fox, the WB, UPN) have appealed to smaller groups, we've seen entire channels/networks marketed to African-American, Spanish-language, and other minority audiences. Scholars like Kristal Brent Zook have examined how these industrial changes have had an impact on television's representation of race.[75] Similarly, the reception of the racialized text by viewers has become a major part of television studies of race—employing cultural studies' ethnographic methods to investigate how race and ethnicity affect the audience's understanding of television. Minu Lee and Chon Heup Cho, for example, have researched Korean soap-opera fans in the U.S., while Marie Gillespie has examined television consumption and reception by Punjabi youth living in London.[76] These two studies examine the reading of television by **diasporas**, ethnic groups dispersed as a minority in a larger society. How do the mainstream media represent that diaspora? If an ethnic diaspora's values and beliefs, its clothing, language, food, and so on, are not hidden, ignored, or repressed—as was attempted with Native Americans—then how do they work their way into television? And how do members of the diaspora negotiate these representations?

Race/ethnic studies, feminism, and queer theory share one important commonality. They position some predefined subculture in opposition to the dominant-hegemonic culture and then attempt to understand how that subculture is depicted and understood within this relationship. Whether this subculture is constructed by gender, sexual orientation, race, ethnicity, or some combination of these factors is less relevant than the understanding of how these oppositional groups interact with, are depicted by, and interpreted within the larger surrounding culture and society. Ultimately, these are discussions of ideology more than biology. The boundary between mainstream culture and subcultures, between the dominant and the oppositional, is thus built on the shifting sands of discourses subjected to social, political, and commercial currents. Chon A. Noriega argues that this boundary is itself unstable, leading to hybrid cultures and blurred distinctions and, consequently, that the distinctions among races, among ethnicities, must themselves be interrogated.[77]

Summary

Television studies, as it has evolved since the 1990s, is not as text-centric as it used to be. Political economic research and production studies examine the industrial apparatuses and workers' discourses that function to generate those texts. And, in parallel fashion, there have been attempts to comprehend the viewer for which these texts are designed. Feminism, queer theory, and race and ethnic studies examine this text-viewer relationship for clues to the construction of social identities. And fan studies and third-wave feminist criticism account for what fans do with television texts. The bulk of television-studies methods is still concerned (some would say obsessed) with the text, with television programs in all their broad variety. However, the methods outlined in this chapter contend that the text cannot be understood on its own, that the researcher must examine how it is produced and how it is consumed.

The brevity of this chapter and the previous one has led to simplification (perhaps even oversimplification) of television-studies methods. And we have had to be selective in our choice of methods to present. Some critical methods and theories that have been applied to television but are not considered here include criticism from rhetorical, dialogic, reader-oriented, psychoanalytic, and postmodernism perspectives. The diversity of television studies prohibits sampling all of the critical methods currently being applied to the medium, but it is hoped that our short survey might entice you to engage more fully with particular approaches.

Notes

1 Much contemporary writing on ideology may be traced back to Friedrich Engels and Karl Marx, *The German Ideology*, Parts I and III (New York: International Publishers, 1947)—originally written in 1845, but not published until 1932.
2 Karl Marx and Frederick Engels, *The German Ideology*, Part I, edited and with an Introduction by C. J. Arthur (New York: International Publishers, 1947), 64. Originally written 1845–46.
3 Antonio Gramsci, *Prison Notebooks* (New York: Columbia University Press, 1991).
4 John Fiske, *Television Culture*, 2nd ed. (London: Routledge, 2011; originally published in 1987), 14.
5 See Hall, "Encoding/Decoding," in *Culture, Media, Language*, Stuart Hall, Dorothy Hobson, Andre Lowe, and Paul Willis, eds. (London: Hutchinson, 1980).
6 Ibid., 134.
7 Ibid., 136–37.
8 Richard Johnson, "What Is Cultural Studies Anyway?," *Social Text*, no. 16 (Winter, 1986–87), 58.
9 "Thick description" is a term borrowed from philosopher Gilbert Ryle and applied to anthropology by Clifford Geertz in his influential work *The Interpretation of Cultures: Selected Essays* (New York: Basic Books, 1973), 6.
10 Mark Allen Peterson, *Anthropology & Mass Communication: Media and Myth in the New Millennium* (New York: Berghahn, 2003), 8.

11 See the Organization for Transformative Works' website for more information: tvcrit.com/find/transformative.
12 Henry Jenkins, *Textual Poachers: Television Fans & Participatory Culture* (New York: Routledge, 1992).
13 Karen Hellekson, "Fan Studies 101," *SFRA Review* 287 (Winter 2009), 5.
14 The Organization for Transformative Works, "What Is Vidding?" *MIT TechTV*, tvcrit.com/find/vidding, accessed July 11, 2017.
15 See Henry Jenkins, *Confessions of an Aca-Fan*, tvcrit.com/find/henryjenkins, accessed July 11, 2017.
16 Lévy terms it "a form of *universally distributed intelligence*, constantly enhanced, coordinated in real time, and resulting in the effective mobilization of skills." Pierre Lévy, *Collective Intelligence: Mankind's Emerging World in Cyberspace*, translated by Robert Bononno (Cambridge, MA: Perseus, 1997), 13.
17 An overview of 1990s production studies that use some form of ethnographic research is provided in a table in John Caldwell, "Cultural Studies of Media Production: Critical Industrial Practices," in *Questions of Method in Cultural Studies*, Mimi White and James Schwoch, eds. (Malden, MA: Blackwell, 2006), 119–20.
18 John Thornton Caldwell, *Production Culture: Industrial Reflexivity and Critical Practice in Film and Television* (Durham, NC: Duke University Press, 2008).
19 In Caldwell's words: "textual analysis of trade and worker artifacts; interviews with film/television workers; ethnographic field observation of production spaces and professional gatherings; and economic/industrial analysis." Ibid., 345.
20 Appendix 3 in *Production Culture* is an amusing guide to "industrial doublespeak." Ibid., 368–69.
21 Ibid., 346.
22 Julie D'Acci, *Defining Women: Television and the Case of* Cagney and Lacey (Chapel Hill: University of North Carolina Press, 1994); Arlene Davila, *Latinos, Inc.: The Making of a People* (Berkeley: University of California Press, 2001); Barry Dornfeld, *Producing Public Television, Producing Public Culture* (Princeton, NJ: Princeton University Press, 1998); and Georgina Born, *Uncertain Vision: Birt, Dyke and the Reinvention of the BBC* (London: Secker & Warburg, 2004).
23 Elana Levine, "Toward a Paradigm for Media Production Research: Behind the Scenes at *General Hospital*," *Critical Studies in Media Communication* 18, no. 1 (March 2001), 66–82.
24 Ibid., 68.
25 Robert W. McChesney, "Communication for the Hell of It: The Triviality of U.S. Broadcasting History," *Journal of Broadcasting and Electronic Media* 40, no. 4 (fall 1996), 540, 544. See Aniko Bodroghkozy's comments on this essay in "Media Studies for the Hell of It? Second Thoughts on McChesney and Fiske," *Flow* 2, no. 9, tvcrit.com/find/hell, accessed July 11, 2017.
26 Edward S. Herman and Noam Chomsky, *Manufacturing Consent: The Political Economy of the Mass Media* (New York: Pantheon, 1988).
27 McChesney, 540.
28 Lara O'Reilly, "The 30 Biggest Media Companies in the World," *Business Insider*, May 31, 2016, tvcrit.com/find/conglomerates, accessed July 10, 2017.
29 McChesney, 547.
30 Jürgen Habermas, *The Structural Transformation of the Public Sphere: An Inquiry Into a Category of Bourgeois Society* (Cambridge, MA: MIT Press, 1989). Originally published in 1962.
31 Peter Dahlgren, *Television and the Public Sphere: Citizenship, Democracy and the Media* (Thousand Oaks, CA: Sage Publications, 1995).
32 John Hartley, *Uses of Television* (New York: Routledge, 1999), 217-18.
33 For example, one study by Forrester Research, Inc. found that television viewing decreases as users' Internet speed increases. Surveying TV viewers in the U.S. and Canada, it learned that persons with broadband connections watched television, on average, two hours less per week than those without—12 hours per week contrasted with 14, or 14 percent less. Paul Bond, "Technology 'Optimists' Turn Off TV," *Computerworld*, August 3, 2005, tvcrit.com/find/turnoff, accessed July 11, 2017.
34 Mary Ellen Brown, ed., *Television and Women's Culture: The Politics of the Popular* (London: SAGE Publications, 1990).
35 The Nineteenth Amendment to the United States Constitution, granting women the right to vote, was ratified in 1920 and marked the climax and endpoint of feminism's first wave. A third wave of feminism arrived in the 1990s and has been bolstered by contemporary queer theory and the experiences of women of color, among other influences. See, for example, Daisy Hernández and Bushra Rehman, eds., *Colonize This! Young Women of Color on Today's Feminism* (Emeryville, CA: Seal, 2002).
36 Kate Millett, *Sexual Politics* (Garden City, NY: Doubleday, 1970).
37 In this episode Donna takes umbrage at being called a pushover and the ideal wife by her friends. She tries to prove that she's not perfect by speaking sharply to her family, but, in the end, she just confirms her selfless nature. See the entire episode on Hulu at tvcrit.com/find/donnareed.

38 Nonetheless, television analysis in popular magazines and online publications still favors this image-of-women approach, and academic analyses of stereotypes continue to be published occasionally—e.g., Paul Martin Lester and Susan Dente Ross, eds., *Images That Injure: Pictorial Stereotypes in the Media* (Westport, CT: Praeger, 2003).

39 Chronicled in Charlotte Brunsdon, *The Feminist, the Housewife, and the Soap Opera* (Oxford: Clarendon Press, 2000).

40 Tania Modleski, "The Search for Tomorrow in Today's Soap Operas," in *Loving With a Vengeance* (Hamden, CT: Archon, 1982), 85–109. Originally published in 1979. See also Tania Modleski, "The Rhythms of Reception: Daytime Television and Women's Work," in *Regarding Television: Critical Approaches*, E. Ann Kaplan, ed. (Frederick, MD: University Publications, 1983), 67-75; and Charlotte Brunsdon, "Crossroads: Notes on Soap Opera," in Kaplan, 76–83.

41 Modleski, *Loving*, 105.

42 Lynn Spigel, *Make Room for TV: Television and the Family Ideal in Postwar America* (Chicago: University of Chicago Press, 1992).

43 Butler's "performative theory of gender" was first expounded in *Gender Trouble: Feminism and the Subversion of Identity* (New York: Routledge, 1990). Gender "masquerade" stems from a 1929 essay by psychologist Joan Riviere and has been elaborated upon by Butler and film theorists such as Mary Ann Doane and Stephen Heath. For more information, see Victor Burgin, James Donald, and Cora Kaplan, eds., *Formations of Fantasy* (New York: Methuen, 1986); and Mary Ann Doane, *Femmes Fatales: Feminism, Film Theory, Psychoanalysis* (New York: Routledge, 1991).

44 Butler, 177 (1999 edition).

45 Rachel Dubrofsky, "Ally McBeal as Postfeminist Icon: The Aestheticizing and Fetishizing of the Independent Working Woman," *The Communication Review*, 5, no. 4 (2002), 264–84; "Is Feminism Dead?" *TIME*, June 29, 1998, cover.

46 For more details, see Lisa Duggan and Nan D. Hunter, *Sex Wars: Sexual Dissent and Political Culture* (New York: Routledge, 1995).

47 "The Strange Case of Clarence and Anita" was broadcast November 4, 1991, just weeks after the hearings.

48 Rebecca Walker, "Becoming the Third Wave," *Ms*, January 1, 1992, 40.

49 Merri Lisa Johnson, ed., *Third Wave Feminism and Television: Jane Puts It in a Box* (London; New York: I. B. Tauris, 2007).

50 Ibid., 19.

51 As Claire Snyder explains, "third-wavers claim to be less rigid and judgmental than their mothers' generation, which they often represent as antimale, antisex, antifemininity, and antifun." R. Claire Snyder, "What Is Third-Wave Feminism? A New Directions Essay," *Signs: Journal of Women in Culture and Society* 34, no. 1 (2008), 179.

52 For more on girlie culture, see Jennifer Baumgardner and Amy Richards, *Manifesta: Young Women, Feminism, and the Future* (New York: Farrar, Straus and Giroux, 2000) and the overview of feminism's branches in Rachel Fudge, "Everything You Always Wanted to Know About Feminism but Were Afraid to Ask," *Bitch Media*, 2005, tvcrit.com/find/bitchmedia, accessed July 11, 2017.

53 Carol Siegel, "Female Heterosexual Sadism: The Final Feminist Taboo in *Buffy the Vampire Slayer* and the Anita Blake Vampire Hunter Series," in Johnson, 56–90.

54 Johnson, 15–16.

55 Lynn Spigel, "Theorizing the Bachelorette: 'Waves' of Feminist Media Studies," *Signs* 30, no. 1 (January 2004), 1212.

56 A. Susan Owen, Sarah R. Stein, and Leah R. Vande Berg, *Bad Girls: Cultural Politics and Media Representations of Transgressive Women* (New York: Peter Lang, 2007), 123.

57 According to Jennifer Baumgardner, the fourth wave began approximately in 2008. For more, see *F 'em!: Goo Goo, Gaga, and Some Thoughts on Balls* (Berkeley: Seal Press, 2011).

58 To be precise, "queer theory" as the title of a specific field of study did not exist until 1990, when Teresa de Lauretis coined the term in conjunction with an academic conference. However, gay and lesbian studies existed long before then. See David M. Halperin, "The Normalization of Queer Theory," *Journal of Homosexuality* 45, no. 2/3/4 (2003), 339–43.

59 E. Ann Kaplan, "Feminist Criticism and Television," in *Channels of Discourse, Reassembled*, 2nd ed., Robert C. Allen, ed. (Chapel Hill: University of North Carolina Press, 1992), 271–76. Several pertinent essays are included in Adam Sexton, ed., *Desperately Seeking Madonna: In Search of the Meaning of the World's Most Famous Woman* (New York: Dell, 1993).

60 Kaplan in Allen, 275.

61 Examples of each of these may be found in Charlotte Brunsdon and Lynn Spigel, eds., *Feminist Television Criticism*, 2nd ed. (Maidenhead, UK: Open University Press, 2007).

62 Darrell Y. Hamamoto, *Monitored Peril: Asian Americans and the Politics of TV Representation* (Minneapolis: University of Minnesota Press, 1994), 2-3. Stereotypes in media beyond TV are articulated in Jannette L. Dates and William Barlow, eds., *Split Image: African Americans in the Mass Media* (Washington, DC: Howard University Press, 1990).
63 Donald Bogle, *Toms, Coons, Mulattoes, Mammies, and Bucks: An Interpretive History of Blacks in American Films* (New York: Viking Press, 1973). Reprinted, by Continuum, in 1989.
64 "Our theory of *racial formation* emphasizes the social nature of race, the absence of any essential racial characteristics, the historical flexibility of racial meanings and categories, the conflictual character of race at both the 'micro-' and 'macro-social' levels, and the irreducible political aspect of racial dynamics." Michael Omi and Howard Winant, *Racial Formation in the United States: From the 1960s to the 1990s* (New York: Routledge, 1994), 4. The previous edition was titled *Racial Formation in the United States: From the 1960s to the 1980s*.
65 As Sasha Torres explains, the racial formation perspective "understands race, not as a set of physical characteristics, but rather as the historically-variable *cultural meanings* assigned to such characteristics. . . . Such an approach stresses, first, that race, as a *biological* category, is meaningless. . . . But if race has no biological meaning, it is replete with cultural meaning. Indeed, it is precisely because race cannot be materially fixed in the body that it can be so richly imbued with meanings of other kinds." Sasha Torres, "Television and Race," in *A Companion to Television*, Janet Wasko, ed. (Malden, MA: Wiley-Blackwell, 2010), 403-4.
66 See Toni Morrison, ed., *Race-ing Justice, En-Gendering Power: Essays on Anita Hill, Clarence Thomas, and the Construction of Social Reality* (New York: Pantheon, 1992).
67 For more see Kobena Mercer, "Black Hair/Style Politics," in *Out There: Marginalization and Contemporary Cultures*, Russell Ferguson, Martha Gever, Trinh T. Minh-Ha, and Cornel West, eds. (Cambridge, MA: MIT Press, 1990), 247-65.
68 Mary Beltrán and Camilla Fojas, *Mixed Race Hollywood* (New York: New York University Press, 2008), 3.
69 Herman Gray, *Watching Race: Television and the Struggle for "Blackness"* (Minneapolis: University of Minnesota Press, 1995), 84-91. I have added some recent programs to Gray's original examples.
70 Ibid.
71 Ibid., 85.
72 Ibid., 87.
73 Ibid., 91.
74 See, for example, Chon Noriega's analysis of the historical, social, and political contexts of Chicanos on television: *Shot in America: Television, the State, and the Rise of Chicano Cinema* (Minneapolis: University of Minnesota Press, 2000).
75 Kristal Brent Zook, *Color by Fox: The Fox Network and the Revolution in Black Television* (New York: Oxford University Press, 1999).
76 Minu Lee and Chong Heup Cho, "Women Watching Together: An Ethnographic Study of Korean Soap Opera Fans in the US," *Cultural Studies* 4, no. 1 (January1990), 30-44; Marie Gillespie, *Television, Ethnicity, and Cultural Change* (New York: Routledge, 1995).
77 Noriega.

Further Readings

Several of the general television-studies books and anthologies noted in Chapter 13's further readings contain significant sections on ideological criticism, cultural studies, fan studies, production studies, political economy, feminism, queer theory, race and ethnic studies. Notably, Robert C. Allen, ed., *Channels of Discourse, Reassembled*, provides separate chapters, with detailed bibliographies, on ideological analysis, feminism, and cultural studies.

Each method considered here has a significant number of books devoted to that topic, of course. We present some of the most influential ones here.

Two anthologies devoted specifically to a cultural studies perspective are Stuart Hall, Dorothy Hobson, Andrew Lowe, and Paul Willis, eds., *Culture, Media, Language* (London: Hutchinson, 1980); and Ellen Seiter, Hans Borchers, Gabriele Kreutzner, and Eva-Maria Warth, eds., *Remote Control: Television, Audiences, and Cultural Power* (New York: Routledge, 1989). Janet Staiger assays a broad variety of approaches to media consumption in *Media Reception Studies* (New York: New York University Press, 2005). Henry Jenkins, *Textual Poachers:*

Television Fans and Participatory Culture (New York: Routledge, 1992) was the first book-length academic study of television fans and virtually single-handedly established the field of fan studies. For an anthology of several analyses of online fans, see Karen Hellekson and Kristina Busse, eds., *Fan Fiction and Fan Communities in the Age of the Internet* (Jefferson, NC: McFarland, 2006).

Robert W. McChesney's attack on cultural studies and postmodernism from the position of political economy may be found in "Communication for the Hell of It: The Triviality of U.S. Broadcasting History," *Journal of Broadcasting and Electronic Media* 40, no. 4 (fall 1996), 540–52, which he enlarges upon and updates in *The Problem of the Media: U.S. Communication Politics in the Twenty-First Century* (New York: Monthly Review Press, 2004). For other political economic essays related to television see the "Spaces of Television" section of Robert C. Allen and Annette Hill, eds., *The Television Studies Reader*. Closely related is Peter Dahlgren, *Television and the Public Sphere: Citizenship, Democracy and the Media* (London: Sage, 1995).

The research area of production studies includes industry economics in its analyses but takes a different tack in explaining it than that of the political economists. John Thornton Caldwell, *Production Culture* (Durham, NC: Duke University Press, 2008) is the defining text in this field, but a good sampling of production studies is also available in Jennifer Holt and Alisa Perren, eds., *Media Industries: History, Theory and Method* (Malden, MA: Blackwell, 2009); and Vicki Mayer, Miranda J. Banks, and John T. Caldwell, eds., *Production Studies: Cultural Studies of Media Industries* (New York: Routledge, 2009). The latter has its own "sequel": Miranda Banks, Bridget Conor, and Vicki Mayer, eds., *Production Studies, The Sequel!: Cultural Studies of Global Media Industries* (New York: Routledge, 2015). A similar, ethnographic approach can also be found in Eric W. Rothenbuhler and Mihai Coman, eds., *Media Anthropology* (Thousand Oaks, CA: Sage, 2005). Timothy Havens uses the production-studies lens to analyze globalization and race in TV industries across the globe in *Black Television Travels: African American Media Around the Globe* (New York: New York University Press, 2013). For a nuts-and-bolts picture of the television business that does not incorporate cultural studies, see Howard J. Blumenthal and Oliver R. Goodenough, *This Business of Television*, 3rd ed. (New York: Billboard Books, 2006); or Robert Del Valle, *The One-Hour Drama Series: Producing Episodic Television* (Los Angeles: Silman-James Press, 2008).

Significant feminist TV essays are collected in Charlotte Brunsdon and Lynn Spigel, eds., *Feminist Television Criticism*, 2nd ed. (Maidenhead, UK: Open University Press, 2007). Books providing overviews of feminist work on TV include Bonnie J. Dow, *Prime-Time Feminism: Television, Media Culture, and the Women's Movement Since 1970* (Philadelphia: University of Pennsylvania Press, 1996); Charlotte Brunsdon, *The Feminist, the Housewife, and the Soap Opera* (Oxford: Clarendon Press, 2000); and Mary Beth Haralovich and Lauren Rabinovitz, eds., *Television, History, and American Culture: Feminist Critical Essays* (Durham, NC: Duke University Press, 1999). A call for third-wave feminist action is sounded in Merri Lisa Johnson, ed., *Third Wave Feminism and Television: Jane Puts It in a Box* (New York: I. B. Tauris, 2007). And aspects of the still-evolving fourth wave of feminism are chronicled in Jennifer Baumgardner, *F 'em!: Goo Goo, Gaga, and Some Thoughts on Balls* (Berkeley: Seal Press, 2011).

For a chronicle of gays and lesbians in television, see Stephen Tropiano, *The Prime Time Closet: A History of Gays and Lesbians on TV* (New York: Applause Theatre & Cinema Books, 2002). Ronald Becker, *Gay TV and Straight America* (Brunswick, NJ: Rutgers University Press, 2006) places the programming of the 1990s into the contexts of contemporary social and political events and the changing nature of what he calls neo-network television. And, additionally, Glyn Davis and Gary Needham, eds., *Queer TV: Theories, Histories, Politics* (New York: Routledge, 2009) seeks to extend the queer consideration of TV to include both production and reception. Also, David Gauntlett, *Media, Gender and Identity* (New York: Routledge, 2002) goes beyond television to cover print publication, the Web, and other media. It attempts to boil down feminism and queer theory into their essential components.

Beretta E. Smith-Shomade, *Shaded Lives: African-American Women and Television* (New Brunswick, NJ: Rutgers University Press, 2002), blends feminism with the study of race on television. Sujata Moorti, *Color of Rape: Gender and Race in Television's Public Spheres* (Albany, NY: State University of New York Press, 2002), addresses the same topic but filters it through Habermas's concept of the public sphere. The broadest overview of African Americans in TV remains J. Fred MacDonald's *Blacks and White TV: African Americans in Television Since 1948* (Chicago: Nelson-Hall Publishers, 1992), but it's largely a general, historical study and has not been updated in over 25 years. Bambi Haggins offers a more recent consideration of black performers on TV (and other media) in *Laughing Mad: The Black Comic Persona in Post-Soul America* (New Brunswick, NJ: Rutgers University Press, 2007). For discursive analyses, see Herman Gray, *Watching Race: Television and the Struggle for "Blackness"* (Minneapolis: University of Minnesota Press, 1995); and Darnell M. Hunt, ed., *Channeling Blackness: Studies on Television and Race in America* (New York: Oxford University Press, 2005). For an understanding of how the TV industry handles programming designed for African-American audiences, see Kristal Brent Zook, *Color by Fox: The Fox Network and the Revolution in Black Television* (New York: Oxford University Press, 1999); and Beretta E. Smith-Shomade, *Watching While Black: Centering the Television of Black Audiences* (New Brunswick, NJ: Rutgers University Press, 2013).

Of course, the study of race and ethnicity in television is not limited to African Americans. The interested reader might begin with the following books. Chon A. Noriega, *Shot in America: Television, the State, and the Rise of Chicano Cinema* (Minneapolis: University of Minnesota Press, 2000) chronicles the history of Chicano images in mass media, placing them in the context of political activism, the exhibition and distribution structures of broadcast television and nonbroadcast film/video, and the "mythopoetic" Chicano tradition (its aesthetic and narrative strategies). The construction of the Asian "other" in American television is detailed in Darrell Y. Hamamoto, *Monitored Peril: Asian Americans and the Politics of TV Representation* (Minneapolis: University of Minnesota Press, 1994). Hamad Naficy, *The Making of Exile Cultures: Iranian Television in Los Angeles* (Minneapolis: University of Minnesota Press, 1993), investigates how the Iranian diaspora in Los Angeles is both assimilated and alienated and how those processes are expressed on television. Hamid Naficy and Teshome H. Gabriel, eds., *Otherness and the Media: The Ethnography of the Imagined and the Imaged* (Langhorne, PA: Harwood Academic Publishers, 1993), addresses several different ethnicities as they appear in television, film, and other media.

Appendix I

Sample Analyses and Exercises

Over the course of *Television*, we have suggested a variety of techniques for looking at television critically. In so doing, we have drawn examples from assorted television programs to illustrate analytical theories that remain rather abstract. The best way to make these theories concrete is to apply them to individual television programs. The acid test of any TV-analytical method is whether or not it helps you understand television.

This appendix presents samples of two analytical assignments and two practical, do-it-yourself exercises:

1. narrative analysis
2. non-narrative analysis
3. editing DIY exercise
4. sound-image interaction DIY exercise.

We encourage you to apply the analytical questions below to narrative and non-narrative programs of your own choice and see what results your analysis yields. These analytical questions can also help guide in-class discussions—providing a structure for the dissection of television programs. For sample analyses written by students, please see *Television*'s website: tvcrit.com. The DIY exercises are based on video and sound clips you can download from tvcrit.com. These clips are in the public domain and can be freely used by students and teachers alike.

One great advantage to TV analysis in the digital age is the ability to grab frames from video for illustrations. All of the frames in *Television* were captured using relatively modest Windows and Mac computers. Basically, screen shots are done by acquiring images from DVDs or video files and using image-editing software (for example, Adobe Photoshop or Irfanview) to touch up the images and store them in appropriate formats (JPEG for the Web; TIFF for printing). Then insert the images into your word-processing document to illuminate your discussion of lighting, set design, objective correlatives, performance, and so on.

You'll find a detailed tutorial on doing video screen shots at tvcrit.com/find/grabtut. If you don't have the equipment for doing your own screen shots, you may be able to find suitable images online. Wikipedia, the free encyclopedia, contains hundreds of screen shots that may be used in student analyses. For a listing of them, see tvcrit.com/find/framegrabs.

Sample Assignment: Narrative Analysis

I. Analysis of Polysemy

This is the core portion, the most important part, of your analysis. In this segment you should analyze the ideas that underpin programs.

A. What meanings, what discourses, are encoded on the text, presented for the viewer to decode? Outline the issues involved and then flesh out that skeleton with details from the program.
B. Are some meanings emphasized over others? Are some presented positively and others negatively? How? In other words, what attitude or perspective toward those meanings does the show take? Does the program seem to have a "message"? For example, if it's a program telling a story about a woman getting an abortion, does it support or condemn her decision?
C. What characterizes the preferred viewer of this program? That is, what sort of viewer does this program seem to be designed for? What potential does the program offer for alternative interpretations, for what might be called "against-the-grain readings"?

II. Analysis of Program Structure: Flow, Segmentation, and Interruption

To effectively analyze a text's polysemy you must break down its overall structure and visual/sound style. This is where you explain how a program takes a perspective toward a certain meaning or issue.

A. What recurring dilemma underpins the narrative of every episode? That is, what general dilemma is repeated every week? What is the program's continuing narrative problematic?
B. Using one or two episodes to illustrate your argument, explain how a specific enigma is played out in one narrative on a particular week/day. How does this one individual episode illustrate the general dilemma of the program? How does the narrative come to an (inconclusive) conclusion?
C. How is the program segmented? Where are the commercials inserted? How is the narrative segmented in order to fit between the commercials? (It would probably be useful for you to list the timing of all of the scenes and commercials in this episode as you prepare your analysis.)
D. What do the commercials suggest about the target audience, the preferred viewer, of the program? Does the polysemy of the commercials support or contradict the meanings of the program?

III. Analysis of Visual/Sound Style

Begin by choosing a single scene from one episode of your program. List all of the shots for that scene. Grab frames from each shot to illustrate your list. Draw a bird's-eye-view diagram of the positions of the actors, furniture, and cameras.

A. How does the mise-en-scene contribute to this episode's narrative? In other words, how do the elements of mise-en-scene communicate aspects of the story to the viewer?
B. Which mode of production was used—single-camera or multiple-camera? What advantages/disadvantages does this mode offer the program? How does it affect what the program can and cannot do?

C. How does the organization of space through editing support the narrative?
D. How do elements of music, dialogue, sound perspective, or sync help to construct the story in this episode? What do they emphasize or de-emphasize?
E. What do the credits tell the viewer about the program? Specifically, what do they indicate about the show's narrative or polysemy? What do the credits re-establish each week?

Sample Assignment: Non-Narrative Analysis

I. Analysis of Polysemy

(This portion is essentially the same as for narrative programs as both analyses seek to deconstruct television's meanings.)

A. What meanings, what discourses, are encoded on the text, presented for the viewer to decode? Outline the issues involved and then flesh out that skeleton with details from the program.
B. Are some meanings emphasized over others? Are some presented positively and others negatively? How? In other words, what attitude or perspective toward those meanings does the show take? Does the program seem to have a "message"?

II. Analysis of Non-Narrative Structure

A. Discuss which modes of representation your text utilizes. Be sure to cite specific examples illustrating the mode.
B. Explain the implied relationship between the television world and the historical world in your text.
C. Explain the implied relationship between the text and the viewer.
D. What principles dictate how the text presents its information about the historical world? In other words, how is the text organized?

III. Analysis of Visual/Sound Style

A. Begin by choosing a two-minute segment (shorter, if you choose a commercial) from your text. List all of the shots for that segment. Grab frames from each shot to illustrate your list. If it helps to understand the segment, draw a bird's-eye-view diagram of the positions of the social actors, historical world, and camera.
B. How does the historical world mise-en-scene of this segment contribute to the text's meaning? In other words, how do the elements of mise-en-scene communicate aspects of the text's meaning to the viewer?
C. Which mode of production was used—single-camera or multiple-camera? What advantages/disadvantages does this mode offer the text?
D. How does the editing support the text's meaning? In other words, why were the shots presented in the order that they were? How does that order affect meaning?
E. How, in this segment, does the manipulation of sound help to construct the text's meaning?

Sample DIY Exercise: Editing

One of the best ways to understand the power of editing is to do it yourself by re-editing something. Take, for example, a 1959 Chevrolet commercial. In two minutes, it communicates a story solely through images, with no dialogue. If one rearranges its 44 shots, one can tell different stories and communicate different meanings. On the *Television* companion website, you'll find the original commercial and a disassembled version of it—all 44 shots have been separated into individual video files. They've been bundled into zip and dmg archives for convenient downloading. Many low-cost video-editing applications—for both Mac and Windows computers—can readily import these video files and allow you to re-edit the commercial.

To give you an idea of what can be done, we've already created six variations:

1. The absolute bare minimum necessary to make the sponsor's point—that one should buy a Chevrolet. The 120-second spot has been reduced to 14 seconds.
2. The kids making faces at the mother and not at each other.
3. The girl making faces at the father, who looks, perplexed, at the mother.
4. Mostly the mother's story, with no sign of the boy.
5. The elimination of the mother.
6. The elimination of the father. (Note that what was originally a shot of the mother sitting in the stationary car is now made to look like she is driving the car while it is moving.)

All of the materials for this DIY editing exercise may be found at tvcrit. com/find/editingex.

Sample DIY Exercise: Sound and Image Interaction

An antiquated Dodge commercial provides a similar opportunity for a do-it-yourself experiment. In this exercise the impact of sound on an image is illustrated.

The original commercial is a 120-second spot for Dodge automobiles circa 1960. On the image track are shots of happy production-line workers assembling cars. The accompanying audio includes heroic music and doggerel about the virtues of auto manufacturing: "Gonna take me a press. Gonna take me some steel. Gonna take my two hands and build an automobile!" How are the meaning and impact of these images changed if the music is manipulated? Try pulling this video into a video-editing application, stripping the original music, and then applying something new. Or, in class, one can simply start audio going on a computer (YouTube is great for this) and then display the video file of the commercial. Instant sound-image interaction!

As with our editing exercise above, we've created six variations to prime the creative pump:

1. A plaintive piano piece—Erik Satie, Gymnopedie No. 1.
2. A pro-union song—Bare Knuckles, "Solidarity Forever."
3. A lively Celtic tune—Henri's Notions, "Mrs. Kelly's Chickens/Louis Waltz."
4. An aggressive classical piece—Huxford Symphony Orchestra, Tchaikovsky Symphony No. 4.
5. A singer-songwriter tune about walking—Jake Berry, "Walking."
6. A bombastic piece of "movie music"—"Invaders from Mars" (Fresh Music Library).

All of the materials for this DIY editing exercise may be found at tvcrit.com/find/soundex.

Appendix II

Mass Communication Research

In Part III we surveyed the major approaches to television research that fall into the very general category of "television studies"—focusing either on textual analysis, discourse theory, or identity theory. Before television studies came into its own in the 1990s, however, a broader category of "mass communication research" looked at television through the lens of social science. And this research tradition continues to the present day, both within academia and in the television industry. It may be useful for the television-studies student to come to a basic understanding of the mass-comm approach and how it differs from television studies because several forms of television studies actually borrow quite a bit from the mass-comm approach, although with important methodological distinctions.

Basic Principles and Presumptions

The basic principle of the scientific method underlying mass communication research is that we may understand a phenomenon through observation and experimentation—be it the pollination of tulips, the popularity of a political leader, or the effect of MTV's *Jackass* on children and teenagers.

Several presumptions underpin this approach:

1. Knowledge about an object of study—a particular phenomenon—exists within that object itself; the researcher "uncovers" it through experimentation and informed observation.
2. As a corollary to presumption #1, the researcher is objective; he or she does not *fabricate* data or take a biased attitude toward them but, rather, merely finds them in the object under study.
3. Experiments should be replicable, as in the natural sciences, i.e., if you repeat an experiment by applying the same procedure to similar objects of study, you should be able to get the same results.
4. An object of study will be understood if enough facts about it can be gathered or its fundamental essence discerned.
5. Research results should be quantifiable; that is, they should be measured and expressed in numbers and formulas (this is true of much, but not all, empirical research).
6. Theory is used to generate hypotheses or speculate about facts generated through empirical research. Also, facts or data may themselves inspire theoretical developments.

These six presumptions reflect an approach that aspires toward objectivity and a "scientific" understanding of television. Let us consider how these empirical presumptions manifest themselves in actual research projects. To do so, we've divided these projects based on two main perspectives: the *industry perspective* of individuals making and selling television products and the *academic perspective* of scholars.

The Industry Perspective

The vast majority of empirical research performed on television is commissioned by the TV industry itself. Its principal research questions are:

1. What did viewers watch, and what type of viewers watched which shows?
2. What will viewers watch in the future, and what type of viewers will be watching?

The first question is answered by corporations such as Arbitron and Nielsen Media Research, whose **ratings** are purchased by TV stations and networks so that they may use them to set advertising rates. Ratings not only calculate what was watched, but they also indicate the **demographics** of the audience: gender, age, income bracket, race, and so on. Demographics are meaningful to stations and networks because they are important to advertisers who want to target viewers to maximize the impact of their commercials—as is further discussed in Chapter 5.

The second question posed by the industry is answered through market research techniques such as focus groups, which ask a small number of viewers for their opinions of upcoming programs or commercials to predict the preferences of the viewing public at large.

There are limitations to these approaches. Nielsen and other ratings systems view programs as consumable products, without exploring their meanings. Viewers are not asked *why* they watched a show, only *if* they did. And although some market research will delve into what a program means to its test viewers, it is less concerned with meaning than with viewer preference and behavior. That is, the market researcher might show a test program to a group of viewers and ask them why and what they liked about it, but the main question remains *whether* they liked it enough to watch it regularly (and buy its advertiser's products). In one typical market research technique, known as **auditorium testing**, test viewers assembled in a room receive a device with a dial, numbered 1 to 5 (1 = like; 5 = hate; or some such scale), or keypad. Then the test audience is shown a program. While the program is running, the viewers turn their dials or press buttons to indicate their current enjoyment or annoyance level. This information is fed into a computer that can chart the responses and even superimpose them on a video recording of the program. To approach information gathering in this fashion indicates just what is crucial to market researchers: the appeal of a television product, not what it means to its viewers.

The Academic Perspective

Social-scientific studies of television conducted within academia are closely related to those within the industry. Many professors at colleges and universities hold positions as consultants to the industry. Academic empirical research is not powered by the same market demands as industrial empirical research, however. Academic researchers are relatively free to pursue "pure" knowledge about television, concerned only about review by other scholars. To understand the work they do, we need to distinguish between their *theories* and their *methods*. In this context, a theory attempts to explain how television works and what its essence is. For example, one component of a television theory might be that the medium is popular because it taps basic human desires. A method, in turn, applies a theory to actual TV programs and the people who view them. A method typically contains rules or conventions for analyzing television—testing the effectiveness of a theory against the reality of television. The principles listed above for the empirical approach typify the rules of one method. In order to understand television theories/methods and the abstract concept of the distinction between them, we will sketch a few of them here.

Empirical Research Theories

The initial academic theories of television were particularly attentive to the impact of TV upon the viewer. The **hypodermic needle** concept, which television research inherited from post-World War I studies of propaganda in newspapers and magazines, is one of the earliest of so-called **effects theories**. In this model, we are directly affected by what we see on TV as if we were injected with a hypodermic needle. Or, to borrow a metaphor from Pavlovian psychology, the bell rings and we salivate.

Subsequent theories of the mass media's influence have dismissed the hypodermic needle doctrine as simplistic **behaviorism**.[1] Television programs are more complex stimuli than Pavlov's bell, and our responses are not as predictable or crude as those of a hungry dog. Various attempts to refine the understanding of media impact have evolved: observational learning/social cognitive theory, reinforcement theory, toleration/desensitization theory, cultivation theory, vicarious catharsis theory, and so on. All of these may be gathered under the umbrella term **limited effects theories**. These theories hold that the media do indeed influence viewers and readers, but there are limitations to these effects due to the many variables involved. The hypodermic needle theory says that television will cause us to feel or behave in a certain way; limited effects theories suggest that certain television programs will cause certain viewers, under certain circumstances, to feel or behave in certain ways. The media are still seen to be affecting us, as in all effects studies, but those effects are no longer presumed to be as simple as a hypodermic needle injecting emotions or ideas into a spectator.

Not all social-scientific researchers view the spectator as passive. The **uses-and-gratifications** approach, for instance, attempts to chart the uses that we make of television and to quantify how it gratifies our needs. This style of research emphasizes the way that we employ television, seeking the emotional or intellectual purposes to which we put it. For example, Richard Kilborn studied the uses and gratifications of soap opera and came up with a list that has been summarized by Daniel Chandler:

- regular part of domestic routine and entertaining reward for work;
- launchpad for social and personal interaction;
- fulfilling individual needs: a way of choosing to be alone or of enduring enforced loneliness;
- identification and involvement with characters (perhaps cathartic);
- escapist fantasy (American supersoaps more fantastical);
- focus of debate on topical issues;
- a kind of critical game involving knowledge of the rules and conventions of the genre.[2]

Kilborn explores how viewers take the soaps and put them to use in their daily lives. He looks for ways in which they gratify viewers' needs. He does not conceive viewers as passive couch potatoes upon which soap operas have a simple and direct effect—as advocates of the hypodermic needle theory and related effects theories would. In sum, then, both conventional effects theories and uses-and-gratifications theory focus on viewers, but effects theories see them as passive entities that the medium influences, while uses-and-gratifications theory posits more active viewers who engage with texts and use them for their own needs.[3] If you review Chapter 12's discussion of ethnographic research of TV viewers, you should see several similarities to the uses-and-gratifications approach.

Empirical Research Methods

The above theories have been implemented through particular research methods. In this regard, academic research into television owes much to research in psychology and the social sciences. The methodology of those disciplines is rooted in the **scientific method**:

1. Derive a hypothesis or **research question**, based on a particular theoretical perspective informed by an established body of knowledge.
2. Test the hypothesis with replicable experimentation and/or observation ("replicable" work is research that may be repeated using the same procedure and similar objects of study).
3. Interpret the results.
   - Do they confirm/contradict the hypothesis?
   - Does this suggest a change in the body of knowledge related to this hypothesis? Has the understanding of this phenomenon progressed?

This is the ideal, at least, to which empirical researchers aspire in their analysis of television.

Content analysis is one common empirical method that is modeled on the scientific method. Its procedure is straightforward. A component of a television text (a program or genre) is selected based on the researcher's theoretical interests: e.g., violence on prime-time programs or sickness and death on soap operas.[4] The researcher observes the television text and counts the number of occurrences of this component in a program's **manifest content**: the characters and their actions, or, in the case of non-narrative television, the social actors (i.e., real people appearing in social roles on television, as discussed previously) and their actions. (Content analysis seldom addresses television's stylistic aspects.[5]) These data are then separated into categories. The counting of the data and their separation into categories are commonly known as **coding**. Once coding is completed, the researcher runs various statistical analyses of the data. Finally, the significance of the statistical results is discussed in relation to previous research.

For example, Nancy Signorielli conducted a content analysis titled "Prime-Time Violence 1993–2001: Has the Picture Really Changed?"[6] She selected 13 sets of coders from undergraduate students majoring in communication and had them watch 1,127 programs selected from the 1993 to 2001 TV seasons. Not every coder watched every program; indeed, only three-quarters of the programs were viewed by more than one coder. The students "coded for" (i.e., counted) acts of violence within a program. Additionally, they described several contextual aspects of the violence—for example, its seriousness or humorousness and whether it was intentional, immoral, and/or gratuitous. Signorielli proposed four research questions that her study hoped to answer. Principal among them was: "Has the amount of violence in samples of prime-time network programs broadcast decreased between the spring of 1993 and the fall of 2001?"[7]

In short, Signorielli's study found that violence had *not* decreased on prime-time television between 1993 and 2001. But then, it had not increased either. Each year, approximately 60 percent of the programs had some violence and that number did not change much over the years she studied. Further, there were, on average, 4.5 violent acts per program. We may well find these numbers to be interesting statistics. It may even disturb us to learn that the majority of TV programs rely on violence for their storylines and that, despite attempts by government policy-makers, media watchdog groups, and network executives, that shows no sign of improving. But the main challenge for any content analysis is establishing the significance or meaning of its statistical data. What does a 4.5 acts-per-program rate of violence signify? What does it mean? How do viewers interpret that violence? Empiricism provides effective procedures for gathering information and describing phenomena, but its method of interpretation, of suggesting what these data and descriptions mean, is less well defined.

In Signorielli's case, she interprets her results by placing them in the context of certain mass communication theories:

> From the standpoint of *observational learning/social cognitive theory*, the pervasiveness of violence on television may translate to the acceptance and/or implementation of violent solutions to problems, while from a *cultivation theory* perspective, the steady diet of television violence may increase viewers' conceptions of a mean world and/or alienation and gloom [emphasis added].[8]

Note that this specific study does *not* prove that violence causes viewers to accept "violent solutions to problems" or increase their "conceptions of a mean world." Strictly speaking, the only thing the study has proved is that there are 4.5 acts of violence per program and that that has remained stable for eight years. The researcher must rely upon mass communication theories to explain what that number means and why it's significant.

There is a crucial methodological leap here from *description* to *interpretation*. It might be better understood if we think of an example outside of the realm of television. Let's say researchers stand on a street corner in Tuscaloosa, Alabama, and "code" the passing cars for their color. In 10 hours, they count 45 crimson cars out of 75 total (a slow day on that street corner). This results in a crimson-car rate of 60 percent of total cars or 4.5 crimson cars per hour (CCPH). These data accurately *describe* what the researchers saw on that day, but for this study to have any import the researchers must now *interpret* those data. Just as Signorielli did with her data, we must speculate about the meaning of these numbers. What does 4.5 CCPH signify? Using Signorielli's language, we could argue:

> From the standpoint of observational learning/social cognitive theory, the pervasiveness of crimson-colored cars may translate to car buyers accepting the validity of that color and purchasing crimson cars for themselves. That is, if we see crimson cars on the street, we will be more likely to buy them ourselves.
>
> From a cultivation theory perspective, 4.5 CCPH may increase traffic watchers' belief that crimson is a color in widespread use throughout Tuscaloosa, the home of the University of Alabama Crimson Tide. They will expect that most Tuscaloosa residents wear crimson clothing, live in crimson houses, and stroll on crimson sidewalks. (Subsequent studies might find that these expectations are true on football game days.)

But these are not the only interpretations one might garner from these data. One could also argue:

- Crimson cars attract sexual partners.
- Crimson resembles blood and crimson cars symbolize danger and excitement.
- 60 percent of Tuscaloosa drivers support the Crimson Tide.
- Crimson cars appear less dirty than lighter cars and so drivers choose them over other lighter cars.
- Tuscaloosa car dealerships prefer to sell crimson cars and keep more of them in stock.

Common sense tells us that some of these interpretations are more plausible than others and some have the weight of theory behind them, but that is not the point. The point is that content-analysis researchers must shift gears from description to interpretation when they stop describing their data and begin speculating on its meaning. In so doing, they leave the pure scientific method behind. Science demands that results can be replicated, that different researchers will always come to the same conclusions. As we have illustrated with our crimson car study, the counting of cars could be replicated and different researchers would come to the same numbers if they replicated our study, but the interpretation of the meaning of 4.5 CCPH is not replicable and could lead to numerous different conclusions.

We have poked a bit of fun at content analysis with this fake study, but if we look more seriously at Signorielli's conclusions we can see how different conclusions could be derived from her data. Invoking cultivation theory, she contends that the "steady diet of television violence" makes viewers increasingly gloomy and alienated. But we could posit the reverse interpretation. We could suggest that today's viewers are increasingly gloomy and alienated because of the plummeting value of a worker's salary, the terrorist attacks in the U.S. and the loss of personal freedoms mandated by the U.S. Patriot Act, and the global unrest in places like Iraq and Afghanistan; and that viewers' increased despondency *causes* them to stay home more, to watch more television, and to desire to view more violent acts. It could be argued that U.S. television networks are merely responding to this desire for violence.

Thus, Signorielli employs cultivation theory to posit that TV causes viewers to become more alienated. Our interpretation of the data posits the reverse—that already alienated viewers cause television to respond with violent imagery. Which is correct? Perhaps both, in parts, or neither. Further research could possibly lend credence to one or the other. But the fact that a difference of opinion is even possible violates the scientific method's fundamental principle of reproducible results. Consequently, content analysis is not pure science, not pure empirical method. But this is not a weakness in this method—unless, of course, you are a hardcore scientist. The necessity for content analyses and other empirical analyses of television to interpret their results requires their researchers to incorporate theoretical or *critical* methods into their studies. Thus, content analysis illustrates how "pure" social science and "pure" critical studies (if such things could possibly exist in television analyses) may blend together to construct useful knowledge about television. In content analysis we see a self-proclaimed empirical method that must make use of critical tools.

Notes

1 Essentially, behaviorists think that human and animal behavior may be best explained in terms of physical stimulation and physical response instead of assuming psychological processes. For example, dogs hear a bell (a physical stimulus) and they start to salivate (a physical response). We don't need to know what the dog is thinking in order to understand this response. Similarly, the hypodermic needle theory presumes that television viewers will see/hear something on television (physical stimulation) and respond with certain behaviors (e.g., going to the store and buying a product) without thinking about it.
2 Daniel Chandler, *Why Do People Watch Television?*, September 18, 1995, tvcrit.com/find/watchtv. Chandler summarizes Richard Kilborn, *Television Soaps* (London: Batsford, 1992).
3 David Gauntlett mounts a pointed attack on these approaches when he lists "Ten Things Wrong With the Media 'Effects' Model," in *Approaches to Audiences: A Reader*, Roger Dickinson, Ramaswani Harindranath, and Olga Linné, eds. (London: Arnold, 1998). Available online at tvcrit.com/find/tenthings, accessed July 11, 2017.
4 Nancy Signorielli, "Prime-Time Violence 1993-2001: Has the Picture Really Changed?" *Journal of Broadcasting and Electronic Media* 47, no. 1 (March 2003), 36-57; Mary Cassata, Thomas Skill, and Samuel O. Boadu, "Life and Death in the Daytime Television Serial: A Content Analysis," in *Life on Daytime Television: Tuning-in American Serial Drama*, Mary Cassata and Thomas Skill, eds. (Norwood, NJ: Ablex, 1983), 23-36. The latter is critiqued in Robert C. Allen, *Speaking of Soap Operas* (Chapel Hill: University of North Carolina Press, 1985), 36-38.

5 One content analysis that *does* account for style (here called "form") is Maria Elizabeth Grabe, Shuhua Zhou, and Brooke Barnett, "Explicating Sensationalism in Television News: Content and the Bells and Whistles of Form," *Journal of Broadcasting & Electronic Media* 45, no. 4 (Fall 2001), 635–55.
6 Signorielli.
7 Ibid., 39. The other three questions related to the context of the violence. In order to keep this example simple, we will only examine her first research question.
8 Ibid., 54.

Further Readings

Denis McQuail, *McQuail's Mass Communication Theory*, 6th ed. (Thousand Oaks, CA: Sage, 2010), is a frequently cited textbook in this area. David Gauntlett takes a highly critical view of effects research in "Ten Things Wrong With the Media 'Effects' Model," in Roger Dickinson, Ramaswani Harindranath, and Olga Linné, eds., *Approaches to Audiences: A Reader* (London: Arnold, 1998)—available online at tvcrit.com/find/tenthings. Robert C. Allen looks specifically at the mass-comm research of television in *Speaking of Soap Operas* (Chapel Hill: University of North Carolina Press, 1985); and *Channels of Discourse, Reassembled* (Chapel Hill: University of North Carolina Press, 1992).

GLOSSARY

Originally Compiled by Rosemary McMahill

180° rule An editing principle of the *continuity (or 180°) system*, which dictates that cameras remain on one side of the *axis of action* in order to preserve the scene's spatial continuity and *screen direction*.

180° system See *continuity system*.

A, B, and C cameras The labeling of cameras on a *multiple-camera production*. Even a so-called *single-camera production* will often have A and B cameras.

aca-fans Academic researchers who are also media fans themselves.

act (segment) A portion or segment of the narrative presented between commercial breaks. Consists of one or more *scenes*.

actor movement Typically referred to by the theatrical term *blocking*.

actualities Events from the *historical world* used in news and sports programs.

ad card Short credit for music used in a TV program. Paid for by a record label or in exchange for the reduction of its license fee.

additive color In video, the combination of red, green, and blue *phosphors* to generate all other colors.

ADR See *automatic dialogue replacement*.

Advanced Television Systems Committee (ATSC) Formed in the early 1990s to set standards for U.S. digital television, including HDTV.

aesthetic A philosophy of the beautiful; criteria that define art (or television) as good or bad. Also used to refer to determining factors of television that are neither technological nor economic.

agency In the context of video gaming, the user's control over the game. As users make choices, interact with on-screen characters, and move through the virtual spaces of games, they become agents of their own narrative destinations.

ambient sound Background sounds of a particular room or location.

analog sound An electronic replica of a sound wave on audio tape or videotape; the sound wave is converted into an electronic copy or analog. This type of sound recording has mostly been replaced by *digital sound* recording. Vinyl albums and audio cassettes create sound through an analog process; compact discs, DVDs, and digital audio tape (DAT) store sound digitally.

anamorphic A widescreen film process (under such trademark names as CinemaScope and Panavision) used to create an image wider than conventional television's. The *aspect ratio* of most films made with anamorphic lenses today is 1:2.40 (modified slightly from 1:2.35, which was the standard in the 1950s), while the conventional, *standard-definition television* image's aspect ratio is 1:1.33.

ancillary markets Venues where films can be shown after their initial theatrical run—many of which are on TV. The order of release, although this is currently changing, has long been: home video, premium cable, network television, nonpremium cable, and television syndication.

antagonist Character and/or situation that hinders the protagonist from achieving his or her goal(s).

anti-naturalistic performance Performance style in which the viewer is kept aware that the actor is pretending to be a character.

aperture In terms of a narrative: a conclusion with an ambiguous ending, and/or without resolution, without answering its questions. The opposite of *closure*. In terms of video and film cameras: the opening through which light passes.

arcing A term used in television studio production to refer to the semicircular sideways movement of the camera.

aristocracy In Marxism, the most elite social class—consisting of individuals who do not work and hold power through inheritance: kings, queens, princes, princesses, and so on. According to Marx's analysis of history, the aristocracy controlled European countries until the *bourgeoisie*'s rise to power in the decades after the Renaissance.

ASL See *average shot length*.

aspect ratio The ratio of height to width of a camera screen. The conventional ratio for television has been 1:1.33 (or 3:4), but *high-definition* television introduced a widescreen TV ratio of 1:1.78 (or 9:16).

ATSC See *Advanced Television Systems Committee*.

audio post *Post-production* sound editing and mixing.

auditorium testing A market-research process. Viewers are assembled in an auditorium, shown a TV program or commercial, and asked to evaluate it through a handheld keypad or dial.

augmented reality Video games and other software that add visual/sound elements to the world around us.

auteur theory Posits that a director is the author of a film/television program in the same manner that a writer is the author of a novel. The director is seen as injecting his/her personal artistic vision into a film/television program, and, over time, certain stylistic and thematic tendencies are discernible in the body of the director's work.

automatic dialogue replacement (**ADR**) The replacement of lines of dialogue during post-production. Also known as automated dialogue replacement or looping.

average shot length (**ASL**) Statistical data that indicate the overall pacing of a television show's editing.

axis of action In the *continuity (or 180°) system*, the line of action around which the space of the scene is oriented.

back light In the *three-point lighting* system, the source of illumination placed behind and above the actor. Its main function is to cast light on the actor's head and shoulders, creating an outline of light around the actor to distinguish him or her from the background.

balance In video and film, the blending of three colors (red, green, and blue in video; yellow, magenta, and cyan in film) to produce a spectrum of colors. Different video processes and film stocks favor some colors over others, resulting in various types of color balance.

base In film production terms, the celluloid backing of a piece of film to which the *emulsion* adheres. In Marxist terms, a society's economic system, upon which is built its *superstructure*.

BD See *Blu-ray disc*.

behaviorism The study of human and animal behavior that avoids making presumptions about human/animal thought processes.

binge-watching Viewing several episodes of a TV show at one sitting.

blocking The actor's movement around a set; the director's incorporation of the actor into the *mise-en-scene*.

blogosphere All blogs taken as a whole. That is, the interconnected *public sphere* of online journals and opinion sites.

Blu-ray disc (**BD**) An optical-disc format for distributing television programs and movies in *high-definition*. It may include interactive "bonus" features.

blue screens On a newsroom set, areas of the background that are blue (or green), onto which live images or maps are substituted through the *chroma key* process.

bokeh The aesthetic appearance of the out-of-focus portion of a photographic image.

boom operator The sound technician who physically operates the *overhead boom microphone*.

bourgeoisie In Marxist terms, the middle class; owners of the *means of production* and employers of the *proletariat*.

brand parity In the context of advertising, when all products are essentially the same. Contrast with a product's *unique selling proposition*.

Brechtian performance *Anti-naturalistic*, confrontational performance style based in the theories of German playwright Bertolt Brecht. He demanded that the viewer constantly be made aware of the fact that he or she is watching a play and that he or she should be distanced from the characters (see *distanciation*).

brightness (luminance) In the context of television's image quality, how bright or dark a color is.

broadcast standards and practices (BSP) The units within TV networks that make sure offensive material is not broadcast—TV's internal censors.

BSPSee *broadcast standards and practices*.

bug A small network or station logo superimposed in a corner of the frame.

camera obscura A darkened chamber with a hole in one wall through which light enters, creating an image of the outdoors on the opposite wall. It was the earliest form of a "camera" and is where the name derives from.

camera operator The person who actually handles the film or video camera.

cardioid microphone A *unidirectional* microphone with most of its sensitivity aimed toward the front and a *pickup pattern* that resembles an inverted heart.

cathode ray tube (CRT) A television picture tube. The cathode ray excites the *pixels* to create the video image.

cause-effect chain In narrative structure, the way one event leads to (causes) another and is the result (effect) of a previous event.

CGI See *computer-generated imagery*.

chiaroscuro A *low-key lighting* style, usually in reference to theatrical productions or the dark paintings of Rembrandt.

chroma See *chrominance*.

chroma key An electronic special effects process, specific to video, making a single color (usually blue or green) transparent so that one image may be inserted into another—as in weather maps with a forecaster superimposed over them.

chrominance The level of *saturation* of a color; the color's purity, how much or little grayness is mixed with it.

CinemaScope A *widescreen, anamorphic* film process with an aspect ratio of 2.35 to 1.

cinematographer The person overseeing all aspects of the film image—including lighting and the operation of the camera.

cinematography The process of making a film image, and the characteristics of the film image.

classical Hollywood cinema (Hollywood classicism) A conventional style of filmmaking with a particular model of narrative structure, editing technique, mise-en-scene, dialogue, music, etc. Narrative is presented in a clear cause-and-effect chain, with definite *closure*.

classical period In the history of theatrical cinema, the 1920s to 1950s when the Hollywood studio system of film production held total power and evolved the classical style of filmmaking. In a genre's evolutionary pattern, the stage during which thematics, narrative structure, and audial/visual style are solidified into firm conventions, a recognizable cohesive unit.

close-miking The positioning of a microphone very close to the performer's mouth—often used by radio and TV announcers.

close-up (CU) A framing that presents a close view of an object or person—filling the frame and separating it or her or him from the surroundings. Conventionally, a TV close-up of a person is from the shoulders or neck up.

closure Occurs when enigmas opened at the beginning of a program and throughout are resolved; all of the narrative's questions are answered. The opposite of *aperture*.

code A set of rules; an historically and/or culturally based set of conventions.

coding In *content analysis*, the process of putting data into categories.

collective intelligence Pierre Lévy's concept of group-authored knowledge, distributed through online services such as Wikipedia.

color announcer A type of television sports announcer; often he or she is a former athlete and/or coach with first-hand expertise.

compositing The *post-production* combination of two or more video/film/digital sources in a single image.

compression artifacts Visible blocks or other degradation of the image caused by squeezing digital video in order to reduce the size of the signal. For example, video that has been compressed in order to be quickly downloaded will often have such artifacts.

computer-generated imagery (CGI) Images that are created digitally, usually through computer modeling with *wireframe* objects.

content analysis An *empirical* method of analysis that selects a specific textual component and counts and codes the number of occurrences of this component into a statistical form, resulting in quantifiable data that usually cannot be interpreted beyond the data itself.

continuity editing (**invisible editing**) A style of editing that creates a continuity of space and time out of the fragments of scenes contained in individual shots; the shots are arranged to support the progression of the story, thus the editing technique does not call attention to itself.

continuity person The person in a production responsible for maintaining consistency in all details from one shot to the next, including action, lighting, props, and costumes.

continuity system (**180° system**) Set of editing conventions that evolved from Hollywood classicism; shots are arranged so that the viewer always has a clear sense of where the characters are and when the shot is occurring.

copyright The exclusive legal rights to perform or sell a song, book, script, photograph, etc. To use copyrighted material (e.g., a piece of music) in a TV program, a fee or *royalty* must be paid the copyright holder. If there is no copyright the material may be used for free and is said to be in the *public domain*.

cost per mil (**CPM**) The advertising rate charged to TV sponsors, which is quantified per thousand viewers. "Mil" equals "thousand," from the Latin word *mille*. Thus, the CPM is the cost per thousand viewers.

CPM See *cost per mil*.

crabbing See *trucking*.

craft practices The standardized methods for making television that are employed by its various craftsmen and craftswomen—e.g., set designers, cinematographers, sound designers, and so on.

craning A movement deriving its name from the mechanical crane on which a camera may be placed. A crane shot is one in which the entire camera, mounted on a crane, is swept upward or downward.

critical studies An analytical approach that seeks to understand the meanings, aesthetics, and significance of a medium. Critical studies is rooted in analytical methods applied to literature, art, history, economics, political science, the cinema, and the theater.

cross-fade Akin to a *dissolve*, one sound fades out while the other fades in, resulting in a brief overlap.

CRT See *cathode ray tube*.

CU See *close-up*.

cultural studies A critical approach that argues that viewers decode television texts based on their specific ideological position in society; it looks at the interaction between the ideological *discourses* of the text and those of the viewer and often uses the research method of *ethnography* to investigate this interaction.

data compression The reduction in size of any digital source.

DAW See *digital audio workstation*.

decoding In cultural studies, the reader/viewer's interpretation of a text that has been *encoded* with meaning by its creators.

deep focus When all planes (foreground, middle-ground, and background) of an image are in *focus*.

deep space blocking A type of blocking associated with single-camera productions, particularly those shot on *location*. The depth of the "set" is emphasized by the ability of one actor to be positioned near the camera and another far away; the actors may move toward one another or participate in independent actions.

definition In terms of the image quality of film and television, definition refers to the capability of the visual medium to separate and depict detail. Sometimes termed resolution.

demographics The characteristics of an audience, usually broken down in terms of age, gender, income, race, etc.; used with *ratings* to set advertising rates.

depth of field The range in front of and behind the *focus distance* that is also in focus.

designated market area (**DMA**) Cohesive metropolitan areas that *ratings* companies use to define television markets.

dialogue Speech among characters that does not usually address the viewer. Also, a type of interview in which the voices of the interviewer and the interviewee are both heard, and both persons may be visible on camera.

diaspora The dispersed, scattered community of people of a country, race, religion, or ethnicity outside of their homeland.

diegesis The world in which the narrative is set. In other words, the world fictional characters inhabit.

diegetic sound *Dialogue*, music, and sound effects that occur in the *diegetic space* of the television program, i.e., sound that is part of the characters' world.

diegetic space The physical world in which the narrative action of the television program takes place.

digital audio workstation (DAW) A computer-based system for digitally editing sound.

digital cinema Movie theaters in which digital video is projected instead of film.

digital endemic A classification for media companies built on digital distribution from the very beginning; for example, Facebook, Twitter.

digital sound An audio recording that converts sound into numbers through *sampling*. Starting in the 1980s, digital sound recordings (e.g., CDs and MP3s) have come to replace *analog sound* recordings (e.g., vinyl albums and audio cassettes).

digital television (DTV) Television broadcast in a digital format—in contrast to analog formats such as *NTSC* and PAL. Permits *HDTV*, *multicasting*, and *enhanced TV*.

digital video (DV) Any video format that relies on digital technology for recording and/or editing. For example, video recorded with a digital camera or edited on a *nonlinear editing* system.

digital video effects (DVE) Special effects created with digital, computer-based technology. Compare with *electronic effects*.

direct to disk A form of digital video recording where the video is stored on a hard disk.

director A person who is in charge of a television show, on the set or in a control booth, during the actual production process.

discourse Socially based belief structures. The viewer brings discourses to the *reading* of the television *text*, which contains discourses that match or clash with the viewer's.

dissolve A special effect wherein simultaneously one shot fades out as the next fades in, so that the two images briefly overlap. Often used to shift from one scene to the next.

distanciation A technique of *Brechtian performance* style wherein the actor retains the sense of him/herself as an actor; thus the viewer and actor alike are distanced from the character rather than identifying with it.

DMA See *designated market area*.

docudrama or docusoap A predominantly fictional program that has some basis in a real-life incident, often a sensational one.

dolly A wheeled camera support that permits a rolling camera movement. In conventional television usage, dollying refers to forward or backward movement and *trucking* (which is accomplished with a dolly) refers to sideways movement.

drone (camera mount) Remote-controlled aerial drones are mounted with cameras to achieve camera movements formerly created with cranes and aircraft.

DTV See *digital television*.

dubbing The replacement of one voice for another during post-production.

DV See *digital video*.

DVD An optical-disc format for distributing television programs and movies that may include interactive "bonus" features. There's no consensus on what "DVD" stands for, but when it was introduced to the consumer market in 1997 (U.S.) it was known variously as the "digital video disc" and the "digital versatile disc."

DVE See *digital video effects*.

dynamic range A range of sounds from soft to loud. A measurement of the limits of microphones, recording and playback machines, and other audio equipment.

Editech The first electronic editing system for videotape—invented and marketed by Ampex.

effects theory A type of communication theory (e.g., *hypodermic needle theory*) that proposes that because viewers are passive television directly affects them.

electron gun A mechanical device located in the rear of a television's picture tube that fires an electron beam at the *pixels*, scanning line-by-line across the lines of the television image, causing the pixels to glow and create the television image.

electronic effects Special effects (including *fades*, *dissolves*, and *keying*) created on video using an analog special effects generator. Compare with *digital video effects* (*DVE*).

electronic news gathering (ENG) The video recording of news events or *actualities*.

electronic press kit (EPK) A digital package of text, photographs, and video distributed by studios/networks to promote television programs.

emotional memory Technique of *Method* acting wherein the actor draws upon memories of previous emotions that match the emotions of the character.

empiricism A theoretical approach that advocates the understanding of a problem through systematic and controlled observation/experimentation, with research results measured and expressed in numbers and formulas.

emulsion The mixture of photosensitive chemicals with a gelatin medium attached to the *base* of a piece of film.

encoding In cultural studies, the creation of meaning within a text by a cultural institution such as the television industry. Readers/viewers may *decode* these preferred meanings when exposed to texts, or they may take a position opposing them.

ENG See *electronic news gathering*.

enhanced TV In *digital TV*, the addition of interactive functions to standard TV programs.

epic theater *Brechtian* theory of theatrical presentation in which the viewer is alienated from the character.

EPK See *electronic press kit*.

essentialism In terms of *race* or *gender*, the belief that distinct physical traits can be used to define categories—more so than culturally racialized/gendered traits.

establishing shot A long shot that positions the character within his or her environment and helps to establish the setting.

ethnography/ethnographic method A research method associated with *cultural studies* and anthropology that researches television consumers and producers, commonly through interviews and *participant observation*. The goal of an ethnography is to generate detailed *thick descriptions* and discursive analysis of individuals' experiences, values, and opinions.

expository mode *Mode* of television that presents an argument about the *historical world*; the "facts" of that world are assertively or even aggressively selected and organized and presented to the viewer in a direct address.

exterior scenes Scenes set outdoors, often in particular *location settings*.

extreme close-up (XCU) A framing that presents a view closer than a conventional close-up—e.g., a shot of an eye that fills the entire screen.

extreme long shot (XLS) A framing that presents a distant view of an object or person—e.g., an aerial shot of a car on a street.

eyeline match An editing principle of the *continuity system* that begins with a shot of a character looking in a specific direction, then cuts to a second shot that shows the area toward which the character was looking.

fade out/fade in A special effect often used for scene-to-scene transition. In a fade out the image darkens until the screen is black. In a fade in, the image starts out black and then gradually becomes visible.

false consciousness In Marxist terms, a counterfeit image of the world determined by one's social class.

fan studies The study of viewers who engage in *textual poaching* and their participatory culture.

feminism A critical approach that concentrates on gender *discourse*, the manner in which the male-female relationship is portrayed, and the power structure inherent in it.

fill light In the *three-point lighting* system, a source of illumination used to fill the shadows created by the *key light*. It is directed obliquely toward the actor from the opposite side of the key light, at approximately the same height (or a little lower), and is generally half as bright as the key light.

film stock The specific type of film used to record images.

filter In lighting, a colored *gel* placed in front of a light source. In cinematography or videography, an optical device (colored, polarized, etc.) attached to the lens.

fine grain A type of film stock in which the *grain* is smaller, resulting in a higher image *definition*.

flashback A disruption of the chronological presentation of events in which an event from the past is presented in a program's present. See *flashforward*.

flashforward A disruption of the chronological presentation of events in which an event from the future is presented in a program's present. See *flashback*.

flow Television's sequence of programs, commercials, news breaks, and so on. The overall flow of television is segmented into small parcels, which often bear little logical connection to one another.

focal length The distance from the lens's optical center to its *focal point*, usually measured in millimeters. There are three conventional types of focal length: *wide angle*, *normal*, and *telephoto*.

focal plane The plane within a film camera where the light strikes the film.
focal point In a camera lens, that spot where the light rays, bent by the lens, converge before expanding again and striking the film or electronic pickup at the focal plane.
focus The adjustment of the camera lens so that the image is sharp and clear.
focus distance The distance from the camera to the object being *focused* on.
Foley A *post-production* process wherein *sound effects* are fabricated for a filmed/videotaped scene while the Foley artist watches a shot projected on a screen.
4K video A video format that is currently the highest resolution found on TV sets manufactured for home use—relying on roughly 4,000 (4K) lines of resolution. It is a higher definition than so-called *high-definition television*.
format In film, refers to the film width itself and is measured in millimeters (e.g., super-8, 16mm, and 35mm). In videotape, the combination of the width of the tape, measured in inches, (e.g., 1/2", 3/4", and 1") and the process used to store the images on tape (e.g., VHS, Beta).
framing Determines what the viewer can and cannot see due to the manipulation of the camera frame (the edge of the image).
frequency response A range of sound frequencies from low to high. A measurement of the limits of microphones, recording and playback machines, and other audio equipment.
function In narrative study, a single action or character attribute. Based in Russian Formalism and the work of Vladimir Propp.
gel A piece of plastic or gelatin placed in front of a light source to change its color.
gender, gendered The ideologically loaded, socially determined construction of masculinity and femininity. Gender is not determined by anatomy, hormones, or DNA but, rather, by the characteristics, the *subject* positions, that society labels as masculine and feminine. It may be used as an adjective (gendered) to refer to the process by which a phenomenon is identified as masculine or feminine.
gender identity A container of society's *discourse*-based ideas of what it means to be a woman or a man.
genre Groupings of television programs defined by their narrative structure, thematic content, and style of sound and image.
globalization The spread (some would say imposition) of the developed world's values upon the developing world. Television is often accused of this form of cultural imperialism as programs from the U.S. and UK are broadcast in countries of low-economic status.
grain The silver halide crystals suspended in the *emulsion* of a piece of film. When struck by light and chemically processed, these crystals change color, resulting in the film image. The smaller the grain, the higher the *definition* of the image (i.e., the sharper the image).
handheld A technique in which the camera is held by the camera operator, rather than fixed to a camera mount such as a tripod or *dolly*.
hard light Direct, undiffused light; the result is the casting of harsh, distinct shadows.
hard news Refers to news stories that examine events that affect society as a whole (e.g., national politics and international relations).
HDTV See *high-definition television*.
hegemony When ruling-class values become naturalized so that persons not in the ruling class come to accept them as their own—even if they do not serve their best interests. The concept originated in the work of Marxist theorist Antonio Gramsci.
high angle A shot in which the camera is placed higher than the filmed actor or object, so that the camera looks down on the actor or object.
high-definition television (HDTV) A broadcast technology in which the number of *scan lines* of the video image is increased and the size of the *pixels* decreased—resulting in a clearer, better *defined* image.
high-key lighting A lighting style in which the ratio in intensity of *key light* to *fill light* is small. The result is an evenly lit set, with a low contrast between the bright and dark areas of the set.
historical reality See *historical world*.
historical world (historical reality) The reality that is processed, selected, ordered, and interpreted by nonfiction television programs.
Hollywood classicism See *classical Hollywood cinema*.
households using television (HUT) The number of homes with television sets turned on at a particular time. A statistic used by ratings companies such as Nielsen.
hue A specific color from within the visible spectrum of white light, e.g., red, green, blue.

HUT See *households using television*.
hypercardioid microphone A highly *unidirectional microphone* for which the *pickup pattern* is narrower than that of a *cardioid microphone*. So-called shotgun microphones have a hypercardioid pattern.
hypodermic needle theory An *effects theory* that purports that the viewer is passive and directly and immediately affected by what he/she sees on television.
icon Generally speaking, an object that represents a theme or an aspect of the character or the like. In the specific context of *semiotics*, a type of *sign* wherein the *signifier* physically resembles the *signified*. For example, a photograph (*signifier*) is a mechanical reproduction of what is photographed (*signified*).
iconography The objects that signify character and themes of the narrative.
ident In UK broadcasting, short announcements that identify a channel and promote upcoming programs.
ideological analysis An area of *television studies* concerned with class and gender representation that studies society's competing *discourses* and the position of the individual within society.
ideology A society's system of beliefs about the world. In Marxism, the dominant ideology is propagated and supported by the society's ruling class.
illusion of depth The ability of the two-dimensional television image to create an illusion whereby space seems to recede into the image. A *telephoto lens* creates a small illusion of depth and a *wide-angle lens* creates a large one.
improvisation Technique of *Method* acting style used mostly in rehearsal; the actor puts him/herself into the mind of the character, places the character into imagined situations, and proceeds to invent dialogue and action.
in medias res Latin term for beginning a story in the middle of the action.
index See *indexical sign*.
indexical sign (index) In *semiotics*, a type of *sign* in which the *signifier* is physically caused by the *signified*. For example, where there is smoke, there is fire. Thus the *signifier* (smoke) is physically caused by the *signified* (fire).
infrastructure See the Marxist definition of *base*.
intellectual property Anything that may be copyrighted—music, scripts, books, television programs, and so on.
interactivity The viewers' or users' interactions with what they see on television or computer screens and their ability to affect on-screen elements. Video games have a very high level of interactivity, while network-era television had hardly any interactivity at all.
interior scenes Scenes set inside, in particular on *studio sets*, though also including location interiors.
intertextuality The intertextual, self-reflexive quality—as when one television *text* (e.g., a commercial) refers to another (e.g., a program or commercial) or to other types of *media texts*.
invisible editing See *continuity editing*.
jump cut An editing technique wherein one shot does not match the preceding shot, resulting in a disruptive gap in space and/or time.
key light In the *three-point lighting* system, the main source of illumination and the most intense light on the set. It is normally positioned above the actor's head and several feet in front of him or her.
keying An special effects process, specific to video, in which an image or text is inserted into another image. See *chroma key*.
kinescope A film copy of a television program made by aiming the film camera at a television screen. Used during the early years of television (before videotape and digital recordings) to record programs that were broadcast live.
laugh track A soundtrack of pre-recorded laughter, usually added in the post-production process to a comedy program with no studio audience.
lavaliere microphone A small microphone often clipped to a performer's tie or shirt.
lead In news stories, the reporter's opening comments—designed to capture viewer attention.
legacy media Media industries operating prior to the arrival of digital distribution of media.
letterbox A process by which a *widescreen* film is presented on video. The top and bottom of the video frame are blackened, and the *widescreen* film frame is reduced to fit into this frame-within-the-video-frame. Also used to present *high-definition video* on conventional TV sets.
license fee In the UK, the annual payment made by all television-set owners that funds the British Broadcasting Corporation (BBC).

lighting color Light may be "colored" by placing a filter or gelatin in front of a light source.

lighting diffusion The hardness or softness of a light source. *Hard light* casts a sharp, definite shadow.

lighting direction The positioning of lights relative to the object being shot. The norm for lighting direction is *three-point lighting*.

lighting intensity The power of a light source. Regarding the relative intensity of lighting sources, see *three-point lighting*.

lighting plot A diagram of the lights to be used on a set.

limited effects theory A type of communication theory (e.g., social learning theory, vicarious catharsis theory) that regards media as having conditional influences on the viewer; due to intervening variables, the effects of media on the viewer are limited.

line cut An edited version of a multiple-camera program that is created while the program is being recorded.

linear perspective A method of drawing or painting that converts the three dimensions of reality into two dimensions. Originally developed during the European Renaissance, it formed the foundation for how lenses represent a visual field.

lip sync Synchronizing a performance to recorded speech or music; most frequently found in music videos, wherein the performers mouth the words to the pre-recorded song while they are filmed or videotaped.

live-on-tape A video production that is recorded live, with most of the editing done while the scenes transpire (rather than in *post-production*).

location settings Pre-existing settings that are chosen as backgrounds for television programs.

long shot (LS) A framing that presents entire objects or persons—situating them in a setting.

loudness (volume) How loud or soft a sound is. See *dynamic range*.

low angle A shot in which the camera is lower than the filmed object; thus the camera looks up at the actor/object.

low-definition television When the resolution or *definition* of an image is less than *standard definition*, resulting in a noticeably blurry, distorted image.

low-key lighting A lighting style wherein the *key light* is so much more intense than the *fill light* that there is a high contrast between bright and dark areas. The bright areas are especially bright and the dark areas are very dark.

LS See *long shot*.

luminance The *brightness* or darkness of a color. See *chrominance* and *saturation*.

M and E track See *music and effects track*.

magnetic tape A ribbon of plastic with a coating on it that is sensitive to magnetic impulses created by electricity. In *analog* technology, these magnetic impulses are modulated on the tape in a fashion parallel to the sound wave's modulation. In *digital* technology, magnetic tape is used to record sounds encoded as a string of numbers that will later be converted into sound.

manifest content In a *content analysis* of a television text, the characters and their actions.

masking A non-*anamorphic widescreen* film process. In masked films, blackened horizontal bands are placed across the top and bottom of a 1:1.33 frame, resulting in a wider *aspect ratio* of 1:1.85.

mass communication research An analytical approach that seeks to understand the effects of a medium on individuals and society. Mass-comm research is rooted in analytical methods employed by psychology, sociology, and anthropology.

master rights The right to use a piece of music in a TV program—provided by *performing rights organizations* to *music supervisors*.

master use license Permission from a song's performers for its use in a TV program. See *music clearance* and *synchronization license*.

match cut An editing principle of the *continuity system* that maintains continuity by fitting ("matching") the space and time of one shot to that of the preceding shot.

match-on-action An editing technique of the *continuity system* wherein a cut is placed in the midst of an action, so that the action from one shot continues to the next.

MCU See *medium close-up*.

means of production Marx's term for the locations (factories and the like) at which goods are produced and men and women labor.

mechanical effects Special effects created on the set using mechanical and/or pyrotechnic devices.

media text Any item in the mass media (e.g., a TV commercial or program, film, magazine, interview, public appearance, etc.).

medium close-up (MCU) A framing in between *medium shot* and *close-up*.

medium long shot (MLS) A framing in between *long shot* and *medium shot*.

medium shot (MS) A framing that presents a moderately close view of an object or person. Conventionally, a TV medium shot of a person is from the thighs or knees up. Two common types of medium shots are the *two shot* and the *three shot*.

Method *Naturalistic performance* style that encourages the actor to become the character, at which point the gestures/dialects necessary for the performance will emerge organically; approaches used to achieve this union between actor and character are *emotional memory*, *sense memory*, and *improvisation*.

microphone (mike) Device used to record sound. The *pickup pattern* of a microphone may be *omnidirectional* or *cardioid*. See also *lavaliere microphone* and *hypercardioid microphone*.

mike See *microphone*.

mise-en-scene The staging of the action for the camera. All of the physical objects in front of the camera and the arrangement of those objects by the director. The organization of setting, costuming, lighting, and actor movement.

mixer A machine that blends various sound sources.

MLS See *medium long shot*.

mode of production An aesthetic style of shooting that relies upon a particular technology and is governed by a certain economic system. Television's two principal modes of production are single-camera and multiple-camera.

mode of representation Manner in which a non-narrative television program depicts *historical reality* and addresses itself to the viewer about that version of reality; modes include *expository*, *interactive*, *observational* and *reflexive*.

motion-capture device A system by which the movement of three-dimensional objects or humans is traced by a computer.

motivation In narrative structure, a catalyst that starts the story's progression—a reason for the story to begin (usually a character's lack or desire).

Movie of the Week See *MOW*.

MOW (Movie of the Week) Industry shorthand for any film produced specifically for television and not shown initially in theaters.

MS See *medium shot*.

multicasting In *digital TV*, individual broadcast stations may simultaneously transmit four or more programs.

multiple-camera production, multi-camera production A *mode of production* unique to television wherein two or more cameras are used to record the scene, enabling simultaneous and/or *post-production* editing. The mode used in most sitcoms and all soap operas, game shows, sports programs, and newscasts.

multi-track tape recorder Used in the sound editing process, this recorder holds a tape that is electronically divided into four (or many more) separate *tracks*. On each is a sound category (dialogue, music, effects) separated from the others, allowing the sound editor to manipulate individual soundtracks before producing a finished soundtrack.

music and effects track (M and E track) A version of the sound track that contains all of the music and *sound effects*, but none of the dialogue. Used to make *dubbed*, foreign-language versions.

music clearance The process by which television programs obtain permission to use songs. See *synchronization license* and *master use license*.

music licensors A holder of a *copyright* to a piece of music who leases or sells it for use in a TV program.

music supervisor Person responsible for selecting a program's music and creating its overall music design.

music television Generally refers to a system, such as a cable or satellite service (e.g., MTV, CMT), through which musical broadcast material is delivered.

music video A visual representation of or accompaniment to a song or other musical selection that usually exists independently as a recording.

musical director Person who selects and arranges the music for a program.

mythic analysis An interpretive strategy of *genre* analysis that approaches genres in terms of archetypes, stories shared by large segments of a culture that offer the researcher evidence of that society's thought process.

narration (voiceover) When a character's or omniscient narrator's voice is heard over an image.

narrative enigma A question that underpins a story and will (in classical films) or will not (in soap opera) be answered at the conclusion.

narrative function A specific action or an attribute of a character in a narrative—according to the narrative theory of V. I. Propp.

narrative image A particular representation of a program created by advertising and promotion in order to entice viewers.

narrative problematic The core, repeatable story structure that underpins a television program.

National Television System Committee (NTSC) A committee established by various manufacturers of television equipment in order to develop a set of standards that would render color transmission and reception compatible with black-and-white television sets. The initials NTSC are also commonly used to refer to the 525-line broadcast standard used in the U.S.

naturalistic performance Performance style in which the actor attempts to create a character that the audience will accept as a plausible and believable human being, rather than an actor trying to portray someone.

negotiated reading In cultural studies, the interpretation of the text that partially accepts and partially rejects the meanings that the text emphasizes.

NLE See *nonlinear editing*.

nondiegetic sound Sound that does not occur in the *diegetic space* (the characters' world), such as music that is added in post-production.

nonlinear editing (NLE) Editing performed on a computer, in which shots do not have to be placed one after the other (i.e., in a linear fashion). NLE systems include Final Cut Pro and Avid Media Composer.

non-narrative television Televisual texts (e.g., news and sports programs, game shows, some commercials) that present reality to us without using conventional narrative structures. Instead, non-narrative television relies on *expository*, *interactive*, *observational*, and/or *reflexive modes of representation*.

normal lens A type of *focal length* that seems to most closely approximate the human eye's range of vision (in actuality the range of vision is narrower in a normal focal length lens, with less *illusion of depth*).

NTSC See *National Television System Committee*.

objective correlative An object that comes to represent an aspect of a character—e.g., Bart Simpson's skateboard representing his carefree and spontaneous lifestyle.

observational mode Type of television text wherein a television producer's presence is not obvious to the viewer, and his or her manipulation of the *historical world* is minimal.

omnidirectional microphone A microphone that is able to pick up sound equally from all directions.

oppositional reading In cultural studies, the interpretation of the text that is wholly contrary to the text's dominant meanings.

overhead boom microphone Held on a long arm by a *boom operator*, positioned above the actors' heads and out of view of the camera, it is equipped with a *hypercardioid microphone* so that sound from the direction it is pointed will be recorded and ambient sound will be minimized.

package In television journalism, an 80- to 105-second news story shot in the field and filed by a reporter.

pan-and-scan (scanning) A process by which a widescreen, anamorphic film (1:2.40) is reduced to television's smaller 1:1.33 *aspect ratio*. The most significant part of the original frame is selected, and the pan-and-scan frame can slide, or "scan," left or right across the original frame.

panning The action of physically rotating the camera left and right, on an imaginary vertical axis. Only the tripod head is moved, not the entire support. Pan also refers to the resulting horizontal movement of the image.

pantomime A style of *naturalistic performance* in which the actor presents the character with specific gestures that, through convention, represent specific emotions or actions.

paradigmatic structure In *semiotics*, a manner in which *signs* are organized and meaning created. Paradigmatic structures create meaning through association, in contrast to *syntagmatic* structures, which create meaning through sequence or chronological order.

participant observation An *ethnographic*, *cultural studies* research method where researchers participate with and observe individuals' experiences in the field.

participatory culture A culture inspired by a television program and largely created by the fans themselves. It consists of fan-generated stories, songs, costumes, and other artifacts, as well as the values and shared history of a program's fan community.

participatory mode In the context of documentary TV, a type of television text in which the *historical world* is mixed with that of the video/filmmaker—according to Bill Nichols. This occurs in one of two ways: the *social actor* is brought into a television studio; and/or a representative of television enters the historical world to provoke a response from social actors.

patriarchy A society dominated by men.

pedestaling The raising or lowering of the camera on the vertical post of the camera support. Pedestal is also the term given to the moveable camera support (the shaft in the center of a dolly) used in studio television production.

perfect fit In the study of television stars, a matching of a particular role's characteristics to a star's *polysemy*.

performing rights organizations (**PROs**) Organizations that control music licenses and collect *royalties* for their use on television.

phosphors See *pixels*.

pickup pattern In microphones, the shape of the space in which the microphone is sensitive to sound. Common patterns include *omnidirectional* and *cardioid*.

pillar boxing A process by which a program shot in the standard *aspect ratio* (1.33:1) is displayed on a *widescreen* television set (1.78:1). The left and right sides of the widescreen frame are blackened and the standard-ratio frame is displayed in this frame-within-the-widescreen-frame.

pilot A program, sometimes a made-for-TV movie, which introduces a new *series*.

pitch How high or low a sound is. See *frequency response*.

pitch session A meeting between creative individuals and studio/network executives at which ideas are presented to executives in hopes of them being bought.

pixels (**phosphors**) Phosphorescent dots, arranged in horizontal lines on the television screen, which produce the video image when struck by a beam from the *electron gun*.

play-by-play announcer A type of television sports announcer, usually a professional broadcaster, who functions as narrator of the game's events, keeps track of game time, prompts the comments of the *color announcers*, reiterates the score, modulates the passage of time, and may lead into commercial breaks.

point-of-view shot A shot in which the camera is physically situated very close to a character's position; thus the resulting shot approximates the character's point-of-view.

political economy An analytical approach that examines how broader, even global, economic pressures shape studios' and networks' production of television.

polysemy Literally, many meanings. Refers to television's ability to communicate contradictory or ambivalent meanings simultaneously.

(online) portal A service that provides and organizes Internet-distributed television.

post-production Everything (e.g., editing, *sound effects*) that transpires after the program itself has been shot.

preferred reading In cultural studies, the interpretation of the text that is stressed by the text itself. Marxists presume this reading to align with the *dominant ideology*.

pre-production The written planning stages of the program (script preparation, budgeting, etc.).

PRO See *performing rights organizations*.

problematic fit In the study of television stars, a complete mismatch of a particular role's characteristics with a star's *polysemy*.

product integration (a.k.a. **product placement**) The appearance of a trademarked product (e.g., Budweiser beer or Ford trucks) in a program—when the sponsor pays for such placement.

production The shooting of the program itself.

production designer The person most responsible for designing the set or selecting a location.

production sound The sound recorded on the set during the recording of a program. It is usually manipulated afterward during the *post-production* process.

production studies An analytical approach focusing on television workers and workplaces to better understand the encoding of the TV text by the industry.

proletariat In Marxist terms, the working class; this least powerful group works to survive, selling its labor to the *bourgeoisie*.

promotion A type of *media text* (e.g., an appearance on a talk show) generated by the star and his or her representatives in a deliberate attempt to shape viewer perception of the star.

pseudomonologue Type of interview in which the interviewer and his or her questions are not evident in the text; only the interviewee's answers are included.

public domain Material (e.g., a piece of music) that is not *copyrighted* and may be used in TV programs without paying a fee or *royalty*.

public service television Programs in service to the public—particularly ones designed more to educate than to entertain, although they might do both. A particularly strong component of television broadcasting in Britain, where the BBC is charged, by law, to provide public service programming.

public sphere A realm where members of the public might interact and discuss socio-political and economic matters of shared interest and concern. Proposed initially by critical theorist Jürgen Habermas in the 1960s, it has been applied recently to the function of television in promoting and shaping social discourse and debate.

publicity A type of *media text* (e.g., an unauthorized biography) that presents information outside the control of the star and his or her representatives.

pulling focus See *racking focus*.

queer theory The study of *discourse* surrounding lesbian, gay, bisexual, and transgender (LGBT) identities and their representation in our culture.

race, **racialized**, **raced** The ideologically loaded, socially determined construction of racial identity through the *racial formation*. Racialized and raced are adjectives referring to the process by which a phenomenon is given a particular racial charge.

race and ethnic studies An analytical approach that emphasizes the *discourses* associated with racial and ethnic cultures—asking how these discourses construct identities.

racial formation The process by which social and political meanings are attached to persons of a certain skin color or language or dress or other physical signifier.

racking focus (**pulling focus**) Shifting the *focus* from foreground to background, or vice versa.

rating In the context of Nielsen's measurement of TV viewership, the percentage of all homes with television sets that are tuned to a specific program. Usually used in conjunction with the Nielsen *share*.

ratings An umbrella term for the calculated amount and percentage of viewers watching a particular program on a particular station—reported by Nielsen as a *rating* and a *share*.

RCD See *remote control device*.

reading The viewer's active interpretation of a *text*—whether written (e.g., a book) or visual (e.g., a television program or film).

reality TV A genre with an ostensible base in reality—featuring nonactors in unscripted situations.

reception studies An analytical approach that emphasizes the interaction of television and its viewers—how viewers obtain pleasure and generate meanings from the medium.

re-establishing shot A long shot that once again positions the character(s) within the environment of the scene, helping to re-establish character and/or setting; also used as a transitional device.

reflexive mode Type of non-narrative television text that draws the viewer's attention to the processes, techniques, and conventions of television production.

remote control device (**RCD**) A device that allows one to operate a television without directly touching it.

repertory *Naturalistic performance* style in which the actor constructs a performance by selecting particular gestures and spoken dialects.

research question An hypothesis proposed by an empirical researcher to start a project.

resolution See *definition*.

rhythm The timing of speech, music, *sound effects*, or editing.

royalty A fee paid for the use of *copyrighted* material.

ruling class Marx's term for the social class in control of a society's *means of production*; the class that controls the means of production controls the society overall.

sampling Either the process by which *analog sound* is converted into a *digital sound* recording (by analyzing small slices of the sound waves) or the incorporation of a snippet of a song into a new song.

saturation (**chroma** or **chrominance**) In terms of television's image quality, the level of a color's purity (or how much or little grayness is mixed with the color).

scan line Lines of glowing *pixels* that make up the television image. In the NTSC system used in the United States, there are 486 visible lines in the *standard-definition* TV image. In the U.S. ATSC system, the *high-definition* TV image has 720 or 1080 scan lines. PAL, developed in Germany, and SECAM, from France, are 625-line systems.

scanning See *pan-and-scan*.

scene The smallest piece of the narrative action; a single narrative event that occurs in continuous space over continuous time.

scenic designer See *set designer*.

schema A group of stylistic conventions that are characteristic of a specific genre, director, network, mode of production, and so on.

scientific method An *empirical* approach that advocates developing research questions and hypotheses based on an established body of theoretical knowledge, investigating them with replicable methodology, and explaining the results in terms of its contribution to the established body of knowledge.

screen direction From the camera's perspective, the direction a character is looking and/or an object is moving in a shot.

screen time The duration of a program—which is normally shorter than the time represented in the program's narrative (that is, its *story time*). The story time of one soap-opera episode, for example, is typically a day or two, but its screen time is less than 60 minutes.

screenplay Generally speaking, a written description of a program, wherein the action and dialogue are described scene-by-scene. (Terms used to describe different types of scripts vary considerably within the television and film industries.)

script (a.k.a. screenplay) Written preparation for a TV program that often includes a writer's draft, table draft, network draft, and/or production draft.

SDTV See *standard-definition television*.

segment See *act*.

segue A transition from one sound to another.

selective use In the study of television stars, a use of selected parts of the star's *polysemy* in a particular role.

self-reflexivity A program that refers back to itself or similar programs. In a genre's evolutionary pattern, the stage during which the genre turns inward and uses its own conventions for subject matter, often in the form of a parody.

semiotics An area of *television criticism* that breaks down all forms of communication into individual units of meaning that are studied in terms of their singular characteristics as well as their interaction with other units of meaning. The science of *signs*.

sense memory Technique of *Method* acting style in which the actor draws upon memories of physical sensations of an emotional event in order to generate *emotional memory*.

serial A narrative form of television that presents daily/weekly episodes, with a multiple set of recurring characters and simultaneous storylines. Because each episode specifically links to the next, narrative *closure* is rare.

series A narrative form that presents weekly episodes, usually self-contained, with a defined set of recurring characters.

set designer (scenic designer) Person who builds or selects elements in constructing the setting of a television program.

set-top box Devices that might literally be placed on top of a television set and connected to it in order to provide cable-TV or satellite-TV access or view DVDs or video cassettes.

sexual politics In *feminist* studies, the power relationship between men and women. From the title of a book by Kate Millett.

SFX See *sound effects*.

shallow focus A small *depth of field*, with just one plane (foreground, middle-ground, or background) in *focus*.

shallow space blocking A type of blocking associated with multiple-camera, *studio set* productions, where, due to the shallow sets, the actors mostly move side-to-side, rather than up-and-back.

share In the context of Nielsen's measurement of TV viewership, the percentage of homes with turned-on television sets that are tuned to a specific program. Usually used in conjunction with the Nielsen *rating*.

shooting script Generally speaking, a written description of a program, wherein each scene is described shot-by-shot. (Terms used to describe different types of scripts vary considerably within the television and film industries.)

shot-counter shot (shot-reverse shot) An editing principle of the continuity system that alternates shots, particularly in conversation scenes between two characters. It is a mainstay of the *180° rule* and the *continuity system*.

shot-reverse shot See *shot-counter shot*.

showrunners Producers (often scriptwriters) who are responsible for the ongoing production of a program.

sign In *semiotics*, the smallest unit of meaning—composed of a *signifier* and its *signified*.

signified The meaning communicated by the *signifier*; can be an object, a concept, a visual field, and so on.

signifier The physical aspect of a *sign*, such as ink on a page, chalk on a chalkboard, a blinking light, light emanating from a TV screen, etc.

signs of character The various signifiers—viewer foreknowledge, character name, appearance, *objective correlatives*, dialogue, lighting, videography or cinematography, and action—that communicate the character to the viewer.

signs of performance The actor's facial, gestural, corporeal, and vocal signifiers that contribute to the development of character.

simulacrum See *simulation*.

simulation (or **simulacrum**) A representation of an incident or object. Postmodernist critics argue that simulations have become more important than real objects, that the simulation appears to be "more real" than reality itself, and that television encourages a "society of the spectacle."

simulcasts Programs, particularly in the late 1940s and early 1950s, which are simultaneously broadcast on both radio and television. The process was revived in the 1960s and 1970s in order to transmit stereo sound on FM radio that would accompany television visuals (of, for example, a music concert).

single A commonly used term for a *close-up* of one person.

single-camera production A *mode of production* wherein one camera operates at a time and the shots are done in the most economically efficient order. On television, the main mode used in creating prime-time dramas, made-for-TV movies, music videos, and commercials.

social actor "Real" people as used in nonfiction television programs; people "performing" according to social codes of behavior in order to represent themselves to others.

social media Online services such as Facebook, Twitter, and Instagram that encourage discussion, commentary, gossip, and other interactions—including fan groups of TV programs.

soft focus An entire image that is slightly out-of-*focus*.

soft light A *diffused* light source, resulting in indistinct, blurred outlines and minimal shadows.

soft news News stories that examine the personal, such as gossip, scandal, murder, mayhem, and "human interest" stories.

sound bite In a news *package*, a short piece of audio that was recorded on location.

sound editor Technician who, in *post-production*, manipulates a program's soundtrack.

sound effects (**SFX**) Incidental sounds that are added to a program's *sound mix* during *post-production*.

sound mix, **sound mixer** The *post-production* process of blending speech, music, and *sound effects* into a program's finished soundtrack. Or it can refer to the final product itself—a program's sound mix. The mixer is the sound editor who brings these sound elements together.

sound perspective The audio point-of-view of a shot—how near or far the sound source seems to be.

sound stage A large room designed for the filming or videotaping of programs. Sets are arranged on the stage in a variety of ways, depending mostly upon the presence/absence of a studio audience.

standard-definition television (**SDTV**) A broadcast technology used in conventional television transmissions that are not in *high definition*. This standard, in the U.S., was first set by the *NTSC* at 486 visible *scan lines* and then decreased by the *ATSC* to 480 scan lines for *digital television*.

stand-up A feature of a television news *package* in which the reporter stands before a site significant to the story to narrate it.

star image A representation of an actor that is fabricated through the *media texts* of promotion, publicity, television programs, and criticism.

Steadicam Registered trademark for a gyroscopically balanced camera mount that attaches to a *camera operator*'s body and produces smooth camera movement without the use of a *dolly*.

stereotype A conventionalized character type that is demeaning to a particular social group.

story time The amount of time that transpires within a program's narrative. See *screen time*.

storyboard A written description of a program consisting of small drawings of individual shots.

stripped syndication A programming strategy in which syndicated shows are scheduled Monday through Friday in the same time slot.

structuralism An analytical approach to *texts* that stresses the binary oppositions underpinning them. Originated in the structural anthropology of Claude Lévi-Strauss.

structured polysemy The organization and emphasis/repression of meanings within television's polysemy.

studio set Three-walled, ceilingless set erected on a *sound stage*; this type of set is usually shallow, normally wider than deep, and rectangular rather than square.

stylistics The study of television techniques and their patterns, significance, and beauty.

subject In psychoanalysis, the human psyche—formed chiefly through the Oedipal Complex. In contemporary Marxism, an individual viewed as a psychological construct who enters the ideological world and who must be considered in relationship to this ideology.

subjective shot A shot wherein the camera is positioned as if it were inside a character's head, looking out of his or her eyes.

subtitling The process in which the original dialogue of a film or television program is both heard and printed at the bottom of the screen. Subtitling is often used for foreign-language films. In television it is also used on conventional programs as closed-captions for viewers with impaired hearing.

subtractive color The process wherein, as white light passes through a piece of film, yellow, magenta, and cyan colors are filtered out, leaving the many colors of the spectrum.

superstructure In Marxist terms, a society's ideological constructs, which grow out of its economic *base*.

sweeps Time period during which Nielsen Media Research conducts seasonal *ratings* of network television programs.

sweetening A *post-production sound effects* process wherein the sound editors add more applause and laughter to those of the actual studio audience.

switcher A technical device that allows a director to change between various video cameras while recording a scene.

symbol *symbolic sign*.

symbolic sign (symbol) In *semiotics*, a type of *sign* in which the *signifier* and the *signified* are connected solely through cultural convention. For example, Christianity (a signified) represented by a cross (signifier) or Judaism (signified) by a Star of David (signifier).

sync (or synch) The synchronization of sound and image. See *lip sync*.

synchronization license Permission from a song's copyright holder for its use in a TV program. See *music clearance* and *master use license*.

syndication The distribution or leasing of television programs to stations and networks by their production companies. It refers both to the second run of a program after a network's initial license period (e.g., *I Love Lucy* [1951–57]) and a program that was created specifically for syndication (e.g., *Baywatch* [1989–99]). See *stripped syndication*.

syntagm In *semiotics*, a first-level ordering of signs—e.g., in narrative television, an individual *scene*. The sequence of scenes is their *syntagmatic structure*.

syntagmatic structure In *semiotics*, the linear or temporal ordering of *signs*. A single *syntagm* in narrative television is a program's smallest story segment. See *paradigmatic structure*.

system In *semiotics*, an ordering of *signs* that gives them meaning.

take A single shot, lasting from the starting to the stopping of the camera.

teasers On television news, brief announcements of upcoming stories used to maintain viewer attention.

Technicolor A type of color film process, used mostly from the late 1930s to the 1950s.

telephoto lens A long *focal length* that creates a narrow but magnified view of an object or person.

television apparatus The combined work of all of the various factions (bankers, media corporations, directors, scriptwriters) that create television programs and the viewing experience itself—including the psychological mechanisms at work during TV viewing.

television criticism Used in the popular press to refer to evaluative reviewing of television.

television studies An academic discipline devoted to the analysis of television—usually employing nonempirical methods (e.g., *auteurism*, *genre* study, *semiotics*, and *feminism*). Closely allied with the activity of *television criticism*, but more interpretive than evaluative.

terrestrial broadcasting The delivery of the broadcast signal via earthbound transmitters, as opposed to satellite broadcasting systems.

text A segment of the televisual *flow*, such as an individual program, a commercial, a newscast, even an entire evening's viewing.
textual poaching"Stealing" an element of a television program and transforming it for one's own purposes. Academics who study viewers' textual poaching engage in *fan studies*.
theatrical film Films originally designed to be shown in theaters, as opposed to made-for-TV films (*MOW*s).
thick description The result of an *ethnographic* approach to interviewing television viewers, which generates detailed descriptions of their experience of the medium. It is contrasted with statistical reports on TV-viewing surveys, which might be characterized as "thin" descriptions.
three shot As with the *two shot*, the conventional framing of three characters in a medium shot.
three-point lighting An *aesthetic* convention in which an actor or object is lit from three sources or points of light of varying intensity. There is one main source of illumination (*key light*), one source filling shadows (*fill light*), and one source backlighting the actors (*back light*).
ticker Information moving across the bottom of the screen—such as sports scores and weather updates.
tilting The action of rotating the camera up and down, on a horizontal axis in a stationary body. Tilt also refers to the resulting vertical movements in the image.
timbre (**tone**) A characteristic of television sound referring to the tonal quality of a note and/or voice.
tone See *timbre*.
track An area along the length of recording tape (like the lanes on a highway) in a *multi-track tape recorder* on which speech, music, or *sound effects* are individually recorded. Similarly, computer-based, *nonlinear editing* (*NLE*) also relies on the metaphor of tracks of sound and image.
tracking Any sideways or forward/backward movement of the camera *dolly*—sometimes on actual tracks.
transformative works Videos, images, texts, etc. created by individuals that blend and transform works by other individuals.
transmedia storytelling The construction of narrative worlds across several media platforms.
transnational corporations (**TNCs**) Large corporations with many holdings in several countries and that often control a variety of media companies beyond television networks/stations (e.g., book/magazine publishing, filmmaking).
treatment A written description of a program containing only a basic outline of the action; the first stage of the scriptwriting process.
trucking (**crabbing**) In television studio production, any sideways movement of the camera.
two shot The framing of two characters in a medium shot.
typecasting When the *star image* perfectly fits the character he or she portrays.
unidirectional microphone A microphone that picks up sound from a specific direction.
unique selling proposition (**USP**) Rosser Reeve's term for that certain something that distinguishes one product from all the others.
uses-and-gratifications A research method that sees the viewer as an active user and attempts to chart the way that viewers employ television; this method quantifies how television fulfills viewers' emotional or intellectual needs.
USP See *unique selling proposition*.
variable focal length See *zoom lens*.
vaudeville *Anti-naturalistic performance* style in which the actor reminds the viewer that the character is not a real person, often by directly addressing the viewer.
VCR See *videocassette*.
verisimilitude The impression of truth or reality.
vidders, vidding, fan vids TV fans who edit together shots from their favorite programs and lay popular music over the images. Vidding is the process of creating fan vids.
video-on-demand (**VOD**) Services that provide video material when the viewer requests it, through a cable company's "on-demand" services, Netflix's online streaming, or something similar.
videocassette, videocassette recorder (**VCR**) A once-revolutionary format for distributing movies to the home market and allowing viewers to record television. Introduced in the U.S. in 1976 and subsequently superseded by the *DVD*, the *Blu-ray disc* and online streaming.

videographer The person overseeing all aspects of the video image—including lighting and the operation of the camera.

videography The characteristics of the video camera.

visual effects The manipulation of the image, usually a digital process and sometimes featuring *computer-generated imagery* (CGI).

VOD See *video-on-demand*.

voiceover See *narration*.

volume How loud a sound is. One of three main characteristics of television sound. See *pitch* and *timbre*.

waveform A visual representation of the shape of a sound wave occurring over time.

wide-angle lens A *focal length* that generally provides a wide view of a scene and increases the *illusion of depth* so that some objects seem to be far apart from one another.

widescreen An *aspect ratio* wider than television's original standard of 1.33:1 (that is, 4:3). Television widescreen (a part of the *high-definition* format) is 16:9 or 1.78:1. Common variations of widescreen in theatrical films are *masked* (1.85:1) and *anamorphic* (2.40:1).

wipe A special effect used as a transition device between scenes, in which a line moves across the screen, apparently erasing one shot as the next replaces it.

XCU See *extreme close-up*.

XLS See *extreme long shot*.

zoom in/zoom out A function of the *zoom lens* wherein the *focal length* is varied from *wide angle* to *telephoto* (zoom in), thereby magnifying the object as the angle of view is narrowed—or vice versa (zoom out).

zoom lens (**variable focal length**) A lens with a variable *focal length*, allowing the operator to shift immediately and continuously from *wide angle* to *telephoto* (or vice versa) without switching lenses.

INDEX

Page numbers in *italic* indicate a figure and page numbers in **bold** indicate a table on the corresponding page.